INTRODUCTION TO C PROGRAMMING

SECOND EDITION

Reema Thareja

Assistant Professor
Department of Computer Science
Shyama Prasad Mukherji College for Women
University of Delhi

Oxford University Press is a department of the University of Oxford. It furthers the University's objective of excellence in research, scholarship, and education by publishing worldwide. Oxford is a registered trade mark of Oxford University Press in the UK and in certain other countries.

Published in India by
Oxford University Press
YMCA Library Building, 1 Jai Singh Road, New Delhi 110001, India

First Edition published in 2012
Second Edition published in 2015

ISBN-13: 978-0-19-945205-7
ISBN-10: 0-19-945205-7

Typeset in Times New Roman
by Pee-Gee Graphics, New Delhi

To my family
and
my uncle Mr B. L. Theraja
who is a well-known author

Features of the Book

> **Programming Tip:**
> If you do not place a parenthesis after 'main', a compiler error will be generated.

Programming Tips

Educates the reader about common programming errors and how to avoid them

Notes

These elements highlight important terms and concepts for a quick recap

C is a case-sensitive language. Therefore rno, Rno, RNo, RNO are considered as different identifiers.

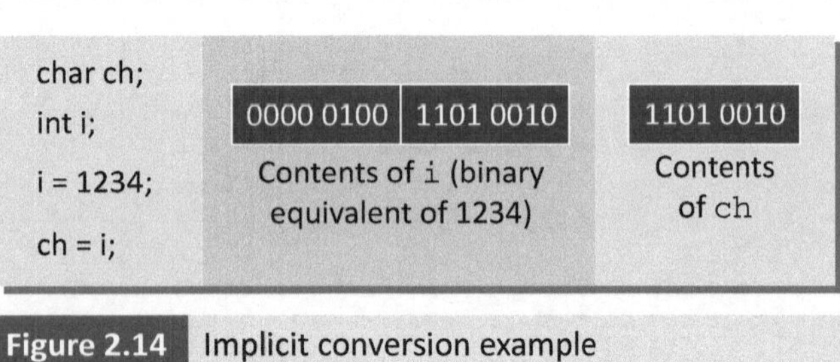

Figure 2.14 Implicit conversion example

Illustrations

The book is visually rich with a number of illustrations to support the explanations, which help clarify the concepts in a clear manner

Solved Examples

Every chapter contains plenty of solved examples to demonstrate the applicability of concepts discussed

Example 8.3 Declare a structure to store information of a particular date.

```
struct date
{
   int day;
   int month;
   int year;
};
```

Preface to the Second Edition

Case Studies

Case studies at the end of select chapters contain detailed programs that reinforce the concepts learnt in chapters

Case Study for Chapters 6 and 7

In C language, a string is nothing but a null-terminated character array and a pointer is a variable that contains the memory location of another variable. Therefore, a pointer is a variable that represents the location of a data item such as a variable or an array element.

Pointers provide an alternate way to access individual elements of the array and they are used to pass arrays and strings as function arguments. Now utilize all these concepts to write a program that performs various operations on a string (using pointers).

```
int option, m, n, length=0;
clrscr();
do
{
    printf("\n 1. Enter the string");
    printf("\n 2. Display the string");
    printf("\n 3. Merge two strings");
    printf("\n 4. Copy n characters from
m^th position");
    printf("\n 5. Calculate length of the
string");
```

Glossary

Contains a list of important terms and their definitions at the end of each chapter for recapitulation of the important concepts learnt

GLOSSARY

Break statement Statement used to terminate the execution of the nearest enclosing loop in which it appears.

Conditional branching Conditional branching statements is used to jump from one part of the program to another depending on whether a particular condition is satisfied or not.

Continue statement Statement that can appear in the body of a loop. When the compiler encounters a `continue` statement then the rest of the statements in the loop are skipped and the control is unconditionally transferred to the loop-continuation portion of the nearest enclosing loop.

Dangling else problem Problem encountered with nesting of `if-else` statements which is created when there is no matching else for every `if` statement.

function and can appear only before one statement in the same function.

If statement Simplest form of decision control statement that is frequently used in decision making.

If-else-if statement Decision control statement that works in the same way as a normal `if` statement. It is also known as `nested if` construct.

If-else statement Decision control statement in which first the test expression is evaluated. If the expression is true, statement `block 1` is executed and statement `block 2` is skipped. Otherwise, if the expression is false, statement `block 2` is executed and statement `block 1` is ignored.

Exercises

Comprehensive exercises at the end of each chapter to facilitate revision

EXERCISES

Fill in the Blanks

1. Structure is a _______ data type.
2. A structure is similar to _______.
3. _______ contains related information of the same data type.

Multiple Choice Questions

1. A data structure that can store related information together is
   (a) array (b) string
   (c) structure (d) all of these
2. A data structure that can store related information of different data types together is
   (a) array (b) string
   (c) structure (d) all of these

State True or False

1. Computer hardware does all the physical work.
2. The computer hardware cannot think and make decisions on its own.

Review Questions

1. Declare a structure(s) that represents the following hierarchical information:
   (a) Student
   (b) Roll Number
   (c) Name
      (i) First name

Preface to the Second Edition

C still continues to be the most popular and widely used programming language, even after four decades of its inception and conceptualization. Its versatility can be drawn from the fact that many advanced languages as well as operating systems like Windows and Unix have inherited the control structures and other basic features of C. Programmers all over the world embrace the C language as it provides them maximum control and incredible efficiency. C programs can produce codes that are compiled directly to a machine's native code. In optimized conditions, a C code can run as fast as a code written in assembly language! C codes are versatile, extensible, portable, and at the same time, extremely easy to learn and practice. Hence, for most of the students, C unquestionably remains the first step towards learning the art of professional programming.

ABOUT THE BOOK

Introduction to C Programming 2e is designed to serve as a textbook for undergraduate-level courses in computer science and engineering and postgraduate-level courses of computer applications. The book explains the fundamental concepts of the C programming language and illustrates the application of these concepts for solving real-world problems with a step-by-step approach.

Unlike existing textbooks on C which concentrate more on the theory of programming in C, this book focuses on its applicability by providing numerous programming examples and a rich set of programming exercises at the end of each chapter. The book will also be useful as a reference and resource to computer professionals operating in the domain of C and other C-like languages.

Every chapter in this book contains multiple programming examples to impart practical knowledge of the concepts. To reinforce the concepts, there are numerous objective, subjective, and programming exercises at the end of each chapter. The salient features of the book include:

- **Lucid style of presentation** that makes the concepts easy to understand
- **Plenty of illustrations** to support the explanations, which help clarify the concepts in a clear manner
- **Solved examples** within the chapters to demonstrate the applicability of concepts discussed
- **Glossary** of important terms at the end of each chapter for recapitulation of the important concepts learnt
- **Comprehensive exercises** at the end of each chapter to facilitate revision
- **Case studies** containing programs that reinforce the concepts learnt in chapters
- **Programming tips** educating readers about common programming errors and how to avoid them
- **Notes** highlighting important terms and concepts for a quick recap

NEW TO THIS EDITION

This second edition presents the following new features:

- How to write and execute C programs in platforms such as Unix, Linux, and Ubuntu
- A section on how to test and build robust C programs
- Detailed discussion on algorithms and how they act as a blueprint for writing effective C programs
- An introductory section on categorization of high-level languages
- New and updated example program codes

ONLINE RESOURCES

The online resource centre provides resources for faculty and students. The following resources are available at http://oupinheonline.com for faculty and students using this text

For Faculty

- Solutions Manual
- PowerPoint Slides

For Students

- Multiple Choice Questions
- Program Codes

Much of the content from the CD that accompanied the first edition has been uploaded to the companion site from where they can be accessed easily.

CONTENT AND STRUCTURE

The text is organized into 11 chapters.

Chapter 1 provides an introduction to computer software. It also provides an insight into different programming languages and the generations through which these languages have evolved.

Chapter 2 discusses the building blocks of the C programming language. The chapter talks about identifiers, constants, variables, and operators supported by the language.

Annexure 1 shows the steps to write, compile, and execute a C program in Unix, Linux and Ubuntu and also discusses some of the bitwise operations.

Chapter 3 deals with special types of statements such as decision control statement, iterative statement, break statement, control statement, and jump statement.

Annexure 2 discusses about algorithms.

Chapter 4 deals with declaring, defining, and calling functions. The chapter also discusses the storage classes as well as variable scope in C. The chapter ends with the important concept of recursive functions and a discussion on the Tower of Hanoi problem.

Annexure 3 explains the usage of user-defined header files.

Chapter 5 provides a detailed explanation of arrays including one-dimensional, two-dimensional, and multi-dimensional arrays. Finally, the operations that can be performed on such arrays are also explained.

Annexure 4 presents some of the widely used sorting techniques.

Chapter 6 unleashes the concept of strings which are better known as character arrays. The chapter not only focuses on reading and writing strings but also explains various operations that can be used to manipulate the character arrays.

Chapter 7 presents a detailed overview of pointers, pointer variables, pointer arithmetic, so and so forth. The chapter also relates the use of pointers with arrays, strings, and functions. This helps the reader to understand how pointers can be used to write efficient programs.

Annexure 5 explains the process of deciphering pointer declarations.

Chapter 8 introduces two user-defined data types. The first is a structure and the second is a union. The chapter includes the use of structures and unions with pointers, arrays, and functions so that the inter-connectivity between the programming techniques can be well understood.

Annexure 6 talks about bit fields and slack bytes.

Chapter 9 discusses how data can be stored in files. The chapter deals with opening, processing, and closing of files through a C program. These files are handled in text mode as well as binary mode for a better clarity of the concepts.

Chapter 10 explains the concept of pre-processor directives. The chapter includes small program codes that illustrate the use of different directives in a C program.

Annexure 7 provides an introduction to data structures.

Chapter 11 introduces linked list which is a preferred data structure when memory needs to be dynamically allocated for the data. The chapter discusses different types of linked lists and the techniques to insert and delete data from a linked list.

ACKNOWLEDGEMENTS

I would like to gratefully acknowledge the feedback and suggestions given by various faculty members for the improvement of the book.

I am obliged to the editorial team at Oxford University Press India for all their support towards revising this book.

Suggestions for improving the presentation and contents can be sent to the publisher through its website www.oup.com or to the author at reemathareja@gmail.com.

Reema Thareja

Preface to the First Edition

C is the most popular and widely used language for developing computer programs. Programmers all over the world embrace the C language as it provides them maximum control and efficiency. One of the major benefits of learning C is its user-friendliness that allows the user to read and write codes for a wide range of platforms, ranging from embedded microcontrollers to advanced scientific systems. The versatility of C is apparent from the fact that many modern operating systems have used C to develop their core.

Developed by Dennis Ritchie in 1972, C has derived numerous features from its precursors such as ALGOL, BCPL, and B. Its tremendous growth resulted in the development of different versions of the language that were similar but incompatible with each other, for example, the traditional C and K&R C. Therefore, the American National Standards Institute (ANSI) in December 1989 defined a standard for the language and renamed it as ANSI C. In 1990, the International Standards Organization (ISO) adopted the ANSI standard. This version of C was known as C89. In 1995, some minor changes were made to C89 and the new modified version was known as C95. During 1990s, C++ and Java became popular among the users and hence the standardization committee felt the need to integrate a few features of C++/Java in C to enhance its usefulness. Some significant changes were made in 1999 and the modified version became C99.

Since C is such a widely accepted and used language, jumping to other modern-day programming languages such as C++ and Java becomes much easier for a person who is well acquainted with C. The programming constructs in C, such as 'if' statements, 'for' and 'while' loops and the types of variables used can be found in many modern languages, therefore the ideas expressed in C are well understood by program developers. Moreover, unlike most of the modern-day languages that apply object-oriented design, C applies a procedural style of design, i.e., it uses procedures such as functions, methods, or routines to call itself or other procedures. However, many applications are still better suited to the procedural style of design, which often goes untaught to many programmers, who focus exclusively on object-oriented design. Learning C provides a strong procedural background, which is a worthy skill-set.

Some other features of C that give it the tag of the most widely used professional language include its *portability*, that is, a C program written on one computer can be made to run on any other computer with little or few modifications and its *extensibility*, that is, any number of functions can be added to the C library and called any number of times in the program, thus making the code easier to write and understand. Therefore, it is not only desirable but also necessary to have a strong fundamental knowledge of the C language.

ACKNOWLEDGEMENTS

I am grateful to my family, friends, and fellow members of the teaching staff at the Institute of Information Technology and Management.

My special thanks would always go to my parents, brother Pallav, sisters Kimi and Rashi, and son Goransh. My sincere thanks go to my uncle Mr B. L. Thareja for his inspiration and guidance in writing this book.

Finally, I would like to acknowledge the technical assistance provided to me by Er Udit Chopra. I would like to thank him for sparing his precious time to help me design and test the programs.

Last but not the least, my acknowledgements will remain incomplete if I do not thank the editorial staff at Oxford University Press, India, who have supported my creative writing activities over the past few years.

Reema Thareja

Brief Contents

Detailed Contents

9. Files 301

10. Preprocessor Directives 336

11. Linked Lists 354

CHAPTER 1

Introduction to Programming

Takeaways

- System Software
- Application Software
- Compiler, Interpreter, Linker, Loader
- Generation of Programming Languages
- Structured and Unstructured Programming
- Logic-oriented Programming
- Object-oriented Programming

1.1 INTRODUCTION TO COMPUTER SOFTWARE

When we talk about a computer, we actually mean two things (Fig. 1.1):

- First is the computer hardware that does all the physical work computers are known for.
- Second is the computer software that commands the hardware what to do and how to do it.

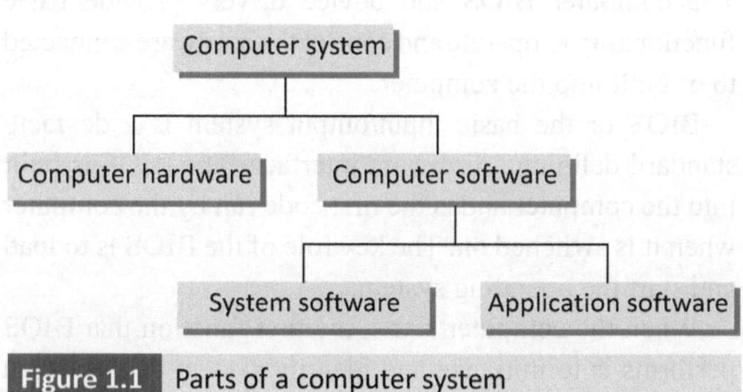

Figure 1.1 Parts of a computer system

If we think of computer as a living being, then the hardware would be the body that does things like seeing with eyes, lifting objects, and filling the lungs with air; the software would be the intelligence which helps in interpreting the images that are seen by the eyes, instructing the arms how to lift objects, and understandable to the filling the lungs with air.

Since the computer hardware is part of a machine, it can only understand two basic concepts: on and off. The on and off concept is called binary. Computer software was developed to make efficient use of binary to instruct the hardware to perform meaningful tasks.

The computer hardware cannot think and make decisions on its own. So, it cannot be used to analyse a given set of data and find a solution on its own. The hardware needs a software (a set of programs) to instruct what has to be done. A program is a set of instructions that is arranged in a sequence to guide a computer to find a solution for the given problem. The process of writing a program is called programming.

Computer software is written by computer programmers using a programming language. The programmer writes a set of instructions (program) using a specific programming language. Such instructions are known as the source code. Another computer program called a compiler is then used on the source code, to transform the instructions into a language that the computer can understand. The result is an executable computer program, which is another name for software.

Examples of computer software include:

- Computer games are widely used as a form of entertainment software that has many genres.
- Driver software which allows a computer to interact with additional hardware devices such as printers, scanners, and video cards.
- Educational software includes programs and games that help in teaching and providing drills to help memorize facts. Educational software can be diversely used—from teaching computer-related activities like typing to higher education subjects like Chemistry.
- Media players and media development software that are specifically designed to play and/or edit digital media files such as music and videos.
- Productivity software is an older term used to denote any program that allows the user to be more productive in a business sense. Examples of such software include word processors, database management utilities, and presentation software.
- Operating system software which helps in coordinating system resources and allows execution of other programs. Some operating systems include Windows Vista, Mac OS X, and Linux.

1.2 CLASSIFICATION OF COMPUTER SOFTWARE

Computer software can be broadly classified into two groups: system software and application software.

- System software [according to Nutt (1997)] provides a general programming environment in which programmers can create specific applications to suit their needs. This environment provides new functions that are not available at the hardware level and performs tasks related to executing the application program.
  System software represents programs that allow the hardware to run properly. System software is transparent to the user and acts as an interface between the hardware of the computer and the application software that users need to run on the computer. Figure 1.2 illustrates the relationship between application software, system software, and hardware.
- Application software is designed to solve a particular problem for users. It is generally what we think of when we say the word computer programs. Examples of application software include spreadsheets, database systems, desktop publishing systems, program development software, games, web browser, among others. Simply put, application software represents programs that allow users to do something besides simply run the hardware.

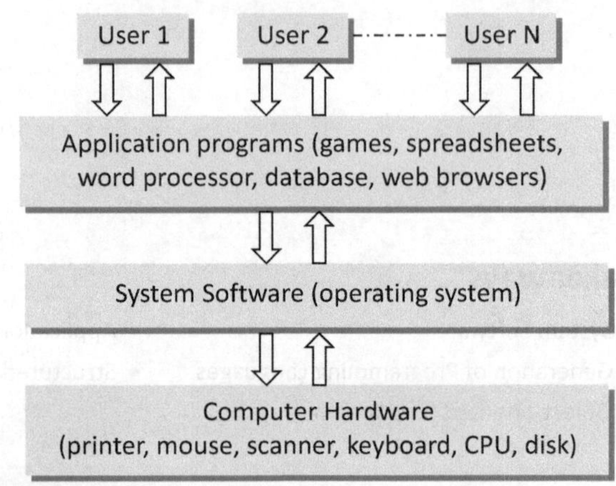

Figure 1.2 Relationship between hardware, system software, and application software

1.2.1 System Software

System software is software designed to operate the computer hardware and to provide and maintain a platform for running application software.

The most widely used system software are discussed in the following sections:

Computer BIOS and Device Drivers

The computer BIOS and device drivers provide basic functionality to operate and control the hardware connected to or built into the computer.

BIOS or the basic input/output system is a de facto standard defining a firmware interface. The BIOS is built into the computer and is the first code run by the computer when it is switched on. The key role of the BIOS is to load and start the operating system.

When the computer starts, the first function that BIOS performs is to initialize and identify system devices such as the video display card, keyboard and mouse, hard disk, CD/DVD drive, and other hardware. In other words, the code in the BIOS chip runs a series of tests called POST (Power On Self Test) to ensure that the system devices are working correctly.

The BIOS then locates software held on a peripheral device such as a hard disk or a CD, and loads and executes that software, giving it control of the computer. This process is known as *booting.*

BIOS is stored on a ROM chip built into the system. A BIOS will also have a user interface like that of a menu (Fig. 1.3) that can be accessed by pressing a certain key on the keyboard when the PC starts. The BIOS menu can enable the user to configure hardware, set the system clock, enable or disable system components, and most importantly, select which devices are eligible to be a potential boot device and set various password prompts.

To summarize, BIOS performs the following functions:

- Initializes the system hardware
- Initializes system registers
- Initializes power management system
- Tests RAM
- Test all the serial and parallel ports
- Initializes floppy disk drive and hard disk controllers
- Displays system summary information

Operating System

The primary goal of an operating system is to make the computer system (or any other device in which it is installed like the cell phone) convenient and efficient to use. The operating system offers generic services to support user applications.

From the user's point of view the primary consideration is always the convenience. Users should find it easy to launch an application and work on it. For example, we use icons which give us a clue about the application. We have a different icon for launching a web browser, e-mail application, or even a document preparation application. In other words, it is the human–computer interface which helps to identify and launch an application. The interface hides a lot of details of the instructions that perform all these tasks.

Similarly, if we examine the programs that help us in using input devices like keyboard/mouse, all the complex details of the character reading program are hidden from the user. We as users simply press buttons to perform the input operation regardless of the complexity of the details involved.

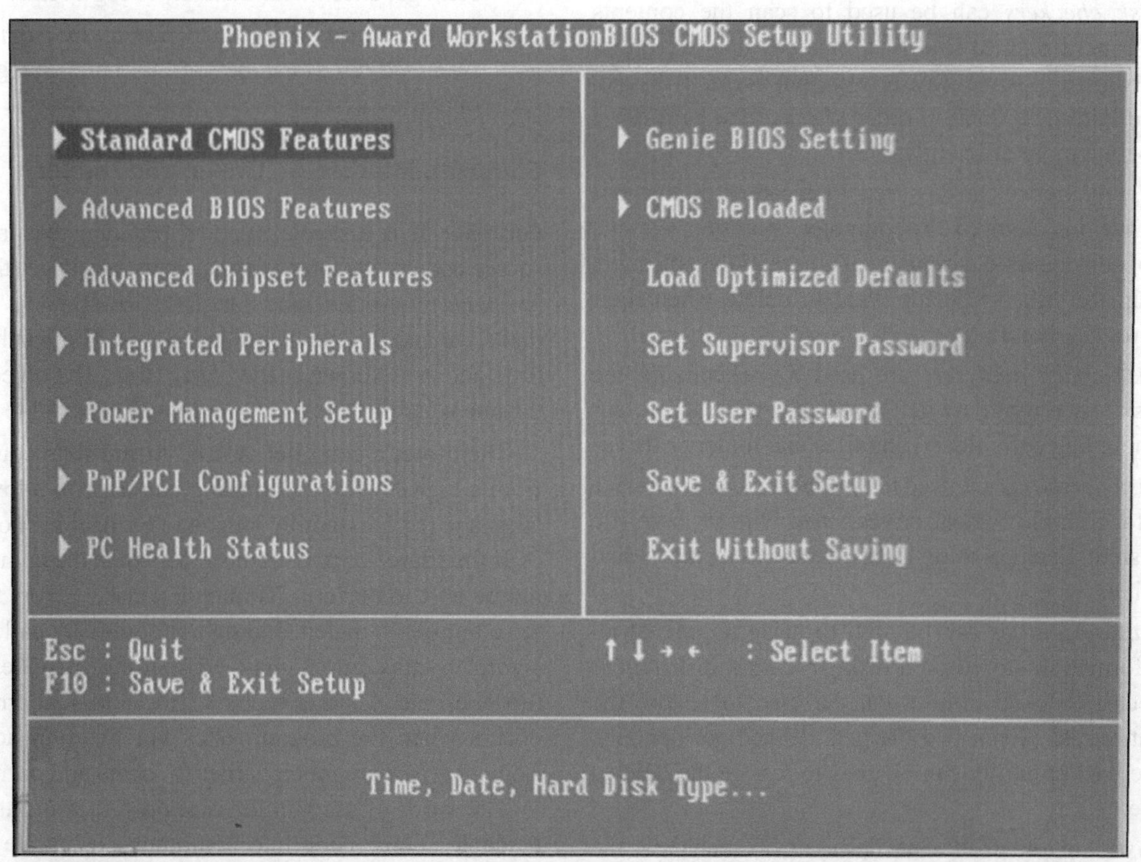

Figure 1.3 BIOS menu

An operating system ensures that the system resources (e.g., CPU, memory, I/O devices, etc.) are utilized efficiently. For example, there may be many service requests on a web server and each user request need to be serviced. Moreover, there may be many programs residing in the main memory. Therefore, the system needs to determine which programs are currently being executed and which programs need to wait for some I/O operation. This information is necessary because the programs that need to wait can be suspended temporarily from engaging the processor. Hence, it is important for an operating system to have a control policy and algorithm to allocate the system resources.

Utility Software

Utility software is used to analyse, configure, optimize, and maintain the computer system. Utility programs may be requested by application programs during their execution for multiple purposes. Some of them are as follows:

- *Disk defragmenters* can be used to detect computer files whose contents are broken across several locations on the hard disk, and move the fragments to one location in order to increase efficiency.
- *Disk checkers* can be used to scan the contents of a hard disk to find files or areas that are either corrupted in some way, or were not correctly saved, and eliminate them in order to make the hard drive operate more efficiently.
- *Disk cleaners* can be used to locate files that are either not required for computer operation, or take up considerable amounts of space. Disk cleaners help the user to decide what to delete when their hard disk is full.
- *Disk space analysers* are used for visualizing the disk space usage by getting the size for each folder (including sub folders) and files in a folder or drive.
- *Disk partitions* are used to divide an individual drive into multiple logical drives, each with its own file system. Each partition is then treated as an individual drive.
- *Backup utilities* can be used to make a copy of all information stored on a disk. In case a disk failure occurs, backup utilities can be used to restore the entire disk. Even if a file gets deleted accidentally, the backup utility can be used to restore the deleted file.
- *Disk compression* can be used to enhance the capacity of the disk by compressing/decompressing the contents of a disk.
- *File managers* can be used to provide a convenient method of performing routine data management tasks such as deleting, renaming, cataloguing, moving, copying, merging, generating, and modifying data sets.
- *System profilers* can be used to provide detailed information about the software installed and hardware attached to the computer.
- *Anti-virus* utilities are used to scan for computer viruses.
- *Data compression* utilities can be used to output a file with reduced file size.
- *Cryptographic utilities* can be used to encrypt and decrypt files.
- *Launcher applications* can be used as a convenient access point for application software.
- *Registry cleaners* can be used to clean and optimize the Windows registry by deleting the old registry keys that are no longer in use.
- *Network utilities* can be used to analyse the computer's network connectivity, configure network settings, check data transfer, or log events.
- *Command line interface (CLI) and Graphical user interface (GUI)* can be used to make changes to the operating system.

Compiler, Interpreter, Linker, and Loader

Compiler It is a special type of program that transforms source code written in a programming language (the *source language*) into machine language comprising just two digits, 1s and 0s (the *target language)*. The resultant code in 1s and 0s is known as the *object code*. The object code is the one which will be used to create an executable program.

Therefore, a compiler is used to translate source code from a high-level programming language to a lower level language (e.g., assembly language or machine code).

If the source code contains errors then the compiler will not be able to perform its intended task. Errors that limit the compiler in understanding a program are called *syntax errors*. Syntax errors may be spelling mistakes, typing mistakes, etc. Another type of error is logical error which occurs when the program does not function accurately. Logical errors are much harder to locate and correct.

The work of a compiler is simply to translate human readable source code into computer executable machine code. It can locate syntax errors in the program (if any) but cannot fix it. Until and unless the syntactical error is rectified the source code cannot be converted into the object code.

Interpreter Like the compiler, the interpreter also executes instructions written in a high-level language. Basically, a program written in a high-level language can be executed in any of the two ways. First by compiling the program and second, to pass the program through an interpreter.

While the compiler translates instructions written in high level programming language directly into the machine language; the interpreter on the other hand, translates the instructions into an intermediate form, which it then executes. This clearly means that the interpreter interprets the source code line by line. This is in striking contrast with the compiler which compiles the entire code in one go.

Usually, a compiled program executes faster than an interpreted program. However, the big advantage of an interpreter is that it does not need to go through the compilation stage during which machine instructions are generated. This process can be time consuming if the program is long. Moreover, the interpreter can immediately execute high-level programs.

All in all, compilers and interpreters both achieve similar purposes, but inherently different as to how they achieve that purpose.

Linker (*link editor binder*), It is a program that combines object modules to form an executable program. Generally, in case of a large program, the programmers prefer to break a code into smaller modules as this simplifies the programming task. Eventually, when the source code of all the modules has been converted into object code, you need to put all the modules together. This is the job of the linker. Usually, the compiler automatically invokes the linker as the last step in compiling a program.

Loader It is a special type of program that copies programs from a storage device to main memory, where they can be executed. However, in this book we will not go into the details of how a loader actually works. This is because the functionality of a loader is generally hidden from the programmer. As a programmer, it suffices to learn that the task of a loader is to bring the program and all its related files into the main memory from where it can be executed by the CPU.

1.2.2 Application Software

Application software is a type of computer software that employs the capabilities of a computer directly to perform a user-defined task. This is in contrast with system software which is involved in integrating a computer's capabilities, but typically does not directly apply them in the performance of tasks that benefit the user.

To better understand application software consider an analogy where hardware would depict the relationship of an electric light bulb (an application) to an electric power generation plant (a system) that depicts the software.

The power plant merely generates electricity which is not by itself of any real use until harnessed to an application like the electric light that performs a service which actually benefits the user.

Typical examples of software applications are word processors, spreadsheets, media players, education software, CAD, CAM, data communication software, statistical and operational research software, etc. Multiple applications bundled together as a package are sometimes referred to as an application suite.

1.3 PROGRAMMING LANGUAGES

A programming language is a language specifically designed to express computations that can be performed by the computer. Programming languages are used to create programs that control the behaviour of a system, to express algorithms, or as a mode of human–computer communication.

Usually, programming languages have a vocabulary of syntax and semantics for instructing a computer to perform specific tasks. The term *programming language* usually refers to high-level languages, such as BASIC, C, C++, COBOL, FORTRAN, Ada, and Pascal to name a few. Each of these languages has a unique set of keywords (words that it understands) and a special syntax for organizing program instructions.

While high-level programming languages are easy for the humans to read and understand, the computer actually understands the machine language that consists of numbers only. Each different type of CPU has its own unique machine language.

In between the machine languages and high-level languages, there is another type of language known as assembly language. Assembly languages are similar to machine languages, but they are much easier to program because they allow a programmer to substitute names for numbers.

However, irrespective of what language the programmer uses, the program written using any programming language has to be converted into machine language so that the computer can understand it. There are two ways to do this: *compile* the program or *interpret* the program.

The question of which language is the best depends on the following factors:

- The type of computer on which the program has to be executed
- The type of program
- The expertise of the programmer

For example, FORTRAN is a particularly good language for processing numerical data, but it does not lend itself very well to organizing large programs. Pascal can be used for writing well-structured and readable programs, but it is not as flexible as the C programming language. C++ goes one step ahead of C by incorporating powerful object-oriented features, but it is complex and difficult to learn.

1.4 GENERATION OF PROGRAMMING LANGUAGES

We now know that programming languages are the primary tools for creating software. As of now, hundreds of programming languages exist in the market, some more used than others, and each claiming to be the best. However, back in 1940s when computers were being developed there was just one language—the machine language.

The concept of generations of programming languages (also known as levels), is closely connected to the advances in technology that brought about computer generations. The four generations of programming languages include:

- machine language
- assembly language
- high-level language (also known as third generation language or 3GL)
- very high-level language (also known as fourth generation language or 4GL).

1.4.1 First Generation: Machine Language

Machine language was used to program the first stored program on computer systems. This is the lowest level of programming language. The machine language is the only language that the computer understands. All the commands and data values are expressed using 1s and 0s, corresponding to the 'on' and 'off' electrical states in a computer.

In the 1950s each computer had its own native language, and programmers had primitive systems for combining numbers to represent instructions such as *add* and *subtract*. Although there were similarities between each of the machine languages a computer could not understand programs written in another machine language (Fig. 1.4).

MACHINE LANGUAGE

This is an example of a machine language program that will add two numbers and find their average. It is in hexadecimal notation instead of binary notation because this is how the computer presented the code to the programmer. The program was run on a VAX/VMS computer, a product of the Digital Equipment Corporation.

```
                                          D000000A   D000
                                          D000000F   D009
                                          D000000B   D009
                                                     D009
                                                     D009
                                                     D0Θ0
FF55   CF      FF54   CF      FF53   CF   C1         DOD0
       FF24    CF     FF27    CF     D2   C7         D00C
                                                     D0E4
                                                     Dd0D
                                                     Dd3D
```

Figure 1.4 A machine language program

In machine language, all instructions, memory locations, numbers, and characters are represented in strings of 1s and 0s. Although machine-language programs are typically displayed with the binary numbers represented in octal (base 8) or hexadecimal (base 16), these programs are not easy for humans to read, write, or debug.

The main advantage of machine language is that the code can run very fast and efficiently, since it is directly executed by the CPU.

However, on the down side, the machine language is difficult to learn and is far more difficult to edit if errors occur. Moreover, if you want to add some instructions into memory at some location, then all the instructions after the insertion point would have to be moved down to make room in memory to accommodate the new instructions.

Last but not the least, the code written in machine language is not portable across systems and to transfer the code to a different computer it needs to be completely rewritten since the machine language for one computer could be significantly different from another computer. Architectural considerations made portability a tough issue to resolve.

1.4.2 Second Generation: Assembly Language

The second generation of programming language includes the assembly language. Assembly languages are symbolic programming languages that use symbolic notation to represent machine-language instructions. These languages are closely connected to machine language and the internal architecture of the computer system on which they are used. Since they are close to the machine, assembly language is also called low-level language. Nearly all computer systems have an assembly language available for use.

Assembly language developed in the mid 1950s was a great leap forward. It used symbolic codes also known as *mnemonic codes* that are easy-to-remember abbreviations, rather than numbers. Examples of these codes include ADD for add, CMP for compare, MUL for multiply, etc.

Assembly language programs consist of a series of individual statements or instructions that instruct the computer what to do. Basically, an assembly language statement consists of a *label*, an *operation code*, and one or more *operands*.

Labels are used to identify and reference instructions in the program. The operation code (opcode) is a mnemonic that specifies the operation that has to be performed such as *move, add, subtract,* or *compare*. The operand specifies the register or the location in main memory from where the data to be processed is located.

However, like the machine language, the statement or instruction in the assembly language will vary from one machine to another because the language is directly related to the internal architecture of the computer and is not designed to be machine independent. This makes the code written in assembly language less portable as the code written for one machine will not run on machines from a different or sometimes even the same manufacturer.

No doubt, the code written in assembly language will be very efficient in terms of execution time and main memory usage as the language is also close to the computer.

Programs written in assembly language need a *translator* often known as the *assembler* to convert them into machine language. This is because the computer will understand only the language of 1s and 0s and will not understand mnemonics like ADD and SUB.

The following instructions are a part of assembly language code to illustrate addition of two numbers:

```
MOV AX,4     Stores the value 4 in the AX
             register of CPU
MOV BX,6     Stores the value 6 in the BX
             register of CPU
ADD AX,BX    Add the contents of AX and BX
             register. Store the result in
             AX register
```

Although assembly languages are much better to work as compared to the machine language, they still require the programmer to think on the machine's level. Even today, some programmers still use assembly language to write parts of applications where speed of execution is critical, such as video games but most programmers today have switched to 3GL or 4GLs to do the same.

1.4.3 Third Generation Programming Language

A third generation programming language (3GL) is a refinement of the second-generation programming language. The 2GL languages brought logical structure to software. The third generation was introduced to make the languages more programmer friendly.

3GLs spurred the great increase in data processing that occurred in the 1960s and 1970s. In these languages, the program statements are not closely related to the internal characteristics of the computer and is therefore often referred to as high-level language.

Generally, a statement written in a high-level programming language will expand into several machine language instructions. This is in contrast to assembly languages, where one statement would generate one machine language instruction. 3GLs made programming easier, efficient, and less prone to errors.

High-level languages fall somewhere between natural languages and machine languages. 3GL includes languages like FORTRAN (FORmula TRANslator) and COBOL (COmmon Business Oriented Language) that made it possible for scientists and business people to write programs using familiar terms instead of obscure machine instructions.

The first widespread use of high-level languages in the early 1960s changed programming into something quite different from what it had been. Programs were written in an English-like manner, making them more convenient to use and giving the programmer more time to address a client's problems.

Although 3GLs relieve the programmer of demanding details they do not provide the flexibility available in low-level languages. However, a few high-level languages like C and FORTRAN combine some of the flexibility of assembly language with the power of high-level languages, but these languages are not well suited to the amateur programmer.

While some high level-languages were designed to serve a specific purpose (such as controlling industrial robots or creating graphics), other languages were flexible and considered to be general-purpose languages. Most of the programmers preferred to use general purpose high-level languages like BASIC (Beginners' All-purpose Symbolic Instruction Code), FORTRAN, PASCAL, COBOL, C++, or Java to write the code for their applications.

Again, a *translator* is needed to translate the instructions written in high-level language into computer-executable machine language. Such translators are commonly known as interpreters and compilers. Each high level language has many compilers.

For example, the machine language generated by one computer's C compiler is not the same as the machine language of some other computer. Therefore, it is necessary to have a C compiler for each type of computer on which the C program has to be executed.

3GLs make it easier to write and debug a program and gives the programmer more time to think about its overall logic. The programs written in such languages are portable between machines. For example, a program written in standard C can be compiled and executed on any computer that has a standard C compiler.

1.4.4 Fourth Generation: Very High-Level Languages

With each generation, programming languages started becoming easier to use and more like natural languages. However, 4GLs is a little different from its prior generation because they are basically non-procedural. When writing code using a procedural language, the programmer has to tell the computer how a task is done—add this, compare that, do this if the condition is true, and so on, in a very specific step-by-step manner. In striking contrast, while using a non-procedural language the programmers define only what they want the computer to do, without supplying all the details of how it has to be done.

There is no standard rule that defines what a fourth-generation language is but certain characteristics of such language include:

- the code comprising instructions are written in English-like sentences;
- they are non-procedural, so users concentrate on 'what' instead of the 'how' aspect of the task;
- the code is easier to maintain;
- 4GL code enhances the productivity of the programmers as they have to type fewer lines of code to get something done. It is said that a programmer becomes 10 times more productive when he writes the code using a 4GL than using a 3GL.

A typical example of a 4GL is the *query language* that allows a user to request information from a database with precisely worded English-like sentences. A query language is used as a database user interface and hides the specific details of the database from the user. For example, when working with Structured Query Language (SQL), the programmer just needs to remember a few rules of **syntax** and **logic**, but it is easier to learn than COBOL or C.

Let us take an example in which a report has to be generated that displays the total number of students enrolled in each class and in each semester. Using a 4GL, the request would look similar to this:

```
TABLE FILE ENROLLMENT

SUM STUDENTS BY SEMESTER BY CLASS
```

So we see that a 4GL is much simpler to learn and work with. The same code if written in C language or any other 3GL would require multiple lines of code to do the same task.

4GLs are still evolving, which makes it difficult to define or standardize them. The only down side of a 4GL is that it does not make efficient use of the machine's resources. However, the benefit of executing a program fast and easily, far outweighs the extra costs of running it.

1.4.5 Fifth Generation Programming Language

5GLs are centred on solving problems using constraints given to the program, rather than using an algorithm written by a programmer. Most constraint-based and logic programming languages and some declarative languages form a part of the fifth-generation languages. 5GLs are widely used in artificial intelligence research. Typical examples of a 5GL include Prolog, OPS5, and Mercury.

Another aspect of a 5GL is that it contains visual tools to help develop a program. A good example of a fifth generation language is Visual Basic.

So taking a forward leap than the 4GLs, 5GLs are designed to make the computer solve a given problem without the programmer. While working with a 4GL, the programmer had to write specific code to do a work but with 5GL, the programmer only needs to worry about what problems need to be solved and what conditions need to be met, without worrying about how to implement a routine or algorithm to solve them.

Generally, 5GLs were built upon Lisp, many originating on the Lisp machine, such as ICAD. Then, there are many frame languages such as KL-ONE.

In the 1990s, 5GLs were considered to be the wave of the future, and some predicted that they would replace all other languages for system development (except the low-level languages). In 1982 to 1993 Japan had put much research and money into their fifth generation computer systems project, hoping to design a massive computer network of machines using these tools. But when larger programs were built, the flaws of the approach became more apparent. Researchers began to observe that starting from a set of constraints for defining a particular problem, then deriving an efficient algorithm to solve the problem is a very difficult task. All these things could not be automated and still requires the insight of a programmer.

However, today the fifth-generation languages are back as a possible level of computer language. Software vendors across the globe currently claim that their software meets the visual 'programming' requirements of the 5GL concept.

1.5 CATEGORIZATION OF HIGH LEVEL LANGUAGES

High level languages can be easily categorized into four groups based on programming paradigm supported by them (refer Fig. 1.5). Programming paradigm refers to the approach the programming language has employed for solving different types of problems.

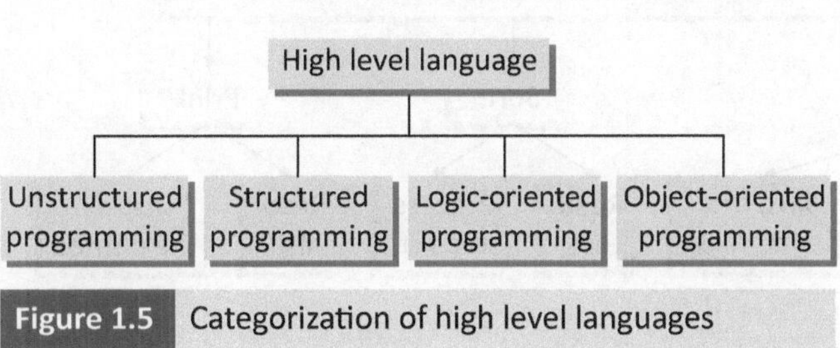

Figure 1.5 Categorization of high level languages

1.5.1 Unstructured Programming

In unstructured programming, programmers write small and simple programs consisting only of one main program. Here the `main()` consisted of *statements* that modifies the data which is *global* throughout the whole program. Refer Fig. 1.6. Though this technique is simple, but is not good for writing large programs. For example, if we need to perform a particular task multiple times in the program, then we need to copy the same sequence of statements at different locations within the program. This has lead to the idea to write functions or procedures. The new technique of using procedures came to be known as procedural programming.

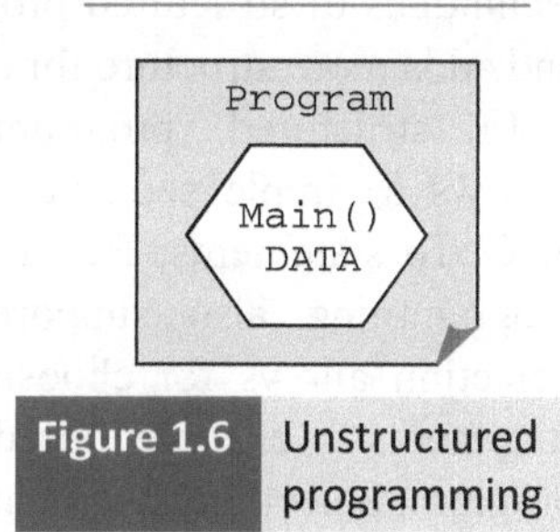

Figure 1.6 Unstructured programming

1.5.2 Structured Programming Language

Structured programming also referred as *modular programming* was first suggested by two mathematicians—Corrado Bohm and Guiseppe Jacopini. It is basically a subset of procedural programming that enforces a logical structure on the program to make it more efficient and easier to understand and modify.

Structured programming employs a top-down approach in which the overall program structure is broken down into separate modules. This allows the code to be loaded into memory more efficiently and also be reused in other programs. Modules are coded separately and once a module is written and tested individually, it is then integrated with other modules to form the overall program structure.

Structured programming is therefore based on modularization which groups related statements together (modules). Modularization makes it easier to write, debug, and understand the program.

Ideally, modules should not be longer than a page. It is always easy to understand a series of 10 single-page modules than it is a single ten-page program.

For some large and complex programs, the overall program structure may further require the need to break the modules into subsidiary pieces. This process continues until an individual piece of code can be written easily.

Almost any language can use structured programming techniques to avoid common pitfalls of unstructured languages. Unstructured programs depend on the programmer's skills to avoid structural problems and are therefore poorly organized. Most modern procedural languages support the concepts of structured programming. Even the object-oriented programming can be thought of as a type of structured programming, as its uses the techniques of structured programming for program flow, and adds more structure for data to the model.

In structured programming, the program flow follows a simple sequence and usually avoids the use of GoTo statements. Besides sequential flow, structured programming also supports selection and repetition. Selection allows for choosing any one of a number of statements to execute, based on the current status of the program. Selection statements contain keywords like "if," "then," "endif," or "switch" that help to identify the order as a logical executable.

In repetition, a selected statement remains active until the program reaches a point where there is a need for some other action to take place. It includes keywords like "repeat," "for," or "do…until." Essentially, the repetition instructs the program how long to continue the function before requesting further instructions.

Advantages

- The goal of structured programming is to write correct programs that are easy to understand and change.
- Modules enhance programmer's productivity by allowing them to look at the big picture first and then focus on details later.
- With modules, many programmers can work on a single, large program, each working on a different module.
- A structured program takes less time to be written than other programs. Modules or procedures written for one program can be reused in other programs also.
- A structured program is easy to debug because in it each procedure is specialized to perform just one task so every procedure can be checked individually for the presence of any error. In striking contrast, unstructured programs consist of a sequence of instructions that are not grouped for specific tasks. Their logic is cluttered with details and therefore difficult to follow.
- Individual procedures are easy to change as well as understand. In a structured program every procedure has meaningful names and has clear documentation to identify the task performed by it. Moreover, a correctly written structured program is self-documenting and can be easily understood by another programmer.

Example Imagine that your institute wants to create a program to manage a name and address list of students.

For this, you would break down the program into the following modules:

1. Enter new names and address.
2. Modify existing entries.
3. Sort entries
4. Printing the list

Now each of the above modules can be further broken down into smaller modules. For example, Enter new entries modules can be subdivided into modules like

- Prompt the user to enter new data
- Read the existing list from the disk
- Add the name and address to the existing list
- Save the updated list to the disk

Similarly, modify existing entries can further be divided into modules like:

- Read the existing list from disk.
- Modify one or more entries.
- Save the updated list to disk.

Observe that two sub-modules: Read the existing list from disk and save the updated list to disk are common to both the modules. So once these sub-modules are written they can be used by both the modules which require the same task to be performed. Structured programming method results in a hierarchical or layered program structure, which is depicted in Fig. 1.7.

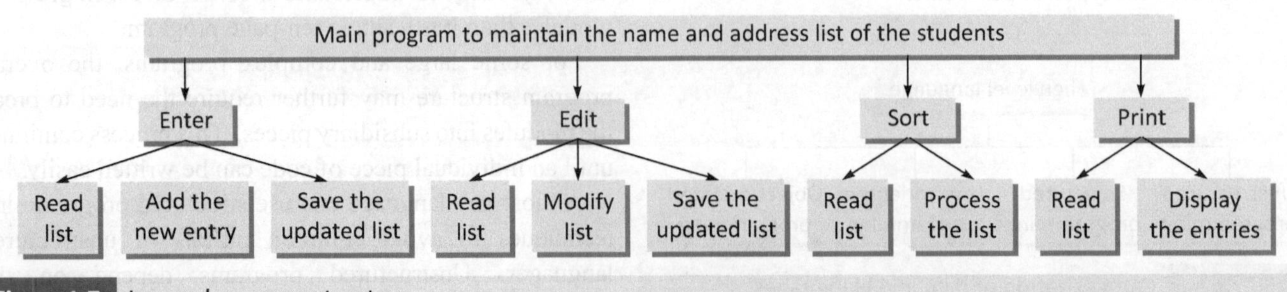

Figure 1.7 Layered program structure

1.5.3 Logic-oriented Programming Language

Logic-oriented programming languages employs a programming paradigm that is based on formal predicate logic. The logic paradigm is remarkably different from the other programming paradigms. The predicate logic describes the nature of a problem by defining relationships between rules and facts. These rules together with an inference algorithm form a program. Prolog, Lisp, and Datalog are few examples of logic-oriented programming languages.
The logical sentence in logic program is given in the form of

```
p(X, Y) if q(X) and r(Y)
```

For example, the *sister* relation can be defined using other simpler relations and properties *father, mother, female* as shown in Fig. 1.8. According to the figure, A can be a sister of B if both A and B have the same father and mother and A is a female.

```
Sister(A, B):-      /* A is the sister of B) if there are two
                       people F and M for which */
Father(F, A),       /* F is the father of A */
Father(F, B),       /* F is the father of B */
Mother(M, A),       /* M is the mother of A */
Mother(M, A),       /* M is the mother of B */
Female(A)           /* A is a female */
```

Figure 1.8 Predicate logic that defines a sister relationship

We have already seen that mathematical (or Boolean) logic has played a vital role in design of logic circuits which forms the basis of any computer system. Therefore, in logic-oriented programming languages, a more advanced construct called predicate logic is used. In these languages, different logical assertions about a situation are made, establishing all known facts. Then queries are made and any deducible solution to the query is returned as output. The role of the computer in this paradigm is thus to maintain data and make logical deductions.

There are two main advantages of using logic-oriented programming. First, the computer solves the problem so the programs are of minimum statements and complexity. Second, the validity of the solution can easily proved.

1.5.4 Object-Oriented Programming

We have seen that unstructured and structured programming paradigms are basically task-based as they focus on the actions the software should accomplish. However, the object-oriented paradigm is task-based and data-based. In the object-oriented paradigm, all the relevant data and tasks are grouped together in entities known as *objects*.

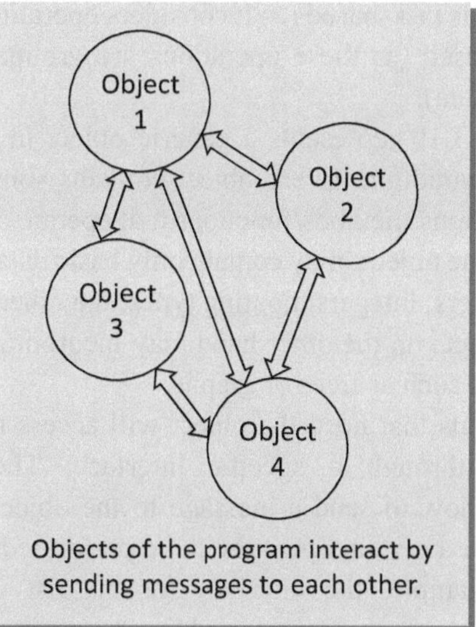

Figure 1.9 Object-oriented paradigm

For example, consider a list of numbers stored in an array. The procedural or modular programming paradigm considers this list as merely a collection of data. Any program that accesses this list must have some procedures/functions to process this list. For example, to find the largest number or to sort the numbers in the list, we needed specific procedures/functions to do the task. Thus, the list is passive entity as it is maintained by a controlling program rather than having the responsibility of maintaining itself.

However, in the object-oriented paradigm, the list and the associated operations are treated as one entity known as an *object*. So, in the object-oriented approach, the list is considered an object consisting of the list together with a collection of routines for manipulating the list. In the list object, there may be routines for adding a number to the list, deleting a number from the list, sorting the list, etc.

The striking difference with traditional approaches is that the program accessing this list does not need to contain procedures for performing tasks rather it uses the routines provided in the object. So in other words, instead of sorting the list as in the procedural paradigm, the program asks the list to sort itself.

Therefore, we can conclude that the object-oriented paradigm is task-based (as it considers operations) as well as data-based (as these operations are grouped with the relevant data).

Figure 1.10 represents a generic object in the object-oriented paradigm. Every object contains some data and the operations/methods/functions that operate on that data. While some objects may contain only basic data types such as characters, integers, floating types, the other object, the other objects on the other hand may incorporate complex data types such as trees or graphs.

Programs that need the object will access the object's methods through a specific interface. The interface specifies how to send a message to the object, that is, a request for a certain operation to be performed.

For example, the interface for the list object may require that any message for adding a new number to the list should include the number to be added. Similarly, the interface might also require that any message for sorting specify whether the sort should be ascending or descending. Hence, an interface specifies how messages can be sent to the object.

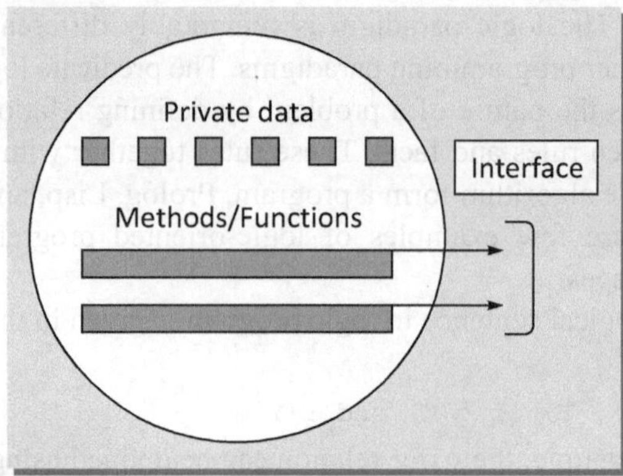

Figure 1.10 Generic Object

OOP is used for simulating real world problems on computers because real world is made of objects.

POINTS TO NOTE

- A computer has two parts—computer hardware which does all the physical work and the computer software which tells the hardware what to do and how to do it.
- A program is a set of instructions that is arranged in a sequence to guide a computer to find a solution for the given problem. The process of writing a program is called programming.
- Computer software is written by computer programmers using a programming language.
- Application software is designed to solve a particular problem for users.
- System software represents programs that allow the hardware to run properly. System software acts as an interface between the hardware of the computer and the application software that users need to run on the computer.
- The key role of the BIOS is to load and start the operating system. The code in the BIOS chip runs a series of tests called POST (Power On Self Test) to ensure that the system devices are working correctly. BIOS is stored on a ROM chip built into the system.
- Utility software is used to analyse, configure, optimize, and maintain the computer system.
- A compiler is a special type of program that transforms source code written in a programming language (the *source language*) into machine language comprising of just two digits—1s and 0s (the *target language)*. The resultant code in 1s and 0s is known as the object code.
- Linker is a program that combines object modules to form an executable program.
- A loader is a special type of program that copies programs from a storage device to main memory, where they can be executed.

EXERCISES

Fill in the Blanks

1. _______ tells the hardware what to do and how to do it.
2. The hardware needs a _______ to instruct what has to be done.
3. The process of writing a program is called _______.
4. _______ is used to write computer software.
5. _______ transforms the source code into binary language.

EXERCISES

6. ________ allows a computer to interact with additional hardware devices such as printers, scanners, and video cards.
7. ________ helps in coordinating system resources and allows other programs to execute.
8. ________ provides a platform for running application software.
9. ________ can be used to encrypt and decrypt files.
10. An assembly language statement consists of a ________, an ________, and ________.

Multiple Choice Questions

1. BIOS is stored in
   (a) RAM (b) ROM
   (c) Hard disk (d) None of these
2. Which language should not be used for organizing large programs?
   (a) C (b) C++
   (c) COBOL (d) FORTRAN
3. Which language is a symbolic language?
   (a) Machine language (b) C
   (c) Assembly language (d) All of these
4. Which language is a 3GL?
   (a) C (b) COBOL
   (c) FORTRAN (d) All of these
5. Which language does not need any translator?
   (a) Machine language (b) 3GL
   (c) Assembly language (d) 4GL
6. Choose the odd one out.
   (a) Compiler (b) Interpreter
   (c) Assembler (d) Linker
7. Which one is a utility software?
   (a) Word processor
   (b) Antivirus
   (c) Desktop publishing tool
   (d) Compiler
8. POST is performed by
   (a) Operating system (b) Assembler
   (c) BIOS (d) Linker
9. Printer, monitor, keyboard, and mouse are examples of
   (a) Operating system
   (b) Computer hardware
   (c) Firmware
   (d) Device drivers
10. Windows VISTA, Linux, Unix are examples of
   (a) Operating system
   (b) Computer hardware
   (c) Firmware
   (d) Device drivers

State True or False

1. Computer hardware does all the physical work.
2. The computer hardware cannot think and make decisions on its own.
3. A software is a set of instructions that is arranged in a sequence to guide a computer to find a solution for the given problem.
4. Word processor is an example of educational software.
5. Desktop publishing system is a system software.
6. BIOS defines firmware interface.
7. Pascal cannot be used for writing well-structured programs.
8. Assembly language is a low-level programming language.
9. Operation code is used to identify and reference instructions in the program.
10. 3GLs are procedural languages.

Review Questions

1. Broadly classify the computer system into two parts. Also make a comparison between a human body and the computer system thereby explaining what each part does.
2. Differentiate between computer hardware and software.
3. Define programming.
4. Define source code.
5. What is booting?
6. What criteria is used to select the language in which the program will be written?
7. Explain the role of operating system.
8. Give some examples of computer software.
9. Differentiate between the source code and the object code.
10. Why are compilers and interpreters used?
11. Is there any difference between a compiler and an interpreter?

EXERCISES

12. What is application software? Give examples.
13. What is BIOS?
14. What do you understand by utility software? Is it a must to have it?
15. Differentiate between syntax errors and logical errors.
16. Can a program written in a high-level language be execute without a linker?
17. Give a brief description of generation of programming languages. Highlight the advantages and disadvantages of languages in each generation.

CHAPTER 2

Introduction to C

Takeaways

- Writing a C Program
- Keywords
- I/O Statements
- Compiling and Executing C Programs
- Identifiers
- Operators
- Basic Data Types
- Variables and Constants
- Type Conversion and Typecasting

2.1 INTRODUCTION

The programming language C was developed in the early 1970s by Dennis Ritchie at Bell Laboratories to be used by the UNIX operating system. It was named 'C' because many of its features were derived from an earlier language called 'B'. Although C was designed for implementing system software, it was later on widely used for developing portable application software.

C is one of the most popular programming languages. It is being used on several different software platforms. In a nutshell, there are a few computer architectures for which a C compiler does not exist.

It is a good idea to learn C because it has been around for a long time which means there is a lot of information available on it. Quite a few other programming languages such as C++ and Java are also based on C which means you will be able to learn them more easily in the future.

2.1.1 Background

Like many other modern languages, C is derived from ALGOL (the first language to use a block structure). Although ALGOL was not accepted widely in the United States but it was widely used in Europe. ALGOL's introduction in the 1960s led the way for the development of structured programming concepts.

Before C, several other programming languages were developed. For example, in 1967 Martin Richards developed a language called BCPL (Basic Combined Programming Language). BCPL was basically a type-less (had no concept of data types) language which facilitated the user with direct access of memory. This made it useful for system programmers. Then in 1970, Ken Thompson developed a language called B. B was used to develop the first version of UNIX. C was developed by Dennis Ritchie in 1972 that took concepts from ALGOL, BCPL, and B. In addition to the concepts of these languages, C also supports the concept of data types. Since UNIX operating system was also developed at Bell Laboratories along with C language, C and UNIX are strongly associated with each other.

For many years, C was mainly used in academic institutions, but with the release of different C compilers for commercial use and popularity of UNIX, C was widely accepted by computer professionals.

C (also known as Traditional C) was documented and popularized in the book *The C Programming Language* by Brian W. Kernighan and Dennis Ritchie in 1978. This book was so popular that the language came to be known as 'K&R C'. The tremendous growth of C language resulted in the development of different versions of the language that were similar but incompatible with each other. Therefore, in the year 1983, the American National

Standards Institute (ANSI) started working on defining the standard for C. This standard was approved in December 1989 and came to be known as ANSI C. In 1990, the International Standards Organization (ISO) adopted the ANSI standard. This version of C came to be known as C89. In 1995, some minor changes were made to C89, the new modified version was known as C95. Figure 2.1 shows the taxonomy of C language. During 1990s C++ and Java programming languages became popular among the users so the standardization committee of C felt that a few features of C++/Java if added to C would enhance its usefulness. So, in 1999 when some significant changes were made to C95, the modified version came to be known as C99. Some of the changes made in the C99 version are as follows:

- Extension to the character types, so that they can support even non-English characters
- Boolean data type
- Extension to the integer data type
- Including type definitions in the `for` statement
- Inclusion of imaginary and complex types
- Addition of //, better known as C++ style line comment

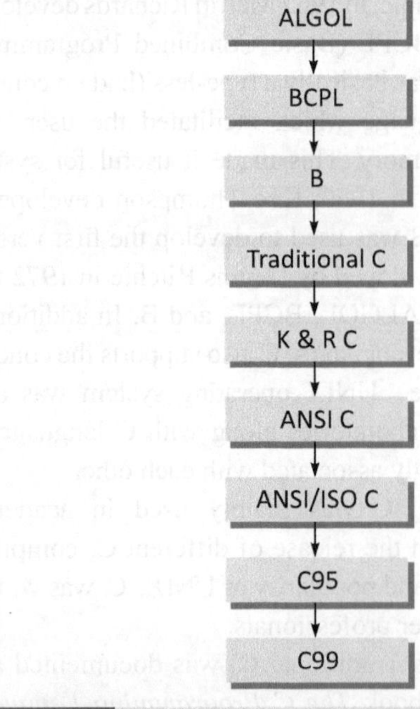

Figure 2.1 Taxonomy of C language

2.1.2 Characteristics of C

C is a robust language whose rich set of built-in functions and operators can be used to write complex programs. The C compiler combines the features of assembly language and high-level language which makes it best suited for writing system software as well as business packages. Some basic characteristics of C language that define the language and have led to its popularity as a programming language are listed below. In this book we will learn all these aspects.

- A high-level programming language enables the programmer to concentrate on the problem at hand and not worry about the machine code on which the program would be run.
- Small size—C has only 32 keywords. This makes it relatively easy to learn as compared to other languages.
- Makes extensive use of function calls.
- C is well suited for structured programming. In this programming approach, C enables the users to think of problem in terms of functions/modules where the collection of all the modules makes up a complete program. This feature facilitates easiness in program debugging, testing, and maintenance.
- Unlike PASCAL it supports loose typing (as a character can be treated as an integer and vice versa).
- Structured language as the code can be organized as a collection of one or more functions.
- Stable language. ANSI C was created in 1983 and since then it has not been revised.
- Quick language: as a well written C program is likely to be as quick as or quicker than a program written in any other language. Since C programs make use of operators and data types, they are fast and efficient. For example, a program written to increment a value from 0–15000 using BASIC would take 50 seconds whereas a C program would do the same in just 1 second.
- Facilitates low level (bitwise) programming.
- Supports pointers to refer computer memory, array, structures, and functions.
- Core language. C is a core language as many other programming languages (such as C++, Java, Perl, etc.) are based on C. If you know C, learning other computer languages becomes much easier.
- C is a portable language, i.e., a C program written for one computer can be run on another computer with little or no modification.
- C is an extensible language as it enables the user to add his own functions to the C library.

- C is often treated as the second best language for any given programming task. While the best language depends on the particular task to be performed, the second best language, on the other hand, will always be C.

2.1.3 Uses of C

C is a very simple language that is widely used by software professionals around the globe. The uses of C language can be summarized as follows.

- C language is primarily used for system programming. The portability, efficiency, the ability to access specific hardware addresses and low runtime demand on system resources makes it a good choice for implementing operating systems and embedded system applications.
- C has been so widely accepted by professionals that compilers, libraries, and interpreters of other programming languages are often implemented in C.
- For portability and convenience reasons, C is sometimes used as an intermediate language for implementations of other languages. Examples of compilers who use C this way are BitC, Gambit, the Glasgow Haskell Compiler, Squeak, and Vala.
  Basically, C was designed as a programming language and was not meant to be used as a compiler target language. Therefore, although C can be used as an intermediate language it is not an ideal option. This led to the development of C-based intermediate languages such as C--.
- C is widely used to implement end-user applications.

2.2 STRUCTURE OF C PROGRAM

C program is composed of preprocessor commands, a global declaration section, and one or more functions (Fig. 2.2).

The preprocessor directives contain special instructions that indicate how to prepare the program for compilation. One of the most important and commonly used preprocessor commands is *include* which tells the compiler that to execute the program, some information is needed from the specified header file.

In this section we will omit the global declaration part and will revisit it in Chapter 7.

A C program contains one or more functions, where a function is defined as a group of C statements that are executed together. The statements in a C program are written in a logical sequence to perform a specific task. The `main()` function is the most important function and is a part of every C program. The execution of a C program begins at this function.

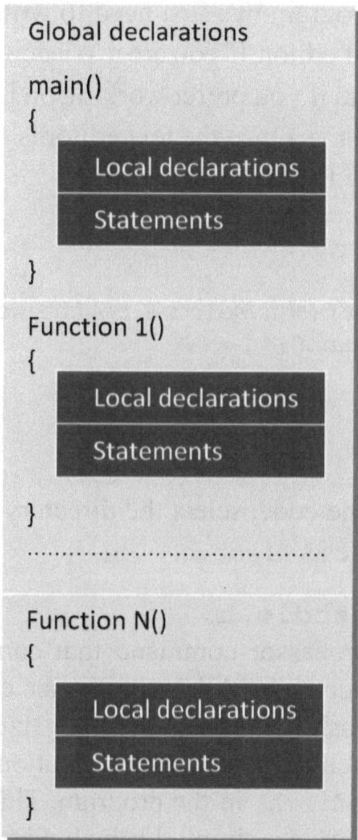

Figure 2.2 Structure of a C program

All functions (including `main()`) are divided into two parts—the declaration section and the statement section. The declaration section precedes the statements section and is used to describe the data that will be used in the function. Note that data declared within a function are known as local declaration as that data will be visible only within that function. Stated in other terms, the life-time of the data will be only till the function ends. The statement section in a function contains the code that manipulates the data to perform a specified task.

From the structure given above we can conclude that a C program can have any number of functions depending on the tasks that have to be performed and each function can have any number of statements arranged according to specific meaningful sequence.

Programmers can choose any name for the functions. It is not mandatory to write `Function1`, `Function2`, etc., but with an exception that every program must contain one function that has its name as `main()`.

2.3 WRITING THE FIRST C PROGRAM

To write a C program, we first need to write the code. For this, open a text editor. If you are a Windows user you may use Notepad and if you prefer working on UNIX/Linux you can use emacs or vi. Once the text editor is opened on your screen, type the following statements:

```
#include <stdio.h>
    int main()
    {
        printf("\n Welcome to the world of C ");
        return 0;
    }
```

Output

```
Welcome to the world of C
```

After writing the code, select the directory of your choice and save the file as `first.c`.

`#include <stdio.h>`

This is a preprocessor command that comes as the first statement in our code. All preprocessor commands start with symbol hash (#). The `#include` statement tells the compiler to include the standard input/output library or header file (`stdio.h`) in the program. This file has some in-built functions. So simply by including this file in our code we can use these functions directly. The standard input/output header file contains functions for input and output of data like reading values from the keyboard and printing the results on the screen.

`int main()`

Every program contains a `main()` function which is the starting point of the program. `int` is the return value of the main function. After all the statements in the program have been written, the last statement of the program will return an integer value to the operating system. The concepts will be clear to us when we read the chapter on Functions. So even if you do not understand certain things, do not worry.

Programming Tip: If you do not place a parenthesis after 'main', a compiler error will be generated.

{ } The two curly brackets are used to group all the related statements of the function `main`. All the statements between the braces form the function body. The function body contains a set of instructions to perform the given task.

`printf("\n Welcome to the world of C ");`

The `printf` function is defined in the `stdio.h` file and is used to print text on the screen. The message that has to be displayed on the screen is enclosed within double quotes and put inside brackets.

Programming Tip: Placing a semi-colon after the parenthesis of main will generate a compiler error.

The message is quoted because in C a text (also known as a string or a sequence of characters) is always put between inverted commas. The `'\n'` is an escape sequence and represents a `newline` character. It is used to print the message on a new line on the screen. Like the `newline` character, the other escape sequences supported by C language are shown in Table 2.1.

Table 2.1 Escape sequences

Escape sequence	Purpose	Escape sequence	Purpose
\a	Audible signal	\?	Question mark
\b	Backspace	\\	Back slash
\t	Tab	\'	Single quote
\n	Newline	\"	Double quote
\v	Vertical tab	\0	Octal constant
\f	New page\ Clear screen	\x	Hexadecimal constant
\r	Carriage return		

Note Escape sequences are actually non-printing control characters that begin with a backslash (\).

`return 0;`

This is a return command that is used to return the value `0` to the operating system to give an indication that there were no errors during the execution of the program.

Every statement in the `main` function ends with a semi-colon (;).

Now that you have written all the statements using the text editor, save the text file as `first.c`. If you are a Windows user then open the command prompt by clicking `Start->Run` and typing 'command' and clicking `Ok`. Using the command prompt, change to the directory in which you had saved your file and then type:

```
C:\>tc first.c
```

In case you are working on UNIX/Linux operating system, then exit the text editor and type

```
$cc first.c -ofirst
```

The -o is for the output file name. If you leave out the -o then the file name a.out is used.

This command is used to compile your C program. If there are any mistakes in the program then the compiler will tell you the mistake you have made and on which line you made it. In case of errors you need to re-open your. c file and correct those mistakes. However, if everything is right then no error(s) will be reported and the compiler will create an exe file for your program. This .exe file can be directly run by typing

```
'hello.exe' for Windows and './hello' for
   UNIX/Linux operating system.
```

When you run the exe file, the output of the program will be displayed on screen. That is,

```
Welcome to the world of C
```

Note: The printf and return statements have been indented or moved away from the left side. This is done to make the code more readable.

2.4 FILES USED IN C PROGRAM

Every C program has four kinds of files associated with it (Fig. 2.3). These include:

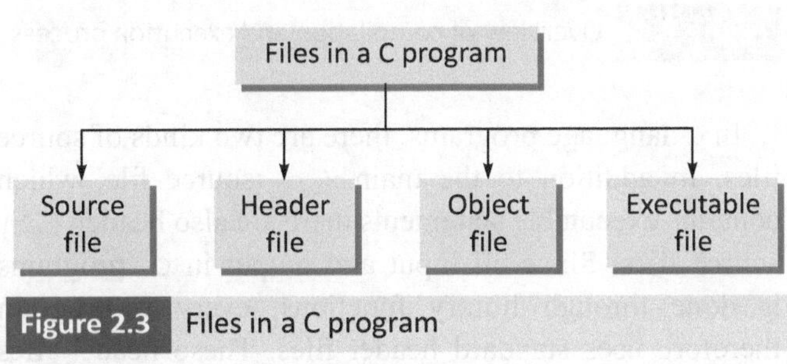

Figure 2.3 Files in a C program

2.4.1 Source Code File

The source code file contains the source code of the program. The file extension of any c source code file is '.c'. This file contains c source code that defines the *main* function and maybe other functions. The main() is the starting point of execution when you successfully compile and run the program. A C program in general may include even other source code files (with the file extension.c).

2.4.2 Header Files

When working with large projects, it is often desirable to separate out certain sub routines from the main() of the program. There also may be a case that the same subroutine has to be used in different programs. In the latter case, one option is to copy the code of the desired sub-routine from one program to another. But copying the code is often tedious as well as error prone and makes maintainability more difficult.

So, another option is to make subroutines and store them in a different file known as header file. The advantage of header files can be realized in the following cases:

- The programmer wants to use the same subroutines in different programs. For this, he simply has to compile the source code of the subroutines once, and then link to the resulting object file in any other program in which the functionalities of these sub-routines are required.
- The programmer wants to change or add subroutines, and have those changes reflected in all the other programs. In this case, he just needs to change the source file for the subroutines, recompile its source code, and then recompile and re-link programs that use them. This way enormous time can be saved as compared to editing the subroutines in every individual program that uses them.

Programming Tip: Missing the inclusion of appropriate header file in the C program will generate an error. Such a program may compile but the linker will give an error message as it will not be able to find the functions used in the program.

Thus, we see that using a header file produces the same results as copying the header file into each source file that needs it. Also when a header file is included, the related declarations appear in only one place. If in future we need to modify the subroutines, we just need to make the changes in one place, and programs that include the header file will automatically use the new version when recompiled later. There is no need to find and change all the copies of the subroutine that has to be changed.

Conventionally, header files names ends with a 'dot h' (.h) extension and its name can use only letters, digits, dashes, and underscores. Although some standard header files are automatically available to c programmers but in addition to those header files, the programmer may have his own user defined header files.

Standard Header Files In all our programs that we had been writing till now, we were using many functions that were not written by us. For example, `strcmp()` function which compares two strings. We just pass string arguments and retrieve the result. We do not know the details of how these functions work. Such functions that are provided by all C compilers are included in standard header files. Examples of these standard header files include:

- `string.h` : for string handling functions
- `stdlib.h` : for miscellaneous functions
- `stdio.h` : for standardized input and output functions
- `math.h` : for mathematical functions
- `alloc.h` : for dynamic memory allocation
- `conio.h` : for clearing the screen

All the header files are referenced at the start of the source code file that uses one or more functions from that file.

2.4.3 Object Files

Object files are generated by the compiler as a result of processing the source code file. Object files contain compact binary code of function definitions. Linker uses this object file to produce an executable file (`.exe` file) by combining the object files together. Object files have a `'.o'` extension, although some operating systems including Windows and MS-DOS have a `'.obj'` extension for the object file.

2.4.4 Binary Executable File

The binary executable file is generated by the linker. The linker links the various object files to produce a binary file that can be directly executed. On Windows operating system, the executable files have `'.exe'` extension.

2.5 COMPILING AND EXECUTING C PROGRAMS

C is a compiled language. So once the C program is written, you must run it through a C compiler that can create an executable file to be run by the computer. While the C program is human-readable, the executable file on the other hand, is a machine-readable file available in an executable form.

The mechanical part of running a C program begins with one or more program source files, and ends with an executable file, which can be run on a computer.

The programming process starts with creating a source file that consists of the statements of the program written in C language. This source file usually contains ASCII characters and can be produced with a text editor, such as Windows notepad, or in an Integrated Design Environment.

The source file is then processed by a special program called a compiler.

Every programming language has its own compiler.

The compiler translates the source code into an object code. The object code contains the machine instructions for the CPU, and calls to the operating system API (Application Programming Interface).

However, even the object file is not an executable file. Therefore, in the next step, the object file is processed with another special program called a linker. While there is a different compiler for every individual language, the same linker is used for object files regardless of the original language in which the new program was written. The output of the linker is an executable or runnable file. The process is shown in Fig. 2.4.

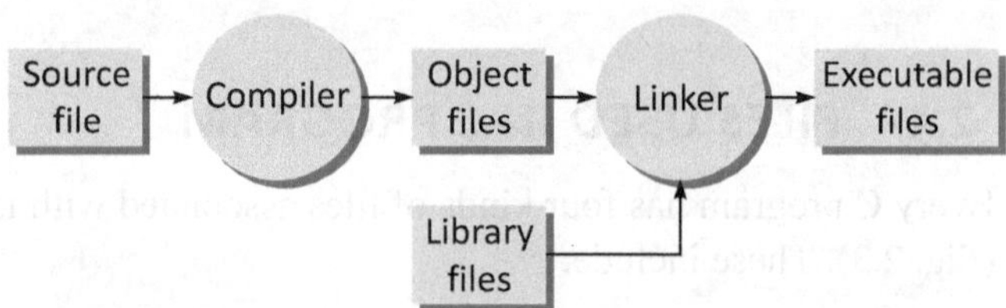

Figure 2.4 Overview of compilation and execution process

In `C` language programs, there are two kinds of source files. In addition to the main (`.c`) source file, which contains executable statements there are also header (`.h`) source files. Since all input and output in `C` programs is done through library functions, every C program therefore uses standard header files. These header files should be written as part of the source code for modular C programs.

The compilation process shown in Fig. 2.5 is done in two steps. In the first step, the preprocessor program reads the source file as text, and produces another text file as output. Source code lines which begin with the # symbol are actually not written in `C` but in the preprocessor language. The output of the preprocessor is a text file which does not contain any preprocessor statements. This file is ready to be processed by the compiler. The linker

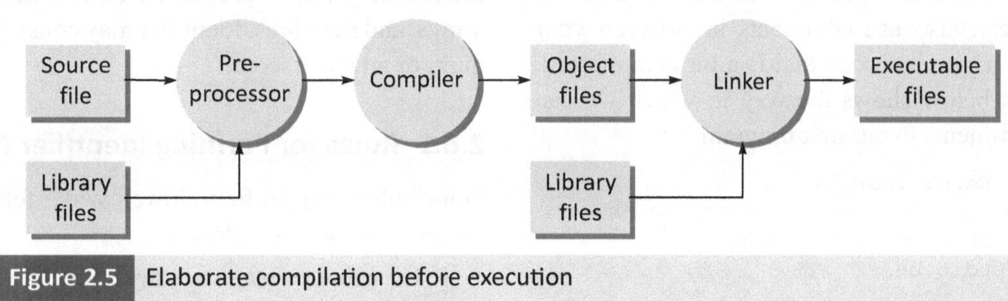

Figure 2.5 Elaborate compilation before execution

combines the object file with library routines (supplied with the compiler) to produce the final executable file.

In modular programming the source code is divided into two or more source files. All these source files are compiled separately thereby producing multiple object files. These object files are combined by the linker to produce an executable file (Fig. 2.6).

2.6 USING COMMENTS

Many a time the meaning or the purpose of the program code is not clear to the reader. Therefore, it is a good programming practice to place some comments in the code to help the reader understand the code clearly. Comments are just a way of explaining what a program does. It is merely an internal program documentation. The compiler ignores the comments when forming the object file. This means that the comments are non-executable statements. C supports two types of commenting.

- // is used to comment a single statement. This is known as a *line comment*. A line comment can be placed anywhere on the line and it does not require to be specifically ended as the end of the line automatically *ends the line*.
- /* is used to comment multiple statements. A /* is ended with */ and all statements that lie within these characters are commented. This type of comment is known as *block comment*.

Note that commented statements are not executed by the compiler. Rather, they are ignored by the compiler as they are simply added in the program to make the code understandable by the programmer as well as other people who read it. It is a good habit to always put a comment at the top of a program that tells you what the program does. This will help in defining the usage of the program the moment you open it.

Programming Tip:
Not putting the */ after the termination of the block comment is a compiler error.

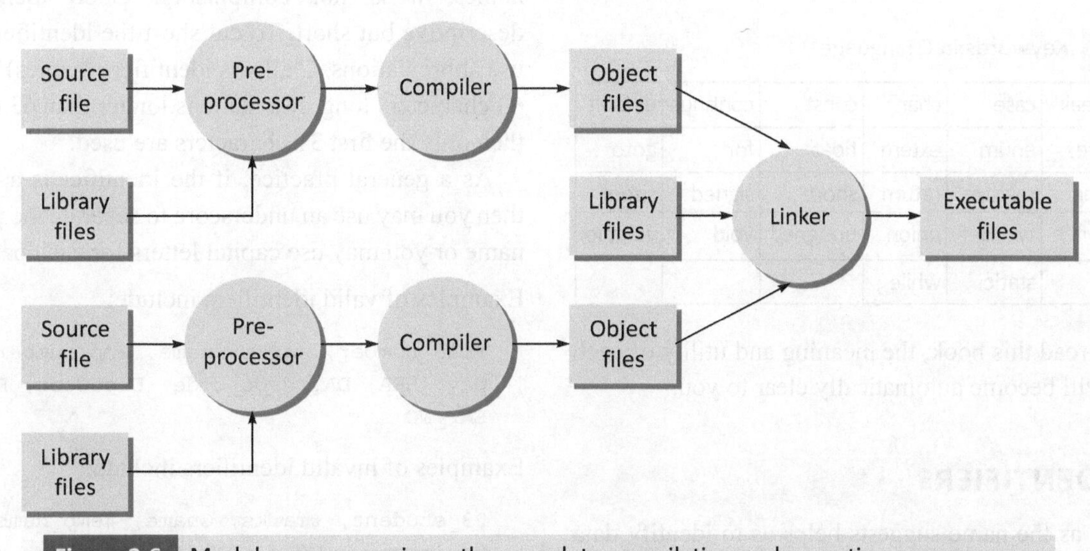

Figure 2.6 Modular programming—the complete compilation and execution process

Commented statements can be used anywhere in the program. You can also use comments in between your code to explain a piece of code that is a bit complicated. The code given below shows the way in which we can make use of comments in our first program.

```
/* Author: Reema Thareja
   Description: To print 'Welcome to the
     world of C' on the screen */
#include <stdio.h>
int main()
{
   printf("\n Welcome to the world of C ");
     // prints message
   return 0; // returns a value 0 to the
     operating system
}
```

Output

```
Welcome to the world of C
```

Since comments are not executed by the compiler, they do not affect the execution speed and the size of the compiled program. Therefore, use comments liberally in your programs so that other users can understand the operations of the program and will serve as an aid to debugging and testing.

2.7 KEYWORDS

Like every computer language, C has a set of reserved words often known as keywords that cannot be used as an identifier. All keywords are basically a sequence of characters that have a fixed meaning. By convention all keywords must be written in lowercase (small) letters. Table 2.2 contains a list of keywords in C.

Table 2.2 Keywords in C language

auto	break	case	char	const	continue	default
double	else	enum	extern	float	for	goto
int	long	register	return	short	signed	sizeof
struct	switch	typedef	union	unsigned	void	volatile
do	if	static	while			

When you read this book, the meaning and utility of each keyword will become automatically clear to you.

2.8 IDENTIFIERS

Identifiers, as the name suggests helps us to identify data and other objects in the program. Identifiers are basically the names given to program elements such as variables, arrays, and functions. Identifier may consist of an alphabet, digit, or an underscore.

2.8.1 Rules for Forming Identifier Names

Some rules have to be followed while forming identifier names. They are as follows:

- It cannot include any special characters or punctuation marks (like `#`, `$`, `^`, `?`, `.`, etc.) except the underscore `'_'`.
- There cannot be two successive underscores.
- Keywords cannot be used as identifiers.
- The case of alphabetic characters that form the identifier name is significant. For example, `"FIRST"` is different from `'first'` and `'First'`.
- The identifier name must begin with an alphabet or an underscore. However, use of underscore as the first character must be avoided because several compiler-defined identifiers in the standard C library have underscore as their first character. Hence, inadvertently duplicated names may cause definition conflicts.
- Identifiers can be of any reasonable length. They should not contain more than 31 characters. It can actually be longer than 31, but the compiler looks at only the first 31 characters of the name.

Programming Tip: C is a case sensitive language. If you type printf function as Printf, then an error will be generated.

Although it is a good practice to use meaningful identifier names, it is not compulsory. Good identifiers are descriptive but short. To cut short the identifier, you may use abbreviations. C allows identifiers (names) to be up to 63 characters long. If a name is longer than 63 characters, then only the first 31 characters are used.

As a general practice, if the identifier is a little long, then you may use an underscore to separate the parts of the name or you may use capital letters for each part.

Examples of valid identifiers include:

```
roll_number, marks, name, emp_number, basic_
pay, HRA, DA, dept_code, DeptCode, RollNo,
EMP_NO
```

Examples of invalid identifiers include:

```
23_student, %marks, @name, #emp_number,
basic.pay, -HRA, (DA), &dept_code, auto
```

C is a case-sensitive language. Therefore rno, Rno, RNo, RNO are considered as different identifiers.

2.9 BASIC DATA TYPES IN C

Data types determine the set of values that a data item can take and the operations that can be performed on the item. C language provides very few basic data types. Table 2.3 lists the data type, their size, range, and usage for a C programmer on a 16-bit computer. Table 2.3 shows the basic data types. In addition to this, we also have variants of `int` and `float` data types.

The char data type is one byte and is used to store single characters. Note that C does not provide any data type for storing text. This is because text is made up of individual characters.

You will be surprised to see that the range of char is given as –128 to 127. The char is supposed to store characters not numbers, so why this range? The answer is that, in memory characters are stored in their ASCII codes. For example, the character `'A'` has the ASCII code 65. In memory we will not store `'A'` but `65` (in binary number format).

Table 2.3 Basic data types in C

Data type	Keyword used	Size in bytes	Range	Use
Character	char	1	–128 to 127	To store characters
Integer	int	2	–32768 to 32767	To store integer numbers
Floating Point	float	4	3.4E–38 to 3.4E+38	To store floating point numbers
Double	double	8	1.7E–308 to 1.7E+308	To store big floating point numbers
Valueless	void	0	Valueless	—

Table 2.4 shows the variants of basic data types in detail.

In Table 2.4, we have `unsigned char` and `signed char`. Do we have negative characters?—no, then why do we have such data types? The answer is that we use signed and unsigned char to ensure portability of programs that store non-character data as char.

While the smaller data types take less memory, the larger types incur a performance penalty. Although the data type we use for our variables does not have a big impact on the speed or memory usage of the application, but we should always try to use `int` unless there is a special need to use any other data type.

Table 2.4 Detailed list of data types

Data type	Size in bytes	Range
char	1	–128 to 127
unsigned char	1	0 to 255
signed char	1	–128 to 127
int	2	–32768 to 32767
unsigned int	2	0 to 65535
signed short int	2	–32768 to 32767
signed int	2	–32768 to 32767
short int	2	–32768 to 32767
unsigned short int	2	0 to 65535
long int	4	–2147483648 to 2147483647
unsigned long int	4	0 to 4294967295
signed long int	4	–2147483648 to 2147483647
float	4	3.4E–38 to 3.4E+38
double	8	1.7E–308 to 1.7E+308
long double	10	3.4E–4932 to 1.1E+4932

When the basic data type is omitted from a declaration, then automatically type `int` is assumed. For example, `longvar; //` `int` is implied.

Last but not the least the void type holds no value. It is primarily used in three cases:

- To specify the return type of a function (when the function returns no value)
- To specify the parameters of the function (when the function accepts no arguments from the caller)
- To create generic pointers. We will read about generic pointers in the chapter on Pointers.

We will discuss the `void` data type in detail in the coming chapters.

Unsigned int/char keeps the sign bit free and makes the entire word available for storage of the non-negative numbers.

Sign bit is the leftmost bit of a memory word which is used to determine the sign of the content stored in that word. When it is 0, the value is positive and when it is 1, the value is negative.

2.9.1 How are Float and Double Stored?

In computer memory, float and double values are stored in mantissa and exponent forms where the exponent represents power of 2 (not 10). The number of bytes used to represent a floating point number generally depends on the precision of the value. While float is used to declare single-precision values, double is used to represent double-precision values.

Floating-point numbers use the IEEE (Institute of Electrical and Electronics Engineers) format to represent mantissa and exponents. According to the IEEE format, a floating point value in its binary form is known as a *normalized form*. In the normalized form, the exponent is adjusted in such a way that the binary point in the mantissa always lies to the right of the most significant non-zero digit.

Example Convert the floating point number 5.32 into an IEEE normalized form.

2	5	R
2	2	1
2	1	0
	0	1

Write the remainders in the reverse order of generation

$0.32 \times 2 = 0.64$	0
$0.64 \times 2 = 1.28$	1
$0.28 \times 2 = 0.56$	0
$0.56 \times 2 = 1.12$	1

Write the whole numbers in the same order of generation

Thus, the binary equivalent of 5.32 = 101.0101.
The normalized form of this binary number is obtained by adjusting the exponent until the decimal point is to the right of the most significant 1.
Therefore, the normalized binary equivalent = 1.010101×2^2.

Moreover, the IEEE format for storing floating point numbers uses a sign bit, mantissa, and the exponent (Fig. 2.7). The sign bit denotes the sign of the value. If the value is positive, the sign bit contains 0 and in case the value is negative it stores 1.

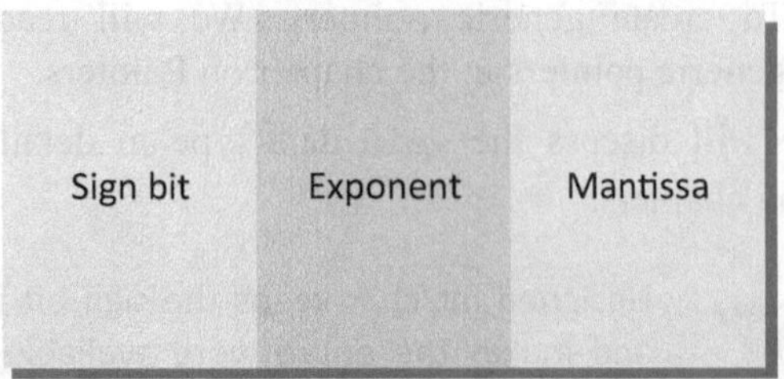

Figure 2.7 IEEE format for storing floating point numbers

Generally, exponent is an integer value stored in unsigned binary format after adding a positive bias. In other words, because exponents are stored in an unsigned form, the exponent is biased by half its possible value. For type float, the bias is 127; for type double, it is 1023. You can compute the actual exponent value by subtracting the bias value from the exponent value. Finally, the normalized binary equivalent is stored in such a way that lower byte is stored at higher memory address. For example, ABCD is actually stored as DCBA.

2.10 VARIABLES

A *variable* is defined as a meaningful name given to the data storage location in computer memory. When using a variable, we actually refer to address of the memory where the data is stored. C language supports two basic kinds of variables—numeric and character.

2.10.1 Numeric Variables

Numeric variables can be used to store either integer values or floating point values. While an integer value is a whole number without a fraction part or decimal point a floating point value can have a decimal point.

Numeric variables may also be associated with modifiers like short, long, signed, and unsigned. The difference between signed and unsigned numeric variables is that signed variables can be either negative or positive but unsigned variables can only be positive. Therefore, by using an unsigned variable we can increase the maximum positive range. When we do not specify the signed/unsigned modifier, C language automatically takes it as a signed variable. To declare an unsigned variable, the unsigned modifier must be explicitly added during the declaration of the variable.

2.10.2 Character Variables

Character variables are just single characters enclosed within single quotes. These characters could be any character from the ASCII character set—letters ('a', 'A'), numerals ('2'), or special characters ('&'). In C, a number that is given in single quotes is not the same as a number without them. This is because 2 is treated as an integral value but '2' is a considered character not an integer.

2.10.3 Declaring Variables

Each variable to be used in the program must be declared. To declare a variable, specify the data type of the variable followed by its name. The data type indicates the kind of data that the variable will store. Variable names should always be meaningful and must reflect the purpose of their usage in the program. The memory location of the variable is of importance to the compiler only and not to the programmer. Programmers must only be concerned with accessing data through their symbolic names. In C, variable declaration always ends with a semicolon, for example:

```
int emp_num;
float salary;
char grade;
double balance_amount;
unsigned short int acc_no;
```

In C variables can be declared at any place in the program but two things must be kept in mind. First, variables should be declared before using them. Second, variables should be declared closest to their first point of use to make the source code easier to maintain.

C allows multiple variables of the same type to be declared in one statement. So the following statement is absolutely legal in C.

```
float temp_in_celsius, temp_in_farenheit;
```

In C variables are declared at three basic places as follows:

- When a variable is declared inside a function it is known as a *local variable*.
- When a variable is declared in the definition of function parameters it is known as *formal parameter* (we will study this in the chapter on Functions).
- When the variable is declared outside all functions, it is known as a *global variable*.

A variable cannot be of type `void`.

2.10.4 Initializing Variables

While declaring the variables, we can also initialize them with some value. For example,

```
int emp_num = 7;
float salary = 9800.99;
char grade = 'A';
double balance_amount = 100000000;
```

The initializer applies only to the variable defined immediately before it. Therefore, the statement

```
int count, flag = 1;
```

initializes the variable `flag` and not `count`. If you want both the variables to be declared in a single statement then write,

```
int count = 0, flag = 1;
```

When variables are declared but not initialized they usually contain garbage values (there are exceptions to this that we will study later).

2.11 CONSTANTS

Constants are identifiers whose value does not change. Variables can change their value at any time but constants can never change their value. Constants are used to define fixed values like `Pi` or the charge on an electron so that their value does not get changed in the program even by mistake.

A constant is an explicit data value specified by the programmer. The value of the constant is known to the compiler at the compile time. C allows the programmer to specify constants of integer type, floating point type, character type, and string type (Fig. 2.8).

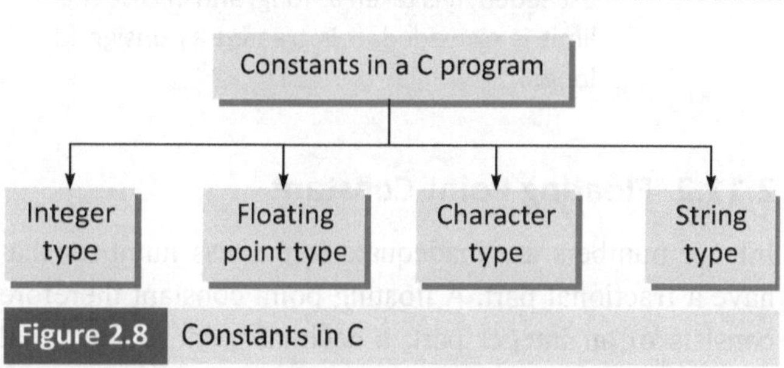

Figure 2.8 Constants in C

2.11.1 Integer Constant

A constant of integer type consists of a sequence of digits. For example, 1, 34, 567, 8907 are valid integer constants. A literal integer like 1234 is of type int by default. For a long integer constant the literal is succeeded with either 'L' or 'l' (like 1234567L). Similarly, an unsigned int literal is written with a 'U' or 'u' suffix (ex, 12U). Therefore, 1234L, 1234l, 1234U, 1234u, 1234LU, 1234ul are all valid integer constants.

Integer literals can be expressed in decimal, octal or hexadecimal notation. By default an integer is expressed in decimal notation. Decimal integers consist of a set of digits, 0 through 9, preceded by an optional – or + sign. Examples of decimal integer constants include: 123, –123, +123, and 0.

While writing integer constants, embedded spaces, commas, and non-digit characters are not allowed. Therefore, integer constants given below are totally invalid in C.

123   456   12,34,567 $123

An integer constant preceded by a zero (0) is an octal number. Octal integers consist of a set of digits, 0 through 7. Examples of octal integers include

012   0   01234

Similarly, an integer constant is expressed in hexadecimal notation if it is preceded with 0x or 0X. Hexadecimal numbers contains digits from 0–9 and alphabets A through F. The alphabets A through F represent numbers 10 through 15. For example, decimal 72 is equivalent to 0110 in octal notation and 0x48 in hexadecimal notation. Examples of hexadecimal integers are 0X12 0x7F 0xABCD 0X1A3B.

In C, a decimal integer constant is treated as an unsigned long if its magnitude exceeds that of signed long. An octal or hexadecimal integer that exceeds the limit of `int` is taken to be unsigned. If even this limit is exceeded, it is taken as long; and in case this limit is exceeded, it is treated as unsigned long.

2.11.2 Floating Point Constant

Integer numbers are inadequate to express numbers that have a fractional part. A floating point constant therefore consists of an integer part, a decimal point, a fractional part, and an exponent field containing an e or E (e means exponent) followed by an integer where the fraction part and integer part are a sequence of digits. However, it is not necessary that every floating point constant must contain all these parts. Some floating point numbers may have certain parts missing. Some valid examples of floating point numbers are: 0.02, –0.23, 123.456, +0.34 123, 0.9, –0.7, +0.8, etc.

A literal like 0.07 is treated as of type double by default. To make it a float type literal, you must specify it using suffix `'F'` or `'f'`. Consider some valid floating point literals given below (Note that suffix `L` is for `long double`).

0.02F   0.34f   3.141592654L   0.002146   2.146E–3

A floating point number may also be expressed in scientific notation. In this notation, the mantissa is either a floating point number or an integer and exponent is an integer with an optional plus or minus sign. Therefore, the numbers given below are valid floating point numbers

0.5e2   14E–2   1.2e+3   2.1E–3   –5.6e–2

Thus, we see that scientific notation is used to express numbers that are either very small or very large. For example,

120000000 = 1.2E8   and   –0.000000025 = –2.5E–8

2.11.3 Character Constant

A character constant consists of a single character enclosed in single quotes. For example, `'a'`, `'@'` are character constants. In computers, characters are stored using machine's character set using ASCII codes. All escape sequences mentioned in Table 2.1 are also character constants.

2.11.4 String Constant

A string constant is a sequence of characters enclosed in double quotes. So `"a"` is not the same as `'a'`. The characters comprising the string constant are stored in successive memory locations. When a string constant is encountered in a C program, the compiler records the address of the first character and appends a null character `('\0')` to the string to mark the end of the string. Thus, length of a string constant is equal to number of characters in the string plus `1` (for the null character). Therefore, the length of string literal `"hello"` is `6`.

2.11.5 Declaring Constants

To declare a constant, precede the normal variable declaration with `const` keyword and assign it a value. For example,

```
const float pi = 3.14;
```

The `const` keyword specifies that the value of `pi` cannot change.

However, another way to designate a constant is to use the pre-processor command `define`. Like other preprocessor commands, `define` is preceded with a # symbol. Although `#define` statements can be placed anywhere in a C program, it is always recommended that these statements be placed at the beginning of the program to make them easy to find and modify at a later stage. Look at the example given below which defines the value of `PI` using define.

```
#define PI 3.14159
#define service_tax 0.12
```

In these examples, the value of `PI` will never change but service tax may change. Whenever the value of the service tax is altered, it can needs to be corrected only in the define statement.

When the preprocessor reformats the program to be compiled by the compiler, it replaces each defined name (such as `PI`, `service_tax`) in the source program with its corresponding value. Hence, it just works like the Find and Replace command available in a text editor.

Let us take a look at some rules that needs to be applied to a `#define` statement which defines a constant.

Rule 1 Constant names are usually written in capital letters to visually distinguish them from other variable names which are normally written in lower case characters. Note that this is just a convention and not a rule.

Rule 2 No blank spaces are permitted in between the # symbol and define keyword.

Rule 3 Blank space must be used between `#define` and constant name and between constant name and constant value.

Rule 4 `#define` is a pre-processor compiler directive and not a statement. Therefore, it does not end with a semi-colon.

2.12 INPUT/OUTPUT STATEMENT IN C

Before going straightaway into performing input and output in C programs let us first understand the concept from scratch. This section deals with the basic understanding of the phenomena involved in accepting input and printing output in C programs.

2.12.1 Streams

A stream acts in two ways. It is the source of data as well as the destination of data. C programs input data and output data from a stream. Streams are associated with a physical device such as the monitor or with a file stored on the secondary memory. C uses two forms of streams—text and binary, as shown in Fig. 2.9.

In a text stream, sequence of characters is divided into lines with each line being terminated with a new-line character `(\n)`. On the other hand, a binary stream contains data values using their memory representation.

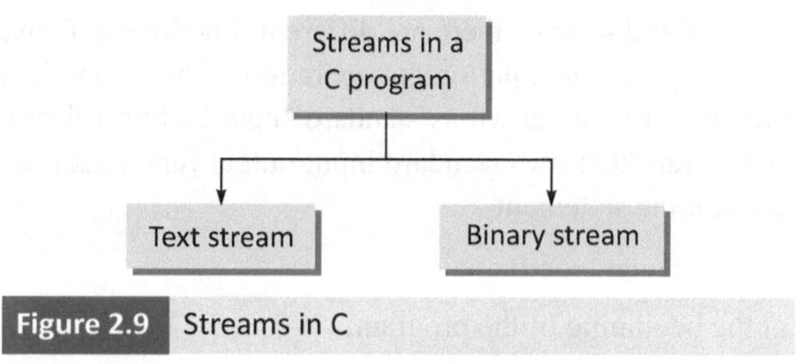

Figure 2.9 Streams in C

We can do input/output from the keyboard/monitor or from any file but in this chapter we will assume that the source of data is the keyboard and destination of the data is the monitor (Fig. 2.10). File handling, i.e., handling input and output via C programs will be discussed later as a separate chapter.

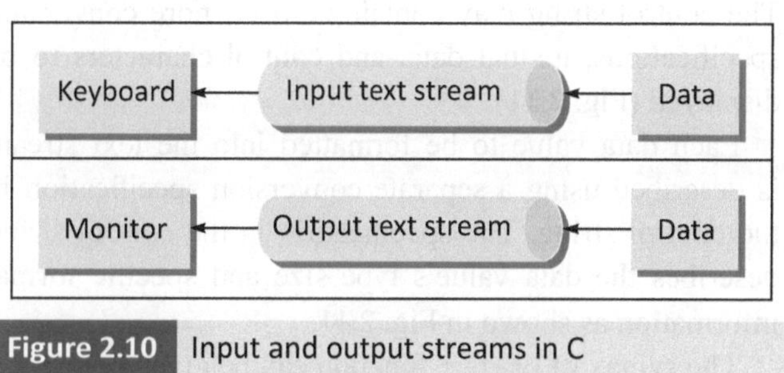

Figure 2.10 Input and output streams in C

2.12.2 Formatting Input/Output

C language supports two formatting functions `printf` and `scanf`. `printf` is used to convert data stored in the program into a text stream for output to the monitor, and `scanf` is used to convert the text stream coming from the keyboard to data values and stores them in program variables. In this section, we will discuss these functions.

Background

The most fundamental operation in a C program is to accept input values to the program from standard input device (keyboard) and output the data produced by the program to a standard output device (monitor). So far we had been assigning values to variables using the assignment operator =. For example,

```
int a = 3;
```

But what if we want to assign value to variable that is inputted by the user at run-time. This is done by using the `scanf` function that reads data from the keyboard. Similarly, for outputting results of the program, `printf` function is used that sends results out to a terminal. Like `printf` and `scanf`, there are different functions in C that can carry out the input/output operations. These functions are collectively known as standard Input/Output Library. A program that uses standard input/output functions must contain the statement

```
#include <stdio.h>
```

at the beginning of the program.

2.12.3 `printf()`

The `printf` function (stands for print formatting) is used to display information required by the user and also prints the values of the variables. For this, the `printf` function takes data values, converts them to a text stream using formatting functions specified in a control string and passes the resulting text stream to the standard output. The control string may contain zero or more conversion specifications, textual data, and control characters to be displayed (Fig. 2.11).

Each data value to be formatted into the text stream is described using a separate conversion specification in the control string. The specification in the control string describes the data value's type size and specific format information as shown in Fig. 2.11.

The syntax of `printf` function can be given as

```
printf ("control string", arg1, arg2, arg3,
    ..., argn);
```

The function accepts two parameters—control string and variable list. The control string may also contain text to be printed like instructions to the user, captions, identifiers, or any other text to make the output readable. In some `printf` statements you may find only a text string that has to be displayed on screen (as seen in the first program that prints `hello world`). The control characters can also be included in the `printf` statement. These control characters include `\n`, `\t`, `\r`, `\a`, etc.

After the control string, the function can have as many arguments as specified in the control string. The parameter control string in the `printf()` is nothing but a C string that contains the text that has to be written on to the standard output device.

Note that there must be enough arguments otherwise, the result will become completely unpredictable. However, if by mistake you specify more number of arguments, the excess arguments will simply be ignored. The prototype of the control string can be as given below.

```
%[flags][width][.precision][length]specifier
```

Each control string must begin with a `%` sign. The `%` character specifies how the next variable in the list of variables has to be printed. After `%` sign follows.

Flags specify output justification such as decimal point, numerical sign, trailing zeros or octal, decimal, or hexadecimal prefixes. Table 2.5 shows the different types of flags with their decription.

Table 2.5 Flags in printf()

Flags	Description
-	Left-justify within the data given field width
+	Displays the data with its numeric sign (either + or –)
#	Used to provide additional specifiers like o, x, X, 0, 0x, or 0X for octal and hexadecimal values, respectively, for values different than zero.
0	The number is left-padded with zeros (0) instead of spaces

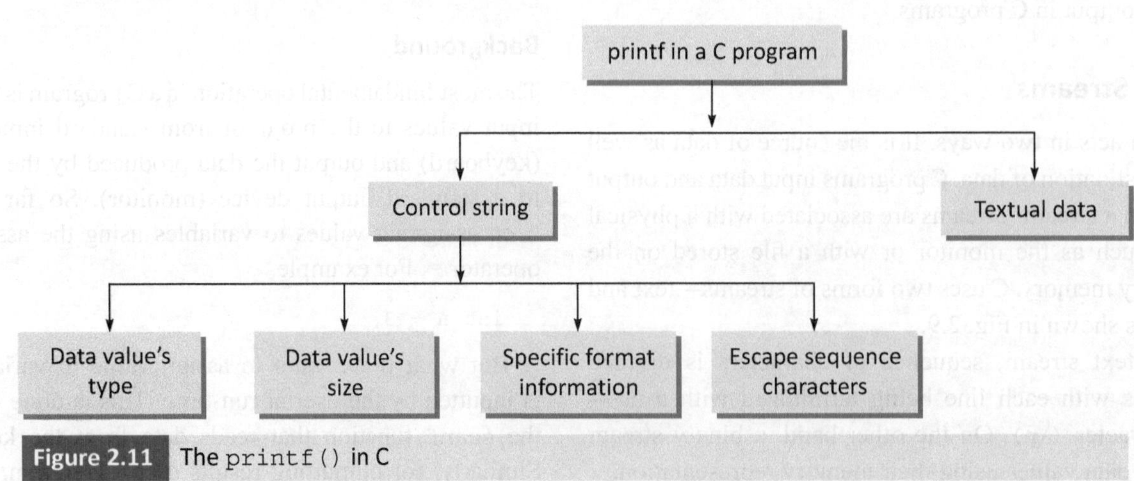

Figure 2.11 The `printf()` in C

Note that when data is shorter than the specified width then by default the data is right justified. To left justify the data use minus sign (–) in the flags field.

When the data value to be printed is smaller than the width specified; then padding is used to fill the unused spaces. By default, the data is padded with blank spaces. If zero is used in the flag field then the data is padded with zeros. One thing to remember here is that zero flag is ignored when used with left justification because adding zeros after a number changes its value.

Width specifies the minimum number of characters to print after being padded with zeros or blank spaces, i.e., it specifies the minimum number of positions in the output. If data needs more space than specified, then `printf` overrides the width specified by the user. Width is a very important field especially when you have to align output in columns. However, if the user does not mention any width then the output will take just enough room for data.

Precision specifies the maximum number of characters to print.

- For integer specifiers (`d, i, o, u, x, X`) : precision flag specifies the minimum number of digits to be written. However, if the value to be written is shorter than this number, the result is padded with leading zeros. Otherwise, if the value is longer, it is not truncated.
- For character strings, precision specifies the maximum number of characters to be printed.
- For floating point numbers, the precision flag specifies the number of decimal places to be printed.

Its format can be given as **.m**, where m specifies the number of decimal digits. When no precision modifier is specified, `printf` prints six decimal positions.

When both width and precision fields are used, width must be large enough to contain the integral value of the number, the decimal point and the number of digits after the decimal point. Therefore, a conversion specification `%7.3f` means print a floating point value of maximum 7 digits where 3 digits are allotted for the digits after the decimal point.

Length field can be explained as given in Table 2.6.

Specifier is used to define the type and the interpretation of the value of the corresponding argument (Table 2.7).

Table 2.6 Length field in `printf()`

Length	Description
h	When the argument is a short int or unsigned short int.
l	When the argument is a long int or unsigned long int for integer specifiers.
L	When the argument is a long double (used for floating point specifiers)

Table 2.7 Specifier field in `printf()`

Type	Qualifying input
c	For single character
d	For decimal values
F	For floating point numbers
E, e	Floating point numbers in exponential format
G, G	Floating point numbers in the shorter of e format
o	For octal number
s	For a sequence of (string of) characters
u	For unsigned decimal value
x, X	For hexadecimal value

Note that if the user specifies a wrong specifier then some strange things will be seen on the screen and the error might propagate to other values in the `printf()` list. The most simple `printf` statement is

```
printf ("Welcome to the world of C
   language");
```

When executed, the function prompts the message enclosed in the quotation to be displayed on the screen.

For `float x = 8900`, the following examples show output under different format specifications:

```
printf ("%f", x);
```

8	9	0	0	.	7	6	8

```
printf ("%10f", x);
```

		8	9	0	0	.	7	6	8

```
printf (%9.2f", x);
```

		8	9	0	0	.	7	7

```
printf ("%6f", x);
```

8	9	0	0	.	7	6	8

```
printf("\n Result: %d%c%f", 12, 'a', 2.3);
Result:12a2.3
printf("\n Result: %d %c %f", 12, 'a', 2.3);
Result:12 a 2.3
printf("\n Result: %d\t%c\t%f", 12, 'a', 2.3);
Result:12   a  2.3
```

```
printf("\n Result: %d\t%c\t%6.2f", 12, 'a',
   245.37154);
```

Result:12 a 245.37

```
printf("\n Result: %5d \t %x \t %#x", 234,
   234, 234);
```

Result: 234 EA 0xEA

```
printf("\n The number is %6d", 12);
```

The number is   12

```
printf("\n The number is %2d", 1234);
```

The number is 1234

```
printf("\n The number is %6d", 1234);
```

The number is   1234

```
printf("\n The number is %-6d", 1234);
```

The number is 1234__ // 2 _ indicates 2 white space

```
printf("\n The number is %06d", 1234);
```

The number is 001234

```
printf("\n The price of this item is %09.2f
   rupees", 123.456);
```

The price of this item is 00123.45 rupees

```
printf("\n This is \'so\' beautiful");
```

This is 'so' beautiful

Programming Tip:
Not placing a comma after the format string in a read or write statement is a compiler error.

```
printf("\n This is \"so\"
beautiful");
```

This is "so" beautiful

```
printf("\n This is \\ so
beautiful ");
```

This is \ so beautiful

```
printf("\n a = |%-+7.2f| b =
   %0+7.2f c = %-0+8.2f", 1.2, 1.2, 1.2);
```

a = +1.20   b = 0001.20 c = 1.20

(Note that in this example, – means left justify, + means display the sign, 7 specifies the width, and 2 specifies the precision.)

```
printf("\n %7.4f \n %7.2f \n %-7.2f \n %f
   \n %10.2e \n %11.4e \n %-10.2e \n %e",
   98.7654, 98.7654, 98.7654, 98.7654,
   98.7654, 98.7654, 98.7654, 98.7654);
```

```
98.7654
  98.77
98.77
98.7654
   9.88e+01
9.8765e+01
9.88e+01
9.876540e+01
```

```
char ch = 'A';
printf("\n %c \n %3c \n %5c", ch, ch, ch);
```

```
A
  A
    A
```

Programming Tip:
Placing an address operator with a variable in the `printf` statement will generate a run-time error.

```
char str[] = "Good Morning";
printf("\n %s", str);
printf("\n %20s", str);
printf("\n %20.10s", str);
printf("\n %.7s", str);
printf("\n %-20.10s", str);
printf("\n %7s", str);
```

```
Good Morning
        Good Morning
          Good Morni
Good Mo
Good Morni
Good Morning
```

(Note that in the last `printf` statement the complete string "Good Morning" is printed. This is because if data needs more space than specified, then `printf` overrides the width specified by the user.)

2.12.4 scanf()

The function `scanf()` stands for scan formatting and is used to read formatted data from the keyboard. The `scanf` function takes a text stream from the keyboard, extracts and formats data from the stream according to a format control string and then stores the data in specified program variables. The syntax of the `scanf()` can be given as,

```
scanf("control string", arg1, arg2, arg3,
………….argn);
```

The minimum field width and precision specifiers are usually constants. However, they may also be provided by arguments to `printf()`. This is done by using the * modifier as shown in the `printf()` statement below.

```
printf("%*.*f", 10, 4, 1234.34);
```

Here, the minimum field width is 10, the precision is 4, and the value to be displayed is 1234.34.

The *control string* specifies the type and format of the data that has to be obtained from the keyboard and stored in the memory locations pointed by the arguments `arg1, arg2,…, argn`, i.e., the arguments are actually the variable addresses where each piece of data are to be stored.

The prototype of the control string can be given as:

```
[=%[*][width][modifiers]type=]
```

Here * is an optional argument that suppresses assignment of the input field, i.e., it indicates that data should be read from the stream but ignored (not stored in the memory location).

Width is an optional argument that specifies the maximum number of characters to be read. However, fewer characters will be read if the `scanf` function encounters a white space or an inconvertible character because the moment scanf encounters a white space character it will stop processing further.

Modifiers is an optional argument that can be `h`, `l`, or fields `L` for the data pointed by the corresponding additional arguments. Modifier **h** is used for `short int` or `unsigned short int`, **l** is used for `long int`, `unsigned long int`, or `double` values. Finally, **L** is used for `long double` data values.

Type specifies the type of data that has to be read. It also indicates how this data is expected to be read from the user. The type specifiers for `scanf` function are given in Table 2.8.

Table 2.8 Type specifiers for `scanf()`

Type	Qualifying input
c	For single character
d	For decimal values
F	For floating point numbers
E, e	Floating point numbers in exponential format
G, G	Floating point numbers in the shorter of e format
o	For octal number
s	For a sequence of (string of) characters
u	For unsigned decimal value
x, X	For hexadecimal value

The `scanf` function ignores any blank spaces, tabs, and new lines entered by the user. The function simply returns the number of input fields successfully scanned and stored.

We will not discuss functions in detail in this chapter. So understanding `scanf` function in depth will be a bit difficult here, but for now just understand that the `scanf` function is used to store values in memory locations associated with variables. For this, the function should have the address of the variables. The address of the variable is denoted by an '&' sign followed by the name of the variable.

Whenever data is read from the keyboard, there is always a return character from a previous read operation. So we should always code at least one white space character in the conversion specification in order to flush that whitespace character. For example, to read two or more data values together in a single scanf statement, we must insert a white space between two fields as shown below:

```
scanf("%d %c", &i, &ch);
```

Now let us quickly summarize the rules to use a `scanf` function in our C programs.

Rule 1: The `scanf` function works until:

(a) the maximum number of characters has been processed,

(b) a white space character is encountered, or

(c) an error is detected.

Rule 2: Every variable that has to be processed must have a conversion specification associated with it. Therefore, the following `scanf` statement will generate an error as `num3` has no conversion specification associated with it.

```
scanf("%d %d", &num1, &num2, &num3);
```

Rule 3: There must be a variable address for each conversion specification. Therefore, the following `scanf` statement will generate an error as no variable address is given for the third conversion specification.

```
scanf("%d %d %d", &num1, &num2);
```

Remember that the ampersand operator `(&)` before each variable name specifies the address of that variable name.

Rule 4: A fatal error would be generated if the format string is ended with a white space character.

Rule 5: The data entered by the user must match the character specified in the control string (except white space or a conversion specification), otherwise an error will be generated and `scanf` will stop its processing. For example, consider the `scanf` statement given below.

```
scanf("%d / %d", &num1, &num2);
```

Here, the slashes in the control string are neither white space characters nor a part of conversion specification, so the users must enter data of the form `21/46`.

Rule 6: Input data values must be separated by spaces.

Rule 7: Any unread data value will be considered as a part of the data input in the next call to scanf.

Rule 8: When the field width specifier is used, it should be large enough to contain the input data size.

Look at the code given below that shows how we input values in variables of different data types.

```
int num;
scanf(" %4d ", &num);
```

The `scanf` function reads a four-digit value into the address or the memory location pointed by `num`.

```
float salary;
scanf(" %f ", &salary);
```

The `scanf` function reads a floating point number (because the type specifier is `%f`) into the address or the memory location pointed by `salary`.

```
char ch;
scanf(" %c ", &ch);
```

The `scanf` function reads a single character (because the type specifier is `%c`) into the address or the memory location pointed by `ch`.

```
char str[10];
scanf(" %s ", str);
```

The `scanf` function reads a string or a sequence of characters (because the type specifier is `%s`) into the address or the memory location pointed by `str`. Note that in case of reading string, we do not use the `&` sign in the `scanf` function. This will be discussed in Chapter 6.

Programming Tip: A compiler error will be generated if the read and write parameters are not separated by commas.

Look at the code given below which combines reading of variables of different data types in one single statement.

```
int num;
float fnum;
char ch;
char str[10];
scanf("%d %f %c %s", &num, &fnum, &ch, str);
```

Look at the `scanf` statement given below for the same code. The statement ignores the character variable and does not store it (as it is preceded by *).

```
scanf("%d %f %*c %s", &num, &fnum, &ch, str);
```

Remember that if an attempt is made to read a value that does not match the expected data type, the `scanf` function will not read any further and would immediately return the values read.

2.12.5 Examples printf/scanf

Look at the code given of below that shows how we output values of variables of different data types.

```
int num;
scanf(" %d ", &num);
printf("%d", num);
```

The `printf` function prints an integer value (because the type specifier is `%d`) pointed by `num` on the screen.

```
float salary;
scanf(" %f ", &salary);
printf(".2%f", salary);
```

The `printf` function prints the floating point number (because the type specifier is `%f`) pointed by salary on the screen. Here, the control string specifies that only two digits must be displayed after the decimal point.

Programming Tip: A float specifier cannot be used to read an integer value.

```
char ch;
scanf(" %c ", &ch);
printf("%c", ch);
```

The `printf` function prints a single character (because the type specifier is `%c`) pointed by ch on the screen.

```
char str[10];
scanf(" %s ", str);
```

The `printf` function prints a string or a sequence of characters (because the type specifier is `%s`) pointed by str on the screen.

```
scanf("%2d %5d", &num1, &num2);
```

The `scanf` statement will read two integer numbers. The first integer number will have two digits while the second can have maximum of 5 digits.

Look at the code given below which combines printing all these variables of different data types in one single statement.

```
int num;
float fnum;
char ch;
char str[10];
double dnum;
```

```
short snum;
long int lnum;
printf("\n Enter the values : ");
scanf("%d %f %c %s %e %hd %ld", &num, &fnum,
   &ch, str, &dnum, &snum, &lnum);
printf("\n num = %d \n fnum = %f \n ch = %c
   \n str = %s \n dnum = %e \n snum = %hd \n
   lnum = %ld", num, fnum, ch, str, dnum,
   snum, lnum);
```

In the printf statement, '\n', is called the newline character and is used to print the succeeding text on the new line. The following output will be generated on execution of the print function.

```
Enter the values
2 3456.443 a abcde 24.321E-2 1 12345678
num = 2
fnum = 3456.44
ch = a
str = abcde
dnum = 0.24321
snum = 1
lnum = 12345678
```

Remember one thing that `scanf` terminates as soon as it encounters a white space character so if your enter the string as `abc def`, then only abc is assigned to `str`.

2.1 Find out the output of the following program.

```
#include <stdio.h>
main()
{
   int a, b;
   printf("\n Enter two four digit numbers : ");
   scanf("%2d %4d", &a, &b);
   printf("\n The two numbers are : %d and
     %d", a, b);
   return 0;
}
```

Output

Programming Tip: Using an incorrect specifier for the data type being read or written will generate a run-time error.

```
Enter two four digit
numbers : 1234 5678
The two numbers are : 12
and 34
```

Here, the variable `a` is assigned the value 12 because it is specified as `%2d`, so it will accept only the first two digits. The rest of the number will be assigned to `b`. The value 5678 that is unread will be assigned to the first variable in the next call to the `scanf` function.

The `%n` specifier is used to assign the number of characters read till the point at which the `%n` was encountered to the variable pointed to by the corresponding argument. The code fragment given below illustrates its usage.

```
int count;
printf("Hello %n World!", &count);
printf("%d", count);
```

The output would be—Hello World! 6 because 6(H, e, l, l, o,) is the number of characters read before the %n modifier.

2.2 Write a program to demonstrate the use of `printf` statement to print values of variables of different data types.

```
#include <stdio.h>
main()
{
   // Declare and initialize variables
   int num = 7;
   float amt = 123.45;
   char code = 'A';
   double pi = 3.1415926536;
   long int population_of_india =
   10000000000;
   char msg[] = "Hi";

   // Print the values of variables
   printf("\n NUM = %d \t AMT = %f \t CODE
   = %c \n PI = %e \t POPULATION OF INDIA =
   %ld \n MESSAGE = %s", num, amt, code, pi,
   population_of_india, msg);
   return 0;
}
```

Output

```
NUM = 7
AMT - 123.45000
CODE = A
PI = 3.141590e+00
POPULATION OF INDIA = 10000000000
MESSAGE = Hi
```

2.3 Write a program to demonstrate the use of `printf` and `scanf` statements to read and print values of variables of different data types.

```
#include <stdio.h>
main()
{
   int num;
   float amt;
   char code;
   double pi;
   long int population_of_india;
   char msg[10];

   printf("\n Enter the value of num : ");
   scanf("%d", &num);
   printf("\n Enter the value of amt : ");
   scanf("%f", &amt);
   printf("\n Enter the value of pi : ");
   scanf("%e", &pi);
   printf("\n Enter the population of india : ");
   scanf("%ld", &population_of_india);
   printf("\n Enter the value of code : ");
   scanf("%c", &code);
   printf("\n Enter the message : ");
   scanf("%s", msg);

   printf("\n NUM = %d \n AMT = %f \n PI =
     %e \n POPULATION OF INDIA = %ld \n CODE
     = %c \n MESSAGE = %s", num, amt, code,
     pi, population_of_india, msg);
   return 0;
}
```

Output

```
Enter the value of num : 5
Enter the value of amt : 123.45
Enter the value of pi : 3.14159
Enter the population of india : 12345
Enter the value of code : c
Enter the message : Hello

NUM = 5
AMT = 123.45000
PI = 3.141590e+00
POPULATION OF INDIA = 12345
CODE = c
MESSAGE = Hello
```

2.4 Write a program to calculate the area of a triangle using Hero's formula.

```
#include <stdio.h>
#include <conio.h>
#include <math.h>
int main()
{
   float a, b, c, area, S;

   printf("\n Enter the lengths of the three
     sides of the triangle : ");
   scanf("%f %f %f", &a, &b, &c);
   S = ( a + b + c)/2;

   // sqrt is a mathematical function defined
     in math.h header file
   area = sqrt(S*(S-a)*(S-b)*(S-c));
   printf("\n Area = %f", area);
   return 0;
}
```

Output

```
Enter the lengths of the three sides of the
  triangle : 12 16 20
Area = 96
```

2.5 Write a program to calculate the distance between two points.

```
#include <stdio.h>
#include <conio.h>
#include <math.h>

int main()
{
   int x1, x2, y1, y2;
   float distance;
   printf("\n Enter the x and y coordinates
     of the first point : ");
   scanf("%d %d", &x1, &y1);
   printf("\n Enter the x and y coordinates
     of the second point :");
   scanf("%d %d", &x2, &y2);

   // sqrt and pow are mathematical
     functions defined in math.h header file
   distance = sqrt(pow((x2-x1),
     2)+pow((y2-y1), 2));
   printf("\n Distance = %f", distance);
   return 0;
}
```

Output

```
Enter the x and y coordinates of the first
  point : 2 5
Enter the x and y coordinates of the second
  point : 3 7
Distance = 2.236068
```

2.12.6 Detecting Errors During Data Input

When the `scanf` function completes reading all the data values, it returns number of values that are successfully read. This return value can be used to determine whether there was any error while reading the input. For example, the statement,

```
scanf("%d %f %c", &a, &b, &c);
```

will return 3 if the user enters, say,

```
12 12.34 A
```

It will return 1 if the user enters erroneous data like

```
12 ABC 12.34
```

This is because a string was entered while the user was expecting a floating point value. So, the scanf reads only first data value correctly and then terminates as soon as it encounters a mismatch between the type of data expected and the type of data entered.

2.13 OPERATORS IN C

An operator is defined as a symbol that specifies the mathematical, logical, or relational operation to be performed. C language supports a lot of operators to be used in expressions. These operators can be categorized into the following major groups:

- Arithmetic operators
- Relational operators
- Equality operators
- Logical operators
- Unary operators
- Conditional operators
- Bitwise operators
- Assignment operators
- Comma operator
- Sizeof operator

In this section, we will discuss about all these operators.

2.13.1 Arithmetic Operators

Consider three variables declared as,

```
int a=9, b=3, result;
```

We will use these variables to explain arithmetic operators. Table 2.9 shows the arithmetic operators, their syntax, and usage in C language.

Table 2.9 Arithmetic operators

Operation	Operator	Syntax	Comment	Result
Multiply	*	a * b	result = a * b	27
Divide	/	a / b	result = a/b	3
Addition	+	a + b	result = a + b	12
Subtraction	–	a – b	result = a – b	6
Modulus	%	a % b	result = a % b	0

In Table 2.9, a and b (on which the operator is applied) are called operands. Arithmetic operators can be applied to any integer or floating-point number. The addition, subtraction, and multiplication (+, -, and *) operators perform the usual arithmetic operations in C programs, so you are already familiar with these operators.

However, the operator % must be new to you. The modulus operator (%) finds the remainder of an integer division. This operator can be applied only to integer operands and cannot be used on float or double operands. Therefore, the code given below generates a compiler error.

```
#include <stdio.h>
#include <conio.h>
int main()
{
    float c = 20.0;
    printf("\n Result = %f", c % 5);
// WRONG. Modulus operator is being applied
    to a float operand
    return 0;
}
```

While performing modulo division, the sign of the result is always the sign of the first operand (the dividend). Therefore,

16 % 3 = 1 – 16 % 3 = –1
16 % –3 = 1 – 16 % –3 = –1

When both operands of the division operator (/) are integers, the division is performed as an integer division. Integer division always results in an integer result. So, the result is always rounded-off by ignoring the remainder. Therefore,

9 / 4 = 2   and   –9/4 = –3

From the above observation, we can conclude two things. If op1 and op2 are integers and the quotient is not an integer, then we have two cases:

- If op1 and op2 have the same sign, then op1/op2 is the largest integer less than the true quotient.
- If op1 and op2 have opposite signs, then op1/op2 is the smallest integer greater than the true quotient.

Note that it is not possible to divide any number by zero. This is an illegal operation that results in a run-time division-by-zero exception, thereby terminating the program.

Except for modulus operator, all other arithmetic operators can accept a mix of integer and floating point numbers. If both operands are integers, the result will be an integer. If one or both operands are floating point numbers, then the result would also be a floating point number.

All the arithmetic operators bind from left to right. As in mathematics the multiplication, division, and modulus operators have higher precedence over the addition and subtraction operators, i.e., if an arithmetic expression consists of a mix of operators, then multiplication, division, and modulus will be carried out first in a left to right order, before any addition and subtraction could be performed. For example,

```
3 + 4 * 7
= 3 + 28
= 31
```

2.6 Write a program to perform addition, subtraction, division, integer division, multiplication, and modulo division on two integer numbers.

```
#include <stdio.h>
#include <conio.h>
int main()
{

   int num1, num2;
   int add_res=0, sub_res=0, mul_res=0,
      idiv_res=0, modiv_res=0;
   float fdiv_res=0.0;
   clrscr();
   printf("\n Enter the first number : ");
   scanf("%d", &num1);
   printf("\n Enter the second number : ");
   scanf("%d", &num2);

   add_res= num1 + num2;
   sub_res=num1 - num2;
   mul_res = num1 * num2;
   idiv_res = num1/num2;
   modiv_res = num1%num2;
   fdiv_res = (float)num1/num2;
   printf("\n %d + %d = %d", num1, num2,
      add_res);
   printf("\n %d - %d = %d", num1, num2,
      sub_res);
   printf("\n %d × %d = %d", num1, num2,
      mul_res);
   printf("\n %d / %d = %d (Integer
      Division)", num1, num2, idiv_res);
   printf("\n %d %% %d = %d (Moduluo
      Division)", num1, num2, modiv_res);
   printf("\n %d / %d = %.2f (Normal
      Division)", num1, num2, fdiv_res);
   return 0;
}
```

Output

```
Enter the first number: 9
Enter the second number : 7
9 + 7 = 16
9 - 7 = 2
9 * 7 = 63
9 / 7 = 1 (Integer division)
9 % 7 = 2 (Modulo division)
9 / 7 = 1.29 (Normal division)
```

2.7 Write a program to find the number of hours and minutes, if the user inputs some minutes.

```
#include<stdio.h>
main()
{
   int mins, hrs, minutes;
   printf("\n Enter the minutes : ");
   scanf("%d", &minutes);

   hrs = minutes/60;
   mins = minutes%60;
   printf("\n %d minutes = %d hrs and %d
   mins ", minutes, hrs, mins);
}
```

Output

```
Enter the minutes : 134
134 minutes = 2 hrs and 14 mins
```

2.8 Write a program to subtract two long integers.

```
#include <stdio.h>
#include <conio.h>
int main()
{
   long int num1= 1234567, num2, diff=0;
   clrscr();
   printf("\n Enter the number: ");
   scanf("%ld", &num2);
   diff = num1 - num2;
   printf("\n Difference = %ld", diff);
   return 0;
}
```

Output

```
Enter the number: 1234
Difference = 1233333
```

2.13.2 Relational Operators

A relational operator, also known as a comparison operator, is an operator that compares two values. Expressions that contain relational operators are called *relational expressions.* Relational operators return true or false value, depending on whether the conditional relationship between the two operands holds or not.

For example, to test the expression, if `x` is less than `y`, relational operator `<` is used as `x < y`. This expression will return TRUE if `x` is less than `y`; otherwise the value of the expression will be FALSE.

Relational operators can be used to determine the relationships between the operands. These relationships are illustrated in Table 2.10.

Table 2.10 Relational operators

Operator	Meaning	Example
<	Less than	3 < 5 gives 1
>	Greater than	7 > 9 gives 0
>=	Less than or equal to	100 >= 100 gives 1
<=	Greater than equal to	50 >= 100 gives 0

The relational operators are evaluated from left to right. The operands of a relational operator must evaluate to a number. Characters are considered valid operands since they are represented by numeric values in the computer system. So, if we say, `'A' < 'B'`, where A is 65 and B is 66 then the result would be `1` as `65 < 66`.

When arithmetic expressions are used on either side of a relational operator, then first the arithmetic expression will be evaluated and then the result will be compared. This is because arithmetic operators have a higher priority over relational operators.

However, relational operators should not be used for comparing strings as this will result in comparing the address of the string and not their contents. You must be wondering why so? The answer to this question will be clear to you in the later chapters. A few examples of relational operators are given below.

<table>
<tr><td colspan="2">If x=1, y=2, and z = 3, then</td></tr>
<tr><td>Expressions that evaluate to TRUE
Note that these expressions are true because their value is not zero.</td><td>Expressions that evaluate to FALSE
Note that these expressions are false because their value is zero.</td></tr>
<tr><td>(x)
(x + y)
(z * 9)
(z + 10 - 5 * a)
(z - x + y)</td><td>(x - 1)
(!(z))
(0 * y)
(y == 1)
(y % 2)</td></tr>
</table>

Although blank spaces are allowed between an operand and an operator, no space is permitted between the components of an operator (like > = is not allowed, it should be >=). Therefore, writing, x==y is correct but writing x = = y is not acceptable in C language.

2.9 Write a program to show the use of relational operators.

```
#include <stdio.h>
main ()
{
    int x=10, y=20;
    printf("\n %d < %d = %d", x, y, x<y);
    printf("\n %d == %d = %d", x, y, x==y);
    printf("\n %d != %d = %d", x, y, x!=y);
    printf("\n %d > %d = %d", x, y, x>y);
    printf("\n %d >= %d = %d", x, y, x>=y);
    printf("\n %d <= %d = %d", x, y, x<=y);
    return 0;
}
```

Output

```
10 < 20 = 0
10 == 20 = 1
10 != 20 = 1
10 > 20 = 0
10 >= 20 = 0
10 <= 20 = 1
```

2.13.3 Equality Operators

C language supports two kinds of equality operators to compare their operands for strict equality or inequality. They are equal to `(==)` and not equal to `(!=)` operators. The equality operators have lower precedence than the relational operators.

The equal-to operator `(==)` returns **`true`** `(1)` if operands on both the sides of the operator have the same value; otherwise, it returns **`false`** `(0)`. On the contrary, the not-equal-to operator `(!=)` returns **`true(1)`** if the operands do not have the same value; else it returns **`false (0)`**. Table 2.11 summarizes equality operators.

Table 2.11 Equality operators

Operator	Meaning
==	Returns 1 if both operands are equal, 0 otherwise
!=	Returns 1 if operands do not have the same value, 0 otherwise

2.13.4 Logical Operators

C language supports three logical operators—logical AND (`&&`), logical OR (`||`), and logical NOT (`!`). As in case of arithmetic expressions, the logical expressions are evaluated from left to right.

Logical AND

Logical AND is a binary operator which simultaneously evaluates two values or relational expressions. If both are true, then the whole expression is true. If both or one of the operands is false, then the whole expression evaluates to false. The truth table of logical AND operator is given in Table 2.12.

Table 2.12 Truth table of logical AND

A	B	A &&B
0	0	0
0	1	0
1	0	0
1	1	1

For example,

```
(a < b) && (b > c)
```

The whole expression is true only if both expressions are true, i.e., if `b` is greater than `a` and `c`.

Logical OR

Logical OR returns a false value if both the operands are false. Otherwise it returns a true value. The truth table of logical OR operator is given in Table 2.13.

Table 2.13 Truth table of logical OR

A	B	A || B
0	0	0
0	1	1
1	0	1
1	1	1

For example,

```
(a < b) || (b > c)
```

The whole expression is true if either `b` is greater than `a` or `b` is greater than `c` or `b` is greater than both `a` and `c`.

Logical NOT

The logical NOT operator takes a single expression and negates the value of the expression. That is, logical NOT produces a `zero` if the expression evaluates to a non-zero value and produces a `1` if the expression produces a zero. In other words, it just reverses the value of the expression. The truth table of logical NOT operator is given in Table 2.14.

Table 2.14 Truth table of logical NOT

A	! A
0	1
1	0

For example,

```
int a = 10, b;
b = !a;
```

Now the value of `b = 0`. This is because value of `a = 10`. `!a = 0`. The value of `!a` is assigned to `b`, hence, the result.

Logical expressions operate in a short cut fashion and stop the evaluation when it knows for sure what the final outcome would be. For example, in a logical expression involving logical AND, if the first operand is false, then the second operand is not evaluated as it is for sure that the result will be false. Similarly, for a logical expression involving logical OR, if the first operand is true, then the second operand is not evaluated as it is for sure that the result will be true.

But this approach has a side effect. For example, consider the following expression:

```
(x > 9) && (y > 0)
```

OR

```
(x > 9) || (y > 0)
```

In the above logical AND expression if the first operand is false then the entire expression will not be evaluated and thus the value of `y` will never be incremented. Same is the case with the logical OR expression. If the first expression is true then the second will never be evaluated and value of `y` will never be incremented.

2.13.5 Unary Operators

Unary operators act on single operands. C language supports three unary operators unary minus, increment, and decrement operators.

Unary Minus

Unary minus (–) operator is strikingly different from the binary arithmetic operator that operates on two operands and subtracts the second operand from the first operand. When an operand is preceded by a minus sign, the unary operator negates its value. For example, if a number is positive then it becomes negative when preceded with a unary minus operator. Similarly, if the number is negative, it becomes positive after applying the unary minus operator. For example,

```
int a, b = 10;
a = -(b);
```

The result of this expression is `a = -10`, because a variable `b` has a positive value. After applying unary minus operator `(-)` on the operand `b`, the value becomes `–10`, which indicates it as a negative value.

Increment Operator (++) and Decrement Operator (– –)

The increment operator is a unary operator that increases the value of its operand by `1`. Similarly, the decrement operator decreases the value of its operand by 1. For example, `--x` is equivalent to writing `x = x - 1`.

The increment/decrement operators have two variants—**prefix** and **postfix**. In a prefix expression `(++x or --x)`, the operator is applied before an operand is fetched for computation and thus, the altered value is used for the computation of the expression in which it occurs. On the contrary, in a postfix expression `(x++ or x--)` an operator is applied after an operand is fetched for computation. Therefore, the unaltered value is used for the computation of the expression in which it occurs.

Therefore, an important point to note about unary increment and decrement operators is that `++x` is not the same as `x++`. Similarly, `--x` is not the same as `x--`. Both `++x` and `x++` increment the value of `x` by `1`. In the former case, the value of `x` is returned before it is incremented whereas, in the latter case, the value of `x` is returned after it is incremented. For example,

```
int x = 10, y;
y = x++;
```

is equivalent to writing

```
y = x;
x = x + 1;
```

whereas,

```
y = ++x;
```

is equivalent to writing

```
x = x + 1;
y = x;
```

The same principle applies to unary decrement operators. The unary operators have a higher precedence than the binary operators. If in an expression we have more than one unary operator then unlike arithmetic operators, they are evaluated from right to left.

When applying the increment or decrement operator, the operand must be a variable. This operator can never be applied to a constant or an expression. Therefore the following codes will generate a compiler error.

When postfix ++ or – – is used with a variable in an expression, then the expression is evaluated first using the original value of the variable and then the variable is incremented or decremented by one.
Similarly, when prefix ++ or – – is used with a variable in an expression, then the variable is first incremented or decremented and then the expression is evaluated using the new value of the variable.

2.10 Write a program to illustrate the use of unary prefix increment and decrement operators.

```
#include <stdio.h>
main()
{
    int num = 3;
    // Using unary prefix increment operator
    printf("\n The value of num = %d", num);
    printf("\n The value of ++num = %d", ++num);
    printf("\n The new value of num = %d", num);
    // Using unary prefix decrement operator
    printf("\n\n The value of num = %d", num);
    printf("\n The value of --num = %d", --num);
    printf("\n The new value of num = %d", num);
```

```
    return 0;
}
```

Output

```
The value of num = 3
The value of ++num = 4
The new value of num = 4

The value of num = 4
The value of --num = 3
The new value of num = 3
```

2.11 Write a program to illustrate the use of unary postfix increment and decrement operators.

```
#include <stdio.h>
main()
{
    int num = 3;
    // Using unary postfix increment operator
    printf("\n The value of num = %d", num);
    printf("\n The value of num++ = %d", num++);
    printf("\n The new value of num = %d", num);
    // Using unary postfix decrement operator
    printf("\n\n The value of num = %d", num);
    printf("\n The value of num = %d", num--);
    printf("\n The new value of num = %d", num);
    return 0;
}
```

Output

```
The value of num = 3
The value of num++ = 3
The new value of num = 4
The value of num = 4
The value of num-- = 4
The new value of num = 3
```

2.13.6 Conditional Operator

The conditional operator or the ternary (?:) is just like an `if–else` statement that can be within expressions. Such an operator is useful in situations in which there are two or more alternatives for an expression. The syntax of the conditional operator is

```
exp1 ? exp2 : exp3
```

`exp1` is evaluated first. If it is true, then `exp2` is evaluated and becomes the result of the expression, otherwise `exp3` is evaluated and becomes the result of the expression. For example,

```
large = ( a > b) ? a : b
```

The conditional operator is used to find largest of two given numbers. First `exp1`, that is (a > b) is evaluated. If a is greater than b, then `large` = a, else `large` = b. Hence, `large` is equal to either a or b but not both.

Hence, conditional operator is used in certain situations, replacing `if-else` condition phrases. Conditional operators make the program code more compact, more readable, and safer to use, as it is easier to check any error (if present) in one single line itself. Conditional operator is also known as ternary operator as it is neither a unary nor a binary operator; it takes *three* operands.

Since a conditional operator is itself an expression, it can be used as an operand of another conditional operation. That means C allows you to have nested conditional expressions. Consider the expression given below which illustrates this concept.

```
int a = 5, b = 3, c= 7, small;
small = (a<b? (a<c?a:c) : (b<c?b:c));
```

2.12 Write a program to determine whether a person is eligible to vote using conditional operator.

```
#include<stdio.h>
#include<conio.h>
main()
{
    int age;
    char ch;
    clrscr();
    printf("\n Enter your age : ");
    scanf("%d", &age);
    ch = (age >= 18)?'y':'n';
    printf("\n Eligible to vote : %c", ch);
}
```

Output

```
Enter your age : 27
Eligible to vote : y
```

2.13 Write a program to find the largest of three numbers using ternary operator.

```
#include <stdio.h>
#include <conio.h>
int main()
```

```
{
    int num1, num2, num3, large;
    clrscr();
    printf("\n Enter the first number: ");
    scanf("%d", &num1);
    printf("\n Enter the second number: ");
    scanf("%d", &num2);
    printf("\n Enter the third number: ");
    scanf("%d", &num3);
    large = num1>num2?(num1>num3?num1:num3):
      (num2>num3?num2:num3);
    printf("\n The largest number is: %d",
      large);
    return 0;
}
```

Output

```
Enter the first number: 12
Enter the second number: 34
Enter the third number: 23
The largest number is:  34
```

2.13.7 Bitwise Operators

As the name suggests, bitwise operators are those operators that perform operations at bit level. These operators include : bitwise AND, bitwise OR, bitwise XOR, and shift operators. The bitwise operators expect their operands to be integers and treat them as a sequence of bits.

Bitwise AND

The bitwise AND operator (&) is a small version of the boolean AND (&&) as it performs operation on bits instead of bytes, chars, integers, etc. When we use the bitwise AND operator, the bit in the first operand is ANDed with the corresponding bit in the second operand. The truth table is same as we had seen in logical AND operation, i.e., the bitwise AND operator compares each bit of its first operand with the corresponding bit of its second operand. If both bits are 1, the corresponding bit in the result is 1 and 0 otherwise. For example,

```
10101010 & 01010101 = 00000000
```

In a C program, the & operator is used as follows.

```
int a = 10, b = 20, c=0;
c= a&b;
```

Bitwise OR

The bitwise OR operator (|) is a small version of the boolean OR (||) as it performs operation on bits instead of bytes, chars, integers, etc. When we use the bitwise OR operator, the bit in the first operand is ORed with the corresponding bit in the second operand. The truth table is same as we had seen in logical OR operation, i.e., the bitwise OR operator compares each bit of its first operand with the corresponding bit of its second operand. If one or both bits are 1, the corresponding bit in the result is 1 and 0 otherwise. For example,

```
10101010 & 01010101 = 11111111
```

In a C program, the | operator is used as follows.

```
int a = 10, b = 20, c=0;
c= a|b
```

Bitwise XOR

The bitwise XOR operator (^) performs operation on individual bits of the operands. When we use the bitwise XOR operator, the bit in the first operand is XORed with the corresponding bit in the second operand. The truth table of bitwise XOR operator is as shown in Table 2.15.

The bitwise XOR operator compares each bit of its first operand with the corresponding bit of its second operand. If one of the bits is 1, the corresponding bit in the result is 1 and 0 otherwise. For example,

```
10101010 ^ 01010101 = 11111111
```

Table 2.15 Truth table of bitwise XOR

A	B	A ^ B
0	0	0
0	1	1
1	0	1
1	1	0

In a C program, the ^ operator is used as follows:

```
int a = 10, b = 20, c=0;
c= a^b
```

Bitwise NOT

The bitwise NOT, or complement, is a unary operation that performs logical negation on each bit of the operand. By performing negation of each bit, it actually produces the 1s complement of the given binary value. Bitwise NOT operator sets the bit to 1 if it was initially 0 and sets it to 0 if it was initially 1. For example,

```
~10101011 = 01010100
```

Bitwise operators are used for testing the bits or shifting them left or right. Always remember that bitwise operators cannot be applied to float or double variables.

Shift Operator

C supports two bitwise shift operators. They are shift-left (<<) and shift-right (>>). These operations are simple and are responsible for shifting bits either to the left or to the right. The syntax for a shift operation can be given as

```
operand op num
```

where the bits in operand are shifted left or right depending on the operator (left if the operator is << and right if the operator is >>) by the number of places denoted by num.

For example, if we have x = 0001 1101, then

x << 1 produces 0011 1010

When we apply a left-shift, every bit in x is shifted to the left by one place. So, the MSB (most significant bit) of x is lost, the LSB of x is set to 0.

Therefore, if we have x = 0001 1101, then

x << 3 produces 1010 0000.

If you observe carefully, you will notice that shifting once to the left multiplies the number by 2. Hence, multiple shifts of 1 to the left, results in multiplying the number by 2 over and over again.

On the contrary, when we apply a shift-right operator, every bit in x is shifted to the right by one place. So, the LSB (least significant bit) of x is lost, the MSB of x is set to 0. For example, if we have x = 0001 1101, then

x >> 1 produces = 0000 1110

Similarly, if we have x = 0001 1101, then

x << 3 produces 0000 0001.

If you observe carefully, you will notice that shifting once to the right divides the number by 2. Hence, multiple shifts of 1 to the right, results in dividing the number by 2 over and over again.

2.13.8 Assignment Operators

In C, the assignment operator is responsible for assigning values to the variables. While the equal sign (=) is the fundamental assignment operator, C language also supports other assignment operators that provide shorthand ways to represent common variable assignments.

When an equal sign is encountered in an expression, the compiler processes the statement on the right side of the sign and assigns the result to the variable on the left side. For example,

```
int x;
x = 10;
```

assigns the value 10 to variable x. If we have,

```
int x = 2, y = 3, sum = 0;
sum = x + y;
then sum = 5.
```

The assignment operator has right-to-left associativity, so the expression

```
a = b = c = 10;
```

is evaluated as

```
(a = (b = (c = 10)));
```

First 10 is assigned to c, then the value of c is assigned to b. Finally, the value of b is assigned to a.

The operand to the left of the assignment operator must always be a variable name. C does not allow any expression, constant, or function to be placed to the left of the assignment operator. Therefore, the statement a + b = 0, is invalid in C language.

To the right of the assignment operator you may have an arbitrary expression. In that case, the expression would be evaluated and the result would be stored in the location denoted by the variable name.

Other Assignment Operators

C language supports a set of shorthand assignment operators of the form

```
variable op = expression
```

where op is a binary arithmetic operator.

Table 2.16 contains a list of other assignment operators that are supported by C.

The advantage of using shorthand assignment operators are as follows:

- Shorthand expressions are easier to write as the expression on the left side need not be repeated.
- The statement involving shorthand operators are easier to read as they are more concise.
- The statement involving shorthand operators are more efficient and easy to understand.

2.14 Write a program to demonstrate the use of assignment operators.

```
#include <stdio.h>
main()
{
   int num1 = 3, num2 = 5;
```

Table 2.16 Assignment operators

Operator	Syntax	Equivalent to	Meaning	Example

/=	variable /= expression	variable = variable / expression	Divides the value of a variable by the value of an expression and assigns the result to the variable.	float a = 9.0;
				float b = 3.0;
				a /= b;

/=	variable /= expression	variable = variable / expression	Divides the value of a variable by the value of an expression and assigns the integer result to the variable.	int a= 9;
				int b = 3;
				a /= b;

*=	variable *= expression	variable = variable * expression	Multiplies the value of a variable by the value of an expression and assigns the result to the variable.	int a = 9;
				int b = 3;
				a *= b;

+=	variable += expression	variable = variable + expression	Adds the value of a variable to the value of an expression and assigns the result to the variable.	int a = 9;
				int b = 3;
				a += b;

−=	variable −= expression	variable = variable – expression	Subtracts the value of the expression from the value of the variable and assigns the result to the variable.	int a = 9;
				int b = 3;
				a −= b;

&=	variable &= expression	variable = variable & expression	Perform the bitwise AND with the value of variable and value of the expression and assign the result in the variable.	int a = 10;
				int b = 20;
				a &= b;

^=	variable ^= expression	variable = variable ^ expression	Perform the bitwise XOR with the value of variable and value of the expression and assign the result in the variable.	int a = 10;
				int b = 20;
				a ^= b;

<<=	variable <<= amount	variable = variable << amount	Performs an arithmetic left shift (amount times) on the value of a variable and assigns the result back to the variable.	int a = 9;
				int b = 3;
				a <<= b;

>>=	variable >>= amount	variable = variable >> amount	Performs an arithmetic right shift (amount times) on the value of a variable and assigns the result back to the variable.	int a = 9;
				int b = 3;
				a >>= b;

```
    printf("\n Initial value of num1 = %d and
      num2 = %d", num1, num2);
    num1 += num2 * 4 - 7;
    printf("\n After the evaluation of the
      expression num1 = %d and num2 = %d",
      num1, num2);
    return 0;
}
```

Output

```
Initial value of num1 = 3 and num2 = 5
After the evaluation of the expression num1
   = 16 and num2 = 5
```

2.13.9 Comma Operator

The comma operator in C takes two operands. It works by evaluating the first and discarding its value, and then evaluates the second and returns the value as the result of the expression. Comma separated operands when chained together are evaluated in left-to-right sequence with the rightmost value yielding the result of the expression. Among all the operators, the comma operator has the lowest precedence.

Therefore, when a comma operator is used, the entire expression evaluates to the value of the right expression. For example, the following statement first increments `a`, then increments `b`, and then assigns the value `b` to `x`.

```
int a=2, b=3, x=0;
x = (++a, b+=a);
```

Now, the value of `x = 6`.

2.13.10 `Sizeof` Operator

The operator `sizeof` is a unary operator used to calculate the size of data types. This operator can be applied to all data types. When using this operator, the keyword `sizeof` is followed by a type name, variable, or expression. The operator returns the size of the variable, data type, or expression in bytes, i.e., the `sizeof` operator is used to determine the amount of memory space that the variable/expression/data type will take.

When a type name is used, it is enclosed in parentheses, but in case of variable names and expressions they can be specified with or without parentheses. A `sizeof` expression returns an unsigned value that specifies the space in bytes required by the data type, variable, or expression. For example, `sizeof(char)` returns 1, i.e., the size of a character data type. If we have,

```
int a = 10;
unsigned int result;
result = sizeof(a);
```

then `result = 2`, which is the space required to store the variable `a` in memory. Since `a` is an integer, it requires 2 bytes of storage space.

2.13.11 Operator Precedence Chart

C operators have two properties: *priority* and *associativity*. When an expression has more than one operator then it is the relative priorities of the operators with respect to each other that determine the order in which the expression will be evaluated. Associativity defines the direction in which the operator having the same precedence acts on the operands. It can be either left-to-right or right-to-left. Priority is given precedence over associativity to determine the order in which the expressions are evaluated. Associativity is then applied, if the need arises.

Table 2.17 lists the operators that C language supports in the order of their *precedence* (highest to lowest). The *associativity* indicates the order in which the operators of equal precedence in an expression are evaluated.

Table 2.17 Operator precedence

Operator	Associativity	Operator	Associativity
() [] . ++(postfix) --(postfix)	left-to-right	^	left-to-right
++(prefix) --(prefix) +(unary) - (unary) ! ~ (type) *(indirection) &(address) sizeof	right-to-left	|	left-to-right
* / %	left-to-right	&&	left-to-right
+ -	left-to-right	||	left-to-right
<< >>	left-to-right	?:	right-to-left
< <= > >=	left-to-right	= += -= *= /= %= &= ^= |= <<= >>=	right-to-left
== !=	left-to-right	,	left-to-right
&	left-to-right		

You must be wondering why the priority of the assignment operator is so low. This is because the action of assignment is performed only when the entire computation is done. It is not uncommon for a programmer to forget the priority of the operators while writing any program. So it is recommended that you use the parentheses operator to override default priorities. From Table 2.17 you can see that the parenthesis operator has the highest priority. So any operator placed within the parenthesis will be evaluated before any other operator.

Example Expressions Using the Precedence Chart

1. ```
x = 3 * 4 + 5 * 6
  = 12 + 5 * 6
  = 12 + 30
  = 42
```
2. ```
x = 3 * (4 + 5) * 6
  = 3 * 9 * 6
  = 27 * 6
  = 162
```
3. ```
x = 3 * 4 % 5 / 2
  = 12 % 5 / 2
  = 2 / 2
  = 1
```
4. ```
x = 3 * (4 % 5) / 2
  = 3 * 4 / 2
  = 12 / 2
  = 6
```
5. ```
x = 3 * 4 % (5 / 2)
  = 3 * 4 % 2
  = 12 % 2
  = 0
```
6. ```
x = 3 * ((4 % 5) / 2)
  = 3 * (4 / 2)
  = 3 * 2
  = 6
```

Take the following variable declaration,

```
int a = 0, b = 1, c = -1;
float x = 2.5, y = 0.0;
```

If we write,

`a = b = c = 7;`

Since the assignment operator works from right-to-left, therefore

`c = 7`. Then since `b = c`, therefore `b = 7`. Now `a = b`, so `a = 7`.

7. `a += b -= c * 10`

This is expanded as

```
a = a + (b = b - (c = c * 10))
  = a + ( b = 1 - (-10)
  = a + ( b = 11)
  = 0 + 11
  = 11
```

8. ```
--a * (5 + b) / 2 - c++ * b
= --a * 6 / 2 - c++ * b
= --a * 6 / 2 - -1 * b
```

(Value of c has been incremented but its altered value will not be visible for the evaluation of this expression)

```
= -1 * 6 / 2 - -1 * 1
```

(Value of a has been incremented and its altered value will be used for the evaluation of this expression)

```
= -1 * 3 - -1 * 1
= -3 - -1 * 1
= -3 - -1
= -2
```

9. ```
a * b * cs
= (a * b) * c (because associativity of *
is from left-to-right)
= 0
```
10. ```
a && b
= 0
```
11. ```
a < b && c < b
= 1
```
12. ```
b + c || ! a
= ( b + c) || (!a)
= 0 ||1
= 1
```
13. ```
x * 5 && 5 || (b / c)
= ((x * 5) && 5) || (b / c)
= (12.5 && 5) || (1/-1)
= 1
```
14. ```
a <= 10 && x >= 1 && b
= ((a <= 10) && (x >= 1)) && b
= (1 && 1) && 1
= 1
```
15. ```
!x || !c || b + c
= ((!x) || (!c)) || (b + c)
= (0 || 0) || 0
= 0
```
16. ```
x * y < a + b || c
= ((x * y) < (a + b)) || c
= (0 < 1) || -1
= 1
```
17. ```
(x > y) + !a || c++
= ((x > y) + (!a)) || (c++)
= (1 + 1) || 0
= 1
```

2.14 Programming Examples

2.15 Write a program to calculate the area of a circle.

```
#include <stdio.h>
```

```
#include <conio.h>
int main()
{
   float radius;
   double area, circumference;
   clrscr();
   printf("\n Enter the radius of the circle: ");
   scanf("%f", &radius);
   area = 3.14 * radius * radius;
      circumference = 2 * 3.14 * radius;
   printf(" Area = %.2le", area);
      printf("\n CIRCUMFERENCE = %.2e",
   circumference);
   return 0;
}
```

Output

```
Enter the radius of the circle:
Area = 153.86
CIRCUMFERENCE = 4.40e+01
```

2.16 Write a program to print the ASCII value of a character.

```
#include <stdio.h>
#include <conio.h>
int main()
{
   char ch;
   clrscr();
   printf("\n Enter any character: ");
   scanf("%c", &ch);
   printf("\n The ascii value of %c is:
     %d",ch,ch);
   return 0;
}
```

Output

```
Enter any character: A
The ascii value of A is: 65
```

2.17 Write a program to read a character in upper case and then print it in lower case.

```
#include <stdio.h>
#include <conio.h>
int main()
{
   char ch;
   clrscr();
   printf("\n Enter any character in upper
     case: ");
   scanf("%c", &ch);
   printf("\n The character in lower case
     is: %c", ch+32);
   return 0;
}
```

Output

```
Enter any character: A
The character in lower case is: a
```

2.18 Write a program to print the digit at ones place of a number.

```
#include <stdio.h>
#include <conio.h>
main()
{
   int num, digit_at_ones_place;
   clrscr();
   printf("\n Enter any number: ");
   scanf("%d", &num);
   digit_at_ones_place = num % 10;
   printf("\n The digit at ones place of %d
     is %d", num, digit_at_ones_place);
   return 0;
}
```

Output

```
Enter any number: 123
The digit at ones place of 123 is 3
```

2.19 Write a program to swap two numbers using a temporary variable.

```
#include <stdio.h>
#include <conio.h>
int main()
{
   int num1, num2, temp;
   clrscr();
   printf("\n Enter the first number: ");
   scanf("%d",&num1);
   printf("\n Enter the second number: ");
   scanf("%d",&num2);
   temp = num1;
   num1 = num2;
   num2=temp;
   printf("\n The first number is %d", num1);
   printf("\n The second number is %d", num2);
   return 0;
}
```

Output

```
Enter the first number : 3
Enter the second number : 5
The first number is 5
The second number is 3
```

2.20 Write a program to swap two numbers without using a temporary variable.

```
#include <stdio.h>
#include <conio.h>
int main()
{
   int num1, num2;
   clrscr();
   printf("\n Enter the first number: ");
   scanf("%d",&num1);

   printf("\n Enter the second number: ");
   scanf("%d",&num2);

   num1 = num1 + num2;
   num2= num1 - num2;
   num1 = num1 - num2;

   printf("\n The first number is %d", num1);
   printf("\n The second number is %d", num2);
   return 0;
}
```

Output

```
Enter the first number: 3
Enter the second number: 5
The first number is 5
The second number is 3
```

2.21 Write a program to convert degrees Fahrenheit into degrees celsius.

```
#include <stdio.h>
#include <conio.h>
main()
{
   float fahrenheit, celsius;
   printf("\n Enter the temperature in
     fahrenheit: ");
   scanf("%f", & fahrenheit);
   celsius = (0.56) * (fahrenheit - 32);
   printf("\n Temperature in degrees celsius
     = %f", celsius);
   return 0;
}
```

2.22 Write a program that displays the size of every data type.

```
#include <stdio.h>
#include <conio.h>
int main()
{
   clrscr();
   printf("\n The size of short integer is:
     %d", sizeof(short int));
   printf("\n The size of unsigned integer
     is: %d", sizeof(unsigned int));
   printf("\n The size of signed integer is:
     %d", sizeof(signed int));
   printf("\n The size of integer is: %d",
     sizeof(int));
   printf("\n The size of long integer is:
     %d", sizeof(long int));

   printf("\n The size of character is: %d",
     sizeof(char));
   printf("\n The size of unsigned character
     is: %d", sizeof(unsigned char));
   printf("\n The size of signed character
     is: %d", sizeof(signed char));

   printf("\n The size of floating point
     number is: %d", sizeof(float));
   printf("\n The size of double number is:
     %d", sizeof(double));
   return 0;
}
```

Output

```
The size of short integer is: 2
The size of unsigned integer is: 2
The size of signed integer is: 2
The size of integer is: 2
The size of long integer is: 2

The size of character is: 1
The size of unsigned character is: 1
The size of signed character is: 1

The size of floating point number is: 4
The size of double number is: 8
```

2.23 Write a program to calculate the total amount of money in the piggybank, given the coins of Rs 10, Rs 5, Rs 2, and Re 1.

```
#include <stdio.h>
#include <conio.h>
main()
{
   int num_of_10_coins, num_of_5_coins, num_
     of_2_coins, num_of_1_coins;
   float total_amt = 0.0;
   clrscr();
```

```
    printf("\n Enter the number of Rs10 coins
      in the piggybank: ");
    scanf("%d", &num_of_10_coins);
    printf("\n Enter the number of Rs5 coins
      in the piggybank: ");
    scanf("%d", &num_of_5_coins);
    printf("\n Enter the number of Rs2 coins
      in the piggybank: ");
    scanf("%d", &num_of_2_coins);
    printf("\n Enter the number of Re1 coins
      in the piggybank: ");
    scanf("%d", &num_of_1_coins);

    total_amt = num_of_10_coins * 10 + num_
      of_5_coins * 5 + num_of_2_coins * 2 +
      num_of_1_coins;

    printf("\n Total amount in the piggybank
      = %f", total_amt);
    getch();
    return 0;
}
```

Output

```
Enter the number of Rs10 coins in the
   piggybank: 10
Enter the number of Rs5 coins in the
   piggybank: 23
Enter the number of Rs2 coins in the
   piggybank: 43
Enter the number of Re1 coins in the
   piggybank: 6
Total amount in the piggybank = 307
```

2.24 Write a program to calculate the bill amount for an item given its quantity sold, value, discount, and tax.

```
#include <stdio.h>
#include <conio.h>
main()
{
    float total_amt, amt, sub_total,
      discount_amt, tax_amt, qty, val,
      discount, tax;
    printf("\n Enter the quantity of item
      sold: ");
    scanf("%f", &qty);
    printf("\n Enter the value of item: ");
    scanf("%f", &val);
    printf("\n Enter the discount percentage: ");
    scanf("%f", &discount);
    printf("\n Enter the tax: ");
    scanf("%f", &tax);

    amt = qty * val;
    discount_amt = (amt * discount)/100.0;
    sub_total = amt - discount_amt;
    tax_amt = (sub_total * tax) /100.0;
    total_amt = sub_total + tax_amt;

    printf("\n\n\n ****** BILL ******");
    printf("\n Quantity Sold: %f", qty);
    printf("\n Price per item: %f", val);
    printf("\n -------------");
    printf("\n Amount: %f", amt);
    printf("\n Discount: - %f", discount_amt);
    printf("\n Discounted Total: %f", sub_total);
    printf("\n Tax: + %f", tax_amt);
    printf("\n -------------");
    printf("\n Total Amount %f", total_amt);
    return 0;
}
```

Output

```
Enter the quantity of item sold: 20
Enter the value of item: 300
Enter the discount percentage: 10
Enter the tax: 12
************* BILL **************"
Quantity Sold :              20
Price per item :             300
                        ---------------
Amount :                     6000
Discount :                 -  600
Discounted Total :           5400
Tax :                      +  648
                         -------------
Total Amount                 6048
```

2.15 TYPE CONVERSION AND TYPECASTING

Till now we have assumed that all the expressions involved data of the same type. But what happens when expressions involve two different data types, like multiplying a floating point number and an integer. Such type of situations are handled either through type conversion or typecasting.

Type conversion or typecasting of variables refers to changing a variable of one data type into another. Type conversion is done implicitly whereas, typecasting has to be done explicitly by the programmer. We will discuss both of them here.

2.15.1 Type Conversion

Type conversion is done when the expression has variables of different data types. To evaluate the expression, the data type is promoted from lower to higher level where the hierarchy of data types (from higher to lower) can be given as: double, float, long, int, short, and char. Figure 2.12 shows the conversion hierarchy of data types.

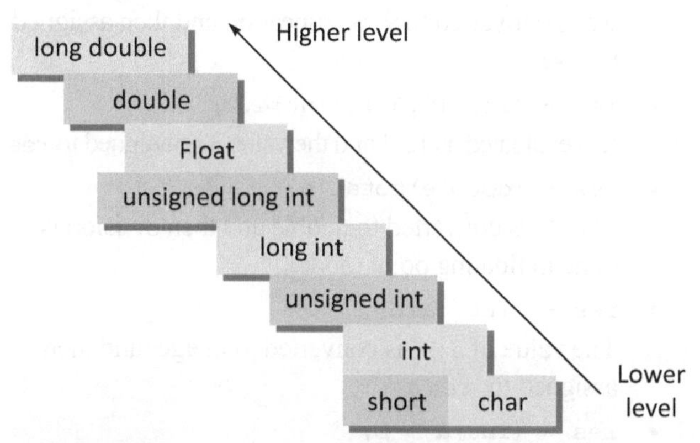

Figure 2.12 Conversion hierarchy of data types

Type conversion is automatically done when we assign an integer value to a floating point variable. Consider the code given below in which an integer data type is promoted to float. This is known as *promotion* (when a lower level data type is promoted to a higher type).

```
float x;
int y = 3;
x = y;
```

Now, `x = 3.0`, as automatically integer value is converted into its equivalent floating point representation. In some cases, when an integer is converted into a floating point number, the resulting floating point number may not exactly match the integer value. This is because the floating point number format used internally by the computer cannot accurately represent every possible integer number. So even if the value of `x = 2.99999995`, you must not worry. The loss of accuracy because of this feature would be always insignificant for the final result. Let us summarize how promotion is done:

- `float` operands are converted to `double`.
- `char` or `short` operands whether signed or unsigned are converted to `int`.
- If any one operand is `double`, the other operand is also converted to `double`. Hence, the result is also of type `double`.
- If any one operand is `long`, the other operand is also converted to `long`. Hence, the result is also of type `long`.

Figure 2.13 exhibits type conversions in an expression.

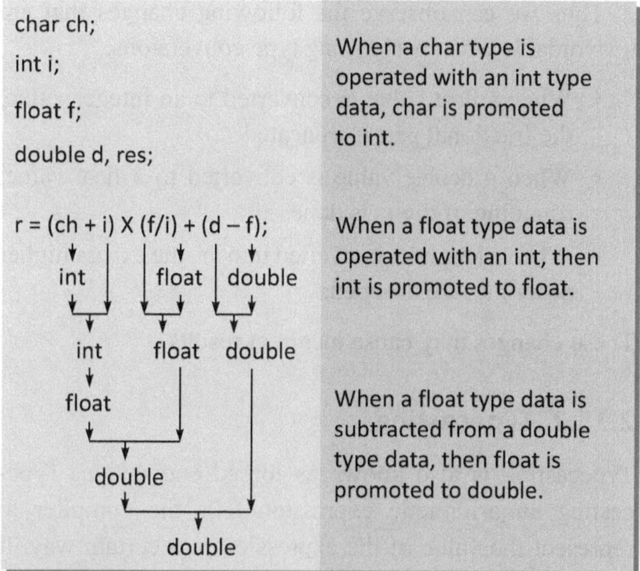

Figure 2.13 Type conversion

Consider the following group of statements.

```
float f = 3.5;
int i;
i = f;
```

The statement `i = f` results in f to be demoted to type `int`, i.e., the fractional part of `f` will be lost and `i` will contain 3 (not 3.5). In this case demotion takes place, i.e., a higher level data type is converted into a lower type. Whenever demotion occurs, some information is lost. For example, in this case the fractional part of the floating point number is lost.

Similarly, if we convert an integer to a short integer or a `long int` to `int`, or `int` to `char`, the compiler just drops the extra bits (Fig. 2.14).

No compile time warning message is generated when information is lost while demoting the type of data.

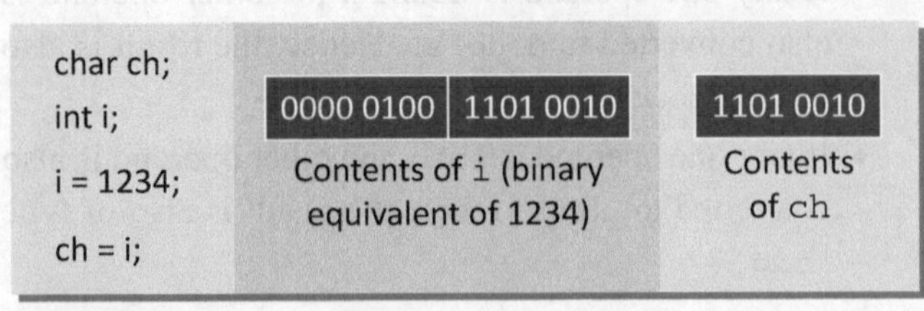

Figure 2.14 Implicit conversion example

Thus we can observe the following changes that are unavoidable when performing type conversions.

- When a float value is converted to an integer value, the fractional part is truncated.
- When a double value is converted to a float value, rounding of digits is done.
- When a long int is converted into int, the excess higher order bits are dropped.

These changes may cause incorrect results.

2.15.2 Typecasting

Typecasting is also known as forced conversion. Typecasting an arithmetic expression tells the compiler to represent the value of the expression in a certain way. It is done when the value of a higher data type has to be converted into the value of a lower data type. But this cast is under the programmer's control and not under compiler's control. For example, if we need to explicitly typecast an integer variable into a floating point variable, then the code to perform typecasting can be given as,

```
float salary = 10000.00;
int sal;
sal = (int) salary;
```

When floating point numbers are converted to integers (as in type conversion), the digits after the decimal are truncated. Therefore, data is lost when floating point representations are converted to integral representations. So in order to avoid such type of inaccuracies, int type variables must be typecast to float type.

As we see in the code, typecasting can be done by placing the destination data type in parentheses followed by the variable name that has to be converted. Hence, we conclude that typecasting is done to make a variable of one data type to act like a variable of another type.

We can also typecast integer values to its character equivalent (as per ASCII code) and vice versa. Typecasting is also done in arithmetic operations to get correct result. For example, when dividing two integers, the result can be of floating type. Also when multiplying two integers the result can be of long int. So to get correct precision value, typecasting can be done. For instance:

```
int a = 500, b = 70 ;
float res;
res = (float) a/b;
```

Let us look at some more examples of typecasting:

- `res = (int)9.5;`
  9.5 is converted to 9 by truncation and then assigned to `res`.
- `res = (int)12.3 / (int)4.2;`
  It is evaluated as 12/4 and the value 3 is assigned to `res`.
- `res = (double)total/n;`
  `total` is converted to double and then division is done in floating point mode.
- `res = (int)(a+b);`
  The value of `a+b` is converted to integer and then assigned to `res`.
- `res = (int)a + b;`
  `a` is converted to int and then added with `b`.
- `res = cos((double)x);`
  It converts `x` to `double` before finding its cosine value.

2.25. Write a program to convert a floating point number into the corresponding integer.

```
#include <stdio.h>
#include <conio.h>
int main()
{
    float f_num;
    int i_num;
    clrscr();
    printf("\n Enter any floating point number: ");
    scanf("%f", &f_num);
    i_num = (int)f_num;
    printf("\n The integer variant of %f is =
      %d", f_num, i_num);
    return 0;
}
```

Output

```
Enter any floating point number: 23.45
The integer variant of 23.45 is = 23
```

2.26. Write a program to convert an integer into the corresponding floating point number.

```
#include <stdio.h>
```

```
#include <conio.h>
int main()
{
    float f_num;
    int i_num;
    clrscr();
    printf("\n Enter any integer: ");
    scanf("%d", &i_num);
    f_num = (float)i_num;
    printf("\n The floating point variant of
      %d is = %f", i_num, f_num);
    return 0;
}
```

Output

```
Enter any integer: 12
The floating point variant of 12 is =
   12.00000
```

2.27. Write a program to calculate a student's result based on two examinations, one sports event, and three activities conducted. The weightage of activities = 30%, sports = 20%, and examination = 50%.

```
#include <stdio.h>
#include <conio.h>
#define ACTIVITIES_WEIGHTAGE 30
#define SPORTS_WEIGHTAGE 20
#define EXAMS_WEIGHTAGE 50
#define EXAMS_TOTAL 200
#define ACTIVITIES_TOTAL 60
#define SPORTS_TOTAL 50
main()
{
    int exam_score1, activities_score1,
      sports_score;
    int exam_score2, activities_score2,
      activities_score3;
    float exam_total, activities_total;
    float total_percent, exam_percent,
      sports_percent, activities_percent;
    clrscr();
    printf("\n Enter the score obtained in
      two examination (out of 100): ");
    scanf("%d %d", &exam_score1, &exam_
      score2);
    printf("\n Enter the score obtained in
      sports events (out of 50): ");
    scanf("%d", &sports_score);
    printf("\n Enter the score obtained in
      three activities (out of 20): ");
    scanf("%d %d %d", &activities_score1,
      &activities_score2, &activities_
      score3);

    exam_total = exam_score1 + exam_score2;
    activities_total = (activities_score1 +
      activities_score2 + activities_score3);

    exam_percent = (float)exam_total * EXAMS_
      WEIGHTAGE / EXAMS_TOTAL;
    sports_percent = (float)sports_score *
      SPORTS_WEIGHTAGE / SPORTS_TOTAL;
    activities_percent = (float)activities_
      total * ACTIVITIES_WEIGHTAGE /
      ACTIVITIES_TOTAL;

    total_percent = exam_percent + sports_
      percent + activities_percent;


    printf("\n\n **********************
      RESULT *************************");
    printf("\n Total percent in examintaion :
      %f", exam_percent);
    printf("\n Total percent in activities :
      %f", activities_percent);
    printf("\n Total percent in sports :
      %f", sports_percent);
    printf("\n ------------------------------
      ----------------------------");
    printf("\n Total percentage : %f", total_
      percent);

    return 0;
}
```

Output

```
Enter the score obtained in two examination
   (out of 100): 78 89
Enter the score obtained in sports events
   (out of 50): 34
Enter the score obtained in three activities
   (out of 20): 19 18 17
****************** RESULT *****************
Total percent in examintaion: 41.75
Total percent in activities : 27
Total percent in sports       : 13
-------------------------------------------
Total percentage              : 82%
```

POINTS TO NOTE

- C was developed in the early 1970s by Dennis Ritchie at Bell Laboratories.
- A function is defined as a group of C statements that are executed together. The execution of a C program begins at this function.
- Every word in a C program is either a keyword or an identifier. C has a set of reserved words often known as keywords that cannot be used as an identifier.
- The difference between signed and unsigned numeric variables is that signed variables can be either negative or positive but unsigned variables can only be positive. By default, C takes a signed variable.
- The statement return 0; returns the value 0 to the operating system to give an indication that there no errors were encountered during the execution of the program.
- The conditional operator or the ternary (?:) is just like an if–else statement that can be within expressions. Conditional operator is also known as ternary operator as it is neither a unary nor a binary operator; it takes three operands.
- The bitwise NOT, or complement, produces the 1s complement of the given binary value.
- The comma operator evaluates the first expression and discards its value, and then evaluates the second and returns the value as the result of the expression.
- sizeof is a unary operator used to calculate the size of data types. This operator can be applied to all data types.
- While type conversion is done implicitly, typecasting has to be done explicitly by the programmer. Type-casting is done when the value of a higher data type has to be converted to a lower data type.

GLOSSARY

ANSI C American National Standards Institute's definition of the C programming language. It is the same as the ISO definition.

Constant A value that cannot be changed.

Data type Definition of the data. For example, int, char, float.

Escape sequence Control codes that comprises of combinations of a backslash followed by letters or digits which represent non-printing characters.

Expression A sequence of operators and operands that may yield a single value as the result of its computation.

Executable program Program which will run in the environment of the operating system or within an appropriate run time environment.

Floating-point number Number that comprises of a decimal place and exponent.

Format specification A string which controls the manner in which input or output of values has to be done.

Identifier The names used to refer to stored data values as in case of constants, variables, or functions.

Integer A number that has no fractional part.

Keyword A word which has a predefined meaning to a C compiler and therefore must not be used for any other purpose.

Library file The file which comprises of compiled versions of commonly used functions that can be linked to an object file to make an executable program.

Library function A function whose source code is stored in the external library file.

Linker The tool that connects object code and libraries to form a complete, executable program.

Operator precedence The order in which operators are applied to operands during the evaluation of an expression.

Preprocessor A processor that manipulates the initial directives of the source file. The source file contains instructions that specifies how the source file shall be processed and compiled.

Preprocessor directive Instructions in the source file that specifies how the file shall be processed and compiled.

Program A text file that contains the source code to be compiled.

Runtime error A program that is encountered when a program is executed.

Source code A text file that contains the source code to be compiled.

Statement A simple statement in C language that is followed by a semicolon.

Syntax error An error or mistake in the source code that prevents the compiler from converting it into object code.

Variable An identifier (and storage) for a data type. The value of a variable may change as the program runs.

EXERCISES

Fill in the Blanks

1. C was developed by ________.
2. ________ is a group of C statements that are executed together.
3. Execution of the C program begins at ________.
4. In memory characters are stored as ________.
5. The statement return 0, returns 0 to the ________.
6. ________ finds the remainder of an integer division.
7. ________ operator reverses the value of the expression.
8. sizeof is a ________ operator used to calculate the size of data types.
9. ________ is also known as forced conversion.
10. The function scanf() returns ________.
11. ________ is executed when the value of the variable does not match with any of the values of the case statement.
12. ________ function prints data on the monitor.
13. ________ establishes the original value for a variable.
14. Character constants are quoted using ________.
15. A C program ends with a ________.
16. ________ file contains mathematical functions.
17. ________ causes the cursor to move to the next line.
18. Floating point values denote ________ values by default.
19. A variable can be made constant by declaring it with the qualifier ________ at the time of initialization.
20. The sign of the result is positive in modulo division if ________.
21. Associativity of operators defines ________.
22. ________ can be used to change the order of evaluation expressions.
23. ________ operator returns the number of bytes occupied by the operand.
24. The ________ specification is used to read/write a short integer.
25. The ________ specification is used to read/write a hexadecimal integer.
26. To print the data left-justified, ________ specification is used.

Multiple Choice Questions

1. The operator which compares two values is
   (a) assignment (b) relational
   (c) unary (d) equal
2. Which operator is used to simultaneously evaluate two expressions with relational operators?
   (a) AND (b) OR
   (c) NOT (d) all of these
3. Ternary operator operates on how many operands?
   (a) 1 (b) 2
   (c) 3 (c) 4
4. Which operator produces the 1s complement of the given binary value?
   (a) logical AND (b) bitwise AND
   (c) logical OR (c) bitwise OR
5. Which operator has the lowest precedence?
   (a) sizeof (b) unary
   (c) assignment (d) comma
6. Short integer has which conversion character associated with it
   (a) %c (b) %d
   (c) %hd (d) %f
7. Which of the following is not a character constant?
   (a) 'A' (b) "A"
   (c) ' ' (d) '*'
8. Which of the following is not a floating point constant?
   (a) 20 (b) -4.5
   (c) 'a' (d) pi

EXERCISES

9. Identify the invalid variable names.
   (a) Initial.Name (b) A+B
   (c) $amt (d) Floats
10. Which operator cannot be used with float operands?
   (a) + (b) –
   (c) % (d) *
11. Identify the erroneous expression.
   (a) x=y=2, 4; (b) res = ++a * 5;
   (c) res = /4; (d) res = a++ –b *2

State True or False

1. We can have only one function in a C program.
2. Header files are used to store program's source code.
3. Keywords are case sensitive.
4. Variable first is same as First.
5. An identifier can contain any valid printable ASCII character.
6. Signed variables can increase the maximum positive range.
7. Commented statements are not executed by the compiler.
8. $amount is a valid identifier in C.
9. Comments cannot be nested.
10. The equality operators have higher precedence than the relational operators.
11. Shifting once to the left multiplies the number by 2.
12. printf("%d", scanf("%d", & num)); is a valid C statement.
13. 1,234 is a valid integer constant.
14. A `printf` statement can generate only one line of output.
15. `stdio.h` is used to store the source code of the program.
16. The closing brace of `main()` is the logical end of the program.
17. The declaration section gives instructions to the computer.
18. Any valid printable ASCII character can be used for a variable name.
19. Declaration of variables can be done anywhere in the program.
20. Underscore can be used anywhere in the variable name.
21. The variable amt is same as AMT in C.
22. void is a data type in C.
23. The function scanf can be used to read only one value at a time.
24. All arithmetic operators have same precedence.
25. The modulus operator can be used only with integers.
26. The expression containing all integer operands is called an integer expression.

Review Questions

1. What are header files? Why are they important? Can we write a C program without using any header file?
2. What are variables?
3. Explain the difference between declaration and definition.
4. How is memory reserved using a declaration statement?
5. What does the data type of a variable signify?
6. Give the structure of a C program.
7. What do you understand by identifiers and keywords?
8. Write a short note on basic data types that the C language supports.
9. Why do we need signed and unsigned char?
10. Explain the terms variables and constants. How many type of variables are supported by C?
11. Why do we include `<stdio.h>` in our programs?
12. Write a short note on operators available in C language.
13. Give the operator precedence chart.
14. Evaluate the expression: (x > y) + ++a || !c
15. Differentiate between typecasting and type conversion.
16. Write a program to read an integer. Then display the value of that integer in decimal, octal, and hexadecimal notation.
17. Write short notes on `printf` and `scanf` functions.
18. Explain the utility of `#define` and `#include` statements.
19. Write a program that prints floating point value in exponential format with the following specifications:
   (a) correct to two decimal places;

EXERCISES

(b) correct to four decimal places; and

(c) correct to eight decimal places.

20. Write a program to read 10 integers. Display these numbers by printing three numbers in a line separated by commas.
21. Write a program to print the count of even numbers between 1 and 200. Also print their sum.
22. Write a program to count number of vowels in a text.
23. Write a program to read the address of a user. Display the result by breaking it into multiple lines.
24. Write a program to read two floating point numbers. Add these numbers and assign the result to an integer. Finally display the value of all the three variables.
25. Write a program to read a floating point number. Display the rightmost digit of the integral part of the number.
26. Write a program to calculate simple interest and compound interest.
27. Write a program to calculate salary of an employee, given his basic pay (to be entered by the user), HRA = 10% of the basic pay, TA = 5% of basic pay. Define HRA and TA as constants and use them to calculate the salary of the employee.
28. Write a program to prepare a grocery bill. For that enter the name of the items purchased, quantity in which it is purchased, and its price per unit. Then display the bill in the following format.

```
************** B I L L **************
Item    Quantity     Price       Amount
______________________________________
Total Amount to be paid
______________________________________
```

29. Write a C program using `printf` statement to print BYE in the following format.

```
BBB    Y   Y   EEEE
B  B    Y Y    E
BBB      Y     EEEE
B  B     Y     E
BBB      Y     EEEE
```

30. Find errors in the following declaration statements:

```
Int n;
float a b;
double = a, b;
complex a b;
a,b : INTEGER
long int a;b;
```

31. Find error(s) in the following code.

```
int a = 9;
float y = 2.0;
a = b % a;
printf("%d", a);
```

32. Find error(s) in the following scanf statement.

```
scanf("%d%f", &marks, &avg);
```

Give the output of the following programs.

1.
```
#include <stdio.h>
main()
{
   int x=3, y=5, z=7;
   int a, b;

   a = x * 2 + y / 5 - z * y;
   b = ++x * (y - 3) / 2 - z++ * y;
   printf("\n a = %d", a);
   printf("\n b = %d", b);
   return 0;
}
```

2.
```
#include <stdio.h>
main()
{
   int a, b =3;
   char c = 'A';
   a = b + c;
   printf("\n a = %d", a);
   return 0;
}
```

3.
```
#include <stdio.h>
main()
{
   int a;
   printf("\n %d", 1/3 + 1/3);
   printf("\n %f", 1.0/3.0 + 1.0/3.0);
   a = 15/10.0 + 3/2;
   printf("\n %d", a);
   return 0;
}
```

4.
```
#include <stdio.h>
int main()
{
   int a = 4);
```

EXERCISES

```
    printf("\n %d ", 10 + a++);
    printf("\n %d ", 10 + ++a);
    return 0;
}
```

5.
```
#include <stdio.h>
main()
{
    int a = 4, b = 5, c= 6;
    a = b == c;
    printf("\n a = %d ", a);
    return 0;
}
```

6.
```
#include <stdio.h>
#include <conio.h>
main()
{
    int a=1, b=2, c=3, d=4, e=5, res;
    clrscr();
    res = a + b /c - d * e;
    printf("\n Result = %d" res);
    res = (a + b) /c - d * e;
    printf("\n Result = %d",res);
    res = a + ( b / (c -d)) * e;
    printf("\n Result = %d",res);
    return 0;
}
```

7.
```
#include <stdio.h>
main()
{
    int a = 4, b = 5;
    printf("\n %d ", (a > b)? a: b);
    return 0;
}
```

8.
```
#include <stdio.h>
int main()
{
    int a = 4, b = 12, c= -3, res;
    res = a > b && a < c;
    printf("\n %d ", res);
    res = a == c || a < b;
    printf("\n %d ", res);
    res = b >10 || b && c < 0 || a > 0;
    printf("\n %d ", res);
    res = (a/2.0 == 0.0 && b/2.0 != 0.0) || c < 0.0;
    printf("\n %d ", res);
    return 0;
}
```

9.
```
#include <stdio.h>
int main()
{
    int a = 20, b = 5, result;
    float c = 20.0, d= 5.0;
    printf("\n10 + a / 4 * b = %d", 10 + a / 4 * b);
    printf("\nc/d*b+a-b=%d",c/d*b+a-b);
    return 0;
}
```

10.
```
#include <stdio.h>
int main()
{
    int a, b;
    printf("\n a = %d \t b = %d \t a + b
      = %d", a, b, a+b);
    return 0;
}
```

11.
```
#include <stdio.h>
int main()
{
    printf("\n %d", 'F');
    return 0;
}
```

12.
```
#include <stdio.h>
int main()
{
    int n = 2;
    n = !n;
    printf("\n n = %d", n);
    return 0;
}
```

13.
```
#include <stdio.h>
int main()
{
    int a = 100, b = 3;
    float c;
    c = a/b;
    printf("\n c = %f", c);
    return 0;
}
```

14.
```
#include <stdio.h>
int main()
{
```

EXERCISES

```
   int n = -2;
   printf("\n n = %d", -n);
   return 0;
}
```

15.
```
#include <stdio.h>
int main()
{
   int a = 2, b = 3, c, d;
   c = a++;
   d = ++b;
   printf("\n c = %d d = %d", c, d);
   return 0;
}
```

16.
```
#include <stdio.h>
int main()
{
   int _ = 30;
   printf("\n _ = %d", _);
   return 0;
}
```

17.
```
#include <stdio.h>
int main()
{
   int a = 2, b = 3, c, d;
   a++;
   ++b;
   printf("\n a = %d b = %d", a, b);
   return 0;
}
```

18.
```
#include <stdio.h>
int main()
{
   int a = 2, b = 3;
   printf("\n %d", ++(a - b));
   return 0;
}
```

19.
```
#include <stdio.h>
int main()
{
   int a = 2, b = 3;
   printf("\n %d", ++a - b);
   return 0;
}
```

20.
```
#include <stdio.h>
int main()
{
   int a = 2, b = 3;
   printf("\n a * b = %d", a*b);
   printf("\n a / b = %d", a/b);
   printf("\n a % b = %d", a%b);
   printf("\n a && b = %d", a*&&b);
   return 0;
}
```

21.
```
#include <stdio.h>
int main()
{
   int a = 2;
   a = a + 3*a++;
   printf("\n a= %d", a);
   return 0;
}
```

22.
```
#include <stdio.h>
int main()
{
   int result;
   result = 3 + 5 - 1 * 17 % -13;
   printf("%d", result);
   result = 3 * 2 + ( 15 / 4 % 7);
   printf("%d", result);
   result = 18 / 9 / 3 * 2 * 3 * 5 % 10 / 4;
   printf("%d", result);
   return 0;
}
```

23.
```
#include <stdio.h>
int main()
{
   int n = 2;
   printf("\n %d %d %d", n++, n, ++n);
   return 0;
}
```

24.
```
#include <stdio.h>
int main()
{
   int a = 2, b = 3, c = 4;
   a=b==c;
   printf("\n a = %d",a);
   return 0;
}
```

25.
```
#include <stdio.h>
int main()
{
   int num = 070;
   printf("\n num = %d", num);
   printf("\n num = %o", num);
   printf("\n num = %x", num);
```

EXERCISES

```
    return 0;
}
```

26.
```
#include <stdio.h>
int main()
{
    printf("\n %40.27s Welcome to C
      programming");
    printf("\n %40.20s Welcome to C
      programming");
    printf("\n %40.14s Welcome to C
      programming");

    printf("\n %-40.27s Welcome to C
      programming");
    printf("\n %-40.20s Welcome to C
      programming");
    printf("\n %-40.14s Welcome to C
      programming");

    return 0;
}
```

27.
```
#include <stdio.h>
main()
{
    int a = -21, b = 3;
    printf("\n %d", a/b + 10);
    b = -b;
    printf("\n %d", a/b + 10);
    return 0;
}
```

28.
```
#include <stdio.h>
main()
{
    int a;
    float b;
    printf("\n Enter four digit number: ");
    scanf("%2d", &a);
    printf("\n Enter any floating point
      number: ");
    scanf("%f", &b);
    printf("\n The numbers are : %d and
      %f", a, b);
    return 0;
}
```

29.
```
#include <stdio.h>
main()
{
    char a, b, c;
    printf("\n Enter three characters : ");
    scanf("%c %c %c", &a, &b, &c);
    a++; b++; C==;
    printf("\n a = %c b = %c and d = %c",
      a, b, c);
    return 0;
}
```

30.
```
#include <stdio.h>
{
    int x=10, y=20, res;
    res = y++ + x++;
    res += ++y + ++x;
    printf("\n x = %d  y = %d  RESULT =
      %d", x,y, res");
    return 0;
}
```

31.
```
#include <stdio.h>
{
    int x=10, y=20, res;
    res = x+++b;
    printf("\n x = %d  y = %d  RESULT =
      %d", x,y, res");
    return 0;
}
```

ANNEXURE 1

A1.1 HOW TO WRITE, COMPILE, AND EXECUTE A C PROGRAM IN UNIX, LINUX, AND UBUNTU

Writing, Compiling, and Executing a C Program in Unix and Linux

To execute a C program first make sure that C compiler gcc is installed on your machine. This is done by writing the *$ whereis cc* or *$ which cc* command in the command shell. If gcc is present then the complete path of the compiler will be displayed on screen. In case the compiler is present, follow the steps given below to write and execute the program.

Step 1: Open the Vim editor and type the program. For this first type the following command in the command shell.

```
$ vim firstprog.c
```

Now when the editor gets opened type the program given below.

```
#include<stdio.h>
main()
{
 printf("Welcome to the World of Programming
 ....");
}
```

Step 2: Compile the program using cc or gcc command. The command will create the a.out file.

```
$ cc firstprog.c
```

Step 3: Execute the C Program. The program can be executed in two ways. First, by executing the *a.out* to see the output. Second, by renaming it to another file and executing it as shown below.

```
$ ./a.out
or
$ mv a.out firstprogram
$ ./firstprogram
```

This will print `Welcome to the World of Programming ....` on the screen.

Writing, Compiling, and Executing a C Program on Ubuntu

Step 1: Open a text editor to write the C program. You can choose Vim, or gedit, or any other editor available to you.

Step 2: Type the code as shown below and save it in a file (e.g., firstprog.c)

```
#include<stdio.h>
main()
{
 printf("Welcome to the World of Programming
 ....");
}
```

Step 3: Compile the program using gcc. GCC is a compiler that is installed by default in Ubuntu. For compiling write the following command:

```
gcc firstprog.c -o firstprogram
```

In the above command, gcc is the compiler; firstprog.c is the name of the file to be compiled and the filename following –o specifies the filename of the output. When you execute this command, the compiler will generate an executable file in case there are no syntax or semantic errors in the program. If there are errors, the compiler will notify you about the errors and you will then have to fix them before re-compiling the code.

Step 4: Execute the program simply by typing the command given below.

```
./firstprogram
```

A1.2 BIT LEVEL PROGRAMMING

A C programmer usually does not need to care about operations at the bit level. He has to think only in terms of int and double, or even higher level data types composed of a combination of these. However, at times it becomes necessary to go to the level of an individual bit. For example, in case of exclusive-OR (XOR) encryption or when dealing with data compression, a programmer needs to operate on individual bits of the data and thus needs to do programming at the bit level. Moreover, bit operations can be used to speed up your program.

Thinking About Bits

The byte is the lowest level at which data can be accessed. C does not support bit type. Therefore, we cannot perform any operation on an individual bit. Even a bitwise operator will be applied to, at a minimum, an entire byte at a time.

We have already studied bitwise NOT, AND, OR, and XOR operators in Chapter 1. To summarize:

- The bitwise NOT ("), or complement, is a unary operator used to perform logical negation on each bit thereby resulting in 1s complement of the given binary value. Digits that were 0s become 1s, and vice versa. For example:

```
"(1010) = 0101
```

- A bitwise OR (|) takes two bit patterns of equal length, and produces another one of the same length by performing the logical inclusive OR operation on each pair of corresponding bits. In each pair, the result is 1 if the first bit is 1 OR the second bit is 1 OR both bits are 1, and otherwise the result is 0.

```
1001 | 0101 = 1101
```

- A bitwise exclusive or (`^`) takes two bit patterns of equal length and performs the logical XOR operation on each pair of corresponding bits. In the result, a bit is set to `1` if the two bits are different, and `0` if they are the same.

  The XOR operation is generally used by assembly language programmers as a short-cut to set the value of a register to zero. Performing `XOR` on a value against itself always results in zero. The `XOR` operation requires fewer `CPU` clock cycles when compared with the sequence of operations that has to be performed to load a zero value and save it to the register. The bitwise `XOR` is also used to toggle flags in a set of bits. For example,

```
1010 ^ 0011 = 1001
```

- A `bitwise AND (&)` takes two bit patterns of equal length and performs the logical AND operation on each pair of corresponding bits. In each pair, the resultant bit is set to `1` if the first bit is `1 AND` the second bit is `1`. Otherwise, it is set to `0`. For example:

```
1010 & 0011 = 0010
```

  The `bitwise AND` is commonly used to perform *bit masking*. This is done to isolate part of a string of bits, or to determine whether a particular bit is 1 or 0. For example, to determine if the second bit is 1, you can straightaway do a bitwise AND to it and another bit pattern containing 1 in the second bit. For example,

```
1010 & 0010 = 0010
```

  Since the result is `0010` (non-zero), it clearly indicates that the second bit in the original pattern was `1`. Such an operation is called *bit masking* because it *masks* the portions that should not be altered or which are not of interest. In this case, the `0` values mask the bits that are not of interest.

  The `bitwise AND` can also be combined with the `bitwise NOT` to *clear* bits.

A1.3 BITWISE SHIFT OPERATORS

In bitwise shift operations, the digits are moved, or *shifted*, to the left or right. The CPU registers have a fixed number of available bits for storing numerals, so when perform shift operations; some bits will be '*shifted out*' of the register at one end, while the same number of bits are '*shifted in*' from the other end.

In an *arithmetic shift*, the bits that are shifted out of either end are discarded. There are two types of arithmetic shift: left arithmetic shift and a right arithmetic shift.

In a left arithmetic shift, zeros are shifted in on the right. For example, consider the register with the following bit pattern:

1	1	0	0	0	1	0	1	← 0
7	6	5	4	3	2	1	0	

1	0	0	0	1	0	1	0
7	6	5	4	3	2	1	0

Note that in arithmetic shift left, the leftmost digit was shifted past the end of the register, and a new `0` was shifted into the rightmost position. The general form of doing a left shift can be given as

```
op << n
```

Here, `op` is an integer expression that has to be shifted and `n` is the number of bit positions to be shifted. For example, if we write

```
unsigned int x = 11000101;
Then x << 2 = 00010100
```

If a right arithmetic shift is performed on an unsigned integer then zeros are shifted on the left.

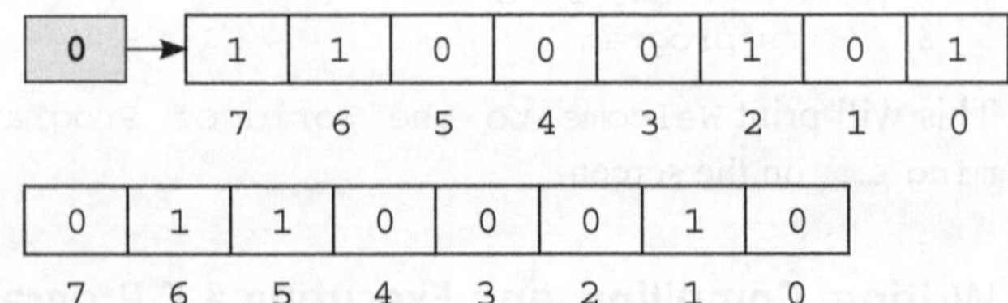

The general form of an arithmetic right shift can be given as:

```
op >> n
```

Here, op is an integer expression that has to be shifted and n is the number of bit positions to be shifted. For example, if we write

```
unsigned int x = 11000101;
```

Then x >> 2 = 00110001

Points to Remember

- op and n can be constants or variables.
- n cannot be negative.
- n should not exceed the number of bits used to represent op.
- Left shifting is the equivalent of multiplying by a power of 2.
- Right shift will be the equivalent of integer division by 2.

Note that in arithmetic shift right operation, bits in op are shifted to right by n positions. In this process, the rightmost n bits will be lost and zeros will be shifted in the leftmost n bits. *(This is true for unsigned integers, for signed integers the shift right operation is machine dependent).*

The left and right shift operators will result in significantly faster code than calculating and then multiplying by a power of two.

Have you wondered what will happen if you shift a number like 128 and storing it in a single byte: 10000000? Since, 128 * 2 = 256, and a register is incapable of storing a number that is bigger than a single byte, so it should not be surprising that the result is 00000000.

CHAPTER 3

Decision Control and Looping Statements

Takeaways

- Decision Control Statements
- Conditional Branching Statements
- Iterative Statements
- Nested Loops
- Break, Continue, and Goto Statements

3.1 INTRODUCTION TO DECISION CONTROL STATEMENTS

Till now we know that the code in the C program is executed sequentially from the first line of the program to its last line, i.e., the second statement is executed after the first, the third statement is executed after the second, and so on.

Although this is true, but in some cases we want only selected statements to be executed. Such type of conditional processing extends the usefulness of programs. It allows the programmers to build programs that determine which statements of the code should be executed and which should be ignored.

C supports two types of decision control statements that can alter the flow of a sequence of instructions. These include conditional type branching and unconditional type branching. Figure 3.1 shows the categorization of decision control statements in C language.

3.2 CONDITIONAL BRANCHING STATEMENTS

The conditional branching statements help to jump from one part of the program to another depending on whether a particular condition is satisfied or not. These decision control statements include:

- `if` statement
- `if-else` statement
- `if-else-if` statement
- `switch` statement

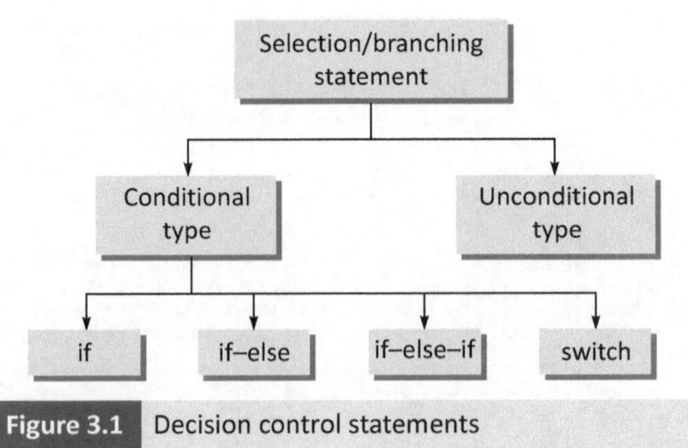

Figure 3.1 Decision control statements

3.2.1 `if` Statement

The `if` statement is the simplest form of decision control statements that is frequently used in decision making. The general form of a simple `if` statement is shown in Fig. 3.2.

The `if` structure may include one statement or `n` statements enclosed within curly brackets. First the test expression is evaluated. If the test expression is true, the statement of if block (statement 1 to n) are executed otherwise these statements will be skipped and the execution will jump to statement x.

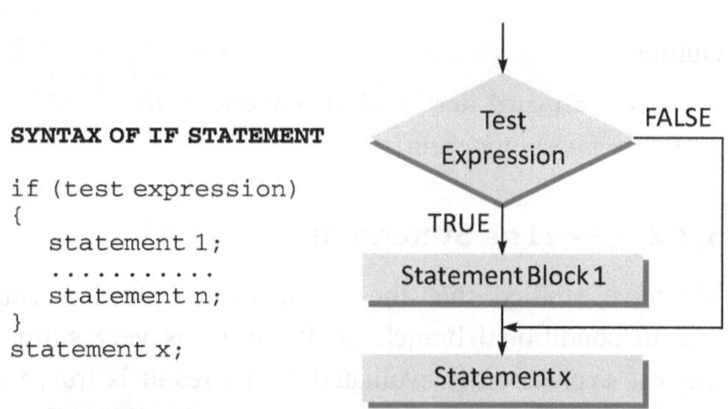

Figure 3.2 if statement construct

The statement in an if construct is any valid C language statement and the test expression is any valid C language expression that may include logical operators. Note that there is no semicolon after the test expression. This is because the condition and statement should be put together as a single statement.

Programming Tip: Properly indent the statements that are dependent on the previous statements.

```
#include <stdio.h>
int main()
{
int x=10; // Initialize the value of x
if ( x>0) // Test the value of x
x++;      // Increment x if it is > 0
printf("\n x = %d", x);
   // Print the value of x
return 0;
}
```

Output

```
x = 11
```

In the above code, we take a variable x and initialize it to 10. In the test expression we check if the value of x is greater than 0. If the test expression evaluates to true then the value of x is incremented. Then the value of x is printed on the screen. The output of this program is

```
x = 11
```

Observe that the printf statement will be executed even if the test expression is false.

3.1 Write a program to determine whether a person is eligible to vote.

```
#include <stdio.h>
#include <conio.h>
main()
{
int age;
printf("\n Enter the age: ");
scanf("%d", &age");
if(age >= 18)
printf("\n You are eligible to vote");
getch()
return 0;
}
```

Output

```
Enter the age: 28
You are eligible to vote
```

In case the statement block contains only one statement, putting curly brackets becomes optional. If there is more than 1 statement in the statement block, putting curly brackets becomes mandatory.

3.2 Write a program to determine the character entered by the user.

```
#include <stdio.h>
#include <ctype.h>
#include <conio.h>
main()
{
char ch;
printf("\n Press any key: ");
scanf("%c", &ch);
if(isalpha(ch)>0)
printf("\n The user has entered a
   character");
if(isdigit(ch)>0)
printf("\n The user has entered a digit");
if(isprint(ch)>0)
printf("\n The user has entered a printable
   character");
if(ispunct(ch)>0)
printf("\n The user has entered a
   punctuation mark");
if(isspace(ch)>0)
printf("\n The user has entered a white
   space character");
getch();
return 0;
}
```

Output

```
Press any key: 3
The user has entered a digit
```

Now let us write a program to detect errors during data input. But before doing this we must remember that when the `scanf()` function completes its action, it returns the number of items that are successfully read. We can use this returned value to test if any error has occurred during data input. For example, consider the following function:

```
scanf("%d %f %c", &a, &b, &c);
```

If the user enters:

```
1 1.2 A
```

then the `scanf()` will return `3`, since three values have been successfully read. But had the user entered,

```
1 abc A
```

then the `scanf()` will immediately terminate when it encounters `abc` as it was expecting a floating point value and print an error message. So after understanding this concept, let us write a program code to detect an error in data input.

```
#include <stdio.h>
main()
{
int num;
char ch;
printf("\n Enter an int and a char value: ");
// Check the return value of scanf()
if(scanf("%d %c", &num, &ch)==2)
printf("\n Data read successfully");
else
printf("\n Error in data input");
}
```

Output

```
Enter an int and a char value: 2 A
Data read successfully
```

3.2.2 `if-else` Statement

We have studied that the `if` statement plays a vital role in conditional branching. Its usage is very simple, the test expression is evaluated, if the result is true, the statement(s) followed by the expression is executed else if the expression is false, the statement is skipped by the compiler.

> **Programming Tip:** Align the matching `if-else` clause vertically.

But what if you want a separate set of statements to be executed if the expression returns a zero value? In such cases we use an `if-else` statement rather than using simple `if` statement. The general form of a simple `if-else` statement is shown in Fig. 3.3.

In the above syntax, we have written statement block. A statement block may include one or more statements. According to the `if-else` construct, first the test expression is evaluated. If the expression is true, `statement block 1` is executed and `statement block 2` is skipped. Otherwise, if the expression is false, statement block 2 is executed and `statement block 1` is ignored. Now in any case after the `statement block 1` or `2` gets

SYNTAX OF IF–ELSE STATEMENT

```
if (test expression)
{
   statement block 1;
}
else
{
   statement block 2;
}
statement x;
```

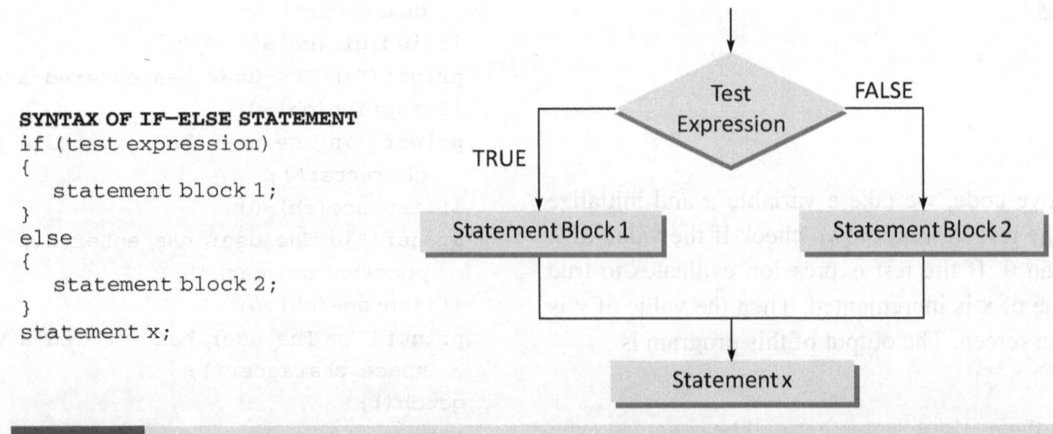

Figure 3.3 If-else statement construct

executed the control will pass to `statement x`. Therefore, `statement x` is executed in every case.

3.3 Write a program to calculate x = (md – bn)/(ad – cb).

```
#include<stdio.h>
#include<conio.h>
main()
{
    int a, b, c, d, m, n;
    float x;
    clrscr();
    printf("\n Enter the values for a,b,c,d,m
    and n : ");
    scanf("%d %d %d %d %d %d", &a, &b, &c,
    &d, &m, &n);
    if(a*d - c*b != 0)
       x = (float)(m*d - b*n)/(float)(a*d - c*b);
    printf("\n The value of expression = %.2f", x);
}
```

Output

```
Enter the values for a,b,c,d,m and n : 5 2 4 3 6 3
The value of expression = 1.71
```

3.4 Write a program to find the number of people who voted.

```
#include<stdio.h>
#include<conio.h>
main()
{
    int age, count=0;
    char ch;
    clrscr();
    for(i=0;i<20;i++)
    {
       scanf("%d %c", &age, &ch);
       if(age>=18 && ch=='n')
          count++;
    }
    printf("\n Total persons surveyed = 20");
    printf("\n No. of people who were
    eligible to vote but did not vote = %d",
    count);
}
```

Output

```
12 n 23 y 56 y 34 n 78 y 90 n 27 y 45 n
18 n 56 y 47 n 44 y 25 n 69 y 52 n 79 y 42
n 63 y 72 n 87 n
Total persons surveyed = 20
No. of people who were eligible to vote but
did not vote = 10
```

3.5 Write a program to find whether the given number is even or odd.

```
#include <stdio.h>
#include <conio.h>
main()
{
int num;
clrscr();
printf("\n Enter any number: ");
scanf("%d",&num);

if(num%2 == 0)
printf("\n %d is an even number", num);
else
printf("\n %d is an odd number", num);
return 0;
}
```

Output

```
Enter any number: 11
11 is an odd number
```

3.6 Write a program to enter any character. If the entered character is in lower case then convert it into upper case and if it is a lower case character then convert it into upper case.

```
#include <stdio.h>
#include <conio.h>
int main()
{
char ch;
clrscr();
printf("\n Enter any character: ");
scanf("%c", &ch);

if(ch >='A' && ch<='Z')
printf("\n The entered character was in
   upper case. In lower case it is: %c",
   (ch+32));
else
printf("\n The entered character was in
   lower case. In upper case it is: %c",
   (ch-32));
return 0;
}
```

Output

```
Enter any character: a
The entered character was in lower case. In
   upper case it is: A
```

3.7 Write a program to enter a character and then determine whether it is a vowel or not.

```
#include <stdio.h>
#include <conio.h>
main()
```

```
{
char ch;
clrscr();

printf("\n Enter any character: ");
scanf("%c", &ch);

if(ch ='a' ||ch =='e' ||ch=='i' ||ch=='o'
   ||ch=='u' || ch=='A' ||ch=='E' ||ch=='I'
   ||ch=='O' ||ch=='U' )
   printf("\n %c is a VOWEL", ch);
else
   printf("\n %c is not a vowel");

getch();
return 0;
}
```

Output

```
Enter any character: v
v is not a vowel
```

3.8 Write a program to find whether a given year is a leap year or not.

```
#include <stdio.h>
#include <conio.h>
int main()
{
int year;
clrscr();
printf("\n Enter any year: ");
scanf("%d",&year);
if((year%4 == 0) && ((year%100 !=0) ||
   (year%400 == 0)))
   printf("\n Leap Year");
else
   printf("\n Not A Leap Year");
return 0;
}
```

Output

```
Enter any year: 1996
Leap Year
```

Pitfall A very common pitfall is to use assignment operator (`=`) instead of comparison operator (`==`). For example, consider the statement

```
if(a = 10)
   printf("%d", a);
```

Here, the statement does not test whether `a` is equal to `10` or not. Rather the value 10 is assigned to `a` and then the value is returned to the `if` construct for testing. Since the value of `a` is non-zero, the `if` construct returns a `1`.

Programming Tip: Do not use floating point numbers for checking for equality in the test expression.

The compiler cannot detect such kinds of errors and thus the programmer should carefully use the operators. The program code given below shows the outcome of mishandling the assignment and the comparison operators.

```
#include <stdio.h>
main()
{
int x = 2, y = 3;
if(x = y)
   printf("\n EQUAL");
else
   printf("\n NOT EQUAL");
}
```

Output

```
EQUAL
```

```
#include <stdio.h>
main()
{
int x = 2, y = 3;
if(x == y)
   printf("\n EQUAL");
else
   printf("\n NOT EQUAL");
}
```

Output

```
NOT EQUAL
```

3.2.3 `if-else-if` Statement

C language supports `if-else-if` statements to test additional conditions apart from the initial test expression. The `if-else-if` construct works in the same way as a normal `if` statement. `if-else-if` construct is also known as nested `if` construct. Its construct is given in Fig. 3.4.

It is not necessary that every `if` statement should have an `else` block as C supports simple `if` statements. After the first test expression or the first `if` branch, the programmer can have as many `else-if` branches as he wants depending on the expressions that have to be tested. For example, the following code tests whether a number entered by the user is negative, positive, or equal to zero.

Programming Tip: Braces must be placed on separate lines so that the block of statements can be easily identified.

```
SYNTAX OF IF-ELSE-IF STATEMENT
if ( test expression 1)
{
   statement block 1;
}
else if ( test expression 2)
{
   statement block 2;
}
   ........................
else
{
   statement Block X;
}
Statement Y;
```

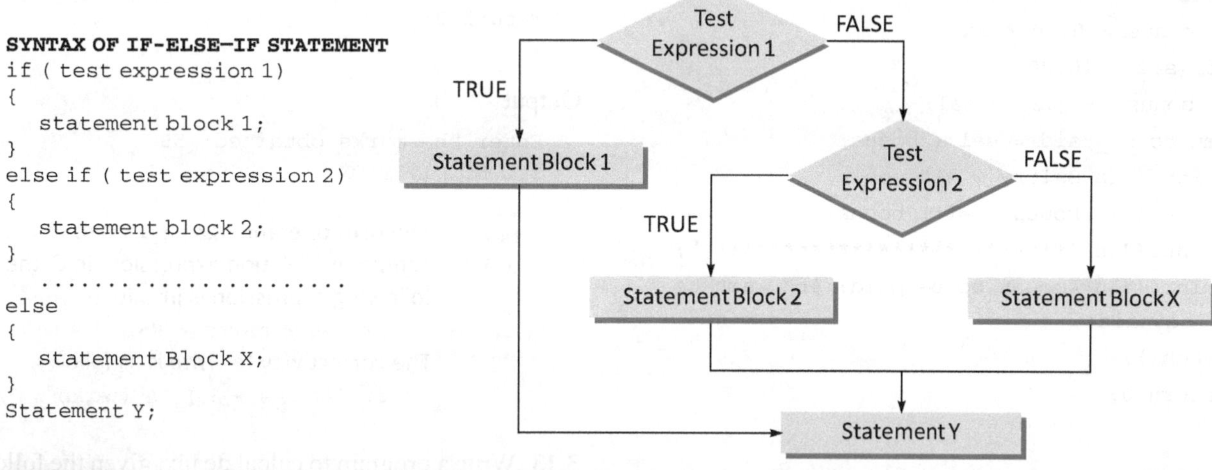

Figure 3.4 `if-else-if` statement construct

3.9 Write a program to demonstrate the use of nested `if` structure.

```
#include <stdio.h>
main()
{
int x, y;
printf("\n Enter two numbers: ");
scanf("%d %d", &x, &y);
if(x == y)
printf("\n The two numbers are equal");
else if(x > y)
printf("\n %d is greater than %d", x, y);
else
printf("\n %d is less than %d", x, y);
return 0;
}
```

Output

```
Enter two numbers: 12 23
12 is less than 23
```

3.10 Write a program to test whether a number entered is positive, negative or equal to zero.

```
#include <stdio.h>
main()
{
int num;
printf("\n Enter any number: ");
scanf("%d", &num);
if(num==0)
printf("\n The value is equal to zero");
else if(num>0)
printf("\n The number is positive");
else
printf("\n The number is negative");
return 0;
}
```

Programming Tip: Keep the logical expressions simple and short. For this, you may use nested if statements.

Output

```
Enter any number: 0
The number is equal to zero
```

3.11 A company decides to give bonus to all its employees on Diwali. A 5% bonus on salary is given to the male workers and 10% bonus on salary to the female workers. Write a program to enter the salary and sex of the employee. If the salary of the employee is less than Rs 10,000 then the employee gets an extra 2% bonus on salary. Calculate the bonus that has to be given to the employee and display the salary that the employee will get.

```
#include <stdio.h>
#include <conio.h>
main()
{
char ch;
float sal, bonus, amt_to_be_paid;
printf("\n Enter the sex of the employee (m
  or f: ");
scanf("%c", &ch);
printf("\n Enter the salary of the employee: ");
scanf("%f", &sal);
if(ch == 'm')
```

```
    bonus = 0.05 * sal;
else
    bonus = 0.10 * sal;
if (sal < 10000)
    bonus += 0.20 * sal;
amt_to_be_paid = sal + bonus;
printf("\n Salary = %f", sal);
printf("\n Bonus = %f", bonus);
printf("\n ***************************");
printf("\n Amount to be paid: %f", amt_to_
    be_paid);
getch();
return 0;
}
```

Output

```
Enter the sex of the employee (m or f): f
Enter the salary of the employee: 12000
Salary = 12000
Bonus = 1200
***************************
Amount to be paid: 13200
```

In the program to test whether a number is positive or negative, if the first test expression evaluates a true value then rest of the statements in the code will be ignored and after executing the `printf` statement which displays `"The value is equal to zero"`, the control will jump to `return 0` statement. Consider the following example which shows usage of the `if-else-if` statement.

3.12 Write a program to display the examination result.

```
#include <stdio.h>
main()
{
int marks;
printf("\n Enter the marks obtained: ");
scanf("%d", &marks);
if ( marks >= 75)
    printf("\n DISTINCTION");
else if ( marks >= 60 &&
marks <75)
    printf("\n FIRST
DIVISION");
else if ( marks >= 50 &&
marks < 60)
    printf("\n SECOND
DIVISION");
else if ( marks >= 40 &&
marks < 50)
    printf("\n THIRD
DIVISION");
else
    printf("\n FAIL");
return 0;
}
```

Programming Tip: Try to use the most probable condition first so that unnecessary tests are eliminated and the efficiency of the program is improved.

Output

```
Enter the marks obtained: 55
SECOND DIVISION
```

The AND operand (&&) is used to form a compound relation expression. In C, the following expression is invalid.

```
if (60 ≤ marks ≤ 75)
```

The correct way to write is as follows:

```
if ((marks ≥ 60) && (marks ≤ 75)
```

3.13 Write a program to calculate tax, given the following conditions:

- if income is less than 150,000 then no tax
- if taxable income is in the range 150,001–300,000 then charge 10% tax
- if taxable income is in the range 300,001–500,000 then charge 20% tax
- if taxable income is above 500,001 then charge 30% tax

```
#include <stdio.h>
#include <conio.h>
#define MIN1 150001
#define MAX1 300000
#define RATE1 0.10
#define MIN2 300001
#define MAX2 500000
#define RATE2 0.20
#define MIN3 500001
#define RATE3 0.30

main()
{
double income, taxable_income;
clrscr();
printf("\n Enter the income: ");
scanf("%lf", &income);

taxable_income = income - 150000;
if(taxable_income <= 0)
    printf("\n NO TAX");
else if(taxable_income >= MIN1 && taxable_
    income < MAX1)
    tax = (taxable_income - MIN1) * RATE1;
else if(taxable_income >= MIN2 && taxable_
    income < MAX2)
```

```
    tax = (taxable_income - MIN2) * RATE2;
else
    tax = (taxable_income - MIN3) * RATE3;
printf("\n TAX = %lf", tax);
getch();
return 0;
}
```

Output

```
Enter the income: 900000
TAX = 74999.70
```

3.14 Write a program to find the greatest among three numbers.

```
#include <stdio.h>
#include <conio.h>
int main()
{
int num1, num2, num3, big=0;
clrscr();
printf("\n Enter the first number: ");
scanf("%d", &num1);
printf("\n Enter the second number: ");
scanf("%d", &num2);
printf("\n Enter the third number: ");
scanf("%d", &num3);

if(num1>num2)
{
if(num1>num3)
printf("\n %d is greater than %d and %d",
    num1, num2, num3);
else
printf("\n %d is greater than %d and %d",
    num3, num1, num2);
}
else if(num2>num3)
printf("\n %d is greater than %d and %d",
    num2, num1, num3);
else
printf("\n %d is greater
than %d and %d", num3,
num1, num2);
return 0;
}
```

Programming Tip: It is always recommended to indent the statements in the block by at least three spaces to the right of the braces.

Output

```
Enter the first number: 12
Enter the second number: 23
Enter the third number: 9
23 is greater than 12 and 9
```

3.15 Write a program to input three numbers and then find largest of them using && operator.

```
#include <stdio.h>
#include <conio.h>
main()
{
int num1, num2, num3;
clrscr();
printf("\n Enter the first number: ");
scanf("%d", &num1);
printf("\n Enter the second number: ");
scanf("%d", &num2);
printf("\n Enter the third number: ");
scanf("%d", &num3);

if(num1>num2  &&  num1>num3)
printf("\n %d is the largest number", num1);
if(num2>num1  &&  num2>num3)
printf("\n %d is the largest number", num2);
else
printf("\n %d is the largest number", num3);
getch();
return 0;
}
```

Output

```
Enter the first number: 12
Enter the second number: 23
Enter the third number: 9
23 is the largest number
```

3.16 Write a program to enter the marks of a student in four subjects. Then calculate the total, aggregate, and display the grades obtained by the student.

```
#include <stdio.h>
#include <conio.h>
main()
{
int marks1, marks2, marks3, marks4, total = 0;
float avg =0.0;
clrscr();

printf("\n Enter the marks in Mathematics: ");
scanf("%d", &marks1);
printf("\n Enter the marks in Science: ");
scanf("%d", &marks2);
printf("\n Enter the marks in Social
    Science: ");
scanf("%d", &marks3);
printf("\n Enter the marks in Computer
    Science: ");
```

```
scanf("%d", &marks4);
total = marks1 + marks2 + marks3 + marks4;
avg = total/4;
printf("\n Total = %d", total);
printf("\n Aggregate = %.2f", avg);

if(avg >= 75)
  printf("\n DISTINCTION");
else if(avg>=60 && avg<75)
  printf("\n FIRST DIVISION");
else if(avg>=50 && avg<60)
  printf("\n SECOND DIVISION");
else if(avg>=40 && avg<50)
  printf("\n THIRD DIVISION");
else
  printf("\n FAIL");
return 0;
}
```

Output

```
Enter the marks in Mathematics: 90
Enter the marks n Science: 91
Enter the marks in Social Science: 92
Enter the marks in Computer Science: 93
TOTAL = 366
AGGREGATE = 91.00
DISTINCTION
```

3.17 Write a program to calculate the roots of a quadratic equation.

```
#include <stdio.h>
#include <math.h>
#include <conio.h>
void main()
{
   int a, b, c;
   float D, deno, root1, root2;
   clrscr();
   printf("\n Enter the values of a, b, and c :");
   scanf("%d %d %d", &a, &b, &c);
   D = (b * b) - (4 * a * c);
   deno = 2 * a;
   if(D > 0)
   {
      printf("\n REAL ROOTS");
      root1 = (-b + sqrt(D)) / deno;
      root2 = (-b - sqrt(D)) / deno;
      printf("\n ROOT1 = %f \t ROOT 2 = %f",
         root1, root2);
   }
   else if(D == 0)
   {
      printf("\n EQUAL ROOTS");
      root1 = -b/deno;
      printf("\n ROOT1 = %f \t ROOT 2 = %f",
         root1, root2);
   }
   else
      printf("\n IMAGINARY ROOTS");
   getch();
}
```

Output

```
Enter the values of a, b, and c : 3 4 5
IMAGINARY ROOTS
```

Let us now summarize the rules for using `if`, `if-else`, and `if-else-if` statements.

Rule 1: The expression must be enclosed in parentheses.

Rule 2: No semicolon is placed after the `if/if-else/if-else-if` statement. Semicolon is placed only at the end of statements in the statement block.

Rule 3: A statement block begins and ends with a curly brace. No semicolon is placed after the opening/closing braces.

Dangling Else Problem

With nesting of `if-else` statements, we often encounter a problem known as *dangling else problem*. This problem is created when there is no matching else for every `if` statement. In such cases, C always pair an `else` statement to the most recent unpaired `if` statement in the current block. Consider the following code which shows such a scenario:

> **Programming Tip:** While forming the conditional expression, try to use positive statements rather than using compound negative statements.

```
if(a > b)
if(a > c)
  printf("\n a is greater than b and c");
else
  printf("\n a is not greater than b and c");
```

The problem is that both the outer `if` statement and the inner `if` statement might conceivably own the `else` clause. The C solution to pair the `if`-construct with the nearest `if` may not always be correct. So the programmer must always see that every `if` statement is paired with an appropriate `else` statement.

Comparing Floating Point Numbers

Never test floating point numbers for exact equality. This is because floating point numbers are just approximations, so it is always better to test floating point numbers for 'approximately equal' rather than testing for exactly equal.

We can test for approximate equality by subtracting the two floating point numbers (that are to be tested) and comparing their absolute value of the difference against a very small number, epsilon. For example, consider the code given below which compares two floating point numbers. Note that epsilon is chosen by the programmer to be small enough so that the two numbers can be considered equal.

```
#include <stdio.h>
#include <math.h>
#define EPSILON 1.0e-5
main()
{
double num1 = 10.0, num2 = 9.5;
double res1, res2;
res1 = num2 / num1 * num1;
res2 = num2;

/* fabs() is a C library function that
returns the floating point absolute value */
if(fabs(res2 - res1) < EPSILON)
   printf("EQUAL");
else
   printf("NOT EQUAL");
return 0;
}
```

Also note that adding a very small floating point value to a very large floating point value or subtracting floating point numbers of widely differing magnitudes may not have any effect. This is because adding/subtracting two floating point numbers that differ in magnitude by more than the precision of the data type used will not affect the larger number.

3.2.4 Switch Case

A switch case statement is a multi-way decision statement that is a simplified version of an if-else block that evaluates only one variable. The general form of a switch statement is shown in Fig. 3.5.

Programming Tip:
It is always recommended to use default label in a switch statement.

Table 3.1 compares general form of a switch statement with that of an if–else statement.

Syntax of Switch Statement

```
switch ( variable )
{
case value1:
  Statement Block 1;break;
  break;
case value2:
  Statement Block 2;break;
  break;
..............................
case value N:
  Statement Block N;break;
  break;
default:
  Statement Block D;
  break;break;
}
Statement X;
```


Figure 3.5 The switch statement construct

Table 3.1 Comparison between the `switch` and `if-else` construct

Generalized `switch` statement	Generalized `if-else` statement

`switch(x) {`
`case 1: // do this`
`case 2: // do this`
`case 3: // do this`
`....`
`default:`
`//do this`
`}`
	`if(exp1) {`
	`  // do this`
	`} else if(exp2) {`
	`  // do this`
	`} else if(exp3) {`
	`  // do this`
	`}`

Here, statement blocks refer to statement lists that may contain zero or more statements. *These statements in the block are not enclosed within opening and closing braces.*

The power of nested `if-else` statements lies in the fact that it can evaluate more than one expression in a single logical structure. Switch statements are mostly used in two situations:

- When there is only one variable to evaluate in the expression.
- When many conditions are being tested for.

When there are many conditions to test, using the `if` and `else-if` construct becomes a bit complicated and confusing. Therefore, `switch` case statements are often used as an alternative to long `if` statements that compare a variable to several *integral* values (integral values are those values that can be expressed as an integer, such as the value of a char). Switch statements are also used to handle the input given by the user.

We have already seen the syntax of the `switch` statement. The `switch` case statement compares the value of the variable given in the `switch` statement with the value of each case statement that follows. When the value of the switch and the case statement matches, the statement block of that particular case is executed.

Did you notice the keyword default in the syntax of the `switch` case statement? Default is also a case that is executed when the value of the variable does not match with any of the values of the case statement, i.e., the default case is executed when there is no match found between the values of switch and case statements and thus there are no statements to be executed. Although the default case is optional, it is always recommended to include it as it handles any unexpected cases.

In the syntax of the switch case statement, we have used another keyword `break`. The `break` statement must be used at the end of each case because if it were not used, then all the cases from the one met will be executed. For example, if the value of `switch` statement matched with that of case 2, then all the statements in case 2 as well as rest of the cases including default will be executed. The `break` statement tells the compiler to jump out of the switch case statement and execute the statement following the switch case construct. Thus, the keyword `break` is used to break out of the case statements. It indicates the end of a case and prevents the program from falling through and executing the code in all the rest of the case statements.

> **Programming Tip:**
> C supports decision control statements that can alter the flow of a sequence of instructions. A switch-case statement is a multi-way decision statement that is a simplified version of an if–else block that evaluates only one variable.

Consider the following example of `switch` statement:

```
char grade = 'C';
switch(grade)
{
case 'O':
   printf("\n Outstanding");
   break;

case 'A':
   printf("\n Excellent");
   break;
case 'B':
   printf("\n Good");
   break;
case 'C':
   printf("\n Fair");
   break;
case 'F':
   printf("\n Fail");
   break;
default:
   printf("\n Invalid Grade");
   break;
}
```

Output

```
Fair
```

3.18 Write a program to demonstrate the use of `switch` statement without a break.

```
#include <stdio.h>
main()
{
int option = 1;
```

```
switch(option)
{
case 1: printf("\n In case 1");
case 2: printf("\n In case 2");
default: printf("\n In case default");
}
return 0;
}
```

Output

```
In case 1
In case 2
In case default
```

Had the value of option been 2, then the output would have been

```
In case 2
In case default
```

And if option was equal to 3 or any other value then only the default case would have been executed, thereby printing

```
In case default
```

To summarize the `switch case` construct, let us go through the following rules:

- The control expression that follows the keyword `switch` must be of integral type (i.e., either be an integer or any value that can be converted to an integer.
- Each case label should be followed with a constant or a constant expression.
- Every case label must evaluate to a unique constant expression value.
- Case labels must end with a colon.
- Two case labels may have the same set of actions associated with it.
- The default label is optional and is executed only when the value of the expression does not match with any labelled constant expression. It is recommended to have a default case in every `switch case` statement.

Programming Tip: Keep the logical expressions simple and short. For this, you may use nested `if` statements.

Programming Tip: Default is also a case that is executed when the value of the variable does not match with any of the values of the case statement.

- The default label can be placed anywhere in the `switch` statement. But the most appropriate position of default case is at the end of the `switch case` statement.
- There can be only one default label in a `switch` statement.
- C permits nested `switch` statements, i.e., a `switch` statement within another `switch` statement.

3.19 Write a program to determine whether an entered character is a vowel or not.

```
#include <stdio.h>
int main()
{
char ch;
printf("\n Enter any character: ");
scanf("%c", &ch);
switch(ch)
{
case 'A':
case 'a':
   printf("\n%c is VOWEL", ch);
   break;
case 'E':
case 'e':
   printf("\n%c is VOWEL", ch);
   break;
case 'I':
case 'i':
   printf("\n % c is VOWEL", ch);
   break;
case 'O':
case 'o':
   printf("\n % c is VOWEL", ch);
   break;
case 'U':
case 'u':
   printf("\n % c is VOWEL", ch);
   break;
default: printf("%c is not a vowel", ch);
}
return 0;
}
```

Output

```
Enter any character: E
E is a VOWEL
```

3.20 Write a program to enter a number from 1–7 and display the corresponding day of the week using `switch case` statement.

```
#include <stdio.h>
#include <conio.h>
int main()
{
int day;
clrscr();
printf("\n Enter any number from 1 to 7: ");
scanf("%d",&day);

switch(day)
{
case 1: printf("\n SUNDAY");
break;
case 2: printf("\n MONDAY");
break;
case 3: printf("\n TUESDAY");
break;
case 4: printf("\n WEDNESDAY");
break;
case 5: printf("\n THURSDAY");
break;
case 6: printf("\n FRIDAY");
break;
case 7: printf("\n SATURDAY");
break;
default: printf("\n Wrong Number");
}
return 0;
}
```

Output

```
Enter any number from 1 to 7: 5
THURSDAY
```

3.21 Write a program that accepts a number from 1 to 10. Print whether the number is even or odd using a `switch case` construct.

```
#include <stdio.h>
main()
{
int num;
printf("\n Enter any number (1 to 10): ");
scanf("%", &num);
switch(num)
{
case 1:
case 3:
case 5:
case 7:
case 9:
  printf("\n ODD");
  break;
case 2:
case 4:
case 6:
case 8:
case 10:
  printf("\n EVEN");
default :
  printf("\n INVALID INPUT");
  break;
}
}
```

OR

```
#include <stdio.h>
main()
{
int num, rem;
printf("\n Enter any number (1 to 10): ");
scanf("%", &num);
rem = num%2;
switch(rem)
{
case 0:
  printf("\n EVEN");
  break;
case 1:
  printf("\n ODD");
  break;
}
}
```

Output

```
Enter any number from 1 to 10: 7
ODD
```

Note that there is no `break` statement after `case A`, so if the character `'A'` is entered, then the control will execute the statements given in `case 'a'`.

For example, consider a simple calculator program that can be used to add, multiply, subtract, and divide two integers.

Advantages of using a `Switch Case` Statement

`Switch case` statement is preferred by programmers due to the following reasons:

- Easy to debug.
- Easy to read and understand.
- Ease of maintenance as compared with its equivalent `if-else` statements.

- Like `if-else` statements, `switch` statements can also be nested.
- Executes faster than its equivalent `if-else` construct.

3.3 ITERATIVE STATEMENTS

Iterative statements are used to repeat the execution of a list of statements, depending on the value of an integer expression. C language supports three types of iterative statements also known as looping statements. They are:

- `While` loop
- `Do-while` loop
- `For` loop

In this section, we will discuss all these statements.

3.3.1 `while` loop

The `While` loop provides a mechanism to repeat one or more statements while a particular condition is true. Figure 3.6 shows the syntax and general form of representation of a `While` loop.

Programming Tip:
Iterative statements are used to repeat the execution of a list of statements, depending on the value of an integer expression.

In the `while` loop, the condition is tested before any of the statements in the statement block is executed. If the condition is true, only then the statements will be executed otherwise if the condition is false, the control will jump to statement `y`, which is the immediate statement outside the `while` loop block.

From the flowchart diagram, it is clear that we need to constantly update the condition of the `while` loop. It is this condition which determines when the loop will end. The `while` loop will execute as long as the condition is true. Note if the condition is never updated and the condition never becomes false then the computer will run into an infinite loop which is never desirable.

Programming Tip:
Check that the relational operator is not mistyped as an assignment operator.

A `while` loop is also referred to as a top-checking loop since control condition is placed as the first line of the code. If the control condition evaluates to false, then the statements enclosed in the loop are never executed.

For example, look at the following code which prints first 10 numbers using a `while` loop.

```
#include <stdio.h>
int main()
{
int i = 0;          // initialize loop variable
while(i<=10)        // test the condition
{                   // execute the loop
                       statements
printf(" %d", i);
i = i + 1;          // condition updated
}
getch();
return 0;
}
```

Output

```
0 1 2 3 4 5 6 7 8 9 10
```

Initially `i = 0` and is less than 10, i.e., the condition is true, so in the `while` loop the value of `i` is printed and the condition is updated so that with every execution of the

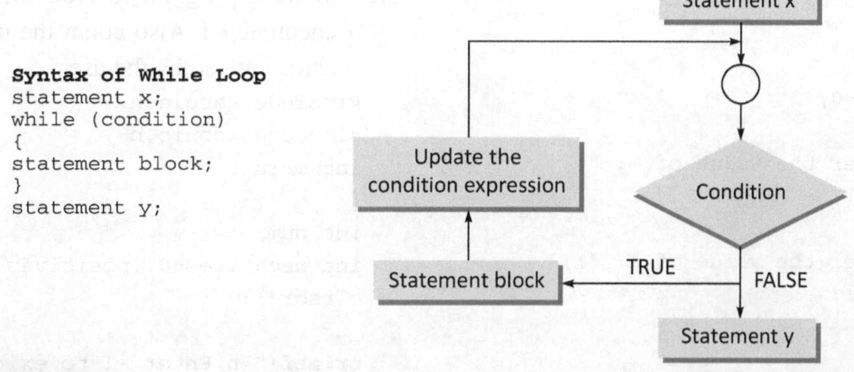

Figure 3.6 The `while` loop construct

loop, the condition becomes more approachable. Let us look at some more programming examples that illustrate the use of `while` loop.

3.22 Write a program to calculate the sum of first 10 numbers.

```
#include <stdio.h>
int main()
{
int i = 0, sum = 0;
while(i<=10)
{
sum = sum + i;
i = i + 1;      // condition updated
}
printf("\n SUM = %d", sum);
return 0;
}
```

Output

```
SUM = 55
```

3.23 Write a program to print 20 horizontal asterisks(*).

```
#include <stdio.h>
main()
{
int i=1;
while (i<=20)
{
printf("*");
i++;
}
return 0;
}
```

Output

```
********************
```

3.24 Write a program to calculate the sum of numbers from m to n.

```
#include <stdio.h>
int main()
{
int n, m, sum =0;
clrscr();
printf("\n Enter the value of m: ");
scanf("%d", &m);

printf("\n Enter the value of n: ");
scanf("%d", &n);

while(m<=n)
{
   sum = sum + m;
   m = m + 1;
}
printf("\n SUM = %d", sum);
return 0;
}
```

Output

```
Enter the value of m: 7
Enter the value of n: 11
SUM = 45
```

3.25 Write a program to display the largest of 6 numbers using ternary operator.

```
#include <stdio.h>
#include <conio.h>
int main()
{
int i=0, large = -1, num;
clrscr();

while(i<=5)
{
printf("\n Enter the number: ");
scanf("%d",&num);
large = num>large?num:large;
i++;
}
printf("\n The largest of five numbers
   entered is: %d", large);
return 0;
}
```

Output

```
Enter the number : 29
Enter the number : 15
Enter the number : 17
Enter the number : 19
Enter the number : 25
The largest of five numbers entered is: 29
```

3.26 Write a program to read the numbers until –1 is encountered. Also count the negative, positive, and zeros entered by the user.

```
#include <stdio.h>
#include <conio.h>
int main()
{
int num;
int negatives=0, positives=0, zeros=0;
clrscr();

printf("\n Enter -1 to exit….");
printf("\n\n Enter any number: ");
scanf("%d",&num);
```

```
while(num != -1)
{
   if(num>0)
      positives++;
   else if(num<0)
      negatives++;
   else
      zeros++;
   printf("\n\n Enter any number: ");
   scanf("%d",&num);
}
printf("\n Count of positive numbers entered
   = %d", positives);
printf("\n Count of negative numbers entered
   = %d", negatives);
printf("\n Count of zeros entered = %d",
   zeros);
getch();
return 0;
}
```

Output

```
Enter any number: -12
Enter any number: 108
Enter any number: -24
Enter any number: 99
Enter any number: -23
Enter any number: 101
Enter any number: -1
Count of positive numbers entered = 3
Count of negative numbers entered = 3
Count of zeros entered = 0
```

3.27 Write a program to calculate the average of numbers entered by the user.

```
#include <stdio.h>
int main()
{
int num, sum = 0, count = 0;
float avg;
printf("\n Enter any number.
Enter -1 to STOP: ");
scanf("%d", &num);
while(num != -1)
{
count++;
sum = sum + num;
printf("\n Enter any number.
Enter -1 to STOP: ");
scanf("%d", &num);
}
avg = (float)sum/count;
printf("\n SUM = %d", sum);
printf("\n AVERGAE = %f", avg);
return 0;
}
```

Programming Tip: Placing a semicolon after the `while`/`for` loop in not a syntax error. So it will not be reported by the compiler. However, it is considered to be a logical error as it changes the output of the program.

Output

```
Enter any number. Enter -1 to STOP: 23
Enter any number. Enter -1 to STOP: 13
Enter any number. Enter -1 to STOP: 3
Enter any number. Enter -1 to STOP: 53
Enter any number. Enter -1 to STOP: 4
Enter any number. Enter -1 to STOP: 63
Enter any number. Enter -1 to STOP: -23
Enter any number. Enter -1 to STOP: -6
Enter any number. Enter -1 to STOP: -1
SUM = 130
AVERAGE = 16.25
```

Thus, we see that `while` loop is very useful for designing interactive programs in which the number of times the statements in the loop has to be executed is not known in advance. The program will execute until the user wants to stop by entering `-1`.

Now look at the code given below which makes the computer hang up in an infinite loop. The code given below is supposed to calculate the average of first 10 numbers, but since the condition never becomes false, the output will not be generated and the intended task will not be performed.

```
#include <stdio.h>
int main()
{
int i = 0, sum =0;
float avg = 0.0;

while(i<=10)
{
  sum = sum + i;
}
avg = sum/10;
printf("\n The sum of first 10 numbers =
   %d", sum);
printf("\n The average of first 10 numbers =
   %f", avg);
return 0;
}
```

3.3.2 do-while Loop

The do-while loop is similar to the while loop. The only difference is that in a do-while loop, the test condition is tested at the end of the loop. Now that the test condition is tested at the end, this clearly means that the body of the loop gets executed at least one time (even if the condition is false). Figure 3.7 shows the syntax and general form of representation of a do-while loop.

Note that the test condition is enclosed in parentheses and followed by a semicolon. The statements in the statement block are enclosed within curly brackets. The curly bracket is optional if there is only one statement in the body of the do-while loop.

Like the while loop, the do-while loop continues to execute whilst a condition is true. There is no choice whether to execute the loop or not because the loop will be executed at least once irrespective of whether the condition is true or false. Hence, entry in the loop is automatic. There is only one choice: to continue or to exit. The do-while loop will continue to execute while the condition is true and when the condition becomes false, the control will jump to statement following the do-while loop.

Similar to the while loop, the do-while is an indefinite loop as the loop can execute until the user wants to stop. The number of times the loop has to be executed can thus be determined at the run time. However, unlike the while loop, the do-while loop is a bottom-checking loop, since the control expression is placed after the body of the loop.

The major disadvantage of using a do-while loop is that it always executes at least once, even if the user enters some invalid data, the loop will execute. One complete execution of the loop takes place before the first comparison is actually done. However, do-while loops are widely used to print a list of options for a menu-driven program. For example, look at the following code.

```
#include <stdio.h>
int main()
{
int i = 0;
do
{
   printf("\n %d", i);
   i = i + 1;
} while(i<=10);
return 0;
}
```

What do you think will be the output? The code will print numbers from 0-11 and not till 10.

3.28 Write a program to calculate the average of first n numbers.

> **Programming Tip:** Do not forget to place a semicolon at the end of the do-while statement.

```
#include <stdio.h>
int main()
{
int n, i = 0, sum =0;
float avg = 0.0;
printf("\n Enter the value of n: ");
scanf("%d", &n);
```

```
Syntax of do-while Loop
statement x;
do
{
statement block;
}while (condition);

statement y;
```

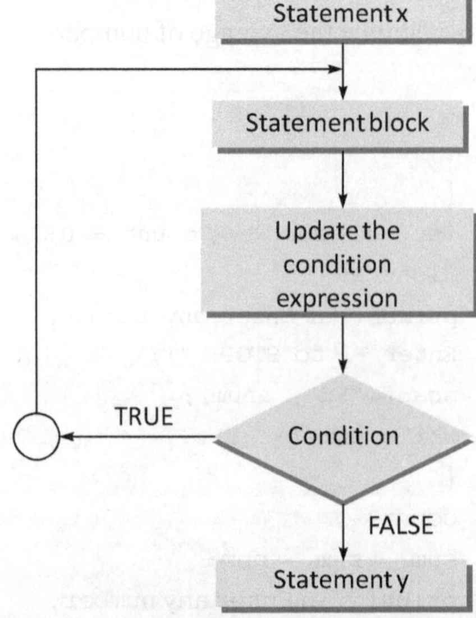

Figure 3.7 do-while construct

```
do
{
   sum = sum + i;
   i = i + 1;
} while(i<=n);

avg = sum/n;
printf("\n The sum of first n numbers = %d",
   sum);
printf("\n The average of first %d numbers =
   %f", n, avg);
return 0;
}
```

Output

```
Enter the value of n: 18
The sum of first n numbers = 171
The average of first %d numbers = 9.00
```

3.29 Write a program using do-while loop to display the square and cube of first n natural numbers.

```
#include <stdio.h>
#include <conio.h>
#include <math.h>
int main()
{
int i, n;
clrscr();

printf("\n Enter the value of n: ");
scanf("%d", &n);
printf("\n -----------------------------");
i=1;
do
{
printf("\n | \t %d \t | \t
%d \t | \t %ld \t |", i,
pow(i,2), pow(i,3));
i++;
} while(i<n);
printf("\n ---------------
-------------------");
return 0;
}
```

Programming Tip: Avoid using do-while loop for implementing pre-test loops and prefer to use the do-while loop for post-test loops.

Output

```
Enter the value of n: 5
--------------------------------------------
|    1    |    1    |    1    |
|    2    |    4    |    8    |
|    3    |    9    |    27   |
|    4    |    16   |    64   |
|    5    |    25   |    125  |
--------------------------------------------
```

3.30 Write a program to list all the leap years from 1900 to 2100.

```
#include <stdio.h>
#include <conio.h>
int main()
{
int m=1900, n=2100;
clrscr();

do
{
if(i%4 == 0)
printf("\n %d is a leap
year",m);
else
printf("\n %d is not a
leap year", m);
m = m+1;
}while(m<=n);
return 0;
}
```

Programming Tip: If you want that the body of the loop must get executed at least once, then use the do–while loop.

3.31 Write a program to read a character until a * is encountered. Also count the number of upper case, lower case, and numbers entered by the users.

```
#include <stdio.h>
#include <conio.h>
int main()
{
char ch;
int lowers = 0, uppers = 0, numbers = 0;
clrscr();

printf("\n Enter any character: ");
scanf("%c, &ch);

do
{
if(ch >='A' && ch<='Z')
   uppers++;
if(ch >='a' && ch<='z')
   lowers++;
if(ch >='0' && ch<='9')
   numbers++;

fflush(stdin);
/* The function is used to clear the
   standard input file. */
printf("\n Enter another character. Enter *
   to exit.");
scanf("%c", &ch);
} while(ch != '*');
```

```
printf("\n Total count of lower case
   characters entered = %d", lowers);
printf("\n Total count of upper case
   characters entered = %d", uppers);
printf("\n Total count of numbers entered =
   %d", numbers);
return 0;
}
```

Output

```
Enter any character: O
Enter another character. Enter * to exit. x
Enter another character. Enter * to exit. F
Enter another character. Enter * to exit. o
Enter another character. Enter * to exit. R
Enter another character. Enter * to exit. d
Enter another character. Enter * to exit. *

Total count of lower case characters entered = 3
Total count of upper case characters entered = 3
Total count of numbers entered = 0
```

3.32 Write a program to read the numbers until –1 is encountered. Also calculate the sum and mean of all positive numbers entered and the sum and mean of all negative numbers entered separately.

```
#include <stdio.h>
#include <conio.h>
int main()
{
int num;
int sum_negatives=0, sum_positives=0;
int positives = 0, negatives = 0;
float mean_positives = 0.0, mean_negatives
   = 0.0;
clrscr();

printf("\n Enter -1 to exit….");
printf("\n\n Enter any number: ");
scanf("%d",&num);

do
{
if(num>0)
{
   sum_positives += num;
   positives++;
}
else if(num<0)
{
   sum_negatives += num;
   negatives++;
}
printf("\n\n Enter any number: ");
scanf("%d",&num);
} while(num != -1);

mean_positives = sum_positives/positives;
mean_negatives = sum_negatives/negatives;

printf("\n Sum of all positive numbers
   entered = %d", sum_positives);
printf("\n Mean of all positive numbers
   entered = %f", mean_positives);

printf("\n Sum of all negative numbers
   entered = %d", sum_negatives);
printf("\n Mean of all negative numbers
   entered = %f", mean_negatives);
return 0;
}
```

Output

```
Enter -1 to exit….
Enter any number: 9
Enter any number: 8
Enter any number: 7
Enter any number: -6
Enter any number: -5
Enter any number: -4
Enter any number: -1
Sum of all positive numbers entered = 24
Mean of all positive numbers entered = 8.000
Sum of all negative numbers entered = -15
Mean of all negative numbers entered =
   -5.000
```

3.3.3 `for` Loop

Like the `while` and `do-while` loop, the `for` loop provides a mechanism to repeat a task until a particular condition is true. `for` loop is usually known as a determinate or definite loop because the programmer knows exactly how many times the loop will repeat. The number of times the loop has to be executed can be determined mathematically by checking the logic of the loop. The syntax and general form of a `for` loop is as given in Fig. 3.8.

When a `for` loop is used, the loop variable is initialized only once. With every iteration of the loop, the value of the loop variable is updated and the condition is checked. If the condition is true, the statement block of the loop is executed, else the statements comprising the statement block of the `for` loop are skipped and the control jumps to the immediate statement following the `for` loop body.

In the syntax of the `for` loop, initialization of the loop variable allows the programmer to give it a value.

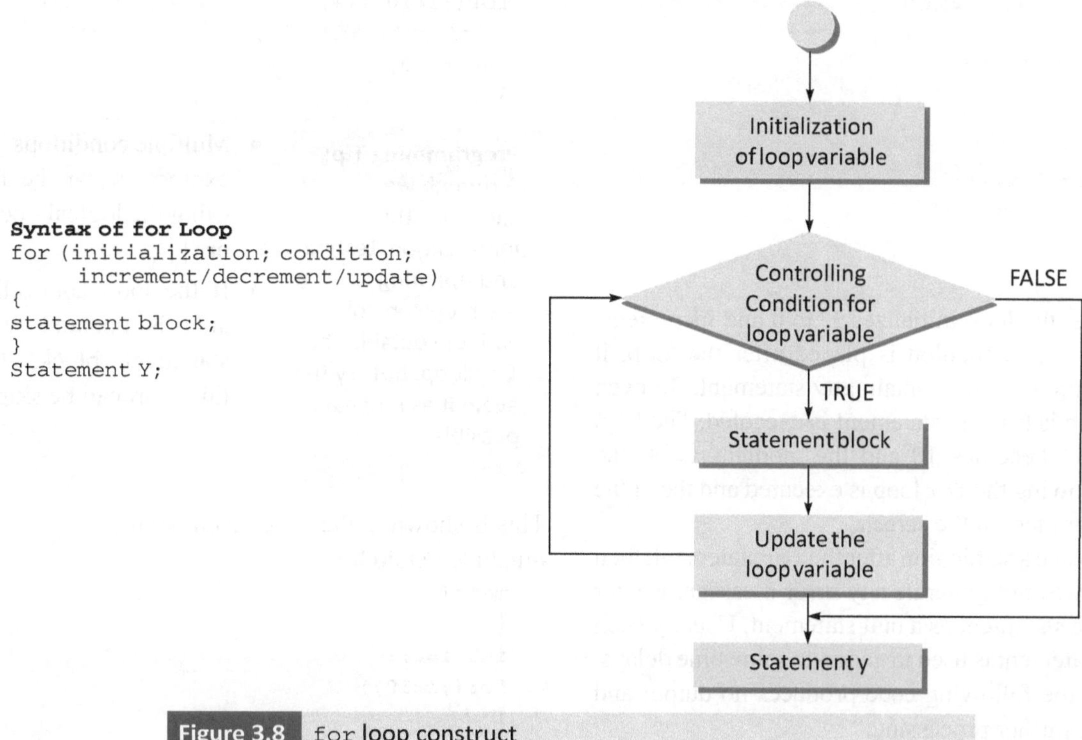

Figure 3.8 `for` loop construct

Second, the condition specifies that while the conditional expression is TRUE the loop should continue to repeat itself. Every iteration of the loop must make the condition near to approachable. So, with every iteration, the loop variable must be updated. Updating the loop variable may include incrementing the loop variable, decrementing the loop variable or setting it to some other value like, `i +=2`, where `i` is the loop variable.

Note that every section of the `for` loop is separated from the other with a semicolon. It is possible that one of the sections may be empty, though the semicolons still have to be there. However, if the condition is empty, it is evaluated as TRUE and the loop will repeat until something else stops it.

The `for` loop is widely used to execute a single or a group of statements a limited number of times. Another point to consider is that in a `for` loop, condition is tested before the statements contained in the body are executed. So if the condition does not hold true, then the body of the `for` loop may never get executed.

Look at the following code which prints the first n numbers using a `for` loop.

```
#include <stdio.h>
int main()
{
int i, n;
printf("\n Enter the value of n :");
scanf("%d", &n);

for(i=0;i<=n;i++)
   printf("\n %d", i);
return 0;
}
```

In the code, `i` is the loop variable. Initially, it is initialized with value zero. Suppose the user enters `10` as the value for `n`. Then the condition is checked, since the condition is true as `i` is less than `n`, the statement in the `for` loop is executed and the value of `i` is printed. After every iteration, the value of `i` is incremented. When `i=n`, the control jumps to the `return 0` statement.

Points to Remember About `for` Loop

- In a `for` loop, any or all the expressions can be omitted. In case all the expressions are omitted, then there must be two semicolons in the `for` statement.
- There must be no semicolon after a `for` statement. If you do that, then you are sure to get

> **Programming Tip:** It is a logical error to update the loop control variable in the body of the `for` loop as well as in the `for` statement.

some unexpected results. Consider the following code.

```
#include <stdio.h>
main()
{
int i;
for(i=0;i<10;i++);
   printf("  %d", i);
return 0;
}
```

In this code, the loop initializes `i` to 0 and increments its value. Since a semicolon is placed after the loop, it means that loop does not contain any statement. So even if the condition is true, no statement is executed. The loop continues till `i` becomes 10 and the moment `i=10`, the statement following the `for` loop is executed and the value of `i` (10) is printed on the screen.

When we place a semicolon after the `for` statement, then the compiler will not generate any error message. Rather it will treat the statement as a null statement. Usually such type of null statement is used to generate some time delays. For example, the following code produces no output and simply delays further processing.

```
#include <stdio.h>
main()
{
int i;
for(i=10000;i>0;i--);
   printf("  %d", i);
return 0;
}
```

- Multiple initializations must be separated with a comma operator as shown in the following code segment.

```
#include <stdio.h>
main()
{
int i, sum;
for(i=0, sum=0;i<10;i++)
   sum += i;
printf(" %d", sum);
return 0;
}
```

- If there is no initialization to be done, then the initialization statement can be skipped by giving only a semicolon. This is shown in the following code.

```
#include <stdio.h>
main()
{
int i=0;
for(;i<10;i++)
   printf("%d", i);
return 0;
}
```

Programming Tip: Although we can place the initialization, testing and updating the loop control variable outside the `for` loop, but try to avoid it as much as possible.

- Multiple conditions in the test expression can be tested by using the logical operator (`&&` or `||`).
- If the loop controlling variable is updated within the statement block, then the third part can be skipped.

This is shown in the code given below.

```
#include <stdio.h>
main()
{
int i=0;
for(;i<10;)
{
   printf("  %d", i);
   i = i + 1;
}
return 0;
}
```

- Multiple statements can be included in the third part of the `for` statement by using the comma operator. For example, the `for` statement given below is valid in C.

```
for(i=0, j=10;i<j; i++, j--)
```

Programming Tip: Although placing an arithmetic expression in initialization and updating section of the `for` loop is permissible, but try to avoid them as they may cause some round-off and/or truncation errors.

- The controlling variable can also be incremented/decremented by values other than 1. This is shown in the code below which prints all odd numbers from 0 to 10.

```
#include <stdio.h>
main()
{
int i;
for(i=1;i<=10;i+=2)
   printf(" %d", i);
return 0;
}
```

- If the `for` loop contains nothing but two semicolons, that is no initialization, condition testing and updating of the loop control variable then the `for` loop may become an infinite loop if no stopping condition is specified in the body of the loop. For example, the following code will infinitely print `C Programming` on the computer screen.

```
#include <stdio.h>
main()
{
for(;;)
printf(" C Programming");
return 0;
}
```

- Never use a floating point variable as the loop control variable. This is because floating point values are just approximations and therefore may result in imprecise values and thus inaccurate test for termination. For example, the following code will result in an infinite loop because of inaccuracies of floating point numbers.

```
#include <stdio.h>
main()
{
float i;
for(i=100;i>=10;)
{
   printf(" %f", i);
   i = (float)i/10;
}
return 0;
}
```

Selecting an appropriate loop Loops can be entry-controlled (also known as pre-test) or entry-controlled (also known as post-test). While in entry-controlled loop, condition is tested before the loop starts, the exit-controlled loop, on the other hand, tests the condition after the loop is executed. If the condition is not met in entry-controlled loop, then the loop will never execute. However, in case of post-test, the body of the loop is executed unconditionally for the first time.

If your requirement is to have a pre-test loop, then choose either `for` loop or `while` loop. In case you need to have a post-test loop then choose a `do-while` loop.

Look at Table 3.2 which shows a comparison between a pre-test loop and a post-test loop.

When we know in advance the number of times, the loop should be executed, we use a counter-controlled loop. The counter is a variable that must be initialized, tested, and updated for performing the loop operations. Such a counter-controlled loop in which the counter is assigned a constant or a value is also known as a definite repetition loop.

Table 3.2 Comparison of pre-test and post-test loops

Feature	Pre-test Loop	Post-test Loop
Initialization	1	1
Number of tests	N+1	N
Statements executed	N	N
Loop control variable update	N	N
Minimum iterations	0	1

When we do not know in advance the number of times the loop will be executed, we use a sentinel controlled loop. In such a loop, a special value called the sentinel value is used to change the loop control expression from true to false. For example, when data is read from the user, the user may be notified that when they want the execution to stop, they may enter `-1`. This `-1` is called the *sentinel value*. A sentinel-controlled loop is often useful for indefinite repetition loops.

If your requirement is to have a counter-controlled loop, then choose `for` loop, else if you need to have a sentinel-controlled loop, then go for either a `while` loop or a `do-while` loop. Although a sentinel-controlled loop can be implemented using `for` loop, but `while` and `do-while` loop offers better option.

3.4 NESTED LOOPS

C allows its users to have nested loops, i.e., loops that can be placed inside other loops. Although this feature will work with any loop like `while`, `do-while`, and `for` but it is most commonly used with the `for` loop, because this is easiest to control. A `for` loop can be used to control the number of times that a particular set of statements will be executed. Another outer loop could be used to control the number of times that a `while` loop is repeated.

In C, loops can be nested to any desired level. However, the loops should be properly indented in order to enable the reader to easily determine which statements are contained within each `for` statement. To see the benefit of nesting loops, we will see some programs that exhibit the use of nested loops.

3.33 Write a program to print the following pattern.

Pass 1- 1 2 3 4 5
Pass 2- 1 2 3 4 5
Pass 3- 1 2 3 4 5
Pass 4- 1 2 3 4 5
Pass 5- 1 2 3 4 5

```
#include <stdio.h>
main()
{
int i, j;
for(i=1;i<=5;i++)
{
   printf("\n Pass %d- ",i);
   for(j=1;j<=5;j++)
      printf(" %d", j);
}
return 0;
}
```

3.34 Write a program to print the following pattern.

```
**********
**********
**********
**********
**********
```

```
#include <stdio.h>
main()
{
int i, j;
for(i=1;i<=5;i++)
{
 printf("\n");
   for(j=1;j<=5;j++)
      printf("*");
}
return 0;
}
```

3.35 Write a program to print the following pattern.

```
*
**
***
****
*****
```

```
#include <stdio.h>
main()
{
int i, j;
for(i=1;i<=5;i++)
{
   printf("\n");
   for(j=1;j<=i;j++)
      printf("*");
}
return 0;
}
```

3.36 Write a program to print the following pattern.

1
12
123
1234
12345

```
#include <stdio.h>
main()
{
int i, j;
for(i=1;i<=5;i++)
{
   printf("\n");
   for(j=1;j<=i;j++)
      printf("%d", j);
}
return 0;
}
```

3.37 Write a program to print the following pattern.

1
22
333
4444
55555

```
#include <stdio.h>
main()
{
int i, j;
for(i=1;i<=5;i++)
{
   printf("\n");
   for(j=1;j<=i;j++)
      printf("%d", i);
}
return 0;
}
```

3.38 Write a program to print the following pattern.

0
12
345
6789

```
#include <stdio.h>
main()
{
```

```
int i, j, count=0;
for(i=1;i<=5;i++)
{
   printf("\n");
   for(j=1;j<=i;j++)
      printf("%d", count++);
}
return 0;
}
```

3.39 Write a program to print the following pattern.

```
A
AB
ABC
ABCD
ABCDE
ABCDEF
```

```
#include <stdio.h>
main()
{
char i, j;
for(i=65;i<=70;i++)
{
   printf("\n");
   for(j=65;j<=i;j++)
      printf("%c", j);
}
return 0;
}
```

3.40 Write a program to print the following pattern.

```
        1
      1 2
    1 2 3
  1 2 3 4
1 2 3 4 5
```

```
#include <stdio.h>
#define N 5
main()
{
int i, j, k;
for(i=1;i<=N;i++)
{
for(k=N;k>=i;k--)
   printf(" ");
   for(j=1;j<=i;j++)
      printf("%d", j);
      printf("\n");
}
return 0;
}
```

3.41 Write a program to print the following pattern.

```
        1
      1 2 1
    1 2 3 2 1
  1 2 3 4 3 2 1
1 2 3 4 5 4 3 2 1
```

```
#include <stdio.h>
#define N 5
main()
{
int i, j, k, l;
for(i=1;i<=N;i++)
{
for(k=N;k>=i;k--)
   printf(" ");
      for(j=1;j<=i;j++)
      printf("%d", j);
         for(l=j-2;l>0;l--)
         printf("%d", l);
         printf("\n");
}
return 0;
}
```

3.42 Write a program to print the following pattern.

```
1
2 2
3 3 3
4 4 4 4
5 5 5 5 5
```

```
#include <stdio.h>
#define N 5
main()
{
int i, j, k, count=5, c;
for(i=1;i<=N;i++)
{
for(k=1;k<=count;k++)
   printf(" ");
   for(j=1;j<=i;j++)
      printf("%2d", i);
      printf("\n");
      c--;
}
return 0;
}
```

3.43 Write a program to print the multiplication table of n, where n is entered by the user.

```
#include <stdio.h>
int main()
```

```
{
int n, i;
printf("\n Enter any number: ");
scanf("%d", &n);

printf("\n Multiplication table of %d", n);
printf("\n ***********************");
for(i=0;i<=20;i++)
printf("\n %d X %d = %d", n, i, (n * i));
return 0;
}
```

Output

```
Enter any number: 2
Multiplication table of 2
***********************
2 X 0 = 0
2 X 1 = 2
.....
2 X 20 = 40
```

3.44 Write a program using `for` loop to print all the numbers from m to n, thereby classifying them as even or odd

```
#include <stdio.h>
#include <conio.h>
int main()
{
int i, m, n;
clrscr();

printf("\n Enter the value of m: ");
scanf("%d", &m);
printf("\n Enter the value n: ");
scanf("%d", &n);
for(i=m;i<=n;i++)
{
   if(i%2 == 0)
      printf("\n %d is even",i);
   else
   printf("\n %d is odd", i);
}
return 0;
}
```

Output

```
Enter the value of m: 5
Enter the value of n: 7
5 is odd
6 is even
7 is odd
```

3.45 Write a program to count the numbers in the range 1 to 100 that are divisible by 2 but not by 3.

```
#include<stdio.h>
#include<conio.h>
main()
{
   int num, i, count=0;
   clrscr();
   for(i=1;i<=100;i++)
      if(i%2==0 && i%3!=0)
         count++;
   printf("\n Count = %d", count);
}
```

Output

```
Count = 34
```

3.46 Write a program using `for` loop to calculate the average of first n natural numbers.

```
#include <stdio.h>
#include <conio.h>
int main()
{
int n, i, sum =0;
float avg = 0.0;
clrscr();

printf("\n Enter the value of n: ");
scanf("%d", &n);

for(i=1;i<=n;i++)
   sum = sum + i;
avg = sum/n;
printf("\n The sum of first n natural
   numbers = %d", sum);
printf("\n The average of first n natural
   numbers = %f", avg);
return 0;
}
```

Output

```
Enter the value of n: 10
The sum of first n natural numbers = 55
The average of first n natural numbers =
   5.500
```

3.47 Write a program using `for` loop to calculate factorial of a number.

```
#include <stdio.h>
#include <conio.h>
int main()
{
int fact = 1, num;
clrscr();

printf("\n Enter the number: ");
```

```
scanf("%d",&num);

if(num == 0)
   fact = 1;
else
{
for(int i=1; i<=num;i++)
   fact = fact * i;
}
printf("\n Factorial of %d is: %d ", num,
   fact);
return 0;
}
```

Output

```
Enter the number: 5
Factorial of 5 is: 120
```

3.48 Write a program to classify a given number as prime or composite.

```
#include <stdio.h>
#include <conio.h>
int main()
{
int flag = 0, i, num;
clrscr();

printf("\n Enter any number: ");
scanf("%d", &num);
for(i=2; i<num/2;i++)
{
   if(num%i == 0)
   {
      flag =1;
      break;
   }
}
if(flag == 1)
   printf("\n %d is a composite number", num);
else
   printf("\n %d is a prime number", num);
   return 0;
}
```

Output

```
Enter the number: 5
5 is a prime number
```

3.49 Write a program using `do-while` loop to read the numbers until –1 is encountered. Also count the number of prime numbers and composite numbers entered by the user

```
#include <stdio.h>
#include <conio.h>
int main()
{
int num, i;
int primes=0, composites=0, flag=0;
clrscr();

printf("\n Enter -1 to exit….");
printf("\n\n Enter any number:");
scanf("%d",&num);

do
{
   for(i=2;i<=num%2;i++)
   {
   if(num%i==0)
      {
         flag=1;
         break;
      }
   }
if(flag==0)
   primes++;
else
   composites++;

flag=0;
printf("\n\n Enter any number: ");
scanf("%d",&num);
} while(num != -1);
printf("\n Count of prime numbers entered =
   %d", primes);
printf("\n Count of composite numbers
   entered = %d", composites);
return 0;
}
```

3.50 Write a program to calculate pow(x,n), i.e., to calculate x^n.

```
#include <stdio.h>
#include <conio.h>
#include <math.h>
int main()
{
int i, num, n;
long int result =1;
clrscr();

printf("\n Enter the number: ");
scanf("%d", &num);
printf("\n Till which power to calculate: ");
```

```
scanf("%d", &n);

for(i=1;i<=n;i++)
result = result * num;

printf("\n pow(%d, %d) = %ld", num, n,
   result);
return 0;
}
```

Output

```
Enter the number: 2
Till which power to calculate: 5
pow(2, 5) = 32
```

3.51 Write a program to print the reverse of a number.

```
#include <stdio.h>
#include <conio.h>
int main()
{
int num, temp;
clrscr();

printf("\n Enter the number: ");
scanf("%d", &num);
printf("\n The reversed number is: ");
while(num != 0)
{
   temp = num%10;
   printf("%d",temp);
   num = num/10;
}
return 0;
}
```

Output

```
Enter the number: 123
The reversed number is: 321
```

3.52 Write a program to enter a number and then calculate the sum of its digits.

```
#include <stdio.h>
#include <conio.h>
int main()
{
int num, temp, sumofdigits = 0;
clrscr();
printf("\n Enter the number: ");
scanf("%d", &num);

while(num != 0)
{
   temp = num%10;
   sumofdigits += temp;
   num = num/10;
}
printf("\n The sum of digits = %d",
   sumofdigits);
return 0;
}
```

Output

```
Enter the number: 123
The sum of digits = 6
```

3.53 Write a program to enter a decimal number. Calculate and display the binary equivalent of this number.

```
#include <stdio.h>
#include <conio.h>
#include <math.h>

int main()
{
int decimal_num, remainder, binary_num = 0,
   i = 0;
clrscr();

printf("\n Enter the decimal number: ");
scanf("%d", &decimal_num);
while(decimal_num != 0)
{
remainder = decimal_num%2;
binary_num += remainder*pow(10,i);
decimal_num = decimal_num/2;
i++;
}
printf("\n The binary equivalent = %d",
   binary_num);
return 0;
}
```

Output

```
Enter the decimal number: 7
The binary equivalent = 111
```

3.54 Write a program to enter a decimal number. Calculate and display the octal equivalent of this number.

```
#include <stdio.h>
#include <conio.h>
#include <math.h>

int main()
{
int decimal_num, remainder, octal_num = 0,
   i = 0;
clrscr();
```

```
printf("\n Enter the decimal number: ");
scanf("%d", &decimal_num);
while(decimal_num != 0)
{
remainder = decimal_num%8;
octal_num += remainder*pow(10,i);
decimal_num = decimal_num/8;
i++;
}
printf("\n The octal equivalent = %d",
   octal_num);
return 0;
}
```

Output

```
Enter the decimal number: 18
The octal equivalent = 22
```

3.55 Write a program to enter a binary number. Calculate and display the decimal equivalent of this number.

```
#include <stdio.h>
#include <conio.h>
#include <math.h>

int main()
{
int decimal_num = 0, remainder, binary_num,
   i = 0;
clrscr();

printf("\n Enter the binary number: ");
scanf("%d", &binary_num);
while(binary_num != 0)
{
remainder = binary_num%10;
decimal_num += remainder*pow(2,i);
binary_num = binary_num/10;
i++;
}
printf("\n The decimal equivalent of = %d",
   decimal_num);
return 0;
}
```

Output

```
Enter the binary number : 111
The decimal equivalent = 7
```

3.56 Write a program to enter an octal number. Calculate and display the decimal equivalent of this number.

```
#include <stdio.h>
#include <conio.h>
#include <math.h>
int main()
{
int decimal_num= 0, remainder, octal_num,
   i = 0;
clrscr();

printf("\n Enter the octal number: ");
scanf("%d", &octal_num);
while(octal_num != 0)
{
remainder = octal_num%10;
decimal_num += remainder*pow(8,i);
octal_num = octal_num/10;
i++;
}
printf("\n The decimal equivalent = %d",
   decimal_num);
return 0;
}
```

Output

```
Enter the octal number: 22
The decimal equivalent = 18
```

3.57 Write a program to enter a hexadecimal number. Calculate and display the decimal equivalent of this number.

```
#include <stdio.h>
#include <conio.h>
#include <math.h>

int main()
{
int decimal_num= 0, remainder, hex_num, i
   =0;
clrscr();

printf("\n Enter the hexadecimal number: ");
scanf("%d", &hex_num);
while(hex_num != 0)
{
remainder = hex_num%10;
decimal_num += remainder*pow(16,i);
hex_num = hex_num/10;
i++;
}
printf("\n The decimal equivalent = %d",
   decimal_num);
return 0;
}
```

Output

```
Enter the hexadecimal number : 39
The decimal equivalent = 57
```

3.58 Write a program to calculate GCD of two numbers.

```
#include <stdio.h>
#include <conio.h>
int main()
{
int num1, num2, temp;
int dividend, divisor, remainder;
clrscr();

printf("\n Enter the first number: ");
scanf("%d", &num1);
printf("\n Enter the second number: ");
scanf("%d", &num2);

if(num1>num2)
{
dividend = num1;
divisor = num2;
}
else
{
dividend = num2;
divisor = num1;
}

while(divisor)
{
remainder = dividend%divisor;
dividend = divisor;
divisor = remainder;
}
printf("\n GCD of %d and %d is = %d", num1,
   num2, dividend);
return 0;
}
```

Output

```
Enter the first number: 64
Enter the second number: 14
GCD of 64 and 14 is = 2
```

3.59 Write a program to sum the series $1+\frac{1}{2}+\frac{1}{3}\cdots+\frac{1}{n}$.

```
#include <stdio.h>
#include <conio.h>
main()
{
int n;
float sum=0.0, a, i;
clrscr();

printf("\n Enter the value of n: ");
scanf("%d", &n);

for(i=1.0;i<=n;i++)
{  a=1/i;
sum = sum +a;
}
printf("\n The sum of series 1/1 + 1/2 +
   .... + 1/%d = %f",n,sum);
return 0;
}
```

Output

```
Enter the value of n: 5
The sum of series 1/1 + 1/2 + .... + 1/5 = 2.2838
```

3.60 Write a program to sum the series $\frac{1}{1^2}+\frac{1}{2^2}+\cdots\frac{1}{3^2}$.

```
#include <stdio.h>
#include <math.h>
#include <conio.h>
main()
{
int n;
float sum=0.0, a, i;
clrscr();
printf("\n Enter the value of n: ");
scanf("%d", &n);
for(i=1.0;i<=n;i++)
{  a=1/pow(i,2);
sum = sum +a;
}
printf("\n The sum of series 1/1² + 1/ 2² +
   .... 1/n²   = %f",sum);
return 0;
}
```

Output

```
Enter the value of n: 5
The sum of series 1/1² + 1/ 2² + .... 1/n²  = 1.4636
```

3.61 Write a program to sum the series $\frac{1}{2}+\frac{2}{3}\cdots\frac{n}{(n+1)}$.

```
#include <stdio.h>
#include <conio.h>
main()
{
int n;
float sum=0.0, a, i;
clrscr();
printf("\n Enter the value of n: ");
scanf("%d", &n);
for(i=1.0;i<=n;i++)
{  a= i/(i+1);
```

```
sum = sum +a;
}
printf("\n The sum of series 1/2 + 2/3 +
   .... = %f",n,n+1,sum);
return 0;
}
```

Output

```
Enter the value of n :5
The sum of series 1/2 + 2/3 + .... = 2.681+E
```

3.62 Write a program to sum the series $\frac{1}{1}+\frac{2^2}{2}+\frac{3^2}{3}+\cdots$

```
#include <stdio.h>
#include <conio.h>
#include <math.h>
main()
{
int n, NUM;
float i,sum=0.0;
clrscr();
printf("\n Enter the value of  n: ");
scanf("%d", &n);
for(i=1.0;i<=n;i++)
{
NUM = pow(i,i);
sum += (float)NUM/i;
}
printf("\n 1/1 + 4/2 + 27/3 + .... = %f",
  sum);
return 0;
}
```

Output

```
Enter the value of n:5
1/1 + 4/2 + 27/3 + .... = 701.000
```

3.63 Write a program to calculate sum of cubes of first n numbers.

Programming Tip: It is a logical error to skip the updating of loop control variable in the while/do-while loop. Without an update statement, the loop will become an infinite loop.

```
#include <stdio.h>
#include <conio.h>
#include <math.h>

main()
{
int i, n;
int term, sum = 0;
clrscr();
printf("\n Enter the value
of n: ");
scanf("%d", &n);
for(i=1;i<=n;i++)
{
term = pow(i,3);
sum += term;
}
printf("\n 1³ + 2³ + 3³ + ...... = %d", sum);
return 0;
}
```

Output

```
Enter the value of n:5
1³ + 2³ + 3³ + ...... = 225
```

3.64 Write a program to calculate sum of squares of first n even numbers.

```
#include <stdio.h>
#include <conio.h>
#include <math.h>

main()
{
int i, n;
int term, sum = 0;
clrscr();
printf("\n Enter the value of n: ");
scanf("%d", &n);
for(i=1;i<=n;i++)
{
if(i%2 == 0)
   { term = pow(i,2);
     sum += term;
   }
}
printf("\n 2² + 4² + 6² + ...... = %d", sum);
return 0;
}
```

Output

```
Enter the value of n: 5
2² + 4² + 6² + ...... = 20
```

3.65 Write a program to find whether the given number is an Armstrong number or not.

```
#include <stdio.h>
#include <conio.h>
#include <math.h>
main()
{
int num, sum=0, r, n;
clrscr();
printf("\n Enter the number: ");
scanf("%d", &num);
n=num;
while(n>0)
{
```

```
    r=n%10;
    sum += pow(r,3);
    n=n/10;
  }
  if(sum==num)
  printf("\n %d is an Armstrong number", num);
  else
  printf("\n %d is not an Armstrong number",
    num);
  return 0;
  }
```

Output

```
  Enter the number : 432
  432 is not an Armstrong number
```

3.66 Write a program to print the multiplication table.

```
#include <stdio.h>
#include <conio.h>
int main()
{
int i, j;
clrscr();

for(i=1;i<=20;i++)
{
printf("\n\n\n\t\t Multiplication table of
  %d",  i);
printf("\n ******************************");
for(j=1;j<=20;j++)
printf("\t %d X %d = %d",i,j, (i*j));
}
getch();
return 0;
}
```

Output

```
Multiplication table of 1
*********************
1 *1 = 1     1 * 2 = 2   1 * 3 = 3    1 * 4 = 4
```

3.67 Write a program using `for` loop to calculate the value of an investment, given the initial value of investment and the annual interest. Calculate the value of investment over a period of time.

```
#include <stdio.h>
main()
{
double initVal, futureVal, ROI;
int yrs, i;
printf("\n Enter the investment value: ");
scanf("%lf", &initVal);
printf("\n Enter the rate of interest: ");
scanf("%lf", &ROI);
printf("\n Enter the number of years for
  which investment has to be done: ");
scanf("%d", &yrs);

futureVal=initVal;
printf("\n YEAR \t\t VALUE");
printf("\n ______________________");
for(i=1;i<=yrs;i++)
{
futureVal = futureVal * (1 + ROI/100.0);
printf("\n   %d \t  %lf", i, futureVal);
}
return 0;
}
```

Output

```
Enter the investment value: 20000
Enter the rate of interest: 12
Enter the number of years for which
  investment has to be done: 5
YEAR        VALUE
______________________

1             22400.00
2             25088.00
3             28098.56
4             31470.38
5             35246.83
```

3.68 Write a program to generate calendar of a month given the start day of the week and the number of days in that month.

```
#include <stdio.h>
main()
{
int i, j, startDay, num_of_days;
printf("\n Enter the starting day of the
  week (1 to 7): ");
scanf("%d", &startDay);
printf("\n ENter the number of days in that
  month: ");
scanf("%d", &num_of_days);

printf(" Sun Mon Tue Wed Thurs Fri Sat\n");
printf("\n ____________________________");
for(i=0;i<startDay-1;i++)
printf("     ");
for(j=1;j<=num_of_days;j++)
{
if(i>6)
{
  printf("\n");
```

```
    i=1;
  }
  else
    i++;
    printf("%2d  ", j);
  }
  return 0;
  }
```

Output

```
Enter the starting day of the week (1 to 7): 5
ENter the number of days in that month : 31

Sun Mon Tue Wed Thurs Fri Sat
1   2   3   4   5   6   7
```

3.5 break AND continue STATEMENTS

3.5.1 break Statement

In C, the break statement is used to terminate the execution of the nearest enclosing loop in which it appears. We have already seen its usage in the switch statement. The break statement is widely used with for loop, while loop, and do-while loop. When compiler encounters a break statement, the control passes to the statement that follows the loop in which the break statement appears. Its syntax is quite simple, just type keyword break followed with a semicolon.

> **Programming Tip:** The **break** statement is used to terminate the execution of the nearest enclosing loop in which it appears.

```
break;
```

In switch statement, if the break statement is missing then every case from the matched case label till the end of the switch, including the default, is executed. This example given below shows the manner in which break statement is used to terminate the statement in which it is embedded.

```
#include <stdio.h>
int main()
{
int i = 0;
while(i<=10)
{
   if (i==5)
   break;
   printf("\n %d", i);
   i = i + 1;
}
return 0;
}
```

Note that the code is meant to print first 10 numbers using a while loop, but it will actually print only numbers from 0 to 4. As soon as i becomes equal to 5, the break statement is executed and the control jumps to the statement following the while loop.

Hence, the break statement is used to exit a loop from any point within its body, bypassing its normal termination expression. When the break statement is encountered inside a loop, the loop is immediately terminated, and program control is passed to the next statement following the loop. Figure 3.9 shows the transfer of control when the break statement is encountered.

```
while(...)
{
.....
if(condition)
break;
......
}
......
```
Transfers control out of the while loop

```
do
{
.....
if(condition)
break;
......
}while(...);
......
```
Transfers control out of the do-while loop

```
for(...)
{
.....
if(condition)
break;
......
}
......
```
Transfers control out of the for loop

```
for(...)
{
...........
  for(...)
  {
  ........
  if(condition)
  break;
  ........
  }
........
}
```
Transfers control out of inner for loop

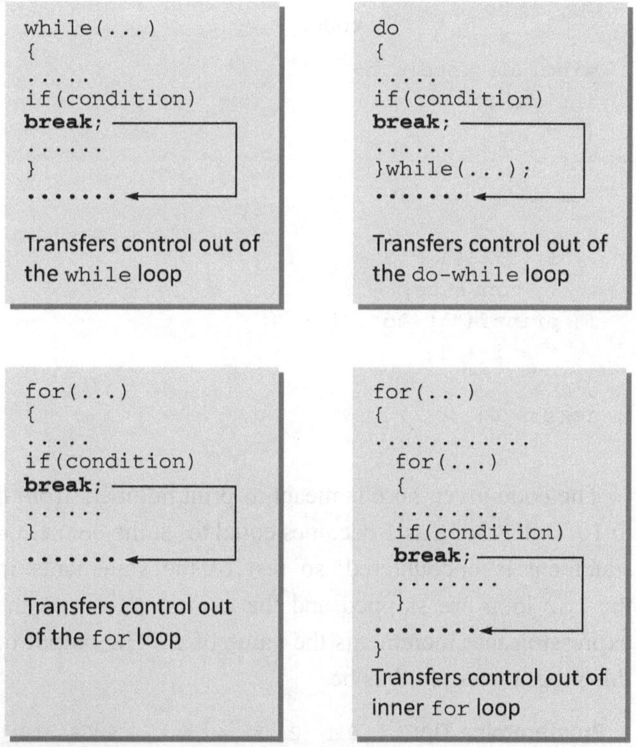

Figure 3.9 break statement

3.5.2 continue Statement

Like the break statement, the continue statement can only appear in the body of a loop. When the compiler encounters a continue statement then the rest of the statements in the loop are skipped and the control is unconditionally transferred to the loop-continuation portion of the nearest enclosing loop. Its syntax is quite simple, just type keyword `continue` followed with a semicolon.

```
continue;
```

> **Programming Tip:** When the compiler encounters a continue statement, then the rest of the statements in the loop are skipped and the control is unconditionally transferred to the loop-continuation portion of the nearest loop.

Again like the break statement, the continue statement cannot be used without an enclosing for, while, or do-while statements. When the continue statement is encountered in the while loop and in the do-while, the control is transferred to the code that tests the controlling expression. However, if placed with a for loop, the continue statement causes a branch to the code that updates the loop variable. For example, look at the following code.

```
#include <stdio.h>
int main()
{
int i;
for(i=0; i<= 10; i++)
{
   if (i==5)
      continue;
   printf("\t %d", i);
   i = i + 1;
}
return 0;
}
```

The code given here is meant to print numbers from 0 to 10. But as soon as i becomes equal to 5, the continue statement is encountered, so rest of the statements in the for loop are skipped and the control passes to the expression that increments the value of i. The output of this program would thus be

> **Programming Tip:** As far as possible, try not to use goto, break, and continue statements as they violate the rules of structured programming.

```
0 1 2 3 4 6 7 8 9 10
```

(Note that there is no 5 in the series. It could not be printed, as continue caused early incrementation of i and skipping of the statement that printed the value of i on screen).

Figure 3.10 illustrates the use of continue statement in loops.

```
while(...)
{
.....
if(condition)
continue;
......
}
.......
```

(Transfers the control to the condition expression of the while loop)

```
do
{
.....
if(condition)
continue;
......
}while(...);
.......
```

(Transfers the control to the condition expression of the do-while loop)

```
for(...)
{
.....
if(condition)
continue;
......
}
.......
```

(Transfers the control to the condition expression of the for loop)

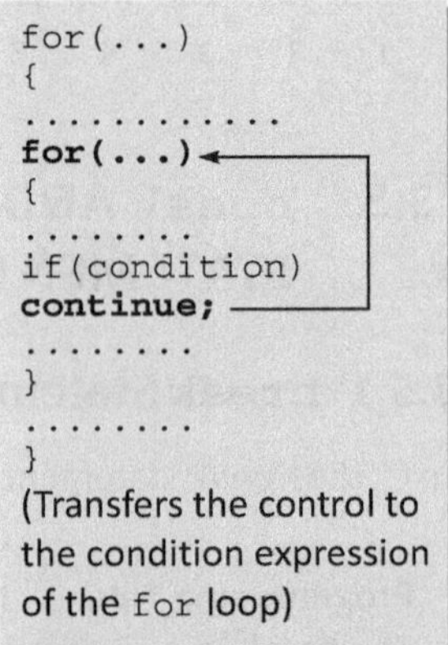

```
for(...)
{
...........
for(...)
{
.......
if(condition)
continue;
.......
}
........
}
```

(Transfers the control to the condition expression of the for loop)

Figure 3.10 The continue statement

Hence, we conclude that the continue statement is somewhat the opposite of the break statement. It forces the next iteration of the loop to take place, skipping any code in between itself and the test condition of the loop. The continue statement is usually used to restart a statement sequence when an error occurs. Look at the program code given below that demonstrates the use of break and continue statements.

69. Write a program to calculate square root of a number.

```
#include <stdio.h>
#include <math.h>
main()
{
int num;
do
{
printf("\n Enter any number. Enter 999 to
   stop: ");
scanf("%d", &num);
if(num == 999)
break;      // quit the loop
if (num < 0)
```

```
{
printf("\n Square root of negative numbers
   is not defined");
continue; // skip the following statements
}
printf("\n The square root of %d, is %f",
   num, sqrt(num));
}while(1);
return 0;
}
```

3.6 goto STATEMENT

The **goto** statement is used to transfer control to a specified `label`. However, the `label` must reside in the same function and can appear only before one statement in the same function. The syntax of `goto` statement is as shown in Fig. 3.11.

Here, `label` is an identifier that specifies the place where the branch is to be made. `label` can be any valid variable name that is followed by a colon (`:`). The `label` is placed immediately before the statement where the control has to be transferred.

The `label` can be placed anywhere in the program either before or after the `goto` statement. Whenever the `goto` statement is encountered the control is immediately transferred to the statements following the `label`. Therefore, `goto` statement breaks the normal sequential execution of the program. If the `label` is placed after the `goto` statement, then it is called a *forward jump* and in case it is located before the `goto` statement, it is said to be a *backward jump*.

```
goto label
.........
.........
label:
   statements
```

Forward jump

```
label:
   statements
.........
.........
goto label
```

Backward jump

Figure 3.11 The goto statement

The `goto` statement is often combined with the `if` statement to cause a conditional transfer of control.

```
if condition then goto label
```

In this book, we will not use the `goto` statement because computer scientists usually avoid this statement in favour of the 'structured programming' paradigm. Some scientists think that the `goto` statement should be abolished from higher-level languages because they complicate the task of analysing and verifying the correctness of programs (particularly those involving loops).

Moreover, structured program theorem proves that the availability of the `goto` statement is not necessary to write programs, as combination of sequence, selection, and repetition constructs are sufficient to perform any computation. The code given below demonstrates the use of a `goto` statement. The program calculates the sum of all positive numbers entered by the user.

> **Programming Tip:** Follow proper indentation for better clarity, readability, and understanding of the loops.

```
#include <stdio.h>
main()
{
int num, sum=0;
read:    // label for goto statement
printf("\n Enter the number. Enter 999 to
   end: ");
scanf("%d", &num);
if (num != 999)
{
   if(num < 0)
      goto read; // jump to label- read
   sum += num;
   goto read;     // jump to label- read
}
printf("\n Sum of the numbers entered by the
   user is = %d", sum);
return 0;
}
```

Conclusion

- It is not necessary to use `goto` statement, as it can always be eliminated by rearranging the code.
- Using the `goto` statement violates the rules of structured programming.
- It is good programming style to use the `break`, `continue`, and `return` statements in preference to `goto` whenever possible.

- goto statements make the program code complicated and render the program unreadable.

One must avoid the use of break, continue, and goto statements as much as possible as they are techniques used in unstructured programming.

In structured programming, you must prefer to use `if` and `if-else` construct to avoid such statements. For example, look at the following code which calculates the sum of numbers entered by the user. The first version uses the `break` statement. The second version replaces `break` by `if-else` construct.

```
// Uses break statement
#include <stdio.h>
main()
{
int num, sum=0;
while(1)
{
printf("\n Enter any number. Enter 999 to
   stop: ");
scanf("%d", &num);
if(num==999)
break;  // quit the loop
sum+=num;
}
printf("\n SUM = %d", sum);
return 0;
}
```

```
// Same program without using break
   statement
#include <stdio.h>
main()
{
int num, sum=0, flag=1;
// flag will be used to exit from the loop
while(flag==1)  // loop control variable
{
printf("\n Enter any number. Enter 999 to
   stop: ");
scanf("%d", &num);
if(num!=999)
sum+=num;
else
flag=0;  // to quit the loop
}
printf("\n SUM = %d", sum);
return 0;
}
```

Now let us see how we can eliminate `continue` statement from our programs. Let us first write a program that calculates the average of all non-zero numbers entered by the user using the `continue` statement. The second program will do the same job but without using `continue`.

```
#include <stdio.h>
main()
{
int num, sum=0, flag=1, count=0;
float avg;
// flag will be used to exit from the loop
while(flag==1)
{
printf("\n Enter any number. Enter 999 to
   stop: ");
scanf("%d", &num);
if(num==0)
continue;  // skip the following statements
if(num!=999)
{
sum+=num;
count++;
}
else
flag=0;
// set loop cntl var to jump out of loop
}
printf("\n SUM = %d", sum);
avg = (float) sum/count;
printf("\n Average = &f", avg);
return 0;
}
```

```
// Same program without using continue statement
#include <stdio.h>
main()
{
int num, sum=0, flag=1, count=0;
float avg;
// flag will be used to exit from the loop
while(flag==1)
{
printf("\n Enter any number. Enter 999 to
   stop: ");
```

```
scanf("%d", &num);
if(num!=0)
{
   if(num!=999)
   {
      sum+=num;
      count++;
   }
   else
      flag=0;
   }
}
printf("\n SUM = %d", sum);
avg = (float) sum/count;
printf("\n Average = &f", avg);
return 0;
}
```

3.7 BUILDING A ROBUST C PROGRAM

Even a small and simple program that is executing properly may have some defects in it. For example, the program executing without errors may give a result that is completely unexpected or incorrect. So, the programmers must test the program to ensure that the program is giving correct result with any input. For example, if you have written a program that accepts numbers from 1 to 1000, then it is not possible to observe the outputs for all the valid values and even the ones that are invalid. So, two simple strategies that can be followed are given below.

First Strategy

Step 1: Divide the input data in three classes. The first class will comprise of all the valid values. The second class contains input data below the lower limit. The third class contains input data above the maximum limit.

Step 2: Pick any one data value from each class. Execute the program with these three data values and check if the result is correct.

If the result is correct in all three cases, the program has high probability to give accurate results with any input value. But if the result differs from the one that is expected, the programmer knows specially the source and reason for defect. So, in the above example the program can be checked with three values like –1, 500, and 1100.

Second Strategy

The second strategy emphasizes checking program at the extreme ends (boundaries) of input domain as most of the errors occur there. In this technique perform the steps given below.

- First, check the program with any value within the input domain say, 500.
- Second, check the program with an input of 1 and 1000 as both these values form the boundary of the input domain.
- Third, check the program with values just below the extreme values. For example, with input values 0 and 999.
- Fourth, check the program with values just above the extreme values. For example, with input values 2 and 1001.

Make sure that every program that you write is tested simultaneously as per these guidelines.

POINTS TO NOTE

- C supports conditional type branching and unconditional type branching. The conditional branching statements help to jump from one part of the program to another depending on whether a particular condition is satisfied or not.
- With nesting of `if-else` statements, we often encounter a problem known as dangling else problem. This problem is created when there is no matching else for every `if` statement. In such cases, C always pairs an `else` statement to the most recent unpaired `if` statement in the current block.
- `Switch case` statements are often used as an alternative to long `if` statements that compare a variable to several integral values. `Switch` statements are also used to handle the input given by the user.
- Default is a case that is executed when the value of the variable does not match with any of the values of the `case` statement.

GLOSSARY

Break statement Statement used to terminate the execution of the nearest enclosing loop in which it appears.

Conditional branching Conditional branching statements is used to jump from one part of the program to another depending on whether a particular condition is satisfied or not.

Continue statement Statement that can appear in the body of a loop. When the compiler encounters a `continue` statement then the rest of the statements in the loop are skipped and the control is unconditionally transferred to the loop-continuation portion of the nearest enclosing loop.

Dangling else problem Problem encountered with nesting of `if-else` statements which is created when there is no matching else for every `if` statement.

Do-while loop The `do-while` loop is similar to the `while` loop. The only difference is that in a `do-while` loop, the test condition is tested at the end of the loop.

For loop: The mechanism used to repeat a task until a particular condition is true. `For` loop is usually known as a determinate or definite loop because the programmer knows exactly how many times the loop will repeat.

Goto statement It is used to transfer control to a specified label. However, the label must reside in the same function and can appear only before one statement in the same function.

If statement Simplest form of decision control statement that is frequently used in decision making.

If-else-if statement Decision control statement that works in the same way as a normal `if` statement. It is also known as `nested if` construct.

If-else statement Decision control statement in which first the test expression is evaluated. If the expression is true, statement `block` 1 is executed and statement `block` 2 is skipped. Otherwise, if the expression is false, statement `block` 2 is executed and statement `block` 1 is ignored.

Iterative statement Statements used to repeat the execution of a list of statements, depending on the value of an integer expression.

Nested loop Loops placed inside other loops.

Switch case statement A `switch case` statement is a multi-way decision statement that is a simplified version of an `if-else` block that evaluates only one variable.

While loop The mechanism used to repeat one or more statements while a particular condition is true.

EXERCISES

Fill in the Blanks

1. Dangling else problem occurs when ___________.
2. The `switch-case` control expression must be of ___________ type.
3. In a `do-while` loop, if the body of the loop is executed n times, the test condition is evaluated ___________ times.
4. The ___________statement is used to skip statements in a loop.
5. A loop that always satisfies the test condition is known as a ___________ loop.
6. In a counter-controlled loop, ___________ variable is used to count the number of times the loop will execute.
7. ___________ statements help to jump from one part of the program to another depending on whether a particular condition is satisfied or not.
8. The control expression that follows the keyword `switch` must be of ___________ type.
9. ___________ statements are used to repeat the execution of a list of statements.
10. In ___________ loop, the entry is automatic and there is only a choice to continue it further or not.
11. When we do not know in advance the number of times the loop will be executed, we use a ___________loop.
12. The ___________statement is used to transfer control to a specified label.
13. ___________statement violates the rules of structured programming.

State True or False

1. Decision control statements are used to repeat the execution of a list of statements.
2. The expression in a selection statement can have no side effects.

EXERCISES

3. An expression in an `if` statement must be enclosed within parentheses.
4. No two case labels can have the same value.
5. The case labelled constant can be a constant or a variable.
6. The `if-else` statement requires integral values in its expressions.
7. There can be only one default case in the `switch-case` statement
8. The `do-while` loop checks the test expression and then executes the statements placed within its body.
9. In a `while` loop, if the body is executed n times, then the test expression is executed (n + 1) times.
10. The number of times the loop control variable is updated is equal to the number of times the loop iterates.
11. In the `for` loop, the value of the loop control variable must be less than that of its ending value.
12. It is necessary to have initialization, testing, and updating expressions within the `for` statement
13. In a pre-test loop, the test condition is checked after the body of the loop.
14. Post-test loops get executed at least for one time.
15. In a `while` loop, the loop control variable is initialized in the body of the loop.
16. The loop control variable may be updated before or after the loop iterates.
17. The number of times the loop control variable is updated is equal to the number of times the loop is executed.
18. Counter-controlled loop must be designed as pre-test loops.
19. The `do-while` loop is a post-test loop.
20. The `for` loop and `while` loop are pre-test loops.
21. Every case label must evaluate to a unique constant expression value.
22. Two case labels may have the same set of actions associated with it.
23. The default label can be placed anywhere in the `switch` statement.
24. C does not permit nested `switch` statements.
25. When we place a semicolon after the `for` statement, the compiler will generate an error message.

Review Questions

1. What are decision control statements? Explain in detail.
2. Compare the use of `if-else` construct with that of ternary operator.
3. Explain the importance of a `switch case` statement. In which situations is a switch case desirable? Also give its limitations.
4. How is comma operator useful in a `for` loop? Explain with the help of relevant examples.
5. Write a short note on `goto` statement. As a programmer would you prefer to use this statement? Justify your answer.
6. With the help of an example explain the dangling `if-else` problem.
7. Why should floating point numbers not used for equality in expressions?
8. Explain the usefulness of default statement in `switch case` statement.
9. Give the points of similarity and differences between a `while` loop and a `do-while` loop.
10. Distinguish between the `break` and the `continue` statements.
11. Write a short note on `iterative` statements that C language supports.
12. Write a program to read a floating point number and an integer. If the value of the floating point number is greater than 3.14 then add 10 to the integer.
13. Enter two integers as dividend and divisor. If the divisor is greater than zero then divide the dividend by the divisor. Assign their result to an integer variable rem and their quotient to a floating point number quo.
14. When will you prefer to work with a `switch` statement?
15. Write a program to print the prime factors of a number.
16. Write a program to test if a given number is a power of 2.

    Hint: A number x is a power of 2 if x != 0 and x & (x - 1)) == 0
17. Write a program to print the Floyd's triangle.
18. Write a program to read two numbers. Then find out whether the first number is a multiple of the second number.
19. Write a program using `switch case` to display a menu that offers 5 options—read three numbers, calculate total, calculate average, display the smallest, and display the largest value.

EXERCISES

20. Write a program to display the sin(x) value where x ranges from 0 to 360 in steps of 15.
21. Write a program to display the cos(x), tan(x) value where x ranges from 0 to 360 in steps of 15.
22. Write a program to calculate electricity bill based on the following information.

Consumption Unit	Rate of Charge
0 – 150	Rs 3 per unit
151 – 350	Rs 100 plus Rs 3.75 per unit exceeding 150 units
301 – 450	Rs 250 plus Rs 4 per unit exceeding 350 units
451 – 600	Rs 300 plus Rs 4.25 per unit exceeding 450 units
Above 600	Rs 400 plus Rs 5 per unit exceeding 600 units

23. Write a program to read an angle from the user and then display its quadrant.
24. Write a program that accepts the current date and the date of birth of the user. Then calculate the age of the user and display it on the screen. Note that the date should be displayed in the format specified as dd/mm/yy.
25. A class has 50 students. Every student is supposed to give three examinations. Write a program to read the marks obtained by each student in all three examinations. Calculate and display the total marks and average of each student in the class.
26. Write a program in which the control variable is updated in the statements of the `for` loop.
27. What is a `null` statement? How can it be useful in our programs?
28. Write a short note on `goto` statement. Why should it be avoided?
29. Write a program which demonstrates the use of `goto`, `break`, and `continue` statements
30. In what situation will you prefer to use `for`, `while` and, `do-while` loop?
31. Can we use a `for` loop when the number of iterations is not known in advance? If yes, give a program that illustrates how this can be done.
32. Write a program that displays all the numbers from 1–100 that are not divisible by 2 as well as by 3.
33. Write a program to calculate parking charges of a vehicle. Enter the type of vehicle as a character (like c for car, b for bus, etc.) and number of hours then calculate charges as given below:
    - Truck/bus – 20 Rs per hour
    - Car – 10 Rs per hour
    - Scooter/ Cycle/ Motor cycle – 5 Rs per hour
34. Modify the above program to calculate the parking charges. Read the hours and minutes when the vehicle enters the parking lot. When the vehicle is leaving, enter its leaving time. Calculate the difference between the two timings to calculate the number of hours and minutes for which the vehicle was parked. Finally calculate the charges based on following rules and then display the result on the screen.

Vehicle Name	Rate till 3 hours	Rate after 3 hours
Truck/bus	20	30
Car	10	20
Cycle/ Motor cycle/ Scooter	5	10

35. Write a program to read month of the year as an integer. Then display the name of the month.
36. Write a program to print the sum of all odd numbers from 1 to 100.
37. Write an interactive program to read an integer. If it is positive then display the corresponding binary representation of that number. The user must enter 999 to stop. In case the user enters a negative number then ignore that input and ask the user to re-enter any different number.
38. Write a program to print 20 asterisks.
39. Change the following `for` loop into a `while` loop. Also convert the `for` loop into a `do-while` loop.

```
int i;
for(i=10;i>0;i--)
printf("%d", i);
```

40. Change the following `do-while` loop into a `for` loop. Also re-write the code by changing the `do-while` loop into a `for` loop.

```
int num;
printf("\n Enter any number. Enter 999
   to stop : ");
scanf("%d", &num);
```

EXERCISES

```
do
{
printf("%d", x);
printf("\n Enter any number. Enter 999
  to stop : ");
scanf("%d", &num);
}while(num != 999);
```

41. Write a program that accepts any number and prints the number of digits in that number.

42. Change the following `while` loop into a `do-while` loop. Also convert the `while` loop into a `for` loop.

```
int num;
printf("\n Enter any number. Enter 999
  to stop : ");
scanf("%d", &num);
while(num != 999)
{
printf("%d", x);
printf("\n Enter any number. Enter 999
  to stop : ");
scanf("%d", &num);
}
```

43. The following `for` loops are written to print numbers from 1 to 10. Are these loops correct? Justify your answer.

(a)
```
int i;
  for(i=0;i<10;i++)
  printf("%d", i);
```

(b)
```
int i, num;
  for(i=0;i<10;i++)
  {
  num = i+1;
  printf("%d", num);
  }
```

(c)
```
int i;
  for(i=1;i<=10;i++)
  {
  printf("%d", i);
  i++;
  }
```

44. Write a program to generate the following pattern:

```
* * * * *
*       *
*       *
*       *
* * * * *
```

45. Write a program to generate the following pattern:

```
$ * * * *
* $     *
*   $   *
*     $ *
* * * * $
```

46. Write a program to generate the following pattern:

```
$ * * * $
* $   $ *
*   $   *
* $   $ *
$ * * * $
```

47. Write programs to implement the following sequence of numbers.

```
1, 8, 27, 64,…
-5, -2, 0, 3, 6, 9, 12, …
-2, -4, -6, -8, -10, -12, …
1, 4, 7, 10, …
```

48. Write a program that reads integers until the user wants to stop. When the user stops entering numbers, display the largest of all the numbers entered.

49. Write a program to print the sum of the following series:

$-x + x^2 - x^3 + x^4 + \ldots$

$1 + (1+2) + (1+2+3) + \ldots$

$1 - x + x^2/2! - x^3/3! + \ldots$

50. Write a program to print the following pattern:

```
*
* *
* * *
* * * *
* * * * *
* * * *
* * *
* *
*
```

51. Write a program to print the following pattern:

```
1
2 1 2
3 2 1 2 3
```

52. Write a program to read a 5-digit number and then display the number in the following formats. For example, the user entered 12345, the result should be

12345	1
2345	12
345	123
45	1234
5	12345

EXERCISES

Program Output

Give the output of the following program codes.

1.
```
include <stdio.h>
main()
{
int a = 2, b = 3, c = 4;
if( c!= 100)
  a = 10;
else
  b = 10;
 if(a + b > 10)
  c = 12;
  a = 20;
  b = ++c;
printf(" \n a = %d \t b = %d \t c = %d"
  , a, b, c);
return 0;
}
```

2.
```
#include <stdio.h>
main()
{
int a = 2, b = 3, c = 4;
if(b==2)
  a=10;
else
  c=10;
printf("\n a= %d \t b = %d \t c = %d",
  a, b, c);
return 0;
}
```

3.
```
#include <stdio.h>
main()
{
int a = 2, b = 3, c = 4;
if(a&&b)
  c=10;
else
  c=20;
printf("\n a = %d \t b = %d \t c = %d" ,
  a, b, c);
return 0;
}
```

4.
```
#include <stdio.h>
main()
{
int a = 2, b = 3, c = 4;
if(a || b || c)
  c=10;
else
  c=20;
printf("\n a = %d \t b = %d \t c = %d",
  a, b, c);
return 0;
}
```

5.
```
#include <stdio.h>
main()
{
int a = 2, b = 3, c = 4;
if(a)
if(b)
  c=10;
else
  c=20;
printf(" \n a = %d \t b = %d \t c = %d",
  a, b, c);
return 0;
}
```

6.
```
#include <stdio.h>
main()
{
int a = 2, b = 3, c = 4;
if(a == 0 || b >= c && c > 0)
if(a && b)
  c=10;
else
  c=20;
printf(" \n a = %d \t b = %d \t c = %d",
  a, b, c);
return 0;
}
```

7.
```
#include <stdio.h>
main()
{
int a = 2, b = 3, c = 4;
if( a= b)
  c++;
printf(" \n a = %d \t b = %d \t c = %d"
  , a, b, c);
return 0;
}
```

8.
```
#include <stdio.h>
main()
{
int a = 2, b = 3, c = 4;
if( a= b < c)
```

EXERCISES

```
    {
    c++;
    a--;
    }
++b;
printf(" \n a = %d \t b = %d \t c = %d",
    a, b, c);
return 0;
}
```

9.
```
switch(ch)
{
case 'a':
case 'A':
    printf("\n A");
case 'b':
case 'B':
    printf("\n B");
default:
printf("\n DEFAULT");
}
```

10.
```
switch(ch)
{
case 'a':
case 'A':
    printf("\n A");
case 'b':
case 'B':
    printf("\n B");
break;
default:
    printf("\n DEFAULT");
}
```

11.
```
switch(ch)
{
case 'a':
case 'A':
    printf("\n A");
    break;
case 'b':
case 'B':
    printf("\n B");
    break;
default:
    printf("\n DEFAULT");
}
```

12.
```
#include <stdio.h>
void main()
{
int num = 10;
printf("\n %d", a>100);
}
```

13.
```
#include <stdio.h>
main()
{
printf("HELLO");
if (-1)
    printf("WORLD");
}
```

14.
```
#include <stdio.h>
main()
{
int a = 3;
if(a < 10)
    printf("\n LESS");
if(a < 20)
    printf("\n LESS");
if(a < 30)
    printf("\n LESS");
}
```

15.
```
#include <stdio.h>
main()
{
int a=10, b=20, c=30, d=40);
if( c < d)
if ( c < b)
    printf("\n c");
else if(a < c)
    printf("\n a");
if(a > b)
    printf("\n b");
else
    printf("\n d");
}
```

16.
```
#include <stdio.h>
main()
{
char ch = 'Y';
switch(ch)
{
default:
    printf("\n YES OR NO");
case 'Y':
    printf("YES");
    break;
case 'N':
    printf("NO");
    break;
```

EXERCISES

```
    }
}
```

17.
```
#include <stdio.h>
main()
{
int num=10;
for(num++;num++;num++)
printf(„ %d", num);
return 0;
}
```

18.
```
#include <stdio.h>
main()
{
int num=10;
for(;--num;)
printf(" %d", num);
return 0;
}
```

19.
```
#include <stdio.h>
main()
{
int num=10;
for(;!num;num++)
printf(" %d", num);
return 0;
}
```

20.
```
#include <stdio.h>
main()
{
float PI = 3.14, area;
int r = 7;
while(r>=0)
{
area = PI * r * r;
printf("\n Area = %f", area);
}
return 0;
}
```

21.
```
#include <stdio.h>
main()
{
int i=0, n=10;
while(i==0)
{
if(n<10)
break;
n--;
}
printf("\n i=%d and n=%d", i,n);
}
```

22.
```
#include <stdio.h>
main()
{
int i=0;
do
   {
   printf("\n %d",i);
   i++;
   }while(i<=0);
printf("\n STOP");
}
```

23.
```
#include <stdio.h>
main()
{
int i, j;
for(i=0;i<=10;i++)
{
printf("\n");
for(j=0;j<=i0;j++)
printf(" ");
printf("\n %d", j);
}
}
```

24.
```
#include <stdio.h>
void main()
{
int num = 10;
printf("\n %d", a>10);
}
```

25.
```
#include <stdio.h>
main()
{
printf("HELLO");
if (!1)
   printf("WORLD");
}
```

26.
```
#include <stdio.h>
main()
{
int x=-1;
unsigned int y=1;
if(x < y)
```

EXERCISES

```
    printf("\n SMALL");
  else
    printf("\n LARGE");
  }
```

27.
```
#include <stdio.h>
main()
{
char ch = -63;
int num = -36;
unsigned int unum = -18;
if(ch > num)
{
  printf("A");
  if(ch > unum)
    printf("B");
  else
    printf("C");
}
  else
  {
  printf("D");
  if(num < unum)
  printf("E");
  else
  printf("F");
  }
}
```

28.
```
#include <stdio.h>
main()
{
int num=10;
for(;++num;num-=2)
printf(" %d", num);
return 0;
}
```

29.
```
#include <stdio.h>
main()
{
int num=10;
for(;;)
printf("HI!!");
return 0;
}
```

30.
```
#include <stdio.h>
main()
{
int num=10;
for(num++; num<=100; num=100)
printf(„ %d", num);
return 0;
}
```

31.
```
#include <stdio.h>
main()
{
while(1);
printf("Hi");
return 0;
}
```

32.
```
#include <stdio.h>
main()
{
int i=0;
char c ='0';
while(i<10)
{
printf("%c", c + i);
i++;
}
return 0;
}
```

33.
```
#include <stdio.h>
main()
{
int i=0;
do
{
if(i>10)
continue;
i++;
}while(i<20);
printf("\n i=%d", i);
}
```

34.
```
#include <stdio.h>
main()
{
int i=1;
for(;i<=1;i++)  {
printf("\n %d",i);
printf("\n STOP");
}
```

35.
```
#include <stdio.h>
main ()
int i, j;
for(i=10;i>=0;i--)
```

EXERCISES

```
{
printf("\n");
for(j=i;j>=0;j--)
printf("%d", j);
}
}
```

Give the functionality of the following loops given.

1.
```
int i=1, sum=0;
while(i!=10)
{
sum +=i;
i = i+2;
}
```

2.
```
int i, sum=0;
for (i=1;i<=10)
sum+=i;
```

3.
```
int i;
for (i=1;i<=10;i++)
i--;
```

4.
```
int i=10;
do
{  printf("%d", i);
} while(i>0);
```

5.
```
int i=10;
do
{  printf("%d", i);
} while(i<5);
```

6.
```
int i=1, n=10, sum=0;
while(i<=n)
{
sum+=i;
i++;
}
```

7.
```
int i, sum=0;
for (i=1;;i++)
sum+=i;
```

8.
```
int i=10;
while(i-->0)
printf("%d", i);
```

9.
```
int i;
for (i=10;i>5;i-=2)
printf("%d", i);
```

10.
```
int i;
for (i=10;i>5;)
printf("%d", i);
```

Find errors in the following codes.

1.
```
#include <stdio.h>
main()
{
int i=1;
while(i<=10)
   {
   i=1;
   printf("%d", i);
   i++;
   }
}
```

2.
```
include <stdio.h>
main()
{
int i;
for(i=0,i<=10;i++)
printf("%d", i);
}
```

3.
```
#include <stdio.h>
main()
{
int i=1;
do
{
   printf("%d", i);
   i++;
}while(i=10)
}
```

4.
```
#include <stdio.h>
main()
{
int i,j;
for(i=1,j=0;i+j<=10;i++)
printf("%d", i);
j+=2;
}
```

ANNEXURE 2

A2.1 ALGORITHM

The typical meaning of 'algorithm' is a formally defined procedure for performing some calculation. If a procedure is formally defined, then it must be implemented using some formal language, and such a language is often known as a *programming language*. In general terms, an algorithm provides a blueprint to write a program to solve a particular problem. It is considered to be an effective procedure for solving a problem in finite number of steps. That is, a well-defined algorithm always provides an answer and is guaranteed to terminate.

Algorithms are mainly used to achieve software re-use. Once we have an idea or a blueprint of a solution, we can implement in any high level language like C, C++, Java, so on and so forth.

An algorithm is basically a set of instructions that solve a problem. It is not uncommon to have multiple algorithms to tackle the same problem but the choice of a particular algorithm must depend on the time and space complexity of the algorithm. In this section, we will read how we can analyse algorithms to determine which one is the most efficient, but first let us look at few examples of algorithm.

A2.2 STATEMENTS IN AN ALGORITHM

Any algorithm has a finite number of steps and some steps may involve decision making, repetition. Broadly speaking, an algorithm exhibits three key features that can be given as:

- Sequence
- Decision
- Repetition

Sequence

Sequence means that each step of the algorithm is executed in the specified order. Let us write an algorithm to add two numbers. This algorithm performs the steps in a purely sequential order. Refer Fig. A.2.1.

Algorithm to add two numbers

```
Step 1: Input the first number as A
Step 2: Input the second number as B
Step 3: SET SUM = A + B
Step 4: PRINT SUM
Step 5: END
```

Figure A2.1 Algorithm to add two numbers

Decision

Decision statements are used when the outcome of the process depends on some condition. For example, if `x = y`, then print `"EQUAL"`. So the general form of `IF` construct can be given as:

```
IF condition then process
```

A condition in this context is any statement that may evaluate either to a true value or a false value. In the above example, a variable `x` can either be equal to `y` or not equal to `y`. However, it cannot be both true and false. If the condition is true then the process is executed.

A decision statement can also be stated in the following manner:

```
IF condition
   Then process1
ELSE process2
```

This form is popularly known as the `if-else` construct. Here, if the condition is true then `process1` is executed else `process2` is executed. Look at Fig. A2.2 that shows an algorithm to check if two numbers are equal.

Algorithm to check if two numbers are equal

```
Step 1: Input the first number as A
Step 2: Input the second number as B
Step 3: IF A = B
            Then PRINT "EQUAL"
        ELSE
            PRINT "NOT EQUAL"
Step 4: END
```

Figure A2.2 Algorithm to test for equality of two numbers

Repetition

Repetition which involves executing one or more steps for a number of times can be implemented using constructs like the `while`, `do-while`, and `for` loops. These loops executed one or more steps until some condition is true.

Figure A2.3 shows an algorithm that prints first 10 natural numbers.

Algorithm to print first 10 natural numbers

```
Step 1: [INITIALIZE] SET I = 0, N = 10
Step 2: Repeat Step while I<=N
Step 3:        PRINT I
Step 4: END
```

Figure A2.3 Algorithm to print first 10 natural numbers

A2.3 SOME MORE ALGORITHMS

Let us write some more algorithms

Write an algorithm for interchanging/swapping two values.

```
Step 1: Input first number as A
Step 2: Input second number as B
Step 3: SET TEMP = A
Step 4: SET A = B
Step 5: SET B = TEMP
Step 6: PRINT A, B
Step 7: END
```

Write an algorithm to find larger of two numbers.

```
Step 1: Input first number as A
Step 2: Input second number as B
Step 3: IF A>B
           then PRINT A
      ELSE
           IF A<B
              then PRINT B
           ELSE
              PRINT "The numbers are equal"
Step 4: END
```

Write an algorithm to find whether a number is even or odd.

```
Step 1: Input the first number as A
Step 2: IF A%2 =0
        Then Print "EVEN"
     ELSE
        PRINT "ODD"
Step 3: END
```

Write an algorithm to print the grade obtained by a student using the following rules.

```
Step 1: Enter the Marks obtained as M
Step 2: IF M>75
        then PRINT O
Step 3: IF M>=60 AND M<75
        then PRINT A
Step 4: IF M>=50 AND M<60
        then PRINT B
Step 5: IF M>=40 AND M<50
        then PRINT C
     ELSE
        PRINT D
Step 6: END
```

Marks	Grade
Above 75	O
60-75	A
50-60	B
40-50	C
Less than 40	D

Write an algorithm to find sum of first N natural numbers.

```
Step 1: Input N
Step 2: SET I = 0, SUM = 0
Step 3: Repeat Steps 3 and 4 while I <= N
Step 4:     SET SUM = SUM + I
        SET I = I + 1
Step 5: PRINT SUM
Step 6: END
```

A2.4 TIME AND SPACE COMPLEXITY OF ALGORITHM

To analyse an algorithm means determining the amount of resources (such as time and storage) needed to execute it. Algorithms are generally designed to work with an arbitrary number of inputs, so the efficiency or complexity of an algorithm is stated in terms of time complexity and space complexity.

The time complexity of an algorithm is basically the running time of the program as a function of the input size. On similar grounds, space complexity of an algorithm is the amount of computer memory required during the program execution, as a function of the input size.

In other words, the number of machine instructions which a program executes during its execution is called its time complexity. This number is primarily dependant on the size of the program's input and the algorithm used.

Generally, the space needed by a program depends on two main parts:

- Fixed part, that varies with problem to problem. It includes space needed for storing instructions, constants, variables and structured variables (such as arrays, structures).
- Variable part, that varies from program to program. It includes space needed for recursion stack and for structured variables that are allocated space dynamically during the run-time of the program.

However, running time requirements are more critical than memory requirements. Therefore, do not worry much about the memory requirement. In this section, we will thus concentrate on running time efficiency of the algorithm.

Expressing Time and Space Complexity

The time and space complexity can be expressed using a function `f(n)` where `n` is the input size for a given instance of the problem being solved. Expressing the complexity is badly needed when:

- We want to predict the rate of growth of complexity as the size of the problem increases.
- When there are multiple algorithms that find a solution to a given problem and we need to find the algorithm that is most efficient.

The most widely used notation to express this function `f(n)` is `Big Oh notation`. The `Big Oh notation` provides the upper bound for the complexity.

Algorithm Efficiency

If a function is linear (without any loops or recursions), the efficiency of that algorithm or the running time of that algorithm can be given as the number of instructions it contains. However, if an algorithm contains certain loops or recursive functions then the efficiency of that algorithm may vary depending on the number of loops and the running time of each loop in the algorithm. The efficiency of an algorithm is expressed in terms of the number of elements that has to be processed. So, if `n` is the number of elements, then the efficiency can be stated as

```
f(n) = efficiency
```

Let us consider different cases in which loops determine the efficiency of the algorithm.

Linear Loops

To calculate the efficiency of an algorithm that has a single loop, we need to first determine the number of times the statements in the loop will be executed. This is because the number of iterations is directly proportional to the loop factor. Higher the loop factor more is the number of iterations. For example, consider the loop given below.

```
for(i=0;i<100;i++)
   statement block;
```

Here 100 is the loop factor. We have said above that efficiency is directly proportional to the number of iterations. Hence the general formula in case of linear loops may be given as

```
f(n) = n
```

But, calculating efficiency is not as simple as given in the example above. Consider the loop given below.

```
for(i=0;i<100;i+=2)
   statement block;
```

Here the number of iterations is just half the number of the loop factor. So, here the efficiency can be given as

```
f(n) = n/2
```

Logarithmic Loops

We have seen that in linear loops, the loop update either adds or subtracts. However in logarithmic loops, the loop controlling variable is either multiplied or divided during each iteration of the loop. For example, look at the loops given below.

```
for(i=1;i<100;i*=2)           for(i=0;i<100;i/=2)
   statement block;              statement block;
```

If we consider the first `for` loop in which the loop controlling variable `i` is multiplied by 2 after each iteration of the loop, the loop will be executed only 10 times and not 100 times. Therefore, putting this analysis in general terms, we can conclude that the iterations in loops that divides/multiplies the loop controlling variables, the efficiency can be given as

```
f(n) = log n
```

Nested Loops

Loops that contain loops are known as nested loops. In order to analyse nested loops, we need to determine the number of iterations each loop completes. The total is then obtained as the product of the number of iterations in the inner loop and in the outer loop.

```
Total no. of iterations = no. of iterations
   in inner loop * no. of iterations in
   outer loop
```

In case of nested loops, we will analyse the efficiency of the algorithm based on whether it's a linear logarithmic, quadratic or dependent quadratic nested loop.

Linear Logarithmic

Consider the code given below in which the loop controlling variable of the inner loop is multiplied after each iteration. The number of iterations in the inner loop is `log 10`. This inner loop is controlled by an outer loop which iterates 10 times. Therefore, according to the formula, the number of iterations for this code can be given as

```
10 log 10
```

```
for(i=0;i<10;i++)
    for(j=1; j<10;j*=2)
        statement block;
```

Talking in more general terms, the efficiency of such loops can be given as `f(n) = n log n`.

Quadratic Loop

In a quadratic loop, the number of iterations in the inner loop is equal to that in the outer loop. Consider the code given below in which the outer loop executes 10 times and for each iteration of the outer loop, the inner loop also executes 10 times. Therefore, the efficiency here is 100.

```
for(i=0;i<10;i++)
    for(j=1; j<10;j++)
        statement block;
```

The generalized formula for quadratic loop can be given as, $f(n) = n^2$.

Dependent Quadratic

In a dependent quadratic loop, the number of iterations in the inner loop is dependent on the outer loop. Consider the code given below which shows such an example.

```
for(i=0;i<10;i++)
    for(j=1; j<i;j++)
        statement block;
```

In this code, the inner loop will execute just once in the first iteration, twice in the second iteration, thrice in the third iteration, so on and so forth. In this way the number of iterations can be calculated as,

```
1 + 2 + 3 + 4 + 5 + … + 9 + 10 = 55
```

If we calculate the average of this loop (55/10 = 5.5), we will observe that it is equal to the number of iterations in the outer loop (10) plus 1 divided by 2. In general terms, the inner loop iterates `(n + 1)/2` times. Therefore, the efficiency of such a code (number of iterations in inner loop * no. of iterations in outer loop) can be given as

```
f(n) = n (n + 1)/2
```

Case Study for Chapters 2 and 3

We have learnt the basics of programming in C language and the concepts to write decision-making programs, let us now apply our learning to write some useful programs.

Program on Roman Numerals

Roman numerals are written as combinations of the seven letters. These letters include:

I = 1	C = 100
V = 5	D = 500
X = 10	M = 1000
L = 50	

If smaller numbers follow larger numbers, the numbers are added. Otherwise, if a smaller number precedes a larger number, the smaller number is subtracted from the larger. For example, to convert 1,100 in Roman numerals, you would write M for 1000 and then a C after it for 100. Therefore, 1100 = MC in Roman numerals. Some more examples include:

- VII = 5+2= 7
- IX = 10-1 = 9
- XL = 50-10 = 40
- CX= 100+10 = 111
- MCMLXXXIV = 1000+(1000-100)+50+30+(5-1) = 1984

Roman Numeral Table

1	I	14	XIV	27	XXVII	150	CL
2	II	15	XV	28	XXVIII	200	CC
3	III	16	XVI	29	XXIX	300	CCC
4	IV	17	XVII	30	XXX	400	CD
5	V	18	XVIII	31	XXXI	500	D
6	VI	19	XIX	40	XL	600	DC
7	VII	20	XX	50	L	700	DCC
8	VIII	21	XXI	60	LX	800	DCCC
9	IX	22	XXII	70	LXX	900	CM
10	X	23	XXIII	80	LXXX	1000	M
11	XI	24	XXIV	90	XC	1600	MDC
12	XII	25	XXV	100	C	1700	MDCC
13	XIII	26	XXVI	101	CI	1900	MCM

1. Write a program to show the Roman number representation of a given number.

```
#include <stdio.h>
#include <conio.h>
main()
{
    int number;
    int ones, tens, hundreds, thousand;
    clrscr();
    printf("\n Enter any number (1-3000): ");
    scanf("%d",&number);
    if(number==0||number>3000)
          printf ("\n INVALID NUMBER");
    thousand = number/1000;
    hundreds = ((number/100)%10);
    tens = ((number/10)%10);
    ones = ((number/1)%10);

    if (thousand ==1)
         printf("M");
    else if (thousand ==2)
```

```
    printf("MM");
else if (thousand ==3)
    printf("MMM");

if (hundreds == 1)
    printf("C");
else if (hundreds == 2)
    printf("CC");
else if (hundreds == 3)
    printf("CCC");
else if (hundreds == 4)
    printf("CD");
else if (hundreds ==5)
    printf("D");
else if (hundreds == 6)
    printf("DC");
else if (hundreds == 7)
    printf("DCC");
else if (hundreds ==8)
    printf("DCCC");
else if (hundreds == 9)
    printf("CM");

if (tens == 1)
    printf("X");
else if (tens == 2)
    printf("XX");
else if (tens == 3)
    printf("XXX");
else if (tens == 4)
    printf("XL");
else if (tens ==5)
    printf("L");
else if (tens == 6)
    printf("LX");
else if (tens == 7)
    printf("LXX");
else if (tens ==8)
    printf("LXXX");
else if (tens == 9)
    printf("XC");

if (ones == 1)
    printf("I");
else if (ones == 2)
    printf("II");
else if (ones == 3)
    printf("III");
else if (ones == 4)
    printf("IV");
else if (ones ==5)
    printf("V");
else if (ones == 6)
    printf("VI");
else if (ones == 7)
    printf("VII");
else if (ones ==8)
    printf("VIII");
else if (ones == 9)
    printf("IX");
getch();
}
```

Output

```
Enter any number (1-3000): 139
CXXXIX
```

Program to Find the Day of a given Date

Given below is an algorithm to calculate the day of the week:

1. *Centuries:* Use the centuries table given below to calculate the century.

Centuries table

1700 – 1799	4
1800 – 1899	2
1900 – 1999	0
2000 – 2099	6
2100 – 2199	4
2200 – 2299	2
2300 – 2399	0
2400 – 2499	6
2500 – 2599	4
2600 – 2699	2

2. *Years:* We know that there are 365 days in a year, that is, 52 weeks plus 1 day. Each year starts on the day of the week after that starting the preceding year. Each leap year has one more day than a common year.

   If we know on which day a century starts (from above), and we add the number of years elapsed since the start of the century, plus the number of leap years that have elapsed since the start of the century, we get the day of the week on which the year starts. Where *year* is the last two digits of the year.
3. *Months:* Use the months table to find the day of the week a month starts.

Months table

January	1 (in leap year 6)
February	4 (in leap year 2)
March	4
April	0
May	2
June	5
July	0
August	3
September	6
October	1
November	4
December	6

4. *Day of the month:* Once we know on which day of the week the month starts, we simply add the day of the month to find the final result.

Days table

Sunday	1
Monday	2
Tuesday	3
Wednesday	4
Thursday	5
Friday	6
Saturday	7

Let us calculate the day of April 24, 1982.

1. Find the century value of 1900s from the centuries table: 0
2. Last two digits give the value of year: 82
3. Divide the 82 by 4: 82/4 = 20.5 and drop the fractional part: 20
4. Find the value of April in the months table: 0
5. Add all numbers from steps 1–4 to the day of the month (in this case, 24): 0+82+20+6+24=132.
6. Divide the result of step 5 by 7 and find the remainder: 132/7=18 remainder 6.
7. Look up the days table for the remainder obtained. 6=Friday.

That the values in the centuries table, months table, and days table are pre-determined. We will only be using them to calculate the day of a particular date.

2. Write a program to find out the day for a given date.

```
#include <stdio.h>
#include <stdlib.h>
#include <conio.h>
main()
{
    int dd,mm,yy,year,month,day,i,n;
    clrscr();
    printf("\n Enter the date: ");
    scanf("%d %d %d",&dd,&mm,&yy);
    if( dd>31 || mm>12)
    {
        printf(" INVALID INPUT ");
        getch();
        exit(0);
    }
    year = yy-1900;
    year = year/4;
    year = year+yy-1900;
    switch(mm)
    {
        case 1:
        case 10:
            month = 1;
            break;
        case 2:
        case 3:
        case 11:
            month = 4;
            break;
        case 7:
        case 4:
            month = 0;
            break;
        case 5:
            month = 2;
            break;
        case 6:
            month = 5;
            break;
        case 8:
            month = 3;
            break;
        case 9:
        case 12:
            month = 6;
            break;
}
year = year+month;
year = year+dd;
day  = year%7;
switch(day)
```

```
{
    case 0:
    // Since 7%7 = 0, case 0 means it's
a Saturday
        printf("\n  SATURDAY");
        break;
    case 1:
        printf("\n SUNDAY");
        break;
    case 2:
        printf("\n MONDAY");
        break;
    case 3:
        printf("\n TUESDAY");
        break;
    case 4:
        printf("\n WEDNESDAY");
        break;
    case 5:
        printf("\n THURSDAY");
        break;
    case 6:
        printf("\n FRIDAY");
        break;
}
getch();
return 0;
}
```

Output

```
Enter the date: 29 10 1981
THURSDAY
```

CHAPTER 4

Functions

Takeaways

- Function Declaration
- Function Definition
- Function Call
- Call-by-Value and Call-by-Reference
- Variable Scope
- Storage Classes
- Recursion

4.1 INTRODUCTION

C enables programmers to break up a program into segments commonly known as *functions*, each of which can be written more or less independently of the others. Every function in the program is supposed to perform a well-defined task. Therefore, the program code of one function is completely insulated from the other functions.

Every function interfaces to the outside world in terms of how information is transferred to it and how results generated by the function are transmitted back from it. This interface is basically specified by the function name. For example, look at Fig. 4.1 which explains how the `main()` calls another function to perform a well-defined task.

From the figure we see that `main()` calls the function named `func1()`. Therefore, `main()` is known as the *calling function* and `func1()` is known as the *called function*. The moment the compiler encounters a function call, instead of executing the next statement in the calling function, the control jumps to the statements that are a part of the called function. After the called function is executed, the control is returned back to the calling program.

It is not necessary that the `main()` can call only one function, it can call as many functions as it wants and as many times as it wants. For example, a function call placed within a `for` loop, `while` loop, or `do-while` loop may call the same function multiple times until the condition holds true.

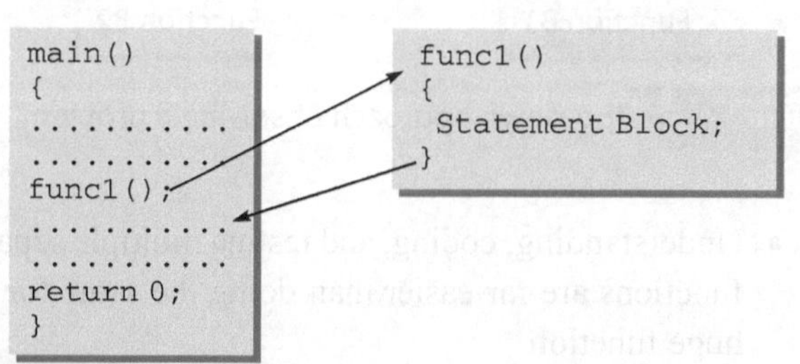

Figure 4.1 The function `main()` calls `func1()`

Another point is that it is not only the `main()` that can call other functions. A function can call any other function. For example, look at Fig. 4.2 which shows one function calling another, and this function in turn calling some other function. From this we see that every function encapsulates a set of operations and when called it returns information to the calling program.

4.1.1 Why are Functions Needed?

Let us analyse the reasons for segmenting a program into manageable chunks as it is an important aspect to programming.

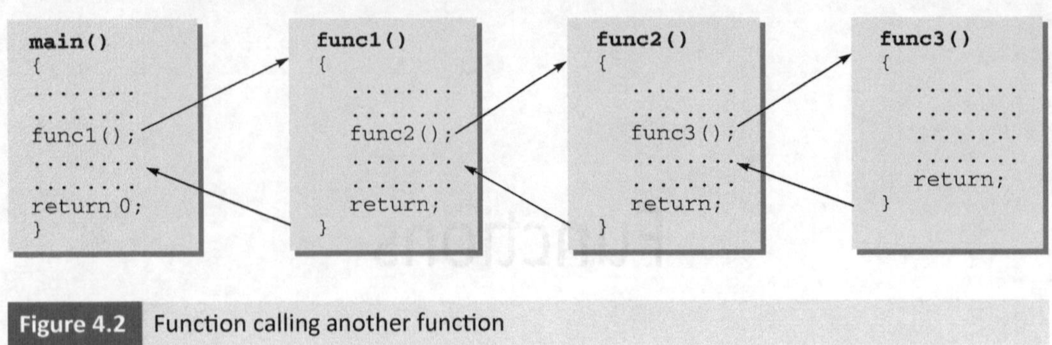

Figure 4.2 Function calling another function

- Dividing the program into separate well-defined functions facilitates each function to be written and tested separately. This simplifies the process of getting the total program to work. Figure 4.3 shows that the `main()` calls other functions for dividing the entire code into smaller sections (or functions). This approach is referred to as the *top-down* approach.

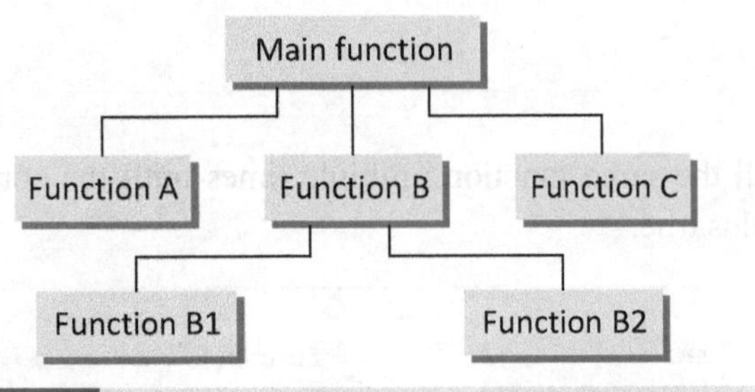

Figure 4.3 Top-down approach of solving a problem

- Understanding, coding, and testing multiple separate functions are far easier than doing the same for one huge function.
- If a big program has to be developed without the use of any function other than `main()`, then there will be countless lines in the `main()` and maintaining this program will be very difficult. A large program size is a serious issue in micro-computers where memory space is limited.
- All the libraries in C contain a set of functions that the programmers are free to use in their programs. These functions have been pre-written and pre-tested, so the programmers can use them without worrying about their code details. This speeds up program development, by allowing the programmer to concentrate only on the code that he has to write.
- When a big program is broken into comparatively smaller functions, then different programmers working on that project can divide the workload by writing different functions.
- Like C libraries, programmers can also write their functions and use them from different points in the main program or any other program that needs its functionalities.

Consider a program that executes a set of instructions repeatedly n times, though not continuously. In case the instructions had to be repeated continuously for n times, they can better be placed within a loop. But if these instructions have to be executed abruptly from anywhere within the program code, then instead of writing these instructions wherever they are required, a better idea is to place these instructions in a function and call that function wherever required. Figure 4.4 explains this concept.

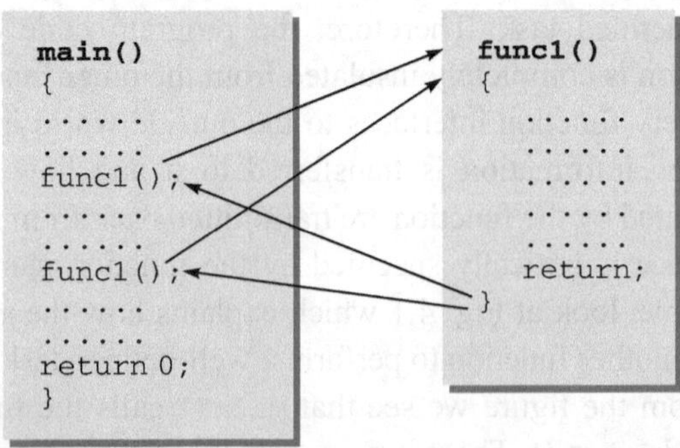

Figure 4.4 Function `func1()` called twice from `main()`

4.2 USING FUNCTIONS

In the first chapter we have said that when we execute a C program, the operating system calls the `main()` function of the program which marks the entry point for the execution. When the program is executed, the `main()` returns some value to the operating system.

Any function (including `main`) can be compared to a black box that takes in input, processes it, and then produces the result. However, we may also have a function that does not take any inputs at all, or the one that does not return anything at all.

While using functions we will be using the following terminologies:

- A function f that uses another function g, is known as the *calling function* and g is known as the *called function*.
- The inputs that the function takes are known as *arguments/parameters*.
- When a called function returns some result back to the calling function, it is said to *return* that result.
- The calling function may or may not pass *parameters* to the called function. If the called function accepts arguments, the calling function will pass parameters, else it will not do so.
- *Function declaration* is a declaration statement that identifies a function with its name, a list of arguments that it accepts, and the type of data it returns.
- *Function definition* consists of a function header that identifies the function, followed by the body of the function containing the executable code for that function.

4.3 FUNCTION DECLARATION/ FUNCTION PROTOTYPE

Before using the function, the compiler must know about the number of parameters and type of parameters that the function expects to receive and the data type of the value that it will return to the calling program. Placing the function declaration statement prior to its use enables the compiler to make a check on the arguments used while calling that function.

The general format for declaring a function that accepts some arguments and returns some value as a result can be given as:

```
return_data_type function_name(data_type
    variable1, data_type variable2,...);
```

Here, `function_name` is a valid name for the function. Naming a function follows the same rules as naming variables. A function should have a meaningful name that must clarify the task that the function will perform. The function name is used to call it for execution in a program. Every function must have a different name that indicates the particular job that the function does.

`return_data_type` specifies the data type of the value that will be returned to the calling function as a result of the processing performed by the called function.

`data_type variable1, data_type variable2, ...` is a list of variables of specified data types. These variables are passed from the calling function to the called function. They are also known as *arguments* or *parameters* that the called function accepts to perform its task. Table 4.1 shows examples of valid function declarations in C.

Table 4.1 Valid function declarations

Function Declaration	Use of the Function
Return data type ↓ char convert_to_ uppercase (char ch);	Converts a character to upper case. The function receives a character as an argument, converts it into upper case and returns the converted character back to the calling program.
Function name ↓ float avg (int a, int b);	Calculates average of two numbers a and b received as arguments. The function returns a floating point value.
int find_largest (int a, int b, int c); ↑ Data type of variable	Finds the largest of three numbers—a, b, and c received as arguments. An integer value which is the largest of the three numbers is returned to the calling function.
double multiply (float a, float b); ↑ Variable 1	Multiplies two floating point numbers a and b that are received as arguments and returns a double value.
void swap (int a, int b);	Swaps or interchanges the value of integer variables a and b received as arguments. The function returns no value, therefore the data type is void.
void print(void);	The function is used to print information on screen. The function neither accepts any value as argument nor returns any value. Therefore, the return type is void and the argument list contains void data type.

Things to remember about function declaration

- After the declaration of every function, there should be a semicolon. If the semicolon is missing, the compiler will generate an error message.

- The function is declaration global. Therefore, the declared function can be called from any point in the program.

Programming Tip: Though optional, use argument names in the function declaration.

- Use of argument names in the function declaration statement is optional. So both declaration statements are valid in C.

```
int func(int, char, float);
```

or

```
int func(int num, char ch, float fnum);
```

- A function cannot be declared within the body of another function.
- A function having void as its return type cannot return any value.
- A function having void as its parameter list cannot accept any value. So the function declared as

```
void print(void);
```

or

```
void print()
```

does not accept any input/arguments from the calling function.

- If the function declaration does not specify any return type, then by default, the function returns an integer value. Therefore when a function is declared as

```
sum(int a, int b);
```

then the function `sum` accepts two integer values from the calling function and in turn returns an integer value to the caller.

- Some compilers make it compulsory to declare the function before its usage while other compilers make it optional. However, it is good to always declare the function before its usage as it allows error checking on the arguments in the function call.

4.4 FUNCTION DEFINITION

When a function is defined, space is allocated for that function in the memory. A function definition comprises two parts:

Programming Tip: It is an error to place a semicolon after the function header in the function definition.

- Function header
- Function body

The syntax of a function definition can be given as:

```
return_data_type function_name(data_type
    variable1, data_type variable2,...)
{
    .......
    statements
    .......
    return( variable);
}
```

Programming Tip: The parameter list in the function definition as well as function declaration must match.

The number of arguments and the order of arguments in the function header must be same as that given in the function declaration statement.

While `return_data_type function_name(data_type variable1, data_type variable2,..)` is known as the function header, the rest of the portion comprising of program statements within { } is the function body which contains the code to perform the specific task.

The function header is same as that of function declaration. The only difference between the two is that a function header is not followed by a semicolon. The list of variables in the function header is known as the *formal parameter list*. The parameter list may have zero or more parameters of any data type. The function body contains instructions to perform the desired computation in a function.

Programming Tip: A function can be defined either before or after the main().

The function definition itself can act as an implicit function declaration. So the programmer may skip the function declaration statement in case the function is defined before being used.

The argument names in the function declaration and function definition need not be the same. However, the data types of the arguments must match with that specified in function declaration as well as function definition.

4.5 FUNCTION CALL

The function call statement invokes the function. When a function is invoked the compiler jumps to the called function to execute the statements that are a part of that function. Once the called function is executed, the program control passes back to the calling function.

Function call statement has the following syntax:

```
function_name(variable1, variable2, ...);
```

When the function declaration is present before the function call, the compiler can check if the correct number and type of arguments are used in the function call and the returned value, if any, is being used reasonably.

Function definitions are often placed in a separate header file which can be included in other C source files that wish to use the functions. For example, the header file `stdio.h` contains the definition of `scanf` and `printf` functions. We simply include this header file and call these functions without worrying about the code to implement their functionality.

List of variables used in function call is known as actual parameter list. The actual parameter list may contain variable names, expressions, or constants.

4.5.1 Points to Remember While Calling a Function

The following points are to be kept in mind while calling a function:

- Function name and the number and type of arguments in the function call must be same as that given in the function declaration and function header of the function definition.

Programming Tip: A logic error will be generated if the arguments in the function call are placed in the wrong order.

- If by mistake the parameters passed to a function are more than what it is specified to accept then the extra arguments will be discarded.
- If by mistake the parameters passed to a function are less than what it is specified to accept then the unmatched argument will be initialized to some garbage value.
- Names (and not the types) of variables in function declaration, function call, and header of function definition may vary.
- If the data type of the argument passed does not match with that specified in the function declaration then either the unmatched argument will be initialized to some garbage value or compile time error will be generated.
- Arguments may be passed in the form of expressions to the called function. In such cases, arguments are first evaluated and converted to the type of formal parameter and then the body of the function gets executed.
- The parameter list must be separated with commas.
- If the return type of the function is not void, then the value returned by the called function may be assigned to some variable as shown in the following statement.

```
variable_name = function_name(variable1,
   variable2, ...);
```

Let us now try writing a program using function.

4.1 Write a program to add two integers using functions.

```
#include <stdio.h>
// FUNCTION DECLARATION
int sum(int a, int b);
int main()
{
   int num1, num2, total = 0;
   printf("\n Enter the first number: ");
   scanf("%d", &num1);
   printf("\n Enter the second number: ");
   scanf("%d", &num2);
   total = sum(num1, num2);
     // FUNCTION CALL
   printf("\n Total = %d", total);
   return 0;
}

// FUNCTION DEFINITION
int sum (int a, int b)    // FUNCTION HEADER
{                        // FUNCTION BODY
   int result;
   result = a + b;
   return result;
}
```

Output

```
Enter the first number: 20
Enter the second number: 30
Total = 50
```

Programming Tip: It is an error to use void as the return type when the function is expected to return a value to the calling function.

The variables declared within the function and its parameters are local to that function. The programmer may use same names for variables in other functions. This eliminates the need for thinking and keeping unique names for variables declared in all the functions in the program.

In the function `sum()`, we have declared a variable result just like any other variable. Variables declared within a function are called *automatic local variables* because of two reasons.

- First, they are local to the function. So, their effect (in terms of scope, lifetime, or accessibility) is limited to the function. Any change made to these variables is visible only in that function.

- Second, they are automatically created whenever the function is called and they cease to exist at the end of the function.

A function cannot be used on the left side of an assignment statement. Therefore writing, `func(10) = 100;` is invalid in C, where func is a function that accepts an integer value.

4.6 return STATEMENT

The `return` statement is used to terminate the execution of a function and returns control to the calling function. When the `return` statement is encountered, the program execution resumes in the calling function at the point immediately following the function call. Refer Fig. 4.2 in which the control passes from the called function to the calling function when the return statement is encountered.

Programming Tip: It is an error to use a return statement in a function that has void as its return type.

A `return` statement may or may not return a value to the calling function. The syntax of `return` statement can be given as

```
return <expression>;
```

Here `expression` is placed in between angular brackets because specifying an expression is optional. The value of `expression`, if present, is returned to the calling function. However, in case `expression` is omitted, the return value of the function is undefined.

The expression, if present, is converted to the type returned by the function. A function that has `void` as its return type cannot return any value to the calling function. So a function that has been declared with return type `void`, a `return` statement containing an expression generates a warning and the expression is not evaluated.

For functions that have no `return` statement, the control automatically returns to the calling function after the last statement of the called function is executed. In other words an implicit return takes place upon completion of the last statement of the called function, and control automatically returns to the calling function.

The programmer may or may not place the expression in a `return` statement within parentheses angular brackets. By default, the return type of a function is `int`.

A function may have more than one `return` statement. For example, consider the program given below.

Programming Tip: When the value returned by a function is assigned to a variable, then the returned value is converted to the type of the variable receiving it.

```
#include <stdio.h>
#include <conio.h>
int check_relation(int a, int b);
// FUNCTION DECLARATION
main()
{
    int a=3, b=5, res;
    clrscr();
    res = check_relation(a, b);
// FUNCTION CALL
    if(res==0) // Test the returned value
        printf("\n EQUAL");
    if(res==1)
        printf("\n a is greater than b");
    if(res==-1)
        printf("\n a is less than b");
    getch();
    return 0;
}
int check_relation(int a, int b)
// FUNCTION DEFINITION
{
    if(a==b)
        return 0;
    if(a>b)
        return 1;
    else if (a<b)
        return -1;
}
```

Programming Tip: An error is generated when the function does not return data of the specified type.

Output

```
a is less than b
```

In the above program there are multiple return statements, but only one of them will get executed depending upon the condition. The `return` statement, like the `break` statement, is used to cause a premature termination of the function.

An expression appearing in a `return` statement is converted to the return type of the function in which the statement appears. If no implicit conversion is possible, the `return` statement is invalid. Since the return type of the function `check_relation()` is `int`, so the result either `0`, `1`, or `-1` is evaluated as an integer.

Programming Tip: A function that does not return any value cannot be placed on the right side of the assignment operator.

We have mentioned earlier that the variables declared inside the function cease to exist after the last statement of the function is executed. So how can we return the value of sum in the program that adds two integers using a function? The answer to this question is that a copy of the value being returned is made automatically and this copy is available to the return point in the program.

4.6.1 Using Variable Number of Arguments

Some functions have a variable number of arguments and data types that cannot be known at the compile time. Typical examples of such functions include the `printf()` and `scanf()` functions. ANSI C offers a symbol called ellipsis to handle such functions. The ellipsis consists of three periods (...). It can be used as

```
int func(char ch, ...);
```

The function declaration statement given above states that `func` is a function that has an arbitrary number and type of argument. However, one must ensure that both the function declaration and function definition should use the ellipsis symbol.

4.7 PASSING PARAMETERS TO THE FUNCTION

When a function is called, the calling function may have to pass some values to the called function. We have been doing this in the programming examples given so far. We will now learn the technicalities involved in passing arguments/parameters to the called function.

Basically, there are two ways in which arguments or parameters can be passed to the called function. They include:

- **Call by value** in which values of the variables are passed by the calling function to the called function. The programs that we have written so far all call the function using call by value method of passing parameters.
- **Call by reference** in which address of the variables are passed by the calling function to the called function.

4.7.1 Call by Value

Till now, we had been calling functions and passing arguments to them using call by value method. In the call-by-value method, the called function creates new variables to store the value of the arguments passed to it. Therefore, the called function uses a copy of the actual arguments to perform its intended task.

If the called function is supposed to modify the value of the parameters passed to it, then the change will be reflected only in the called function. In the calling function no change will be made to the value of the variables. This is because all the changes were made to the copy of the variables and not on the actual variables.

> **Programming Tip:**
> It is legal to have multiple return statements in C.

To understand this concept, consider the code given below. The function `add()` accepts an integer variable `num` and adds `10` to it. In the calling function, the value of `num = 2`. In `add()`, the value of `num` is modified to `12` but in the calling function the change is not reflected.

```
#include <stdio.h>
void add(int n);    // FUNCTION DECLARATION
int main()
{
    int num = 2;

    printf("\n The value of num before
      calling the function = %d", num);
    add(num);     // FUNCTION CALL
    printf("\n The value of num after calling
      the function = %d", num);
    return 0;
}

void add(int n)  // FUNCTION DEFINITION
{
    n = n + 10;
    printf("\n The value of num in the called
      function = %d", n);
}
```

Output

```
The value of num before calling the function = 2
The value of num in the called function = 12
The value of num after calling the function = 2
```

Since the called function uses a copy of num, the value of num in the calling function remains untouched. This concept can be more clearly understood from Fig. 4.5.

In the above program, the called function could not directly modify the value of the argument that was passed to it. In case the value has to be changed, then the programmer may use the return statement. This is shown in the following code.

```
#include <stdio.h>
int add (int n);  // FUNCTION DECLARATION
```

```
int main()
{
  int num = 2;
  printf("\n The value of num before
    calling the function = %d", num);
  num = add(num); // FUNCTION CALL
  printf("\n The value of num after calling
    the function = %d", num);
  return 0;
}

int add(int n)   // FUNCTION DEFINITION
{
  n = n + 10;
  printf("\n The value of num in the called
    function = %d", n);
     return n;
}
```

Output

```
The value of num before calling the function = 2
The value of num in the called function = 12
The value of num after calling the function = 12
```

2	2
num in the calling function	num in the calling function, is known as n in the called function
2	12
num in the calling function remains unchanged	n is modified in the called function

Figure 4.5 Call-by-value method of argument passing

The following points are to be noted while passing arguments to a function using call-by-value method.

- When arguments are passed by value, the called function creates new variables of the same data type as the arguments passed to it.
- The values of the arguments passed by the function are copied into the newly created variables.
- Arguments are called by value when the function does not need to modify the values of the original variables in the calling program.
- Values of the variables in the calling functions remain unaffected when the arguments are passed using call by value technique.

Therefore, call by value method of passing arguments to a function must be used only in two cases:

- When the called function does not modify the value of the actual parameter. It simply uses the value of the parameters to perform its task.
- When you want that the called function should only temporarily modify the value of the variables and not permanently. So although the called function may modify the value of the variables, but these variables remain unchanged in the calling program.

Pros and Cons

The biggest advantage of using call by value technique to pass arguments to the called function is that arguments can be variables (e.g., x), literals (e.g., 6), or expressions (e.g., x+1). The disadvantage is that copying data consumes additional storage space. In addition, it can take a lot of time to copy, thereby resulting in performance penalty, especially if the function is called many times.

> **Programming Tip:** Using call by value method of passing values must be preferred to avoid inadvertent changes to variables of the calling function in the called function.

4.7.2 Call by Reference

When the calling function passes arguments to the called function using call by value method, the only way to return the modified value of the argument to the caller is explicitly using the return statement. The better option when a function wants to modify the value of the argument is to pass arguments using call-by-reference technique. In call by reference, we declare the function parameters as references rather than normal variables. When this is done any changes made by the function to the arguments it receives are visible to the calling program.

To indicate that an argument is passed using call by reference, an ampersand sign (&) is placed after the type in the parameter list. This way, changes made to the parameter in the called function body will then be reflected in its value in the calling program.

Hence, in call-by-reference method, a function receives an implicit reference to the argument, rather than a copy of its value. Therefore, the function can modify the value of the variable and that change will be reflected in the calling function as well. The following program uses this concept. To understand this concept, consider the code given below.

```
#include <stdio.h>
void add (int *n);
```

```
int main()
{
   int num = 2;
   printf("\n The value of num before
     calling the function = %d", num);
   add(&num);
   printf("\n The value of num after calling
     the function = %d", num);
   return 0;
}

void add( int *n)
{
   *n = *n + 10;
   printf("\n The value of num in the called
     function = %d", n);
}
```

Output

```
The value of num before calling the function = 2
The value of num in the called function = 12
The value of num after calling the function = 12
```

Pros and Cons

The advantages of using call-by-reference technique of passing arguments are as follows:

- Since arguments are not copied into new variables, it provides greater time- and space-efficiency.
- The function can change the value of the argument and the change is reflected in the caller.
- A function can return only one value. In case we need to return multiple values, pass those arguments by reference so that modified values are visible in the calling function.

However, the side-effect of using this technique is that when an argument is passed using call by address, it becomes difficult to tell whether that argument is meant for input, output, or both.

Now let us write a few programs that use the call-by-value and the call-by-reference mechanisms.

4.2 Write a function to swap the value of two variables.

```
#include <stdio.h>
void swap_call_by_val(int, int);
void swap_call_by_ref(int *, int *);
main()
   {
      int a=1, b=2, c=3, d=4;
      printf("\n In main(), a = %d and b = %d",
        a, b);
      swap_call_by_val(a, b);
      printf("\n In main(), a = %d and b = %d",
        a, b);
      printf("\n\n In main(), c = %d and d =
        %d", c, d);
      swap_call_by_ref(&c, &d);
         // address of the variables is passed
      printf("\n In main(), c = %d and d =
         %d", c, d);
      return 0;
   }
void swap_call_by_val(int a, int b)
{
   int temp;
   temp = a;
   a = b;
   b = temp;
   printf("\n In function (Call By Value
      Method) a = %d and b = %d", a, b);
}
void swap_call_by_ref(int *c, int *d)
{
   int temp;
   temp = *c;
      // *operator used to refer to the value
   *c = *d;
   *d = temp;
   printf("\n In function (Call By Reference
      Method) c = %d and d = %d", *c, *d);
}
```

Output

```
In main(), a = 1 and b = 2
   In function (Call By Value Method) a = 2
   and b = 1
In main(), a = 1 and b = 2

In main(), c = 3 and d = 4
   In function (Call By Reference Method) c
   = 4 and d = 3
   In main(), c = 4 and d = 3
```

4.3 Write a program to find biggest of three integers using functions.

```
#include <stdio.h>
int greater(int a, int b, int c);

int main()
{
   int num1, num2, num3, large;

   printf("\n Enter the first number: ");
   scanf("%d", &num1);
   printf("\n Enter the second number: ");
   scanf("%d", &num2);
   printf("\n Enter the third number: ");
   scanf("%d", &num3);

   large = greater(num1, num2, num3);
   printf("\n Largest number = %d", large);
   return 0;
```

```
}
int greater(int a, int b, int c)
{
   if(a>b && a>c)
      return a;
   if(b>a && b>c)
      return b;
   else
      return c;
}
```

Output

```
Enter the first number : 45
Enter the second number: 23
Enter the third number : 34
Largest number = 45
```

4.4 Write a program to calculate area of a circle using function.

```
#include <stdio.h>
float cal_area(float r);

int main()
{
   float area, radius;
   printf("\n Enter the radius of the
        circle: ");
   scanf("%f", &radius);
   area = cal_area(radius);
   printf("\n Area of the circle with radius
        %f = %f", radius, area);
   return 0;
}
float cal_area(float radius)
{
   return (3.14 * radius * radius);
}
```

Output

```
Enter the radius of the circle: 7
Area of the circle with radius 7 = 153.83
```

4.5 Write a program to convert time to minutes.

```
#include <stdio.h>
#include <conio.h>
int convert_time_in_mins(int hrs, int
   minutes);
main()
{
   int hrs, minutes, total_mins;
   printf("\n Enter hours and minutes: ");
   scanf("%d %d", &hrs, &minutes);
   total_mins = convert_time_in_mins(hrs,
       minutes);
   printf("\n Total minutes = %d", total_
       mins);
   getch();
   return 0;
}
int convert_time_in_mins(int hrs, int minutes)
{
   int mins;
   mins = hrs*60 + minutes;
   return mins;
}
```

Output

```
Enter the hours and minutes: 4 30
Total minutes = 270
```

4.6 Write a program to calculate P(n/r).

```
#include <stdio.h>
#include <conio.h>
int Fact(int);
main()
{
   int n, r;
   float result;
   clrscr();
   printf("\n Enter the value of n: ");
   scanf("%d", &n);
   printf("\n Enter the value of r: ");
   scanf("%d", &r);
   result = (float)Fact(n)/Fact(r);
   printf("\n P(n/r): P(%d)/(%d) = %f", n,
       r, result);
   getch();
   return 0;
}
int Fact(int num)
{
   int f=1, i;
   for(i=num;i>=1;i--)

      f = f*i;
   return f;
}
```

Output

```
Enter the value of n: 4
Enter the value of r: 2
P(n/r): P(12)/(3) = 12.00
```

4.7 Write a program to calculate C(n/r).

```
#include <stdio.h>
```

```
#include <conio.h>
int Fact(int);
main()
{
   int n, r;
   float result;
   clrscr();
   printf("\n Enter the value of n: ");
   scanf("%d", &n);
   printf("\n Enter the value of r: ");
   scanf("%d", &r);
   result = (float)Fact(n)/(Fact(r)*Fact(n-r));
   printf("\n C(n/r) : C(%d/%d) = %.2f", n,
       r, result);
   getch();
   return 0;
}
int Fact(int num)
{
   int f=1, i;
   for(i=num;i>=1;i--)
      f = f*i;
   return f;
}
```

Output

```
Enter the value of n: 4
Enter the value of r: 2
C(n/r): C(12)/(3) = 6.00
```

4.8 Write a program to sum the series—1/1! + 1/2! + 1/3! + ... + 1/n!

```
#include <stdio.h>
#include <conio.h>
int Fact(int);
main()
{
   int n, f, i;
   float result=0.0;
   clrscr();
   printf("\n Enter the value of n: ");
   scanf("%d", &n);
   for(i=1;i<=n;i++)
   {
      f=Fact(i);
      result += 1/(float)f;
   }
   printf("\n The sum of the series 1/1! +
       1/2! + 1/3!... = %f", result);
   getch();
   return 0;
}
int Fact(int num)
{
   int f=1, i;
   for(i=num;i>=1;i--)

      f = f*i;
   return f;
}
```

Output

```
Enter the value of n: 2
The sum of the series 1/1! + 1/2! + 1/3!... = 1.5
```

4.9 Write a program to sum the series—1/1! + 4/2! + 27/3! + ...

```
#include <stdio.h>
#include <conio.h>
#include <math.h>
int Fact(int);
main()
{
   int n, i, NUM, DENO;
   float sum=0.0;
   clrscr();
   printf("\n ");
   scanf("%d",&n);
   for(i=1;i<=n;i++)
   {

      NUM = pow(i,i);

      DENO = Fact(i);

      sum += (float)NUM/DENO;
   }
   printf("\n 1/1! + 4/2! + 27/3! + ....=
        %f", sum);
   getch();
   return 0;
}
int Fact(int n)
{
   int f=1, i;
   for(i=n;i>=1;i--)

      f=f*i;
   return f;
}
```

Output

```
Enter the value of n: 2
1/1! + 4/2! + 27/3! + ....= 3
```

4.8 SCOPE OF VARIABLES

In C, all constants and variables have a defined scope. By scope we mean the accessibility and visibility of the variables at different points in the program. A variable or a constant in C has four types of scope: block, function, file, and program scope.

4.8.1 Block Scope

We have studied that a statement block is a group of statements enclosed within opening and closing curly brackets ({ }). If a variable is declared within a statement block then, as soon as the control exits that block, the variable will cease to exist. Such a variable also known as a local variable is said to have a *block scope*.

So far we had been using local variables. For example, if we declare an integer x inside a function, then that variable is unknown to the rest of the program outside (i.e., outside that function).

Programming Tip:
It is an error to use the name of a function argument as the name of a local variable.

Blocks of statements may be placed one after the other in a program; such blocks that are placed at the same level are known as *parallel blocks*. However, a program may also contain a nested block, like a `while` loop inside `main()`. If an integer `x` is declared and initialized in the `main()`, and then re-declared and re-initialized in the `while` loop, then the integer variable x will occupy different memory slots and will be considered as different variables. The following code reveals this concept.

```
#include <stdio.h>
int main()
{
    int x = 10;
    int i=0;
    printf("\n The value of x outside the
         while loop is %d", x);

    while (i<3)
    {
       int x = i;
       printf("\n The value of x inside the
          while loop is %d", x);
       i++;
    }

    printf("\n The value of x outside the
         while loop is %d", x);
    return 0;
}
```

Output

```
The value of x outside the while loop is 10
The value of x inside the while loop is 0
The value of x inside the while loop is 1
The value of x inside the while loop is 2
The value of x outside the while loop is 10
```

Programming Tip:
Try to avoid variable names that hide variables in outer scope.

You may get an error message while executing this code. This is because some C compilers make it mandatory to declare all the variables first before you do anything with i.e., they permit declaration of variables right after the curly brackets of `main()` starts.

Hence, we can conclude two things:

- Variables declared with same names as those in outer block mask the outer block variables while executing the inner block.
- In nested blocks, variables declared outside the inner blocks are accessible to the nested blocks, provided these variables are not re-declared within the inner block.

In order to avoid error, a programmer must prefer to use different names for variables not common to inner as well as outer blocks.

4.8.2 Function Scope

Function scope indicates that a variable is active and visible from the beginning to the end of a function. In C, only the `goto` label has function scope. In other words function scope is applicable only with `goto` label names. This means that the programmer cannot have the same label name inside a function.

Using `goto` statements is not recommended as it is not considered to be a good programming practice. We will not discuss the `goto` statement in detail here but, we will take a look at an example of code that demonstrates the function scope.

```
int main()
{
     .
     .
     loop:   /* A goto label has function
     scope */
     .
     .
     .
     goto loop;  /* the goto statement */
     .
     .
     return 0;
}
```

In this example, the label loop is visible from the beginning to the end of the `main()` function. Therefore, there should not be more than one label having the same name within the `main()` function.

4.8.3 Program Scope

Till now we have studied that variables declared within a function are local variables. These local variables (also known as internal variables) are automatically created when they are declared in the function and are usable only within that function. The local variables are unknown to other functions in the program. Such variables cease to exist after the last statement in the function in which they are declared and are re-created each time the function is called.

Programming Tip: The value of a global variable can be used from anywhere in the program whereas the local variable cease to exist outside the function in which it is declared.

However, if you want a function to access some variables which are not passed to them as arguments, then declare those variables outside any function blocks. Such variables are commonly known as *global variables* and can be accessed from any point in the program.

Lifetime Global variables are created at the beginning of program execution and remain in existence throughout the period of execution of the program. These variables are known to all the functions in the program and are accessible to them for usage. Global variables are not limited to a particular function so they exist even when a function calls another function. These variables retain their value so that they can be used from every function in the program.

Place of Declaration The global variables are declared outside all the functions including `main()`. Although there is no specific rule that states where the global variables must be declared, it is always recommended to declare them on top of the program code.

Name Conflict If we have a variable declared in a function that has same name as that of the global variable, then the function will use the local variable declared within it and ignore the global variable. However, the programmer must not use names of global variables as the names of local variables, as this may lead to confusion and lead to erroneous result.

If a global variable is not initialized during its initialization then it is automatically initialized to zero by default.

Consider the following program.

```
#include <stdio.h>
int x = 10;
void print();
int main()
{
    printf("\n The value of x in the main() =
        %d", x);
    int x = 2;
    printf("\n The value of local variable x
        in the main() = %d", x);
    print();
    return 0;
}
void print()
{
    printf("\n The value of x in the print()
        = %d", x);
}
```

Output

```
The value of x in the main() = 10
The value of local variable x in the main() = 2
The value of x in the print() = 10
```

From the code we see that local variables overwrite the value of global variables. In big programs use of global variables is not recommended until it is very important to use them because there is a big risk of confusing them with any local variables of the same name.

Functions are considered to be self-contained and independent modules. So they need to be isolated from the rest of the code, but using global variables loose this idea behind making functions.

4.8.4 File Scope

When a global variable is accessible until the end of the file, the variable is said to have *file scope*. To allow a variable to have file scope, declare that variable with the static keyword before specifying its data type, as shown:

```
static int x = 10;
```

A global static variable can be used anywhere from the file in which it is declared but it is not accessible by any other files. Such variables are useful when the programmer writes his own header files.

4.9 STORAGE CLASSES

The *storage class* of a variable defines the scope (visibility) and lifetime of variables and/or functions declared within a C program. In addition to this, the storage class gives the following information about the variable or the function.

- The storage class of a function or a variable determines the part of memory where storage space will be allocated for that variable or function (whether the variable/function will be stored in a register or in RAM).
- It specifies how long the storage allocation will continue to exist for that function or variable.
- It specifies the scope of the variable or function, i.e., the storage class indicates the part of the C program

in which the variable name is visible or the part in which it is accessible. In other words, whether the variable/function can be referenced throughout the program or only within the function, block, or source file where it has been defined.

- It specifies whether the variable or function has internal, external, or no linkage.
- It specifies whether the variable will be automatically initialized to zero or to any indeterminate value.

C supports four storage classes: automatic, register, external, and static. The general syntax for specifying the storage class of a variable can be given as

```
<storage_class_specifier> <data type>
    <variable name>
```

4.9.1 `auto` Storage Class

The auto storage class specifier is used to explicitly declare a variable with *automatic storage*. It is the default storage class for variables declared inside a block. For example, if we write

```
auto int x;
```

then `x` is an integer that has automatic storage. It is deleted when the block in which `x` was declared exits.

The auto storage class can be used to declare variables in a block or the names of function parameters. However, since the variable names or names of function parameters by default have automatic storage, the auto storage class specifier is therefore treated as redundant while declaring data.

Important things to remember about variables declared with auto storage class include:

- All local variables declared within a function belong to automatic storage class by default.
- They should be declared at the start of the program block. (Right after the opening curly bracket {)
- Memory for the variable is automatically allocated upon entry to a block and freed automatically upon exit from that block.
- The scope of the variable is local to the block in which it is declared. These variables may be declared within a nested block.
- Every time the block (in which the automatic variable is declared) is entered, the value of the variable declared with initializers is initialized.
- The auto variables are stored in the primary memory of the computer.
- If auto variables are not initialized at the time of declaration, then they contain some garbage value.

The following code uses an `auto` integer that is local to the function in which it is defined.

```
#include <stdio.h>
void func1()
{
  int a=10;
  printf("\n a = %d", a);
      // auto integer local to func1()
}
void func2()
{
  int a=20;
  printf("\n a = %d", a);
      // auto integer local to func2()
}
void main()
{
  int a=30  // auto integer local to main()
  func1();
  func2();
  printf("\n a = %d", a);
}
```

Output

```
a = 10
a = 20
a = 30
```

4.9.2 `register` Storage Class

When a variable is declared using `register` as its storage class, it is stored in a CPU register instead of RAM. Since the variable is stored in RAM, the maximum size of the variable is equal to the register size. One drawback of using a register variable is that they cannot be operated using the unary `'&'` operator because it does not have a memory location associated with it. A register variable is declared in the following manner:

```
register int x;
```

`register` variables are used when quick access to the variable is needed. It is not always necessary that the `register` variable will be stored in the `register`. Rather, the `register` variable might be stored in a `register` depending on the hardware and implementation restrictions.

Hence, programmers can only suggest the compiler to store those variables in the registers which are used repeatedly or whose access times are critical. However, for the compiler, it is not an obligation to always accept such requests. In case the compiler rejects the request to store the variable in the register, the variable is treated as having the storage class specifier `auto`.

Like auto variables, register variables also have automatic storage duration. That is, each time a block is entered, the storage for register variables defined in that block are accessible and the moment that block is exited, the variables becomes no longer accessible for use. Now let us have a look at the following code that uses a `register` variable.

```
#include <stdio.h>
int exp(int a, int b); // FUNCTION DECLARATION
main()
{
   int a=3, b=5, res;
   res = exp(a, b);// FUNCTION CALL
   printf("\n %d to the power of %d = %d",
         a, b, res);
   getch();
   return 0;

}
int exp(int a, int b)  // FUNCTION DEFINITION
{
   register int res=1;
   int i;
   for(i=1;i<=b;i++)
      res = res*b;
   return res;
}
```

Output

```
3 to the power of 5 = 243
```

4.9.3 `extern` Storage Class

A large C program can be broken down into smaller programs. When these smaller programs are compiled, they are joined together to form a large program. However, these smaller programs may need to share certain variables for processing. For such situations C language provides an external storage class that is specified using the keyword `extern`.

The storage class `extern` is used to give a reference of a global variable that is visible to all the program files. Such global variables are declared like any other variable in one of the program file. When there are multiple files in a program and you need to use a particular function or variable in a file apart from which it is declared, then use the keyword `extern`. To declare a variable `x` as `extern` write,

```
extern int x;
```

External variables may be declared outside any function in a source code file as any other variable is declared. But usually external variables are declared and defined at the beginning of a source file.

Memory is allocated for external variables when the program begins execution, and remains allocated until the program terminates. External variables may be initialized while they are declared. However, the initializer must be a constant expression. The compiler will initialize its value only once during the compiler time. In case the `extern` variable is not initialized, it will be initialized to zero by default.

External variables have global scope, i.e., these variables are visible and accessible from all the functions in the program. However, if any function has a local variable with the same name and types as that of the global or extern variable, then references to the name will access the local variable rather than the extern variable. Hence extern variables are overwritten by local variables.

Let us now write a program in which we will use the `extern` keyword.

```
// FILE 1.C
#include <stdio.h>
#include <FILE2.C>
   // Programmer's own header file
int x;
void print(void);
int main()
{
   x = 10;
   printf("\n x in FILE1 = %d", x);
   print();
   return 0;
}
// END OF FILE1.C
// FILE2.C
#include <stdio.h>

extern int x;
void print()
{
   printf(«\n x in FILE 2 = %d», x);
}
main()
{
// Statements
}
// END OF FILE2.C
```

Output

```
x in FILE1 = 10
x in FILE2 = 10
```

In the program, we have used two files—`File1` and `File2`. `File1` has declared a global variable `x`. `File1` also includes File2 which has a print function that uses the external variable x to print its value on the screen.

The extern specifier tells the compiler that the variable has already been declared elsewhere and therefore it should not allocate storage space for that variable again. During compilation of the program, the linker will automatically resolve the reference problem.

In a multi-file program, the global variable must be declared only once (in any one of the files) without using the extern keyword. This is because, otherwise the linker will have a conflict as to which variable to use and therefore in such a situation it raises a warning message.

4.9.4 static Storage Class

While auto is the default storage class for all local variables, static is the default storage class for all global variables. Static variables have a lifetime over the entire program, i.e., memory for the static variables is allocated when the program begins running and is freed when the program terminates. To declare an integer x as static, write,

```
static int x = 10;
```

Here x is a local static variable. Static local variables when defined within a function are initialized at the runtime. The difference between an auto variable and a static variable is that the static variable when defined within a function is not re-initialized when the function is called again and again. It is initialized just once and further calls of the function share the value of the static variable. Hence, the static variable inside a function retains its value during various calls.

When a static variable is not explicitly initialized by the programmer then it is automatically initialized to zero when memory is allocated for them. Although static automatic variables exist even after the block in which they are defined terminates, their scope is local to the block in which they are defined.

Static storage class can be specified for auto as well as extern variables. For example, we can write

```
static extern int x;
```

When we declare a variable as external static variable, then that variable is accessible from all the functions in this source file.

Static variables can be initialized while they are being declared. But this initialization is done only once at the compile time when memory is being allocated for the static variable. Also the value with which the static variable is initialized must be a constant expression.

Look at the following code which clearly differentiates between a static variable and a normal variable.

```
#include <stdio.h>
void print(void);  // FUNCTION DECLARATION
int main()
{
    printf("\n First call of print()");
    print();        // FUNCTION CALL
    printf("\n\n Second call of print()");
    print();        // FUNCTION CALL
    printf("\n\n Third call of print()");
    print();        // FUNCTION CALL
    return 0;
}

void print()  // FUNCTION DEFINITION
{
    static int x;
    int y = 0;
    printf("\n Static integer variable, x =
         %d", x);
    printf("\n Integer variable, y = %d", y);
    x++;
    y++;
}
```

Output

```
First call of print()
Static integer variable, x = 0
Integer variable, y = 0

Second call of print()
Static integer variable, x = 1
Integer variable, y = 0

Third call of print()
Static integer variable, x = 2
Integer variable, y = 0
```

4.9.5 Comparison of Storage Classes

Table 4.2 compares the key features of all the storage classes.

Table 4.2 Comparison of storage classes

FEATURE	STORAGE CLASS			
	`auto`	`extern`	`register`	`static`
Accessibility	Accessible within the function or block in which it is declared.	Accessible within all program files that are a part of the program.	Accessible within the function or block in which it is declared.	Local: Accessible within the function or block in which it is declared. Global: Accessible within the program in which it is declared.
Storage	Main memory	Main memory	CPU register	Main memory
Existence	Exists when the function or block in which it is declared is entered. Ceases to exist when the control returns from the function or the block in which it was declared.	Exists throughout the execution of the program.	Exists when the function or block in which it is declared is entered. Ceases to exist when the control returns from the function or the block in which it was declared.	Local: Retains value between function calls or block entries. Global: Preserves value in program files.
Default value	Garbage	Zero	Garbage	Zero

4.10 RECURSIVE FUNCTIONS

A *recursive function* is defined as a function that calls itself to solve a smaller version of its task until a final call is made which does not require a call to itself. Every recursive solution has two major cases, they are

- *Base case,* in which the problem is simple enough to be solved directly without making any further calls to the same function.
- *Recursive case,* in which first the problem at hand is divided into simpler sub-parts. Second the function calls itself but with sub parts of the problem obtained in the first step. Third, the result is obtained by combining the solutions of simpler sub-parts.

Therefore, recursion is defining large and complex problems in terms of a smaller and more easily solvable problem. In recursive function, a complex problem is defined in terms of simpler problems and the simplest problem is given explicitly.

To understand recursive functions, let us take an example of calculating factorial of a number. To calculate `n!`, what we have to do is multiply the number with factorial of the number that is 1 less than that number. In other words, `n! = n × (n-1)!`

Let us say we need to find the value of `5!...`

```
5! = 5 × 4 × 3 × 2 × 1
   = 120
```

This can be written as

```
5! = 5 × 4! , where 4!= 4 × 3!
```

Therefore,

```
5! = 5 × 4 × 3!
```

Similarly, we can also write,

```
5! = 5 × 4 × 3 × 2!
```

Expanding further

```
5! = 5 × 4 × 3 × 2 × 1!
```

We know, `1! = 1`

Therefore, the series of problem and solution can be given as shown in Fig. 4.6.

PROBLEM	SOLUTION
5!	5 × 4 × 3 × 2 × 1!
= 5 × 4!	= 5 × 4 × 3 × 2 × 1
= 5 × 4 × 3!	= 5 × 4 × 3 × 2
= 5 × 4 × 3 × 2!	= 5 × 4 × 6
= 5 × 4 × 3 × 2 × 1!	= 5 × 24
	= 120

Figure 4.6 Recursive factorial function

Now if you look at the problem carefully, you can see that we can write a recursive function to calculate the factorial of a number. Every recursive function must have a base case and a recursive case. For the factorial function,

Programming Tip: Every recursive function must have at least one base case. Otherwise, the recursive function will generate an infinite sequence of calls thereby resulting in an error condition known as an infinite stack.

- **Base case** is when `n = 1`, because if `n = 1`, the result will be 1 as 1! = 1.
- **Recursive case** of the factorial function will call itself but with a smaller value of `n`, this case can be given as

  factorial(n) = n × factorial (n–1)

Look at the following code which calculates the factorial of a number recursively.

```
#include <stdio.h>
int Fact(int);   // FUNCTION DECLARATION
main()
{
    int num;
    printf("\n Enter the number: ");
    scanf("%d", &num);
    printf("\n Factorial of %d = %d", num,
       Fact(num));// FUNCTION CALL
    return 0;
}

int Fact( int n)// FUNCTION DEFINITION
{
    if(n==1)
       return 1;
    return (n * Fact(n-1));  // FUNCTION CALL
}
```

From the above example, let us analyse the basic steps of a recursive program.

Step 1: Specify the base case which will stop the function from making a call to itself.

Step 2: Check to see whether the current value being processed matches with the value of the base case. If yes, process and return the value.

Step 3: Divide the problem into a smaller or simpler sub-problem.

Step 4: Call the function from the sub-problem.

Step 5: Combine the results of the sub-problems.

Step 6: Return the result of the entire problem.

The base case of a recursive function acts as the terminating condition. So, in the absence of an explicitly-defined base case, a recursive function would call itself indefinitely.

4.10.1 Greatest Common Divisor

The greatest common divisor of two numbers (integers) is the largest integer that divides both the numbers. We can find the GCD of two numbers recursively by using the *Euclid's algorithm* that states

$$\text{GCD(a, b)} = \begin{cases} \text{b, if b divides a} \\ \text{GCD(b, a mod b), otherwise} \end{cases}$$

GCD can be implemented as a recursive function because if `b` does not divide `a`, then we call the same function (GCD) with another set of parameters that are smaller and simpler than the original ones. Here we assume that `a > b`. However if `a < b`, then interchange `a` and `b` in the formula given above.

Working

Assume `a = 62` and `b = 8`

```
GCD(62, 8)
   rem = 62 % 8 = 6
   GCD(8, 6)
      rem = 8 % 6 = 2
      GCD(6, 2)
         rem = 6 % 2 = 0
      Return 2
   Return 2
Return 2
```

4.10. Write a program to calculate GCD using recursive functions.

```
#include <stdio.h>
int GCD(int, int);  // FUNCTION DECLARATION
main()
{
    int num1, num2, res;
    printf("\n Enter the two numbers: ");
    scanf("%d %d", &num1, &num2);
    res = GCD(num1, num2);  // FUNCTION CALL
    printf("\n GCD of %d and %d = %d", num1,
       num2, res);
    return 0;
}

int GCD(int x, int y) // FUNCTION DEFINITION
{
    int rem;
    rem = x%y;
    if(rem==0)
       return y;
    else
       return (GCD(y, rem)); // FUNCTION CALL
}
```

4.10.2 Finding Exponents

We can find a solution to find exponent of a number using recursion. To find x^y, the base case would be when `y=0`, as we know that any number raised to the power `0` is `1`. Therefore, the general formula to find x^y can be given as

$$\text{EXP}(x, y) = \begin{cases} 1, & \text{if } y == 0 \\ x * \text{EXP}(x^{y-1}), & \text{otherwise} \end{cases}$$

Working

```
exp_rec(2, 4) = 2 * exp_rec( 2, 3)
    exp_rec(2, 3) =  2 * exp_rec( 2, 2)
      exp_rec(2, 2)  2 * exp_rec( 2, 1)
         exp_rec(2, 1)  = 2 * exp_rec( 2, 0)
            exp_rec( 2, 0) = 1
         exp_rec( 2, 1) = 2 * 1 = 2
      exp_rec( 2, 2) = 2 * 2 = 4
   exp_rec( 2, 3) = 2 * 4 = 8
exp_rec( 2, 4) = 2 * 8 = 16
```

4.11. Write a program to calculate `exp(x,y)` using recursive functions.

```
#include <stdio.h>
int exp_rec(int, int);
main()
{
   int num1, num2, res;
   printf("\n Enter the two numbers: ");
   scanf("%d %d", &num1, &num2);
   res = exp_rec(num1, num2);
   printf ("\n RESULT = %d", res);
   return 0;
}

int exp_rec(int x, int y)
{
   if( y==0)
      return 1;
   else
      return ( x * exp_rec( x, y-1));
}
```

4.10.3 Fibonacci Series

The Fibonacci series can be given as

`0 1 1 2 3 5 8 13 21 34 55 ......`

That is, the third term of the series is the sum of the first and second terms. On similar grounds, fourth term is the sum of second and third terms, and so on. Now we will design a recursive solution to find the nth term of the Fibonacci series. The general formula to do so can be given as

$$\text{FIB}(n) = \begin{cases} 1, & \text{if } n<=2 \\ \text{FIB}(n-1) + \text{FIB}(n-2), & \text{otherwise} \end{cases}$$

As per the formula, `FIB(1) =1` and `FIB(2) = 1`. So we have two base cases. This is necessary because every problem is divided into two smaller problems (Fig. 4.7).

4.12. Write a program to print the Fibonacci series using recursion.

```
#include <stdio.h>
int Fibonacci(int);
main()
{
   int n;
   printf("\n Enter the number of terms in
           the series: ");
   scanf("%d", &n);
   for(int i=0;i<n;i++)
```

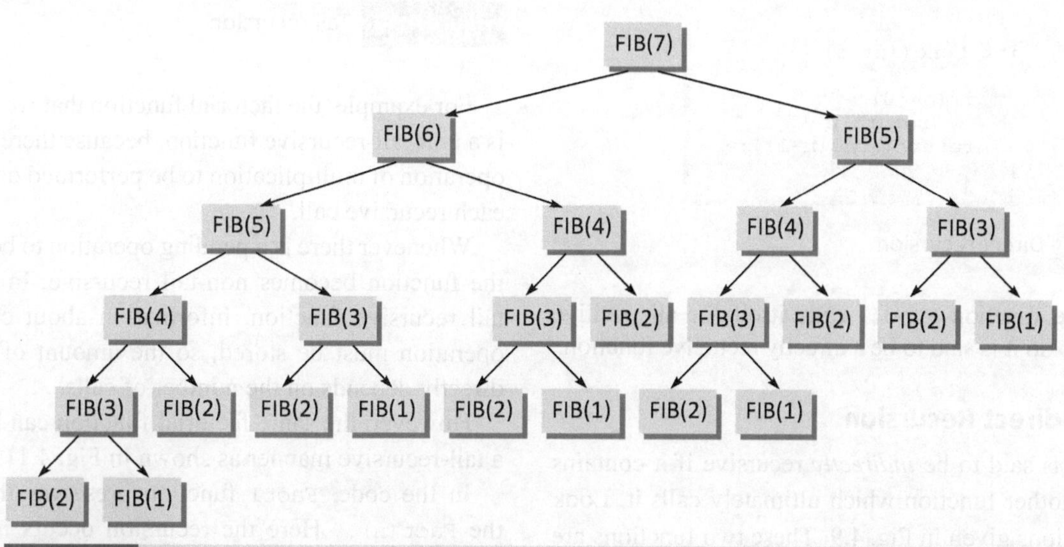

Figure 4.7 Recursion structure of `fib` function

```
    printf("\n Fibonacci (%d) = %d", i,
      Fibonacci(i));
  return 0;
}

int Fibonacci(int num)
{
  if(num <= 2)
    return 1;
  return (Fibonacci (num - 1) +
      Fibonacci(num - 2));
}
```

4.11 TYPES OF RECURSION

Recursion is a technique that breaks a problem into one or more sub-problems that are similar to the original problem. Any recursive function can be characterized based on:

- whether the function calls itself directly or indirectly (*direct or indirect recursion*),
- whether any operation is pending at each recursive call (*tail-recursive* or not), and
- the structure of the calling pattern (*linear or tree-recursive*).

In this section, we will read about all these types of recursions.

4.11.1 Direct Recursion

A function is said to be *directly* recursive if it explicitly calls itself. For example, consider Fig. 4.8.

```
int Func(int n)
{
    if(n==0)
        return n;
    return(Func(n-1));
}
```

Figure 4.8 Direct recursion

Here, the function `Func()` calls itself for all positive values of `n`, so it is said to be a directly recursive function.

4.11.2 Indirect Recursion

A function is said to be *indirectly* recursive if it contains a call to another function which ultimately calls it. Look at the functions given in Fig. 4.9. These two functions are indirectly recursive as they both call each other.

```
int Func1(int n)
{
    if(n==0)
        return n;
    return Func2(n);
}

int Func2(int x)
{
    return Func1(x-1);
}
```

Figure 4.9 Indirect recursion

4.11.3 Tail Recursion

A recursive function is said to be *tail recursive* if no operations are pending to be performed when the recursive function returns to its caller (Fig. 4.10). When the called function returns, the returned value is immediately returned from the calling function. Tail recursive functions are highly desirable because they are much more efficient to use as the amount of information that has to be stored on the system stack is independent of the number of recursive calls.

```
int Fact(int n)
{
    if(n==1)
        return 1;
    return (n * Fact(n-1));
}
```

Figure 4.10 Tail recursion

For example, the factorial function that we have written is a non-tail-recursive function, because there is a pending operation of multiplication to be performed on return from each recursive call.

Whenever there is a pending operation to be performed, the function becomes non-tail recursive. In such a non-tail recursive function, information about each pending operation must be stored, so the amount of information directly depends on the number of calls.

However, the same factorial function can be written in a tail-recursive manner as shown in Fig. 4.11.

In the code, `Fact1` function preserves the syntax of the `Fact(n)`. Here the recursion occurs in the `Fact1` function and not in `Fact` function. Carefully observe that

`Fact1` has no pending operation to be performed on return from recursive calls. The value computed by the recursive call is simply returned without any modification. So in this case, the amount of information to be stored on the system stack is constant (just the value of `n` and `res` needs to be stored) and is independent of the number of recursive calls.

```
int Fact(n)
{
return Fact1(n, 1);
}
int Fact1(int n, int res)
{
    if (n==1)
        return res;
    return Fact1(n-1, n*res);
}
```

Figure 4.11 Tail-recursive and non-tail-recursive function

Converting Recursive Functions to Tail Recursive

A non-tail recursive function can be converted into a tail-recursive function by using an *auxiliary parameter* as we did in case of the Factorial function. The auxiliary parameter is used to form the result. When we use such a parameter, the pending operation is incorporated into the auxiliary parameter so that the recursive call no longer has a pending operation. We generally use an auxiliary function while using the auxiliary parameter. This is done to keep the syntax clean and to hide the fact that auxiliary parameters are needed.

4.11.4 Linear and Tree Recursion

Recursive functions can also be characterized depending on the way in which the recursion grows in a linear fashion or forming a tree structure (Fig. 4.12).

In simple words, a recursive function is said to be *linearly* recursive when the pending operation (if any) does not make another recursive call to the function. For example, observe the last line of recursive factorial function. The factorial function is linearly recursive as the pending operation involves only multiplication to be performed and does not involve another recursive call to `Fact`.

On the contrary, a recursive function is said to be *tree* recursive (or *non-linearly* recursive) if the pending operation makes another recursive call to the function. For example, the `Fibonacci` function `Fib` in which the pending operations recursively calls the `Fib` function.

```
int Fibonacci(int num)
{
  if(num <= 2)
    return 1;
  return ( Fibonacci (num - 1) + Fibonacci(num - 2));
}
```

Observe the series of function calls. When the function returns, the pending operations in turn calls the function

Fibonacci(7) = Fibonacci(6) + Fibonacci(6) = Fibonacci(5) + Fibonacci(4)
Fibonacci(5) = Fibonacci(4) + Fibonacci(3)
Fibonacci(4) = Fibonacci(3) + Fibonacci(2)
Fibonacci(3) = Fibonacci(2) + Fibonacci(1)

Now we have, Fibonacci(3) = 1 + 1 = 2

Fibonacci(4) = 2 + 1 = 3
Fibonacci(5) = 3 + 2 = 5
Fibonacci(6) = 3 + 5 = 8
Fibonacci(7) = 5 + 8 = 13

Figure 4.12 Tree recursion

4.12 TOWER OF HANOI

The tower of Hanoi is one of the main applications of a recursion. It says, 'if you can solve `n-1` cases, then you can easily solve the nth case'.

Look at Fig. 4.13 which shows three rings mounted on pole A. The problem is to move all these rings from pole A to pole C while maintaining the same order. The main issue is that the smaller disk must always come above the larger disk.

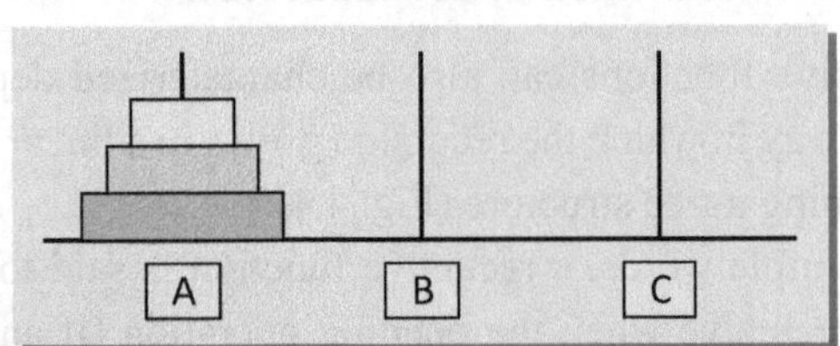

Figure 4.13 Tower of Hanoi

We will be doing this using a spare pole. In our case, A is the source pole, C is the destination pole, and B is the spare pole. To transfer all the three rings from A to C, we will first shift the upper two rings (`n-1 rings`) from the source pole to the spare pole. We move the first two rings from pole A to B as shown in Fig. 4.14.

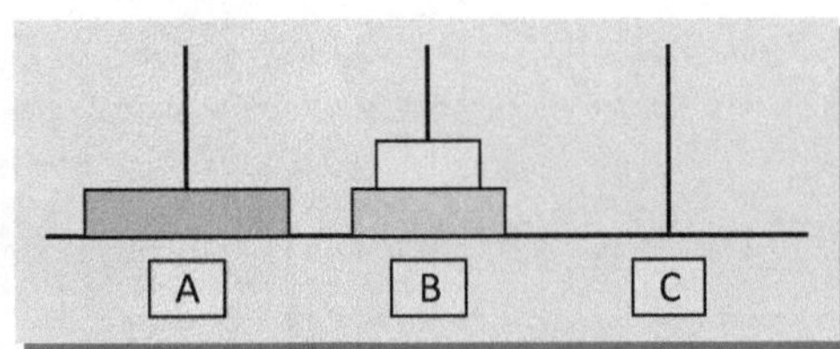

Figure 4.14 Move rings from A to B

Now that `n-1` rings have been removed from pole A, the source pole, the nth ring can be easily moved from the source pole (A) to the destination pole (C). Figure 4.15 shows this step.

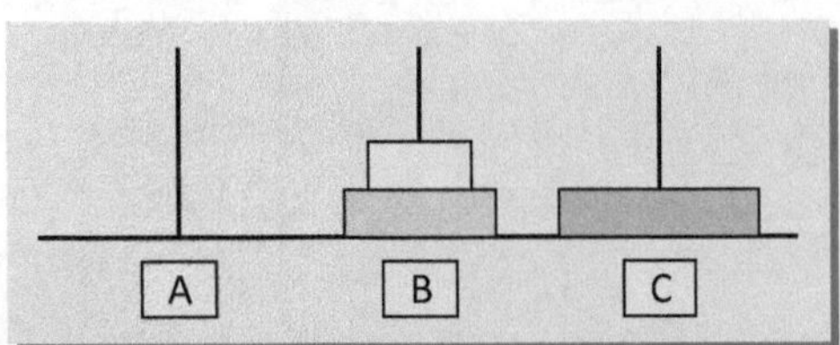

Figure 4.15 Move ring from A to C

The final step is to move the `n-1` rings from the spare pole (B) to the destination pole (C). This is shown in Fig. 4.16.

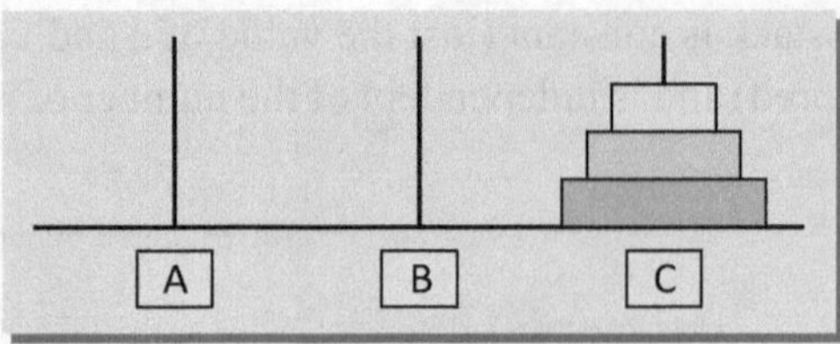

Figure 4.16 Move rings from B to C

To summarize, the solution to our problem of moving n rings from A to C using B as spare can be given as:

Base case: `if n=1`

- Move the ring from A to C using B as spare

Recursive case:

- Move `n-1` rings from A to B using C as spare
- Move the one ring left on A to C using B as spare
- Move `n-1` rings from B to C using A as spare

The following code implements the solution of the Tower of Hanoi problem.

```
#include <stdio.h>
int main()
{
    int n;
    printf("\n Enter the number of rings: ");
    scanf("%d", &n);
    move(n,'A', 'C', 'B');
    return 0;
}

void move(int n, char source, char dest, char
    spare)
{
    if (n==1)
      printf("\n Move from %c to
          %c",source,dest);
    else
    {
      move(n-1,source,spare,dest);
      move(1,source,dest,spare);
      move(n-1,spare,dest,source);
    }
}
```

Let us look at the Tower of Hanoi problem in detail using the program given above. Figure 4.17 on the next page explains the working of the program using one, then two, and finally three rings.

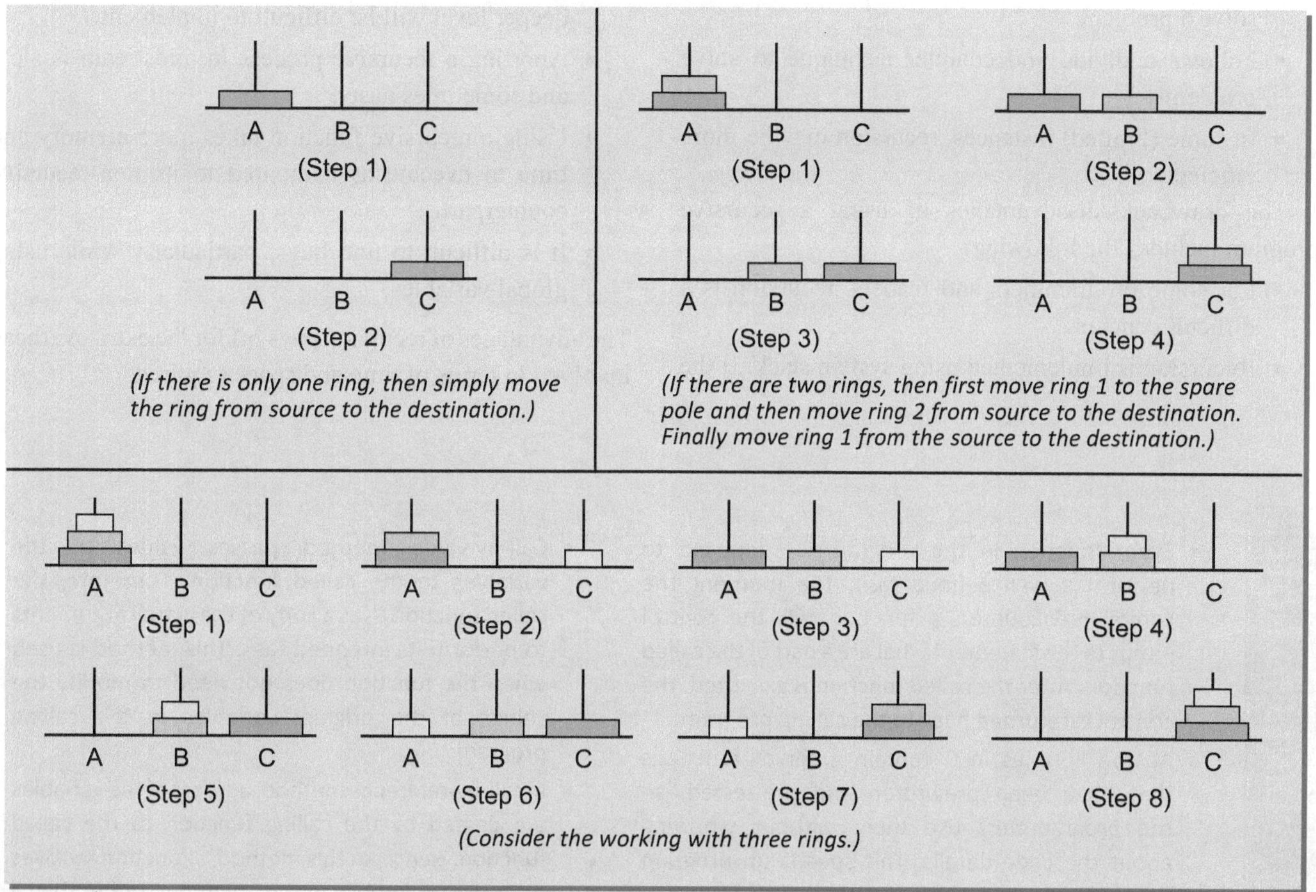

Figure 4.17 Working of Tower of Hanoi with one, two and three rings

4.13 RECURSION VERSUS ITERATION

Recursion is more of a top-down approach to problem solving in which the original problem is divided into smaller sub-problems. On the contrary, iteration follows a bottom-up approach that begins with what is known and then constructing the solution step by step.

Recursion is an excellent way of solving complex problems especially when the problem can be defined in recursive terms. For such problems, a recursive code can be written and modified in a much simpler and clearer manner.

However, recursive solutions are not always the best solutions. In some cases, recursive programs may require substantial amount of run-time overhead. Therefore, when implementing a recursive solution, there is a trade-off involved between the time spent in constructing and maintaining the program and the cost incurred in running-time and memory space required for the execution of the program.

Whenever a recursive function is called, some amount of overhead in the form of a runtime stack is always involved. Before jumping to the function with a smaller parameter, the original parameters, the local variables, and the return address of the calling function are all stored on the system stack. Therefore, while using recursion a lot of time is needed to first push all the information on the stack when the function is called and then time is again involved in retrieving the information stored on the stack once the control passes back to the calling function.

To conclude, one must use recursion only to find solution to a problem for which no obvious iterative solution is known. To summarize the concept of recursion let us briefly discuss the pros and cons of recursion.

The advantages of using a recursive program includes the following:

- Recursive solutions often tend to be shorter and simpler than non-recursive ones.
- Code is clearer and easier to use.

- Recursion works similar to the original formula to solve a problem.
- Follows a divide and conquer technique to solve problems.
- In some (limited) instances, recursion may be more efficient.

The drawbacks/disadvantages of using a recursive program includes the following:

- For some programmers and readers, recursion is a difficult concept.
- Recursion is implemented using system stack. If the stack space on the system is limited, recursion to a deeper level will be difficult to implement.
- Aborting a recursive process in midstream is slow and sometimes nasty.
- Using a recursive function takes more memory and time to execute as compared to its non-recursive counterpart.
- It is difficult to find bugs, particularly while using global variables.

The advantages of recursion pays off for the extra overhead involved in terms of time and space required.

POINTS TO NOTE

- Every function in the program is supposed to perform a well defined task. The moment the compiler encounters a function call, the control jumps to the statements that are a part of the called function. After the called function is executed, the control is returned back to the calling program.
- All the libraries in C contain a set of functions that have been prewritten and pre-tested, so the programmers use them without worrying about the code details. This speeds up program development.
- While function declaration statement identifies a function with its name, a list of arguments that it accepts and the type of data it returns, the function definition, on the other hand, consists of a function header that identifies the function, followed by the body of the function containing the executable code for that function.
- `main()` is the function that is called by the operating system and therefore, it is supposed to return the result of its processing to the operating system.
- Placing the function declaration statement prior to its use enables the compiler to make a check on the arguments used while calling that function.
- A function having void as its return type cannot return any value. Similarly, a function having void as its parameter list cannot accept any value.
- When a function is defined, space is allocated for that function in the memory. A function definition comprises of two parts: function header and function body.
- Call-by-value method passes values of the variables to the called function. Therefore, the called function uses a copy of the actual arguments to perform its intended task. This method is used when the function does not need to modify the values of the original variables in the calling program.
- In call-by-reference method, address of the variables are passed by the calling function to the called function. Hence, in this method, a function receives an implicit reference to the argument, rather than a copy of its value. This allows the function to modify the value of the variable and that change will be reflected in the calling function as well.
- Scope means the accessibility and visibility of the variables at different points in the program. A variable or a constant in C has four types of scope: block, function, file, and program scope.
- The storage class of a variable defines the scope (visibility) and life time of variables and/or functions declared within a C program.
- The auto storage class is the default storage class for variables declared inside a block. The scope of the variable is local to the block in which it is declared. When a variable is declared using register as its storage class, it is stored in a CPU register instead of RAM. Extern is used to give a reference of a global variable that is visible to all the program files. Static is the default storage class for global variables.

GLOSSARY

Argument A value passed to the called function by the calling function.

Block A sequence of definitions, declarations, and statements, enclosed within curly brackets.

Divide and conquer Solving a problem by dividing it into two or more smaller instances. Each of these smaller instances is recursively solved, and the solutions are combined to produce a solution for the original problem.

Iteration Solving a problem by repeatedly working on successive parts of the problem.

Recursion An algorithmic technique where a function calls itself with a smaller of the task in order to solve that task.

Recursion termination The point at which base condition is met and a recursive algorithm stops calling itself and begins to return values.

Recursion tree Technique to analyse the complexity of an algorithm by diagramming the recursive function calls.

Tail recursion A form of recursion in which the last operation of a function is a recursive call.

Tower of Hanoi Given three towers or poles and *n* disks of decreasing sizes, move the disks from one pole to another one by one without putting a larger disk on a smaller one.

EXERCISES

Fill in the Blanks

1. _______ provides an interface to use the function.
2. After the function is executed, the control passes back to the _______.
3. A function that uses another function is known as the _______.
4. The inputs that the function takes are known as _______.
5. `main()` is called by the _______.
6. Function definition consists of _______ and _______.
7. In _______ method, address of the variable is passed by the calling function to the called function.
8. Function scope is applicable only within _______.
9. Function that calls itself is known as a _______ function.
10. Recursive functions are implemented using _______.
11. _______ function is defined as a function that calls itself.
12. The function `int func();` takes _______ arguments.
13. _______ variables can be accessed from all functions in the program.
14. The execution of a program starts at _______.
15. By default, the return type of a function is _______.
16. Parameters used in function call are called _______.
17. Variable declared inside a function is known as _______.

Multiple Choice Questions

1. The function that is invoked is known as
   (a) calling function (b) caller function
   (c) called function (d) invoking function
2. Function declaration statement identifies a function with its
   (a) name
   (b) arguments
   (c) data type of return value
   (d) all of these
3. Which return type cannot return any value to the caller?
   (a) int (b) float
   (c) void (d) double
4. Memory is allocated for a function when the function is
   (a) declared (b) defined
   (c) called (d) returned
5. Which keyword allows a variable to have file scope?
   (a) auto (b) static
   (c) register (d) extern
6. The default storage class of global variables is
   (a) auto (b) static
   (c) register (d) extern

EXERCISES

7. Which variable retains its value in-between function calls?
   (a) auto (b) static
   (c) register (d) extern
8. The default storage class of a local variable is
   (a) auto (b) static
   (c) register (d) extern

State True or False

1. The calling function must pass parameters to the called function.
2. Function header is used to identify the function.
3. The name of a function is global.
4. No function can be declared within the body of another function.
5. The function call statement invokes the function.
6. Auto variables are stored inside CPU registers.
7. Extern variables are initialized by default.
8. The default storage class of local variables is `extern`.
9. Recursion follows a divide-and-conquer technique to solve problems.
10. Local variables overwrite the value of global variables.
11. A C function can return only one value.
12. A function must have at least one argument.
13. A function can be declared and defined before the `main()`.
14. A function can be defined in the `main()`.
15. Variable names in the function definition must match with those specified in the function declaration.
16. Specifying variable names in the function declaration is optional.
17. The `main()` is a user-defined function.

Review Questions

1. Define a function. Why are they needed?
2. Explain the concept of making function calls.
3. Differentiate between function declaration and function definition.
4. Differentiate between formal parameters and actual parameters.
5. How many types of storage classes C language supports? Why do we need different types of such classes?
6. Give the features of each storage class.
7. Explain the concept of recursive functions with example.
8. Differentiate between an iterative function and a recursive function. Which one will you prefer to use and in what circumstances?
9. What will happen when the actual parameters are less than formal parameters in a function?
10. What will happen when data type of a variable in the function declaration does not match with the corresponding variable in the function header?
11. What will happen when a function returns a value that does not match with the return type of the function?
12. Write a program to calculate factorial of a number using recursion. Also write a non-recursive procedure to do the same job.
13. Explain the Tower of Hanoi problem.
14. Write a program using function that calculates the hypotenuse of a right-angled triangle.
15. Write a function that accepts a number `n` as input and returns the average of numbers from 1 to `n`.
16. Differentiate between call-by-value and call-by-reference using suitable examples.
17. What do you understand by scope of a variable? Explain in detail with suitable examples.
18. Why function declaration statement is placed prior to function definition?
19. Write a function to reverse a string using recursion.
20. Write a function is_prime that returns a 1 if the argument passed to it is a prime number and a 0 otherwise.
21. Write a function that accepts an integer between 1–12 to represent the month number and displays the corresponding month of the year (e.g., if month = 1, then display JANUARY).
22. Write a function is_leap_year which takes the year as its argument and checks whether the year is a leap year or not and then displays an appropriate message on the screen.
23. Write a program to concatenate two strings using recursion.
24. Write a program to read an integer number. Print the reverse of this number using recursion.
25. Write a program to swap two variables that are defined as global variables.
26. Write a program to compute `F(x, y)` where

EXERCISES

```
F(x, y) = F(x-y, y) + 1 if y≤x
And F(x, y) = 0 if x<y
```

27. Write a program to compute `F(n, r)` where `F(n, r)` can be recursively defined as

```
F(n, r) = F(n-1, r) + F(n-1, r-1)
```

28. Write a program to compute Lambda(n) for all positive values of n where Lambda(n) can be recursively defined as

```
Lambda(n) = Lambda(n/2) + 1 if n>1
AND Lambda(n) = 0 if n =1
```

29. Write a program to compute `F(M, N)` where `F(M, N)` can be recursively defined as

```
F(M,N) = 1 if M=0 or M≥N≥1
AND F(M,N) = F(M-1,N) + F(M-1, N-1)
   otherwise
```

30. Write a menu-driven program to add, subtract, multiply, and divide two integers using functions.
31. Write a program to find the smallest of three integers using functions.
32. Write a program to calculate area of a triangle using function.
33. Write a program to find whether a number is divisible by 2 or not using functions.
34. Write a program to illustrate call-by-value technique of passing arguments to a function.
35. Write a program to illustrate call-by-reference technique of passing arguments to a function.
36. Write a program to swap two integers using call-by-value method of passing arguments to a function.
37. Write a program using function to calculate x to the power of y, where y can be either negative or positive.
38. Write a program using function to calculate compound interest given the principal, rate of interest and number of years.
39. Write a program to swap two integers using call-by-reference method of passing arguments to a function.
40. Write a program to calculate factorial of a number (a) using recursion (b) without using recursion.
41. Write a program to convert the given string "hello world" to "dlrow olleh" without using recursion.
42. Write a program to find HCF of two numbers (a) using recursion (b) without using recursion.
43. Write a program to calculate x^y (a) using recursion (b) without using recursion.
44. Write a program to print the Fibonacci series (a) using recursion (b) without using recursion.
45. Write a program using functions to perform calculator operations.
46. Write a function that converts temperature given in Celsius into Fahrenheit.
47. Write a function that prints the conversion table of Degrees Fahrenheit into Degrees Celsius ranging from 32-212 degrees Celsius.
48. Write a function to draw the following pattern on the screen

```
********
!      !
!      !
!      !
********
```

49. Write a function to print a table of binomial coefficients which is given by the formula-

```
B(m, x) = m!/ (x! (m-x)!) where m > x
```

Hint: `B(m,0) = 1, B(0,0) = 1 and`
`B(m,x) = B(m, x-1) * [( m - x + 1)/x]`

50. Write a program to evaluate

$f(x) = x - x^3/3! + x^5/5! - x^7/7! + \ldots$

Program Output

Find the output of the following codes:

1.
```
#include <stdio.h>
int func();
main()
{
   printf("%d", func());
   printf("%d", func());
   printf("%d", func());
   printf("%d", func());
   return 0;
}
int func()
{
   int counter=0;
   return counter;
}
```

2.
```
#include <stdio.h>
int func();
main()
{
   printf("%d", func());
   printf("%d", func());
   printf("%d", func());
   printf("%d", func());
```

```
    return 0;
  }
  int func()
  {
    static int counter=0;
    return counter;
  }
```

3.
```
#include <stdio.h>
int func();
int counter = 5;
main()
{
  printf("%d", func());
  printf("%d", func());
  printf("%d", func());
  printf("%d", func());
  return 0;
}
int func()
{
  return counter++;
}
```

4.
```
#include <stdio.h>
int add(int, int);
main()
{
  int a=2, b=3;
  printf("%d %d %d", a, b, add(a, b));
  return 0;
}
int add(int a, int b)
{
  int c;
  c = a+b
  return;
}
```

5.
```
#include <stdio.h>
int add(int, int);
main()
{
  int a=2, b=3;
  printf("%d %d %d", a, b, add(a, b));
  return 0;
}
int add(int a, int b)
{
  int c;
  c = a+b
}
```

6.
```
#include <stdio.h>
int func(int);
main()
{
  int a=2;
  printf("%d", func(a));
  return 0;
}
int func(int a)
{
  if(a>1)
  return func(--a) + 10;
  else
  return 0;
}
```

7.
```
#include <stdio.h>
void func(int);
main()
{
  int a=127;
      printf("%d", a);
      func(a);
  return 0;
}
void func(int a)
{
  a++;
      printf("%d", a);
}
```

8.
```
#include <stdio.h>
void func(int);
auto int a;
main()
{
  int a=10;
      printf("%d", a);
      func(a);
  return 0;
}
void func(int a)
{
  a++;
      printf("%d", a);
}
```

9.
```
#include <stdio.h>
static int add(int val)
(
      static int sum;
      sum += val;
```

EXERCISES

```
        return sum;
    }
    main()
    {
        int i, n=10;
            for(i=0;i<10;i++)
                add(i);
            printf("\n SUM = %d", func(0));
        return 0;
    }
```

10.
```
#include <stdio.h>
int func(int);
main()
{
    int a=2;
    printf("%d", func(a));
    return 0;
}
int func(int a)
{
    {
            ;
        }
        {
        { ;
        }
        return a;
    }
}
```

11.
```
#include <stdio.h>
void func(int);
int a=10;
main()
{
    int a=2;
        printf("%d", a);
        func(a);
    printf("%d", a);
    return 0;
}
void func(int a)
{
    a=20;
}
```

12.
```
#include <stdio.h>
void func(char);
main()
{
    char ch=256;
        func(ch);
    return 0;
}
void func(char a)
{
        printf("%d", a);
}
```

13.
```
#include <stdio.h>
int a;
static int func()
(
        return a++;
}
main()
{
    a=10;
        printf("%d", func());
        a *= 10;
        printf("%d", func());
    return 0;
}
```

14.
```
#include <stdio.h>
int prod(int x, int y)
{
    return (x*y);
}
main()
{
    int x=2, y=3, z;
    z = prod(x,prod(x,y));
    printf("%d", z);
    return 0;
}
```

ANNEXURE 3

A3.1 USER DEFINED HEADER FILES

At times the programmer may need a function that provides additional processing capabilities and may want to create a separate source code file to contain that function. This would help to segregate the function from rest of the *main* source code. In such a situation, the user may create a user defined header file so that the compiler knows how to call this function.

For example, if we want the factorial function to be stored in a user defined header file, then write the code of the factorial function in a file and save it as "`fact.h`". Then in the main program file, we will include the `fact.h` file and call the function in the same way as we call other functions. Look at the code given below which illustrates this concept.

```
int factorial(int num)
{
    long int f=1;
    for(;num >= 1;num--)
        f = f * num;
    return f;
}

// Contents for the main file
#include <stdio.h>
#include <conio.h>
#include"fact.h"
main()
{
    int num, f;
    clrscr();
    printf("\n Enter any number: ");
    scanf("%d", &num);
    f = factorial(num);
    printf("\n FACTORIAL of %d = %d", num, f);
    getch();
    return 0;
}
```

In the above code, a user defined header file—`fact.h` has been used. The name of the header file has been enclosed within quotes to tell the compiler not to look along the standard library path, but to look in the same path as the source file.

Note that you will compile the file that contains the source code, that is the file contains the `main()`. The compiler will compile it into object code. As long as the C program is syntactically correct, the object code will be created.

The linker will combine the object code, library files, and create the executable. It is the header file that links the definition of the function with the implementation.

CHAPTER 5

Arrays

Takeaways

- Array Declaration
- Array Operations
- Array Length
- 2D Arrays
- Using Arrays with Functions
- Multi-dimensional Arrays
- Sparse Matrices

5.1 INTRODUCTION

Take a situation in which we have 20 students in a class and we are asked to write a program that reads and prints the marks of all these 20 students. In this program, we will need 20 integer variables with different names, as shown in Fig. 5.1.

Marks1	Marks5	Marks9	Marks13	Marks17
Marks2	Marks6	Marks10	Marks14	Marks18
Marks3	Marks7	Marks11	Marks15	Marks19
Marks4	Marks8	Marks12	Marks16	Marks20

Figure 5.1 Twenty variables with different names

Now to read values for these 20 different variables, we must have 20 read statements. Similarly, to print the value of these variables, we need 20 write statements. If it is just a matter of 20 variables, then it might be acceptable for the user to follow this approach. But imagine, will it be possible to follow this approach if we had to read and print marks of the students

- in the entire course (say 100 students)
- in the entire college (say 500 students)
- in the entire university (say 10000 students)

The answer is no, definitely not. To process large amount of data, we need a data structure known as *array.*

Programming Tip:
In an array of size n, the index ranges from 0 to n – 1.

An array is a collection of similar data elements. These data elements have the same data type. The elements of the array are stored in consecutive memory locations and are referenced by an index (also known as the subscript). The subscript is an ordinal number which is used to identify an element of the array. Some examples where the concept of an array can be used include:

- List of temperatures recorded on every day of the month
- List of employees in a company
- List of students in a class
- List of products sold
- List of customers

5.2 DECLARATION OF ARRAYS

We have already seen that every variable must be declared before it is used. The same concept is true in case of array variables also. An array must be declared before being used. Declaring an array means specifying three things:

- Data type—what kind of values it can store, for example `int, char, float, double.`
- Name—to identify the array.
- Size—the maximum number of values that the array can hold.

Arrays are declared using the following syntax:

```
type name[size];
```

Here the type can be either `int, float, double, char` or any other valid data type. The number within brackets indicates the size of the array, i.e., the maximum number of elements that can be stored in the array. The size of the array is a constant and must have a value at compilation time. For example, if we write,

Programming Tip:
To declare and define an array, you must specify its name, type, and size.

```
int marks[10];
```

The above statement declares a `marks` variable to be an array containing 10 elements. In C, the array `index` (also known as subscripts) starts from `zero`. This means that the array `marks` will contain 10 elements in all. The first element will be stored in `marks[0]`, the second element in `marks[1]`, and so on. Therefore, the last element, i.e., the 10th element will be stored in `marks[9]`. Note that 0, 1, 2, 3 written within square brackets are subscripts/index. In memory, the array will be stored as shown in Fig. 5.2.

Points to Remember

- Note that C does not allow declaring an array whose number of elements is not known at the compile time.

Therefore, the following array declarations are illegal in C.

```
int arr[];
int n, arr[n];
```

- Generally it is a good programming practice to define the size of an array as a symbolic constant as shown in the following code.

```
#include <stdio.h>
#define N 100
main()
{
   int arr[N];
   ..........
}
```

- The size of the array can be specified using an expression. However, the components of the expression must be available for evaluation of the expression when the program is compiled. Therefore, the following array declarations are valid in C language.

```
#include <stdio.h>
#define N 100
main()
{
   int i=10;
   int arr[N+10], my_arr[i-5*10];
   .........
}
```

C array indices start from 0. So for an array with N elements, the index of the last element is N – 1.

- C never checks the validity of the array index—neither at compile time nor at run time. So even if you declare an array as

```
int arr[N];
```

The C compiler will not raise any error but the result of running such code is totally unpredictable. Even if you declare an array of 10 elements and later on by mistake try to access the 11th element, no error will be generated. But the results will be unpredictable as the memory occupied by the (so-called) 11th element may be storing data of another object.

1st element	2nd element	3rd element	4th element	5th element	6th element	7th element	8th element	9th element	10th element
marks[0]	marks[1]	marks[2]	marks[3]	marks[4]	marks[5]	marks[6]	marks[7]	marks[8]	marks[9]

Figure 5.2 Memory representation of an array of 10 elements

5.3 ACCESSING ARRAY ELEMENTS

For accessing an individual element of the array, the array subscript must be used. For example, to access the fourth element of the array, you must write `arr[3]`. The subscript/index must be an integral value or an expression that evaluates to an integral value.

Although storing the related data items in a single array enables the programmers to develop concise and efficient programs there is no single operation that can operate on all the elements of the array. To access all the elements of the array, you must use a loop. That is, we can access all the elements of the array by varying the value of the subscript into the array. But note that the subscript must be an integral value or an expression that evaluates to an integral value. As shown in Fig. 5.2, the first element of the array `marks[10]` can be accessed by writing, `marks[0]`. Now to process all the elements of the array, we will use a loop as shown in Fig. 5.3.

> **Programming Tip:**
> To access all the elements of the array, you must use a loop. There is no single statement that can do the work.

```
// Set each element of the array to -1

int i, marks[10];
for(i=0;i<10;i++)
        marks[i] = -1;
```

Figure 5.3 Code to initialize each element of the array to –1

The code accesses every individual element of the array and sets its value to –1. In the `for` loop, first the value of `marks[0]` is set to –1, then the value of the index `(i)` is incremented and the next value, i.e., `marks[1]` is set to –1. The procedure is continued until all the `10` elements of the array are set to –1.

The name of the array is a symbolic reference for the address to the first byte of the array. Therefore, whenever we use the array name, we are actually referring to the first byte of that array. The index specifies an offset from the beginning of the array to the element being referenced.

> There is no single statement that can read, access, or print all the elements of the array. To do this, we have to do it using a `for/while/do-while` loop to execute the same statement with different index values.

5.3.1 Calculating the Address of Array Elements

You must be wondering, how C knows where an individual element of the array is located in the memory? The answer is that the array name is a symbolic reference for the address to the first byte of the array. When we use the array name, we are actually referring to the first byte of the array.

The subscript or the index represents the offset from the beginning of the array to the element being referenced. With just the array name and the index, C can calculate the address of any element in the array.

An array stores all its data elements in consecutive memory locations. So, storing just the base address, i.e., the address of the first element in the array is sufficient. The address of other data elements can simply be calculated using the base address. The formula for doing this calculation is,

```
Address of data element, A[k] = BA(A) + w(k
- lower_bound)
```

Here, `A` is the array, `k` is the index of the element for which we have to calculate the address, `BA` is the base address of the array `A`, `w` is the word size of one element in memory (e.g., size of `int` is 2), and `lower_bound` is the index of the first element in the array.

Example 5.1

Given an array `int marks[]` = {99, 67, 78, 56, 88, 90, 34, 85}. Calculate the address of `marks[4]` if base address = 1000.

Solution

	99	67	78	56	88	90	34	85
Marks	[0]	[1]	[2]	[3]	**[4]**	[5]	[6]	[7]
	1000	1002	1004	1006	**1008**	1010	1012	1014

We know that storing an integer value requires 2 bytes, therefore here, word size is 2 bytes.

```
Marks[4]= 1000 + 2(4 - 0)
        = 1000 + 2(4) = 1008
```

Example 5.2 Given an array,

`float avg[] = {99.0, 67.0, 78.0, 56.0, 88.0, 90.0, 34.0, 85.0}`. Calculate the address of `avg[4]` if base address = 1000.

We know that storing a floating point number requires 4 bytes, therefore, word size is 4 bytes.

99.0	67.0	78.0	56.0	88.0	90.0	34.0	85.0
avg [0]	[1]	[2]	[3]	[4]	[5]	[6]	[7]
1000	1004	1008	1012	1016	1020	1024	1028

```
Avg[4] = 1000 + 4(4 - 0)
       = 1000 + 4(4) = 1016
```

Note: When we write arr[i], the compiler interprets it as the contents of memory slot which is i slots away from the beginning of the array arr.

5.4 STORING VALUES IN ARRAYS

When we declare and define an array, we are just allocating space for the elements; no values are stored in the array. To store values in the array, there are three ways. First, to initialize the array elements during declaration; second, to input values for individual elements from the keyboard; third, to assign values to individual elements. This is shown in Fig. 5.4.

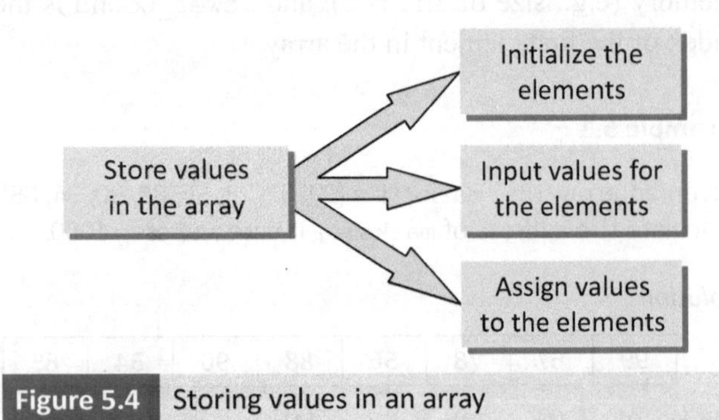

Figure 5.4 Storing values in an array

5.4.1 Initialization of Arrays

Elements of the array can also be initialized at the time of declaration as in the case of every other variable. When an array is initialized, we need to provide a value for every element in the array. Arrays are initialized by writing,

Programming Tip: By default, the elements of the array are not initialized. They may contain some garbage value, so before using the array you must initialize the array or read some meaningful data into it.

```
type array_name[size]={list of values};
```

The values are written with curly brackets and every value is separated by a comma. It is a compiler error to specify more number of values than the number of elements in the array. When we write,

```
int marks[5]={90, 82, 78, 95, 88};
```

an array with name `marks` is declared that has space that is enough to store 5 elements. The first element, i.e., `marks[0]` is assigned with the value `90`. Similarly, the second element of the array, i.e., `marks[1]` has been assigned `82`, and so on.

While initializing the array at the time of declaration, the programmer may omit to mention the size of the array. For example,

```
int marks[]= {98, 97, 90};
```

The above statement is absolutely legal. Here, the compiler will allocate enough space for all initialized elements. If the number of values provided is less than the number of elements in the array, the un-assigned elements are filled with zeros. Figure 5.5 illustrates initialization of arrays.

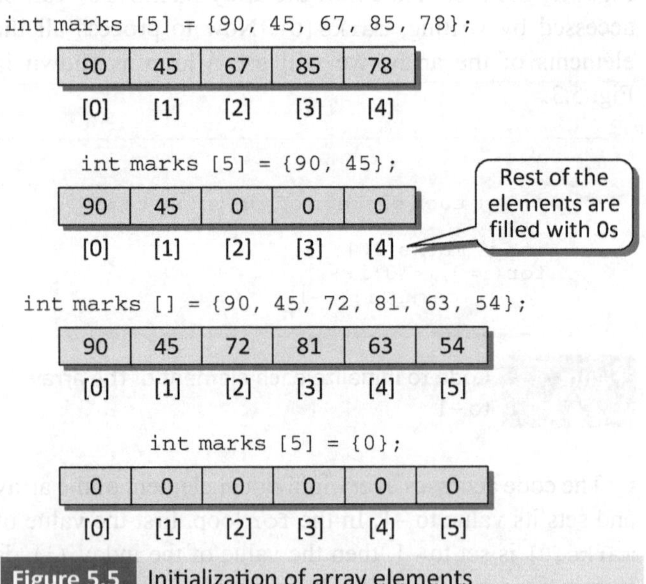

Figure 5.5 Initialization of array elements

Note: If we have more initializers than the declared size of the array, then a compile time error will be generated. For example, the following statement will result in a compiler error.
int marks[3] = {1,2,3,4};

5.4.2 Inputting Values

An array can be filled by inputting values from the keyboard. In this method, a `while/do-while` or a `for` loop is executed to input the value for each element of the array. For example, look at the code shown in Fig. 5.6.

```
// Input value of each element of the array

int i, marks[10];
for(i=0;i<10;i++)
    scanf("%d", &marks[i]);
```

Figure 5.6 Code for inputting each element of the array

In the code, we start with the index `i` at `0` and input the value for the first element of the array. Since the array can have `10` elements, we must input values for elements whose index varies from `0` to `9`. Therefore, in the `for` loop, we test for condition `(i<10)` which means the number of elements in the array.

5.4.3 Assigning Values

The third way to assign values to individual elements of the array is by using the assignment operator. Any value that evaluates to an appropriate data type as that of the array can be assigned to the individual array element. A simple assignment statement can be written as,

```
marks[3] = 100;
```

Here, `100` is assigned to the fourth element of the array which is specified as `marks[3]`.

We cannot assign one array to another array, even if the two arrays have the same type and size. To copy an array, you must copy the value of every element of the first array into the element of the second array. Figure 5.7 illustrates the code to copy an array.

```
// Copy an array at the individual element level

int i, arr1[10], arr2[10];
arr1[10] = {0,1,2,3,4,5,6,7,8,9}
for(i=0;i<10;i++)
    arr2[i] = arr1[i];
```

Figure 5.7 Code to copy an array at the individual element level

In Fig. 5.7, the code accesses each element of the first array and simultaneously assigns its value to the corresponding element of the second array. Finally, the index value `i` is incremented to access the next element in succession. Therefore, when this code is executed, `arr2[0] = arr1[0], arr2[1] = arr1[1], arr2[2] = arr1[2]`, and so on.

We can also use a loop to assign a pattern of values to the array elements. For example, if we want to fill an array with even integers starting (from `0`), then we will write the code as shown in Fig. 5.8.

```
// Fill an array with even numbers

int i, arr[10];
for(i=0;i<10;i++)
    arr[i] = i*2;
```

Figure 5.8 Code for filling an array with even numbers

In the code, we assign to each element value equal to twice of its index, where index starts from zero. So after executing this code we will have, `arr[0] = 0, arr[1] = 2, arr[2] = 4`, and so on.

5.5 LENGTH OF AN ARRAY

Length of the array is given by the number of elements stored in it. The general formula to calculate the length of the array is,

```
Length = upper_bound - lower_bound + 1
```

where `upper_bound` is the index of the last element and `lower_bound` is the index of the first element in the array.

Usually, `lower_bound` is zero but this is not a compulsion as we can have an array whose index may start from any non-zero value.

Example 5.3 Let Age be an array of integers such that

```
Age[0] = 2     Age[1] = 5     Age[2] = 3
Age[3] = 1     Age[4] = 7
```

Solution

Show the memory representation of the array and calculate its length.

Memory representation of the array `Age` is as given

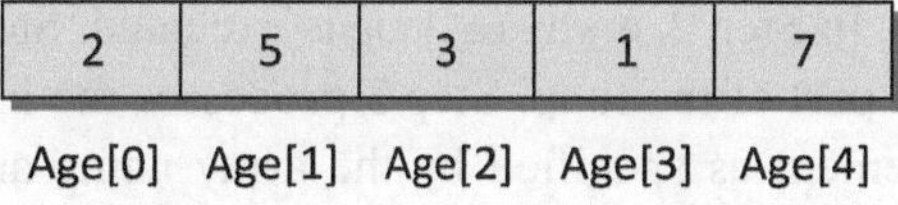


```
Length = upper_bound - lower_bound + 1
```

Here, lower_bound = 0, upper_bound = 4
Therefore, length = 4 – 0 + 1 = 5

5.6 ARRAY OPERATIONS

There are a number of operations that can be performed on arrays. These operations include:

- Traversal
- Insertion
- Search
- Deletion
- Merging
- Sorting

We will study all these operations in detail in this section.

5.6.1 Traversal

Traversing the array element means accessing each and every element of the array for a specific purpose. We have already seen this while reading about accessing array elements. This is just a re-visit of the topic.

If A is an array of homogeneous data elements, then traversing the data elements can include printing every element, counting the total number of elements, or performing any processing on these elements. Since an array is a linear data structure (because all its elements form a sequence), traversing its elements is very simple and straightforward. The algorithm for array traversal is given in Fig. 5.9.

```
Step 1: [Initialization] Set I = lower_bound
Step 2: Repeat steps 3 to 4 while I <= upper_bound
Step 3: Apply Process to A[I]
Step 4: Set  I = I + 1
     [End of Loop]
Step 5: Exit
```

Figure 5.9 Algorithm for array traversal

In Step 1, we initialize index to the lower bound of the array. In Step 2, a while loop is executed. Steps 3 and 4 form a part of the loop. Step 3 processes the individual array element as specified by the array name and index value. Step 4 increments the index value so that the next array element could be processed. The while loop in Step 2 is executed until all the elements in the array are processed. In other words, the while loop will be executed until i is less than or equal to the upper bound of the array.

Example 5.4 Assume that there is an array Marks[ ], such that the index of the array specifies the roll number of the student and the value of a particular element denotes the marks obtained by the student. For example, if it is given Marks[4] = 78, then the student whose roll number is 4 has obtained 78 marks in the examination. Now, write an algorithm to:

(a) Find the total number of students who have secured 80 or more marks.
(b) Print the roll number and marks of all the students who have got distinction.

Solution

(a) *Step 1:* [Initialization] Set I = I + 1
Step 2: Repeat for I = lower_bound to upper_bound
If Marks[I] >= 80, then: Set Count = Count + 1
End of Loop]
Step 3: Exit

(b) *Step 1:* [Initialization] Set I = I + 1
Step 2: Repeat for I = lower_bound to upper_bound
If Marks[I] >= 75, Write: I, Marks[I]
[End of Loop]
Step 3: Exit

5.1 Write a program to read and display n numbers using an array.

```
#include <stdio.h>
#include <conio.h>
int main()
{
  int i=0, n, arr[20];
  clrscr();
  printf("\n Enter the number of elements:");
  scanf("%d", &n);
  for(i=0;i<n;i++)
```

```
    {
        printf("\n Arr[%d] = ", i);
        scanf("%d", &arr[i]);
    }
    printf("\n The array elements are ");
    for(i=0;i<n;i++)

        printf("Arr[%d] = %d\t", i, arr[i]);
    return 0;
}
```

Output

```
Enter the number of elements: 5
Arr[0] = 1
Arr[1] = 2
Arr[3] = 3
Arr[4] = 4
Arr[5] = 5
The array elements are
Arr[0] = 1    Arr[1] = 2    Arr[3] = 3
Arr[4] = 4    Arr[5] = 5
```

5.2 Write a program to read and display n random numbers using an array.

```
#include <stdio.h>
#include <conio.h>
#include <stdlib.h>
#define MAX 10
main()
{
    int arr[MAX], i,RandNo;
    for(i=0;i< MAX;i++)
    {
        /* Scale the random number in the range
               0 to MAX-1 */
        RandNo = rand() % MAX;
        // rand() is a pre-defined function
        arr[i] = RandNo;
    }
    printf("\n The contents of the array are:
            \n");
    for(i=0;i<MAX;i++)
        printf("\t %d", arr[i]);
    getch();
    return 0;
}
```

Output

```
The contents of the array are:
6   0   8   4   7   1   0   2   7   3
```

5.3 Write a program to print the position of the smallest of n numbers using arrays.

```
#include <stdio.h>
#include <conio.h>
int main()
{
    int i, n, arr[20], small =1234, pos = -1;
    clrscr();

    printf("\n Enter the number of elements in
                the array: ");
    scanf("%d", &n);
    for(i=0;i<n;i++)
        scanf("%d",&arr[i]);
    for(i=0;i<n;i++)
    {
        if(arr[i]<small)
        {
        small = arr[i];
        pos = i;
        }
    }
    printf("\n The smallest of element is :
                %d", small);
    printf("\n The position of the smallest
                number in the array is: %d", pos);
    return 0;
}
```

Output

```
Enter the number of elements: 5
1 2 3 4 5
The smallest number is: 1
The position of the smallest number in the
array is: 0
```

5.4 Write a program to interchange the largest and the smallest number in the array.

```
#include <stdio.h>
#include <conio.h>
int main()
{
    int i, n, arr[20], temp;
    int small = 9999, small_pos =0;
    int large = -9999, large_pos = 0;
    clrscr();
    printf("\n Enter the number of elements in
                the array: ");
    scanf("%d", &n);

    for(i=0;i<n;i++)
    {
```

```
    printf("\n Enter the value of element
        %d: ",i);
    scanf("%d",&arr[i]);
  }
  for(i=0;i<n;i++)
  {
    if(arr[i]<small)
    {
      small = arr[i];
      small_pos = i;
    }
    if(arr[i]>large)
    {
      large = arr[i];
      large_pos = i;
    }
  }
  printf("\n The smallest of these numbers
        is : %d", small);
  printf("\n The position of the smallest
        number in the array is: %d",small_
        pos);
  printf("\n The largest of these numbers
        is: %d", large);
  printf("\n The position of the largest
        number in the array is: %d",large_
        pos);
  temp = arr[large_pos];
  arr[large_pos] =arr[small_pos];
  arr[small_pos] = temp;
  printf("\n The new array is: ");
  for(i=0;i<n;i++)
    printf(" \n arr[%d] = %d ", i, arr[i]);
  return 0;
}
```

Output

```
Enter the number of elements: 5
1 2 3 4 5
Enter the value of elements 1:1
Enter the value of elements 2:2
Enter the value of elements 3:3
Enter the value of elements 4:4
Enter the value of elements 5:5
The smallest of these numbers is : 1
The position of the smallest number in the
array is: 0
The largest of these numbers is: 5
The position of the largest number in the
array is: 4
The new array is:
5  4  3  2   1
```

5.5 Write a program to find the second biggest number using an array of n numbers.

```
#include <stdio.h>
#include <conio.h>
int main()
{
  int i, n, arr[20], large =-1111, second_
  large = -1234;
  clrscr();

  printf("\n Enter the number of elements
    in the array: ");
  scanf("%d", &n);

  for(i=0;i<n;i++)
  {
    printf("\n Enter the number: ");
    scanf("%d",&arr[i]);
  }
  for(i=0;i<n;i++)
  {
    if(arr[i]>large)
    large = arr[i];
  }
  for(i=0;i<n;i++)
  {
    if(arr[i] != large)
    {
    if(arr[i]>second_large)
    second_large = arr[i];
    }
  }
  printf("\n The numbers you entered are: ");
  for(i=0;i<n;i++)
    printf("%d ", arr[i]);
  printf("\n The largest of these numbers
  is: %d",large);
  printf("\n The second largest of these
  numbers is: %d",second_large);
  return 0;
}
```

Output

```
Enter the number of elements in the array: 5
Enter the number: 1
Enter the number: 2
Enter the number: 3
Enter the number: 4
Enter the number: 5
The numbers you entered are in the array:
1  2  3  4   5
The largest of these numbers is: 5
The second largest of these numbers is: 4
```

5.6 Write a program to enter n number of digits. Form a number using these digits.

```
#include <stdio.h>
#include <conio.h>
#include <math.h>
int main()
{
    int number=0, digit[10], numofdigits,i;
    clrscr();

    printf("\n Enter the number of digits: ");
    scanf("%d", &numofdigits);
    for(i=0;i<numofdigits;i++)
    {
        printf("\n Enter the %d th digit: ", i);
        scanf("%d", &digit[i]);
    }
    i=0;
    while(i<numofdigits)
    {
        number = number + digit[i] * pow(10,i);
        i++;
    }
    printf("\n The number is: %d", number);
    return 0;
}
```

Output

```
Enter the number of digits: 3
Enter the 0th digit: 3
Enter the 1th digit: 4
Enter the 2th digit: 5
The number is: 543
```

5.7 Write a program to find whether the array of integers contain a duplicate number.

```
#include <stdio.h>
#include <conio.h>
int main()
{
    int array1[10], i, n, j, flag=0;
    clrscr();

    printf("\n Enter the size of the array:");
    scanf("%d", &n);
    for(i=0;i<n;i++)
    {
        scanf("%d", &array1[i]);
    }
    for(i=0;i<n;i++)
    {
        for(j= i+1;j<n;j++)
        {
        if(array1[i] == array1[j] && i!=j)
        {
            flag=1;
            printf("\n Duplicate number %d found
                at location %d and %d", array1[i],
                i, j);
        }

        }
    }
    if(flag==0)
        printf("\n No Duplicate");
    return 0;
}
```

Output

```
Enter the size of the array: 5
1 2 3 4 5
No Duplicate
```

5.8 Write a program to read marks of 10 students in the range of 0–100. Then make 10 groups: 0–10, 10–20, 20–30, etc. Count the number of values that fall in each group and display the result.

```
#include <stdio.h>
#include <conio.h>
main()
{
    int marks[50], i;
    int group[10]={0};
    printf("\n Enter the marks of 10 students
    : \n");
    for(i=0;i<10;i++)
    {
        printf("\n MARKS[%d] = ", i);
        scanf("%d", &marks[i]);
        ++group[(int)(marks[i])/10];
    }
    printf("\n\n *************************");
    printf("\n GROUP \t\t FREQUENCY");
    for(i=0;i<10;i++)
        printf("\n    %d \t\t %d", i, group[i]);
    getch();
    return 0;
}
```

Output

```
Enter the marks of 10 students:
MARKS[0] = 95
MARKS[1] = 88
MARKS[2] = 67
```

```
MARKS[3] = 78
MARKS[4] = 81
MARKS[5] = 98
MARKS[6] = 55
MARKS[7] = 45
MARKS[8] = 72
MARKS[9] = 90
*************************
GROUP      FREQUENCY
0          0
1          0
2          0
3          0
4          1
5          1
6          1
7          2
8          2
9          3
```

5.9 Write a program to enter the number of days a programmer takes to code a module. Then categorize it in different groups to analyse the data.

```
#include<stdio.h>
#include<conio.h>
main()
{
   int i,n, start, end,arr[20];
   int group[11] = {0};
   clrscr();
   printf("\n Enter the number of
   programmers : ");
   scanf("%d", &n);
   for(i=0;i<n;i++)
   {  printf("\n In how many days did
      programmer %d code the project? : ",
      i+1);
      scanf("%d", &arr[i]);
      ++group[(int)(arr[i]/10)];
   }
   printf("\n ************* THE FREQUENCY
   TABLE ****************\n");
   for(i=0;i<10;i++)
   {
      start = i*10;
      if(i!=10)
         end = start+9;
      else
         end = 100;
      printf(" %d \t \t %d \t to \t %d \t
      %d\n", i+1, start, end, group[i]);
   }
}
```

Output

```
***** THE FREQUENCY TABLE ******
   1    0 to 9   2
   2   10 to 19  3
   3   20 to 29  1
   4   30 to 39  2
   5   40 to 49  3
   6   50 to 59  2
   7   60 to 69  4
   8   70 to 79  2
   9   80 to 89  3
  10   90 to 99  2
```

5.10 Modify the above program to display frequency histograms of each group.

```
#include <stdio.h>
main()
{
   int marks[10], i;
   int group[10]={0};
   printf("\n Enter the marks of 10 students
   : \n");
   for(i=0;i<10;i++)
   {
      printf("\n MARKS[%d] = ", i);
      scanf("%d", &marks[i]);
      ++group[(int)(marks[i])/10];
   }
   printf("\n\n *************************");
   printf("\n GROUP \t\t FRQUENCY");
   for(i=0;i<10;i++)
      printf("\n %d \t\t %d", i, group[i]);
        i=0;
   printf("\n\n FREQUENCY HISTOGRAM");
   for(index=0;index<10;index++)
   {
      printf("\n GROUP %d | ",index);
      for(i=0;i<group[index];i++)
      printf(" *");
   }
   getch();
   return 0;
}
```

Output

```
Enter the marks of 10 students:
MARKS[0] = 95
MARKS[1] = 88
MARKS[2] = 67
MARKS[3] = 78
MARKS[4] = 81
MARKS[5] = 98
```

```
MARKS[6] = 55
MARKS[7] = 45
MARKS[8] = 72
MARKS[9] = 90
************************
GROUP    FREQUENCY
0        0
1        0
2        0
3        0
4        1
5        1
6        1
7        2
8        2
9        3
FREQUENCY HISTOGRAM
GROUP 0 |
GROUP 1 |
GROUP 2 |
GROUP 3 |
GROUP 4 |
GROUP 5 | *
GROUP 6 | *
GROUP 7 | * *
GROUP 8 | * *
GROUP 9 | * * *
```

5.11 Write a program to read a sorted list of floating point values and then calculate and display the median of the values.

```
#include <stdio.h>
#include <conio.h>
main()
{
  int i, j, n;
  float median, values[10];
  printf("\n Enter the size of the array: ");
  scanf("%d", &n);
  printf("\n Enter the values: ");
  for(i=0;i<n;i++)
     scanf("%f", &values[i]);
  if(n%2==0)
     median = (values[n/2]+values[n/2+1])/2.0;
  else
     median = values[n/2 + 1];
  printf("\n MEDIAN = %f", median);
  getch();
  return 0;
}
```

Output

```
Enter the size of the array: 5
Enter the values:
12 34 56 78 89
MEDIAN = 56.00
```

5.12 Write a program to feed a list of numbers and calculate its mean, standard deviation, and variance.

```
#include<stdio.h>
#include<conio.h>
#include<math.h>
main()
{
  int i, n;
  float arr[20], std_dev, sum=0, sum_sqr=0,
  mean, variance, deviation;
  clrscr();
  printf("\n Enter the number of values :
  ");
  scanf("%d", &n);
  for(i=0;i<n;i++)
  {
     scanf("%f", &arr[i]);
     sum += arr[i];
  }
  mean = sum/(float)n;
  for(i=0;i<n;i++)
  {
     deviation = arr[i] - mean;
     sum_sqr += deviation * deviation;
  }
  varience = sum_sqr/(float)n;
  std_dev = sqrt(variance);
  printf("\n Mean : %.2f", mean);
  printf("\n Standard Deviation : %.2f",
  std_dev);
  printf("\n Variance : %.2f", variance);
}
```

Output

```
Enter the number of values : 10
12 23 34 45 56 67 78 89 90 35
Mean = 52.90
Standard Deviation = 26.12
Variance = 682.49
```

5.6.2 Insertion

Inserting an element in the array means adding a new data element in an already existing array. If the element has to be inserted at the end of the existing array, then the task of inserting is quite simple. We just have to add 1 to the `upper_bound` and assign the value. Here we assume that the memory space allocated for the array is still available. For example, if an array is declared to contain 10 elements, but currently it is having only 8 elements, then obviously there is space to accommodate two more elements. But if it already has 10 elements, then we will not be able to add another element to it.

Figure 5.10 shows an algorithm to insert a new element to the end of the array.

```
Step 1: Set upper_bound = upper_bound + 1
Step 2: Set A[upper_bound] = VAL
Step 3: EXIT
```

Figure 5.10 Algorithm to append a new element to an existing array

In Step 1 of the array, we increment the value of the upper_bound. In Step 2, the new value is stored at the position pointed by upper_bound.

For example, if we have an array that is declared as

```
int marks[60];
```

The array is declared to store marks of all the students in the class. Now suppose there are 54 students and a new student comes and is asked to given the same test. The marks of this new student would be stored in marks[55]. Assuming that the student secured 68 marks, we will assign the value as,

```
marks[55] = 68;
```

However, if we have to insert an element in the middle of the array, then this is not a trivial task. On an average, we might have to move as much as half of the elements from its position in order to accommodate space for the new element.

For example, consider an array whose elements are arranged in ascending order. Now, if a new element has to be added, it will have to be added probably somewhere in the middle of the array. To do this, what we will have to do is, first find the location where the new element will be inserted and then move all the elements (that have a value greater than that of the new element) one space to the right so that space can be created to store the new value.

Example 5.5 Data[] is an array that is declared as int Data[20]; and contains the following values:

```
Data[] = {12, 23, 34, 45, 56, 67, 78, 89, 90, 100};
```

(a) Calculate the length of the array.
(b) Write the upper bound and lower bound.
(c) Give the memory representation of the array.
(d) If a new data element with value 75 has to be inserted, find its position.
(e) Insert the new data element and then give the memory representation of the array.
(f) length of the array = number of elements
Therefore, length of the array = 10
(g) By default, lower_bound = 0, (it can be set to any value) and upper_bound = 9

12	23	34	45	56	67	78	89	90	100
[0]	[1]	[2]	[3]	[4]	[5]	[6]	[7]	[8]	[9]

(h) Since the elements of the array are stored in ascending order, the new data element will be stored after 67, i.e., at the 6th location. So, all the array elements from the 6th position will be moved one space towards the right to accommodate the new value.

12	23	34	45	56	67	75	78	89	90	100
[0]	[1]	[2]	[3]	[4]	[5]	[6]	[7]	[8]	[9]	[10]

Algorithm to insert an element in the middle of the array

The algorithm INSERT will be declared as INSERT (A, N, POS, VAL). The arguments are

(a) A, the array in which the element has to be inserted
(b) N, the number of elements in the array
(c) POS, the position at which the element has to be inserted and
(d) VAL, the value that has to be inserted.

In the algorithm given in Fig. 5.11, in Step 1, we first initialize I with the total number of elements in the array.

```
Step 1: [INITIALIZATION] SET I = N
Step 2: Repeat Steps 3 and 4 while I >= POS
Step 3:             SET A[I + 1] = A[I]
Step 4:             SET I = I - 1
        [End of Loop]
Step 5: SET N = N + 1
Step 6: SET A[POS] = VAL
Step 7: EXIT
```

Figure 5.11 Algorithm to insert a new element at a specified position

In Step 2, a while loop is executed which will move all the elements that have index greater than POS one space towards right to create space for the new element. In Step 5, we increment the total number of elements in the array by `1` and finally in Step 6, the new value is inserted at the desired position.

Now, let us visualize this algorithm by taking an example. Initial `Data[]` is given as shown in Fig. 5.12. Calling `INSERT (Data, 6, 3, 100)` will lead to the following processing in the array:

45	23	34	12	56	20	20
Data[0]	Data[1]	Data[2]	Data[3]	Data[4]	Data[5]	Data[6]

45	23	34	12	56	56	20
Data[0]	Data[1]	Data[2]	Data[3]	Data[4]	Data[5]	Data[6]

45	23	34	12	12	56	20
Data[0]	Data[1]	Data[2]	Data[3]	Data[4]	Data[5]	Data[6]

45	23	34	10	12	56	20
Data[0]	Data[1]	Data[2]	Data[3]	Data[4]	Data[5]	Data[6]

Figure 5.12 Inserting a new value in an existing array

5.13 Write a program to insert a number at a given location in an array.

```
#include <stdio.h>
#include <conio.h>
int main()
{
   int i, n, num, pos, arr[10];
   clrscr();
   
   printf("\n Enter the number of elements
   in the array: ");
   scanf("%d", &n);
   
   for(i=0;i<n;i++)
   {
      printf("\n Arr[%d] = : ", i);
      scanf("%d", &arr[i]);
   }
   printf("\n Enter the number to be
   inserted: ");
   scanf("%d", &num);
   printf("\n Enter the position at which
   the number has to be added: ");
   scanf("%d", &pos);
   
   for(i=n;i>=pos;i--)
      arr[i+1] = arr[i];
   arr[pos] = num;
   n++;
   printf("\n The array after insertion of
   %d is: ", num);
   
   for(i=0;i<n+1;i++)
      printf("\n Arr[%d] = %d", i, arr[i]);
   getch();
   return 0;
}
```

Output

```
Enter the number of elements in the array: 5
Enter the values:
1 2 3 4 5
Enter the number to be inserted: 7
Enter the position at which the number has
to be added: 3
The array after insertion of 7 is:
1 2 3 7 4 5
```

5.14 Write a program to insert a number in an array that is already sorted in ascending order.

```
#include <stdio.h>
#include <conio.h>
int main()
{
   int i, n, j, num, arr[10];
   clrscr();
   printf("\n Enter the number of elements
   in the array: ");
   scanf("%d", &n);
    printf("\n Enter the array elements:");
    for(i=0;i<n;i++)
       scanf("%d", &arr[i]);
   printf("\nEnter the number to be inserted: ");
   scanf("%d", &num);
   for(i=0;i<n;i++)
   {
      if(arr[i] > num)
      {
         for(j = n-1; j>=i; j--)
            arr[j+1] = arr[j];
         arr[i] = num;
         break;
      }
```

```
    }
    n++;
    printf("\n The array after insertion of
    %d is: ", num);
    for(i=0;i<n+1;i++)
        printf("\t %d", arr[i]);
    getch();
    return 0;
}
```

Output

```
Enter the number of elements in the array: 5
1 2 3 4 5
Enter the number to be inserted: 6
The array after insertion of 6 is:
1 2 3 4 5 6
```

5.6.3 Deletion

Deleting an element from the array means removing a data element from an already existing array. If the element has to be deleted from the end of the existing array, then the task of deletion is quite simple. We just have to subtract 1 from the upper_bound. Figure 5.13 shows an algorithm to delete an element from the end of the array.

```
Step 1: Set upper_bound = upper_bound - 1
Step 2: EXIT
```

Figure 5.13 Algorithm to delete the last element of an array

For example, if we have an array that is declared as

```
int marks[];
```

The array is declared to store marks of all the students in the class. Now suppose there are 54 students and the student with roll number 54 leaves the course. The marks of this student were therefore stored in `marks[54]`. We just have to decrement the `upper_bound`. Subtracting `1` from the upper bound will indicate that there are `53` valid data in the array.

However, if we have to delete the element from the middle of the array, then this task is not trivial. On an average, we might have to move as much as half of the elements from its position in order to occupy the space of the deleted element.

For example, consider an array whose elements are arranged in ascending order. Now, if an element has to be deleted probably from somewhere middle in the array. To do this, what we will have to do is, first find the location from where the element has to be deleted and then move all the elements (that have a value greater than that of the element) one space towards the left so that space vacated by the deleted element be occupied by rest of the elements.

Example 5.6 `Data[]` is an array that is declared as `int Data[10];` and contains the following values:

```
Data[] = {12, 23, 34, 45, 56, 67, 78, 89, 90, 100};
```

(a) Calculate the length of the array.
(b) Write the upper bound and lower bound.
(c) Give the memory representation of the array.
(d) If a data element with value 56 has to be deleted, find its position.

Solution

(a) `length of the array = number of elements`
Therefore, `length of the array = 10`

12	23	34	45	56	67	78	89	90	100

(b) By default, `lower_bound = 0` (it can be set to any value) and `upper_bound= 9`.

(c) Data[0] Data[1] Data[2] Data[3] Data[4] Data[5] Data[6] Data[7] Data[8] Data[9]

(d) Since the elements of the array are stored in ascending order, we will compare the value that has to be deleted from the value of every element in the array. As soon as `VAL = Data[I]`, where `I` is the index or subscript of the array, we will get the position from which the element has to be deleted. For example, if we see this array, here `VAL = 56`. `Data[0] = 12` which is not equal to 56. Like this, we will compare and finally get the value of `POS = 4`.

Algorithm to delete an element from the middle of the array

The algorithm `DELETE` will be declared as `DELETE(A, N, POS)`. The arguments are as follows:

(a) `A`, the array from which the element has to be deleted
(b) `N`, the number of elements in the array
(c) `POS`, the position from which the element has to be deleted.

Figure 5.14 shows the algorithm in which we first initialize `I` with the position from which the element has to be deleted. In Step 2, a `while` loop is executed which will move all the elements that have index greater than `POS` one space towards left to occupy the space vacated by the deleted element. When we say that we are deleting an element, actually we are overwriting the element with the value of its successive element. In Step 5, we decrement the total number of elements in the array by 1.

```
Step 1: [INITIALIZATION] SET I = POS
Step 2: Repeat Steps 3 and 4 while I <= N - 1
Step 3: SET A[I] = A[I + 1]
Step 4: SET I = I + 1
        [End of Loop]
Step 5: SET N = N - 1
Step 6: EXIT
```

Figure 5.14 Algorithm to delete an element from the middle of the array

Now, let us visualize this algorithm by taking an example and having a look at Fig. 5.14.
Initial Data[] is given as shown in Fig. 5.15.
Calling DELETE (Data, 6, 2) will lead to the following processing in the array:

45	23	34	12	56	20
Data[0]	Data[1]	Data[2]	Data[3]	Data[4]	Data[5]

(a)

45	23	12	12	56	20
Data[0]	Data[1]	Data[2]	Data[3]	Data[4]	Data[5]

(b)

45	23	12	56	56	20
Data[0]	Data[1]	Data[2]	Data[3]	Data[4]	Data[5]

(c)

45	23	12	56	20	20
Data[0]	Data[1]	Data[2]	Data[3]	Data[4]	Data[5]

(d)

45	23	12	56	20
Data[0]	Data[1]	Data[2]	Data[3]	Data[4]

(e)

Figure 5.15 Deleting elements from the array

5.15. Write a program to delete a number from a given location in an array.

```
#include <stdio.h>
#include <conio.h>
int main()
{
    int i, n, pos, arr[10];
    clrscr();

    printf("\n Enter the size of the array:");
    scanf("%d", &n);
    printf("\n Enter the elements of the
    array : ");
    for(i=0;i<n;i++)
        scanf("%d", &arr[i]);
    printf("\n Enter the position from which
    the number has to be deleted: ");
    scanf("%d", &pos);

    for(i= pos; i<n;i++)
        arr[i] = arr [i+1];
    n--;
    printf("\n The array after deletion is:");
    for(i=0;i<n;i++)
        printf("\n Arr[%d] = %d", i, arr[i]);
    getch();
    return 0;
}
```

Output

```
Enter the size of the array: 5
Enter the elements of the array:
1 2 3 4 5
Enter the position from which the number has
to be deleted: 3
The array after deletion is:
Arr[0] = 1
Arr[1] = 2
Arr[2] = 3
Arr[3] = 5
```

5.16. Write a program to delete a number from an array that is already sorted in ascending order.

```
#include <stdio.h>
#include <conio.h>
int main()
{
    int i, n, j, num, arr[10];
    clrscr();
    printf("\n Enter the number of elements
    in the array : ");
    scanf("%d", &n);

    for(i=0;i<n;i++)
        scanf("%d", &arr[i]);
    printf("\n Enter the number to be deleted : ");
```

```
    scanf("%d", &num);
    for(i=0;i<n;j++)
    {
       if(arr[i] == num)
       {
       for(j=i; j<n;i++)
       arr[j] = arr[j+1];
       }
    }
    printf("\n The array after deletion is:
    ");
    for(i=0;i<n-1;i++)
       printf("\t%d", arr[i]);
    getch();
    return 0;
}
```

Output

```
Enter the number of elements in the array:
5
1 2 3 4 5
Enter the number to be deleted: 3
The array after deletion is: 1 2 4 5
```

5.6.4 Merging

Merging two arrays in a third array means first copying the contents of the first array into the third array and then copying the contents of the second array into the third array. Hence, the merged array contains contents of the first array followed by the contents of the second array.

If the arrays are unsorted then merging the arrays is very simple as one just needs to copy the contents of one array into another. But merging is not a trivial task when the two arrays are sorted and the merged array also needs to be sorted. Let us first discuss the merge operation on unsorted arrays. This operation is shown in Fig. 5.16.

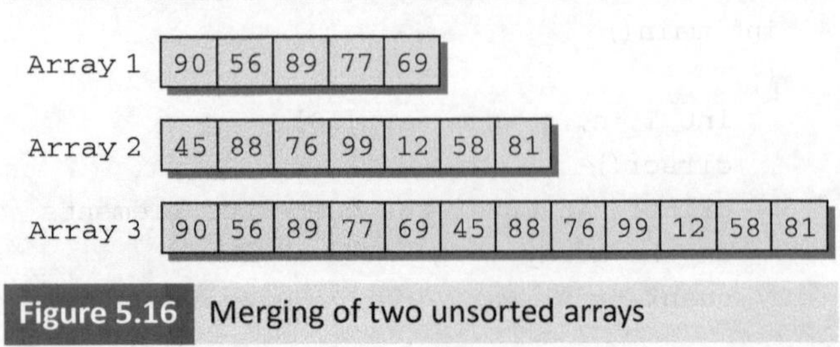

Figure 5.16 Merging of two unsorted arrays

5.17 Write a program to merge two unsorted arrays.

```
#include <stdio.h>
#include <conio.h>
main()
{
    int arr1[10], arr2[10], arr3[20];
    int i, n1, n2, m, index=0;
    clrscr();
    printf("\n Enter the number of elements
    in array 1: ");
    scanf("%d", &n1);
    printf("\n\n Enter the Elements of the
    first array");
    printf("\n ****************************");
    for(i=0;i<n1;i++)
       scanf("%d", &arr1[i]);

    printf("\n Enter the number of elements
    in array 2: ");
    scanf("%d", &n2);
    printf("\n\n Enter the Elements of the
    second array");
    printf("\n ****************************");
    for(i=0;i<n2;i++)
       scanf("%d", &arr2[i]);
    m = n1+n2;
    for(i=0;i<n1;i++)
    {
       arr3[index] = arr1[i];
       index++;
    }
    for(i=0;i<n2;i++)
    {
       arr3[index] = arr2[i];
       index++;
    }
    printf("\n\n The merged array is");
    printf("\n *********************");
    for(i=0;i<m;i++)
       printf("\t Arr[%d] = %d", i, arr3[i]);
    getch();
    return 0;
}
```

Output

```
Enter the number of elements in array 1: 3
Enter the Elements of the first array
10 20 30 ****************
Enter the number of elements in array 2: 3
Enter the Elements of the second array
15 25 35 ************
```

```
The merged array is
**********
Arr[0]= 10      Arr[1]  = 20    Arr[3]  = 30
Arr[4]  = 15    Arr[5]  = 25    Arr[6]  = 35
```

If we have two sorted arrays and the resultant merged array also needs to be a sorted one, then the task of merging the arrays becomes a little difficult. The task of merging can be explained using Fig. 5.17.

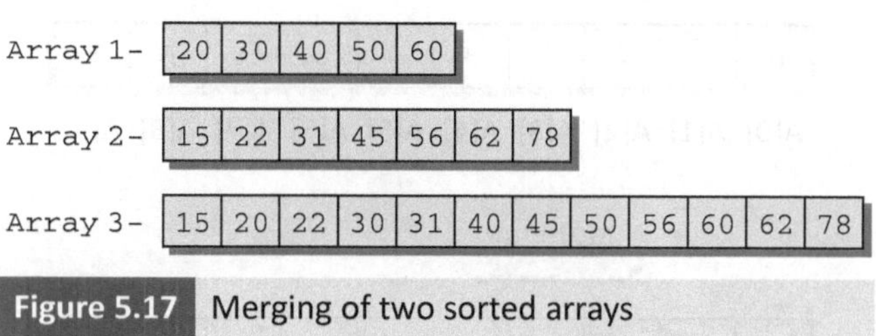

Figure 5.17 Merging of two sorted arrays

The figure shows how the merged array is formed using two sorted arrays. Here, we first compare the 1st element of `Array 1` with the 1st element of `Array 2`, put the smaller element in the merged array. Since `20 > 15`, we put `15` as the first element in the merged array. We then compare the 2nd element of the second array with the 1st element of the first array. Since `20 < 22`, now `20` is stored as the second element of the merged array. Next, 2nd element of the first array is compared with the 2nd element of the second array. Since `30 > 22`, we store `22` as the third element of the merged array. Now, we will compare the 2nd element of the first array with 3rd element of the second array. As `30 < 31`, we store `30` as the 4th element of the merged array. This procedure will be repeated until elements of both the arrays are placed in the right location in the merged array.

5.18 Write a program to merge two sorted arrays.

```
#include <stdio.h>
#include <conio.h>
main()
{
   int arr1[10], arr2[10], arr3[20];
   int i, n1, n2, m, index=0;
   int index_first = 0, index_second = 0;
   clrscr();
   printf("\n Enter the number of elements
   in array1: ");
   scanf("%d", &n1);
   printf("\n\n Enter the elements of the
   first array");
   printf("\n ****************************");
   for(i=0;i<n1;i++)
      scanf("%d", &arr1[i]);
   printf("\n Enter the number of elements
   in array2 : ");
   scanf("%d", &n2);
   printf("\n\n Enter the elements of the
   second array");
   printf("\n ****************************");
   for(i=0;i<n2;i++)
      scanf("%d", &arr2[i]);
   m = n1+n2;
   while(index_first < n1 && index_second < n2)
   {
      if(arr1[index_first]<arr2[index_second])
      {
         arr3[index] = arr1[index_first];
         index_first++;
      }
      else
      {
         arr3[index] = arr2[index_second];
         index_second++;
      }
      index++;
   }

   /* if elements of the first array is over
      and the second array has some elements */

   if(index_first == n1)
   {
      while(index_second<n2)
      {
         arr3[index] = arr2[index_second];
         index_second++;
         index++;
      }
   }
   /* if elements of the second array is over
      and the first array has some elements */

   else if(index_second == n2)
   {
      while(index_first<n1)
      {
         arr3[index] = arr1[index_first];
         index_first++;
         index++;

      }
   }
   printf("\n\n The contents of the merged
   array are");
   printf("\n ****************************");
   for(i=0;i<m;i++)
      printf("\n Arr[%d] = %d", i, arr3[i]);
```

```
    getch();
    return 0;
}
```

Output

```
Enter the number of elements in array1: 3
Enter the Elements of the first array
*******
10 20 30
Enter the number of elements in array2: 3
Enter the Elements of the second array
***********
15 25 35
The contents of the merged array is
***********
Arr[0]= 10      Arr[1]  = 15    Arr[3]  = 20
Arr[4]  = 25    Arr[5]  = 30    Arr[6]  = 35
```

5.6.5 Searching

Searching means to find whether a particular value is present in the array or not. If the value is present in the array then searching is said to be successful and the searching process gives the location of that value in the array. Otherwise, if the value is not present in the array, the searching process displays the appropriate message and in this case searching is said to be unsuccessful.

There are two popular methods for searching the array elements. One is *linear search* and the second is *binary search*. The algorithm that should be used depends entirely on how the values are organized in the array. For example, if the elements of the array are arranged in ascending order, then binary search should be used as it is more efficient for sorted list in terms of complexity. We will discuss these two methods in detail in this section.

Linear Search

Linear search, also called sequential search is a very simple method used for searching an array for a particular value. It works by comparing every element of the array one by one in sequence until a match is found. Linear search is mostly used to search an unordered list of elements (array in which data elements are not sorted). For example, if an array `A[]` is declared and initialized as,

```
int A[] = { 10, 8, 2, 7, 3, 4, 9, 1, 6, 5};
```

and `VAL = 7`, then searching means to find out whether the value `'7'` is present in the array or not. If yes, then the search is successful and it returns the position of occurrence of `VAL`. Here, the `POS = 3` (index starting from 0). Figure 5.18 illustrates this concept.

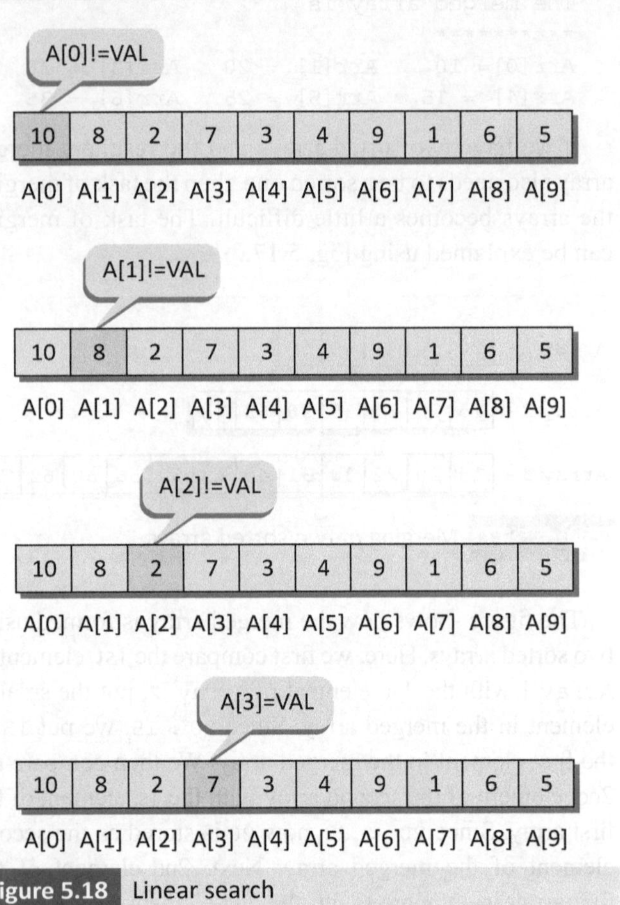

Figure 5.18 Linear search

Thus, we see that linear search executes in `O(n)` time where `n` is the number of elements in the array. Obviously, the best case of linear search is when `VAL` is equal to the first element of the array. In this case, only one comparison will be made.

Likewise, the worst case will happen when either `VAL` is not present in the array or it is equal to the last element of the array. In both the cases, `n` comparisons will have to be made. However, the performance of the linear search algorithm (Fig. 5.19) can be improved by using a sorted array.

In Step 1 and Step 2 of the algorithm, we initialize the value of `POS` and `I`. In Step 3, a `while` loop is executed that would be executed until `I` is less than `N` (total number of elements in the array). In Step 4, a check is made to see if a match is found between the current array element and the `VAL`. If a match is found, then the position of the array element is printed else the value of `I` is incremented to match the next element with `VAL`. However, if all the arrays elements have been compared with `VAL`, and no match is found then it means that the `VAL` is not present in the array.

```
LINEAR_SEARCH(A, N, VAL, POS)

Step 1: [INITIALIZE] SET POS = -1
Step 2: [INITIALIZE] SET I = 0
Step 3:      Repeat Step 4 while I<N
Step 4:                IF A[I] = VAL, then
                            SET POS = I
                            PRINT POS
                            Go to Step 6
             [END OF IF]
         [END OF while LOOP]
Step 5: PRINT "Value Not Present In The Array"
Step 6: EXIT
```

Figure 5.19 Algorithm for linear search

5.19 Write a program to implement linear search.

```
#include <stdio.h>
#include <conio.h>
main()
{
   int arr[10], num, i, n, found = 0, pos = -1;
   clrscr();

   printf("\n Enter the number of elements
   in the array : ");
   scanf("%d", &n);

   printf("\n Enter the elements -");
   for(i=0;i<n;i++)
      scanf("%d", &arr[i]);

   printf("\n Enter the number that has to
   be searched : ");
   scanf("%d", &num);

   for(i=0;i<n;i++)
   {
      if(arr[i] == num)
      {
         found =1;
         pos=i;
         printf("\n %d is found in the array
            at position = %d", num, i);
         break;
      }
   }
   if (found == 0)
      printf("\n %d DOES NOT EXIST in the
         array", num);
   getch();
   return 0;
}
```

Output

```
Enter the number of elements in the array:
5
Enter the elements: 1 2 3 4 5
Enter the number that has to be searched: 7
7 DOES NOT EXIST in the array
```

Binary Search

We have seen that the linear search algorithm is very slow. If we have an array with 1 million entries then to search a value from that array, we would need to make 1 million comparisons in the worst case. However, if the array is sorted, we have a better and efficient alternative, known as binary search.

Binary search is a searching algorithm that works efficiently with a *sorted list*. The algorithm finds out the position of a particular element in the array. The mechanism of binary search can be better understood by using the analogy of a telephone directory. When we are searching for a particular name in the directory, we will first open the directory from the middle and then decide whether to look for the name in the first part of the directory or in the second part of the directory. Again we will open some page in the middle and the whole process will be repeated until we finally find the name.

Take another analogy. How do we find words in a dictionary? We first open the dictionary somewhere in the middle. Then we compare the first word on that page with the desired word whose meaning has to be found. If the word comes before the word that appear on the page we will look in the first half of the dictionary else we will look in the second half. Again, we will open up some page in the first half of the dictionary pages. Compare the first word on that page with the desired word and repeat the same procedure until we finally get the word. The same mechanism is applied in binary search.

Now let us consider how this mechanism will be applied to search for a value in a sorted array. Given an array that is declared and initialized as,

```
int A[] = {0, 1, 2, 3, 4, 5, 6, 7, 8, 9, 10};
```

and `VAL = 9`, the algorithm (Fig. 5.20) will proceed in the following manner.

```
BEG = 0, END = 10, MID = (0 + 10)/2 = 5
```

Now, `VAL = 9` and `A[MID] = A[5] = 5`

`A[5]` is less than `VAL`, therefore, we will now search for the value in the later half of the array. So, we change the values of `BEG` and `MID`.

Now, `BEG = MID + 1 = 6, END = 10, MID = (6 + 10)/2 =16/2 = 8`

Now, `VAL = 9 and A[MID] = A[8] = 8`

`A[8]` is less than `VAL`, therefore, we will now search for the value in the later half of the array. So, again we change the values of `BEG` and `MID`.

Now, `BEG = MID + 1 = 9, END = 10, MID = (9 + 10)/2 = 9`

Now `VAL = 9 and A[MID] = 9.`

Now `VAL = 9 and A[MID] = 9.`

In this algorithm we see that `BEG` and `END` are the beginning and ending positions of the segment that we are looking to search for the element. `MID` is calculated as `(BEG + END)/2`. Initially, `BEG = lower_bound` and `END = upper_bound`. The algorithm will terminate when `A[MID] = VAL`. When the algorithm ends, we will set `POS = MID`. `POS` is the position at which the value is present in the array.

However, if `VAL` is not equal to `A[MID]`, then the values of `BEG`, `END`, and `MID` will be changed depending on whether `VAL` is smaller or greater than `A[MID]`.

(a) If `VAL < A[MID]`, then `VAL` will be present in the left segment of the array. So, the value of `END` will be changed as, `END = MID - 1`

(b) If `VAL > A[MID]`, then `VAL` will be present in the right segment of the array. So, the value of `BEG` will be changed as, `BEG = MID + 1`

Finally, if that `VAL` is not present in the array, then eventually, `END` will be less than `BEG`. When this happens, the algorithm should terminate as it will indicate that the element is not present in the array and the search will be unsuccessful.

Let us consider another example.

```
int A[] = {0, 1, 2, 3, 4, 5, 6, 7, 8, 9,
   10}; and VAL = 2
Step 1: BEG = 0, END = 10, MID = 5
   A[MID] > VAL
Step 2: BEG = 0, END = MID - 1 = 4, MID = 2
   A[MID] = VAL
```

Figure 5.20 shows an algorithm for binary search.

In Step 1, we initialize the value of variables—`BEG`, `END`, and `POS`. In Step 2, a `while` loop is executed until `BEG` is less than or equal to `END`. In Step 3, value of `MID` is calculated. In Step 4, we check if the value of `MID` is equal to `VAL` (item to be searched in the array). If a match is found then value of the `POS` is printed and the algorithm exits. However, if a match is not found then if the value of `A[MID]` is greater than `VAL`, then the value of `END` is modified otherwise if `A[MID]` is less than `VAL`, then value of `BEG` is altered. In Step 5, if the value of `POS = -1`, then it means `VAL` is not present in the array and an appropriate message is printed on the screen before the algorithm exits.

The complexity of the binary search algorithm can be expressed as `f(n)`, where `n` is the number of elements in the array. The complexity of the algorithm is calculated depending on the number of comparisons that are made. In binary search algorithm, we see that with each comparison, the size of the segment where search has to be made is

```
BINARY_SEARCH(A, lower_bound, upper_bound, VAL, POS)

Step 1: [INITIALIZE] SET BEG = lower_bound, END = upper_bound, POS = -1
Step 2: Repeat Step 3 and Step 4 while BEG <= END
Step 3:         SET MID = (BEG + END)/2
Step 4:         IF A[MID] = VAL, then
                     POS = MID
                     PRINT POS
                     Go to Step 6
                IF A[MID] > VAL then;
                     SET END = MID - 1
                ELSE
                     SET BEG = MID + 1
                [END OF IF]
        [END OF while LOOP]
Step 5: IF POS = -1, then
            PRINTF "VAL IS NOT PRESENT IN THE ARRAY"
        [END OF IF]
Step 6: EXIT
```

Figure 5.20 Algorithm for binary search

reduced to half. Thus, we can say that, in order to locate a particular `VAL` in the array, total number of comparisons that will be made is given by,

$2^{f(n)} > n$ or $f(n) = \log_2 n$

5.20 Write a program to implement binary search.

```
#include <stdio.h>
#include <conio.h>
main()
{
   int arr[10], num, i, n, beg, end, mid,
   found =0;
   clrscr();

   printf("\n Enter the number of elements
   in the array: ");
   scanf("%d", &n);
   printf("\n Enter the elements: ");
   for(i=0;i<n;i++)
   {
      scanf("%d", &arr[i]);
   }
   printf("\n Enter the number that has to
   be searched: ");
   scanf("%d", &num);

   beg = 0, end = n-1;
   while(beg ≤ end)
   {
      mid = (beg + end)/2;
      if (arr[mid] == num)
      {
      printf("\n %d is present in the array
         at position = %d", num, mid);
      found=1;
      break;
      }
      if (arr[mid]>num)
         end = mid-1;
      else if (arr[mid] < num)
         beg = mid+1;
   }
   if ( beg > end && found == 0)
      printf("\n %d DOES NOT EXIST IN THE
         ARRAY", num);
   getch();
   return 0;
}
```

Output

```
Enter the number of elements in the array: 5
Enter the elements: 1 2 3 4 5
Enter the number that has to be searched: 7
7 DOES NOT EXIST in the array
```

5.7 ONE-DIMENSIONAL ARRAYS FOR INTER-FUNCTION COMMUNICATION

Like variables of other data types, we can also pass an array to a function. While in some situations, you may want to pass individual elements of the array, and in other situations you may want to pass the entire array. In this section, we will discuss both these cases. Look at Fig. 5.21 which will make the concept easier to understand.

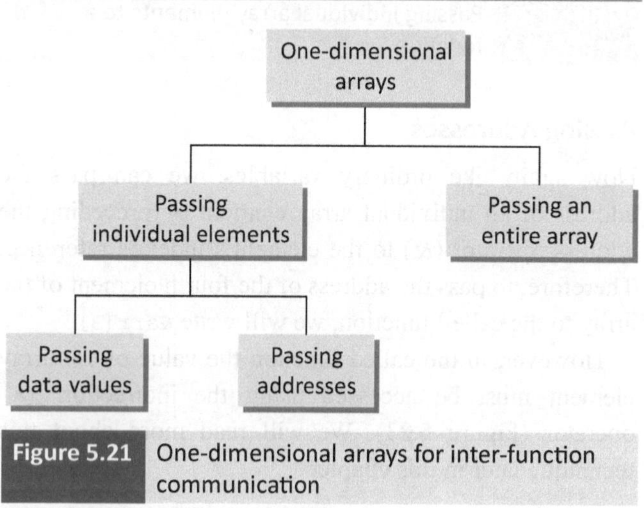

Figure 5.21 One-dimensional arrays for inter-function communication

Passing Individual Elements

The individual elements of an array can be passed to a function either by passing their addresses or their data values.

Passing Data Values

The individual elements can be passed in the same manner as we pass variables of any other data type. The condition is just that the data type of the array element must match the type of the function parameter. Figure 5.22 shows the code to pass an individual array element by passing data value.

In the above example, only one element of the array is passed to the called function. This is done by using the index expression. So `arr[3]` actually evaluates to a single integer value. The called function hardly bothers whether a normal integer variable is passed to it or an array value is passed.

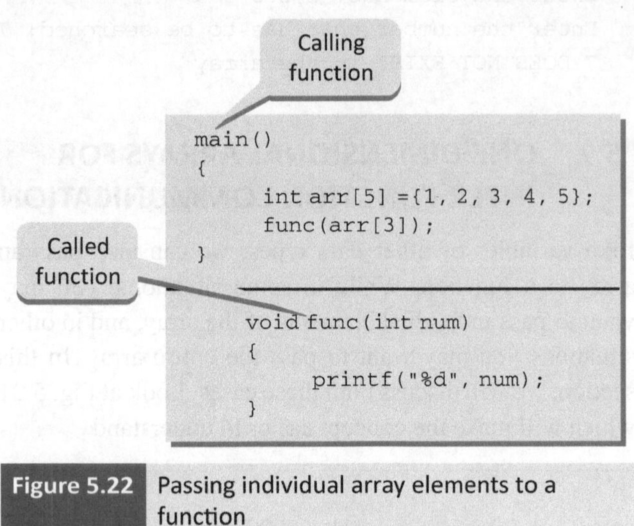

Figure 5.22 Passing individual array elements to a function

Passing Addresses

Now again like ordinary variables, we can pass the address of an individual array element by preceding the address operator (&) to the element's indexed reference. Therefore, to pass the address of the fourth element of the array to the called function, we will write `&arr[3]`.

However, in the called function the value of the array element must be accessed using the indirection (*) operator (Figure 5.23). We will read more about this technique later in this chapter.

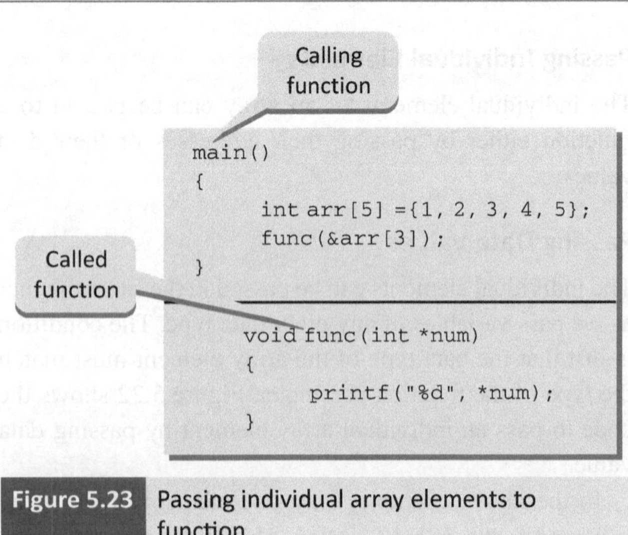

Figure 5.23 Passing individual array elements to function

Passing the Entire Array

We have studied that in C, the array name refers to the first byte of the array in memory. The address of rest of the elements in the array can be calculated using the array name and the index value of the element. Therefore, when we need to pass an entire array to a function, we can simply pass the name of the array. Figure 5.24 illustrates the code which passes the entire array to the called function.

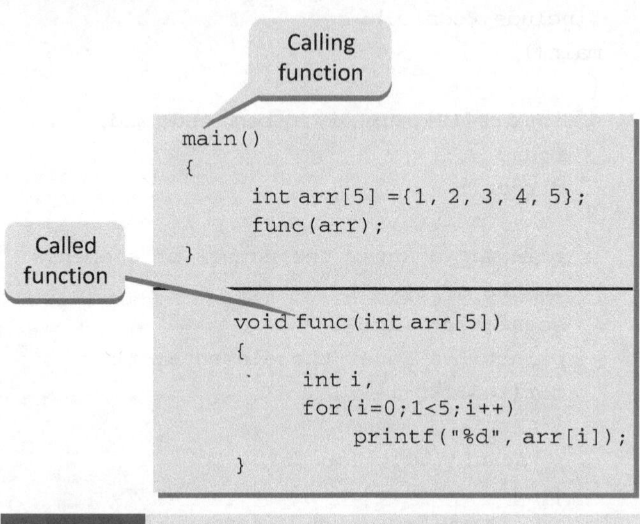

Figure 5.24 Passing entire array to function

In cases where we do not want the called function to make any changes to the array, the array must be received as a constant array by the called function. This prevents any type of un-intentional modifications of the array elements. To declare the array as a constant array, simply add the keyword `const` before the data type of the array.

Programming Tip: When an entire array is to be sent to the called function, the calling function just needs to pass the name of the array.

5.21 Write a program to read and print an array of n numbers.

```
#include <stdio.h>
#include <conio.h>
void read_array( int arr[], int);
void display_array( int arr[], int);

int main()
{
   int num[10], n;
   clrscr();
   printf("\n Enter the size of the array:");
   scanf("%d", &n);
   read_array(num, n);
   display_array(num, n);
   getch();
```

```
    return 0;
}
void read_array( int arr[10], int n)
{
    int i;
    for(i=0;i<n;i++)
    {
        printf("\n array[%d] = ", i);
        scanf("%d", &arr[i]);
    }
}
void display_array( int arr[10], int n)
{
    for(int i=0;i<n;i++)
    printf("\n array[%d] = %d", i, arr[i]);
}
```

Output

```
Enter the size of the array: 5
1 2 3 4 5
1 2 3 4 5
```

5.22 Write a program to merge two integer arrays. Also display the merged array in reverse order.

```
#include <stdio.h>
#include <conio.h>
void read_array(int my_array[], int);
void display_array(int my_array[], int);
void merge_array(int my_array3[], int, int
    my_array1[], int, int my_array2[], int);
void reverse_array(int my_array[], int);
int main()
{
    int arr1[10], arr2[10], arr3[20], n, m, t;
    clrscr();

    printf("\n Enter the number of elements
    in the first array: ");
    scanf("%d", &m);
    read_array(arr1, m);
    printf("\n Enter the number of elements
    in the second array: ");
    scanf("%d", &n);
    read_array(arr2, n);
    t = m + n;
    merge_array(arr3, t, arr1, m, arr2, n);

    printf("\n The merged array is : ");
    display_array(arr3, t);

    printf("\n The merged array in reverse
    order is: ");
    reverse_array(arr3, t);
    getch();
    return 0;
}
void read_array(int my_array[10], int n)
{
    int i;
    for(i=0;i<n;i++)
        scanf("%d", &my_array[i]);
}
void merge_array(int my_array3[], int t, int
    my_array1[], int m, int my_array2[], int n)
{
    int i, j=0;
    for(i=0; i<m; i++)
    {
        my_array3[j] = my_array1[i];
        j++;
    }
    for(i=0; i<n; i++)
    {
        my_array3[j] = my_array2[i];
        j++;
    }
}
void display_array(int my_array[], int n)
{
    int i;
    for(i=0;i<n;i++)
        printf("\n arr[%d] = %d", i,
            my_array[i]);
}
void reverse_array(int my_array[], int m)
{
    int i, j;
    for(i=m-1, j=0;i>=0;i--, j++)
        printf("\n arr[%d] = %d", j,
            my_array[i]);
}
```

Output

```
Enter the number of elements in the first
array: 3
10 20 30
Enter the number of elements in the second
array: 3
15 25 35
The merged array is:
Arr[0]= 10    Arr[1] = 20    Arr[2] = 30
Arr[3] = 15   Arr[4] = 25    Arr[5] = 35
The merged array in reverse order is:
Arr[0] = 35  Arr[1] = 25  Arr[2] = 15
Arr[3] = 30  Arr[4] = 20  Arr[5] = 10
```

5.23 Write a program to interchange the biggest and the smallest number in the array.

```
#include <stdio.h>
#include <conio.h>

void read_array(int my_array[], int);
void display_array(int my_array[], int);
void interchange(int arr[], int);
int find_biggest_pos(int my_array[10], int n);
int find_smallest_pos(int my_array[10], int n);
int main()
{
   int arr[10], n;
   clrscr();

   printf("\n Enter the size of the array:");
   scanf("%d", &n);
   read_array(arr, n);
   display_array(arr, n);
   interchange(arr, n);
   display_array(arr, n);
   getch();
   return 0;
}
void read_array(int my_array[10], int n)
{
   int i;
   for(i=0;i<n;i++)
      scanf("%d", &my_array[i]);
}
void display_array(int my_array[10], int n)
{
   int i;
      printf("n");
   for(i=0;i<n;i++)
      printf("\t array[%d] = %d", i, my_
   array[i]);
}
void interchange(int my_array[10], int n)
{
   int temp, big_pos, small_pos;
   big_pos = find_biggest_pos(my_arr, n);
   small_pos = find_smallest_pos(my_arr,n);
   temp = my_array[big_pos];
   my_array[big_pos] = my_array[small_pos];
   my_array[small_pos] = temp;
}
int find_biggest_pos(int my_array[10], int n)
{
   int i, large = -123456, pos=-1;
   for(i=0;i<n;i++)
   {
      if (my_array[i] > large)
      {
         large = my_array[i];
         pos=i;
      }
   }
   return pos;
}
int find_smallest_pos(int my_array[10], int
   n)
{
   int i, small = 123456, pos=-1;
   for(i=0;i<n;i++)
   {
      if (my_array[i] < small)
      {
         small = my_array[i];
         pos=i;
      }
   }
   return pos;
}
```

Output

```
Enter the size of the array: 5
1 2 3 4 5
Arr[0] = 1    Arr[1] = 2    Arr[2] = 3
Arr[3] = 4    Arr[4] = 5
Arr[0] = 5    Arr[1] = 2    Arr[2] = 3
Arr[3] = 4    Arr[4] = 1
```

If a function receives an array that does not change it, then the array should be received as a constant array. This would ensure that the contents of the array are not accidentally changed. To declare an array as constant, prefix its type with the `const` keyword, as shown below.

```
int sum(const int arr[ ], int n);
```

5.8 TWO-DIMENSIONAL ARRAYS

Till now we have read only about one-dimensional arrays. A one-dimensional array is organized linearly and only in one direction. But at times, we need to store data in the form of matrices or tables. Here the concept of one-dimensional array is extended to incorporate two-dimensional data structures. A two-dimensional array is specified using two subscripts where one subscript denotes row and the other denotes column. C considers the two-dimensional array as an array of a one-dimensional array. Figure 5.25 shows a two-dimensional array which can be viewed as an array of arrays.

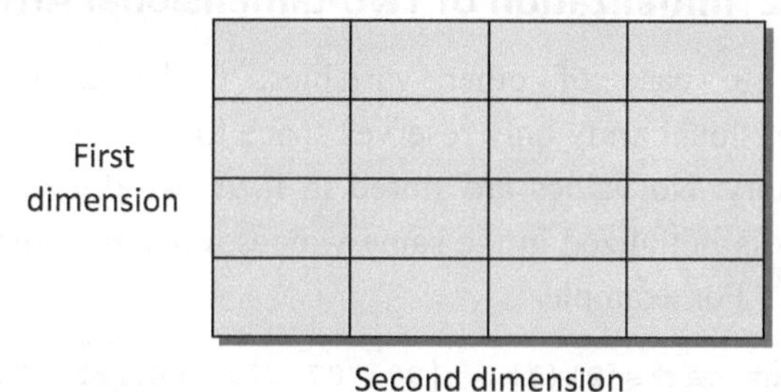

Figure 5.25 Two-dimensional array

5.8.1 Declaration of Two-dimensional Arrays

Similar to one-dimensional arrays, two-dimensional arrays must be declared before being used. The declaration statement tells the compiler the name of the array, the data type of each element in the array, and the size of each dimension. A two-dimensional array is declared as:

```
data_type array_name[row_size][column_size];
```

Therefore, a two-dimensional `m` × `n` array is an array that contains `m` × `n` data elements and each element is accessed using two subscripts, `i` and `j` where `i<= m` and `j<= n`.

For example, if we want to store the marks obtained by 3 students in 5 different subjects, then we can declare a two-dimensional array as

```
int marks[3][5]
```

A two-dimensional array called `marks` is declared that has `m(3)` rows and `n(5)` columns. The first element of the array is denoted by `marks[0][0]`, the second element as `marks[0][1]`, and so forth. Here, `marks[0][0]` stores the marks obtained by the first student in the first subject, `marks[1][0]` stores the marks obtained by the second student in the first subject, and so on.

> **Note** Each dimension of the two-dimensional array is indexed from zero to its maximum size minus one. The first index selects the row and the second selects the column.

The pictorial form of a two-dimensional array is given in Fig. 5.26.

Hence, we see that a `2D` array is treated as a collection of `1D` arrays. The elements of the `2D` array comprises `1D` array (the rows). To understand this, we can also see the representation of a two-dimensional array as shown in Fig. 5.27.

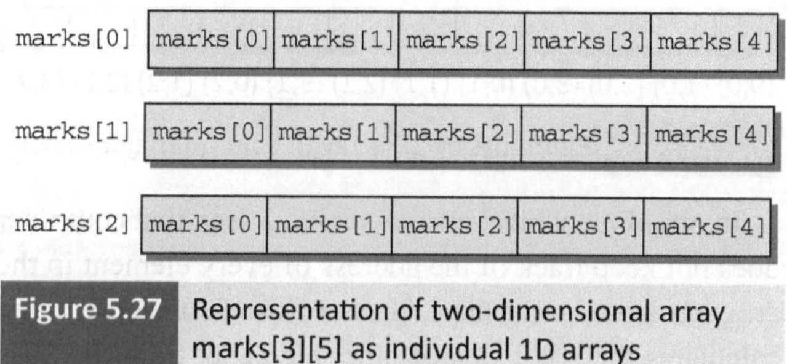

Figure 5.27 Representation of two-dimensional array marks[3][5] as individual 1D arrays

Although Fig. 5.27 shows a rectangular picture of a two-dimensional array, these elements will be actually stored sequentially in memory. Since computer memory is basically one-dimensional, a multidimensional array cannot be stored in memory as a grid.

Basically, there are two ways of storing a two-dimensional array in memory. The first way is *row major order* and the second is *column major order*. Let us see how the elements of a 2D array are stored in a row major order. Here, the elements of the first row are stored before the elements of the second and third row, i.e., the elements of the array are stored row by row where `n` elements of

Row/Columns	Column 0	Column 1	Column 2	Column 3	Column 4
Row 0	marks[0][0]	marks[0][1]	marks[0][2]	marks[0][3]	marks[0][4]
Row 1	marks[1][0]	marks[1][1]	marks[1][2]	marks[1][3]	marks[1][4]
Row 2	marks[2][0]	marks[2][1]	marks[2][2]	marks[2][3]	marks[2][4]

Figure 5.26 Two-dimensional array

the first row will occupy the first nth locations. This is illustrated in Fig. 5.28.

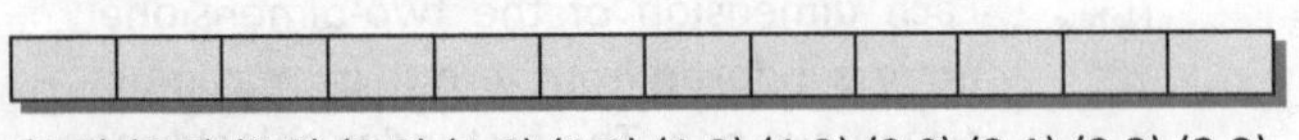

Figure 5.28 Elements of 2D array in row major order

When we store the elements in a column major order, the elements of the first column are stored before the elements of the second and third column, i.e., the elements of the array are stored column by column where n elements of the first column will occupy the first nth locations. This is illustrated in Fig. 5.29.

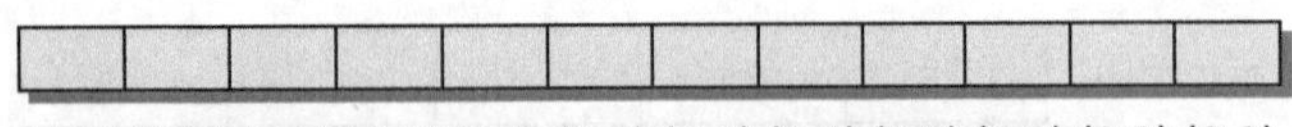

Figure 5.29 Elements of 2D array in column major order

In one-dimensional arrays, we have seen that computer does not keep track of the address of every element in the array. It stores only the address of the first element and calculates the addresses of other elements from the base address (address of the first element). Same is the case with a two-dimensional array. Here also, the computer stores the base address and the address of the other elements is calculated using the following formula.

`Address(A[I][J] = B_A + w{M(J - 1) + (I - 1)}`, if the array elements are stored in column major order, and

`Address(A[I][J] = B_A + w{N (I - 1) + (J - 1)}`, if the array elements are stored in row major order.

where, `w` is the number of words stored per memory location, `N` is the number of columns, `M` is the number of rows, `I` and `J` are the subscripts of the array element, and `B_A` is the base address.

Example 5.7 Consider a 20 × 5 two-dimensional array Marks which has base address = 1000 and number of words per memory location of the array = 2. Now compute the address of the element `Marks[18, 4]` assuming that the elements are stored in row major order.

```
Address(A[I][J]
    = Base_Address + w{N (I - 1) + (J - 1)}
Address(Marks[18,4])
    = 1000 + 2{5(18 - 1) + (4 - 1) }
    = 1000 + 2 { 5(17) + 3}
    = 1000 + 2 (88)
    = 1000 + 176 = 1176
```

5.8.2 Initialization of Two-dimensional Arrays

Like in case of other variables, declaring a two-dimensional array only reserves space for the array in the memory. No values are stored in it. A two-dimensional array is initialized in the same way as a one-dimensional array. For example,

```
int marks[2][3] = {90, 87, 78, 68, 62, 71};
```

The initialization of a two-dimensional array is done row by row. The above statement can also be written as

```
int marks[2][3]={{90,87,78},{68, 62, 71}};
```

The given two-dimensional array has 2 rows and 3 columns. Here, the elements in the first row are initialized first and then the elements of the second row are initialized. Therefore,

```
marks[0][0] = 90      marks[0][1] = 87
marks[0][2] = 78      marks[1][0] = 68
marks[1][1] = 62      marks[1][2] = 71
```

Therefore, in the above example, each row is defined as a one-dimensional array of three elements that are enclosed in braces. Commas are used to separate the elements in the row as well as to separate the elements of two rows.

In case of one-dimensional array, if the array is completely initialized, we may omit the size of the array. Same concept can be applied to a two-dimensional array, except that only the size of the first dimension can be omitted. Therefore, the declaration statement given below is valid.

```
int marks[][3]={{90,87,78},{68, 62, 71}};
```

In order to initialize the entire two-dimensional array to zero, simply specify the first value as zero, i.e., simply write

```
int marks[2][3] = {0};
```

If some values are missing in the initializer then it is automatically set to zero. For example, the statement given below will initialize the values in the first row but the elements of the second row will be initialized to zero.

```
int marks[2][3] ={ {50, 60, 70}};
```

Note: An un-initialized array contains unpredictable contents.

5.8.3 Accessing the Elements

The elements in a multidimensional array are stored in contiguous memory locations. While accessing the elements, remember that the last subscript varies most rapidly whereas the first varies least rapidly.

In case of one-dimensional arrays we used a single `for` loop to vary the index `i` in every pass, so that all the elements could be scanned. Similarly, since a two-dimensional array contains two subscripts, we will use two `for` loops to scan the elements. The first `for` loop will loop for each row in the 2D array and the second `for` loop will scan individual columns for every row in the array.

However, individual elements of a two-dimensional array can be initialized using the assignment operator as shown below.

```
marks[1][2] = 79; or
marks[1][2] = marks[1][1] + 10;
```

In order to input the values from the keyboard, you must use the following code.

```
for(i=0;i<2;i++)
   for(j=0;j<2;j++)
      scanf("%d", &arr[i][j]);
```

Look at the code given below which prints the elements of a 2D array on the screen.

5.24 Write a program to print the elements of a 2D array.

```
#include <stdio.h>
#include <conio.h>
main()
{
   int arr[2][2] = {12, 34, 56,32};
   int i, j;
   for(i=0;i<2;i++)
   {
      printf("\n");
      for(j=0;j<2;j++)
      printf("%d\t", arr[i][j]);
   }
   return 0;
}
```

Output

```
12 34
56 32
```

5.25 Write a program to generate Pascal's triangle.

```
#include <stdio.h>
#include <conio.h>
main()
{
   int arr[7][7]={0};
   int row=2, col, i, j;
   arr[0][0] = arr[1][0] = arr[1][1] = 1;
   while(row <= 7)
   {
      arr[row][0] = 1;
      for(col = 1;col <= row;col++)
      arr[row][col] = arr[row-1][col-1] +
            arr[row-1][col];
      row++;
   }
   for(i=0;i<7;i++)
   {
      printf("\n");
      for(j=0;j<=i;j++)
         printf("\t %d", arr[i][j]);
   }
   getch();
   return 0;
}
```

Output

```
1
1  1
1  2  1
1  3  3  1
1  4  6  4  1
1  5  10 10 5  1
1  6  15 20 15 6  1
```

5.26 In a small company there are 5 salesmen. Each salesman is supposed to sell 3 products. Write a program using two-dimensional array to print (i) the total sales by each salesman and (ii) total sales of each item.

```
#include <stdio.h>
#include <conio.h>
main()
{
   int sales[5][3], i, j, total_sales=0;
   //INPUT DATA
   printf("\n ENTER THE DATA");
   printf("\n *****************");
   for(i=0;i<5;i++)
   {
      printf("\n Enter the sales of 3 items
            sold by salesman %d: ", i);
      for(j=0;j<3;j++)
```

```
        scanf("%d", &sales[i][j]);
    }
    // PRINT TOTAL SALES BY EACH SALESMAN
    for(i=0;i<5;i++)
    {
      total_sales = 0;
      for(j=0;j<3;j++)
        total_sales += sales[i][j];
      printf("\n Total Sales By Salesman %d
                = %d",i, total_sales);
    }
    // TOTAL SALES OF EACH ITEM
    for(i=0;i<3;i++) // for each item
    {
      total_sales=0;
      for(j=0;j<5;j++) // for each salesman
        total_sales += sales[j][i];
      printf("\n Total sales of item %d
                = %d", i, total_sales);
    }
    getch();
    return 0;
}
```

Output

```
ENTER THE DATA
*****************
Enter the sales of 3 items sold by saleman
0: 23 23 45
Enter the sales of 3 items sold by salesman
1: 34 45 63
Enter the sales of 3 items sold by salesman
2: 36 33 43
Enter the sales of 3 items sold by salesman
3: 33 52 35
Enter the sales of 3 items sold by salesman
4: 32 45 64
Total Sales By Salesman 0 = 91
Total Sales By Salesman 1 = 142
Total Sales By Salesman 2 = 112
Total Sales By Salesman 3 = 120
Total Sales By Salesman 4 = 141
Total sales of item 0 = 158
Total sales of item 1 = 198
Total sales of item 2 = 250
```

5.27 In a class there are 10 students. Each student is supposed to appear in 3 tests. Write a program using two-dimensional arrays to print

(i) the marks obtained by each student in different subjects

(ii) total marks and average obtained by each student

(iii) store the average of each student in a separate 1D array so that it can be used to calculate the class average.

```
#include <stdio.h>
#include <conio.h>
main()
{
  int marks[10][3], i, j;
  int total_marks[10]={0};;
  float class_avg=0.0, total_avg = 0.0;
  float avg[10];

  //INPUT DATA
  printf("\n ENTER THE DATA");
  printf("\n *****************");
  for(i=0;i<10;i++)
  {
  printf("\n Enter the marks of student %d
        in 3 subjects : ", i);
    for(j=0;j<3;j++)
      scanf("%d", &marks[i][j]);
  }

  // CALCULATE TOTAL MARKS OF EACH STUDENT
  for(i=0;i<10;i++)
  {
    for(j=0;j<3;j++)
      total_marks[i] += marks[i][j];
  }
  // CALCULATE AVERAGE OF EACH STUDENT
  for(i=0;i<10;i++)
  {
    for(j=0;j<3;j++)
      avg[i] = (float)total_marks[i]/3.0;
  }
  // CALCULATE CLASS AVERAGE
  for(i=0;i<10;i++)
    total_avg += avg[i];
  class_avg = (float)total_avg/10;
  // DISPLAY RESULTS
  printf("\n\n STUD NO. MARKS OBTAINED IN
  THREE SUBJECTS TOTAL MARKS \t AVERAGE");
  printf("
  \n*************************************");
  for(i=0;i<10;i++)
  { printf("\n %4d", i);
    for(j=0;j<3;j++)
      printf("   %d", marks[i][j]);
    printf("%4d \t%2.2f", total_marks[i],
        avg[i]);
  }
  printf("\n\n CLASS AVERAGE = %f", class_
  avg);
  getch();
```

```
    return 0;
}
```

Output

```
ENTER THE DATA
*****************
Enter the marks of student 0 in 3 subjects:
78 89 90
Enter the marks of student 1 in 3 subjects:
98 87 76
Enter the marks of student 2 in 3 subjects:
67 78 89
Enter the marks of student 3 in 3 subjects:
90 87 65
Enter the marks of student 4 in 3 subjects:
56 87 97
Enter the marks of student 5 in 3 subjects:
45 67 89
Enter the marks of student 6 in 3 subjects:
66 77 88
Enter the marks of student 7 in 3 subjects:
76 87 98
Enter the marks of student 8 in 3 subjects:
67 88 66
Enter the marks of student 9 in 3 subjects:
66 75 78
STUD NO. MARKS OBTAINED IN THREE SUBJECTS
TOTAL MARKS   AVERAGE
***************
0    78    89    90    257   85.67
1    98    87    76    261   87.00
2    67    78    89    234   78.00
3    90    87    65    242   80.67
4    56    87    97    240   80.00
5    45    67    89    201   67.00
6    66    77    88    231   77.00
7    76    87    98    261   87.00
8    67    88    66    221   73.67
9    66    75    78    210   73.00
CLASS AVERAGE = 78.90
```

5.28 Write a program to read a two-dimensional array marks which stores marks of 5 students in 3 subjects. Write a program to display the highest marks in each subject.

```
#include <stdio.h>
#include <conio.h>
main()
{
   int marks[5][3], i, j, max_marks;
   for(i=0;i<5;i++)
   {
      printf("\n Enter the marks obtained by
            student %d",i);
      for(j=0;j<3;j++)
      {
         printf("\n marks[%d][%d] = ", i, j);
         scanf("%d", &marks[i][j]);
      }
   }
   for(j=0;j<3;j++)
   {
      max_marks = -999;
      for(i=0;i<5;i++)
      {
         if(marks[i][j]>max_marks)
         max_marks = marks[i][j];
      }
      printf("\n The highest marks obtained
            in the subject %d= %d", j,
            max_marks);
   }
   getch();
   return 0;
}
```

Output

```
Enter the marks obtained by student 0
marks[0][0] = 89
marks[0][1] = 76
marks[0][2] = 100
Enter the marks obtained by student 1
marks[1][0] = 99
marks[1][1] = 90
marks[1][2] = 89
Enter the marks obtained by student 2
marks[2][0] = 67
marks[2][1] = 76
marks[2][2] = 56
Enter the marks obtained by student 3
marks[3][0] = 88
marks[3][1] = 77
marks[3][2] = 66
Enter the marks obtained by student 4
marks[4][0] = 67
marks[4][1] = 78
marks[4][2] = 89
The highest marks obtained in the subject 0
= 99
The highest marks obtained in the subject 1
= 90
The highest marks obtained in the subject 2
= 100
```

5.9 OPERATIONS ON TWO-DIMENSIONAL (2D) ARRAYS

Two-dimensional arrays can be used to implement the mathematical concept of matrices. In mathematics, a matrix is a grid of numbers, arranged in rows and columns. Thus, using two-dimensional arrays, we can perform the following operations on an m × n matrix:

Transpose: Transpose of a m × n matrix A is given as a n × m matrix B where,

$$B_{i,j} = A_{j,i}$$

Sum: Two matrices that are compatible with each other can be added together thereby storing the result in the third matrix. Two matrices are said to be compatible when they have the same number of rows and columns. Elements of the matrices can be added by writing:

$$C_{i,j} = A_{i,j} + B_{i,j}$$

Difference: Two matrices that are compatible with each other can be subtracted thereby storing the result in the third matrix. Two matrices are said to be compatible when they have the same number of rows and columns. Elements of the matrices can be subtracted by writing:

$$C_{i,j} = A_{i,j} - B_{i,j}$$

Product: Two matrices can be multiplied with each other if the number of columns in the first matrix is equal to the number of rows in the second matrix. Therefore, m × n matrix A can be multiplied with a p × q matrix if n = q. Elements of the matrices can be multiplied by writing:

$$C_{i,j} = \sum A_{i,k}B_{j,k} \text{ for } k=1 \text{ to } k < n$$

5.29 Write a program to read and display a 3 × 3 matrix.

```
#include <stdio.h>
#include <conio.h>
int main()
{
   int i, j, mat[3][3];
   clrscr();

   printf("\n Enter the elements of the
   matrix ");
   printf("\n ************************");

   for(i=0;i<3;i++)
   {
      for(j=0;j<3;j++)
         scanf("%d",&mat[i][j]);
   }
   printf("\n The elements of the matrix are ");
   printf("\n ************************");

   for(i=0;i<3;i++)
   {
      printf("\n");
      for(j=0;j<3;j++)
         printf("\t %d%d%d",i, j, mat[i][j]);
   }
   return 0;
}
```

Output

```
Enter the elements of the matrix
************************
1 2 3 4 5 6 7 8 9
The elements of the matrix are
************************
1 2 3
4 5 6
7 8 9
```

5.30 Write a program to transpose a 3 × 3 matrix.

```
#include <stdio.h>
#include <conio.h>
int main()
{
   int i, j, mat[3][3], transposed_mat[3][3];
   clrscr();

   printf("\n Enter the elements of the
   matrix");
   printf("\n ************************");
   for(i=0;i<3;i++)
   {
      for(j=0;j<3;j++)
      {
         printf("\n mat[%d][%d] = ",i, j);
         scanf("%d", &mat[i][j]);
      }
   }
   printf("\n The elements of the matrix are ");
   printf("\n ************************");

   for(i=0;i<3;i++)
   {
      printf("\n");
      for(j=0;j<3;j++)
         printf("\t mat[%d][%d] = %d", i, j,
            mat[i][j]);
   }
   for(i=0;i<3;i++)
   {
      for(j=0;j<3;j++)
         transposed_mat[i][j] = mat[j][i];
   }
   printf("\n The elements of the transposed
   matrix are ");
   printf("\n ************************");

   for(i=0;i<3;i++)
   {
```

```
        printf("\n");
        for(j=0;j<3;j++)
            printf("\t transposed_mat[%d][%d]
                  = %d",i, j, transposed_ mat[i]
                  [j]);
    }
    return 0;
}
```

Output

```
Enter the elements of the matrix
************************
1 2 3 4 5 6 7 8 9
The elements of the matrix are
************************
1 2 3
4 5 6
7 8 9
The elements of the transposd matrix are
************************
1 4 7
2 5 8
7 8 9
```

5.31 Write a program to input two m × n matrices and then calculate the sum of their corresponding elements and store it in a third m × n matrix.

```
#include <stdio.h>
#include <conio.h>
int main()
{
    int i, j;
    int rows1, cols1, rows2, cols2, rows_sum,
    cols_sum;
    int mat1[5][5], mat2[5][5], sum[5][5];
    clrscr();

    printf("\n Enter the numbers of rows in
    the first matrix: ");
    scanf("%d",&rows1);

    printf("\n Enter the numbers of columns
    in the first matrix: ");
    scanf("%d",&cols1);

    printf("\n Enter the numbers of rows in
    the second matrix: ");
    scanf("%d",&rows2);
    printf("\n Enter the numbers of columns
    in the second matrix:");
    scanf("%d",&cols2);

    if(rows1 != rows2 || cols1 != cols2)
    {
        printf("\n The number of rows and
            columns of both the matrices must
            be equal");
        getch();
        exit();
    }
    rows_sum = rows1;
    cols_sum = cols1;

    printf("\n Enter the elements of the
    first matrix");
    printf("\n ************************");

    for(i=0;i<rows1;i++)
    {
        for(j=0;j<cols1;j++)
            scanf("%d",&mat1[i][j]);
    }
    printf("\n Enter the elements of the
    second matrix");
    printf("\n ************************");

    for(i=0;i<rows2;i++)
    {
        for(j=0;j<cols2;j++)
            scanf("%d",&mat2[i][j]);
    }
    for(i=0;i<rows_sum;i++)
    {
        for(j=0;j<cols_sum,j++)
            sum[i][j] = mat1[i][j] + mat2[i][j];
    }
    printf("\n The elements of the resultant
    matrix are");
    printf("\n ************************");

    for(i=0;i<rows_sum;i++)
    {
        printf("\n");
        for(j=0;j<cols_sum;j++)
            printf("\t %d", sum[i][j]);
    }
    return 0;
}
```

Output

```
Enter the numbers of rows in the first
matrix: 2
Enter the numbers of columns in the first
matrix: 2
Enter the numbers of rows in the second
matrix: 2
Enter the numbers of columns in the second
matrix: 2
Enter the elements of the first matrix
*************************
1 2 3 4
Enter the elements of the second matrix
*************************
5 6 7 8
The elements of the resultant matrix are
*************************
6   8
10 12
```

5.10 TWO-DIMENSIONAL ARRAYS FOR INTER-FUNCTION COMMUNICATION

There are three ways of passing parts of the two-dimensional array to a function (process). First, we can pass individual elements of the array. This is exactly same as we passed element of a one-dimensional array. Second, we can pass a single row of the two-dimensional array. This is equivalent to passing the entire one-dimensional array to a function. This has already been discussed in the previous section. Third, we can pass the entire two-dimensional array to the function. Refer Fig. 5.30 which shows the three ways of using two-dimensional arrays for inter-function, interprocess communication.

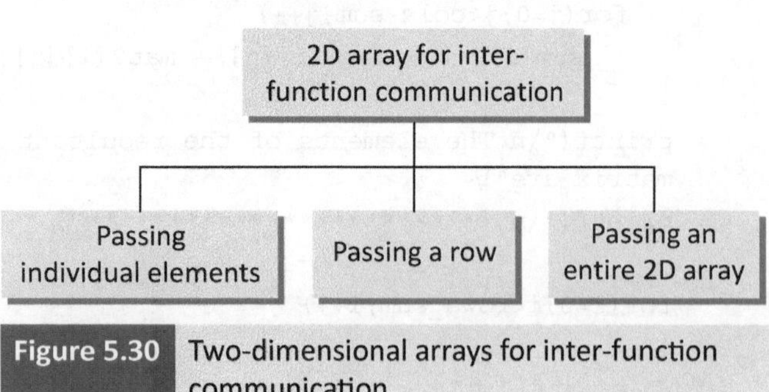

Figure 5.30 Two-dimensional arrays for inter-function communication

5.10.1 Passing a Row

A row of a two-dimensional array can be passed by indexing the array name with the row number. When we send a single row of a two-dimensional array, then the called function receives a one-dimensional array. Figure 5.31 illustrates how a single row of a two-dimensional array is passed to the called function.

Calling function

```
main()
{
    int arr[2][3]= ( {1, 2, 3}, {4, 5, 6}};
    func(arr[1]);
}
```

Called function

```
void func(int arr[])
{
    int i;
    for(i=0;i<5;i++)
      printf("%d", arr[i] * 10);
}
```

Figure 5.31 Passing two-dimensional arrays for inter-function communication

5.10.2 Passing an Entire 2D Array

> **Programming Tip:** A compiler error will be generated if you omit the array size in the parameter declaration for any array dimension other than the first.

To pass a two-dimensional array to a function, we use the array name as the actual parameter. (The same we did in case of a 1D array). However, the parameter in the called function must indicate that the array has two dimensions.

5.32 Write a menu-driven program to read and display an m × n matrix. Also find the sum, transpose, and product of two m × n matrices.

```
#include <stdio.h>
#include <conio.h>
void read_matrix(int mat[2][2], int, int);
void sum_matrix(int mat1[2][2], int mat2[2]
   [2], int, int);
void mul_matrix(int mat1[2][2], int mat2[2]
   [2], int, int);
void transpose_matrix(int mat2[2][2], int,
   int);
void display_matrix(int mat[2][2], int r,
   int c);
```

```
int main()
{
   int option, row, col;
   int mat1[2][2], mat2[2][2];
   clrscr();

   do
   {

      printf("\n ******* MAIN MENU ********");
      printf("\n 1. Read the two matrices");
      printf("\n 2. Add the matrices");
      printf("\n 3. Multiply the matrices");
      printf("\n 4. Transpose the matrix");
      printf("\n 5. EXIT");

      printf("\n\n Enter your option: ");
      scanf("%d", &option);
      switch(option)
      {
         case 1:
               printf("\n Enter the number of
                     rows and columns of
                     the matrix: ");
               scanf("%d %d", &row, &col);
               printf("\n Enter the first
                     matrix: ");
               read_matrix(mat1, row, col);
               printf("\n Enter the second
                     matrix: ");
               read_matrix(mat2, row, col);
               break;
      case 2:
               sum_matrix(mat1, mat2, row,
                  col);
               break;
      case 3:
               if(col == row)
               mul_matrix(mat1, mat2, row,
                  col);
               else
               printf("\n To multiply two
                  matrices, number of
                  columns in the first
                  matrix must be equal to
                  number of rows in the
                  second matrix");
               break;
      case 4:
               transpose_matrix(mat1, row, col);
               break;
      }
   }while(option != 5);
   getch();
   return 0;
}
void read_matrix(int mat[2][2], int r, int c)
{
   int i, j;
   for(i = 0;i < r;i++)
   {  printf("\n");
      for(j = 0;j < c;j++)
      {
      printf("\t mat[%d][%d] = ",i,j);
      scanf("%d", &mat[i][j]);
      }
   }
}
void sum_matrix(int mat1[2][2], int mat2[2]
   [2], int r, int c)
{
   int i, j, sum[2][2];
   for(i=0;i<r;i++)
   {
      for(j=0;j<c;j++)
      sum[i][j] = mat1[i][j] + mat2[i][j];
   }
   display_matrix(sum, r, c);
}
void mul_matrix(int mat1[2][2], int mat2[2]
   [2], int r, int c)
{
   int i, j, k, prod[2][2];
   for(i=0;i<r;i++)
   {
      for(j=0;j<c;j++)
      {
      prod[i][j] = 0;
      for(k=0;k<c;k++)
      prod[i][j] += mat1[i][k] * mat2[k][j];
      }
   }
   display_matrix(prod, r, c);
}
void transpose_matrix(int mat[2][2], int r,
   int c)
{
   int i, j, tp_mat[2][2];
   for(i=0;i<r;i++)
   {
      for(j=0;j<c;j++)
         tp_mat[j][i] = mat[i][j];
   }
   display_matrix(tp_mat, r, c);
}

void display_matrix(int mat[2][2], int r,
   int c)
```

```
{
  int i, j;
  for(i=0;i<r;i++)
  {
     printf("\n");
     for(j=0;j<c;j++)
        printf("\t mat[%d][%d] = %d", i, j,
               mat[i][j]);
  }
}
```

Output

```
******* MAIN MENU ********
1. Read the two matrices
2. Add the matrices
3. Multiply the matrices
4. Transpose the matrix
5. EXIT
Enter your option: 1
Enter the number of rows and columns of the
matrix:  2 2
Enter the first matrix:
mat[0][0] = 1    mat[0][1] = 2
mat[1][0] = 3    mat[1][0] = 4
Enter the second matrix :
mat[0][0] = 2    mat[0][0] = 3
mat[0][0] = 4    mat[0][0] = 5
******* MAIN MENU ********
1. Read the two matrices
2. Add the matrices
3. Multiply the matrices
4. Transpose the matrix
5. EXIT
Enter your option: 2
mat[0][0] = 3    mat[0][0] = 5
mat[0][0] = 7    mat[0][0] = 9
......
```

5.33 Write a program to fill a square matrix with value zero on the diagonals, 1 on the upper right triangle, and –1 on the lower left triangle.

```
#include <stdio.h>
#include <conio.h>
void read_matrix(int mat[5][5], int);
void display_matrix(int mat[5][5], int);
int main()
{
  int row;
  int mat1[5][5], mat2[5][5];
  clrscr();
  printf("\n Enter the number of rows and
  columns of the matrix ");
  scanf("%d", &row);
  read_matrix(mat1, row);
  display_matrix(mat1, row);
  getch();
  return 0;
}

void read_matrix(int mat[5][5], int r)
{
  int i, j;
  for(i = 0;i < r;i++)
  {
    for(j = 0;j < r;j++)
    {
      if(i==j)
        mat[i][j] = 0;
      if(i>j)
        mat[i][j] = -1;
      else if [i > j]
        mat[i][j] = 1;
    }
  }
}
void display_matrix(int mat[5][5], int r)
{
  int i, j;
  for(i=0;i<r;i++)
  {
    printf("\n");
    for(j=0;j<r;j++)
      printf("\t mat[%d][%d] = %d", i, j,
             mat[i][j]);
  }
}
```

Output

```
Enter the number of rows and columns of
the matrix: 2
 0   1
-1   0
```

5.11 MULTIDIMENSIONAL ARRAYS

A multidimensional array in simple terms is an array of arrays. Like we have one index in a one-dimensional array, two indices in a two-dimensional array, in the same way we have n indices in a, n-dimensional array or multi-dimensional array. Conversely, an n-dimensional array is specified using n indices. An n-dimensional $m_1 \times m_2 \times m_3 \times ... m_n$ array is a collection $m_1 * m_2 * m_3 * ... * m_n$ elements. In a multi-dimensional array, a particular element is specified by using n subscripts as $A[I_1][I_2][I_3]...[I_n]$, where,

$I_1 <= M_1 \quad I_2 < = M_2 \quad I_3 <= M_3 \ldots\ldots \quad I_n <= M_n$

A multi-dimensional array can contain as many indices as needed and the requirement of the memory increases with the number of indices used. However, practically speaking we will hardly use more than three indices in any program. Figure 5.32 shows a three-dimensional array. The array has three pages, four rows, and two columns.

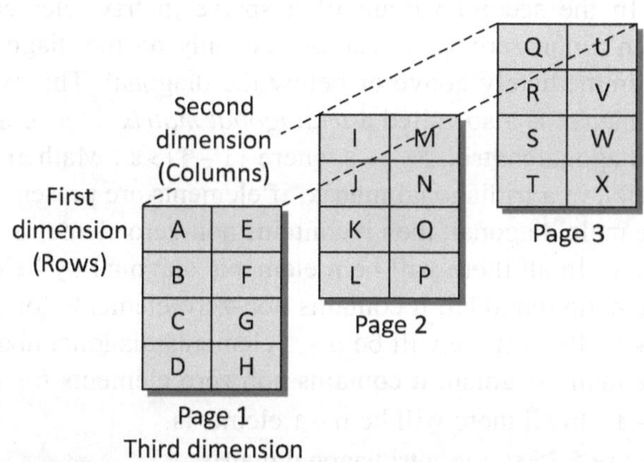

Figure 5.32 Three-dimensional array

A multi-dimensional array is declared and initialized similar to one- and two-dimensional arrays.

Example 5.8 Consider a three-dimensional array defined as int A[2][2][3]. Calculate the number of elements in the array. Also give the memory representation of the array in row major order and column major order.

> **Note** A three-dimensional array consists of pages. Each page in turn contains m rows and n columns.

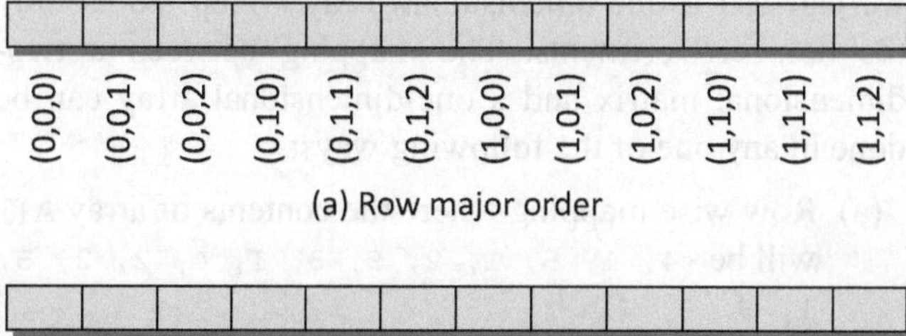

(a) Row major order

(b) Column major order

The three-dimensional array will contain 2 × 2 × 3 = 12 elements.

5.34 Write a program to read and display a 2 × 2 × 2 array.

```
#include <stdio.h>
#include <conio.h>
int main()
{
   int array1[2][2][2], i, j, k;
   clrscr();

   printf("\n Enter the elements of the
         matrix");
   printf("\n ******************************");
   for(i = 0;i < 2;i++)
   {
     for(j = 0;j < 2;j++)
     {
       for(k = 0;k < 2;k++)
       {
         printf("\n array[%d][ %d][ %d]
                = ", i, j, k);
         scanf("%d", &array1[i][j][k]);
       }
     }
   }
   printf("\n The matrix is: ");
   printf("\n ******************************");
   for(i = 0;i < 2;i++)
   {
     printf("\n\n");
     for(j = 0;j < 2;j++)
     {
       printf("\n");
       for(k = 0;k < 2;k++)
   printf("\tarray[%d][%d] %d] = %d", i, j,
         k, array1[i][j][k]);
     }
   }
   getch();
   return 0;
}
```

Output

```
Enter the elements of the matrix
******************************
1 2 3 4 5 6 7 8
arr[0][0][0] = 1          arr[0][0][1] = 2
arr[0][1][0] = 3          arr[0][1][1] = 4
arr[1][0][0] = 5          arr[1][0][1] = 6
arr[1][1][0] = 7          arr[1][1][1] = 8
```

5.12 SPARSE MATRICES

Sparse matrix is a matrix that has many elements with a value zero. In order to efficiently utilize the memory, specialized algorithms and data structures that take advantage of the sparse structure of the matrix should be used. If we apply operations using standard matrix structures and algorithms to sparse matrices, then execution will slow down and the matrix will consume large amounts of memory. Sparse data can be easily compressed which in turn can significantly reduce memory usage.

Basically, there are two types of sparse matrices. In the first type of sparse matrix, all elements above the main diagonal have a value zero. This type of sparse matrix is also called a *lower triangular matrix* because if you see it pictorially, all the elements with a non-zero value appear below the diagonal. In a lower triangular matrix, $A_{i,j} = 0$ where `i >= j`. An `n` × `n` lower triangular matrix `A` has one `non zero` element in the first row, two non-zero element, in the second row and likewise, `n` non-zero elements in the nth row. Figure 5.33 shows a lower triangular matrix.

$$\begin{bmatrix} 1 & & & & \\ 5 & 3 & & & \\ 2 & 7 & 1 & & \\ 3 & 1 & 4 & 2 & \\ 9 & 2 & 8 & 1 & 7 \end{bmatrix}$$

Figure 5.33 Lower triangular matrix

To store the lower triangular matrix efficiently in memory, we can use a one-dimensional array which stores only the non-zero elements. The mapping between a two-dimensional matrix and a one-dimensional array can be done in any one of the following ways:

(a) Row wise mapping—here the contents of array `A[]` will be `{1, 5, 3, 2, 7, -1, 3, 1, 4, 2, -9, 2, -8, 1, 7}`

(b) Column wise mapping—here the contents of array `A[]` will be `{1, 5, 2, 3, -9, 3, 7, 1, 2, -1, 4, -8, 2, 1, 7}`

Like a lower triangular matrix, we also have an *upper triangular matrix* in which $A_{i,j} = 0$ where `i<=j`. An `n` × `n` upper triangular matrix A has n non zero element in the first row, `n-1` non zero element in the second row and likewise, `1` non zero elements in the nth row. Figure 5.34 shows an upper triangular matrix.

$$\begin{bmatrix} 1 & 2 & 3 & 4 & 5 \\ & 3 & 6 & 7 & 8 \\ & & -1 & 9 & 1 \\ & & & 9 & 3 \\ & & & & 7 \end{bmatrix}$$

Figure 5.34 Upper triangular matrix

In the second variant of a sparse matrix, elements with a non-zero value can appear only on the diagonal or immediately above or below the diagonal. This type of matrix is also called a *tridiagonal matrix*. Hence in a tridiagonal matrix, $A_{i,j} = 0$ where `|i - j| > 1`. Mathematically, in a tridiagonal matrix, if elements are present on the main diagonal, then it contains non-zero elements for `i = j`. In all there will be n elements diagonal by below the main diagonal, it contains non-zero elements for `i = j + 1`. In all there will be `n - 1` elements diagonal above the main diagonal, it contains non zero elements for `i = j - 1`. In all there will be `n - 1` elements.
Figure 5.35 shows a tridiagonal matrix.

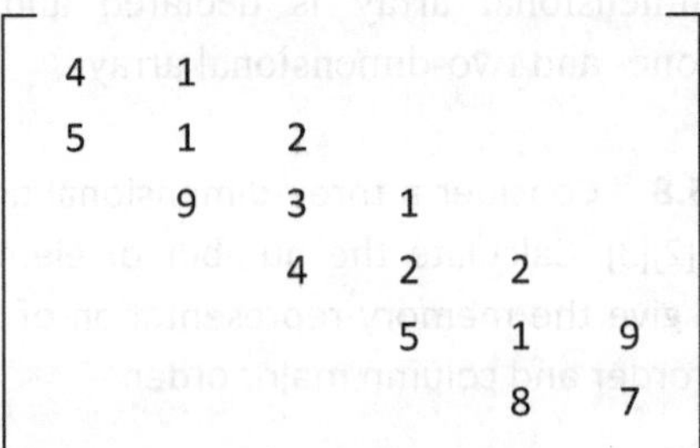

Figure 5.35 Tridiagonal matrix

To store the tridiagonal matrix efficiently in memory, we can use a one-dimensional array which stores only the non-zero elements. The mapping between a two-dimensional matrix and a one-dimensional array can be done in any one of the following ways:

(a) Row wise mapping—here the contents of array `A[]` will be `{4, 1, 5, 1, 2, 9, 3, 1, 4, 2, 2, 5, 1, 9, 8, 7}`

(b) Column wise mapping—here the contents of array `A[]` will be `{4, 5, 1, 1, 9, 2, 3, 4, 1, 2, 5, 2, 1, 8, 9, 7}`

(c) Diagonal wise mapping—here the contents of array `A[]` will be `{5, 9, 4, 5, 8, 4, 1, 3, 2, 1, 7, 1, 2, 1, 2, 9}`

POINTS TO NOTE

- An array is a collection of similar data elements of the same data type.
- The elements of the array are stored in consecutive memory locations and are referenced by an index (also known as the subscript). Subscript indicates an ordinal number of the elements counted from the beginning of the array.
- Declaring an array means specifying three things: data type, name, and its size.
- The name of the array is a symbolic reference for the address of the first byte of the array. Therefore, whenever we use the array name, we are actually referring to the first byte of that array. The index specifies an offset from the beginning of the array to the element being referenced.
- A two-dimensional array is specified using two subscripts where one subscript denotes row and the other denotes column. C considers the two-dimensional array as an array of a one-dimensional array.
- A multi-dimensional array in simple terms is an array of arrays. Like we have one index in a one-dimensional array, two indices in a two-dimensional array, in the same way we have n indices in an n-dimensional or multi-dimensional array. Conversely, an n-dimensional array is specified using n indices.
- Sparse matrix is a matrix that has many elements with a value zero. Basically, there are two types of sparse matrices. In the first type of sparse matrix, all elements above the main diagonal have a value zero. This type of sparse matrix is called a lower triangular matrix.
- In the second variant of a sparse matrix, elements with a non-zero value can appear only on the diagonal or immediately above or below the diagonal. This type of sparse matrix is called a tri-diagonal matrix.

GLOSSARY

Array An array is a collection of similar data elements.

Array index Location of an item in an array.

Binary search Search a sorted array by repeatedly dividing the search interval in half. Begin with an interval covering the whole array. If the value of the search key is less than the item in the middle of the interval, narrow the interval to the lower half. Otherwise narrow it to the upper half. Repeatedly check until the value is found or the interval is empty.

k-dimensional array An array with exactly *k* orthogonal axes or *k* dimensions.

Linear search Search an array by checking elements one at a time.

Lower triangular matrix A matrix A_{ij} forms a lower triangular when $i \geq j$.

Matrix A two-dimensional array in which the first index is the row and the second index is the column.

One-dimensional array An array with one dimension or one subscript/index.

Rectangular matrix An $n \times m$ matrix whose size may not be the same in both dimensions.

Sparse matrix A matrix that has relatively few non-zero elements.

Three-dimensional array An array with three dimensions or three subscripts/indices.

Two-dimensional array An array with two dimensions or two subscripts/indices.

Upper triangular matrix A matrix A_{ij} forms an upper triangular when $i \leq j$.

EXERCISES

Fill in the Blanks

1. An array is a ________.
2. Every element is accessed using a ________.
3. An expression that evaluates to an ________ value may be used as an index.
4. The elements of an array are stored in ________ memory locations.
5. An n-dimensional array contains ________ subscripts.
6. Name of the array acts as a ________.
7. Declaring an array means specifying the ________, ________ and ________.

EXERCISES

8. The subscript or the index represents the offset from the beginning of the array to _________.
9. _________ is used to access an element in the array.
10. _________ is the address of the first element in the array.
11. Length of the array is given by the number of _________.
12. _________ means accessing each element of the array for a specific purpose.
13. Performance of the linear search algorithm can be improved by using a _________.
14. The complexity of linear search algorithm is _________.
15. An array occupies _________ memory locations.
16. An array name is often known to be a _________ pointer.
17. A multi-dimensional array in simple terms is an _________.
18. arr[3] = 10; initializes the _________ element of the array with value 10.
19. The _________ search locates the value by starting at the beginning of the array and moving towards its end.

Multiple-Choice Questions

1. If an array is declared as `arr[] = {1,3,5,7,9};` then what is the value of sizeof(arr[ ])?

   (a) 10 (b) 20
   (c) 30 (d) 40
2. If an array is declared as arr[] = {1,3,5,7,9}; then what is the value of arr[3]?

   (a) 1 (b) 7
   (c) 9 (d) 5
3. If an array is declared as double arr[50], how many bytes will be allocated to it?

   (a) 50 (b) 100
   (c) 200 (d) 400
4. If an array is declared as int arr[50], how many elements can it hold?

   (a) 49 (b) 50
   (c) 51 (d) 0
5. If an array is declared as int arr[5][5], how many elements can it store?

   (a) 5 (b) 25
   (c) 10 (d) 0
6. The worst case complexity is _____ when compared with the average case complexity of a binary search algorithm.

   (a) equal (b) greater
   (c) less (d) none of these
7. The complexity of binary search algorithm is

   (a) O(n) (b) $O(n^2)$
   (c) O(n log n) (d) O(log n)
8. In linear search, when VAL is equal to the first element of the array, which case is it?

   (a) worst case (b) average case
   (c) best case (d) amortized case
9. Given an integer array, arr[]; the ith element can be accessed by writing

   (a) (arr+i) (b) *(i + arr)
   (c) arr[i] (d) all of these

State True or False

1. An array is used to refer to multiple memory locations having the same name.
2. An array need not be declared before being used.
3. An array contains elements of the same data type.
4. A loop is used to access all the elements of the array.
5. All the elements of the array are automatically initialized to zero when the array is defined.
6. An array stores all its data elements in non-consecutive memory location.
7. To copy an array, you must copy the value of every element of the first array into the element of the second array.
8. Lower bound is the index of the last element in the array.
9. Merged array contains contents of the first array followed by the contents of the second array.
10. Binary search is also called sequential search.
11. Linear search is performed on a sorted array.
12. Binary search is the best searching algorithm for all types of arrays.
13. It is possible to pass entire array as a function argument.
14. arr[i] is equivalent to writing *(arr+i).

EXERCISES

15. Array name is equivalent to the address of its last element.
16. When an array is passed to a function, C passes the value for each element.
17. When an array is passed to a function, it is always passed by call-by-reference method.
18. Linear search can be used to search a value in any array.
19. Linear search is recommended for small arrays.
20. A two-dimensional array is nothing but an array of one-dimensional arrays.
21. A two-dimensional array contains data of two different types.
22. When an array is declared, all its elements are automatically initialized to zero.
23. A char type variable can be used as a subscript in an array.
24. By default, the first subscript of the array is zero.
25. A long int value can be used as an array subscript.
26. The maximum number of dimensions that an array can have is 4.

Review Questions

1. Why are arrays needed?
2. What does array name signify?
3. How is an array represented in memory?
4. How is a two-dimensional array represented in memory?
5. How can arrays be used for inter-function communication?
6. How are multi-dimensional arrays useful?
7. What happens when an array is initialized with
   (a) fewer initializers as compared to its size?
   (b) more initializers as compared to its size?
8. Explain sparse matrix.
9. Why does storing of sparse matrices need extra consideration? How are sparse matrices stored efficiently in the computer's memory?
10. For an array declared as int arr[50], calculate the address of arr[35], if Base(arr) = 1000 and w=2.
11. Consider a 10 X 5 two dimensional array `Marks` which has base address = 2000 and the number of words per memory location of the array = 2. Now compute the address of the element- `Marks[8, 5]` assuming that the elements are stored in row major order.
12. Given an array, int arr[] = {9, 18, 27, 36, 45, 54, 63, 72, 81, 90, 99}; Trace the steps of binary search algorithm to find value 90 and 17 from the array.
13. Which technique of searching an element in the array do you prefer to use and in which situation?
14. Write a program which deletes all duplicate elements from the array.
15. Write a program that tests the equality of two one-dimensional arrays.
16. Write a program that reads an array of 100 integers. Display all pairs of elements whose sum is 50.
17. Write a program to input an array of 10 numbers and swap the value of the largest and smallest number.
18. Write a program to interchange second element with the second last element.
19. Write a program that calculates the sum of squares of the elements.
20. Write a program to calculate the number of duplicate entries in the array.
21. Write a program to arrange the values of an array in such a way that even numbers precede the odd numbers.
22. Given a sorted array of integers; calculate the sum, mean, variance and standard deviation of the numbers in the array.
23. Write a program to compute the sum and mean of the elements of a two-dimensional array.
24. Write a program to read and display a 3X3 matrix.
25. Write a program to transpose a 3X3 matrix.
26. Write a program that computes the sum of elements that are stored on the main diagonal of a matrix using pointers.
27. Write a program to count the total number of non-zero elements in a two-dimensional array.
28. Write a program to read and display an array of 10 floating point numbers.
29. Write a program to read and display an array of 10 floating point numbers using functions.
30. Write a program to read an array of 10 floating point numbers. Display the mean of these numbers till two decimal places.
31. Write a program to read an array of 10 floating point numbers. Display the position of the largest number.

EXERCISES

32. Write a program to read an array of 10 floating point numbers. Display the smallest number and its position in the array.
33. Write a program to input the elements of a two-dimensional array. Then from this array make two arrays—one that stores all odd elements of the two-dimensional array and the other stores all even elements of the array.
34. Write a program to merge two integer arrays. Also display the merged array in reverse order.
35. Write a program to transpose a 3X3X3 matrix.
36. Write a program to multiply two mXn matrices.
37. Write a menu driven program to add, subtract, and transpose two matrices.
38. Write a program that reads a matrix and displays the sum of its diagonal elements.
39. Write a program that reads a matrix and displays the sum of the elements above the main diagonal.

    Hint: Calculate sum of elements of array A, where A_{ij} *and i<j*
40. Write a program that reads a matrix and displays the sum of the elements below the main diagonal.

    Hint: Calculate sum of elements of array A, where A_{ij} *and i>j*

    Hint: Calculate sum of elements of array A where A_{ij} *and i>j*
41. Write a program that reads a square matrix of size n x n. Write a function

    `int is Upper Triangular(int a[] [], int n)` that returns 1 if the matrix is upper triangular.

    Hint: Array A is upper triangular if A_{ij}*= 0 for i>j*
42. Write a program that reads a square matrix of size nxn. Write a function

    `int is Lower Triangular(int a[] [], int n)` that returns 1 if the matrix is lower triangular.

    Hint: Array A is lower triangular if A_{ij}*= 0 for i<j*
43. Write a program that reads a square matrix of size nxn. Write a function `int isSymmetric(int a[] [], int n)` that returns 1 if the matrix is upper triangular.

    Hint: Array A is symmetric if A_{ij}*=* A_{ji} *for all values of i and j*
44. Write a program to calculate XA + YB where A and B are matrices and X = 2 and Y = 3.
45. Write a program to find a given number from an unsorted array.
46. Write a program to find a given number from a sorted array.
47. Write a program to read an array of 10 floating point numbers. Display the position of the second largest number.
48. Write a program to enter five single digit numbers in an array. Form a number using the array elements.
49. Write a program to find whether number 3 is present in the array arr[]= {1,2,3,4,5,6,7,8}.
50. Write a program to read a floating point array. Update the array to insert a new number at the specified location.
51. Write a program to read a sorted floating point array. Update the array to insert a new number.
52. Write a program to read a floating point array. Update the array to delete the number from the specified location.
53. Write a program to read a sorted floating point array. Update the array to delete the given number.
54. Modify the linear search program so that it operates on a sorted array.
55. Write a program to build an array of 100 random numbers in the range 1 to 100. Perform the following operations on the array:
    (a) Count the number of elements that are completely divisible by 3.
    (b) Display the elements of the array by displaying a maximum of 10 elements in one line.
    (c) Display only the even elements of the array by displaying a maximum of 10 elements in one line.
    (d) Count the number of odd elements.
    (e) Find the smallest element in the array.
    (f) Find the position of the largest value in the array.
56. Write a program to read two floating point arrays. Merge these arrays and display the resultant array.
57. Write a program to read two sorted floating point arrays. Merge these arrays and display the resultant array.
58. How can one-dimensional array be used for inter-process communication?
59. Write a program to read and display a p*q*r array.
60. Write a program to initialize all diagonal elements of a two-dimensional array to zero.

61. Consider a 10 X 10 two-dimensional array which has base address = 1000 and the number of words per memory location of the array = 2. Now compute the address of the element arr[8][5] assuming that the elements are stored in row major order. Then calculate the same assuming the elements are stored in column major order.
62. Consider an array MARKS[20][5] which stores the marks obtained by 20 students in 5 subjects. Now write a program to
    (a) find the average marks obtained in each subject
    (b) find the average marks obtained by every student
    (c) find the number of students who have scored below 50 in their average
    (d) display the scores obtained by every student
63. Consider the array given below:

Adam	Charles	Dicken	Esha	Georgia	Hillary	Mishael
Name[0]	Name[1]	Name[2]	Name[3]	Name[4]	Name[5]	Name[6]

(a) How many elements would be moved if the name Andrew has to be added in it?
    (i) 7 (ii) 4
    (iii) 5 (iv) 6

(b) How many elements would be moved if the name Esha has to be deleted from it?
    (i) 3 (ii) 4
    (iii) 5 (iv) 6

(c) How many comparisons need to be made to search for the name Hillary?
    (i) 3 (ii) 4
    (iii) 5 (iv) 6

Program Output

Identify errors, if any, in the following declaration statements.

(a) int marks(10);
(b) int marks[10, 5];
(c) int marks[10],[5];
(d) int marks[10];
(e) int marks[ ];
(f) int marks[10] [5];
(g) int marks[9+1][6-1];

Identify errors, if any, in the following initialization statements.

(a) int marks[ ] = {0,0,0,0};
(b) int marks[2][3] = {10,20,30,40};
(c) int marks[2,3] = {10, 20,30},{40,50,60}};
(d) int marks[10]={0};

Find out the output of the following codes.

1.
```
#include <stdio.h>
    main()
{
    int i, arr[10];
    for(i=0;i<10;i++)
        arr[i*2] = 1;
    for(i=0;i<10;i++)
        arr[i*2+1] = -1;
    for(i=0;i<10;i++)
        printf("\t %d", arr[i]);
    return 0;
}
```

2.
```
#include <stdio.h>
main()
{
    int arr[]={0,1,2,0,1,2,0,1,2};
    printf("\\n %d",arr[3]);
    printf("\\n %d",arr[arr[3]]);
    printf("\\n %d",arr[arr[3]+arr[1]]);
    printf("\\n %d",
    arr[arr[arr[arr[1]]]]);
    return 0;
}
```

3.
```
#include <stdio.h>
main()
{
    int arr1[]={0,1,2,0,1,2,0,1,2,0};
    int i, arr2[10];
    for(i=0;i<10;i++)
        arr2[i] = arr1[9-i];
    for(i=0;i<10;i++)
        printf("\t %d", arr2[i]);
    return 0;
}
```

ANNEXURE 4

A4.1 INTRODUCTION TO SORTING

The term *sorting* means arranging the elements of the array in some relevant order which may either be ascending or descending, i.e., if A is an array, then the elements of A are arranged in sorted order (ascending order) in such a way that, `A[0] < A[1] < A[2] < ... < A[N]`.

For example, if we have an array that is declared and initialized as,

```
int A[] = {21, 34, 11, 9, 1, 0, 22};
```

Then the sorted array (ascending order) can be given as,

```
A[] = {0, 1, 9, 11, 21, 22, 34}.
```

A *sorting algorithm* is defined as an algorithm that puts elements of a list in a certain order (that can either be numerical, lexicographical, or any user-defined order).

A4.2 BUBBLE SORT

Bubble sort is a very simple method that sorts the array elements by repeatedly moving the largest element to the highest index position of the array (case of arranging elements in ascending order). In bubble sorting, consecutive adjacent pairs of elements in the array are compared with each other. If the element at the lower index is greater than the element at the higher index, the two elements are interchanged so that the smaller element is placed before the bigger one. This process is continued till the list of unsorted elements gets exhausted.

This procedure of sorting is called bubble sorting because the smaller elements 'bubble' to the top of the list. At the end of the first pass, the largest element in the list will be placed at the end of the list. Bubble sort is also referred to as sinking sort.

If the elements are to be sorted in descending order, then with each pass the smallest element is moved to the lowest index of the array.

Bubble Sort Example

To discuss the bubble sort let us consider an array that has the following elements:

```
A[] = {30, 52, 29, 87, 63, 27, 18, 54}
```

Pass 1:

(a) Compare 30 and 52. Since 30 < 52, then no swapping is done.

(b) Compare 52 and 29. Since 52 > 29, swapping is done. 30, **29, 52,** 87, 63, 27, 19, 54

(c) Compare 52 and 87. Since 52 < 87, no swapping is done.

(d) Compare, 87 and 63. Since, 87 > 83, swapping is done. 30, 29, 52, **63, 87**, 27, 19, 54

(e) Compare 87 and 27. Since 87 > 27, swapping is done. 30, 29, 52, 63, **27, 87**, 19, 54

(f) Compare 87 and 19. Since 87 > 19, swapping is done. 30, 29, 52, 63, 27, 19, 87, 54

(g) Compare 87 and 54. Since 87 > 54, swapping is done. 30, 29, 52, 63, 27, 19, **54, 87**

Observe that after the end of the first pass, the largest element is placed at the highest index of the array. All the other elements are still unsorted.

Pass 2:

(a) Compare 30 and 29. Since 30 > 29, swapping is done. **29, 30**, 52, 63, 27, 19, 54, 87

(b) Compare 30 and 52. Since 30 < 52, no swapping is done.

(c) Compare 52 and 63. Since 52 < 63, no swapping is done.

(d) Compare 63 and 27. Since 63 > 27, swapping is done. 29, 30, 52, **27, 63**, 19, 54, 87

(e) Compare 63 and 19. Since 63 > 19, swapping is done. 29, 30, 52, 27, **19, 63**, 54, 87

(f) Compare 63 and 54. Since 63 > 54, swapping is done. 29, 30, 52, 27, 19, **54, 63**, 87

Observe that after the end of the second pass, the second largest element is placed at the second highest index of the array. All the other elements are still unsorted.

Pass 3:

(a) Compare 29 and 30. Since 29 < 30, no swapping is done.

(b) Compare 30 and 52. Since 30 < 52, no swapping is done.

(c) Compare 52 and 27. Since 52 > 27, swapping is done. 29, 30, **27, 52**, 19, 54, 63, 87

(d) Compare 52 and 19. Since 52 > 19, swapping is done. 29, 30, 27, **19, 52**, 54, 63, 87

(e) Compare 52 and 54. Since 52 < 54, no swapping is done.

Observe that after the end of the third pass, the third largest element is placed at the third highest index of the array. All the other elements are still unsorted.

Pass 4:

(a) Compare 29 and 30. Since 29 < 30, no swapping is done.

(b) Compare 30 and 27. Since 30 > 27, swapping is done.
29, **27, 30**, 19, 52, 54, 63, 87

(c) Compare 30 and 19. Since 30 > 19, swapping is done.
29, 27, **19, 30**, 52, 54, 63, 87

(d) Compare 30 and 52. Since 30 < 52, no swapping is done.

Observe that after the end of the fourth pass, the fourth largest element is placed at the fourth highest index of the array. All the other elements are still unsorted.

Pass 5:

(a) Compare 29 and 27. Since 29 > 27, swapping is done.
27, 29, 19, 30, 52, 54, 63, 87

(b) Compare 29 and 19. Since 29 > 19, swapping is done.
27, **19, 29**, 30, 52, 54, 63, 87

(c) Compare 29 and 30. Since 29 < 30, no swapping is done.

Observe that after the end of the fifth pass, the fifth largest element is placed at the fifth highest index of the array. All the other elements are still unsorted.

Pass 6:

(a) Compare 27 and 19. Since 27 > 19, swapping is done.
19, 27, 29, 30, 52, 54, 63, 87

(b) Compare 27 and 29. Since 27 < 29, no swapping is done.

Observe that after the end of the sixth pass, the sixth largest element is placed at the sixth largest index of the array. All the other elements are still unsorted.

Pass 7:

(a) Compare 19 and 27. Since 19 < 27, no swapping is done.

Observe that the entire list is sorted now.

A4.1 Write a program to enter n numbers in an array. Redisplay the array with elements being sorted in ascending order.

```
#include <stdio.h>
#include <conio.h>
int main()
{
  int i, n, temp, j, arr [10];
  clrscr();
  printf("\n Enter the number of elements
  in the array: ");
  scanf("%d", &n);
  printf("\n Enter the elements ");
  for(i = 0;i < n;i++)
     scanf("%d", &arr [i]);
  for(i = 0;i < n;i++)
  {
     for(j = 0;j < n-i;j++)
     {
     if(arr [j] > arr [j+1])
     {
     temp = arr [j];
     arr [j] = arr [j+1];
     arr [j+1] = temp;
     }
     }
  }
  printf("\n The array sorted in ascending
  order is: \n");
  for(i = 0;i < n;i++)
     printf("\t %d", i, arr[i]);
  getch();
  return 0;
}
```

Output

```
Enter the number of elements in the
array: 6
Enter the elements 27 72 36 63 45 54
The array sorted in ascending order is:
27 36 45 54 63 72
```

A4.3 INSERTION SORT

Insertion sort is a very simple sorting algorithm, in which the sorted array (or list) is built one element at a time. We all are familiar with this technique of sorting as we usually use it for ordering a deck of cards while playing bridge.

The main idea behind insertion sort is that it inserts each item into its proper place in the final list. To save memory, most implementations of the insertion sort algorithm work by moving the current data element past the already sorted values and repeatedly interchanging it with the preceding value until it is in its correct place.

Although insertion sort is less efficient when compared with other more advanced algorithms such as quick sort, heap sort, and merge sort, we will still read about its technique to gain an understanding of the subject.

The Technique

Insertion sort works as follows:

- The array of values to be sorted is divided into two sets. One that stores sorted values and the other contains unsorted values.
- The sorting algorithm will proceed until there are elements in the unsorted set.
- Suppose there are n elements in the array. Initially the element with index 0 (assuming `LB, Lower Bound = 0`) is in the sorted set, rest of the elements are in the unsorted set.
- The first element of the unsorted partition has array index 1 (if `LB = 0`).
- During each iteration of the algorithm, the first element in the unsorted set is picked up and inserted into the correct position in the sorted set.

Example A4.1 Consider an array of integers given below. Sort the values in the array using insertion sort.

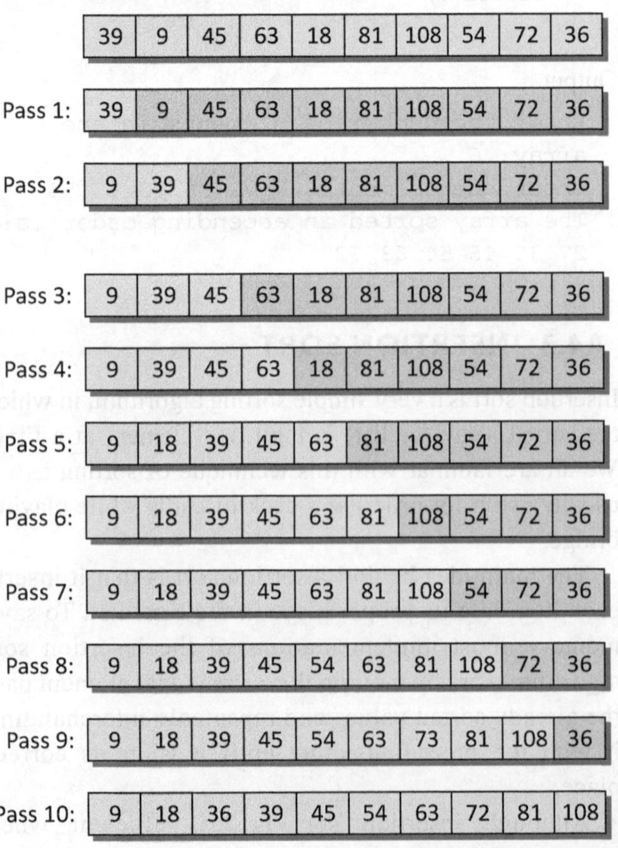

	39	9	45	63	18	81	108	54	72	36
Pass 1:	39	9	45	63	18	81	108	54	72	36
Pass 2:	9	39	45	63	18	81	108	54	72	36
Pass 3:	9	39	45	63	18	81	108	54	72	36
Pass 4:	9	39	45	63	18	81	108	54	72	36
Pass 5:	9	18	39	45	63	81	108	54	72	36
Pass 6:	9	18	39	45	63	81	108	54	72	36
Pass 7:	9	18	39	45	63	81	108	54	72	36
Pass 8:	9	18	39	45	54	63	81	108	72	36
Pass 9:	9	18	39	45	54	63	73	81	108	36
Pass 10:	9	18	36	39	45	54	63	72	81	108

In Pass 1, `A[0]` is the only element in the sorted set. In Pass 2, `A[1]` will be placed either before or after `A[0]`, so that the array `A` is sorted. In Pass 3, `A[2]` will be placed either before `A[0]`, in-between `A[0]` and `A[1]` or after `A[1]`, so that the array is sorted. In Pass 4, `A[4]` will be placed in its proper place so that the array `A` is sorted. In Pass N, A[N–1] will be placed in its proper place so that the array A is sorted.

Therefore, to insert the element `A[K]` in the sorted list `A[0], A[1], ...., A[K-1]`, we need to compare `A[K]` with `A[K-1]`, then with `A[K-2]`, then with `A[K-3]` until we meet an element `A[J]` such that `A[J] <= A[K]`.

In order to insert `A[K]` in its correct position, we need to move each element `A[K-1]`, `A[K-2]`, ..., `A[J]` by one position and then `A[K]` is inserted at the `(J+1)`th location. The algorithm for insertion sort is given in Fig. A 4.1.

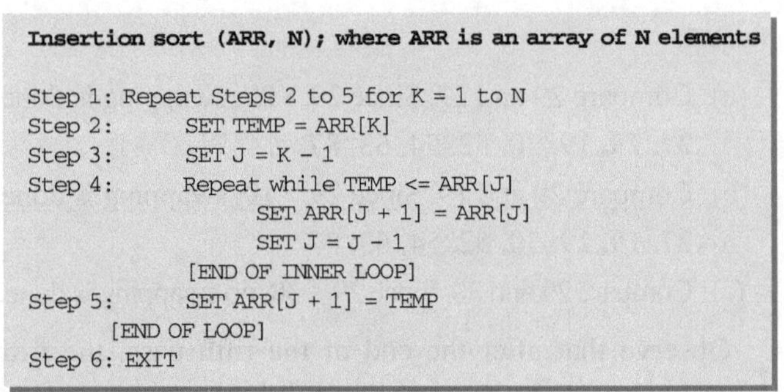

```
Insertion sort (ARR, N); where ARR is an array of N elements

Step 1: Repeat Steps 2 to 5 for K = 1 to N
Step 2:        SET TEMP = ARR[K]
Step 3:        SET J = K - 1
Step 4:        Repeat while TEMP <= ARR[J]
                      SET ARR[J + 1] = ARR[J]
                      SET J = J - 1
                  [END OF INNER LOOP]
Step 5:        SET ARR[J + 1] = TEMP
               [END OF LOOP]
Step 6: EXIT
```

Figure A4.1 Algorithm for insertion sort

In the algorithm, Step 1 executes a `for` loop which will be repeated for each element in the array. In Step 2, we store the value of `K`th element in `TEMP`. In Step 3, we set the `J`th index in array. In Step 4, a `for` loop is executed that will create space for the new element from the unsorted list to be stored in the list of sorted elements. Finally, in Step 5, the element is stored at the `J`th location.

Advantages of Insertion Sort

The advantages of this sorting algorithm are as follows:

- Easy to implement.
- Efficient to use on small sets of data.
- Efficient implementation on data sets that are already substantially sorted.
- Performs better than algorithms such as selection sort and bubble sort. Insertion sort algorithm is much simpler than the shell sort, with only a small trade-off in efficiency. While, the insertion sort is twice as

fast as the bubble sort, it is almost 40% faster than the selection sort.

- Requires less memory space.
- Considered to be online as it can sort a list as and when it receives new elements.

A4.2 Write a program to sort an array ARR using insertion sort algorithm.

```
#include <stdio.h>
#include <conio.h>
void insertion_sort(int arr[],int n);
void main()
{
   int arr[10], i, n, j, k;
   clrscr();
   printf("\n Enter the number of elements
   in the array: ");
   scanf("%d", &n);
   printf("\n Enter the elements of the
   array");
   for(i = 0;i < n;i++)
   {
      printf("\n arr[%d] = ", i);
      scanf("%d", &arr[i]);
   }
   insertion_sort(arr,n);
   printf("\n The sorted array is: \n");
   for(i = 0;i < 10;i++)
      printf("%d\t", arr[i]);
   getch();
}
void insertion_sort(int arr[], int n)
{
   int i, j, temp;
   for(i = 0;i < n;i++)
   {
      temp = arr[i];
      j = i-1;
      while((temp < arr[j]) && (j>=0))
      {
      arr[j+1] = arr[j];
      j--;
      }
      arr[j+1] = temp;
   }
}
```

Output

```
Enter the number of elements in the array: 6
Enter the elements of the array 27 72 36 63
45 54
The sorted array is:
27 36 45 54 63 72
```

A4.4 SELECTION SORT

Selection sort is a sorting algorithm that has quadratic running time complexity given as $O(n^2)$ thereby making it inefficient to be used on large lists. Although, selection sort performs worse than insertion sort algorithm it is noted for its simplicity, and also has performance advantages over more complicated algorithms in certain situations. Selection sort is generally the preferred choice for sorting files with very large objects (records) and small keys.

The Technique

Consider an array `ARR` with `N` elements. The selection sort takes N–1 passes to sort the entire array and works as follows. First find the smallest value in the array and place it in the first position. Then find the second smallest value in the array and place it in the second position. Repeat this procedure until the entire array is sorted. Therefore,

In Pass 1, find the position `POS` of the smallest value in the array and then swap `ARR[POS]` and `ARR[0]`. Thus, `ARR[0]` is sorted.

In Pass 2, find the position `POS` of the smallest value in sub-array of `N-1` elements. Swap `ARR[POS]` with `ARR[1]`. Now, `A[0]` and `A[1]` is sorted.

In Pass 3, find the position `POS` of the smallest value in sub-array of `N–2` elements. Swap `ARR[POS]` with `ARR[2]`. Now `ARR[0]`, `ARR[1]`, and `ARR[2]` is sorted.

In Pass N–1, find the position POS of the smaller of the elements `ARR[N-2]` and `ARR[N-1]`. Swap `ARR[POS]` and `ARR[N-2]` so that `ARR[0]`, `ARR[1]`, …, `ARR[N-1]` is sorted.

The algorithm for selection sort is shown in Fig. A 4.2. In the algorithm, during the Kth pass we need to find the position `POS` of the smallest elements from `ARR[K]`, `ARR[K+1]`, ..., `ARR[N]`. To find the smallest element we will use a variable `SMALL` to hold the smallest value in the sub-array ranging from `ARR[K]` to `ARR[N]`. Then swap `ARR[K]` with `ARR[POS]`. This procedure is repeated until all the elements in the array are sorted.

```
SMALLEST (ARR, K, N, POS)

Step 1: [Initialize] SET SMALL = ARR[K]
Step 2: [Initialize] SET POS = K
Step 3: Repeat for J = K+1 to N
          IF SMALL > ARR[J], then
          SET SMALL = ARR[J]
          SET POS = J
          [END OF IF]
          [END OF LOOP]
Step 4: Exit
```

```
Selection Sort to sort an array ARR with N elements

Step 1: Repeat Steps 2 and 3 for K =1 to N-1
Step 2: CALL SMALLEST(ARR, K, N, POS)
Step 3: SWAP A[K] with ARR[POS]
        [END OF LOOP]
Step 4: Exit
```

Figure A4.2 Algorithm for selection sort

The advantages of the selection sort algorithm are as follows:

- simple and easy to implement
- can be used for small data sets
- 60% more efficient than bubble sort algorithm

The disadvantage is that it is inefficient for large data sets. Insertion sort is considered to be better than selection sort and bubble sort.

A4.3 Write a program to sort an array using selection sort algorithm.

```
#include <stdio.h>
#include <conio.h>
int smallest(int arr[], int k, int n);
void selection_sort(int arr[], int n);
void main()
{
    int arr[10], i, n, j,k;
    clrscr();
    printf("\n Enter the number of elements
    in the array: ");
    scanf("%d", &n);
    printf("\n Enter the elements of the
    array");
    for(i = 0;i < n;i++)
    {
        printf("\n arr[%d] = ", i);
        scanf("%d", &arr[i]);
    }
    selection_sort(arr, n);
    printf("\n The sorted array is: \n");
    for(i = 0;i<n;i++)
        printf("%d\t", arr[i]);
    getch();
}
int smallest(int arr[], int k, int n)
{
    int pos = k, small=arr[k], i;
    for(i = k+1;i < n;i++)
    {
        if(arr[i]< small)
        {
        small = arr[i];
        pos = i;
        }
    }
    return pos;
}
void selection_sort(int arr[],int n)
{
    int k, pos, temp;
    for(k = 0;k < n;k++)
    {
        pos = smallest(arr, k, n);
        temp = arr[k];
        arr[k]  = arr[pos];
        arr[pos]  = temp;
    }
}
```

Output

```
Enter the number of elements in the array: 6
Enter the elements of the array  27 72 36 63
45 54
The sorted array is:
27 36 45 54 63 72
```

Example A4.2 Sort the array given below using selection sort

39	9	81	45	90	27	72	18

PASS	LOC	ARR[0]	ARR[1]	ARR[2]	ARR[3]	ARR[4]	ARR[5]	ARR[6]	ARR[7]
1	1	9	39	81	45	90	27	72	18
2	7	9	18	81	45	90	27	72	39
3	5	9	18	27	45	90	81	72	39
4	7	9	18	27	39	90	81	72	45
5	7	9	18	27	39	45	81	72	90
6	6	9	18	27	39	45	72	81	90

CHAPTER 6

Strings

Takeaways

- Reading and Writing Strings
- Array of Strings
- Suppressing Input
- Strings and Character Functions
- String Operations

6.1 INTRODUCTION

Nowadays, computers are widely used for word processing applications such as creating, inserting, updating, and modifying textual data. Besides this we need to search for a particular pattern within a text, delete it, or replace it with another pattern. So there are actually a lot we as users do to manipulate the textual data.

Programming Tip: Character constants are enclosed in single quotes. String constants are enclosed in double quotes.

In C language, a string is nothing but a null-terminated character array. This means that after the last character, a null character ('\0') is stored to signify the end of the character array. For example, if we write,

```
char str[] = "HELLO";
```

We are declaring a character array that has five usable characters namely, H, E, L, L, and O. Apart from these characters, a null character ('\0') is stored at the end of the string. So, the internal representation of the string becomes HELLO'\0'. To store a string of length 5, we need 5 + 1 locations (1 extra for the null character). The name of the character array (or the string) is a pointer to the beginning of the string. Figure 6.1 shows the difference between character storage and string storage.

If we had declared str as,

```
char str[5] = "HELLO";
```

Then the null character will not be appended automatically to the character array. This is because, str can hold only 5 characters and the characters in HELLO have already filled the space allocated to it.

Note When the compiler assigns a character string to a character array, it automatically appends a null character to the end of the string. Therefore, the size of the string should be equal to maximum number of characters in the string plus one.

Programming Tip: When allocating memory space for a character array, reserve space to hold the null character also.

Like we use subscripts (also known as index) to access the elements of an array, the same subscripts are also used to access the elements of the character array. The subscript starts with a zero (0). All the characters of a string array are stored in successive memory locations. Figure 6.2 shows how str[] is stored in memory.

Thus we see that in simple terms a string is a sequence of characters. In Fig. 6.2, 1000, 1001, 1002, and so on are the memory addresses of individual characters. From the figure, we see that H is stored at memory location 1000

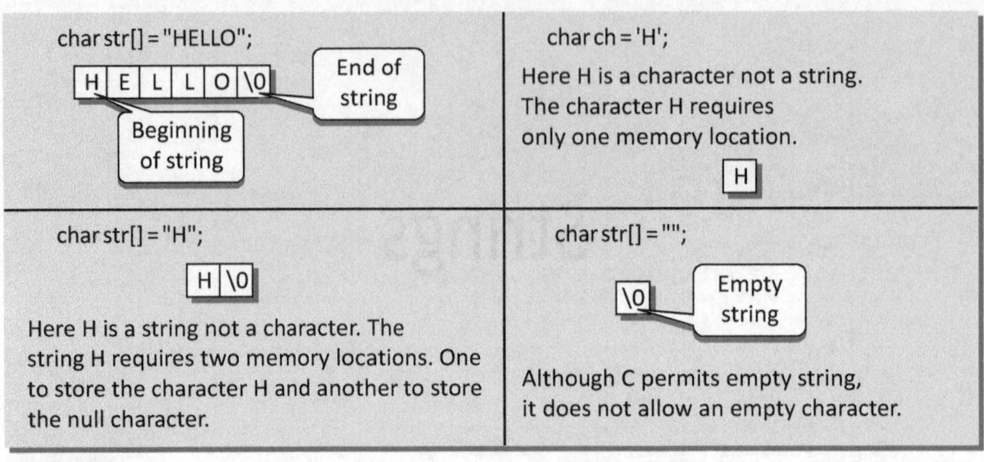

Figure 6.1 Difference between character storage and string storage

but in reality the ASCII codes of characters are stored in memory and not the character itself, i.e., at address `1000`, `72` will be stored the ASCII code for `H` is `72`.

```
char str[] = "HELLO";
```

str[0]	1000	H
str[1]	1001	E
str[2]	1002	L
str[3]	1003	L
str[4]	1004	O
str[5]	1005	\0

Figure 6.2 Memory representation of a character array

The above statement declares a constant string as we have assigned value to it while declaring the string. However, the general form of declaring a string is,

```
char str[size];
```

When we declare the string in this way, we can store `size -1` characters in the array because the last character would be the null character. For example, `char mesg[100];` can store maximum `99` usable characters.

Till now we have seen one way of initializing strings. The other way to initialize a string is to initialize it as an array of characters, like

```
char str[] = {'H', 'E', 'L', 'L', 'O', '\0'};
```

In this example, we have explicitly added the null character. Also observe that we have not mentioned the size of the string (or the character array). Here, the compiler will automatically calculate the size based on the number of elements initialized. So, in this example 6 memory slots will be reserved to store the string variable, `str`.

We can also declare a string with size much larger than the number of elements that are initialized. For example, consider the statement below.

```
char str[10] = "HELLO";
```

In such cases, the compiler creates a character array of size 10; stores the value `"HELLO"` in it and finally terminates the value with a null character. Rest of the elements in the array are automatically initialized to NULL. Figure 6.3 shows the memory representation of such a string.

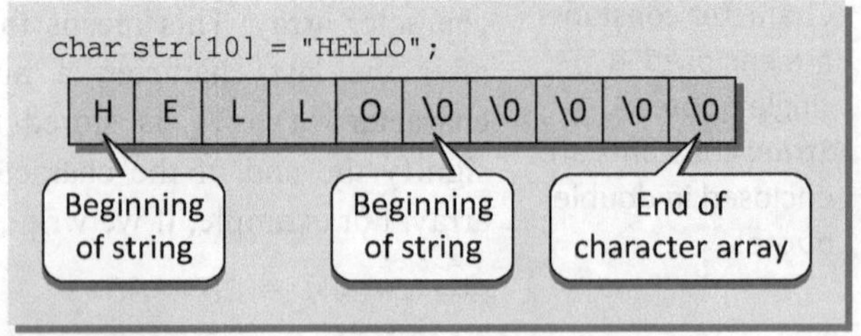

Figure 6.3 Memory representation of a string

However, the following declaration is illegal in C and would generate a compile time error because of two reasons. First, the array is initialized with more elements than it can store. Second, initialization cannot be separated from declaration.

```
char str[3];
str = "HELLO";
```

Note: An array name cannot be used as the left operand of an assignment operator. Therefore, the following statement is illegal in C.

```
char str2, str1[]="HI";
str2 = str1;
```

6.1.1 Reading Strings

If we declare a string by writing

```
char str[100];
```

Then `str` can be read from the user by using three ways:

1. using `scanf` function
2. using `gets()` function
3. using `getchar()`, `getch()`, or `getche()` function repeatedly

The string can be read using `scanf()` by writing

```
scanf("%s", str);
```

Although the syntax of `scanf()` function is well known and easy to use, the main pitfall with this function is that the function terminates as soon as it finds a blank space. For example, if the user enters `Hello World`, then `str` will contain only `Hello`. This is because the moment a blank space is encountered, the string is terminated by the `scanf()` function. You may also specify a field width to indicate the maximum number of characters that can be read in. Remember that extra characters are left unconsumed in the input buffer.

Programming Tip: Using & operand with a string variable in the `scanf` statement is optional as string variable is a character array and denotes the address where the array begins.

Unlike `integer, float,` and `characters, %s` format does not require the ampersand before the variable `str`.

Note: When `scanf()` encounters a white space character, it terminates reading further and appends a null character to the string that has been read. The white space character is left in the input stream and might be mistakenly read by the next `scanf()` statement. So in order to delete the white space character from the input stream, either use a space in the format string before the next conversion code or FLUSH the input stream by using the `fflush` function by writing `fflush(stdin);`.

The next method of reading a string is by using `gets()` function. The string can be read by writing

```
gets(str);
```

`gets()` is a simple function that overcomes the drawbacks of the `scanf()`. The `gets()` takes the starting address of the string which will hold the input. The string inputted using `gets()` is automatically terminated with a `null` character.

Last but not the least, the string can also be read by calling the `getchar()` repeatedly to read a sequence of single characters (unless a terminating character is entered) and simultaneously storing it in a character array as shown below.

```
i=0;
ch=getchar(); // Get a character
while(ch != '*')
{
   str[i] = ch;
      // Store the read character in str
   i++;
   ch=getchar(); // Get another character
}
str[i] = '\0';
   // terminate str with null character
str[i] = '\0';
```

Programming Tip: A compile time error will be generated if a string is assigned to a character variable.

Note that in this method, you have to deliberately append the characters with a null character. The other two functions automatically do this.

6.1.2 Writing Strings

The string can be displayed on screen using three ways:

1. using `printf()` function
2. using `puts()` function
3. using `putchar()` function repeatedly

The string can be displayed using `printf()` by writing

```
printf("%s", str);
```

We use the conversion character `'s'` to output a string. Observe carefully that there is no `&` character used with the string variable. We may also use width and precision specifications along with `%s` (as discussed in Chapter 1). The `width` specifies the minimum output field width. If the string is short, extra space is either left padded or right padded. The precision specifies the maximum number of characters to be displayed. A negative width left pads short string rather than the default right justification. If the string is long, the extra characters are truncated. For example,

```
printf("%5.3s", str);
```

The above statement would print only the first three characters in a total field of five characters. Also these three characters are right justified in the allocated width. To make the string left justified, we must use a minus sign. For example,

```
printf("%-5.3s", str);
```

When the field width is less than the length of the string, the entire string will be printed. Also if the number of characters to be printed is specified as zero, then nothing is printed on the screen.

The next method of writing a string is by using `puts()` function. The string can be displayed by writing

```
puts(str);
```

`puts()` is a simple function that overcomes the drawbacks of the `printf()`. The function `puts()` writes a line of output on the screen. It terminates the line with a newline character (`'\n'`). It returns an `EOF (-1)` if an error occurs and returns a positive number on success.

Last but not the least, the string can also be written by calling the `putchar()` repeatedly to print a sequence of single characters.

```
i=0;
while(str[i] != '\0')
{
  putchar(str[i]);
    // Print the character on the screen
  i++;
}
```

Note one interesting point from the given fragment.

```
char str = "Hello";
printf("\n %s", str); // prints Hello
printf("\n %s", &str); // prints Hello
printf("\n %s", &str[2]); // prints llo
```

This is possible because a string is an array of characters.

6.1.3 Summary of Functions Used to Read and Write Characters

Table 6.1 contains a list of functions that are used to read characters from the keyboard and write characters to the screen.

Table 6.1 Function to read and write characters

Function	Operation
getchar()	Used to read a character from the keyboard; waits for carriage return (enter key). It returns an integer, in which the low-order byte contains the character. The getchar() can be used to input any key, including RETURN, TAB, and ESC.
getch()	Getch() is an alternative for the getchar(). Unlike getchar(), the getch() waits for a keypress, after which it returns immediately.
getche()	Similar to getch(). The only difference is that getche() echoes the character on screen.
putchar()	Used to write a character to the screen. It accepts an integer parameter of which only the low-order byte is output to the screen. Putchar() returns the character written, or EOF (–1) if an error occurs.

6.1 Write a program to display a string using `printf()`.

```
#include <stdio.h>
#include <conio.h>
main()
{
  char str[] = "Introduction to C";
  clrscr();
  printf("\n |%s|", str);
  printf("\n |%20s|", str);
  printf("\n |%-20s|", str);
  printf("\n |%.4s|", str);
  printf("\n |%20.4s|", str);
  printf("\n |%-20.4s|", str);
  getch();
  return 0;
}
```

Output

```
|Introduction to C|
|   Introduction to C|
|Introduction to C   |
|Intr|
|                Intr|
|Intr                |
```

6.2 Write a program to read and display a string.

```
#include <stdio.h>
#include <conio.h>
main()
{
  char str[50];
```

```
    printf("\n Enter the string: ");
    scanf("%s", str);
    clrscr();
    printf("\n |%s|", str);
    printf("\n |%20s|", str);
    printf("\n |%-20s|", str);
    printf("\n |%.4s|", str);
    printf("\n |%20.4s|", str);
    printf("\n |%-20.4s|", str);
    getch();
    return 0;
}
```

Output

```
Enter the string:
 |Introduction|
 |        Introduction|
 |Introduction        |
 |Intr|
 |                Intr|
 |Intr                |
```

The printf function in UNIX supports specification of variable field width or precision, i.e., if we write,

```
printf("\n %*.s*, w, p, str);
```

the printf statement will print first p characters of str in the field width of w.

6.3 Write a program to print the following pattern.

```
H
H E
H E L
H E L L
H E L L O
H E L L O
H E L L
H E L
H E
H
```

```
#include <stdio.h>
#include <conio.h>
main()
{
    int i, w, p;
    char str[] = "HELLO";
    printf("\n");
    for(i=0;i<=5;i++)
    {
        p = i+1;
        printf("\n %-5.*s", p, str);
    }
    printf("\n");
    for(i=5;i>=0;i--)
    {
        p = i+1;
        printf("\n %-5.*s", p, str);
    }
    getch();
    return 0;
}
```

6.4 Write a program to print the following pattern.

```
        H
      H E
    H E L
  H E L L
H E L L O
H E L L O
  H E L L
    H E L
      H E
        H
```

```
#include <stdio.h>
#include <conio.h>
main()
{
    int i, w, p;
    char str[] = "HELLO";
    printf("\n");
    for(i = 0;i <= 5;i++)
    {
        p = i+1;
        printf("\n %5.*s", p, str);
    }
    printf("\n");
    for(i = 5;i >= 0;i--)
    {
        p = i+1;
        printf("\n %5.*s", p, str);
    }
    getch();
    return 0;
}
```

sprintf() Function

The library function sprintf() is similar to printf(). The only difference is that the formatted output is written to a memory area rather than directly to a standard output (screen). The sprintf() is useful in situation when formatted strings in memory has to be transmitted over a communication channel or to a special device.

The syntax of `sprintf()` can be given as

```
int sprintf( char * buffer, const char *
    format [ , argument , ...] );
```

Here, `buffer` is the place to store the resulting string from using the function. The `argument` command is an ellipsis so you can put as many types of arguments as you want. Finally, the `format` is the string that contains the text to be printed. The string may contain format tags.

```
#include < stdio.h>
main()
{
    char buf[100];
    int num = 10;
    sprintf(buf, "num = %3d", num);
}
```

6.2 SUPPRESSING INPUT

The function `scanf()` can be used to read a field without assigning it to any variable. This is done by preceding that field's format code with a `*`. For example, given:

```
scanf("%d*c%d", &hr, &min);
```

The time can be read as `9:05` as a pair. Here the colon would be read but not assigned to anything. Therefore, assignment suppression is particularly useful when part of what is input needs to be suppressed.

6.2.1 Using a Scanset

The ANSI standard added the new scanset feature to the C language. A *scanset* is used to define a set of characters which may be read and assigned to the corresponding string. A scanset is defined by placing the characters inside square brackets prefixed with a `%`, as shown in the example:

```
%["aeiou"]
```

When we use the above scanset, `scanf()` will continue to read characters and put them into the string until it encounters a character that is not specified in the scanset. For example, consider the code given below.

```
#include <stdio.h>
int main()
{
    char str[10];
    printf("\n Enter string: " );
    scanf("%[aeiou]", str );
    printf( "The string is: %s", str);
    return 0;
}
```

The code will stop accepting a character as soon as the user enters a character that is not a vowel.

However, if the first character in the set is a ^ (caret symbol), then `scanf()` will accept any character that is not defined by the scanset. For example, if you write

```
scanf("%[^aeiou]", str);
```

Then, `str` can contain characters other than those specified in the scanset, i.e., it will accept any non-vowel character. However, the caret and the closing bracket can be included in the scanset anywhere. They have a predefined meaning only when they are included as the first character of the scanset. So if you want to accept a text from the user that contain caret and opening bracket then make sure that they are not the first characters in the scanset. This is shown in the following example:

```
scanf("%[0123456789.^[]()_+-$%&*]", str);
```

In the given example, `str` can accept any character enclosed in the opening and closing square brackets (including ^ and `[`).

The user can also specify a range of acceptable characters using a hyphen. This is shown in the statement given below.

```
scanf("%[a-z]", str );
```

Here, `str` will accept any character from small `a` to small `z`. Always remember that scansets are case sensitive. However, if you want to accept a hyphen then it must either be the first or the last character in the set.

Example 6.1 To better understand the scanset try the following code with different inputs:

```
#include <stdio.h>
int main()
{
    char str[10];
    printf("\n Enter string: " );
    scanf("%[A-Z]", str );
      // Reads only upper case characters
    printf( "The string is : %s", str);
    return 0;
}
```

A major difference between the scanset and the string conversion codes is that scanset does not skip leading white spaces. If the white space is a part of the scanset, then scanset accepts any white space character otherwise, it terminates if a white space character is entered without being specified in the scanset.

The scanset may also terminate if a field width specification is included and the maximum number of characters that can be read has been reached. For example, the statement given below will read maximum 10 vowels. So the `scanf` statement will terminate if 10 characters has been read or if a non-vowel character is entered.

```
scanf("%10[aeiou]", str );
```

`sscanf()` Function

The `sscanf` function accepts a string from which to read input. It accepts a template string and a series of related arguments. The `sscanf` function is similar to `scanf` function except that the first argument of `sscanf` specifies a string from which to read, whereas `scanf` can only read from standard input. Its syntax is given as

```
sscanf(const char *str, const char *format, [p1, p2, ...]);
```

Here the `sscanf()` reads data from `str` and stores them according to the parameter format into the locations given by the additional arguments. Locations pointed by each additional argument are filled with their corresponding type of value specified in the format string.
Consider the `sscanf` example given below.

```
sscanf(str, "%d", &num);
```

Here, `sscanf` takes three arguments. The first is `str` that contains data to be converted. The second is a string containing a format specifier that determines how the string is converted. Finally, the third is a memory location to place the result of the conversion. When the sscanf function completes successfully it returns the number of items successfully read.

Similar `scanf()`, the `sscanf()` will terminate as soon as it encounters a space, i.e., if data continues till it comes across a blank space.

6.3 STRING TAXONOMY

In C, we can store a string either in fixed-length format or in variable-length format as shown in Fig. 6.4.

Fixed-length string When storing a string in a fixed length format, you need to specify an appropriate size for the string variable. If the size is too small, then you will not be able to store all the elements in the string. On the other hand, if the string size is large, then unnecessarily memory space will be wasted.

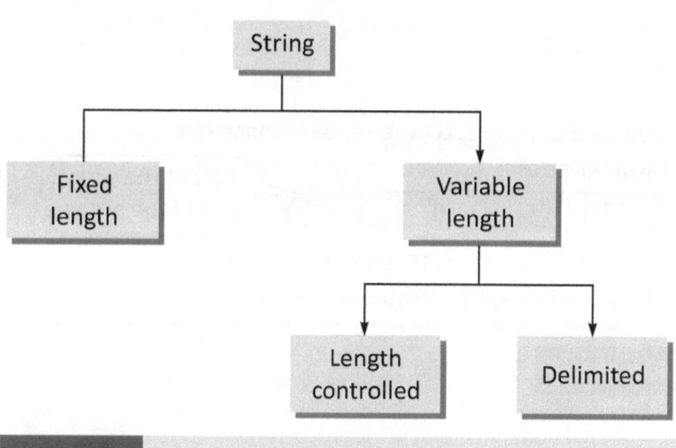

Figure 6.4 String taxonomy

Variable-length string A better option is to use a variable length format in which the string can be expanded or contracted to accommodate the elements in it. For example, if you declare a string variable to store the name of a student. If a student has a long name of say 20 characters, then the string can be expanded to accommodate 20 characters. On the other hand, a student name has only 5 characters, then the string variable can be contracted to store only 5 characters. However, to use a variable length string format you need a technique to indicate the end of elements that are a part of the string. This can be done either by using length-controlled string or a delimiter.

Length-controlled string In length-controlled string, you need to specify the number of characters in the string. This count is used by string manipulation functions to determine the actual length of the string variable.

Delimited string In this format, the string is ended with a delimiter. The delimiter is then used to identify the end of the string. For example, in English language every sentence is ended with a full-stop (.). Similarly, in C we can use any character such as comma, semicolon, colon, dash, null character, etc. as the delimiter of a string. However, null character is the most commonly used string delimiter in the C language.

You must be having some confusion when we use the term string and character array. Basically a string is stored in an array of characters. If we are using the null character as the string delimiting character then we treat the part of the array from the beginning to the null character as the string and ignore the rest. Figure 6.5 illustrates this concept.

In C, a string is a variable length array of characters that is delimited by the null character.

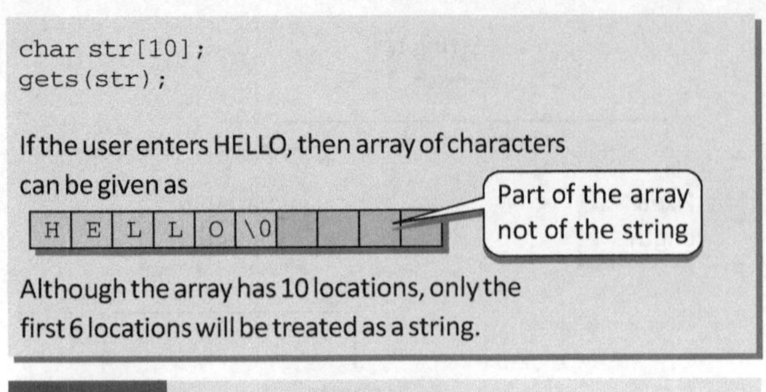

Figure 6.5 Delimited string

6.4 STRING OPERATIONS

In this section, we will learn about different operations that are performed on character arrays. But before we start with these operations, we must understand the way arithmetic operators can be applied to characters.

In C, characters can be manipulated in the same way as we do with numbers. When we use a character constant or a character variable in an expression, it is automatically converted into an integer value, where the value depends on the local character set of the system. For example, if we write,

```
int i;
char ch = 'A';
i = ch;
printf("%d", i);
// Prints 65, ASCII value of ch that is 'A'
```

C also enables programmers to perform arithmetic operations on character variables and character constants. So, if we write,

```
int i;
char ch = 'A';
i = ch + 10;
printf("%d", i);
// Prints 75, ASCII value of ch that is 'A' + 10
```

Character variables and character constants can be used with relational operators as shown in the example,

```
char ch = 'C';
if(ch >= 'A' && ch <= 'Z')
printf("The character is in upper case");
```

6.4.1 Length

The number of characters in the string constitutes the length of the string. For example, `LENGTH("C PROGRAMMING IS FUN")` will return 20. Note that even blank spaces are counted as characters in the string.

`LENGTH('0') = 0` and `LENGTH('') = 0` because both the strings do not contain any character and the ASCII code of `'\0'` is zero. Therefore, both the strings are empty and of zero length. Figure 6.6 shows an algorithm that calculates the length of a string.

```
Step 1: [INITIALIZE] SET I = 0
Step 2: Repeat Step 3 while STR[I] != '\0'
Step 3:                         SET I = I + 1
            [END OF LOOP]
Step 4: SET LENGTH = I
Step 5: END
```

Figure 6.6 Algorithm to calculate the length of a string

In this algorithm, I is used as an index of the string `STR`. To traverse each and every character of `STR` we increment the value of `I`. Once the null character is encountered, the control jumps out of the `while` loop and initialize length with the value of `I`. This is because the number of characters in the string constitutes its length.

There is a library function `strlen(s1)` that returns the length of `s1`. It is defined in `string.h`.

6.5 Write a program to find the length of a string.

```
#include <stdio.h>
#include <conio.h>
int main()
{
    char str[100], i = 0, length;
    clrscr();
    printf("\n Enter the string :");
    gets(str);
    while(str[i] != '\0')
      i++;
    length = i;
    printf("\n The length of the string is :
    %d", length);
    getch();
}
```

Output

```
Enter the string : HELLO
The length of the string is : 5
```

6.4.2 Converting Characters of a String into Upper Case

We have already seen that in memory the ASCII codes are stored instead of the real value. The ASCII code for `A-Z` varies from `65 to 91` and the ASCII code for `a-z` ranges from `97 to 123`. So if we have to convert a lower case character to upper case, then we just need to subtract `32` from the ASCII value of the character. Figure 6.7 shows an algorithm that converts characters of a string into upper case.

Note: There is a library function `toupper()` that converts a character into upper case. It is defined in `ctype.h`

```
Step1: [Initialize] SET I=0
Step 2: Repeat Step 3 while STR[I] != '\0'
Step 3:         IF STR[I] > 'a' AND STR[I] < 'z'
                        SET Upperstr[I] = STR[I] - 32
                ELSE
                        SET Upperstr[I] = STR[I]
        [END OF IF]
        [END OF while LOOP]
Step 4: SET Upperstr[I] = '\0'
Step 5: EXIT
```

Figure 6.7 Algorithm to convert characters of a string into upper case.

In the algorithm, we initialize `I` to `zero`. Using `I` as the index of `STR`, we traverse each character from step 2 to 3. If the character is already in upper case, then it is copied in the `Upperstr` string else the lower case character is converted into upper case by subtracting `32` from its ASCII value. The upper case character is then stored in `Upperstr`. Finally, when all the characters have been traversed a null character is appended to the `Upperstr` (as done in Step 4).

6.6 Write a program to convert characters of a string to upper case.

```
#include <stdio.h>
#include <conio.h>
int main()
{
   char str[100], upper_str [100];
   int i=0, j=0;
   clrscr();
   printf("\n Enter the string:");
   gets(str);
   while(str[i] != '\0')
   {
      if(str[i]>='a' && str[i]<='z')
      upper_str[i] = str[i] -32;
      else
      upper_str[i] = str[i];
      i++; j++;
   }
   upper_str[j] = '\0';
   printf("\n The string converted into
   upper case is : ");
   puts(upper_str);
   return 0;
}
```

Output

```
Enter the string: hello
The string converted into upper case is:
HELLO
```

6.4.3 Converting Characters of a String Into Lower Case

The ASCII code for `A-Z` varies from `65 to 91` and the ASCII code for `a-z` ranges from `97` to `123`. So if we have to convert an upper case character into lower case, then we just need to add `32` to its `ASCII` value. Figure 6.8 shows an algorithm that converts characters of a string into lower case.

Note: In C, there is a library function `tolower()` that converts a character into lower case. It is defined in `ctype.h`

```
Step 1: [Initialize] SET I=0
Step 2: Repeat Step 3 while STR[I] != '\0'
Step 3: IF STR[1] > 'A' AND STR[I] < 'Z'
                        SET Lowerstr[I] = STR[I] + 32
                ELSE
                        SET Lowerstr[I] = STR[I]
        [END OF IF]
        [END OF while LOOP]
Step 4: SET Lowerstr[I] = '\0'
Step 5: EXIT
```

Figure 6.8 Algorithm to convert characters of a string into lower case.

In the algorithm, we initialize `I` to `zero`. Using `I` as the index of `STR`, we traverse each character from Steps 2 to 3. If the character is already in lower case, then it is copied in the `Lowerstr` string else the upper case character is converted into lower case by adding `32` to its ASCII value. The lower case character is then stored in `Lowerstr`. Finally, when all the characters have been traversed a null character is appended to the `Lowerstr` (as done in Step 4).

6.7 Write a program to convert characters of a string into lower case.

```
#include <stdio.h>
#include <conio.h>
int main()
{
   char str[100], lower_str [100];
   int i = 0, j = 0;
   clrscr();
   printf("\n Enter the string :");
   gets(str);
   while(str[i] != '\0')
   {
      if(str[i]>='A' && str[i]<='Z')
      lower_str[j] = str[i] + 32;
      else
      lower_str[i] = str[i];
      i++; j++;
   }
   lower_str[j] = '\0';
   printf("\n The string converted into
   lower case is : ");
   puts(lower_str);
   return 0;
}
```

Output

```
Enter the string : HeLLo
The string converted into lower case is:
hello
```

6.4.4 Concatenating Two Strings to form a New String

IF `S1` and `S2` are two strings, then *concatenation* operation produces a string which contains characters of `S1` followed by the characters of `S2`. Figure 6.9 shows an algorithm that concatenates two strings.

In this algorithm, we first initialize the two counters `I` and `J` to zero. To concatenate the strings, we have to copy the contents of the first string followed by the contents of the second string in a third string, `new_str`. Steps 2 to 4 copies the contents of the first string in the `new_str`. Likewise, Steps 6 to 8 copy the contents of the second string in the `new_str`. After the contents have been copied a null character is appended at the end of the `new_str`.

```
Step 1: Initialize I = 0 and J = 0
Step 2: Repeat Step 3 to 4 while I <= LENGTH(str1)
Step 3:         SET new_str[J] = str1[I]
Step 4:         Set I = I+1 and J = J+1
    [END of Step 2]
Step 5: SET I=0
Step 6: Repeat Steps 6 to 7 while I <= LENGTH(str2)
Step 7:         SET new_str[J] = str1[I]
Step 8:         Set I = I+1 and J = J+1
    [END of step 5]
Step 9: SET new_str[J] = '\0'
Step 10: EXIT
```

Figure 6.9 Algorithm to concatenate two strings

6.8 Write a program to concatenate two strings.

```
#include <stdio.h>
#include <conio.h>
int main()
{
   char str1[100], str2[100], str3[100];
   int i=0, j=0;
   clrscr();
   printf("\n Enter the first string : ");
   gets(str1);
   printf("\n Enter the second string : ");
   gets(str2);
   while(str1[i] != '\0')
   {
      str3[j] = str1[i];
      i++;
      j++;
   }
   i=0;
   while(str2[i] != '\0')
   {
      str3[j] = str2[i];
      i++;
      j++;
   }
   str3[j] = '\0';
   printf("\n The concatenated string is:");
   puts(str3);
   getch();
   return 0;
}
```

Output

```
Enter the first string : Hello,
Enter the second string: How are you?
The concatenated string is: Hello, How are
you?
```

6.4.5 Appending

Appending one string to another string involves copying the contents of the source string at the end of the destination string. For example, if S1 and S2 are two strings, then appending S1 to S2 means we have to add the contents of S1 to S2. Here S1 is the source string and S2 is the destination string. The appending operation would leave the source string S1 unchanged and destination string S2 = S2 + S1. Figure 6.10 shows an algorithm that appends two strings.

There is a library function `strcat(s1, s2)` that concatenates s2 to s1. It is defined in `string.h`.

```
Step 1: [Initialize] SET I =0 and J=0
Step 2: Repeat Step 3 while Dest_Str[I] != '\0'
Step 3:     SET I + I + 1
             [END OF LOOP]
Step 4: Repeat Step 5 to 7 while Source_Str[J] != '\0'
Step 5:     Dest_Str[I] = Source_Str[J]
Step 6:     SET I = I + 1
Step 7:     SET J = J + 1
           [END OF LOOP]
Step 8: SET Dest_Str[I] = '\0'
Step 9: EXIT
```

Figure 6.10 Algorithm to append two strings

In this algorithm, we first traverse through the destination string to reach its end, i.e., reach the position where a `null` character is encountered. The characters of the source string are then copied into the destination string starting from that position. Finally, a `null` character is added to terminate the destination string.

6.9 Write a program to append a string to another string.

```
#include <stdio.h>
#include <conio.h>
main()
{
    char Dest_Str[100], Source_Str[50];
    int i = 0, j = 0;
    clrscr();
    printf("\n Enter the source string : ");
    gets(Source_Str);
    printf("\n Enter the destination string:");
    gets(Dest_Str);
    while(Dest_Str[i] != '\0')
        i++;
    while(Source_Str[j] != '\0')
    {
        Dest_Str[i] = Source_Str[j];
        i++;
        j++;
    }
    Dest_Str[i] = '\0';
    printf("\n After appending, the
    destination string is: ");
    puts(Dest_Str);
    getch();
    return 0;
}
```

Output

```
Enter the source string: How are you?
Enter the destination string: Hi,
After appending, the destination string is:
Hi, How are you?
```

6.4.6 Comparing Two Strings

If S1 and S2 are two strings then comparing two strings will give either of these results:

(a) S1 and S2 are equal

(b) S1 > S2, when in dictionary order S1 will come after S2

(c) S1 < S2, when in dictionary order S1 precedes S2

To compare the two strings, each and every character is compared from both the strings. If all the characters are same then the two strings are said to be equal. Figure 6.11 shows an algorithm that compares two strings.

There is a library function `strcmp (s1, s2)` that compares s2 with s1. It is defined in `string.h`.

In this algorithm, we first check whether the two strings are of same length. If not, then there is no point in moving ahead as it straightaway means that the two strings are not same. However, if the two strings are of the same length, then we compare character by character to check if all the characters are same. If yes, then variable SAME is set to 1 else if SAME = 0, then we check which string precedes the other in dictionary order and print the corresponding message.

6.10 Write a program to compare two strings.

```
#include <stdio.h>
#include <conio.h>
#include <string.h>
main()
{
```

```
    char str1[50], str2[50];
    int i=0, len1 = 0, len2 = 0, same= 0;
    clrscr();
    printf("\n Enter the first string : ");
    gets(str1);
    printf("\n Enter the second string : ");
    gets(str2);
    len1 = strlen(str1);
    len2 = strlen(str2);
    if(len1 == len2)
    {
      while(i<len1)
      {
      if(str1[i] == str2[i])
      i++;
      else break;
      }
      if(i==len1)
     {
      same=1;
      printf("\n The two strings are equal");
     }
    }
    if(len1!=len2)
      printf("\n The two strings are not
    equal");
    if(same == 0)
    {
    if(str1[i]>str2[i])
      printf("\n String1 is greater than
    string2");
      else if(str1[i]<str2[i])
      printf("\n String2 is greater than
    string1");
    }
    getch();
    return 0;
}
```

Output

```
Enter the first string: Hello
Enter the second string: Hello
The two strings are equal
```

```
Step 1: [Initialize] SET I=0, SAME =0
Step 2: SET Len1 = Length(STR1), Len2 = Length(STR2)
Step 3: IF len1 != len2, then
            Write "Strings Are Not Equal"
        ELSE
            Repeat while I<Len1
                IF STR1[I] == STR2[I]
                    SET I = I + 1
                ELSE
                    Go to Step
                [END OF IF]
            [END OF LOOP]
            IF I = Len1, then
                SET SAME = 1
                Write "Strings are equal"
            [END OF IF]
Step 4: IF SAME = 0, then
            IF STR1[I] > STR2[I], then
                Write "String1 is greater than String2"
                    ELSE IF STR1[I] < STR2[I], then
                Write "String2 is greater than String1"
            [END OF IF]
        [END OF IF]
Step 5: EXIT
```

Figure 6.11 Algorithm to compare two strings

6.4.7 Reversing a String

If `S1= "HELLO"`, then reverse of `S1 = "OLLEH"`. To reverse a string we just need to swap the first character with the last, second character with the second last character, so on and so forth. Figure 6.12 shows an algorithm that reverses a string.

There is a library function `strrev(s1)` that reverses all the characters in the string except the null character. It is defined in `string.h`.

```
Step 1: [Initialize] SET I=0, J= Length(STR)
Step 2: Repeat Step 3 and 4 while I< Length(STR)
Step 3: SWAP( STR(I), STR(J))
Step 4: SET I = I + 1, J = J – 1
        [END OF LOOP]
Step 5: EXIT
```

Figure 6.12 Algorithm to reverse a string

In Step 1, `I` is initialized to zero and `J` is initialized to the length of the string `STR`. In Step 2, a `while` loop is executed until all the characters of the string are accessed. In Step 3, we swap the `ith` character of `STR` with its `jth` character. (As a result, the first character of `STR` will be replaced with the last character, the second character will be replaced with the second last character of `STR`, and so on). In Step 4, the value of `I` is incremented and `J` is decremented to traverse `STR` in the forward and backward direction, respectively.

6.11 Write a program to reverse the given string.

```
#include <stdio.h>
#include <conio.h>
#include <string.h>
int main()
{
```

```
    char str[100], temp;
    int i = 0, j = 0;
    clrscr();
    printf("\n Enter the string: ");
    gets(str);
    j=strlen(str)-1;
    while(i<j)
    {
        temp = str[j];
        str[j] = str[i];
        str[i] = temp;
        i++;
        j--;
    }
    printf("\n The reversed string is: ");
    puts(str);
    getch();
    return 0;
}
```

Output

```
Enter the string: Hi there
The reversed string is: ereht iH
```

6.4.8 Extracting a Substring from Left

In order to extract a substring from the main string we need to copy the content of the string starting from the first position to the nth position where n is the number of characters to be extracted. For example, if `S1 = "Hello World"`,

then `Substr_Left(S1, 7) = Hello W`

Figure 6.13 shows an algorithm that extracts the first `n` characters from a string.

```
Step 1: [Initialize] SET I=0
Step 2: Repeat Step 3 while STR[I] != '\0' AND I<N
Step 3:     SET Substr[I] = STR[I]
Step 4:     SET I = I + 1
          [END OF LOOP]
Step 5: SET Substr[I] ='\0'
Step 6: EXIT
```

Figure 6.13 Algorithm to extract first `n` characters from a string

In Step 1, we initialize the index variable `I` with `zero`. In Step 2, a `while` loop is executed until all the characters of `STR` have been accessed and `I` is less than `N`. In Step 3, the `I`th character of `STR` is copied in the `I`th character of `Substr`. In Step 4, the value of `I` is incremented to access the next character in `STR`. In Step 5, the `Substr` is appended with a `null` character.

6.12 Write a program to extract the first N characters of a string.

```
#include <stdio.h>
#include <conio.h>
int main()
{
    char str[100], substr[100];
    int i=0, n;
    clrscr();
    printf("\n Enter the string: ");
    gets(str);
    printf("\n Enter the number of characters
    to be copied: ");
    scanf("%d", &n);
    i = 0;
    while(str[i] != '\0' && i< n)
    {
        substr[i] = str[i];
        i++;
    }
    substr [i] = '\0';
    printf("\n The substring is: ");
    puts(substr);
    getch();
    return 0;
}
```

Output

```
Enter the string: Hi there
Enter the number of characters to be copied: 2
The substring is: Hi
```

6.4.9 Extracting a Substring from Right of the String

In order to extract a substring from the right side of the main string we need to first calculate the position. For example, if `S1 = "Hello World"` and we have to copy 7 characters starting from the right, then we have to actually start extracting characters from the 5th position. This is calculated by, total number of `characters - n`.

For example, if `S1 = "Hello World", then Substr_Right(S1, 7) = o World`

Figure 6.14 shows an algorithm that extracts `n` characters from the right of a string.

In Step 1, we initialize the index variable `I` to zero and `J` to `Length(STR) - N + 1`, so that `J` points to the character from which the string has to be copied in the substring. In Step 2, a `while` loop is executed until the null character in `STR` is accessed. In Step 3, the `J`th character of `STR` is copied in the `I`th character of `Substr`. In Step

4, the value of `I` and `J` is incremented. In Step 5, the `Substr` is appended with a `null` character.

```
Step 1: [Initialize] SET I=0, J = Length(STR) - N + 1
Step 2: Repeat Step 3 while STR[J] != '\0'
Step 3:       SET Substr[I] = STR[J]
Step 4:       SET I = I + 1, J = J + 1
         [END OF LOOP]
Step 5: SET Substr[I] ='\0'
Step 6: EXIT
```

Figure 6.14 Algorithm to extract n characters from the right of a string

6.13 Write a program to extract the last N characters of a string.

```
#include <stdio.h>
#include <conio.h>
int main()
{
   char str[100], substr[100];
   int i=0, j=0, n;
   clrscr();
   printf("\n Enter the string : ");
   gets(str);
   printf("\n Enter the number of characters
   to be copied: ");
   scanf("%d", &n);
   j = strlen(str) – n+1;
   while(str[j] != '\0')
   {
      substr[i] = str[j];
      i++, j++;
   }
   substr [i] = '\0';
   printf("\n The substring is : ");
   puts(substr);
   getch();
   return 0;
}
```

Output

```
Enter the string : Hi there
Enter the number of characters to be
copied : 5
The substring is : there
```

6.4.10 Extracting a Substring from the Middle of a String

To extract a substring from a given string requires information about three things. The main string, the position of the first character of the substring in the given string, and maximum number of characters/length of the substring. For example, if we have a string,

```
str[] = "Welcome to the world of
programming";
```

then,

```
SUBSTRING(str, 15, 5) = world
```

Figure 6.15 shows an algorithm that extracts the substring from a middle of a string .

```
Step 1: [INITIALIZE] Set I = N, J = 0
Step 2: Repeat steps 3 to 6 while str[I] != '0' and N>=0
Step 3:        SET substr[J] = str[I]
Step 4:        SET I = I + 1
Step 5:        SET J = J + 1
Step 6:        SET N = N - 1
         [END of loop]
Step 7: SET substr[J] = '\0'
Step 8: EXIT
```

Figure 6.15 Algorithm to extract a substring from the middle of a string

In this algorithm, we initialize a loop counter `I` to `M`, i.e., the position from which the characters have to be copied. Steps 3 to 6 are repeated until `N` characters have been copied. With every character copied, we decrement the value of `N`. The characters of the string are copied into another string called `substr`. At the end a `null` character is appended to the `substr` to terminate the string.

6.14 Write a program to extract the substring from a given string.

```
#include <stdio.h>
#include <conio.h>
int main()
{
   char str[100], substr[100];
   int i=0, j=0, n, m;
   clrscr();
   printf("\n Enter the main string: ");
   gets(str);
   printf("\n Enter the position from which
   to start the substring: ");
   scanf("%d", &m);
   printf("\n Enter the length of the
   substring: ");
   scanf("%d", &n);
   i=m;
   while(str[i] != '\0' && n>=0)
   {
      substr[j] = str[i];
      i++;
      j++;
      n--;
```

```
    }
    substr[j] = '\0';
    printf("\n The substring is : ");
    puts(str);
    getch();
    return 0;
}
```

Output

```
Enter the main string : Hi there
Enter the position from which to start the
substring: 1
Enter the length of the substring: 7
The substring is : i there
```

6.4.11 Insertion

The insertion operation inserts a string `S`, in the main text `T`, at the `k`th position. The general syntax of this operation is `INSERT(text, position, string)`. For example, `INSERT("XYZXYZ", 3, "AAA") = "XYZAAAXYZ"`

Figure 6.16 shows an algorithm to insert a string in a given text at the specified position.

```
Step 1: [INITIALIZE] SET I=0, J=0 and K=0
Step 2: Repeat steps 3 to 4 while text[I] != '0'
Step 3: IF I = pos, then
        Repeat while str[K] != '\0'
            new_str[j] = str[k]
            SET J=J+1
            SET K = K+1
        [END OF INNER LOOP]
          ELSE
            new_str[[J] = text[I]
            SET J = J+1
Step 4: SET I = I+1
     [END OF OUTER LOOP]
Step 5: SET new_str[J] = '\0'
Step 6: EXIT
```

Figure 6.16 Algorithm to insert a string in a given text at the specified position

> **Programming Tip:** A program must include `stdio.h` for standard I/O operations, `ctype.h` for character handling functions, `string.h` for string functions, and `stdlib.h` for other general utility functions.

This algorithm first initializes the indexes in the string to zero. From Steps 3 to 6, the contents of `new_str` are built. If `I` is exactly equal to the position at which the substring has to be inserted into the text, then the inner loop copies the contents of the substring into the `new_str`. Otherwise, the contents of the text are copied into it.

6.15 Write a program to insert a string in the main text.

```
#include <stdio.h>
#include <conio.h>
main()
{
    char text[100], str[20], ins_text[100];
    int i=0, j=0, k=0,pos;
    clrscr();
    printf("\n Enter the main text : ");
    gets(text);
    printf("\n Enter the string to be
    inserted : ");
    gets(str);
    printf("\n Enter the position at which
    the string has to be inserted: ");
    scanf("%d", &pos);
    while(text[i]!='\0')
    {
        if(i==pos)
        {
        while(str[k]!='\0')
        {
        ins_text[j]=str[k];
        j++;
        k++;
        }
        }
        else
        {
        ins_text[j]=text[i];
        j++;
        }
        i++;
    }
    ins_text[j]='\0';
    printf("\n The new string is: ");
    puts(ins_text);
    getch();
    return 0;
}
```

Output

```
Enter the main text: How you?
Enter the string to be inserted: are
Enter the position at which the string has
to be inserted: 6
The new string is: How are you?
```

6.4.12 Indexing

Index operation returns the position in the string where the string pattern first occurs. For example,

`INDEX("Welcome to the world of programming", "world") = 15`

However, if the pattern does not exist in the string, the `INDEX` function returns `0`. Figure 6.17 shows an algorithm to find the index of the first occurrence of a string within a given text.

```
Step 1:  [Initialize] SET I=0 and
                    MAX = LENGTH(text) - LENGTH(str) +1
Step 2:  Repeat Steps 3 to 6 while I <= MAX
Step 3:  Repeat step 4 for K = 0 To Length(str)
Step 4:       IF str[K] != text[I + K], then GOTO step 6
         [END of inner loop]
Step 5:  SET INDEX = I. Goto step 8
Step 6:  SET I = I+1
         [END OF OUTER LOOP]
Step 7:  SET INDEX = -1
Step 8:  EXIT
```

Figure 6.17 Algorithm to find the index of the first occurrence of a string within a given text

In this algorithm, `MAX` is initialized to `LENGTH(text) – Length(str) + 1`. Take for example, if a text contains `"Welcome To Programming"` and the string contains `"World"`. In the main text we will look for at the most `22 - 5 + 1 = 18` characters because after that there is no scope left for the string to be present in the text.

Steps 3 to 6 are repeated until each and every character of the text has been checked for the occurrence of the string within it. In the inner loop, in Step 3, we check `n` characters of string with `n` characters of text to find if the characters are same. If it is not the case, then we move to Step 6, where `I` is incremented. If the string is found, index is initialized with `I` else set to `-1`. For example, if

```
TEXT = W E L C O M E  T O  T H E  W O R L D
STRING = C O M E
```

In the first pass of the inner loop, we will compare `WELC` with `COME` character by character. As soon as `W` and `C` do not match, the control will move to Step 6 and then `ELCO` will be compared with `COME`. In the next pass, `LCOM` will be compared with `COME`.

We will write the programming code of indexing operation in the operations that follows.

6.4.13 Deletion

The deletion operation deletes a substring from a given text. We write it as, `DELETE(text, position, length)`. For example,

```
DELETE("ABCDXXXABCD", 5, 3) = "ABCDABCD"
```

Figure 6.18 shows an algorithm to delete a substring from a given text.

```
Step 1: [INITIALIZE] SET I=0 and J=0
Step 2: Repeat steps 3 to 6 while text[I] !='\0'
Step 3: IF I=N, then
                   Repeat Step 4 while N>=0
                          SET I = I+1
                          SET N = N - 1
                   [END of inner loop]
           [END OF IF]
Step 4: SET new_str[J] = text[I]
Step 5: SET J= J + 1
Step 6: SET I = I + 1
           [ END of outer loop]
Step 7: SET new_str[J] = '\0'
Step 8: EXIT
```

Figure 6.18 Algorithm to delete a substring from a text

In this algorithm, we first initialize indexes to `zero`. The Steps 3 to 6 are repeated until all the characters of the text are scanned. If `I` is exactly equal to `M`, the position from which deletion has to be done, then the index of the text is incremented and `N` is decremented. `N` is the number of characters that have to be deleted starting from position `M`. However, if `I` is not equal to `M`, then the characters of the text are simply copied into the `new_str`.

Delete operation can also be used to delete a string from a given text. To do this, we first find out the first index at which the string occurs in the text. Then we delete `n` number of characters from the text, where `n` is the number of characters in the string.

6.16 Write a program to delete a substring from a text.

```
#include <stdio.h>
#include <conio.h>
main()
{
   char text[200], str[20], new_text[200];
   int i=0, j=0, found=0, k, n=0, copy_
   loop=0;
   clrscr();
   printf("\n Enter the main text: ");
   gets(text);
   fflush(stdin);
   printf("\n Enter the string to be deleted: ");
   gets(str);
   fflush(stdin);
   while(text[i]!='\0')
   {
      j=0, found= 0, k=i;
       while(text[k]==str[j] && str[j]!='\0')
       {
          k++;
          j++;
       }
       if(str[j]=='\0')
```

```
        copy_loop=k;
        new_text[n] = text[copy_loop];
        i++;
        copy_loop++;
        n++;
        }
    new_str[n]='\0';
    printf("\n The new string is: ");
    puts(new_text);
    getch();
    return 0;
}
```

Output

```
Enter the main text: Hello, how are you?
Enter the string to be deleted: , how are you?
The new string is: Hello
```

6.4.14 Replacement

Replacement operation is used to replace the pattern `P1` by another pattern `P2`. This is done by writing, `REPLACE(text, pattern1, pattern2)`

For example, `("AAABBBCCC", "BBB", "X")` = `AAAXCCC` `("AAABBBCCC", "X", "YYY")= AAABBBCC`.

In the second example, there is no change as `'X'` does not appear in the text. Figure 6.19 shows an algorithm to replace a pattern `P1` with another pattern `P2` in the text.

```
Step 1: [INITIALIZE] SET Pos = INDEX(TEXT, P1)
Step 2: SET TEXT = DELETE(TEXT, Pos, LENGTH(P1))
Step 3: INSERT(TEXT, Pos, P2)
Step 4: EXIT
```

Figure 6.19 Algorithm to replace a pattern P_1 with another pattern P_2 in the text

The algorithm is very simple, where we first find the position `Pos`, at which the pattern occurs in the text, then delete the existing pattern from that position, and insert a new pattern there. String matching refers to finding occurrences of a pattern string within another string.

6.17 Write a program to replace a pattern with another pattern in the text.

```
#include <stdio.h>
#include <conio.h>
main()
{
   char str[200], pat[20], new_str[200],
   rep_pat[100];
   int i=0, j=0, k, n=0, copy_loop=0, rep_
   index=0;
   clrscr();
   printf("\n Enter the string: ");
   gets(str);
   fflush(stdin);
   printf("\n Enter the pattern: ");
   gets(pat);
   fflush(stdin);
   printf("\n Enter the replace pattern: ");
   gets(rep_pat);
   while(str[i]!='\0')
   {
    j=0,k=i;
      while(str[k]==pat[j] && pat[j]!='\0')
      {
         k++;
         j++;
      }
      if(pat[j]=='\0')
      {
         copy_loop=k;
         while(rep_pat[rep_index] !='\0')
         {
            new_str[n] = rep_pat[rep_index];
            rep_index++;
            n++;
         }
      }
    new_str[n] = str[copy_loop];
    i++;
    copy_loop++;
    n++;
   }
   new_str[n]='\0';
   printf("\n The new string is: ");
   puts(new_str);
   getch();
   return 0;
}
```

Output

```
Enter the string: How ARE you?
Enter the pattern: ARE
Enter the pattern: are
The new string is : How are you?
```

6.5 MISCELLANEOUS STRING AND CHARACTER FUNCTIONS

In this section, we will discuss some character and string manipulation functions that are part of `ctype.h`, `string.h`, and `stdlib.h`.

6.5.1 Character Manipulation Functions

Table 6.2 illustrates some character functions contained in `ctype.h`.

Table 6.2 Functions in ctype.h

Function	Usage	Example
isalnum(int c)	Checks whether character c is an alphanumeric character	isalpha('A');
isalpha(int c)	Checks whether character c is an alphabetic character	isalpha('z');
iscntrl(int c)	Checks whether character c is a control character	scanf("%d", &c); iscntrl(c);
isdigit(int c)	Checks whether character c is a digit	isdigit(3);
isgraph()	Checks whether character c is a graphic or printing character. The function excludes the white space character	isgraph('!');
isprint(int c)	Checks whether character c is a printing character. The function includes the white space character	isprint('@');
islower(int c)	Checks whether the character c is in lower case	islower('k');
isupper(int c)	Checks whether the character c is in upper case	isupper('K');
ispunct(int c)	Checks whether the character c is a punctuation mark	ispunct('?');
isspace(int c)	Checks whether the character c is a white space character	isspace(' ');
isxdigit(int c)	Checks whether the character c is a hexadecimal digit	isxdigit('F');
tolower(int c)	Converts the character c to lower case	tolower('K') returns k
toupper(int c)	Converts the character c to upper case	tolower('k') returns K

6.5.2 String Manipulation Functions

In this section we will look at some commonly used string functions present in the `string.h` header file.

`strcat` Function

Syntax:

```
char *strcat(char *str1, const char *str2);
```

Programming Tip: Before using string copy and concatenating functions, ensure that the destination string has enough space to store all the elements so that memory overwriting does not take place.

The `strcat` function appends the string pointed to by `str2` to the end of the string pointed to by `str1`. The terminating null character of `str1` is overwritten. The process stops when the terminating null character of `str2` is copied. The argument `str1` is returned. Note that `str1` should be big enough to store the contents of `str2`.

```
#include <stdio.h>
#include <string.h>
int main()
{
    char str1[50] = "Programming";
    char str2[] = "In C";
    strcat(str1, str2);
    printf("\n str1: %s", str1);
    return 0;
}
```

Output

```
str1: ProgrammingIn C
```

`strncat` Function

Syntax:

```
char *strncat(char *str1, const char *str2,
size_t n);
```

Appends the string pointed to by `str2` to the end of the string pointed to by `str1` up to `n` characters long. The terminating null character of `str1` is overwritten. Copying stops when `n` characters are copied or the terminating null character of `str2` is copied. A terminating null character is appended to `str1` before returning to the calling function.

```
#include <stdio.h>
#include <string.h>
int main()
{
    char str1[50] = "Programming";
```

```
    char str2[] = "In C";
    strncat(str1, str2, 2);
    printf("\n str1: %s", str1);
    return 0;
}
```

Output

```
str1: Programming In
```

strchr Function

Syntax:

```
char *strchr(const char *str, int c);
```

The strchr ( ) function searches for the first occurrence of the character c (an unsigned char) in the string pointed to by the argument str. The function returns a pointer pointing to the first matching character, or null if no match was found.

```
#include <stdio.h>
#include <string.h>
int main()
{
    char str[50] = "Programming In C";
    char *pos;
    pos = strchr(str, 'n');
    if(pos)
        printf("\n n is found in str at
    position %d", pos);
    else
        printf("\n n is not present in the
    string");
    return 0;
}
```

Output

```
n is found in str at position 9
```

strrchr Function

Syntax:

```
char *strrchr(const char *str, int c);
```

The strchr ( ) function searches for the first occurrence of the character c (an unsigned char) beginning at the rear end and working towards the front in the string pointed to by the argument str, i.e., the function searches for the last occurrence of the character c and returns a pointer pointing to the last matching character, or null if no match was found.

```
#include <stdio.h>
#include <string.h>
int main()
{
    char str[50] = "Programming In C";
    char *pos;
    pos = strrchr(str, 'n');
    if(pos)
        printf("\n The last position of n is:
    %d", pos-str);
    else
        printf("\n n is not present in the
    string");
    return 0;
}
```

Output

```
The last position of n is: 13
```

strcmp Function

Syntax:

```
int strcmp(const char *str1, const char
*str2);
```

The strcmp compares the string pointed to by str1 to the string pointed to by str2. The function returns zero if the strings are equal. Otherwise, it returns a value less than zero or greater than zero if str1 is less than or greater than str2, respectively.

```
#include <stdio.h>
#include <string.h>
int main()
{
    char str1[10] = "HELLO";
    char str2[10] = "HEY";
    if(strcmp(str1,str2)==0)
        printf("\n The two strings are
    identical");
    else
        printf("\n The two strings are not
    identical");
    return 0;
}
```

Output

```
The two strings are not identical
```

strncmp Function

Syntax:

```
int strncmp(const char *str1, const char
*str2, size_t n);
```

This function compares at most the first n bytes of str1 and str2. The process stops comparing after the null character is encountered. The function returns zero if the first n bytes of the strings are equal. Otherwise, it returns a value less than zero or greater than zero if str1 is less than or greater than str2, respectively.

```
#include <stdio.h>
#include <string.h>
int main()
{
   char str1[10] = "HELLO";
   char str2[10] = "HEY";
   if(strncmp(str1,str2,2)==0)
      printf("\n The two strings are
   identical");
   else
      printf("\n The two strings are not
   identical");
   return 0;
}
```

Output

```
The two strings are identical
```

strcpy Function

Syntax:

```
char *strcpy(char *st r1, const char *str2);
```

This function copies the string pointed to by str2 to str1 including the null character of str2. It returns the argument str1. Here str1 should be big enough to store the contents of str2.

```
#include <stdio.h>
#include <string.h>
int main()
{
   char str1[10], str2[10] = "HELLO";
   strcpy(str1,str2);
   printf("\n str1: %s", str1);
   return 0;
}
```

Output

```
HELLO
```

strncpy Function

Syntax:

```
char *strncpy(char *st r1, const char *str2,
size_t n);
```

This function copies up to n characters from the string pointed to by str2 to str1. Copying stops when n characters are copied. However, if the null character in str2 is reached then the null characters are continually copied to str1 until n characters have been copied. Finally, a null character must be appended to str1. However, if n is zero or negative then nothing is copied.

Programming Tip:
Do not use string functions on a character array that is not terminated with a null character.

```
#include <stdio.h>
#include <string.h>
int main()
{
   char str1[10], str2[10] = "HELLO";
   strncpy(str1,str2, 2);
   printf("\n str1: %s", str1);
   return 0;
}
```

Output

```
HE
```

To copy the string str2 in str1, a better way is to write

```
strncpy(str1, str2,
   sizeof(str1)-1);
```

This would enforce the copying of only that much characters for which str1 has space to accommodate. We have written size of str1 minus 1 to store the null character.

strlen Function

Syntax:

```
size_t strlen(const char *str);
```

This function calculates the length of the string str up to but not including the null character, i.e., the function returns the number of characters in the string.

```
#include <stdio.h>
#include <string.h>
int main()
{
   char str[] = "HELLO";
   printf("\n Length of str is: %d",
   strlen(str));
   return 0;
}
```

Output

```
Length of str is: 5
```

strstr Function

Syntax:

```
char *strstr(const char *str1, const char
*str2);
```

The function is used to find the first occurrence of string `str2` (not including the terminating null character) in the string `str1`. It returns a pointer to the first occurrence of `str2` in `str1`. If no match is found, then a `null` pointer is returned.

```
#include <stdio.h>
#include <string.h>
int main()
{
   char str1[] = "HAPPY BIRTHDAY TO YOU";
   char str2[] = "DAY";
   char *ptr;
   ptr = strstr(str1, str2);
   if(ptr)
      printf("\n Substring Found");
   else
      printf("\n Substring Not Found");
   return 0;
}
```

Output

```
Substring Found
```

strspn Function

Syntax:

```
size_t strspn(const char *str1, const char *str2);
```

The function returns the index of the first character in `str1` that doesn't match any character in `str2`.

```
#include <stdio.h>
#include <string.h>
int main()
{
   char str1[] = "HAPPY BIRTHDAY TO YOU";
   char str2[] = "HAPPY BIRTHDAY JOE";
   printf("\n The position of first
   character in str2 that does not
   match with that in str1 is %d",
   strspn(str1,str2));
   return 0;
}
```

Output

```
The position of first character in str2
that does not match with that in str1 is 15
```

strcspn Function

Syntax:

```
size_t strcspn(const char *str1, const char *str2);
```

The function returns the index of the first character in `str1` that matches any of the characters in `str2`.

```
#include <stdio.h>
#include <string.h>
int main()
{
   char str1[] = "PROGRAMMING IN C";
   char str2[] = "IN";
   printf("\n The position of first
   character in str2 that matches with that
   in str1 is %d", strcspn(str1,str2));
   return 0;
}
```

Output

```
The position of first character in str2
that matches with that in str1 is 8
```

strpbrk Function

Syntax:

```
char *strpbrk(const char *str1, const char *str2);
```

The function `strpbrk()` returns a pointer to the first occurrence in `str1` of any character in `str2`, or `NULL` if none are present. The only difference between `strpbrk()` and `strcspn` is that `strcspn()` returns the index of the character and `strpbrk()` returns a pointer to the first occurrence of a character in `str2`.

```
#include <stdio.h>
#include <string.h>
int main()
{
   char str1[] = "PROGRAMMING IN C";
   char str2[] = "AB";
   char *ptr = strpbrk(str1,str2);
   if(ptr==NULL)
      printf("\n No character matches in the
   two strings");
   else
      printf("\n Character in str2 matches
   with that in str1");
   return 0;
}
```

Output

```
No character matches in the two strings
```

strtok Function

Syntax:

```
char *strtok( char *str1, const char
  *delimiter );
```

The `strtok()` function is used to isolate sequential tokens in a null-terminated string, `str`. These tokens are separated in the string using delimiters. The first time that `strtok` is called, `str` should be specified; subsequent calls, wishing to obtain further tokens from the same string, should pass a `NULL` pointer instead. However, the delimiter must be supplied each time, though it may change between calls.

The `strtok()` function returns a pointer to the beginning of each subsequent token in the string, after replacing the token itself with a `NULL` character. When all tokens are left, a `null` pointer is returned.

```
#include <stdio.h>
#include <string.h>
main ()
{
   char str[] = "Hello, to, the, world of,
   programming";
   char delim[] = ",";
   char result[20];
   result = strtok(str, delim);
   while(result!=NULL)
   {
      printf("\n %s", result);
      result = strtok(NULL, delim);
   }
   getch();
   return 0;
}
```

Output

```
Hello
to
the
world of
programming
```

strtol Function

Syntax:

```
long strtol(const char *str, char **end, int
base);
```

The `strtol` function converts the string pointed by `str` to a `long` value. The function skips leading white space characters and stops when it encounters the first non-numeric character. `strtol` stores the address of the first invalid character in `str` in `*end`. If there were no digits at all, then the `strtol` function will store the original value of `str` in `*end`. You may pass `NULL` instead of `*end` if you do not want to store the invalid characters anywhere.

Finally, the third argument base specifies whether the number is in `hexa-decimal`, `octal`, `binary`, or `decimal` representation.

```
#include <stdio.h>
#include <stdlib.h>
main ()
{
   long num;
num = strtol("12345 Decimal Value", NULL, 10);
printf("%ld", num);
num = strtol("65432 Octal Value", NULL, 8);
printf("%ld", num);
num = strtol("10110101 Binary Value", NULL, 2);
printf("%ld", num);
num = strtol("A7CB4 Hexadecimal Value",
   NULL, 16);
printf("%ld", num);
getch();
return 0;
}
```

Output

```
12345
27418
181
687284
```

strtod Function

Syntax:

```
double strtod(const char *str, char **end);
```

The function accepts a string `str` that has an optional plus (`'+'`) or minus sign (`'-'`) followed by either:

- a decimal number containing a sequence of decimal digits optionally consisting of a decimal point, or
- a hexadecimal number consisting of a `"0X"` or `"0x"` followed by a sequence of hexadecimal digits optionally containing a decimal point.

In both cases, the number may be optionally followed by an exponent (`'E'` or `'e'` for decimal constants or a `'P'` or `'p'` for hexadecimal constants), followed by an optional plus or minus sign, followed by a sequence of decimal digits. For decimal constants and hexadecimal constants, the exponent indicates the power of 10 and 2, respectively, by which the number should be scaled.

```
#include <stdio.h>
#include <stdlib.h>
main ()
{
   double num;
   num = strtod("123.345abcdefg", NULL);
   printf("%lf", num);
   getch();
   return 0;
}
```

Output

```
123.345000
```

atoi() Function

Till now you must have understood that the value 1 is an integer and '1' is a character. So there is a huge difference when we write the two statements given below

```
int i=1;       // here i =1
int i='1';     // here i =49, the ASCII
   value of character 1
```

Similarly, `123` is an integer number but `'123'` is a string of digits. What if you want to operate some integer operations on the string `'123'`? For this, C provides a function `atoi` that converts a given string into its corresponding integer.

The `atoi()` function converts a given string passed to it as an argument into an integer. The `atoi()` function returns that integer to the calling function. However, the string should start with a number. The `atoi()` will stop reading from the string as soon as it encounters a non-numerical character. The `atoi()` is included in the `stdlib.h` file. So before using this function in your program, you must include this header file. The syntax of `atoi()` can be given as,

```
int atoi( const char *str );
```

Example
```
i = atoi( "123.456" );
RESULT: i = 123.
```

atof() Function

The function `atof()` converts the string that it accepts as an argument into a double value and then return that value to the calling function. However, the string must start with a valid number. One point to remember is that the string can be terminated with any non-numerical character, other than `"E"` or `"e"`. The syntax of `atof()` can be given as,

```
double atof( const char *str );
```

Example
```
x = atof( "12.39 is the answer" );
RESULT: x = 12.39
```

atol() Function

The function `atol()` converts the string into a long int value. The `atol` function returns the converted long value to the calling function. Like `atoi`, the `atol()` will read from a string until it finds any character that should not be in a long. Its syntax can be given as,

```
long atol( const char *str );
```

Example
```
x = atol( "12345.6789" );
RESULT: x = 12345L.
```

> **Note** The functions atoi(), atof(), and atol() are a part of stdlib.h header file.

6.6 ARRAY OF STRINGS

Till now we have seen that a string is an array of characters. For example if we say, char `name[] = "Mohan"`, then name is a string (character array) that has five characters.

Now suppose that there are `20` students in a class and we need a string that stores names of all the `20` students. How can this be done? Here, we need a string of strings or an array of strings. Such an array of strings would store `20` individual strings. An array of string is declared as,

```
char names[20][30];
```

Here, the first index will specify how many strings are needed and the second index specifies the length of every individual string. So here, we allocate space for `20` names where each name can be a maximum of `30` characters long. Hence, the general syntax for declaring a two-dimensional array of strings can be given as,

```
<data type> <array_name> [<row_size>]
[<column_size>];
```

Let us see the memory representation of an array of strings. If we have an array declared as,

```
char name[5][10] = {"Ram", "Mohan", "Shyam",
"Hari", "Gopal"};
```

then in memory the array is stored as shown in Fig. 6.20.

Name[0]	R	A	M	'\0'						
Name[1]	M	O	H	A	N	'\0'				
Name[2]	S	H	Y	A	M	'\0'				
Name[3]	H	A	R	I	'\0'					
Name[4]	G	O	P	A	L	'\0'				

Figure 6.20 Memory representation of a 2D character array

By declaring the array names, we allocate 50 bytes. But the actual memory occupied is 27 bytes. Thus we see, more than half of the memory allocated lies wasted. Figure 6.21 shows an algorithm to process an individual string from an array of strings.

```
Step 1: [Initialize] SET I=0
Step 2: Repeat step 3 while I< N
Step 3: Apply Process to NAMES[I]
        [END OF LOOP]
Step 4: EXIT
```

Figure 6.21 Algorithm to process an individual string from an array of strings

Programming Tip: When accessing elements of a character array, make sure that the elements are within the array boundaries.

In Step 1, we initialize the index variable I to zero. In Step 2, a while loop is executed until all the strings in the array are accessed. In Step 3, each individual string is processed.

6.18 Write a program to read and print the names of n students of a class.

```
#include <stdio.h>
#include <conio.h>
main()
{
   char names[5][10];
   int i, n;
   clrscr();
   printf("\n Enter the number of students:");
   scanf("%d", &n);
   for(i=0;i<n;i++)
   {
      printf("\n Enter the name of
   student %d: ", i+1);
      gets(names[i]);
   }
   printf("\n Names of the students are:\n");
   for(i = 0;i < n;i++)
      puts(names[i]);
   getch();
   return 0;
}
```

Output

```
Enter the number of students: 3
Enter the name of student: Aditya
Enter the name of student: Goransh
Enter the name of student: Sarthak
Names of the students are: Aditya Goransh
Sarthak
```

6.19 Write a program to sort names of students.

```
#include <stdio.h>
#include <conio.h>
main()
{
   char names[5][10], temp[10];
   int i, n, j;
   clrscr();
   printf("\n Enter the number of students: ");
   scanf("%d", &n);
   for(i=0;i<n;i++)
   {
      printf("\n Enter the name of the
   student %d: ", i+1);
      fflush(stdin);
      gets(names[i]);
   }
   for(i = 0;i < n;i++)
   {
      for(j = 0;j < n-i-1;j++)
      {
      if(strcmp(names[j], names[j+1])>0)
      {
      strcpy(temp, names[j]);
      strcpy(names[j], names[j+1]);
      strcpy(names[j+1], temp);
               }
            }
         }
      printf("\n Names of the
   students are: ");
      for(i=0;i<n;i++)
      puts(names[i]);
      getch();
   return 0;
}
```

Programming Tip: Strings cannot be manipulated with arithmetic or other operators available in C boundaries.

Output

```
Enter the number of students: 3
Enter the name of student: Sarthak
Enter the name of student: Goransh
Enter the name of student: Aditya
Names of the students are: Aditya Goransh
Sarthak
```

PROGRAMMING EXAMPLES

6.20 Write a program to read and print the text until a * is encountered. Also count the number of characters in the text entered.

```
#include <stdio.h>
#include <conio.h>
int main()
{
   char str[1000];
   int i=0;
   clrscr();
   printf("\n Enter * to end");
   printf("\n **************");
   printf("\n Enter the text: ");
   scanf("%c", &str[i]);
   while(str[i] != '*')
   {
      i++;
      scanf("%c", &str[i]);
   }
   str[i] = '\0';
   printf("\n The text is: ");
   i=0;
   while(str[i] != '\0')
   {
      printf("%c", str[i]);
      i++;
   }
   printf("\n The count of characters is:
   %d",i-1);
   return 0;
}
```

Output

```
Enter * to end
**************
Enter the sentence: Hi there*
The text is: Hi there
The count of characters is: 7
```

6.21 Write a program to read a sentence. Then count the number of words in the sentence.

```
#include <stdio.h>
#include <conio.h>
int main()
{
   char str[1000];
   int i=0, count=0;
   clrscr();
   printf("\n Enter the sentence: ");
   gets(str);
   while(str[i] != '\0')
   {
      if(str[i] == ' ' && str[i+1] != ' ')
      count++;
      i++;
   }
   printf("\n The total count of words is:
   %d", count);
   return 0;
}
```

Output

```
Enter the sentence: How are you
The total count of words is: 3
```

6.22 Write a program to read multiple lines of text until a * is entered. Then count the number of characters, words, and lines in the text.

```
#include <stdio.h>
#include <conio.h>
int main()
{
   char str[1000];
   int i=0, word_count = 1, line_count =1,
   char_count = 1;
   clrscr();
   printf("\n Enter a * to end");
   printf("\n **************");
   printf("\n Enter the text: ");
   scanf("%c", &str[i]);
   while(str[i] != '*')
   {
      i++;
      scanf("%c", &str[i]);
   }
   str[i] = '\0';
   i=0;
   while(str[i] != '\0')
   {
      if(str[i] == '\n' || i==79)
        line_count++;
      if(str[i] == ' ' &&str[i+1] != ' ')
        word_count++;
      char_count++;
      i++;
   }
   printf("\n The total count of words is:
   %d", word_count);
   printf("\n The total count of lines is:
   %d", line_count);
   printf("\n The total count of characters
   is: %d", char_count);
```

```
    return 0;
}
```

Output

```
Enter the text: Hi there*
The total count of words is: 2
The total count of lines is: 1
The total count of characters is: 7
```

6.23 Write a program to copy n characters of a string from the mth position in another string.

```
#include <stdio.h>
#include <conio.h>
int main()
{
    char str[1000], copy_str[1000];
    int i=0, j=0, m, n;
    clrscr();
    printf("\n Enter the text: ");
    gets(str);
    printf("\n Enter the position from which
    to start: ");
    scanf("%d", &m);
    printf("\n Enter the number of characters
    to be copied: ");
    scanf("%d", &n);
    i = m;
    while(str[i] != '\0' && n>0)
    {
        copy_str[j] = str[i];
        i++;
        j++;
        n--;
    }
    copy_str[j] = '\0';
    printf("\n The copied text is: ");
    puts(copy_str);
    return 0;
}
```

Output

```
Enter the text: How are you?
Enter the position from which to start: 2
Enter the number of characters to be copied:
5
The copied text is: w are
```

6.24 Write a program to enter a text that has commas. Replace all the commas with semicolons and then display the text.

```
#include <stdio.h>
#include <conio.h>
int main()
{
    char str[1000], copy_str[1000];
    int i=0;
    clrscr();
    printf("\n Enter the text: ");
    gets(str);
    while(str[i] != '\0')
    {
        if(str[i] ==',')
        copy_str[i] = ';';
        else
        copy_str[i] = str[i];
        i++;
    }
    copy_str[i] = '\0';
    printf("\n The copied text is: ");
    i=0;
    while(copy_str[i] != '\0')
    {
        printf("%c", copy_str[i]);
        i++;
    }
    return 0;
}
```

Output

```
Enter the text: Hello, How are you
The copied text is: Hello; How are you
```

6.25 Write a program to enter a text that contains multiple lines. Rewrite this text by printing line numbers before the text of the line starts.

```
#include <stdio.h>
#include <conio.h>
int main()
{
    char str[1000];
    int i=0, linecount = 1;
    clrscr();
    printf("\n Enter a * to end");
    printf("\n **************");
    printf("\n Enter the text: ");
    scanf("%c", &str[i]);
    while(str[i] != '*')
    {
        i++;
        scanf("%c", &str[i]);
    }
    str[i] = '\0';
    i=0;
    while(str[i] != '\0')
    {
        if(linecount == 1 && i == 0)
        printf("\n %d\t", linecount);
        if(str[i] == '\n')
        {
        linecount++;
        printf("\n %d\t", linecount);
```

```
        }
        printf("%c", str[i]);
        i++;
    }
    return 0;
}
```

Output

```
Enter a * to end
*************
Enter the text:
Hello
how
are You?
1  Hello
2  how
3  are you?
```

6.26 Write a program to enter a text that contains multiple lines. Display the n lines of text starting from the mth line.

```
#include <stdio.h>
#include <conio.h>
int main()
{
    char str[1000];
    int i = 0, m, n, linecount = 0;
    clrscr();
    printf("\n Enter the text: ");
    scanf("%c", &str[i]);
    while(str[i]!='*')
      { i++;
        scanf("%c", &str[i]);
      }
    str[ii+1] = '\0';
    printf("\n Enter the line number from
    which to copy : ");
    scanf("%d", &m);
    printf("\n Enter the line number till
    which to copy : ");
    scanf("%d", &n);
    i=0,
    while(str[i] != '\0')
    {
      if(linecount == m )
      {
        j = i;
        while(n>0)
        {
        printf("%c", str[j]);
        j++;
        if(str[j] == '\n')
        {
        n--;
        linecount++;
        printf("%d \t", linecount);
        }
        }
        }
      else
      {
        i++;
        if(str[i] == '\n')
        linecount++;
      }
    }
    getch();
    return 0;
}
```

Output

```
Enter the text : Hello
how
are you?
*
Enter the line number from which to copy: 1
Enter the line number till which to copy: 2
Hello 1
how 2
```

6.27 Write a program to enter a text. Then enter a pattern and count the number of times the pattern is repeated in the text.

```
#include <stdio.h>
#include <conio.h>
main()
{
    char str[200], pat[20];
    int i=0, j=0, found=0, k, count=0;
    clrscr();
    printf("\n Enter the string: ");
    gets(str);
    printf("\n Enter the pattern: ");
    gets(pat);
    while(str[i]!='\0')
    {
        j=0, k=i;
    while(str[k]==pat[j] && pat[j]!='\0')
        {
          k++;
          j++;
        }
        if(pat[j]=='\0')
        {
          found=1;
          count++;
        }
        i++;
        }
```

```
        if(found==1)
            printf("\n PATTERN FOUND %d TIMES",
    count);
        else
        printf("\n PATTERN NOT FOUND");
    return 0;
}
```

Output

```
Enter the string: She sells sea shells on
the sea shore
Enter the pattern: sea
PATTERN FOUND 2 TIMES
```

6.28 Write a program to find whether a given string is a palindrome or not.

```
#include <stdio.h>
#include <conio.h>
int main()
{
    char str[100];
    int i = 0, j, length = 0;
    clrscr();
    printf("\n Enter the string: ");
    gets(str);
    while(str[i] != '\0')
    length++;
    i++;
    i=0;
    j = length - 1;
    while(i <= length/2)
    {
        if(str[i] == str[j])
        {
        i++;
        j--;
        }
        else
        break;
    }
    if(i>=j)
        printf("\n PALINDROME");
    else
        printf("\n NOT A PALINDROME");
    return 0;
}
```

Output

```
Enter the string: madam
PALINDROME
```

6.29 Write a program to implement a quiz program.

```
#include <stdio.h>
#include <string.h>
#include <conio.h>
main()
{
    char quest[5][100];
    char option1[3][20],option2[3][20],
    option3[3][20],option4[3][20],
    option5[3][20];
    int response[5], correct_ans[5], option,
    i, marks;
    clrscr();
    strcpy(quest[0],"Name the capital of
    India");
    strcpy(option1[0],"1. Mumbai");
    strcpy(option1[1],"2. New Delhi");
    strcpy(option1[2],"3. Chennai");
    correct_ans[0] = 1;
    strcpy(quest[1],"Name the national bird
    of India");
    strcpy(option2[0],"1. Peacock");
    strcpy(option2[1],"2. Sparrow");
    strcpy(option2[2],"3. Parrot");
    correct_ans[1]=0;
    strcpy(quest[2],"Name the first prime
    minister of India");
    strcpy(option3[0],"1. M D Gandhi");
    strcpy(option3[1],"2. S D Sharma");
    strcpy(option3[2],"3. J L Nehru");
    correct_ans[2]=2;
    strcpy(quest[3],"Name the first female
    president of India");
    strcpy(option4[0],"1. Pratibha Patil");
    strcpy(option4[1],"2. Sonia Gandhi");
    strcpy(option4[2],"3. Indira Gandhi");
    correct_ans[3] = 0;
    strcpy(quest[4],"Name the youngest prime
    minister of India");
    strcpy(option5[0],"1. Rajiv Gandhi");
    strcpy(option5[1],"2. Sanjay Gandhi");
    strcpy(option5[2],"3. Rahul Gandhi");
    correct_ans[4] = 0;
    do
    {
        printf("\n\n\n\n QUIZ PROGRAM");
        printf("\n******************");
        printf("\n 1. Display Questions");
        printf("\n 2. Display Correct Answers");
        printf("\n 3. Display Result");
        printf("\n 4. EXIT");
        printf("\n ************************");
        printf("\n\n\n Enter your option: ");
        scanf("%d", &option);
        switch(option)
        {
```

```
case 1:
printf("\n %s \n", quest[0]);
for(i=0;i<3;i++)
printf("\n %s", option1[i]);
printf("\n\n Enter your answer number: ");
scanf("%d", &response[0]);
printf("\n %s \n", quest[1]);
for(i=0;i<3;i++)
printf("\n %s", option2[i]);
printf("\n\n Enter your answer number: ");
scanf("%d", &response[1]);
printf("\n %s \n", quest[2]);
for(i=0;i<3;i++)
printf("\n %s", option3[i]);
printf("\n\n Enter your answer number: ");
scanf("%d", &response[2]);
printf("\n %s \n", quest[3]);
for(i=0;i<3;i++)
printf("\n %s", option4[i]);
printf("\n\n Enter your answer number: ");
scanf("%d", &response[3]);
printf("\n %s \n", quest[4]);
for(i=0;i<3;i++)
printf("\n %s", option5[i]);
printf("\n\n Enter your answer number: ");
scanf("%d", &response[4]);
break;
case 2:
   printf("\n\n CHECK THE CORRECT ANSWERS");
   printf("\n ************************");
   printf("\n %s \n
%s",quest[0],option1[correct_ans[0]]);
   printf("\n\n %s \n
%s",quest[1],option2[correct_ans[1]]);
   printf("\n\n %s \n
%s",quest[2],option3[correct_ans[2]]);
   printf("\n\n %s \n
%s",quest[3],option4[correct_ans[3]]);
   printf("\n\n %s \n
%s",quest[4],option5[correct_ans[4]]);
   break;
   case 3:
   marks = 0;
   for(i = 0;i <= 4;i++)
   {
   if(correct_ans[i]+1 == response[i])
   marks++;
   }
   printf("\n Out of 5 you score %d",
marks);
   break;
   }
}while(option!=4);
getch();
return 0;
}
```

POINTS TO NOTE

- A string is nothing but a null-terminated character array.
- A string is terminated with a null character ('\0') to signify the end of the character array.
- A string is a character array from which individual characters can be accessed using a subscript that starts from zero.
- All the characters of a string array are stored in successive memory locations.
- A string can be read from the user by using three ways—using `scanf` function, using `gets()` function, or using `getchar()` function repeatedly.
- `scanf` function terminates as soon as it finds a blank space.
- The `gets()` takes the starting address of the string which will hold the input. The string inputted using `gets()` is automatically terminated with a null character.
- The string can also be read by calling the `getchar()` repeatedly to read a sequence of single characters (unless a terminating character is entered).
- A string can be displayed on the screen using three ways—using `printf` function, using `puts()` function or using `putchar()` function repeatedly.
- In `printf()`, the width specifies the minimum output field width. If the string is short, extra space is either left padded or right padded. The precision specifies the maximum number of characters to be displayed. A negative width left pads short string rather than the default right justification. If the string is long, the extra characters are truncated.
- The number of characters in the string constitutes the length of the string.
- Appending one string to another string involves copying the contents of the source string at the end of the destination string. There is a library function `strcat(s1, s2)` that concatenates `s2` to `s1`. It is defined in `string.h`
- To extract a substring from a given string requires information about three things—the main string, the position of the first character of the substring in the given string, and the maximum number of characters/length of the substring.
- Index operation returns the position in the string where the string pattern first occurs.
- Replacement operation is used to replace the pattern P1 by another pattern P2.

GLOSSARY

String An array of characters terminated by a NULL character.

String matching Finding occurrences of a *pattern* string within another *string*.

String taxonomy A string can be stored either in fixed-length or in variable-length format.

EXERCISES

Fill in the Blanks

1. Strings are __________.
2. Every string is terminated with a __________.
3. If a string is given as "AB CD", the length of this string is __________.
4. The subscript of a string starts with __________.
5. Characters of a string are stored in __________ memory locations.
6. char `mesg[100];` can store maximum __________characters.
7. __________ function terminates as soon as it finds a blank space.
8. `LENGTH('')` = __________.
9. The ASCII code for `A-Z` varies from __________.
10. `toupper()` is used to __________.
11. `S1>S2`, means __________.
12. The function to reverse a string is __________.
13. If `S1 = "GOOD MORNING"`, then `Substr_Left (S1, 7)` =
14. `INDEX("Welcome to the world of programming", "world")` = __________.
15. __________ returns the position in the string where the string pattern first occurs.
16. The function `atoi()` is present in __________ header file.
17. `strncat` is used to __________.
18. `strcmp(str1, str2)` returns 1 if __________.
19. __________ function computes the length of a string.
20. Besides `printf()`, __________ function can be used to print a line of text on the screen.

Multiple Choice Questions

1. `LENGTH('0')` =
   (a) –1 (b) 0
   (c) 1 (d) None of these
2. ASCII code for `a–z` ranges from
   (a) 0–26 (b) 35–81
   (c) 97–123 (d) None of these
3. Insert`("XXXYYYZZZ", 1, "PPP")` =
   (a) PPPXXXYYYZZZ (b) XPPPXXYYYZZZ
   (c) XXXYYYZZZPPP
4. Delete`("XXXYYYZZZ", 4,3)` =
   (a) XXYZ (b) XXXYYZZ
   (c) XXXYZZ
5. If `str[] = "Welcome to the world of programming"`, then, `SUBSTRING(str, 15, 5)` =
   (a) world (b) programming
   (c) welcome (d) none of these
6. `strcat()` is defined in which header file?
   (a) ctype.h (b) stdio.h
   (c) string.h (d) math.h
7. A string can be read using which functions?
   (a) `gets()` (b) `scanf()`
   (c) `getchar()` (d) all of these
8. Replace`("XXXYYYZZZ", "XY", "AB")` =
   (a) XXABYYZZZ (b) XABYYYZZZ
   (c) ABXXXYYYZZZ
9. The index of U in Oxford University Press is?
   (a) 5 (b) 6
   (c) 7 (d) 8
10. `s1 = "HI", s2 = "HELLO", s3 = "BYE"`. How can we concatenate the three strings?
    (a) `strcat(s1,s2,s3)`
    (b) `strcat(s1(strcat(s2,s3)))`
    (c) `strcpy(s1, strcat(s2,s3))`
11. `strlen("Oxford University Press")` is ?
    (a) 22 (b) 23
    (c) 24 (d) 25
12. Which function adds a string to the end of another string?
    (a) `stradd()` (b) `strcat()`
    (c) `strtok()` (d) `strcpy()`

EXERCISES

State True or False

1. A string Hello World can be read using `scanf()`
2. Initializing a string as, `char str[]="HELLO";` is incorrect as a null character has not been explicitly added.
3. A string when read using `scanf()` needs an ampersand character.
4. The `gets()` takes the starting address of the string which will hold the input.
5. The `gets()` and `scanf()` automatically appends a null character at the end of the string read from the keyboard.
6. The function `scanf()` can be used to read a line of text that includes white space characters.
7. The function `tolower()` is defined in `ctype.h` header file.
8. Arithmetic operators can be applied to string variables.
9. String variables can be present either on the left or on the right side of the assignment operator.
10. If `S1` and `S2` are two strings, then concatenation operation produces a string which contains characters of `S2` followed by the characters of `S1`.
11. Appending one string to another string involves copying the contents of the source string at the end of the destination string.
12. `S1<S2`, when in dictionary order `S1` precedes `S2`.
13. If `S1` = "`GOOD MORNING`", then `Substr_Right(S1, 5) = MORNING`.
14. Replace `("AAABBBCCC", "X", "YYY")= AAABBBCC`.
15. When a string is initialized during its declaration, the string must be explicitly terminated with a null character.
16. The function `strcmp("and","ant")` will return a positive value.
17. Assignment operator can be used to copy the contents of one string into another.

Review Questions

1. What are strings? Discuss some operations that can be performed on strings.
2. Explain how strings are represented in main memory.
3. Explain operations that can be performed on strings.
4. How are strings read from the standard input device? Explain the different functions used to perform string input operation.
5. Explain how strings can be displayed on the screen.
6. Explain the syntax of `printf()` and `scanf()`.
7. Write a short note on string operations.
8. Differentiate between `gets()` and `scanf()`.
9. Give the drawbacks of `getchar()` and `scanf()`. Which function can be used to overcome the shortcomings of `getchar()` and `scanf()`?
10. How can `putchar()` be used to print a string?
11. Differentiate between a character and a string.
12. Differentiate between a character array and a string.
13. List all the substrings that can be formed from the string "ABCD".
14. What do you understand by pattern matching? Give an algorithm for it.
15. Write a short note on array of strings.
16. How is an array of strings represented in the memory?
17. Explain with an example how an array of strings is stored in main memory.
18. If `Substring` function is given as- `SUBSTRING(string, position, length)` then, find `S(5,9)` if `S = "Welcome to world of C Programming"`.
19. If Index function is given as `INDEX(text, pattern)`, then find the `index(T, P)` where T = "Welcome to `world of C Programming`" and P = "of".
20. Write a program in which a string is passed as an argument to a function.
21. Write a program in C to concatenate first `n` characters of a string to another string.
22. Write a program in C that compares first `n` characters of one string with first `n` characters of another string.
23. Write a program that reads your name and then displays the ASCII value of each character in your name on a separate line.
24. Write a program in C that removes leading and trailing spaces from a string.
25. Write a program to read a word and re-write its characters in alphabetical order.
26. Write a program that accepts an integer value from 0 to 999. Display the value of the number read in words. That is, if the user enters 753, then print Seven Hundred Fifty Three.
27. Write a program to insert a word before a given word in the text.

EXERCISES

28. Write a program to (a) read a name and then display it in abbreviated form, (b) Janak Raj Thareja should be displayed as JRT; (c) Janak Raj Thareja should be displayed as J.R. Thareja.
29. Write a program in C that replaces a given character with another character in the string.
30. Write a program to display the word Hello in the following format:

```
H
H E
H E L
H E L L
H E L L O
```

31. Write a program to display the given string array in reverse order.
32. Write a program to count the number of characters, words, and lines in the given text.
33. Write a program to count the number of digits, upper case characters, lower case characters, and special characters in a given string.
34. Write a program to count the total number of occurrences of a given character in the string.
35. Write a program to accept a text. Count and display the number of times the word "the" appears in the text.
36. Write a program to count the total number of occurrences of a word in the text.
37. Write a program to find the last instance of occurrence of a sub-string within a string.
38. Write a program to insert a sub-string in the middle of a given string.
39. Write a program to input an array of strings. Then reverse the string in the format shown below.

    "HAPPY BIRTHDAY TO YOU" should be displayed as "YOU TO BIRTHDAY HAPPY".
40. Write a program to append a given string in the following format.

    "GOOD MORNING MORNING GOOD"
41. Write a program to trim a string.
42. Write a program to input a text of at least two paragraphs. Interchange the first and second paragraphs and then re-display the text on screen.
43. Write a program to input a text of at least two paragraphs. Construct an array PAR such that PAR[I] contains the location of the Ith paragraph in TEXT.
44. Write a program to find the length of "GOOD MORNING".
45. (a) Write a program to convert the given string "GOOD MORNING" to "good morning".

    (b) Write a program to convert the given string "hello world" to "HELLO WORLD".
46. Write a program to concatenate two given strings "Good Morning" and "World". Display the resultant string.
47. Write a program to append two given strings "Good Morning" and "World". Display the resultant string.
48. Write a program to check whether the two given strings "Good Morning" and "GOOD MORNING" are same.
49. Write a program to convert the given string "hello world" to "dlrow olleh".
50. Write a menu-driven program that demonstrates the use of string functions present in the `string.h` header file.
51. Write a menu-driven program that demonstrates the use of character handling functions present in the `ctype.h` header file.
52. Write a program to extract the string "Good" from the given string "Good Morning".
53. Write a program to extract the string "od Mo" from the given string "Good Morning".
54. Write a program to insert "University" in the given string "Oxford Press" so that the string should read as "Oxford University Press".
55. Write a program to delete "University" from the given string "Oxford University Press" so that the string should read as "Oxford Press".
56. Write a menu-driven program to read a string, display the string, merge two strings, copy n characters from the mth position, calculate the length of the string.
57. Write a program to copy the last n characters of a character array in another character array. Also convert the lower case letters into upper case letters while copying.
58. Write a program to copy "University" from the given string "Oxford University Press" in another string.
59. Write a program to simulate the `strcpy` function.
60. Write a program to program to rewrite the string "Good Morning" to "Good Evening".
61. Write a program to read and display names of employees in a department.
62. Write a program to sort the names of employees alphabetically.

EXERCISES

63. Write a program to read a short story and count the number of characters, words, lines in the story.
64. Write a program to enter a text that has both lower case as well as uppercase characters. Replace all the lower case characters with upper case characters and then display the text.
65. Write a program to read a short story. Display the n lines of story starting from the mth line.
66. Write a program to read a short story. Rewrite the story by printing the line number before the starting of each line.
67. Write a program to display a list of candidates. Prompt 100 users to cast their vote. Finally display the winner in the elections.
68. Write a program to delete the last character of a string.
69. Write a program to delete the first character of a string.
70. Write a program to count the number of times a given character appears in the string.
71. Write a program to insert a new name in the string array `STUD[][]`, assuming that names are sorted alphabetically.
72. Write a program to delete a name in the string array `STUD[][]`, assuming that names are sorted alphabetically.
73. In a class there are 20 students. Each student is supposed to appear in three tests and two quizzes throughout the year. Make an array that stores the names of all these 20 students. Make five arrays that stores marks of three subjects as well as scores of two quizzes for all the students. Calculate the average and total marks of each student. Display the result.

Find errors in the following codes.

```
1. main()
   {
      char str1[]="Programming";
      char str2[] = "In C";
      str1 = str2;
      printf("\n str1 = %s", str1);
   }
2. main()
   {
      char str[]={'H','e','l','l','o'};
      printf("\n str = %s", str);
   }
3. main()
   {
      char str[5]="HELLO";
      printf("\n str = %s", str);
   }
4. main()
   {
      char str[10];
      strncpy(str, "HELLO", 3);
      printf("\n str = %s", str);
   }
5. main()
   {
      char str[10];
      strcpy(str, "Hello there");
      printf("\n str = %s", str);
   }
6. main()
   {
      char str[]= "Hello there";
      if(strstr(str, "Uni")==0)
         printf("\n Substring Found");
   }
7. main()
   {
      char str1[10], str2[10];
      gets(str1, str2);
      printf("\n str1 = %s and str2 = %s",
      str1, str2);
   }
```

Find the output of the following codes.

```
1. main()
   {
      char str1[]= {'H','I'};
      char str2[] = {'H', 'I', '\0'};
      if(strcmp(str1, str2) == 0)
         printf("\n The strings are equal");
      else
         printf("\n Strings are not
      equal");
   }
2. main()
   {
      char str[]= "Programming in C";
      int i;
      while(str[i]!='\0')
      {
         if(i%2==0)
            printf("%c", str[i]);
         i++;
      }
   }
3. main()
   {
      char str[]="GGOD MORNING";
```

EXERCISES

```
    printf("\n %20.10s", str);
    printf("\n %s", str[0]);
    printf("\n %s", &str[5]);
  }
4. main()
  {
    char ch = 'k';
    printf("%c", ch+10);
  }
5. main()
  {
    char str1[]= "Programming";
  chat str2[] = "Is Fun";
    strcpy(str1, str2);
    printf("\n %s", str1);
  }
6. main()
  {
    char str1[]= "Programming";
    chat str2[] = "Is Fun";
    strncpy(str1, str2, 3);
    printf("\n %s", str1);
  }
7. main()
  {
    char str1[]= "Programming";
    chat str2[] = "Project";
    printf("%d", strncmp(str1, str2, 3));
  }
8. main()
  {
    char str[]= "Oxford University Press";
    printf("%s", strstr(str, "Uni"));
  }
```

CHAPTER 7

Pointers

Takeaways

- Pointer Expressions
- Pointers with Functions
- Function Pointers
- Pointer Arithmetic
- Pointers with Arrays
- Dynamic Memory Allocation
- Null and Generic Pointers
- Pointers with Strings

7.1 UNDERSTANDING THE COMPUTER'S MEMORY

Every computer has a primary memory. All data and programs need to be placed in the primary memory for execution. The primary memory or RAM (Random Access Memory which is a part of the primary memory) is a collection of memory locations (often known as cells) and each location has a specific address. Each memory location is capable of storing 1 byte of data (though new computers are able to store 2 bytes of data but in this book we have been talking about locations storing 1 byte of data). Therefore, a `char` type data needs just 1 memory location, an `int` type data needs 2 memory locations. Similarly, `float` and `double` type data need 4 and 8 memory locations, respectively.

Generally, the computer has three areas of memory each of which is used for a specific task. These areas of memory include—stack, heap, and global memory.

Stack A fixed size of stack is allocated by the system and is filled as needed from the bottom to the top, one element at a time. These elements can be removed from the top to the bottom by removing one element at a time, i.e., the last element added to the stack is removed first.

When the program has used the variables or data stored in the stack, it can be discarded to enable the stack to be used for other programs to store its data. We have already read a little bit on the system stack in Functions when we discussed Recursion. We will read more about them in the chapter on Stacks.

Stack is the section of memory that is allocated for automatic variables within functions.

Heap It is a contiguous block of memory that is available for use by the program when the need arises. A fixed size heap is allocated by the system and is used by the system in a random fashion.

The addresses of the memory locations in heap that are not currently allocated to the program for use are stored in a free list. When the program requests a block of memory, the dynamic allocation technique (discussed at the end of this Chapter) takes a block from the heap and assigns it to the program. When the program has finished using the block, it returns the memory block to the heap and the location of the memory locations in that block is added to the free list.

Compared to heaps, a stack is faster but smaller and expensive. When a program begins execution with the `main()`, all variables declared within `main()` are allocated space on the stack. Moreover, all the parametres passed to the called function will be stored on the stack.

Global memory The block of code that is the `main()` program (along with other functions in the program) is stored in the global memory. The memory in the global area is allocated randomly to store the code of different functions in the program in such a way that one function is not contiguous to another function. Besides, the function code, all global variables declared in the program are stored in the global memory area.

Other memory layouts C provides some more memory areas such as text segment, BSS, and shared library segment.

- The text segment is used to store the machine instructions corresponding to the compiled program. This is generally a read-only memory segment.
- BSS (Block Started by Symbol) is used to store un-initialized global variables.
- Shared library segment contains the executable image of shared libraries that are being used by the program.

7.2 INTRODUCTION TO POINTERS

Every variable in C language has a name and a value associated with it. When a variable is declared, a specific block of memory within the computer is allocated to hold the value of that variable. The size of the allocated block depends on the type of the data. Let us write a program to find the size of the various data types on your system. (Note the size of integer may vary from one system to another. In 32 bit systems, integer variable is allocated 4 bytes while on 16 bit systems it is allocated 2 bytes).

7.1 Write a program to find the size of various data types on your system.

```
#include <stdio.h>
int main()
{
    printf("\n The size of short integer is :
    %d", sizeof(short int));
    printf("\n The size of unsigned integer
    is: %d", sizeof(unsigned int));
    printf("\n The size of signed integer is:
    %d", sizeof(signed int));
    printf("\n The size of integer is:%d",
    sizeof(int));
    printf("\n The size of long integer is:
    %d", sizeof(long int));

    printf("\n The size of character is: %d",
    sizeof(char));
    printf("\n The size of unsigned character
    is: %d", sizeof(unsigned char));
    printf("\n The size of signed character
    is: %d", sizeof(signed char));

    printf("\n The size of floating point
    number is: %d", sizeof(float));
    printf("\n The size of double number is:
    %d", sizeof(double));
    return 0;
}
```

Output

```
The size of short integer is: 2
The size of unsigned integer is: 2
The size of signed integer is: 2
The size of integer is: 2
The size of long integer is: 4
The size of character is: 1
The size of unsigned character is: 1
The size of signed character is: 1
The size of floating point number is: 4
The size of double number is: 8
```

Consider the statement below.

```
int x = 10;
```

When this statement executes, the compiler sets aside 2 bytes of memory to hold the value 10. It also sets up a symbol table in which it adds the symbol x and the relative address in memory where those 2 bytes were set aside.

Thus, every variable in C has a value and a memory location (commonly known as address) associated with it. Some texts use the term *rvalue* and *lvalue* for the value and the address of the variable, respectively.

The rvalue appears on the right side of the assignment statement (10 in the above statement) and cannot be used on the left side of the assignment statement. Therefore, writing `10 = k;` is illegal. If we write,

```
int x, y;
x = 10;
y = x;
```

Then in this code we have two integer variables `x` and `y`. Compiler reserves memory for integer variable `x` and stores rvalue `10` in it. When we say y = x, then x is interpreted as its rvalue (since it is on the right-hand side of the assignment operator '='). Here x refers to the value stored at the memory location set aside for `x`, in this case `10`. After this statement is executed, the rvalue of `y` is also `10`.

You must be wondering why we are discussing addresses and lvalues? Actually pointers are nothing but memory addresses. A *pointer* is a variable that contains the memory location of another variable. Therefore, a pointer is a variable that represents the location of a data item, such as a variable or an array element. Pointers are frequently used in C language as they have a number of useful applications. These applications include:

- to pass information back and forth between a function and its reference point
- enable the programmers to return multiple data items from a function via function arguments
- provide an alternate way to access individual elements of the array
- to pass arrays and strings as function arguments
- enable references to functions. So with pointers, the programmer can even pass functions as argument to another function
- to create complex data structures such as trees, linked list, linked stack, linked queue, and graphs
- for dynamic memory allocation of a variable

7.3 DECLARING POINTER VARIABLES

A pointer provides access to a variable by using the address of that variable. A pointer variable is therefore a variable that stores the address of another variable. The general syntax of declaring pointer variables can be given as below.

```
data_type *ptr_name;
```

Programming Tip:
The data type of the pointer variable and the variable to which it points must be the same.

Here, `data_type` is the data type of the value that the pointer will point to. For example,

```
int *pnum;
char *pch;
float *pfnum;
```

In each of the above statements, a pointer variable is declared to point to a variable of the specified data type. Although all these pointers, `pnum`, `pch`, and `pfnum` point to different data types but they will occupy the same amount of space in memory. But how much space they occupy will depend on the platform where the code is going to run. To verify this, execute the following code and observe the result:

```
#include <stdio.h>
main()
{
    int *pnum;
    char *pch;
    float *pfnum;
    double *pdnum;
    long *plnum;
    printf("\n Size of integer pointer =
    %d", sizeof(pnum));
    printf("\n Size of character pointer =
    %d", sizeof(pch));
    printf("\n Size of float pointer = %d",
    sizeof(pfnum));
    printf("\n Size of double pointer = %d",
    sizeof(pdnum));
    printf("\n Size of long pointer = %d",
    sizeof(plnum));
}
```

Output

```
Size of integer pointer = 2
Size of character pointer = 2
Size of float pointer = 2
Size of double pointer = 2
Size of long pointer = 2
```

Now let us declare an integer pointer variable and start using it in our program code.

```
int x= 10;
int *ptr;
ptr = &x;
```

In the above statement, `ptr` is the name of pointer variable. The `'*'` informs the compiler that `ptr` is a pointer variable and the `int` specifies that it will store the address of an integer variable. An integer pointer variable, therefore, *point to* an integer variable. In the last statement, `ptr` is assigned the address of x. The `&` operator retrieves the lvalue (address) of x, and copies that to the contents of the pointer `ptr`.

Programming Tip:
A pointer variable can store only the address of a variable.

Consider the memory cells given in Fig. 7.1.

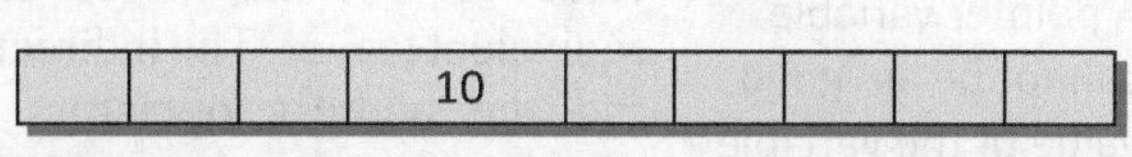

Figure 7.1 Memory representation

Now, since x is an integer variable, it will be allocated 2 bytes. Assuming that the compiler assigns it memory locations 1003 and 1004, we say the value of x = 10 and the address of x (written as &x) is equal to 1003, i.e., the starting address of x in the memory. When we write, ptr = &x, then ptr = 1003.

In C, pointers are not allowed to store memory addresses, but they can store only the addresses of variables of a given type. Therefore writing a statement like int *ptr = 1000; is absolutely illegal in C.

We can *dereference* a pointer, i.e., refer to the value of the variable to which it points, by using unary '*' operator (also known as *indirection operator*) as in *ptr, i.e., *ptr = 10, since 10 is value of x. Therefore, * is equivalent to writing *value at address*. Look at the code below which shows the use of pointer variable.

Programming Tip:
The address of a memory location is a constant, therefore, it cannot be changed in the program code.

```
#include <stdio.h>
int main()
{
    int num, *pnum;
    pnum = &num;
    printf("\n Enter the number: ");
    scanf("%d", &num);
    printf("\n The number that was entered
    is: %d", *pnum);
    printf("\n The address of number in
    memory is: %p", &num);
    return 0;
}
```

Output

```
Enter the number: 10
The number that was entered is: 10
The address of number in memory is: FFDC
```

%p control string prints the argument as a memory address in hexadecimal form. %u prints memory address in decimal form.

Programming Tip:
A pointer variable cannot be assigned value of the variable to which it points.

Can you tell what will be the value of *(&num)? Yes it is equivalent to num. The indirection and the address operators are inverse of each other, so when combined in an expression, they cancel each other.

We can also assign values to variables using pointer variables and modify its value. The code given below shows this.

```
#include <stdio.h>
int main()
{
    int num, *pnum;
    pnum = &num;
    *pnum = 10;
    printf("\n *pnum = %d", *pnum);
    printf("\n num = %d", num);
    *pnum  = *pnum + 1;
    // increments the value of num
    printf("\nAfter increment *pnum = %d", *pnum);
    printf("\n After increment num = %d", num);
    return 0;
}
```

Output

```
*pnum = 10
num = 10
After increment *pnum = 11
After increment num = 11
```

Now can you predict the output of the following code?

```
#include <stdio.h>
int main()
{
    int num, *pnum1, *pnum2;
    pnum1 = &num;
    *pnum1 = 10;
    pnum2 = pnum1;
    printf("\n Value of num using all three
    variables (num, *pnum1, *pnum2) = %d %d
    %d", num, *pnum1, *pnum2);
    printf("\n Address of num using all three
    variables (&num, pnum1, pnum2) = %x %x
    %x", num, pnum1, pnum2);
return 0;
}
```

While the first printf statement will print the value of num, the second printf statement will print address of num. These are just three different ways to refer to the value and address of the same variable.

Any number of pointers can point to the same address.

The address of a variable is the address of the first byte occupied by that variable. Basically, address of the variable is the relative location of the variable with respect to the program's memory space. We cannot change the address of a variable, we can only use them. Although the address of a variable cannot be changed, the variable's address may change during different program runs, i.e., if you try to print the address of `num` today, it may print `4010`. Next time when you run the program, it may print the address as `FA12`.

Programming Tip:
It is an error to assign address of a variable to another variable of the same type. The variable to which the adddress is being assigned must be declared as a pointer variable.

One thing to remember always is that the data type of the pointer variable and the variable whose address it will store must both be of the same type. Therefore, the following code is not valid.

```
int x = 10;
float y = 2.0;
int *px;
float *py;
px = &y;//INVALID
py = &x;//INVALID
```

Also note that it is not necessary that the pointer variable will point to the same variable throughout the program. It can point to any variable as long as the data type of the pointer variable is same as that of the variable it points to. The following code illustrates this concept.

```
#include <stdio.h>
main()
{
   int a=3, b=5;
   int *pnum;
   pnum = &a;
   printf("\n a = %d", *pnum);
   pnum = &b;
   printf("\n b = %d", *pnum);
   return 0;
}
```

Output

```
a = 3
b = 5
```

Using an un-initialized pointer can cause unpredictable results.

7.4 POINTER EXPRESSIONS AND POINTER ARITHMETIC

Like other variables, pointer variables can also be used in expressions. For example, if `ptr1` and `ptr2` are pointers, then the following statements are valid:

```
int num1=2, num2= 3, sum=0, mul=0, div=1;
int *ptr1, *ptr2;
ptr1 = &num1;
ptr2 = &num2;

sum = *ptr1 + *ptr2;
mul = sum * *ptr1;
*ptr2 +=1;
div = 9 + *ptr1/*ptr2 - 30;
```

Programming Tip:
A pointer variable that is declared but not initialized contains garbage value. Hence, such a pointer variable must not be used before it is assigned any variable's address.

In C, the programmer may add or subtract integers from pointers. We can also subtract one pointer from the other. We can also use short hand operators with the pointer variables as we use with other variables.

C also allows to compare pointers by using relational operators in the expressions. For example, `p1 > p2`, `p1 == p2`, and `p1! = p2` are all valid in `C`.

When using pointers, unary increment `(++)` and decrement `(--)` operators have greater precedence than the dereference operator `(*)`. But both these operators have a special behaviour when used as suffix. In that case the expression is evaluated with the value it had before being increased. Therefore, the expression

```
*ptr++
```

is equivalent to `*(ptr++)` as `++` has greater operator precedence than `*`. Therefore, the expression will increase the value of `ptr` so that it now points to the next element. This means the statement `*ptr++` does not perform the intended task. Therefore, to increment the value of the variable whose address is stored in `ptr`, you should write

```
(*ptr)++
```

Now, let us consider another C statement

```
int num1=2, num2=3;
int *p = &num1, *q=&num2;
*p++ = *q++;
```

What will `*p++ = *q++` do? Because ++ has a higher precedence than *, both `p` and `q` are increased, but because the increment operators (++) are used as postfix and not prefix, the value assigned to `*p` is `*q` before

Programming Tip:
It is an error to subtract two pointer variables.

both p and q are increased. Then both are increased. So the statement is equivalent to writing:

```
*p = *q;
++p; ++q;
```

Let us now summarize the rules for pointer operations:

- A pointer variable can be assigned the address of another variable (of the same type).
- A pointer variable can be assigned the value of another pointer variable (of the same type).
- A pointer variable can be initialized with a `NULL` (or `0`) value.
- Prefix or postfix increment and decrement operators can be applied on a pointer variable.
- An integer value can be added or subtracted from a pointer variable.
- A pointer variable can be compared with another pointer variable of the same type using relational operators.
- A pointer variable cannot be multiplied by a constant.
- A pointer variable cannot be added to another pointer variable.

PROGRAMS USING POINTERS

7.2 Write a program to print 'Hello World' using pointers.

```
#include <stdio.h>
int main()
{
    char *ch = "Hello World";
    printf("%s", ch);
    return 0;
}
```

Output

```
Hello World
```

7.3 Write a program to add two floating point numbers. The result should contain only two digits after the decimal.

```
#include <stdio.h>
int main()
{
    float num1, num2, sum = 0.0;
    float *pnum1 = &num1, *pnum2 = &num2,
    *psum = &sum;
    printf("\n Enter the two numbers: ");
    scanf("%f %f", pnum1, pnum2);
    // pnum1 = &num1;
    *psum = *pnum1 + *pnum2;
    printf("\n %f + %f = %.2f", *pnum1,
    *pnum2, *psum);
    return 0;
}
```

Output

```
Enter the two numbers: 2.5 3.4
2.5 + 3.4 = 5.90
```

7.4 Write a program to calculate the area of a circle.

```
#include <stdio.h>
#include <conio.h>
int main()
{
    double radius, area = 0.0;
    double *pradius = &radius, *parea = &area;
    printf("\n Enter the radius of the circle: ");
    scanf("%lf", pradius);
    *parea = 3.14 * (*pradius) * (*pradius);
    printf("\n The area of the circle with
    radius %.2lf = %.2lf", *pradius, *parea);
    return 0;
}
```

Output

```
Enter the radius of the circle: 7.0
The area of the circle with radius 7.0 =
    153.83
```

7.5 Write a program to convert a floating point number into an integer.

```
#include <stdio.h>
int main()
{
    float fnum, *pfnum = &fnum;
    int num, *pnum = &num;
    printf("\n Enter the floating point no.: ");
    scanf("%f", &fnum);
    *pnum = (int)*pfnum;
    printf("\n The integer equivalent of %f =
    %d", *pfnum, *pnum);
    return 0;
}
```

Output

```
Enter the floating point no.: 3.4
The integer equivalent of 3.4000 = 3
```

7.6 Write a program to find the biggest of three numbers.

```
#include <stdio.h>
int main()
```

```
{
   int num1, num2, num3;
   int *pnum1 = &num1, *pnum2 = &num2,
   *pnum3= &num3;
   printf("\n Enter the first number: ");
   scanf("%d", pnum1);
   printf("\n Enter the second number: ");
   scanf("%d", pnum2);
   printf("\n Enter the third number: ");
   scanf("%d", pnum3);
   if(*pnum1 > *pnum2  &&  *pnum1 > *pnum3)
      printf("\n %d is the largest number", *pnum1);
   if(*pnum2 > *pnum1  &&  *pnum2 > *pnum3)
      printf("\n %d is the largest number", *pnum2);
   else
      printf("\n %d is the largest number", *pnum3);
   return 0;
}
```

Output

```
Enter the first number: 5
Enter the second number: 7
Enter the third number: 3
7 is the largest number
```

7.7 Write a program to print a character. Also print its ASCII value and rewrite the character in upper case.

```
#include <stdio.h>
#include <conio.h>
int main()
{
   int ch, *pch = &ch;
   clrscr();
   printf("\n Enter the character: ");
   scanf("%c", &ch);
   printf("\n The char entered is: %c", *pch);
   printf("\n ASCII value of the char is: %d", *pch);
   printf("\n The char in upper case is: %c", *pch - 32);
   getch();
   return 0;
}
```

Output

```
Enter the character: z
The char entered is: z
ASCII value of the char is: 122
The char in upper case is: Z
```

7.8 Write a program which takes an input from the user and then checks whether it is a number or a character. If it is a character, determine whether it is in upper case or lower case.

```
#include <stdio.h>
#include <conio.h>
int main()
{
   char ch, *pch = &ch;
   clrscr();
   printf("\n Enter any character: ");
   scanf("%c", pch);
   if(*pch >='A' && *pch<='Z')
      printf("\n Upper case char was entered");
   if(*pch >='a' && *pch<='z')
      printf("\n Lower case char was entered");
   else if(*pch>='0' && *pch<='9')
      printf("\n You entered a number");
   getch();
   return 0;
}
```

Output

```
Enter any character: 7
You entered a number
```

7.9 Write a program using pointer variables to read a character until * is entered. If the character is in upper case, print it in lower case and vice versa. Also count the number of upper and lower case characters entered.

```
#include <stdio.h>
#include <conio.h>
int main()
{
   char ch, *pch = &ch;
   int upper = 0, lower = 0;
   clrscr();
   printf("\n Enter the character: ");
   scanf("%c", pch);
   while(*pch != '*')
   {
      if(*pch >= 'A' && *pch <= 'Z')
      {
      *pch += 32;
      upper++;
      }
      if(*pch >= 'a' && *pch <= 'z')
      {
      *pch -= 32;
      lower++;
      }
      printf("%c", *pch);
      fflush(stdin);
```

```
        printf("\n Enter the character: ");
        scanf("%c", pch);
    }
    printf("\n Total number of upper case
    characters = %d", upper);
    printf("\n Total number of lower case
    characters = %d", lower);
    getch();
    return 0;
}
```

Output

```
Enter the character: A
A
Enter the character: b
B
Enter the character: c
C
Enter the character: *
Total number of upper case characters = 1
Total number of lower case characters = 2
```

7.10 Write a program to test whether a number is positive, negative, or equal to zero.

```
#include <stdio.h>
int main()
{
    int num, *pnum = &num;
    printf("\n Enter any number: ");
    scanf("%d", pnum);
    if(*pnum>0)
        printf("\n The number is positive");
    else
    {
        if(*pnum<0)
        printf("\n The number is negative");
        else
        printf("\n The number is equal to
    zero");
    }
    return 0;
}
```

Output

```
Enter any number: -1
The number is negative
```

7.11 Write a program to display the sum and average of numbers from m to n.

```
#include <stdio.h>
int main()
{
    int num, *pnum = &num, range;
    int m, *pm = &m;
    int n, *pn = &n;
    int sum = 0, *psum = &sum;
    float avg, *pavg = &avg;
    printf("\n Enter the starting and ending
    limit of the numbers to be summed:");
        scanf("%d %d", pm, pn);
        range = n - m ;
    while(*pm <= *pn)
    {
        *psum = *psum + *pm;
        *pm = *pm + 1;
    }
    printf("\n Sum of numbers = %d , *psum);
    *pavg = *psum / range;
    printf("\n Average of numbers = %f",
    *pavg);
    return 0;
}
```

Output

```
Enter the starting and ending limit of the
    numbers to be summed: 0 10
Sum of numbers = 55
Average of numbers = 5.5
```

7.12 Write a program to print all even numbers from m–n.

```
#include <stdio.h>
#include <conio.h>
int main()
{
    int m, *pm = &m;
    int n, *pn = &n;
    printf("\n Enter the starting and ending
    limit of the numbers: ");
        scanf("%d %d", pm, pn);
    while(*pm <= *pn)
    {
        if(*pm %2 == 0)
        printf("\n %d is even", *pm);
        else
        printf("\n %d is odd", *pm);
        (*pm)++;
    }
    return 0;
}
```

Output

```
Enter the starting and ending limit of the
    numbers: 0 10
0 is even
2 is even
4 is even
6 is even
```

```
8 is even
10 is even
```

7.13 Write a program to read numbers until –1 is entered. Also display whether the number is prime or composite.

```
#include <stdio.h>
int main()
{
    int num, *pnum = &num;
    int i, flag = 0;
    printf("\n ***** ENTER -1 TO EXIT
    ******");
    printf("\n Enter any number: ");
    scanf("%d", pnum);
    while(*pnum != -1)
    {
        if(*pnum == 1)
        printf("\n %d is neither prime nor
    composite", *pnum);
        else if(*pnum == 2)
        printf("\n %d is prime", *pnum);
        else
        {
        for(i=2; i<*pnum/2; i++)
        {
        if(*pnum/i == 0)
        flag =1;
        }
        if(flag == 0)
        printf("\n %d is prime", *pnum);
        else
        printf("\n %d is composite", *pnum);
        }
        printf("\n Enter any number: ");
        scanf("%d", pnum);
    }
    return 0;
}
```

Output

```
***** ENTER -1 TO EXIT ******
Enter any number: 3
3 is prime
Enter any number: 1
I is neither prime nor composite
Enter any number: -1
```

7.5 NULL POINTERS

We have seen that the pointer variable is a pointer to some other variable of the same data type. However, in some cases we may prefer to have *null pointer* which is a special pointer value that does not point anywhere. This means that a `NULL` pointer does not point to any valid memory address.

To declare a `null` pointer you may use the predefined constant `NULL`, which is defined in several standard header files including `<stdio.h>`, `<stdlib.h>`, and `<string.h>`. After including any of these files in your program just write,

```
int *ptr = NULL;
```

You can always check whether a given pointer variable stores address of some variable or contains a `NULL` by writing,

```
if (ptr == NULL)
{
   Statement block;
}
```

You may also initialize a pointer as a null pointer by using a constant 0, as shown below.

```
int ptr,
ptr = 0;
```

Programming Tip:
It is a logical error to dereference a `Null` pointer.

This is a valid statement in C, as even `NULL` which is a preprocessor macro typically has the value, or replacement text, `0`. However, to avoid ambiguity it is always better to use `NULL` to declare a null pointer.

A function that returns pointer values can return a null pointer when it is unable to perform its task.

`Null` pointers are used in situations where one of the pointers in the program points to different locations at different times. In such situations it is always better to set it to a `Null` pointer when it doesn't point anywhere valid, and to test to see if it's a `Null` pointer before using it.

A run time error is generated if you try to dereference a `Null` pointer.

7.6 GENERIC POINTERS

Programming Tip:
A compiler error will be generated if you assign a pointer of one type to a pointer of another type without a cast.

A *generic pointer* is a pointer variable that has `void` as its data type. The `void` pointer, or the generic pointer, is a special type of pointer that can be used to point to variables of any data type. It is declared like a normal pointer variable but using the void keyword as the pointer's data type. For example,

```
void *ptr;
```

In C, since you cannot have a variable of type void, the void pointer will therefore not point to any data and thus, cannot be dereferenced. You need to type cast a void pointer (generic pointer) to another kind of pointer before using it.

> **Programming Tip:**
> A pointer variable of type void * cannot be dereferenced.

Generic pointers are often used when you want a pointer to point to data of different types at different times. For example, look at the code given below.
Here is some code using a void pointer:

```
#include <stdio.h>
int main()
{
    int x=10;
    char ch = 'A';
    void *gp;
    gp = &x;
    printf("\n Generic pointer points to the
    integer value = %d", *(int*)gp);
    gp = &ch;
    printf("\n Generic pointer now points to
    the character %c", *(char*)gp);
    return 0;
}
```

Output

```
Generic pointer points to the integer value
  = 10
Generic pointer now points to the character
  = A
```

It is always recommended to avoid using void pointers unless absolutely necessary, as they effectively allow you to avoid type checking.

7.7 PASSING ARGUMENTS TO FUNCTION USING POINTERS

We have already seen call by value method of passing parametres to a function. Using call by value method, it is impossible to modify the actual parametres in the call when you pass them to a function. Furthermore, the incoming arguments to a function are treated as local variables in the function and those local variables get a *copy* of the values passed from their caller.

Pointers provide a mechanism to modify data declared in one function using code written in another function. In other words: If data is declared in `func1()` and we want to write code in `func2()` that modifies the data in `func1()`, then we must pass the addresses of the variables we want to change.

The calling function sends the addresses of the variables and the called function must declare those incoming arguments as pointers. In order to modify the variables sent by the caller, the called function must dereference the pointers that were passed to it. Thus, passing pointers to a function avoids the overhead of copying data from one function to another. Hence, to use pointers for passing arguments to a function, the programmer must do the following:

> **Programming Tip:**
> While using pointers to pass arguments to a function, the calling function must pass addresses of the variables as arguments and the called function must dereference the arguments to use them in the function body for processing.

- Declare the function parametres as pointers.
- Use the dereferenced pointers in the function body.
- Pass the addresses as the actual argument when the function is called.

It is an error to return a pointer to a local variable in the called function, because when the function terminates , its memory may be allocated to a different program.

PROGRAMMING EXAMPLES

Let us write some programs that pass pointer variables as parametres to functions.

7.14 Write a program to add two integers using functions

```
#include <stdio.h>
#include <conio.h>
void sum (int *a, int *b, int *t);
int main()
{
    int num1, num2, total;
    printf("\n Enter the first number: ");
    scanf("%d", &num1);
    printf("\n Enter the second number: ");
    scanf("%d", &num2);
```

```
    sum(&num1, &num2, &total);
    printf("\n Total = %d", total);
    getch();
    return 0;
}
void sum (int *a, int *b, int *t)
{
    *t = *a + *b;
}
```

Output

```
Enter the first number: 2
Enter the first number: 3
Total = 5
```

7.15 Write a program, using functions, to find the biggest of three integers.

```
#include <stdio.h>
int greater(int *a, int *b, int *c, int *large);
int main()
{
    int num1, num2, num3, large;
    printf("\n Enter the first number: ");
    scanf("%d", &num1);
    printf("\n Enter the second number: ");
    scanf("%d", &num2);
    printf("\n Enter the third number: ");
    scanf("%d", &num3);
    greater(&num1, &num2, &num3, &large);
    return 0;
}
int greater (int *a, int *b,
int *c, int *large)
{
    if(*a > *b && *a > *c)
    *large = *a;
    if(*b > *a && *b > *c)
    *large = *b;
    else
    *large = *c;
    printf("\n Largest number = %d", *large);
}
```

Programming Tip: A compiler error will be generated if you use pointer arithmetic with multiply, divide or modulo operators.

Output

```
Enter the first number: 1
Enter the second number: 7
Enter the third number: 9
Largest number = 9
```

7.16 Write a program to calculate the area of a triangle.

```
#include <stdio.h>
void read(float *b, float *h);
void calculate_area (float *b, float *h,
    float *a);
int main()
{
    float base, height, area;
    read(&base, &height);
    calculate_area(&base, &height, &area);
    printf("\n Area of the triangle with base
    %f and height %f = %f", base, height, area);
    return 0;
}
void read(float *b, float *h)
{
    printf("\n Enter the base of the
    triangle: ");
    scanf("%f", b);
    printf("\n Enter the height of the
    triangle: ");
    scanf("%f", h);
}
void calculate_area (float *b, float *h,
    float *a)
{
    *a = 0.5 * (*b) * (*h);
}
```

Output

```
Enter the base of the triangle: 10
Enter the height of the triangle: 5
Area of the triangle with base 10.0 and
    height 5.0 = 25.00
```

Hence, we see that functions usually return only one value. Pointers can be used to return more than one value to the calling function. This is done by allowing the arguments to be passed by address which enables the function to alter the values pointed to and thus helps to return more than one value.

7.8 POINTERS AND ARRAYS

The concept of array is very much bound to the one of pointer. An array occupies consecutive memory locations. Consider Fig. 7.2. For example, if we have an array declared as,

`int arr[] = {1, 2, 3, 4, 5};`

then in memory it would be stored as shown in Fig. 7.2.

Array notation is a form of pointer notation. The name of the array is the starting address of the array in memory. It is also known as the base address. In other words, base address is the address of the first element in the array or the address of `arr[0]`. Now let us use a pointer variable as given in the statement below.

```
int *ptr;
ptr = &arr[0];
```

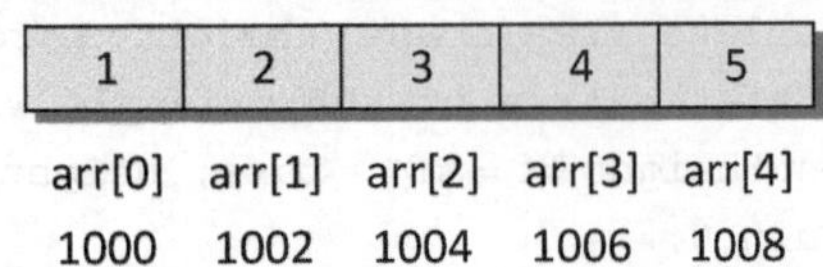

Figure 7.2 Memory representation of arr[]

Here, `ptr` is made to point to the first element of the array. Execute the code given below and observe the output which will make the concept clear to you.

> **Programming Tip:** The name of the array is actually a pointer that points to the first element of the array.

```
main()
{
int arr[]={1,2,3,4,5};
printf("\n Address of
array = %p %p %p", arr,
    &arr[0], &arr);
}
```

Similarly, writing `ptr = &arr[2]`, makes ptr to point to the third element of the array, that has index 2. Figure 7.3 shows `ptr` pointing to the third element of the array.

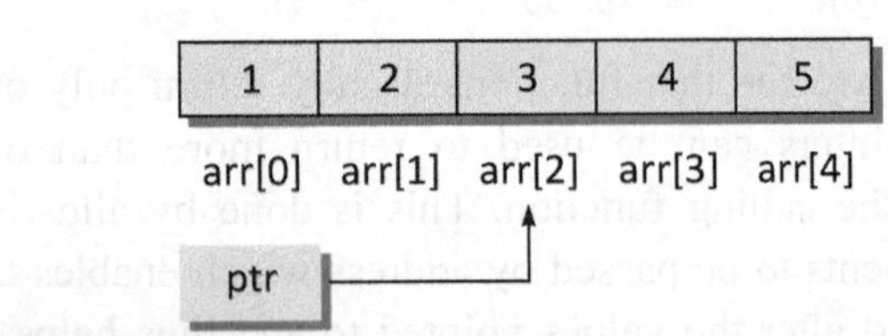

Figure 7.3 Pointer pointing to the third element of the array

If pointer variable `ptr` holds the address of the first element in the array, then the address of successive elements can be calculated by writing `ptr++`.

```
int *ptr = &arr[0];
ptr++;
printf("\n The value of the second element
    of the array is %d", *ptr);
```

The `printf()` function will print the value 2 because after being incremented `ptr` points to the next location. One point to note here is that if x is an integer variable, then `x++`, adds 1 to the value of `x`. But `ptr` is a pointer variable, so when we write `ptr + i`, then adding `i` gives a pointer that points `i` elements further along an array than the original pointer.

> **Programming Tip:** An error is generated if an attempt is made to change the address of the array.

Since `++ptr` and `ptr++` are both equivalent to `ptr + 1`, incrementing a pointer using the unary ++ operator, increments the address it stores by the amount given by `sizeof(type)` where *type* is the data type of the variable it points to (i.e., 2 for an integer). For example, consider Fig. 7.4.

If `ptr` originally points to `arr[2]`, then `ptr++` will make it to point to the next element, i.e., `arr[3]`. This is shown in Fig. 7.4.

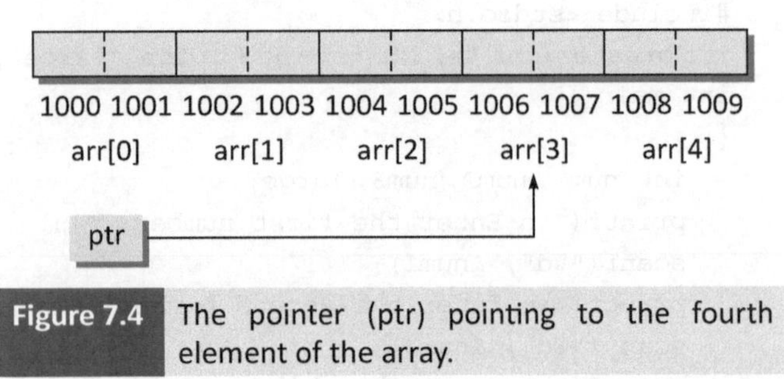

Figure 7.4 The pointer (ptr) pointing to the fourth element of the array.

Had this been a character array, every byte in the memory would have been used to store an individual character. `ptr++` would then add only 1 byte to the address of `ptr`.

When using pointers, an expression like `arr[i]` is equivalent to writing `*(arr+i)`. If `arr` is the array name, then the compiler implicitly takes

```
arr = &arr[0]
```

To print the value of the third element of the array, we can straightaway use the expression `*(arr+2)`. Note that `arr[i] = *(arr + i)`

> **Programming Tip:** When an array is passed to a function, we are actually passing a pointer to the function. Therefore, in the function declaration you must declare a pointer to receive the array name.

Many beginners get confused by thinking of array name as a pointer. For example, while we can write

```
ptr = arr;   // ptr =
&arr[0]
```

We cannot write

```
arr = ptr;
```

This is because while ptr is a variable, arr is a constant. The location at which the first element of arr will be stored cannot be changed once arr[] has been declared. Therefore, an array name is often known to be a constant pointer.

To summarize, the name of an array is equivalent to the address of its first element, as a pointer is equivalent to the address of the element that it points to. Therefore, arrays and pointers use the same concept.

arr[i], i[arr], *(arr+i), *(i+arr) gives the same value.

Look at the following code and understand the result of executing them:

```
main()
{
   int arr[]={1,2,3,4,5};
   int *ptr, i;
   ptr=&arr[2];
   *ptr = -1;
   *(ptr+1) = 0;
   *(ptr-1) = 1;
   printf("\n Array is: ");
   for(i=0;i<5;i++)
      printf(" %d", *(arr+i);
}
```

Output

```
Array is:  1  1  -1  0  5
```

In C we can add or subtract an integer from a pointer to get a new pointer, pointing somewhere other than the original position. C also permits addition and subtraction of two pointer variables. For example, look at the code given below.

```
main()
{
   int arr[]={1,2,3,4,5,6,7,8,9};
   int *ptr1, *ptr2;
   ptr1 = arr;
   ptr2 = ptr+2;
   printf(.%d", ptr2 -ptr1);
}
```

Output

```
2
```

In the code, ptr1 and ptr2 are pointers pointing to the elements of the same array. We may subtract two pointers as long as they point to the same array. Here, the output is 2 because there are two elements between ptr1 and ptr2 in the array arr. Both the pointers must point to the same array or one past the end of the array, otherwise this behaviour cannot be defined.

Moreover, C also allows pointer variables to be compared with each other. Obviously, if two pointers are equal, then they point to the same location in the array. However, if one pointer is less than the other, it means that the pointer points to some element nearer to the beginning of the array. Like with other variables, relational operators (>, >, =, etc.) can also be applied to pointer variables.

7.17 Write a program to display an array of given numbers.

```
#include <stdio.h>
main()
{
   int arr[]={1,2,3,4,5,6,7,8,9};
   int *ptr1, *ptr2;
   ptr1 = arr;
   ptr2 = &arr[8];
   while(ptr1<=ptr2)
   {
      printf("%d", *ptr1);
      ptr1++;
   }
}
```

Output

```
1 2 3 4 5 6 7 8 9
```

An object is a named region of storage; an lvalue is an expression referring to an object.

Table 7.1 summarizes pointer arithmetic.

7.18 Write a program to read and display an array of n integers.

```
#include <stdio.h>
int main()
{
   int i, n;
   int arr[10], *parr = arr;
   printf("\n Enter the number of elements: ");
   scanf("%d", &n);
   printf("\n Enter the elements: ");
   for(i = 0; i < n; i++)
      scanf("%d", parr+i);
   printf("\n The elements entered are: ");
```

```
    for(i=0; i < n; i++)
        printf("\t %d", *(parr+i));
    return 0;
}
```

Output

```
Enter the number of elements: 5
Enter the elements: 1 2 3 4 5
The elements entered are: 1 2 3 4 5
```

7.19 Write a program to find mean of n numbers using arrays.

```
#include <stdio.h>
int main()
{
    int i, n, arr[20], sum =0;
    int *pn = &n, *parr = arr, *psum = &sum;
    float mean = 0.0, *pmean = &mean;
    printf("\n Enter the number of elements
    in the array: ");
    scanf("%d", pn);
    for(i = 0; i < *pn; i++)
    {
        printf("\n Enter the number: ");
        scanf("%d", (parr + i));
    }
    for(i=0; i < *pn; i++)
        *psum += *(arr + i);
    *pmean = *psum / *pn;
    printf("\n The numbers you entered are: ");
    for(i=0; i < *pn; i++)
        printf("%d ", *(arr + i));
    printf("\n The sum is: %d", *psum);
    printf("\n The mean is: %f", *pmean);
    return 0;
}
```

Output

```
Enter the number of elements: 5
Enter the number: 1
Enter the number: 2
Enter the number: 3
Enter the number: 4
Enter the number: 5
The numbers you entered are:
1 2 3 4 5
The sum is: 15
The mean is: 3.00
```

7.20 Write a program to find the largest of n numbers using arrays. Also display its position.

```
#include <stdio.h>
int main()
{
    int i, n, arr[20], large = -1111, pos = 0;
    int *pn = &n, *parr = arr, *plarge =
    &large, *ppos = &pos;
    clrscr();
    printf("\n Enter the number of elements
    in the array: ");
    scanf("%d", pn);
    for(i = 0; i < *pn;i++)
    {
        printf("\n Enter the number: ");
        scanf("%d", parr+i);
```

Table 7.1 Pointer arithmetic

Operation	Condition	Declaration	Description
Assignment	Pointers must be of same type	int *ptr1, *ptr2;	If we write *ptr1 = *ptr2, then both the pointers point to the same location
Addition of an integer		int i, *ptr;	If we write, ptr + i, then ptr will point to ith object after its initial position
Subtraction of an integer		int i, *ptr;	If we write, ptr – i, then ptr will point to ith object before its initial position
Comparison of pointers	Pointers should point to elements of the same array	int *ptr1, *ptr2;	If we write, ptr1 < ptr2, then it would return 1 if ptr1 points to an element that is near to the beginning of the array, i.e., the element comes before the element pointed by ptr2
Subtraction of pointers	Pointers should point to elements of the same array	int *ptr1, *ptr2;	If we write ptr1 – ptr2, then it returns the number of elements between ptr1 and ptr2 (provided ptr1 > ptr2)
Addition of pointers is illegal in C. Therefore, ptr1+ptr2 is not valid in C.			

```
        }
        for(i = 0; i < *pn; i++)
        {
            if(*(parr+i) > *plarge)
            {
            *plarge = *(parr+i);
            *ppos = i;
            }
        }
        printf("\n The numbers you entered are:
        ");
        for(i = 0; i < *pn;i++)
            printf("%d ", *(parr+i));
        printf("\n The largest of these numbers
        is: %d", *plarge);
        printf("\n The position of the largest
        number in the array is: %d", *ppos);
        return 0;
}
```

Output

```
Enter the number of elements: 5
Enter the number: 1
Enter the number: 2
Enter the number: 3
Enter the number: 4
Enter the number: 5
The numbers you entered are:
1 2 3 4 5
The largest of these numbers is: 5
The position of the largest number in the
    array is: 4
```

7.9 PASSING AN ARRAY TO A FUNCTION

An array can be passed to a function using pointers. For this, a function that expects an array can declare the formal parameter in either of the two following ways:

`func(int arr[]);` OR `func(int *arr);`

When we pass the name of the array to a function, the address of the zeroth element of the array is copied to the local pointer variable in the function. Observe the difference; unlike ordinary variables the values of the elements are not copied, only the address of the first element is copied.

When a formal parameter is declared in a function header as an array, it is interpreted as a pointer to a variable and not as an array. With this pointer variable you can access all the elements of the array by using the expression, `array_name + index`. To find out how many elements are there in the array, you must pass the size of the array as another parameter to the function. So for a function that accepts an array as parameter, the declaration should be as follows:

```
func(int arr[], int n);  OR
func(int *arr, int n);
```

Look at the following program which illustrates the use of pointers to pass an array to a function.

7.21 Write a program to read and print an array of n numbers, then find out the smallest number. Also print the position of the smallest number.

```
#include <stdio.h>
void read_array(int *arr, int n);
void print_array(int *arr, int n);
void find_small(int *arr, int n, int *small,
    int *pos);
int main()
{
    int num[10], n, small, pos;
    printf("\n Enter the size of the array: ");
    scanf("%d", &n);
    read_array(num, n);
    print_array(num, n)
    find_small(num, n, &small, &pos);
    printf("\n The smallest number in the
    array is at position %d", small pos);
    return 0;
}
void read_array(int *arr, int n)
{
    int i;
    printf("\n Enter the array elements: ");
    for(i=0;i<n;i++)
        scanf("%d", &arr[i]);
}
void print_array(int *arr, int n)
{
    int i;
    printf("\n The array elements are: ");
    for(i=0;i<n;i++)
        printf("\t %d", arr[i]);
}
void find_small(int *arr, int n, int *small,
    int *pos)
{
    for(i=0;i<n;i++)
    {
        if(*(arr+i)< *small)
        {
        *small = *(arr+i);
        *pos = i;
```

```
        }
    }
}
```

Output

```
Enter the size of the array: 5
Enter the array elements: 1 2 3 4 5
The array elements are: 1 2 3 4 5
The smallest number in the array is = 1 at
   position 0
```

It is not necessary to pass the whole array to a function. We can also pass a part of the array known as a sub-array. A pointer to a sub-array is also an array pointer. For example, if we want to send the array starting from the third element then we can pass the address of the third element and the size of the sub-array, i.e., if there were `10` elements in the array, and we want to pass the array starting from the third element, then only eight elements would be a part of the sub-array. So the function call can be written as

```
func(&arr[2], 8);
```

7.10 DIFFERENCE BETWEEN ARRAY NAME AND POINTER

When memory is allocated for an array, its base address is fixed and it cannot be changed during program execution. In other words, an array name is an address constant. Therefore, its value cannot be changed. To ensure that the address of the array does not get changed even inadvertently, C does not allow array names to be used as an `lvalue`. Hence, array names cannot appear on the left side of the assignment operator.

However, you may declare a pointer variable of appropriate type that points to the first element of the array and use it as `lvalue`. Figure 7.5 shows two sets of codes. The first code gives an error as the array name is being used as an `lvalue` for the `++` operator. The second code shows the correct way of doing the same thing.

Second thing to remember is that an array cannot be assigned to another array. This is because an array name cannot be used as the lvalue.

```
int arr1[]={1,2,3,4,5};
int arr2[5];
arr2 = arr1;    // ERROR
```

But, one pointer variable can be assigned to another pointer variable of the same type.

```
main()
{
    int arr[5], i;
    for(i=0i<5;i++)
    {
        *arr=0;
        arr++;      //ERROR
    }
    for(i = 0; i < 5;i++)
        printf("\n %d", *(arr+i));
}
```

```
main()
{
    int arr[5], i, *parr;
       parr = arr;
    for(i = 0; i < 5;i++)
    {
        *parr=0;
        parr++;
    }
    for(i = 0; i < 5;i++)
        printf("\n %d", *(arr+i));
}
```

Figure 7.5 Array and pointer

Therefore, the following statements are valid in C:

```
int arr1[]={1,2,3,4,5};
int *ptr1, *ptr2;
ptr1 = arr1;
ptr2 = ptr1;
```

When we write `ptr2 = ptr1`, we are not copying the data pointed to. Rather, we are just making two pointers point to the same location. This is shown in Fig. 7.6.

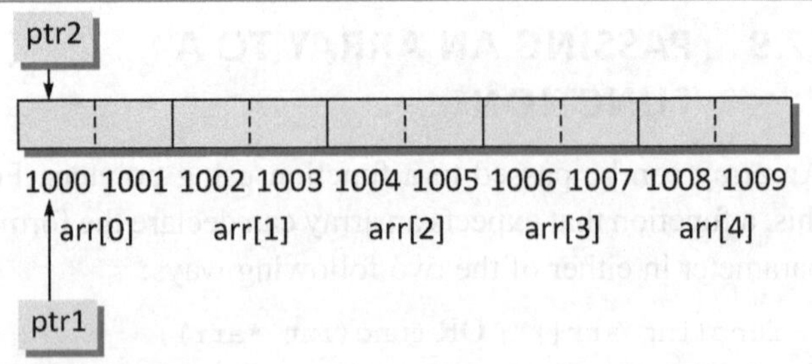

Figure 7.6 Pointers pointing to the same location

Third point of difference lies with the return value of the address operator. The address operator returns the address of the operand. But when an address operator is applied to an array name, it gives the same value as the array reference without the operator. Therefore, `arr` and `&arr` gives the same value. However, this is not true for a pointer variable.

Last but not the least, the `sizeof` operator when applied to an array name returns the number of bytes allocated for the array. But in case of a pointer variable, the `sizeof` operator returns the number of bytes used for the pointer variable (machine dependent). Look at the following code which illustrates this concept.

```
main()
{
   int arr[]={1,2,3,4,5};
   int *ptr;
   ptr=arr;
   printf("\n Size of array = %d", sizeof(arr));
   printf("\n Size of pointer variable = %d",
   sizeof(ptr));
}
```

Output (On Turbo C)

```
Size of array = 10
Size of pointer variable = 2
```

7.11 POINTERS AND STRINGS

In C, strings are treated as arrays of characters that are terminated with a binary zero character (written as `'\0'`). Consider, for example,

```
char str[10];

str[0] = 'H';
str[1] = 'i';
str[2] = '!':
str[3] = '\0';
```

C language provides two alternate ways of declaring and initializing a string. First, you may write:

```
char str[10] = {'H', 'i', '!', '\0',};
```

But this also takes more typing than is convenient. So, C permits:

```
char str[10] = "Hi!";
```

When the double quotes are used, `null` character (`'\0'`) is automatically appended to the end of the string.

When a string is declared like this, the compiler sets aside a contiguous block of memory 10 bytes long to hold characters and initializes its first four characters `Hi!\0`.

Now, consider the following program that prints a text:

```
#include <stdio.h>
int main()
{
   char str[] = "Hello";
   char *pstr;
   pstr = str;
   printf("\n The string is: ");
   while(*pstr != '\0')
   {
      printf("%c', *pstr);
      pstr++;
   }
   return 0;
}
```

Output

```
The string is: Hello
```

In this program, we declare a character pointer `*pstr` to show the string on the screen. We then *point* the pointer `pstr` at `str`. Then we print each character of the string in the `while` loop. Instead of using the `while` loop, we could have straightaway used the function `puts()` as shown.

```
puts(pstr);
```

The function prototype for `puts()` is as follows:

```
int puts(const char *s);
```

Here the `const` modifier is used to assure the user that the function will not modify the contents pointed to by the source pointer. The address of the string is passed to the function as an argument.

The parameter passed to `puts()` is a pointer which is nothing but the address to which it points to, or, simply, an address. Thus by writing `puts(str);` means passing the address of `str[0]`.

Similarly, when we write `puts(pstr);` we are passing the same address, because we have written `pstr = str;`

Now consider the code which displays a string using pointers.

```
#include <stdio.h>
int main(void)
{
   char *str = "Welcome to the world of
   programming";
   char *pstr;      // pointer to character
   pstr = str;
   while(*pstr! = '\0')
   {
      printf("%c", *pstr);
      pstr++;
   }
   return 0;
}
```

Output

```
Welcome to the world of programming
```

In the above code, pstr is assigned the address of the string, str. The pointer pstr can then be used to point to successive characters until the null character is reached.

Consider another program which reads a string and then scans each character to count the number of upper and lower case characters entered.

```
#include <stdio.h>
int main()
{
   char str[100], *pstr;
   int upper = 0, lower = 0;
   printf("\n Enter the string: ");
   gets(str);
   pstr = str;
   while(*pstr != '\0')
   {
      if(*pstr >= 'A' && *pstr <= 'Z')
         upper++;
      else if(*pstr >= 'a' && *pstr <= 'z')
         lower++;
      pstr++;
   }
   printf("\n Total number of upper case
   characters = %d", upper);
   printf("\n Total number of lower case
   characters = %d", lower);
   return 0;
}
```

Output

```
Enter the string: How are you
Total number of upper case characters = 1
Total number of lower case characters = 8
```

7.22 Write a program to read and print a text. Also count the number of characters, words, and lines in the text.

```
#include <stdio.h>
int main()
{
   char str[100], *pstr;
   int chars = 1, lines = 1, words = 1;
   pstr=str;
   printf("\n Enter the string: ");
   gets(str);
   pstr = str;
   while(*pstr != '\0')
   {
      if(*pstr == '\n')
         lines++;
      if(*pstr == ' ' && *(pstr + 1) != ' ')
         words++;
      chars++;
      pstr++;
   }
   printf("\n The string is: ");
   puts(str);
   printf("\n Number of characters = %d", chars);
   printf("\n Number of lines = %d", lines);
   printf("\n Number of words = %d", words);
   return 0;
}
```

Output

```
Enter the string: How are you
Number of characters = 11
Number of lines = 1
Number of words = 3
```

7.23 Write a program to copy a character array in another character array.

```
#include <stdio.h>
#include <conio.h>
int main()
{
   char str[100], copy_str[100];
   char *pstr, *pcopy_str;
   int i = 0;
   clrscr();
   pstr = str;
   pcopy_str = copy_str;
   printf("\n Enter the string: ");
   gets(str);
   while(*pstr != '\0')
   {
      *pcopy_str = *pstr;
      pstr++, pcopy_str++;
   }
   *pcopy_str = '\0';
   printf("\n The copied text is: ");
   pcopy_str = copy_str;
   while(*pcopy_str != '\0')
   {
      printf("%c", *pcopy_str);
      pcopy_str++;
   }
   getch();
   return 0;
}
```

Output

```
Enter the string: C Programming
The copied text is: C Programming
```

7.24 Write a program to copy n characters of a character array from the mth position in another character array.

```
#include <stdio.h>
int main()
```

```
{
   char str[100], copy_str[100];
   char *pstr, *pcopy_str;
   int m, n, i = 0;
   pstr = str;
   pcopy_str = copy_str;
   printf("\n Enter the string: ");
   gets(pstr);
   printf("\n Enter the position from which
   to start: ");
   scanf("%d", &m);
   printf("\n Enter the number of characters
   to be copied: ");
   scanf("%d", &n);
   pstr = pstr + m - 1;
   i=0;
   while(*pstr != '\0' && i <n)
   {
      *pcopy_str = *pstr;
      pcopy_str++;
      pstr++;
      i++;
   }
   *pcopy_str = '\0';
   printf("\n The copied text is: ");
   puts(copy_str);
   return 0;
}
```

Output

```
Enter the string: How are you
Enter the position from which to start: 2
Enter the number of characters to be
   copied: 5
The copied text is: w are
```

7.25 Write a program to copy the last n characters of a character array in another character array. Also convert the lower case letters into upper case letters while copying.

```
#include <stdio.h>
#include <string.h>
int main()
{
   char str[100], copy_str[100];
   char *pstr, *pcopy_str;
   int i = 0, n;
   pstr = str;
   pcopy_str = copy_str;
   printf("\n Enter the string:");
   gets(str);
   printf("\n Enter the number of characters
   to be copied (from the end): ");
   scanf("%d", &n);
   pstr = pstr + strlen(str) - n;
   while(*pstr != '\0')
   {
      *pcopy_str = *pstr - 32;
      pstr++; pcopy_str++;
   }
   *pcopy_str = '\0';
   printf("\n The copied text is: ");
   puts(copy_str);
   return 0;
}
```

Output

```
Enter the string: Hi there
Enter the number of characters to be copied
   (from the end): 5
The copied text is: there
```

7.26 Write a program to read a text, delete all the semi-colons it has, and finally replace all '.' with a ','.

```
#include <stdio.h>
int main()
{
   char str[100], copy_str[100];
   char *pstr, *pcopy_str;
   pstr = str;
   pcopy_str = copy_str;
   printf("\n Enter the string: ");
   gets(str);
   pstr = str;
   while(*pstr != '\0')
   {
      if(*pstr != ';')
      { }  // do nothing
      if (*pstr == '.')
         *pcopy_str = ',';
      else
         *pcopy_str = *pstr;
         pstr++; pcopy_str++;
   }
   *pcopy_str = '\0';
   printf("\n The new text is: ");
   pcopy_str = copy_str;
   while(*pcopy_str != '\0')
   {
      printf("%c", *pcopy_str);
      pcopy_str++;
   }
   return 0;
}
```

Output

```
Enter the string: Introduction to C
   Programming; is a book written by; Reema
   Thareja.
```

```
The new text is: Introduction to C
   Programming is a book written by Reema
   Thareja,
```

7.27 Write a program to reverse a string.

```
#include <stdio.h>
int main()
{
   char str[100], copy_str[100];
   char *pstr, *pcopy_str;
   pstr = str;
   pcopy_str = copy_str;
   printf("\n Enter * to end");
   printf("\n **************");
   printf("\n Enter the string: ");
   scanf("%c", pstr);
   while(*pstr != '*')
   {
     pstr++;
     scanf("%c", pstr);
   }
   *pstr = '\0';
   pstr--;
   while (pstr >= str)
   {
     *pcopy_str = *pstr;
     pcopy_str++;
     pstr--;
   }
   *pcopy_str = '\0';
   printf("\n The new text is: ");
   pcopy_str = copy_str;
   while(*pcopy_str != '\0')
   {
     printf("%c", *pcopy_str);
     pcopy_str++;
   }
   return 0;
}
```

Output

```
Enter * to end
**************
Enter the string: Learning C++
The new text is: ++ C gninraeL
```

7.28 Write a program to concatenate two strings.

```
#include <stdio.h>
int main()
{
   char str1[100], str2[100], copy_str[2000];
   char *pstr1, *pstr2, *pcopy_str;
   clrscr();
   pstr1 = str1;
   pstr2 = str2;
   pcopy_str = copy_str;
   printf("\n Enter the first string: ");
   gets(str1);
   printf("\n Enter the second string: ");
   gets(str2);
   pstr1=str1;
   while(*pstr1 != '\0')
   {
     *pcopy_str = *pstr1;
     pcopy_str++, pstr1++;
   }
   pstr2 = str2;
   while(*pstr2 != '\0')
   {
     *pcopy_str = *pstr2;
     pcopy_str++, pstr2++;
   }
   *pcopy_str = '\0';
   printf("\n The new text is: ");
   pcopy_str = copy_str;
   while(*pcopy_str != '\0')
   {
     printf("%c", *pcopy_str);
     pcopy_str++;
   }
   return 0;
}
```

Output

```
Enter the first string: Introduction to C
   Programming by
Enter the first string: Reema Thareja
The new text is: Introduction to C
   Programming by Reema Thareja
```

7.12 ARRAY OF POINTERS

An array of pointers can be declared as

```
int *ptr[10]
```

The above statement declares an array of `10` pointers where each of the pointer points to an integer variable. For example, look at the code given below.

```
int *ptr[10];
int p = 1, q = 2, r = 3, s = 4, t = 5;
ptr[0] = &p;
ptr[1] = &q;
ptr[2] = &r;
ptr[3] = &s;
ptr[4] = &t
```

Can you tell what will be the output of the following statement?

```
printf("\n %d", *ptr[3]);
```

The output will be 4 because ptr[3] stores the address of integer variable and *ptr[3] will therefore print the value of s that is 4. Now look at another code in which we store the address of three individual arrays in the array of pointers.

```
main()
{
    int arr1[]={1,2,3,4,5};
    int arr2[]={0,2,4,6,8};
    int arr3[]={1,3,5,7,9};
    int *parr[3] = (arr1, arr2, arr3);
    int i;
    for(i = 0;i<3;i++)
        printf("%d", *parr[i]);
}
```

Output

```
1 0 1
```

Surprised with this output? Try to understand the concept. In the for loop, parr[0] stores the base address of arr1 (or, &arr1[0]). So writing *parr[0] will print the value stored at &arr1[0]. Same is the case with *parr[1] and *parr[2].

Now consider an array of character pointers that is pointed to the strings.

```
char *ptr[3];
```

In the ptr array, each element is a character pointer. Therefore, we can assign character pointers to the elements of the array. For example,

```
ptr[0] = str;
```

Another way to initialize an array of characters with three strings can be given as,

```
char *ptr[3] = {"Janak","Raj","Paul"};
```

Here, ptr[0] is Janak, ptr[1] is Raj, and ptr[2] is Paul.

The memory layout of ptr can be given as shown in Fig. 7.7. It requires only 15 bytes to store the three strings.

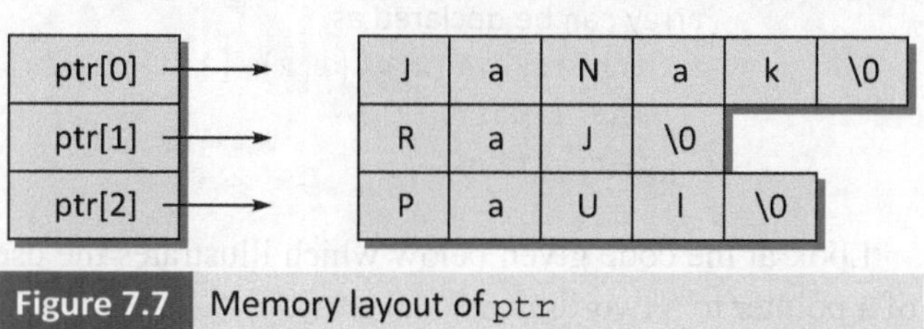

Figure 7.7 Memory layout of ptr

However, char str[3][10] = {"Janak", "Raj", "Paul"}; will behave in the same way as an array of characters. The only difference is the memory layout (Fig. 7.8). While the array of pointers needs only 15 bytes of storage, str will reserve 30 bytes in memory, despite the fact that some memory locations will be reserved but not utilized.

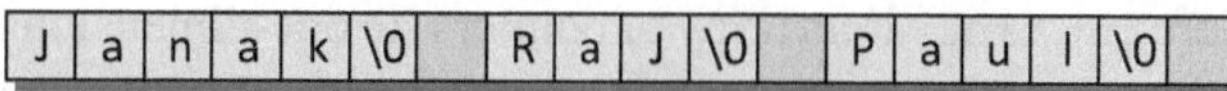

Here, the grey locations represent the uninitialized memory cells

Figure 7.8 Memory layout

Look at the following program that uses an array of characters to display the name of the day corresponding to the number.

```
#include <stdio.h>
char *day_of_week(int);
main()
{
    int day_num;
    char *day;
    printf("\n Enter the day from 1 to 7: ");
    scanf("%d", &day_num);
    day = day_of_week(day_num);
    if(day)
        printf("%s", day);
    else
        printf("\n Invalid Day");
}
char *day_of_week(int d)
{
    char *week_day[7] = {"SUNDAY", "MONDAY",
    "TUESDAY", "WEDNESDAY", "THURSDAY",
    "FRIDAY", "SATURDAY"};
    if(day>=1 || day<=7)
        return week_day[d-1];
    else
        return NULL;
}
```

Output

```
Enter the day from 1 to 7: 3
TUESDAY
```

An array of pointers whose elements point to arrays of varying sizes is called a *ragged array*. Therefore, array of pointers week_day and ptr in the above discussion are better known as ragged arrays.

7.13 POINTERS AND 2-D ARRAYS

Elements of a two-dimensional array are stored in contiguous memory locations. A two-dimensional array is not the same as an array of pointers to one-dimensional arrays. To declare a pointer to a two-dimensional array, you may write

```
int **ptr
```

Here `int **ptr` is an array of pointers (to one-dimensional arrays), while `int mat[5][5]` is a 2D array. They are not the same type and are not interchangeable.
Consider a two-dimensional array declared as

```
int mat[5][5];
```

Individual elements of the array `mat` can be accessed using either:

```
mat[i][j] or
*(*(mat + i) + j) or
*(mat[i]+j);
```

To understand more fully what is going on, let us replace

`*(multi + row)` with `X` so the expression

`*(*(mat + i) + j)` becomes `*(X + col)`

Using pointer arithmetic, we know that the address pointed to by (i.e., value of) `X + col + 1` must be greater than the address `X + col` by an amount equal to `sizeof(int)`.

Since `mat` is a two-dimensional array, we know that in the expression `multi + row` as used above, `multi + row + 1` must increase in value by an amount equal to that needed to *point to* the next row, which in this case would be an amount equal to `COLS * sizeof(int)`.

Thus, in case of a two-dimensional array, in order to evaluate expression (for a row major 2D array), we must know a total of 4 values:

1. The address of the first element of the array, which is given by the name of the array, i.e., `mat` in our case
2. The size of the type of the elements of the array, i.e., `sizeof` integers in our case
3. The specific index value for the row
4. The specific index value for the column

Note that

```
int (*ptr)[10];
```

declares `ptr` to be a pointer to an array of 10 integers. This is different from

```
int *ptr[10];
```

which would make `ptr` the name of an array of 10 pointers to type `int`. You must be thinking how pointer arithmetic works if you have an array of pointers. For example:

```
int * arr[10] ;
int ** ptr = arr
```

In this case, `arr` has type `int **`. Since all pointers have the same size, the address of `ptr + i` can be calculated as:

```
addr(ptr + i) = addr(ptr) + [sizeof(int *) * i]
= addr(ptr) + [2 * i]
```

Since `arr` has type `int **`,

```
arr[0] = & arr[0][0],
arr[1] = & arr[1][0], and in general,
arr[i] = & arr[i][0].
```

According to pointer arithmetic, `arr + i = & arr[i]`, yet this skips an entire row of 5 elements, i.e., it skips complete 10 bytes (5 elements each of 2 bytes size). Therefore, if `arr` is address **1000**, then `arr + 2` is address **1010**. To summarize, `&arr[0][0]`, `arr[0]`, `arr`, and `&arr[0]` point to the base address.

```
&arr[0][0] + 1 points to arr[0][1]
arr[0] + 1 points to arr[0][1]
arr + 1 points to arr[1][0]
&arr[0] + 1 points to arr[1][0]
```

To conclude, a two-dimensional array is not the same as an array of pointers to 1D arrays. Actually a two-dimensional array is declared as:

```
int (*ptr)[ 10 ] ;
```

Here `ptr` is a pointer to an array of 10 elements. The parentheses are not optional. In the absence of these parentheses, `ptr` becomes an array of 10 pointers, not a pointer to an array of 10 ints.

Pointer to a one-dimensional array can be declared as,

```
int arr[]={1,2,3,4,5};
int *parr;
parr = arr;
```

Similarly, pointer to a two-dimensional array can be declared as,

```
int arr[2][2]={{1,2},{3,4}};
int (*parr)[2];
parr=arr;
```

Look at the code given below which illustrates the use of a pointer to a two-dimensional array.

```
#include <stdio.h>
main()
{
   int arr[2][2]={{1,2}.{3,4}};
   int i, (*parr)[2];
   parr = arr;
   for(i = 0; i < 2; i++)
   {
      for(j = 0; j < 2 ;j++)
         printf(" %d", (*(parr+i))[j]);
   }
}
```

Output

```
1 2 3 4
```

The golden rule to access an element of a two-dimensional array can be given as

```
arr[i][j] = (*(arr+i))[j] = *((*arr+i))+j)
   = *(arr[i]+j)
```

Therefore,

```
arr[0][0] = *(arr)[0] = *((*arr)+0)
   = *(arr[0]+0)
arr[1][2] = (*(arr+1))[2] = *((*(arr+1))+2)
   = *(arr[1]+2)
```

If we declare an array of pointer using, `data_type *array_name[SIZE];`	If we declare a pointer to an array using, `data_type (*array_name)[SIZE];`
Here `SIZE` represents the number of rows and the space for columns that can be dynamically allocated.	Here `SIZE` represents the number of columns and the space for rows that may be dynamically allocated.

7.29 Write a program to read and display a 3 × 3 matrix.

```
#include <stdio.h>
int main()
{
   int i, j, mat[3][3];
   clrscr();
   printf("\n Enter elements of the matrix");
   printf("\n ************************");
   for(i=0;i<3;i++)
   {
      for(j=0;j<3;j++)
      {
      printf("\n mat[%d][%d] = ",i,j);
      scanf("%d", &mat[i][j]);
      }
   }
   printf("\n Elements of the matrix are");
   printf("\n ************************");
   for(i=0;i<3;i++)
   {
      printf("\n");
      for(j = 0; j < 3; j++)
      printf("\t mat[%d][%d] = %d",i,j,
   *(*(mat + i)+j));
   }
   return 0;
}
```

OR

```
#include <stdio.h>
int main()
{
   int i, j, mat[3][3];
   clrscr();
   printf("\n Enter elements of the matrix");
   printf("\n ************************");
   for(i=0;i<3;i++)
   {
      for(j=0;j<3;j++)
      {
      printf("\n mat[%d][%d] = ",i,j);
      scanf("%d", (*(mat + i)+j));
      }
   }
   printf("\n The elements of the matrix are ");
   printf("\n ************************");
   for(i=0;i<3;i++)
   {
      printf("\n");
      for(j=0;j<3;j++)
      printf("\t mat[%d][%d] = %d",i,j,
      *(*(mat + i)+j));
   }
   return 0;
}
```

OR

```
#include <stdio.h>
void display(int (*)[3]);
int main()
{
   int i, j, mat[3][3];
   clrscr();
   printf("\n Enter elements of the matrix");
   printf("\n ************************");
   for(i=0;i<3;i++)
   {
      for(j = 0; j < 3; j++)
```

```
        {
        printf("\n mat[%d][%d] = ",i,j);
        scanf("%d", &mat[i][j]);
        }
    }
    display(mat);
}
void display(int (*mat)[3])
{
    int i, j;
    printf("\n elements of the matrix are");
    printf("\n ************************");
    for(i = 0; i < 3; i++)
    {
        printf("\n");
        for(j=0;j<3;j++)
        printf("\t mat[%d][%d] = %d",i,j,
    *(*(mat + i)+j));
    }
    return 0;
}
```

Output

```
Enter the elements of the matrix
********************************
1 2 3 4 5 6 7 8 9
The elements of the matrix
********************************
1 2 3
4 5 6
7 8 9
```

Note

A double pointer cannot be used as a 2D array. Therefore, it is wrong to declare: 'int **mat' and then use 'mat' as a 2D array. These are two very different data types used to access different locations in memory. So running such a code may abort the program with a 'memory access violation' error.

A 2D array is not equivalent to a double pointer. A 'pointer to pointer of T' can't serve as a '2D array of T'. The 2D array is equivalent to a pointer to row of T, and this is very different from pointer to pointer of T.

When a double pointer that points to the first element of an array is used with the subscript notation ptr[0][0], it is fully dereferenced two times and the resulting object will have an address equal to the value of the first element of the array.

7.14 POINTERS AND 3-D ARRAY

In this section, we will see how pointers can be used to access a three-dimensional array. We have seen that pointer to a one-dimensional array can be declared as,

```
int arr[]={1,2,3,4,5};
int *parr;
parr = arr;
```

Similarly, pointer to a two-dimensional array can be declared as,

```
int arr[2][2]={{1,2},{3,4}};
int (*parr)[2];
parr = arr;
```

A pointer to a three-dimensional array can be declared as,

```
int arr[2][2][2]={1,2,3,4,5,6,7,8};
int (*parr)[2][2];
parr = arr;
```

We can access an element of a three-dimensional array by writing,

```
arr[i][j][k] = *(*(*(arr+i)+j)+k)
```

Look at the code given below which illustrates the use of a pointer to a three-dimensional array.

```
#include <stdio.h>
#include <conio.h>
main()
{
  int i,j,k;
  int arr[2][2][2];
  int (*parr)[2][2]= arr;
  clrscr();
    printf("\n Enter the elements of a 2 × 
  2 × 2 array: ");
  for(i = 0; i < 2; i++)
  {
    for(j = 0; j < 2; j++)
    {
      for(k = 0; k < 2; k++)
        scanf("%d", &arr[i][j][k]);
    }
  }
  printf("\n The elements of the 2 × 2 × 2
  array are: ");
  for(i = 0; i < 2; i++)
  {
    for(j = 0; j < 2; j++)
    {
      for(k = 0; k < 2; k++)
        printf("%d", *(*(*(parr+i)+j)+k));
    }
```

```
    }
    getch();
    return 0;
}
```

Output

```
Enter the elements of a 2 × 2 × 2 array: 1
   2 3 4 5 6 7 8
The elements of the 2 × 2 × 2 array are: 1
   2 3 4 5 6 7 8
```

Note: In the `printf` statement, you could also have used `*(*(*(arr+i)+j)+k))` instead of `*(*(*(parr+i)+j)+k))`.

7.15 FUNCTION POINTERS

C allows operations with pointers to functions. We have seen earlier in this chapter that every function code along with its variables is allocated some space in the memory. Thus, every function has an address. *Function pointers* are pointer variables that point to the address of a function. Like other pointer variables, function pointers can be declared, assigned values, and used to access the functions they point to.

This is a useful technique for passing a function as an argument to another function. In order to declare a pointer to a function we have to declare it like the prototype of the function except that the name of the function is enclosed between parentheses `()` and an asterisk `(*)` is inserted before the name. The syntax of declaring a function pointer can be given as,

```
return_type(*function_pointer_name)
    (argument_list);
```

Look at the declaration below in which we declare a pointer to a function that returns an integer value and accepts two arguments—one of type `int` and the other of type `float`.

```
int (*func)(int a, float b);
```

Because of precedence, if you do not put the function name within parenthesis, you will end up declaring a function returning a pointer as shown:

```
/* function returning pointer to int */
int *func(int a, float b);
```

7.15.1 Initializing a Function Pointer

As in case of other pointer variables, a function pointer must be initialized prior to use. If we have declared a pointer to the function, then that pointer can be assigned the address of the correct function just by using its name. Like in the case of an array, a function name is changed into an address when it's used in an expression. It is optional to use the address operator `(&)` in front of the function name.

For example, if `fp` is a function pointer and we have a function `add()` with prototype given as,

```
int add(int, int);
```

Then writing `fp = add;` initializes the function pointer `fp` with the address of `add()`.

7.15.2 Calling a Function Using a Function Pointer

When a pointer to a function is declared, it can be called using one of two forms:

```
(*func)(1,2);
```

or

```
func(1,2);
```

Look at the program given below which makes use of a pointer to a function.

```
#include <stdio.h>
void print(int n);
void (*fp)(int);
main()
{
    fp = print;
    (*fp)(10);
    fp(20);
    return 0;
}
void print(int value)
{
    printf("\n %d", value);
}
```

Output

```
10
20
```

Now let us write another code that illustrates how the contents of `fp` can be changed at run time to point to two different functions during program execution.

```
#include <stdio.h>
float (*func)(float, float);//Define a
   function pointer
float add(float, float);
float sub(float, float);
main()
```

```
{
   func = add;
   // function pointer points to add
   printf("\n Addition = %f", func(9.5, 3.1));
   func = sub;
   // function pointer points to sub
   printf("\n Subtraction = %f", func(9.5, 3.1));
}
float add(float x, float y)
{
   return (x + y);
}
float sub(float x, float y)
{
   return (x - y);
}
```

Output

```
Addition = 12.80000
Subtraction = 8.40000
```

A function pointer can be declared and initialize to `NULL` as shown below:

```
int (*fp)(int) = NULL;
```

7.15.3 Comparing Function Pointers

Comparison operators such as `==` and `!=` can be used the same way as usual. Consider the code given below which checks if `fp` actually contains the address of the function `print(int)`.

```
if(fp >0){ // check if initialized
   if(fp == print)
      printf("\n Pointer points to print");
   else
      printf("\n Pointer not initialized!");
}
```

7.15.4 Passing a Function Pointer as an Argument to a Function

A function pointer can be passed as the calling argument of a function. This is in fact necessary if you want to pass a pointer to a callback function. The following code shows how to pass a pointer to a function which returns an `int` and accepts two `int` values.

Note that in the program below, the function `operate` calls the functions `add` and `subtract` with the following line:

```
result = (*operate_fp) (num1, num2);
```

```
#include <stdio.h>
int add(int, int);
int subt(int, int);
int operate(int (*operate_fp) (int, int),
   int, int);
main()
{
   int result;
   result = operate(add, 9, 7);
   printf ("\n Addition = %d", result);
   result = operate(sub, 9, 7);
   printf ("\n Subtraction = %d", result);
   return 0;
}
int add (int a, int b)
{
   return (a + b);
}
int subtract (int a, int b)
{
   return (a - b);
}
int operate(int (*operate_fp) (int, int),
   int a, int b)
{
   int result;
   result = (*operate_fp) (a,b);
   return result;
}
```

Output

```
Addition = 16
Subtraction = 2
```

7.16 ARRAY OF FUNCTION POINTERS

When an array of function pointers is made, the appropriate function is selected using an index. The code given below shows the way to define and use an array of function pointers in C.

Step 1: Use `typedef` keyword so that 'fp' can be used as type

```
typedef int (*fp)(int, int);
```

Step 2: Define the array and initialize each element to `NULL`. This can be done in two ways:

// with 10 pointers to functions which return an `int` and take two `int`s

1. fp funcArr[10] = {NULL};
2. int (*funcArr[10])(int, int) = {NULL};

Step 3: Assign the function's address—'Add' and 'Subtract' funcArr1[0] = funcArr2[1] = Add;

```
funcArr[0] = &Add;
funcArr[1] = &Subtract;
```

Step 4: Call the function using an index to address the function pointer

```
printf("%d\n", funcArr[1](2, 3));
    // short form
printf("%d\n", (*funcArr[0])(2, 3));
    // correct way
```

7.30 Write a program to add, that uses an array of function pointers, subtract, multiply, or divide two given numbers.

```
#include <stdio.h>
   int sum(int a, int b);
   int subtract(int a, int b);
   int mul(int a, int b);
   int div(int a,int b);

   int (*fp[4]) (int a, int b);

   int main(void)
   {
     int result;
     int num1, num2, op;
     fp[0] = sum;
     fp[1] = subtract;
     fp[2] = mul;
     fp[3] = div;
   printf("\n Enter the numbers: ");
   scanf("%d %d", &num1, &num2);
   do

   {
     printf("\n 0: Add \n 1: Subtract \n
   2: Multiply \n 3: Divide \n 4. EXIT\n");

    printf("\n\n Enter the operation: ");
    scanf("%d", &op);
     result = (*fp[op]) (num1, num2);
     printf("\n Result = %d", result);
   } while(op!=4);
     return 0;
   }
   int sum(int a, int b)
   {
     return a + b;
   }
   int subtract(int a, int b)
   {
     return a - b;
   }
   int mul(int a, int b)
   {
     return a * b;
   }
   int div(int a, int b)
   {
     if(b)
         return a / b;
     else
         return 0;
   }
```

Output

```
Enter the numbers: 2 3
0: Add
1: Subtract
2: Multiply
3: Divide
4. EXIT
Enter the operation: 0
Result = 5
Enter the operation: 4
```

7.17 POINTERS TO POINTERS

In C language you are also allowed to use pointers that point to pointers. The pointers in turn, point to data (or even to other pointers). To declare pointers to pointers, just add an asterisk (*) for each level of reference. For example, if we have:

```
int x = 10;
 int *px; //pointer to an integer
 int **ppx; // pointer to a pointer to an
    integer
 px = &x;
ppx = &px;
```

Assume, that the memory location of these variables is as shown in Fig. 7.9.

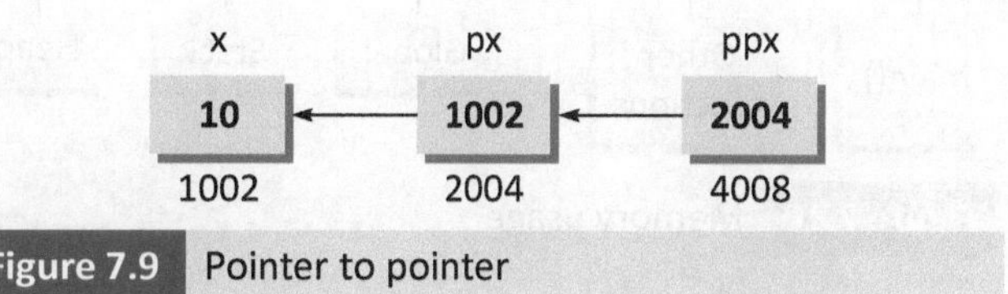

Figure 7.9 Pointer to pointer

Now if we write,

```
printf("\n %d", **ppx);
```

then it will print 10, the value of x.

7.18 MEMORY ALLOCATION IN C PROGRAMS

C supports three kinds of memory allocation through the variables in C programs:

Static allocation When we declare a static or global variable, static allocation is done for the variable. Each static or global variable is allocated a fixed size of memory space. The number of bytes reserved for the variable cannot change during execution of the program. Till now we have been using this technique to define variables, arrays, and pointers.

Automatic allocation When we declare an automatic variable, such as a function argument or a local variable, automatic memory allocation is done. The space for an automatic variable is allocated when the compound statement containing the declaration is entered, and is freed when it exits from a compound statement.

Dynamic allocation A third important kind of memory allocation is known as *dynamic allocation.* In the following sections we will read about dynamic memory allocation using pointers.

7.19 MEMORY USAGE

Before jumping into dynamic memory allocation, let us first understand how memory is used. Conceptually, memory is divided into two—program memory and data memory (Fig. 7.10).

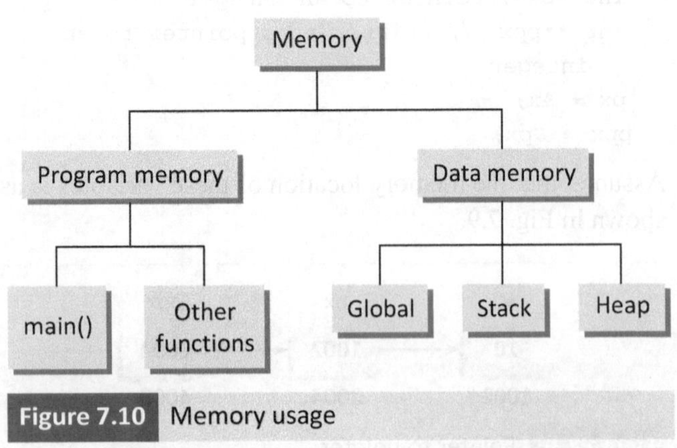

Figure 7.10 Memory usage

The program memory consists of memory used for the `main()` and other called functions in the program, whereas data memory consists of memory needed for permanent definitions such as global data, local data, constants, and dynamic memory data. The way in which C handles the memory requirements is a function of the operating system and the compiler.

When a program is being executed, its `main()` and all other functions are always kept in the memory. However, the local variables of the function are available in the memory only when they are active. When we studied recursive functions, we have seen that the system stack is used to store a single copy of the function and multiple copies of the local variables.

Apart from the stack, we also have a memory allocation known as heap. Heap memory is unused memory allocated to the program and available to be assigned during its execution. When we dynamically allocate memory for variables, heap acts as a memory pool from which memory is allocated to those variables.

However, this is just a conceptual view of memory and implementation of the memory is entirely in the hands of system designers.

7.20 DYNAMIC MEMORY ALLOCATION

The process of allocating memory to the variables during execution of the program or at run time is known as *dynamic memory allocation*. C language has four library routines which allow this function.

Till now whenever we needed an array we had declared a static array of fixed size, say

```
int arr[100];
```

When this statement is executed, consecutive space for 100 integers is allocated. It is not uncommon that we may be using only `10%` or `20%` of the allocated space thereby wasting rest of the space. To overcome this problem and to utilize the memory efficiently `C` language provides a mechanism of dynamically allocating memory so that only the amount of memory that is actually required is reserved. We reserve space only at the run time for the variables that are actually required. Dynamic memory allocation gives best performance in situations in which we do not know memory requirements in advance.

C provides four library routines to automatically allocate memory at the run time. These routines are shown in Table 7.2.

When we have to dynamically allocate memory for variables in our programs then pointers are the only way to go. When we use `malloc()` for dynamic memory allocation, then you need to manage the memory allocated for variables yourself.

Table 7.2 Memory allocation/ de-allocation functions

Function	Task
malloc()	Allocates memory and returns a pointer to the first byte of allocated space
calloc()	Allocates space for an array of elements and initializes them to zero. Like malloc(), calloc() also returns a pointer to the memory
free()	Frees previously allocated memory
realloc()	Alters the size of previously allocated memory

7.20.1 Memory Allocations Process

In computer science, the free memory region is called the heap. The size of heap is not constant as it keeps changing when the program is executed. In the course of program execution, some new variables are created and some variables cease to exist when the block in which they were declared is exited. For this reason it is not uncommon to encounter memory overflow problems during dynamic allocation process. When an overflow condition occurs, the memory allocation functions mentioned above will return a null pointer.

7.20.2 Allocating a Block of Memory

Let us see how memory is allocated using the `malloc()`. `malloc` is declared in `<stdlib.h>`, so we include this header file in any program that calls `malloc`. The `malloc` function reserves a block of memory of specified size and returns a pointer of type `void`. This means that we can assign it to any type of pointer. The general syntax of the `malloc()` is

```
ptr =(cast-type*)malloc(byte-size);
```

where `ptr` is a pointer of type `cast-type`. The `malloc()` returns a pointer (of cast type) to an area of memory with size `byte-size`.

For example,

```
arr=(int*)malloc(10*sizeof(int));
```

This statement is used to dynamically allocate memory equivalent to `10` times the area of `int` bytes. On successful execution of the statement the space is reserved and the address of the first byte of memory allocated is assigned to the pointer `arr` of type `int`.

The function `Calloc()` is another function that reserves memory at the run time. It is normally used to request multiple blocks of storage each of the same size and then sets all bytes to `zero`. `Calloc()` stands for contiguous memory allocation and is primarily used to allocate memory for arrays. The syntax of `calloc()` can be given as:

> **Programming Tip:**
> To use dynamic memory allocation functions, you must include the header file `stdlib.h`.

```
ptr=(cast-type*) calloc(n,elem-size);
```

The above statement allocates contiguous space for n blocks each size of elements size bytes. The only difference between `malloc()` and `calloc()` is that when we use `calloc()`, all bytes are initialized to zero. `Calloc()` returns a pointer to the first byte of the allocated region.

When we allocate memory using `malloc()` or `calloc()`, a `null` pointer will be returned if there is not enough space in the system to allocate. A `null` pointer, points definitely nowhere. It is a *not a pointer* marker; therefore, it is not a pointer you can use. Thus, whenever you allocate memory using `malloc()` or `calloc()`, you must check the returned pointer before using it. If the program receives a null pointer, it should at the very least print an error message and exit, or perhaps figure out some way of proceeding without the memory it asked for. But in any case, the program cannot go on to use the null pointer it got back from `malloc()/calloc()`.

A call to `malloc`, with an error check, typically looks something like this:

```
int *ip = malloc(100 * sizeof(int));
if(ip == NULL)
{
    printf("\n Memory could not  be
    allocated");
    return;
}
```

7.31 Write a program to read and display values of an integer array. Allocate space dynamically for the array.

```
#include <stdio.h>
#include <conio.h>
#include <stdlib.h>
main()
{
    int i, n;
    int *arr;
    clrscr();
    printf("\n Enter the number of elements ");
    scanf("%d", &n);
    arr = (int*)malloc(n * sizeof(int));
```

```
    if(arr == NULL)
    {
        printf("\n Memory Allocation Failed");
        exit(0);
    }
    for(i=0;i<n;i++)
    {
        printf("\n Enter the value %d of the
    array: ", i);
        scanf("%d",&arr[i]);
    }
    printf("\n The array contains \n");
    for(i=0;i<n;i++)
        printf("%d",arr[i]);
        // another way is to write *(arr+i)
    return 0;
}
```

Now let us also see how we can allocate memory using the calloc function. The calloc() function accepts two parametres—num and size, where num is the number of elements to be allocated and size is the size of elements. The following program demonstrates the use of calloc() to dynamically allocate space for an integer array.

```
#include <stdio.h>
#include <stdlib.h>
main ()
{
    int i,n;
    int *arr;
    printf ("\n Enter the number of elements: ");
    scanf("%d",&n);
    arr = (int*) calloc(n,sizeof(int));
    if (arr==NULL)
        exit (1);
    printf("\n Enter the %d values to be
    stored in the array", n);
    for (i = 0; i < n; i++)
        scanf ("%d",&arr[i]);
    printf ("\n You have entered: ");
    for(i = 0; i < n; i++)
        printf ("%d",arr[i]);
    free(arr);
    return 0;
}
```

7.20.3 Releasing the Used Space

When a variable is allocated space during the compile time, then the memory used by that variable is automatically released by the system in accordance with its storage class. But when we dynamically allocate memory then it is our responsibility to release the space when it is not required. This is even more important when the storage space is limited. Therefore, if we no longer need the data stored in a particular block of memory and we do not intend to use that block for storing any other information, then as a good programming practice we must release that block of memory for future use, using the free function. The general syntax of the free() is

```
free(ptr);
```

where ptr is a pointer that has been created by using malloc() or calloc(). When memory is de-allocated using the free(), it is returned back to the free list within the heap.

7.20.4 To Alter the Size of Allocated Memory

At times the memory allocated by using calloc() or malloc() might be insufficient or in excess. In both the situations we can always use realloc() to change the memory size already allocated by calloc() and malloc(). This process is called *reallocation of memory*. The general syntax for realloc() can be given as,

```
ptr = realloc(ptr,newsize);
```

The function realloc() allocates new memory space of size specified by newsize to the pointer variable ptr. It returns a pointer to the first byte of the memory block. The allocated new block may be or may not be at the same region. Thus, we see that realloc() takes two arguments. The first is the pointer referencing the memory and the second is the total number of bytes you want to reallocate. If you pass zero as the second argument, it will be equivalent to calling free(). Like malloc() and calloc(), realloc returns a void pointer if successful, else a NULL pointer is returned.

If realloc() was able to make the old block of memory bigger, it returns the same pointer. Otherwise, if realloc() has to go elsewhere to get enough contiguous memory then it returns a pointer to the new memory, after copying your old data there. However, if realloc() can't find enough memory to satisfy the new request at all, it returns a null pointer. So again you must check before using, that the pointer returned by the realloc() is not a null pointer.

```
/*Example program for reallocation*/
#include < stdio.h>
#include < stdlib.h>
#define NULL 0
main()
{
    char *str;
    /*Allocating memory*/
```

```
    str = (char *)malloc(10);
    if(str==NULL)
    {
       printf("\n Memory could not be allocated");
       exit(1);
    }
    strcpy(str,"Hi");
    printf("\n STR = %s", str);
    /*Reallocation*/
    str = (char *)realloc(str,20);
    if(str==NULL)
    {
       printf("\n Memory could not be
          reallocated");
       exit(1);
    }
    printf("\n STR size modified.\n");
    printf("\n STR = %s\n", str);
    strcpy(str,"Hi there");
    printf("\n STR = %s", str);
    /*freeing memory*/
    free(str);
    return 0;
}
```

Note: With `realloc()`, you can allocate more bytes without losing your data.

Dynamically Allocating a 2-D Array

We have seen how `malloc()` can be used to allocate a block of memory which can simulate an array. Now we can extend our understanding further to do the same to simulate multi-dimensional arrays.

If we are not sure of the number of columns that the array will have, then we will first allocate memory for each row by calling `malloc`. Each row will then be represented by a pointer. Look at the code below which illustrates this concept.

```
#include <stdlib.h>
#include <stdio.h>
main()
{
   int **arr,i,j,ROWS,COLS;
   printf("\n Enter the number of rows and
   columns in the array: ");
   scanf("%d %d",ROWS,COLS);
   arr=(int **)malloc(ROWS * sizeof(int *));
   if(arr == NULL)
   {
      printf("\n Memory could not be
         allocated");
      exit(-1);
   }
   for(i=0; i<ROWS; i++)
   {
      arr[i] = (int *)malloc(COLS * sizeof(int));
      if(arr[i] == NULL)
      {
         printf("\n Memory Allocation Failed");
         exit(-1);
      }
   }
   printf("\n Enter the values of the array: ");
   for(i = 0; i < ROWS; i++)
   {
      for(j = 0; j < COLS; j++)
         scanf("%d",&arr[i][j]);
   }
   printf("\n The array is as follows: ");
   for(i = 0; i < ROWS; i++)
   {
      for(j = 0; j < COLS; j++)
         printf("%d",arr[i][j]);
   }
   for(i = 0; i < ROWS; i++)
      free(arr[i]);
   free(arr);
   return 0;
}
```

Here, `arr` is a pointer-to-pointer-to-`int`: at the first level as it points to a block of pointers, one for each row. We first allocate space for rows in the array. The space allocated to each row is big enough to hold a `pointer-to-int`, or `int *`. If we successfully allocate it, then this space will be filled with pointers to columns (number of `int`s). This can be better understood from Fig. 7.11.

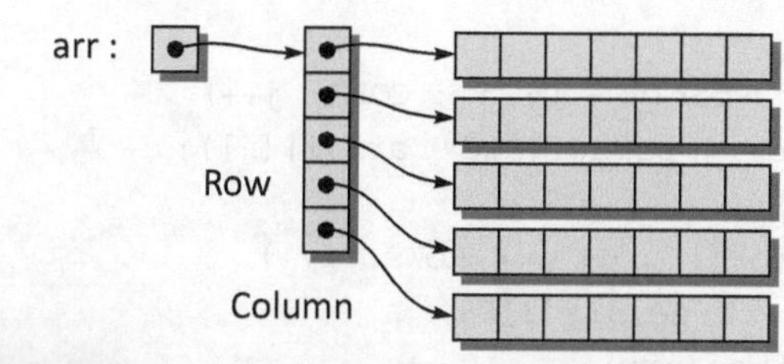

Figure 7.11 Memory allocation of two-dimensional array

Once the memory is allocated for the two-dimensional array, we can use subscripts to access its elements. When we write, `arr[i][j]`, it means we are looking for the `i`th pointer pointed to by `arr`, and then for the `j`th `int` pointed to by that inner pointer.

When we have to pass such an array to a function, then the prototype of the function will be written as

```
func(int **arr, int ROWS, int COLS);
```

In the above declaration, `func` accepts a `pointer-to-pointer-to-int` and the dimensions of the arrays as parametres, so that it will know how many rows and columns there are.

Look at the code given below which illustrates another way of dynamically allocating space for a two-dimensional array.

```
#include <stdlib.h>
#include <stdio.h>
main()
{
   int *arr, i, j, ROWS, COLS;
   printf("\n Enter the number of rows and
   columns in the array: ");
   scanf("%d %d", ROWS, COLS);
   arr = (int *)malloc(ROWS * COLS *
   sizeof(int));
   if(arr == NULL)
   {
      printf("\n Memory could not be
         allocated");
      exit(-1);
   }
   printf("\n Enter the values of the array: ");
   for(i = 0; i < ROWS; i++)
   {
      for(j = 0; j < COLS; j++)
         scanf("%d", &arr[i][j]);
   }
   printf("\n The array is as follows: ");
   for(i = 0; i < ROWS; i++)
   {
      for(j = 0; j < COLS; j++)
         printf("%d", arr[i][j]);
   }
   for(i = 0; i < ROWS; i++)
      free(arr[i]);
   free(arr);
   return 0;
}
```

To dynamically allocate space for a 3-D array, arr[10][20][30], perform the following steps

```
1. int ***arr;
2. arr = (int ***) malloc(10*
   sizeof(int **));
3. for(i=0;i<10;i++) arr[i] = (int
   **) malloc(20*sizeof(int *));
4. for(i=0;i<10;i++) {for(j=0;
   j<20;j++) arr[i][j] = (int *)
   malloc(30 * sizeof(int));
```

7.21 DRAWBACKS OF POINTERS

Although pointers are very useful in C they are not free from limitations. If used incorrectly, pointers can lead to bugs that are difficult to unearth. For example, if you use a pointer to read a memory location but that pointer is pointing to an incorrect location then you may end up reading a wrong value. An erroneous input always leads to an erroneous output, therefore however efficient your program code may be, the output will always be disastrous. Same is the case when writing a value to a particular memory location.

Consider a scenario in which the program code is supposed to read the account balance of a customer, add new amount to it, and then re-write the modified value to that location. If the pointer is pointing to the account balance of some other customer then the account balance of the wrong customer will be updated.

Let us try to find some common errors encountered when using pointers.

```
int x, *px;
 x = 10;
*px = 20;
```

Error un-initialized pointer `px` is pointing to an unknown memory location. Hence it will overwrite that location's contents and store 20 in it. Such a pointer is called a *wild pointer*. A pointer which is not initialized with any address is called a wild pointer. It may contain any garbage address and thus dereferencing a wild pointer can be dangerous.

```
int x, *px;
x = 10;
px = x;
ERROR: it should be px = &x;
```

```
int x = 10, y = 20, *px, *py;
px = &x, py = &y;
if(px < py)      // it should be *px and *py
   printf("\n px is less than py");
else
   printf("\n py is less than px");
```

Look at another code given below.

```
#include <stdio.h>
main()
{
   char *str1, *str2;
   printf("\n Enter the string: ");
   gets(str1);
   while(*str1!='\0')
   {
      *str2 = *str1;
      str2++, str1++;
   }
   *str2='\0';
   printf("\n String is: ");
   while(*str2!='\0')
   {
      printf("%c", *str2);
      str2++;
   }
}
```

Error str2 will not be printed because str2 has moved ahead of its starting location and before displaying the string, it has not been initialized with its starting address.

Memory leak Memory leakage occurs when memory is allocated but not released when it is no longer required. This causes an application to unnecessarily consume memory thereby reducing the memory available for other applications. Although in small programs it is not a big concern but when dealing with large projects, memory leakage may result in slowing down the application or crashing the application when the computer memory resource limits are reached.

For example, if a function dynamically allocates memory for 100 double values and forgets to free the memory and in worst case if that function is called several times within the code then ultimately the system may crash.

Dangling pointer Dangling pointers arise when an object is deleted or de-allocated, without modifying the value of the pointer. As a result, the pointer still points to the memory location of the de-allocated memory.

Once the memory is de-allocated, the system may reallocate that block of freed memory to another process. In case the program then dereferences the (now) dangling pointer, *unpredictable behaviour may result*, as the memory may now contain completely different data.

This problem can become worse when the program writes data to memory pointed by a dangling pointer causing a silent corruption of unrelated data, leading to subtle bugs that can be extremely difficult to find. Moreover, if the overwritten data is bookkeeping data used by the system's memory allocator, the corruption can even cause system instabilities.

Hence, dangling pointer problem occurs when the pointer still points to the same location in memory even though the reference has been deleted and may now be used for other purposes.

A common mistake that we often do in C program is to return address of a stack-allocated local variable. We know that once a called function returns, the space for these variables gets de-allocated and technically they have garbage values. Look at the code below which illustrates how we get a dangling pointer when a called function returns.

```
char *func(void)
{
     Char ch='A';
     /* ... */
     return &ch;
}
```

The above program returns the address of ch. So the calling function may access its value. Any functions called thereafter will overwrite the stack storage allocated for ch with other values and the pointer would no longer work correctly. Therefore, if a pointer to ch must be returned it must be declared as static.

Consider the code below which illustrates another dangling pointer problem.

```
char *ptr1;
char *ptr2 = (char *)malloc(sizeof(char));
ptr1 = ptr2;
free(ptr2);
```

Now ptr1 becomes a dangling pointer. A solution to the above is to assign 0(null) to ptr1 immediately before exiting the block in which it is declared. An alternative solution would be to somehow guarantee that ptr1 will not be used again without further initialization.

Memory corruption Memory corruption often occurs when due to programming errors, the contents of a memory location gets modified unintentionally. When the program uses the contents of the corrupted memory, it either results in program crash or in strange and bizarre behaviour.

Memory corruption is one of the most difficult programming errors to trace mainly because of two reasons:

- The source of the memory corruption and its manifestation may be far apart. Therefore, it may become hard to correlate the cause and the effect of the problem.
- Symptoms of memory corruption problem may appear under unusual conditions thereby making it even harder to consistently reproduce the error.

Memory corruption errors can be broadly classified into following categories:

1. *Using un-initialized memory:* An un-initialized memory contains garbage value. Hence, using the contents of an un-initialized memory can lead to unpredictable program behaviour.
2. *Using un-owned memory:* A common programming mistake is to use pointers for accessing and modifying memory that is not owned by the program. This situation may arise when the pointer happens to be a `null pointer` or a dangling pointer. Using such a pointer to write to a memory location is a serious programming flaw as it may lead to crash another program or even the operating system.
3. *Using beyond allocated memory (buffer overflow):* If the elements of the array are accessed in a loop, with incorrect terminating condition, memory beyond the array bounds may be manipulated. Buffer overflow is a common programming flaw exploited by computer viruses causing serious threat to computer security.
4. *Faulty de-allocation of memory:* Memory leaks and freeing un-allocated memory can also result in memory corruption.

These days, memory debuggers like *Purify*, *Valgrind*, *Insure++* are widely used for detecting memory corruption errors.

POINTS TO NOTE

- All data and programs need to be placed in the primary memory for execution.
- Pointers are nothing but memory addresses. A pointer is a variable that contains the memory address of another variable.
- The '&' operator retrieves the lvalue (address) of the variable. We can dereference a pointer, i.e., refer to the value of the variable to which it points by using unary '*' operator.
- The address of a memory location is a pointer constant, therefore it cannot be changed in the program code.
- Unary increment and decrement operators have greater precedence than the dereference operator (*).
- Null pointer is a special pointer value that is known not to point anywhere. This means that a NULL pointer does not point to any valid memory address. To declare a null pointer you may use the predefined constant `NULL`, You may also initialize a pointer as a null pointer by using a constant 0.
- A generic pointer is a pointer variable that has void as its data type. The generic pointer can be used to point to variables of any data type.
- When the memory for an array is allocated, its base address is fixed and it cannot be changed during program execution.
- When we dynamically allocate memory for variables, heap acts as a memory pool from which memory is allocated to those variables. The process of allocating memory to the variables during execution of the program or at run time is known as dynamic memory allocation.
- `malloc(), calloc(), and realloc` returns a void pointer if successful, else a `NULL` pointer is returned.
- Memory leakage occurs when memory is allocated but not released when it is no longer required.

GLOSSARY

Alias A reference (usually in the form of a pointer) to an object which is also known via other references that may include its own name or other pointers.

Dereference To look up a value referred to. Usually, the 'value referred to' is the value pointed to by a pointer. Therefore, 'dereference a pointer' means to see what it points to. In C, a pointer is dereferenced either using the unary * operator or the array subscripting operator [].

Function pointer A pointer to any function type.

Lvalue An expression that appears on the left-hand sign of an assignment operator, hence, something that can

GLOSSARY

perhaps be assigned to. An lvalue specifies something that has a location, as opposed to a transient value.

Null pointer A pointer value which is not the address of any object or function. A null pointer points to nothing.

Null pointer constant An integral constant expression with value 0 (or such an expression cast to void *), that represents a null pointer.

Pointer Variable that stores addresses.

Rvalue An expression that appears on the right-hand sign of an assignment operator. Generally, rvalue can participate in an expression or be assigned to some other variable.

EXERCISES

Fill in the Blanks

1. Size of character pointer is _______.
2. Allocating memory at run time is known as _______.
3. A pointer to a pointer stores _______ of another _______ variable.
4. _______ pointer does not point to any valid memory address.
5. The size of memory allocated for a variable depends on its _______.
6. On 16-bit systems, integer variable is allocated _______ bytes.
7. The _______ appears on the right side of the assignment statement.
8. Pointers are nothing but _______.
9. _______ enable programmers to return multiple values from a function via function arguments.
10. The _______ operator informs the compiler that the variable is a pointer variable.
11. Data and programs need to be placed in the _______ for execution.
12. When compared with heaps, _____ is faster but also smaller and expensive.
13. All variables declared within `main()` are allocated space on the _______.
14. Shared libraries segment contains _______.
15. The function `malloc()` returns _______.
16. When memory is de-allocated using the `free()`, it is returned back to the _______ within the _______.
17. The functions `malloc()`, `calloc()`, and `realloc` return _______ if successful, else _______ is returned.
18. The function `realloc()` is used to _______.
19. A two-dimensional array is a _______.
20. An un-initialized memory contains _______.
21. Pointer to pointer stores _______.
22. The only integer value that can be assigned to a pointer variable is _______.
23. _______ can be used as parameter declaration to declare an array of integers passed to a function.
24. Dynamically allocated memory can be referred using _______.
25. _______ function returns memory to the heap.
26. Ragged array is implemented using an array of pointers to _______.

Multiple Choice Questions

1. The operator signifies a
   (a) referencing operator
   (b) dereferencing operator
   (c) address operator
   (d) none of these
2. `(&num)` is equivalent to writing
   (a) &num (b) *num
   (c) num (d) none of these
3. Pointers are used to create complex data structures like
   (a) trees (b) linked list
   (c) stack (d) queue
   (e) all of these
4. While declaring pointer variables, which operator do we use?
   (a) address (b) arrow
   (c) indirection (d) dot
5. Which operator retrieves the lvalue of a variable?
   (a) & (b) *
   (c) -> (d) none of these
6. The code of the `main()` program is stored in memory in
   (a) stack (b) heap

EXERCISES

(c) global (d) bss

7. For dynamically allocated variables, memory is allocated from which memory area?

   (a) Stack (b) Heap

   (c) Global (d) BSS

8. The function `malloc()` is declared in which header file

   (a) `stdio.h` (b) `stdlib.h`

   (c) `conio.h` (d) `iostream.h`

9. Which function is used to request memory and set all aloocated bytes to zero?

   (a) `malloc()` (b) `calloc()`

   (c) `realloc()` (d) `free()`

State True or False

1. A pointer is a variable.
2. The `&` operator retrieves the lvalue of the variable.
3. Array name can be used as a pointer.
4. Unary increment and decrement operators have greater precedence than the dereference operator.
5. The generic pointer can be pointed at variables of any data type.
6. A function pointer cannot be passed as a function's calling argument.
7. On 32-bit systems, integer variable is allocated 4 bytes.
8. Lvalue cannot be used on the left side of the assignment statement.
9. Pointers provide an alternate way to access individual elements of the array.
10. Pointer is a variable that represents the contents of a data item.
11. Unary increment and decrement operators have greater precedence than the dereference operator.
12. A fixed size of stack is allocated by the system and is filled as needed from the top to bottom.
13. All the parametres passed to the called function will be stored on the stack.
14. When the memory for an array is allocated, its base address is fixed and it cannot be changed during program execution.
15. An array can be assigned to another array.
16. Memory leakage occurs when memory is allocated but not released when it is no longer required.
17. `mat[i][j]` is equivalent to `*(*(mat + i) + j)`.
18. Dangling pointers arise when an object is deleted or de-allocated, without modifying the value of the pointer.
19. It is possible to add two pointer variables.
20. Pointer constants cannot be changed.
21. The value of a pointer is always an address.
22. *ptr++ will add 1 to the value pointed by ptr.
23. Pointers of different types can be assigned to each other without a cast.
24. Adding 1 to a pointer variable will make it point 1 byte ahead of the memory location to which it is currently pointing.
25. Any arithmetic operator can be used to modify the value of a pointer.
26. Only one call to free() is enough to release the entire array allocated using calloc().
27. Ragged arrays consume less memory space.

Review Questions

1. Explain the difference between a null pointer and a void pointer.
2. Define pointers.
3. Write a short note on pointers.
4. Compare pointer and array name.
5. Explain the result of the following code-

```
int num1 = 2, num2 = 3;
int *p = &num1, *q = &num2;
*p++ = *q++;
```

6. What do you understand by a null pointer?
7. What is an array of pointers? How is it different from a pointer to an array?
8. Write a short note on pointer arithmetic.
9. How are generic pointers different from other pointer variables?
10. What do you understand by the term pointer to a function?
11. Differentiate beween ptr++ and *ptr++.
12. How are arrays related to pointers?
13. Briefly explain array of pointers.
14. Write a program to sort 10 integers using array of pointers.
15. Write a program to illustrate the use of a pointer that points to a 2D array.
16. Give the advantages of using pointers.

EXERCISES

17. Can we have an array of function pointers? If yes, illustrate with the help of a suitable example.
18. Explain the term dynamic memory allocation.
19. Differentiate between `malloc()`, `calloc`, and realloc().
20. Write a short note on pointers to pointers.
21. Differentiate between a function returning pointer to int and a pointer to function returning int.
22. Write a program that illustrates passing of character arrays as an argument to a function (use pointers).
23. Differentiate between pointer to constants and constant to pointers.
24. What is a void pointer?
25. Define null pointer.
26. Explain the call by address technique of passing parameters to function.
27. How are pointers used on two dimensional arrays?
28. Write a program to print Hello world using pointers.
29. Write a program to enter a lowercase character. Print this character in uppercase and also display its ASCII value.
30. Write a program to subtract two integer values.
31. Write a program to calculate area of a circle.
32. Write a program to convert 3.14 into its integral equivalent.
33. Write a program to find smallest of three integer values.
34. Write a program to input a character and categorize it as a vowel or a consonant.
35. Write a program to input 10 values in an array. Categorize each value as positive, negative, or equal to zero.
36. Write a program to input a character. If it is in uppercase print in lowercase and vice versa.
37. Write a program to display the sum and average of numbers from 100–200.
38. Write a program to print all odd numbers from 100–200.
39. Write a program to input 10 values in an array. Categorize each value as prime or composite.
40. Write a program to subtract two floating point numbers using functions.
41. Write a program to calculate the area of a circle.
42. How can you declare a pointer variable?
43. Differentiate between a variable address and a variable's value. How can we access a variable's address and its value using pointers?
44. Give a brief of different memory areas available to the programmer.
45. What do you understand by dereferencing a pointer variable?
46. Write a short note on pointer expressions and pointer arithmetic.
47. What will *p++ = *q++ do?
48. Write a program to add two integers using functions. Use call by address technique of passing parameters.
49. Write a short note on pointer and a three dimensional array.
50. How can a pointer be used to access individual elements of an array? Illustrate with an example.
51. Can we assign a pointer variable to another pointer variable? Justify your answer with the help of an example.
52. What will happen if we add or subtract an integer to or from a pointer variable?
53. Is it possible to compare two pointer variables? Illustrate using an example.
54. Can we subtract two pointer variables?
55. With the help of an example explain how an array can be passed to a function? Is it possible to send just a single element of the array to a function?
56. Can array names appear on the left side of the assignment operator? Why?
57. Differentiate between an array name and an array pointer.
58. Using a program, explain how pointer variables can be used to access strings.
59. Write a program to print "Good Morning" using pointers.
60. Write a program to print the lowercase characters into uppercase and vice versa in the given string "gOOd mORninG".
61. Write a program to copy "University" from the given string "Oxford University Press" in another string.
62. Write a program to copy last five characters from the given string "Oxford University Press" in another string.

EXERCISES

63. Write a menu-driven program to perform various string operations using pointers.
64. How can you have array of function pointers? Illustrate with an example.
65. Briefly discuss memory allocation schemes in C language.
66. Write a program to read and print a floating point array. The space for the array should be allocated at the run time.
67. Write a program to demonstrate working of calloc().
68. Write a short note on realloc(). Give a program to explain its usage.
69. With the help of an example, explain how pointers can be used to dynamically allocate space for two-dimensional and three-dimensional arrays.
70. Write a short note on wild pointers.
71. Give a briefing of memory leakage problem with the help of an example.
72. What is a dangling pointer?
73. Explain memory corruption with the help of suitable examples.
74. Differentiate between *(arr+i) and (arr+i).
75. Write a function to calculate roots of a quadartic equation. The function must accept arguments and return result using pointers.
76. Write a program using pointers to insert a value in an array.
77. Write a program using pointers to search a value from an array.
78. Write a function that accepts a string using pointers. In the function, delete all the occurrences of a given character and display the modified string on the screen.
79. Write a program to reverse a string using pointers.
80. Write a program to compare two arrays using pointers.
81. How can we access the value pointed by a pointer to a pointer?

Program output

Give the output of the following code.

1.
```
main()
{
    int arr[]={1,2,3,4,5};
    int *ptr, i;
    ptr = arr+4;
    for(i = 4; i >= 0;i--)
        printf("\n %d", *(ptr-i));
}
```

2.
```
main()
{
    int arr[]={1,2,3,4,5};
    int *ptr, i;
    ptr = arr+4;
    for(i = 0; i < 5; i++)
        printf("\n %d", *(ptr-i));
}
```

3.
```
#include <stdio.h>
main()
{
    int val=3;
    int *pval=&val;
    printf("%d %d", ++val, *ptr);
}
```

4.
```
#include <stdio.h>
main()
{
    int val=3;
    int *pval=&val;
    printf("%d %d", val, *ptr++);
}
```

5.
```
#include <stdio.h>
main()
{
    int val=3;
    int *pval=&val;
    printf("%d %d", val, ++*ptr);
}
```

6.
```
#include <stdio.h>
main()
{
    int arr[]={1,2,3,4,5};
    printf("%d", ++*arr);
}
```

7.
```
#include <stdio.h>
main()
{
    int arr[]={1,2,3,4,5};
```

EXERCISES

```
   int *parr - arr+2;
   printf("%d %d", ++*parr-1, 1+*-parr);
}
```

8.
```
#include <stdio.h>
main()
{
   int num = 5, *ptr=&a, x=*ptr;
   printf("%d %d %d", ++num, x+2,
   *ptr--);
}
```

9.
```
#include <stdio.h>
main()
{
   int num=5, *ptr=&num;
   printf("\n %d", *&num);
   printf("\n %d", *&*&num);
   printf("\n %d", *&ptr);
   printf("\n %d", **&ptr);
   printf("\n %d", &**&ptr);
}
```

10.
```
main()
{
   int num=5, *ptr=&num;
   printf("%d %d", num, x+2, (*ptr)--);
}
```

11.
```
#include <stdio.h>
main()
{
   int arr[]={1,2,3,4,5}, i, k = 3;
   for(i=0;i<10;i++)
      *(arr+i)=i;
   printf("%d", *(arr[+k-1]);
}
```

12.
```
#include <stdio.h>
main()
{
   int arr[]={1,2,3,4,5};
   int i=1,j=2;
   printf("\n %d", *(arr+1+i));
   printf("\n %d", *(arr+*(arr+1)));
   printf("\n %d", *(arr+i)+*(arr+j);
   printf("\n %d", *(arr+j));
}
```

13.
```
main()
{
   char str[]="ABCDEFGH", *pstr=str;
   pstr++;
   while(*pstr!='H')
      printf("%c", *pstr++);
}
```

14.
```
main()
{
   char str[]="ABCDEFGH";
   printf("%d", (&str[3]-&str[0]);
}
```

15.
```
main()
{
   char *str="ABCDEFGH";
   (*str++);
   printf("%s", str);
}
```

16.
```
main()
{
   char *str="ABCDEFGH";
   str++;
   printf("%s", str);
}
```

17.
```
main()
{
   char *str="AbcDefGh";
   int i=0;
   while(*str)
   {
      if(isupper(*str++))
         i++;
   }
   printf("%d", i);
}
```

18.
```
main()
{
   printf("Hello World"+3);
}
```

19.
```
main()
{
   int arr[][2]={1,2,3,4,5,6,7,8,9};
   printf("%d", sizeof(arr));
}
```

20.
```
main()
{
   int arr[2][3]={1,2,3,4,5,6,7,8,9};
```

EXERCISES

```
    printf("%d", sizeof(arr[1]));
}
```

21. main()

```
{
    int arr[5], *parr=arr;
    while(parr < &arr[5])
    {
        *parr = parr-arr;
        printf("%d", *parr);
        parr++;
    }
}
```

22. main()

```
{
    char *str = "Hello World";
    str[5]='!';
    printf("%s", str);
}
```

23. main()

```
{
    char *str1 = "Hello World";
    char str2[20] = "Hello World";
    char str3[] = "Hello World";
    printf(" %d %d %d", sizeof(str1),
    sizeof(str2), sizeof(str3));
}
```

24. main()

```
{
    register int num = 3, *ptr = &num';
    printf("%d",*ptr);
}
```

25. #include <stdio.h>

```
void func(int (*parr)[3]);
main()
{
    int arr[2][3] = {1,2,3,4,5,6};
    func(arr);
    func(arr + 1);
}
void func(int (*parr)[3])
{
    int i;
    for(i = 0; i < 2; i++)
        printf("%d", (*parr)[i]);
}
```

Find errors if any in the following statements.

- `int ptr, *ptr;`
- `int num, *ptr=num;`
- `int *ptr=10;`
- `int num, **ptr=#`
- `int *ptr1, *ptr2, *ptr3=*ptr1+*ptr2;`
- `int *ptr; scanf("%d", &ptr);`

ANNEXURE 5

A5.1 DECIPHERING POINTER DECLARATIONS

The *right–left* rule is a widely used rule for creating as well as deciphering C declarations. Before starting, let us first understand the meaning of different symbols and the way in which they are read.

Symbol	Read As	Location
*	pointer to	placed on the left side
[]	array of	placed on the right side
()	function returning	placed on the right side

Following are the steps to decipher the declaration:

Step 1: Find the identifier and read as 'identifier is'.

Step 2: Read the symbols on the right of the identifier. For example, if you find '( )', then you know that it is a function declaration. So you can now say, 'identifier is function returning'. Or if you encounter a '[ ]', then read it as 'identifier is array of'.

Continue moving right until you either run out of symbols or you encounter a right parenthesis.

Step 3: Now, check the symbols to the left of the identifier. If it is not a symbol given in the table, then just say it. For example if you encounter `int`, then just say it as it is. Otherwise, translate it into English using the above table. Continue going left until you either run out of symbols or you encounter a left parenthesis.

Step 4: Repeat Steps 2 and 3 until the entire declaration is completely deciphered. Consider some examples:

```
int *ptr[];
```

Step 1: Find the identifier. Here, the identifier is `ptr`. So say,

```
'ptr is'
```

Step 2: Identify the symbols on the right side of the identifier until you run out of symbols or encounter a left parenthesis. Here, the symbol is []. So say

```
'ptr is array of'
```

Step 3: Move to left of the identifier until you run out of symbols or encounter a left parenthesis. Here, the symbol is *. So say,

```
ptr is array of pointer to
```

Step 4: Continue moving left. Here, you find `int`. So say,

```
ptr is array of pointer to int.
```

Now decipher the following declaration:

```
int *(*func())();
```

Step 1: Find the identifier. Here, the identifier is `func`. So say,

```
func is
```

Step 2: Identify the symbols on the right side of the identifier until you run out of symbols or encounter a left parenthesis. Here, the symbol is `()`. So say

```
func is function returning
```

Step 3: Move to left of the identifier until you run out of symbols or encounter a left parenthesis. Here, the symbol is *. So say,

```
func is function returning pointer to
```

Step 4: Can't move left anymore because of the left parenthesis, so now move to right. Here, you will encounter a symbol `()`. So say,

```
func is function returning pointer to
    function returning
```

Step 5: Can't move right anymore as all symbols have exhausted so move to left. Here you will encounter a '*'. So say,

```
func is function returning pointer to
    function returning pointer to
```

Step 6: Continue moving left. Here you will find `int`. So say,

```
func is function returning pointer to
    function returning pointer to int.
```

Some declarations also contain array size and function parametres. So if you encounter a symbol as '[10]', then read it as 'array (size 10)'. If you encounter, something like '(`int *, char`)', then read it as 'function expecting (`int *, char`) and returning...'. Now consider such an example and decipher the following decalaration:

```
int (*(*func)(int *, char))[3][5];
```

Use the steps illustrated below and check your answer.

```
func is pointer to function expecting (int
    *,char) and
returning pointer to array (size 3) of array
    (size 5) of int.
```

Some Illegal Declarations in C

It is quite possible that you end up with some illegal declarations using this rule. So, you must be very clear about what is legal in C and what is not allowed in the language. For example, consider a declaration as shown:

```
int *((*func)())[][];
```

This can be deciphered as, 'func is pointer to function returning array of array of pointer to int'. But did you notice that a function cannot return an array, but only a pointer to an array. Therefore, this declaration is illegal.

Let us look as some more illegal combinations in C language:

```
[]()—C does not permit an array of functions
()()—A function cannot return a function
()[]—A function cannot return an array
```

The table given below lists the declaration, meaning, and its remarks as valid or invalid.

Declaration	Meaning	Remarks
float num;	num is a float	Valid
char *ch;	ch is a pointer to char	Valid
int arr[];	arr is an array of int	Valid
float func();	func is a function returning float	Valid
int **ptr;	ptr is a pointer to pointer to int	Valid
char (*ptr)[];	ptr is a pointer to array of char	Valid
char (*ptr)();	ptr is a pointer to function returning char	Valid
float *ptr[];	ptr is array of pointers to float	Valid
int mat[][];	mat is an array of array of int	Valid
int func[]()	func is an array of function returning int	Invalid
float *func();	func is a function returning pointer to float	Valid
float func()[];	func is a function returning array of float	Invalid
float func()();	func is a function returning function returning float	Invalid
int ***ptr;	ptr is a pointer to pointer to pointer to int	Valid
int (**ptr)[];	ptr is a pointer to pointer to array of int	Valid
float (**func)();	func is a pointer to pointer to a function returning float	Valid
char *(*ptr)[];	ptr is a pointer to array of pointer to char	Valid
float (*ptr)[][];	ptr is a pointer to array of array of float	Valid
float (*ptr)[]();	ptr is a pointer to array of function returning float	Invalid
char *(*(ptr)();	ptr is a pointer to function returning a pointer to char	Valid
char (*ptr)()[];	ptr is a pointer to function returning an array of char	Invalid
int (*ptr)()();	ptr is a pointer to function returning function returning int	Invalid
float **ptr[];	ptr is an array of pointer to pointer to int	Valid
char (*ptr[])[];	ptr is array of pointer to array of char	Valid
char (*ptr[])();	ptr is array of pointer to function returning char	Valid
float *ptr[][];	ptr is array of array of pointer to float	Valid
int arr[][][];	arr is array of array of array of int	Valid

(Contd)

(Contd)

Declaration	Meaning	Remarks
int arr[][]();	arr is array of array of function returning int	Invalid
float *arr[]();	arr is array of function returining pointer to float	Invalid
int arr[]()[];	arr is array of function returning array of int	Invalid
float **func();	func is a function returning pointer to float pointer (or pointer to float)	Valid
char *func()[];	func is a function returning array of char pointer	Invalid
float (*func())[];	func is a function returning pointer to array of float	Valid
float (*func())();	func is a function returning pointer to function returning float	Valid
char func()[][];	func is a function returning array of array of char	Invalid
char func()[]();	func is a function returning array of array of function returning char	Invalid
char *func()();	func is a function returning function returning char pointer	Invalid

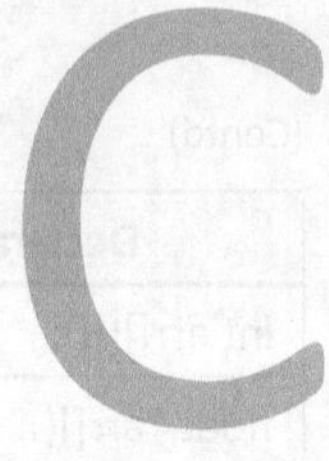

Case Study for Chapters 6 and 7

In C language, a string is nothing but a null-terminated character array and a pointer is a variable that contains the memory location of another variable. Therefore, a pointer is a variable that represents the location of a data item such as a variable or an array element.

Pointers provide an alternate way to access individual elements of the array and they are used to pass arrays and strings as function arguments. Now utilize all these concepts to write a program that performs various operations on a string (using pointers).

1. Write a menu-driven program to read the following operations: 1. a string, 2. display the string, 3. merge two strings, 4. copy n characters from the mth position, 5. calculate the length of the string, 6. count the number of upper case, lower case, numbers and special characters, 7. count the number of words, lines and characters, 8. replace, with; 9. exit.

```
#include <stdio.h>
#include <string.h>
#include <conio.h>
void read_str(char *my_str);
void display_str(char *my_str);
void merge_str(char *my_str1, char *my_str2,
char *my_str3);
void copy(char my_str1[], int m, int n);
int cal_len(char my_str[]);
void count(char my_str[]);
void count_wlc(char my_str[]);
void replace_str(char *my_str);
int main()
{
   char str1[100], str2[100], merged_str[200],
copy_str[100];
   int option, m, n, length=0;
   clrscr();
   do
   {
      printf("\n 1. Enter the string");
      printf("\n 2. Display the string");
      printf("\n 3. Merge two strings");
      printf("\n 4. Copy n characters from mth
position");
      printf("\n 5. Calculate length of the
string");
      printf("\n 6. Count the number of upper
case, lower case, numbers, and special
characters");
      printf("\n 7. Count the number of words,
lines, and characters");
      printf("\n 8. Replace, with ;");
      printf("\n 9. EXIT");

      printf("\n\n Enter your option: ");
      scanf("%d", &option);
      switch(option)
      {
         case 1:
            fflush(stdin);
            read_str(str1);
            break;
         case 2:
            display_str(str1);
            break;
         case 3:
            read_str(str2);
            merge_str(str1, str2, merged_str);
            break;
```

```
        case 4:
          printf("\n Enter the position from
which to copy the text: ");
          scanf("%d", &m);
          printf("\n Enter the number of
characters to be copied: ");
          scanf("%d", &n);
          copy(str1, m, n);
          break;
        case 5:
          length = cal_len(str1);
          printf("\n The length of the
string is: %d", length);
          break;
        case 6:
          count(str1);
          break;
        case 7:
          count_wlc(str1);
          break;
        case 8:
          replace_str(str1);
          break;
      }
   }while (option != 9);
   return 0;
}

void read_str( char *my_str)
{
   fflush(stdin);
   printf("\n Enter the string: ");
   gets(my_str);
}

void display_str(char *my_str)
{

   printf("\n The string is: ");
   while(*my_str != '\0')
   {
     printf("%c", *my_str);
     my_str++;
   }
}

void merge_str(char *my_str1, char *my_str2,
char *my_str3)
{
   strcpy(my_str3,my_str1);
   strcat(my_str3, my_str2);
   display_str(my_str3);
}
```

```
void copy(char my_str1[], int m, int n)
{
   int i = 0;
   char *pstr;
   printf("\n The copied string is: ");
   while(i < n || my_str1[m]!='\0')
   {
     *pstr = my_str1[m];
     m++;i++;
     printf("%c",*pstr);
   }
}

int cal_len(char my_str[])
{       char *str = my_str;
   int len = 0;
   while(*str != '\0')
   {
   str++;
     len++;
   }
    return len;

}

void count(char my_str[])
{
   char *pstr = my_str;
   int upper_case = 0, lower_case = 0, numbers
= 0, spcl_char = 0;
   while (*pstr != '\0')
   {
     if (*pstr >= 'A' && *pstr <= 'Z')
       upper_case++;
     else if (*pstr >= 'a' && *pstr <= 'z')
       lower_case++;
     else if (*pstr >= '0' && *pstr <= '9')
       numbers++;
     else
       spcl_char++;
     pstr++;
   }
   printf("\n Upper case character = %d",
upper_case);
   printf("\n Lower case character = %d",
lower_case);
   printf("\n Numbers = %d", numbers);
   printf("\n Special characters = %d", spcl_
char);
}

void count_wlc(char my_str[])
```

```
{
   char *pstr = my_str;
   int words =1, lines =1, characters = 1;
   while(*pstr != '\0')
   {
     if (*pstr == '\n')
       lines++;
     if (*pstr == ' ' && *(my_str+1) != ' ')
       words++;
     characters++;
     pstr++;
   }
   printf("\n Number of words = %d", words);
   printf("\n Number of lines = %d", lines);
   printf("\n Number of characters = %d",
characters);
}

void replace_str(char my_str[])
{
   char *pstr=my_str;
   while (*pstr != '\0')
   {
     if(*pstr == ',')
       *pstr = ';';
     pstr++;
   }
   display_str(my_str);
}
```

Output

```
1. Enter the string
2. Display the string
3. Merge two strings
4. Copy n characters from mth position
5. Calculate length of the string
6. Count the number of upper case, lower
case, numbers, and special characters
7. Count the number of words, lines, and
characters
8. Replace, with;
9. EXIT
Enter your option: 1
Enter the string: Hi

1. Enter the string
2. Display the string
3. Merge two strings
4. Copy n characters from mth position
5. Calculate length of the string
6. Count the number of upper case, lower
case, numbers and special characters
7. Count the number of words, lines and
characters
8. Replace, with;
9. EXIT
Enter your option: 3
Enter the string: there
The string is Hi there
```

CHAPTER 8

Structure, Union, and Enumerated Data Types

Takeaways

- Structure Declaration, Initialization and Access
- Nested Structures
- Arrays of structures
- Structures and Functions
- Self Referential Structures
- Unions
- Unions Within Structures
- Enumerated Data Types

8.1 INTRODUCTION

A structure is similar to records. It stores related information about an entity. Structure is basically a user-defined data type that can store related information (even of different data types) together. The major difference between a structure and an array is that, an array contains related information of the same data type.

A structure is, therefore, a collection of variables under a single name. The variables within a structure are of different data types and each has a name that is used to select it from the structure.

8.1.1 Structure Declaration

Programming Tip: Do not forget to place a semicolon after the definition of structures and unions.

A structure is declared using the keyword `struct` followed by a structure name. All the variables of the structure are declared within the structure. A structure type is generally declared by using the following syntax:

```
struct struct-name
{
    data_type var-name;
    data_type var-name;
    ...
};
```

For example, if we have to define a structure for a student, then its related information probably would be: `roll_number`, `name`, `course`, and `fees`. This structure can be declared as,

```
struct student
{
    int r_no;
    char name[20];
    char course[20];
    float fees;
};
```

Now, the structure has become a user-defined data type. Each `var-name` declared within a structure is called a member of the structure. The structure declaration, however, does not allocate any memory or consume storage space. It just gives a template that conveys to the C compiler how the structure is laid out in memory and gives details of the member names. Like any other data type, memory is allocated for the structure when we declare a variable of the structure. For example, we can define a variable `student` by writing,

```
struct student stud1;
```

Here, `struct student` is a data type and `stud1` is a variable. Look at another way of declaring variables. In the following syntax, the variable is declared at the time of structure declaration.

```
struct student
{
   int r_no;
   char name[20];
   char course[20];
   float fees;
}stud1, stud2;
```

In this declaration we declare two variables `stud1` and `stud2` of the structure `student`. So if you want to declare more than one variable of the structure, then separate the variables using a comma.

When we declare variables of the structure, separate memory is allocated for each variable. This is shown in Fig. 8.1.

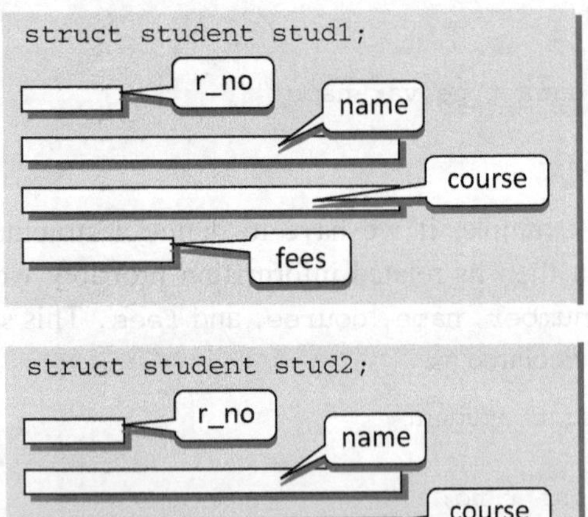

Figure 8.1 Memory allocation for a structure variable

Let us see some more structure declarations.

Example 8.1 Declare a structure to store information about a point in the coordinate system.

```
struct point
{
   int x,y;
};
```

Example 8.2 Declare a structure to store customer information.

```
struct customer
{
   int cust_id;
   char name[20];
   char address[20];
   long int phone_num;
   int DOB;
};
```

Example 8.3 Declare a structure to store information of a particular date.

```
struct date
{
   int day;
   int month;
   int year;
};
```

Example 8.4 Declare a structure to store information of a particular book.

```
struct BOOK
{
   char title[20];
   char author[20];
   int pages;
   float price;
   int yr_of_publication;
};
```

Programming Tip: Use different member names for different structures for clarity.

Example 8.5 Declare a structure to create an inventory record.

```
struct inventory
{
   char prod_name[20];
   float price;
   int stock;
};
```

Note: Structure type and variable declaration of a structure can be either local or global depending on their placement in the code.

Last but not the least, structure member names and names of the structure follow the same rules as laid down for the names of ordinary variables. However, care should be taken to ensure that the name of structure and the name of a structure member should not be the same. Moreover, structure name and its variable name should also be different.

8.1.2 `Typedef` Declarations

Programming Tip: C does not allow declaration of variables at the time of creating a typedef definition. So variables must be declared in an independent statement.

The `typedef` (derived from type definition) keyword enables the programmer to create a new data type name for an existing data type. By using `typedef`, no new data is created, rather an alternate name is given to a known data type.

The general syntax of using the `typedef` keyword is given as:

```
typedef existing data type
new data_type
```

Note that `typedef` statement does not occupy any memory, it simply defines a new type. For example, if we write

```
typedef int INTEGER;
```

then `INTEGER` is the new name of data type `int`. To declare variables using the new data type name, precede the variable name with the data type name (new). Therefore, to define an integer variable, we may now write

```
INTEGER num=5;
```

When we precede a `struct` name with `typedef` keyword, then the `struct` becomes a new type. It is used to make the construct shorter with more meaningful names for types already defined by C or for types that you have declared. A `typedef` declaration is a synonym for the type. For example, writing

```
typedef struct student
{
    int r_no;
    char name[20];
    char course[20];
    float fees;
};
```

Now that you have preceded the structure's name with the keyword `typedef`, the student becomes a new data type. Therefore, now you can straightaway declare variables of this new data type as you declare variables of type `int`, `float`, `char`, `double`, etc., to declare a variable of structure `student` you will just write,

```
student stud1;
```

Note that we have not written `struct student stud1`.

8.1.3 Initialization of Structures

A structure can be initialized in the same way as other data types are initialized. *Initializing a structure* means assigning some constants to the members of the structure. When the user does not explicitly initialize the structure, then C automatically does that. For `int` and `float` members, the values are initialized to zero and `char` and string members are initialized to the `'\0'` by default (in the absence of any initialization done by the user).

The initializers are enclosed in braces and are separated by commas. However, care must be taken to see that the initializers match their corresponding types in the structure definition.

The general syntax to initialize a structure variable is given as follows:

```
struct struct_name
{
    data_type member_name1;
    data_type member_name2;
    data_type member_name3;
    ...............................
}struct_var = {constant1, constant2,
constant 3,...};
```

OR

```
struct struct_name
{
    data_type member_name1;
    data_type member_name2;
    data_type member_name3;
    .......................
    .......
};
struct struct_name struct_var = {constant1,
constant2, constant 3,...};
```

Programming Tip: It is an error to assign a structure of one type to a structure of another type.

For example, we can initialize a student structure by writing

```
struct student
{
    int r_no;
    char name[20];
    char course[20];
    float fees;
}stud1 = {01, "Rahul", "BCA", 45000};
```

or by writing

```
struct student stud1 = {01, "Rahul", "BCA",
45000};
```

Figure 8.2 illustrates how the values will be assigned to the individual fields of the structure.

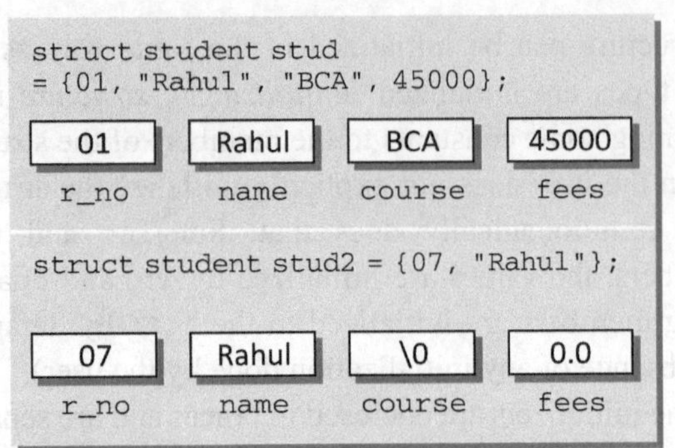

Figure 8.2 Assigning values to structure elements

When all the members of a structure are not initialized, it is called partial initialization. In case of partial initialization, first few members of the structure are initialized and those that are uninitialized are assigned default values.

8.1.4 Accessing the Members of a Structure

Each member of a structure can be used just like a normal variable, but its name will be a bit longer. A structure member variable is generally accessed using a '.' (dot) operator. The syntax of accessing a structure or a member of a structure can be given as:

Programming Tip:
A member of the structure cannot be accessed directly using its name. Rather you must use the structure name followed by the dot operator before specifying the member name.

```
struct_var.member_name
```

The dot operator is used to select a particular member of the structure. For example, to assign value to the individual data members of the structure variable stud1, we may write,

```
stud1.r_no = 01;
stud1.name = "Rahul";
stud1.course = "BCA";
stud1.fees = 45000;
```

To input values for data members of the structure variable stud1, we may write,

```
scanf("%d", &stud1.r_no);
scanf("%s", &stud1.name);
```

Similarly, to print the values of structure variable stud1, we may write,

```
printf("%s", stud1.course);
printf("%f", stud1.fees);
```

Memory is allocated only when we declare variables of the structure. In other words, memory is allocated only when we instantiate the structure. In the absence of any variable, structure definition is just a template that will be used to reserve memory when a variable of type struct is declared.

Once the variables of a structure are defined, we can perform a few operations on them. For example, we can use the assignment operator '=' to assign the values of one variable to another.

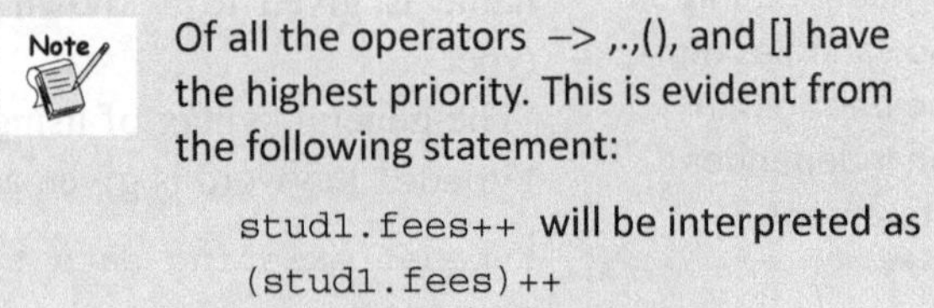

8.1.5 Copying and Comparing Structures

We can assign a structure to another structure of the same type. For example, if we have two structure variables stud1 and stud2 of type struct student given as,

Programming Tip:
An error will be generated if you try to compare two structure variables.

```
struct student stud1 =
{01, "Rahul", "BCA",
45000};
struct student stud2;
```

Then to assign one structure variable to another we will write,

```
stud2 = stud1;
```

This statement initializes the members of stud2 with the values of members of stud1. Therefore, now the values of stud1 and stud2 can be given as shown in Fig. 8.3.

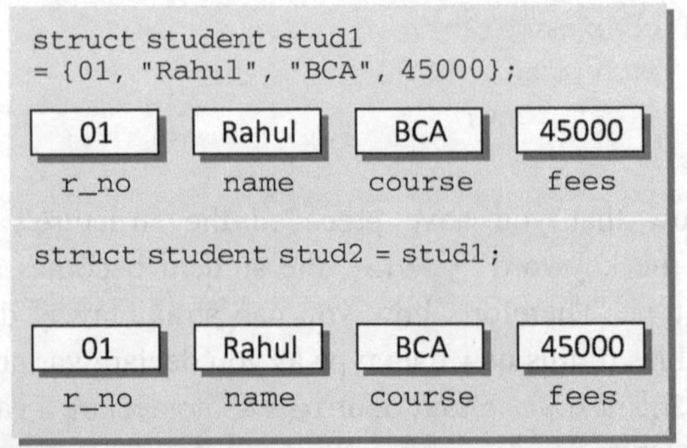

Figure 8.3 Values of structure variables

C does not permit comparison of one structure variable with another. However, individual members of one structure can be compared with individual members of another structure. When we compare one structure member with another structure's member, the comparison will behave like any other ordinary variable comparison. For example, to compare the fees of two students, we will write,

```
if(stud1.fees > stud2.fees)
   Fees of stud1 is greater than stud2
```

8.1 Write a program using structures to read and display the information about a student.

```
#include <stdio.h>
#include <conio.h>
int main()
{
   struct student
   {
      int roll_no;
      char name[80];
      float fees;
      char DOB[80];
   };
   struct student stud1;
   clrscr();
   printf("\n Enter the roll number: ");
   scanf("%d", &stud1.roll_no);
   printf("\n Enter the name: ");
   scanf("%s", stud1.name);
   printf("\n Enter the fees: ");
   scanf("%f", &stud1.fees);
   printf("\n Enter the DOB: ");
   scanf("%s", stud1.DOB);
   printf("\n ********STUDENT'S DETAILS
   *******");
   printf("\n ROLL No. = %d", stud1.roll_no);
   printf("\n NAME = %s", stud1.name);
   printf("\n FEES = %f", stud1.fees);
   printf("\n DOB = %s", stud1.DOB);
   getch();
   return 0;
}
```

Output

```
Enter the roll number: 01
Enter the name: Rahul
Enter the fees: 45000
Enter the DOB: 25-09-1991
********STUDENT'S DETAILS *******
ROLL No. = 01
NAME = Rahul
FEES = 45000.00
DOB = 25-09-1991
```

8.2 Write a program, using structures, to find the biggest of three numbers.

```
#include <stdio.h>
#include <conio.h>
int main()
{
   struct numbers
   {
      int a, b, c;
      int largest;
   };
   struct numbers num;
   clrscr();
   printf("\n Enter the three numbers: ");
   scanf("%d %d %d", &num.a, &num.b, &num.c);
   if (num.a > num.b && num.a > num.c)
      num.largest = num.a;
   if (num.b > num.a && num.b > num.c)
      num.largest = num.b;
   if (num.c > num.a && num.c > num.b)
      num.largest = num.c;
   printf("\n The largest number is: %d",
   num.largest);
   getch();
   return 0;
}
```

Output

```
Enter the three numbers: 7 9 1
The largest number is: 9
```

8.3 Write a program to read, display, add, and subtract two complex numbers.

```
#include <stdio.h>
#include <conio.h>
int main()
{
   typedef struct complex
   {
      int real;
      int imag;
   }COMPLEX;
   COMPLEX c1, c2, sum_c, sub_c;
   int option;
```

```
    clrscr();
    do
    {
        printf("\n *** MAIN MENU ***");
        printf("\n 1. Read the complex nos.");
        printf("\n 2. Display the complex nos.");
        printf("\n 3. Add the complex nos.");
        printf("\n 4. Subtract the complex nos.");
        printf("\n 5. EXIT");
        printf("\n Enter your option: ");
        scanf("%d", &option);
        switch(option)
        {
        case 1:
            printf("\n Enter the real and imaginary
                parts of the first complex number: ");
            scanf("%d %d", &c1.real, &c1.imag);
            printf("\n Enter the real and imaginary
                parts of the second complex number: ");
            scanf("%d %d", &c2.real, &c2.imag);
            break;
        case 2:
            printf("\n The first complex number is:
                %d + %di", c1.real, c1.imag);
            printf("\n The second complex number is:
                %d + %di", c2.real, c2.imag);
            break;
        case 3:
            sum_c.real = c1.real + c2.real;
            sum_c.imag = c1.imag + c2.imag;
            printf("\n The sum of two complex numbers
                is: %d + %di", sum_c.real, sum_c.imag);
            break;
        case 4:
            sub_c.real = c1.real - c2.real;
            sub_c.imag = c1.imag - c2.imag;
            printf("\n The difference between two
                complex numbers is: %d + %di",
                sub_c.real, sub_c.imag);
            break;
        }
    }while(option != 5);
    getch();
    return 0;
}
```

Output

```
******** MAIN MENU *********
1. Read the complex numbers
2. Display the complex numbers
3. Add the complex numbers
4. Subtract the complex numbers
5. EXIT
Enter your option: 1
Enter the real and imaginary parts of the
first complex number: 2 3
Enter the real and imaginary parts of the
second complex number: 4 5
******** MAIN MENU *********
1. Read the complex numbers
2. Display the complex numbers
3. Add the complex numbers
4. Subtract the complex numbers
5. EXIT
Enter your option: 3
The sum of two complex numbers is: 6 + 8i
```

8.4 Write a program to enter two points and then calculate the distance between them.

```
#include <stdio.h>
#include <conio.h>
#include<math.h>
int main()
{
    typedef struct point
    {
        int x, y;
    }POINT;
    POINT p1, p2;
    float distance;
    clrscr();
    printf("\n Enter the coordinates of the
    first point: ");
    scanf("%d %d", &p1.x, &p1.y);
    printf("\n Enter the coordinates of the
    second point: ");
    scanf("%d %d", &p2.x, &p2.y);
    distance = sqrt(pow((p1.x - p2.x), 2) +
    pow((p1.y - p2.y), 2));
    printf("\n The coordinates of the first
    point are: %dx %dy", p1.x, p1.y);
    printf("\n The coordinates of the second
    point are: %dx %dy", p2.x, p2.y);
    printf("\n Distance between p1 and p2 =
    %f", distance);
    getch();
    return 0;
}
```

Output

```
Enter the coordinates of the first point: 2 3
Enter the coordinates of the second point: 9 9
The coordinates of the first point are: 2x 3y
The coordinates of the second point are: 9x 9y
Distance between p1 and p2 = 9.219544
```

8.2 NESTED STRUCTURES

A structure can be placed within another structure, i.e., a structure may contain another structure as its member. A structure that contains another structure as its member is called a *nested structure*.

Let us now see how we declare nested structures or structures that contain structures. Although it is possible to declare a nested structure with one declaration, it is not recommended. The easier and clearer way is to declare the structures separately and then group them in a high-level structure. When you do this, take care to check that nesting must be done from inside out (from lowest level to the most inclusive level), i.e., to say, declare the innermost structure, then the next level structure, working towards the outer (most inclusive) structure.

```
typedef struct
{
   char first_name[20];
   char mid_name[20];
   char last_name[20];
}NAME;

typedef struct
{
   int dd;
   int mm;
   int yy;
}DATE;

typedef struct student
{
   int r_no;
   NAME name;
   char course[20];
   DATE DOB;
   float fees;
};
```

In this example, we see that the structure `student` in turn contains two other structures—`NAME` and `DATE`. Both these structures have their own fields. The structure `NAME` has three fields: `first_name`, `mid_name`, and `last_name`. The structure `DATE` also has three fields: `dd`, `mm`, and `yy`, which specify the day, month, and year of the date. To assign values to the structure fields, we will write,

```
student stud1;
stud1.name.first_name = "Janak";
stud1.name.mid_name = "Raj";
stud1.name.last_name = "Thareja";
stud1.course = "BCA";
stud1.DOB.dd = 15;
stud1.DOB.mm = 09;
stud1.DOB.yy = 1990;
stud1.fees = 45000;
```

In case of nested structures we use the dot operator in conjunction with the structure variables to access the members of the innermost as well as the outermost structures. The use of nested structures is illustrated in the following program:

8.5 Write a program to read and display information of a student, using a structure within a structure.

```
#include <stdio.h>
#include <conio.h>
int main()
{
   struct DOB
   {
      int day;
      int month;
      int year;
   };
   struct student
   {
      int roll_no;
      char name[100];
      float fees;
      struct DOB date;
   };
   struct student stud1;
   clrscr();
   printf("\n Enter the roll number: ");
   scanf("%d", &stud1.roll_no);
   printf("\n Enter the name: ");
   scanf("%s", stud1.name);
   printf("\n Enter the fees: ");
   scanf("%f", &stud1.fees);
   printf("\n Enter the DOB: ");
   scanf("%d %d %d", &stud1.date.day,
   &stud1.date.month, &stud1.date.year);
   printf("\n *** STUDENT'S DETAILS ***");
   printf("\n ROLL No. = %d", stud1.roll_no);
   printf("\n NAME = %s", stud1.name);
```

```
    printf("\n FEES = %f", stud1.fees);
    printf("\n DOB = %d - %d - %d", stud1.
    date.day, stud1.date.month, stud1.date.
    year);
    getch();
    return 0;
}
```

Output

```
Enter the roll number: 01
Enter the name: Rahul
Enter the fees: 45000
Enter the DOB: 25 09 1991
********STUDENT'S DETAILS *******
ROLL No. = 01
NAME = Rahul
FEES = 45000.00
DOB = 25-09-1991
```

8.3 ARRAYS OF STRUCTURES

In the above examples, we have seen how to declare a structure and assign values to its data members. Now we will discuss how to declare an array of a structure. For this purpose, let us first analyse, where we would need array of structures.

In a class, we do not have just one student. But there may be at least 30 students. So the same definition of the structure can be used for all the 30 students. This would be possible when we will make an array of the structure. An array of a structure is declared in the same way as we had declared an array of a built-in data type.

> **Programming Tip:**
> It is an error to omit array subscripts when referring to individual structures of an array of structures.

Another example, where an array of structures is desirable, is in case of an organization. An organization has a number of employees. So, defining a separate structure for every employee is not a viable solution. So here we can have a common structure definition for all the employees. This can again be done by declaring an array of the structure employee.

The general syntax for declaring an array of a structure can be given as,

```
struct struct_name
{
    data_type member_name1;
    data_type member_name2;
    data_type member_name3;
    ....................................
};
struct struct_name struct_var[index];
```

Consider the given structure definition.

```
struct student
{
    int r_no;
    char name[20];
    char course[20];
    float fees;
};
```

A student array can be declared simply by writing,

```
student stud[30];
```

Now, to assign values to the ith student of the class, we will write,

```
stud[i].r_no = 09;
stud[i].name = "RASHI";
stud[i].course = "MCA";
stud[i].fees = 60000;
```

In order to initialize the array of structure variables at the time of declaration, you should write as follows:

```
student stud[3] = {{01, "Aman", "BCA",
45000},{02, "Aryan", "MCA", 60000}, {03,
"John", "BCA", 45000}};
```

8.6 Write a program to read and display the information of all the students in the class.

```
#include <stdio.h>
#include <conio.h>
int main()
{
    struct student
    {
        int roll_no;
        char name[80];
        int fees;
        char DOB[80];
    };
    struct student stud[50];
    int n, i;
    clrscr();
    printf("\n Enter the number of students: ");
    scanf("%d", &n);
    for(i = 0;i < n;i++)
    {
        printf("\n Enter the roll number: ");
        scanf("%d",&stud[i].roll_no);
        fflush(stdin);
```

```
        printf("\n Enter the name: ");
        gets(stud[i].name);
        fflush(stdin);
        printf("\n Enter the fees: ");
        scanf("%d", &stud[i].fees);
        fflush(stdin);
        printf("\n Enter the DOB: ");
        gets(stud[i].DOB);
        fflush(stdin);
    }
    for(i = 0;i < n;i++)
    {
        printf("\n ********DETAILS OF STUDENT
    %d ******", i+1);
        printf("\n ROLL No. = %d", stud[i].
    roll_no);
        printf("\n NAME = %s", stud[i].name);
        printf("\n FEES = %d", stud[i].fees);
        printf("\n DOB = %s", stud[i].DOB);
    }
    getch();
    return 0;
}
```

Output

```
Enter the number of students: 2
Enter the roll number: 1
Enter the name: kirti
Enter the fees: 5678
Enter the DOB: 9 9 91
Enter the roll number: 2
Enter the name: kangana
Enter the fees: 5678
Enter the DOB: 27 8 91
********DETAILS OF STUDENT 1*******
ROLL No. = 1
NAME = kirti
FEES = 5678
DOB = 9 9 91
********DETAILS OF STUDENT 2*******
ROLL No. = 2
NAME = kangana
FEES = 5678
DOB = 27 8 91
```

8.7 Write a program to read and display the information of all the students in the class. Then edit the details of the ith student and redisplay the entire information.

```
#include <stdio.h>
#include <string.h>
#include <conio.h>
int main()
{
    struct student
    {
        int roll_no;
        char name[80];
        int fees;
        char DOB[80];
    };
    struct student stud[50];
    int n, i, rolno, new_rolno;
    int new_fees;
    char new_DOB[80], new_name[80];
    clrscr();
    printf("\n Enter the number of students: ");
    scanf("%d", &n);
    for(i = 0;i < n;i++)
    {
        printf("\n Enter the roll number: ");
        scanf("%d", &stud[i].roll_no);
        fflush(stdin);
        printf("\n Enter the name: ");
        gets(stud[i].name);
        fflush(stdin);
        printf("\n Enter the fees: ");
        scanf("%d", stud[i].fees);
        fflush(stdin);
        printf("\n Enter the DOB: ");
        gets(stud[i].DOB);
        fflush(stdin);
    }
    for(i = 0;i < n;i++)
    {
        printf("\n ********DETAILS OF STUDENT
    %d*******", i+1);
        printf("\n ROLL No. = %d", stud[i].
    roll_no);
        printf("\n NAME = %s", stud[i].name);
        printf("\n FEES = %d", stud[i].fees);
        printf("\n DATE OF BIRTH = %s",
    stud[i].DOB);
    }
    printf("\n Enter the roll no. of the
    student whose record has to be edited: ");
    scanf("%d", &rolno);
    printf("\n Enter the new roll number: ");
    scanf("%d", &new_rolno);
    printf("\n Enter the new name: ");
    scanf("%s", new_name);
    printf("\n Enter the new fees: ");
    scanf("%d", &new_fees);
    printf("\n Enter the new date of birth: ");
    scanf("%s", new_DOB);
```

```
    stud[rolno].roll_no = new_rolno;
    strcpy(stud[rolno].name, new_name);
    stud[rolno].fees = new_fees;
    strcpy(stud[rolno].DOB,new_DOB);
    for(i=0;i<n;i++)
    {
      printf("\n ********DETAILS OF STUDENT
    %d*******", i+1);
      printf("\n ROLL No. = %d", stud[i].
    roll_no);
      printf("\n NAME = %s", stud[i].name);
      printf("\n FEES = %d", stud[i].fees);
      printf("\n DATE OF BIRTH = %s",
    stud[i].DOB);
    }

    getch();
    return 0;
}
```

Output

```
Enter the number of students: 2
Enter the roll number: 1
Enter the name: kirti
Enter the fees: 5678
Enter the DOB: 9 9 91
Enter the roll number: 2
Enter the name: kangana
Enter the fees: 5678
Enter the DOB: 27 8 91
********DETAILS OF STUDENT 1*******
ROLL No. = 1
NAME = kirti
FEES = 5678
DOB = 9 9 91
********DETAILS OF STUDENT 2*******
ROLL No. = 2
NAME = kangana
FEES = 5678
DOB = 27 8 91
Enter the roll number. of the student whose
  record has to be edited: 2
Enter the new roll number: 2
Enter the new name: kangana khullar
Enter the new fees: 7000
Enter the new date of birth: 27 8 92
********DETAILS OF STUDENT 1*******
ROLL No. = 1
NAME = kirti
FEES = 5678
DOB = 9 9 91
********DETAILS OF STUDENT 2*******
ROLL No. = 2
NAME = kangana
FEES = 7000
DOB = 27 8 92
```

8.4 STRUCTURES AND FUNCTIONS

For structures to be fully useful, we must have a mechanism to pass them to functions and return them. A function may access the members of a structure in three ways as shown in Fig. 8.4.

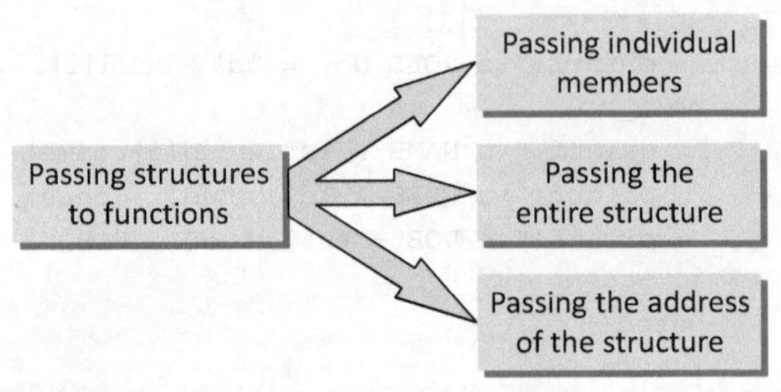

Figure 8.4 Passing structures to a function

8.4.1 Passing Individual Members

To pass any individual member of the structure to a function we must use the direct selection operator to refer to the individual members for the actual parametres. The called program does not know if the two variables are ordinary variables or structure members. Look at the following code that illustrates this concept.

```
#include <stdio.h>
typedef struct
{
  int x;
  int y;
}POINT;
void display(int, int);
main()
{
  POINT p1 = {2, 3};
  display(p1.x, p1.y);
  return 0;
}
void display(int a, int b)
{
  printf("The coordinates of the point are:
  %d %d", a, b);
}
```

Output

```
The coordinates of the point are: 2 3
```

8.4.2 Passing the Entire Structure

Just like any other variable, we can pass an entire structure as a function argument. When a structure is passed as an argument, it is passed using the call by value method, i.e., a copy of each member of the structure is made. This is a very inefficient method especially when the structure is very big or the function is called frequently. In such a situation passing and working with pointers may be more efficient.

The general syntax for passing a structure to a function and returning a structure can be given as,

```
struct struct_name func_name(struct struct_
name struct_var);
```

This syntax can vary as per need. For example, in some situations we may want a function to receive a structure but return a void or value of some other data type. The following code passes a structure to the function using the call by value method.

```
#include <stdio.h>
typedef struct
{
   int x;
   int y;
}POINT;
void display(POINT);
main()
{
   POINT p1 = {2, 3};
   display(p1);
   return 0;
}
void display(POINT p)
{
   printf("%d %d", p.x, p.y);
}
```

8.8 Write a program to read, display, add, and subtract two distances. Distance must be defined using kms and metres.

```
#include <stdio.h>
#include <conio.h>
typedef struct distance
{
   int kms;
   int metres;
}DISTANCE;
DISTANCE add_distance(DISTANCE, DISTANCE);
DISTANCE subtract_distance(DISTANCE,
   DISTANCE);
DISTANCE d1, d2, d3, d4;
int main()
{
   int option;
   clrscr();
   do
   {
     printf("\n *** MAIN MENU ***");
     printf("\n 1. Read the distances ");
     printf("\n 2. Display the distances");
     printf("\n 3. Add the distances");
     printf("\n 4. Subtract the distances");
     printf("\n 5. EXIT");
     printf("\n Enter your option: ");
     scanf("%d", &option);
     switch(option)
     {
     case 1:
     printf("\n Enter the first distance in
   kms and metres: ");
     scanf("%d %d", &d1.kms, &d1.metres);
     printf("\n Enter the second distance
   kms and metres: ");
     scanf("%d %d", &d2.kms, &d2.metres);
     break;
     case 2:
     printf("\n The first distance is: %d
   kms %d metres", d1.kms, d1.metres);
     printf("\n The second distance is: %d
   kms %d metres", d2.kms, d2.metres);
     break;
     case 3:
     d3 = add_distance(d1, d2);
     printf("\n The sum of two distances
   is: %d kms %d metres", d3.kms, d3.metres);
   break;
     case 4:
     d4 = subtract_distance(d1, d2);
     printf("\n The difference between two
   distances is: %d kms %d metres", d4.kms,
   d4.metres);
     break;
     }
   }while(option != 5);
   getch();
   return 0;
}
DISTANCE add_distance(DISTANCE d1, DISTANCE d2)
```

```
{
  DISTANCE sum;
  sum.metres = d1.metres + d2. metres;
  sum.kms = d1.kms + d2.kms;
  if(sum.metres >= 1000)
  {
     sum.metres = sum.metres%1000;
     sum.kms += 1;
  }
  return sum;
}
DISTANCE subtract_distance(DISTANCE d1,
  DISTANCE d2)
{
  DISTANCE sub;
  if(d1.kms > d2.kms)
  {
     sub.metres = d1.metres - d2. metres;
     sub.kms = d1.kms - d2.kms;
  }
  else
  {
     sub.metres = d2.metres - d1. metres;
     sub.kms = d2.kms - d1.kms;
  }
  if(sub.metres < 0)
  {
     sub.kms = sub.kms - 1;
     sub.metres = sub.metres + 1000;
  }
  return sub;
}
```

Output

```
******** MAIN MENU *********
1. Read the distances
2. Display the distances
3. Add the distances
4. Subtract the distances
5. EXIT
Enter your option: 1
Enter the first distance in kms and metres:
5 300
Enter the secont distance in kms and metres:
3 400
1. Read the distances
2. Display the distances
3. Add the distances
4. Subtract the distances
5. EXIT
Enter your option: 3
The sum of two distances is: 8 kms 700 metres
```

8.9 Write a program, using pointer to structure, to initialize the members in the structure. Use functions to print the student's information.

```
#include <stdio.h>
#include <conio.h>
struct student
{
   int r_no;
   char name[20];
   char course[20];
   float fees;
};
void display(struct student *);
main()
{
   struct student *ptr_stud1;
   struct student stud1 = {01, "Rahul",
   "BCA", 45000};
   clrscr();
   ptr_stud1 = &stud1;
   display(ptr_stud1);
   return 0);
}
void display(struct student *ptr_stud1)
{
   printf("\n DETAILS OF STUDENT");
   printf("\n -----------------------------");
   printf("\nROLL NO. = %d", ptr_stud1 -> r_no);
   printf("\nNAME = ", puts(ptr_stud1 -> name));
   printf("\nCOURSE = ", puts(ptr_stud1 -> course));
   printf("\nFEES = %f", ptr_stud1 -> fees);
}
```

Output

```
DETAILS OF STUDENT
------------------------------------------
ROLL NUMBER = 01
NAME  = Rahul
COURSE  = BCA
FEES = 45000.00
```

8.10 Write a program to read, display, add, and subtract two time defined using hour, minutes, and values of seconds.

```
#include <stdio.h>
#include <conio.h>
typedef struct
{
   int hr;
```

```
    int min;
    int sec;
}TIME;
TIME t1, t2, t3, t4;
TIME subtract_time(TIME, TIME);
TIME add_time(TIME, TIME);
int main()
{
    int option;
    clrscr();
    do
    {
        printf("\n **** MAIN MENU *****");
        printf("\n 1. Read time ");
        printf("\n 2. Display time");
        printf("\n 3. Add");
        printf("\n 4. Subtract");
        printf("\n 5. EXIT");
        printf("\n Enter your option: ");
        scanf("%d", &option);
        switch(option)
        {
        case 1:
        printf("\n Enter the first time in
    hrs, mins, and secs: ");
        scanf("%d%d%d", &t1.hr, &t1.min, &t1.sec);
        fflush(stdin);
        printf("\n Enter the second time in
    hrs, mins, and secs: ");
        scanf("%d%d%d", &t2.hr, &t2.min, &t2.sec);
        fflush(stdin);
        break;
        case 2:
        printf("\n The first time is: %d hr %d
    min %d sec", t1.hr, t1.min, t1.sec);
        printf("\n The second time is: %d hr
    %d min %d sec", t2.hr, t2.min, t2.sec);
        break;
        case 3:
        t3 = add_time(t1, t2);
        printf("\n The sum of the two time
    values is: %dhr %dmin %dsec", t3.hr,
    t3.min, t3.sec);
        break;
        case 4:
        t4 = subtract_time(t1, t2);
        printf("\n The difference in time
    is: %d hr %d min %d sec", t4.hr, t4.min,
    t4.sec);
        break;
        }
    }while(option != 5);
    getch();
    return 0;
}
TIME add_time(TIME t1, TIME t2)
{
    TIME sum;
    sum.sec = t1.sec + t2.sec;
    while(sum.sec >= 60)
    {
        sum.sec -=60;
        sum.min++;
    }
    sum.min = t1.min + t2.min;
    while(sum.min >= 60)
    {
        sum.min -=60;
        sum.hr++;
    }
    sum.hr = t1.hr + t2.hr;
    return sum;
}
TIME subtract_time(TIME t1, TIME t2)
{
    TIME sub;
    if(t1.hr > t2.hr)
    {
        if(t1.sec < t2.sec)
        {
        t1.sec += 60;
        t1.min--;
        }
        sub.sec = t1.sec - t2.sec;
        if(t1.min < t2.min)
        {
        t1.min += 60;
        t1.hr--;
        }
        sub.min = t1.min - t2.min;
        sub.hr = t1.hr - t2.hr;
    }
    else
    {
        if(t2.sec < t1.sec)
        {
        t2.sec += 60;
        t2.min--;
        }
        sub.sec = t2.sec - t1.sec;
        if(t2.min < t1.min)
        {
```

```
        t2.min += 60;
        t2.hr--;
        }
        sub.min = t2.min - t1.min;
        sub.hr = t2.hr - t1.hr;
    }
    return sub;
}
```

Output

```
******** MAIN MENU *********
1. Read time
2. Display time
3. Add two time
4. Subtract two time
5. EXIT
Enter your option: 1
Enter the first time in hrs, mins, and secs:
2 30 20
Enter the second time in hrs, mins, and
secs: 3 20 30
******** MAIN MENU *********
1. Read time
2. Display time
3. Add
4. Subtract
5. EXIT
Enter your option: 3
 The sum of the two time value is: 5 hr 50
 min 50 sec
```

Let us summarize some points that must be considered while passing a structure to the called function.

- If the called function is returning a copy of the entire structure then it must be declared as `struct` followed by the structure name.
- The structure variable used as parameter in the function declaration must be the same as that of the actual argument in the called function (and that should be the name of the `struct` type).
- When a function returns a structure then in the calling function the returned structure must be assigned to a structure variable of the same type.

8.4.3 Passing Structures Through Pointers

Passing large structures to function using the call by value method is very inefficient. Therefore, it is preferred to pass structures through pointers. It is possible to create a pointer to almost any type in C, including user-defined types. It is extremely common to create pointers to structures. Like in other cases, a pointer to a structure is never itself a structure, but merely a variable that holds the address of a structure. The syntax to declare a pointer to a structure can be given as,

> **Programming Tip:**
> Using pointers to pass a structure to a function is more efficient than using the call-by-value method.

```
struct struct_name
{
    data_type member_name1;
    data_type member_name2;
    data_type member_name3;
    ...................................
}*ptr;
```

OR

```
struct struct_name *ptr;
```

For our student structure we can declare a pointer variable by writing,

```
struct student *ptr_stud, stud;
```

The next thing to be done is to assign the address of `stud` to the pointer using the address operator `(&)` as we would do in case of any other pointer. So to assign the address, we will write

```
ptr_stud = &stud;
```

To access the members of the structure, one way is to write,

```
/* get the structure, then select a member */
(*ptr_stud).roll_no;
```

Since parenthesis have a higher precedence than `*`, writing this statement would work well. But this statement is not easy for a beginner to work with. So C introduces a new operator to do the same task. This operator is known as the pointing-to operator `(->)`. Here it is being used:

> **Programming Tip:**
> The selection operator (->) is a single token, so do not place any white space between them.

```
/* the roll_no in the structure ptr_stud
points to */
ptr_stud -> roll_no = 01;
```

This statement is far easier than its alternative.

8.11 Write a program, using a pointer to a structure, to initialize the members in the structure.

```
#include <stdio.h>
```

```
#include <conio.h>
struct student
{
   int r_no;
   char name[20];
   char course[20];
   int fees;
};

main()
{
   struct student stud1, stud2, *ptr_stud1,
   *ptr_stud2;
   clrscr();
   ptr_stud1 = &stud1;
   ptr_stud2 = &stud2;
   ptr_stud1->r_no = 01;
   strcpy(ptr_stud1-> name, "Rahul");
   strcpy(ptr_stud1->course, "BCA");
   ptr_stud1->fees = 45000;

   printf("\n Enter the details of the
   second student:");
   printf("\n Enter the Roll Number =");
   scanf("%d", &ptr_stud2->r_no);
   fflush(stdin);
   printf("\n Enter the Name = ");
   gets(ptr_stud2->name);
   fflush(stdin);
   printf("\n Enter the Course = ");
   gets(ptr_stud2->course);
   fflush(stdin);
   printf("\n Enter the Fees = ");
   scanf("%d", &ptr_stud2->fees);
   printf("\n DETAILS OF FIRST STUDENT");
   printf("\n ---------------------------");
   printf("\n ROLL NUMBER = %d",ptr_stud1->r_no);
   printf("\n NAME = %s", ptr_stud1->name);
   printf("\n COURSE = %s",ptr_stud1->course);
   printf("\n FEES = %d", ptr_stud1->fees);
   printf("\n\n\n\n DETAILS OF SECOND
   STUDENT");
   printf("\n ---------------------------");
   printf("\n ROLL NUMBER = %d",ptr_stud2->r_no);
   printf("\n NAME = %s", ptr_stud2->name);
   printf("\n COURSE = %s",ptr_stud2->course);
   printf("\n FEES = %d", ptr_stud2->fees);

   return 0;
}
```

Output

```
Enter the details of the second student:
Enter the Roll Number = 02
Enter the Name = Aditya
Enter the Course = MCA
Enter the Fees = 60000

DETAILS OF FIRST STUDENT
--------------------------------------------
ROLL NUMBER = 01
NAME = Rahul
COURSE = BCA
FEES = 45000.00

DETAILS OF SECOND STUDENT
--------------------------------------------
ROLL NUMBER = 02
NAME = Aditya
COURSE = MCA
FEES = 60000.00
```

8.12 Write a program, using a pointer to a structure, to initialize the members in the structure using an alternative technique.

```
#include <stdio.h>
#include <conio.h>
struct student
{
   int r_no;
   char name[20];
   char course[20];
   float fees;
};

main()
{
   struct student *ptr_stud1;
   struct student stud1 = {01, "Rahul",
   "BCA", 45000};
   clrscr();
   ptr_stud1 = &stud1;
   printf("\n DETAILS OF STUDENT");
   printf("\n ---------------------------");
   printf("\n ROLL NUMBER = %d", ptr_stud1->r_no);
   printf("\n NAME = %s ", ptr_stud1 -> name);
   printf("\n COURSE = %f", ptr_stud1
   ->course);
   printf("\n FEES = %f", ptr_stud1->fees);
   return 0;
}
```

Output

```
DETAILS OF STUDENT
--------------------------------------------
ROLL NUMBER = 01
NAME = Rahul
COURSE = BCA
FEES = 45000.00
```

8.13 Write a program, using an array of pointers to a structure, to read and display the data of a student.

```
#include <stdio.h>
#include <conio.h>
#include <alloc.h>
typedef struct student
{
   int r_no;
   char name[20];
   char course[20];
   int fees;
};
struct student *ptr[10];
main()
{
   int i;
   for(i=0;i<10;i++)
   {
      ptr[i] = (struct student *)malloc(size
   of(struct student));
      printf("\n Enter the data for student
   %d "i+1);
      printf("\n \t ROLL NO.: ");
      scanf("%d", ptr[i]->r_no);
      printf("\n \t NAME: ");
      gets(ptr[i]->name);
      printf("\n \t COURSE: ");
      gets(ptr[i]->course);
      printf("\n \t FEES: ");
      scanf("%d", ptr[i]->fees);
   }
   printf("\n DETAILS OF STUDENT");
   printf("\n ---------------------------");
   for(i=0;i<10;i++)
   {
      printf("\n ROLL NUMBER = %d",
   ptr_stud[i]->r_no);
      printf("\n NAME  = %f",
   ptr_stud[i]->name);
      printf("\n COURSE  = %f",
   ptr_stud[i]->course);
      printf("\n FEES = %d",
   ptr_stud[i]->fees);
   }
   return 0;
}
```

Output

```
Enter the data for the student 1
ROLL NO.: 01
NAME: Rahul
COURSE: BCA
FEES: 45000
```

8.14 Write a program to read, display, add, and subtract two heights. Height should be given in feet and inches.

```
#include <stdio.h>
#include <conio.h>
typedef struct
{
   int ft;
   int inch;
}HEIGHT;

HEIGHT h1, h2, h3;
HEIGHT add_height(HEIGHT *, HEIGHT *);
HEIGHT subtract_height(HEIGHT *, HEIGHT *);
main()
{
   int option;
   clrscr();
   do
   {
      printf("\n *** MAIN MENU ***");
      printf("\n 1. Read height ");
      printf("\n 2. Display height");
      printf("\n 3. Add");
      printf("\n 4. Subtract");
      printf("\n 5. EXIT");
      printf("\n Enter your option: ");
      scanf("%d", &option);
      switch(option)
      {
      case 1:
      printf("\n Enter the first height in
   feet and inches: ");
      scanf("%d %d", &h1.ft, &h1.inch);
      printf("\n Enter the second height in
   feet and inches: ");
      scanf("%d %d", &h2.ft, &h2.inch);
      break;
      case 2:
      printf("\n The first height is: %d ft
   %d inch", h1.ft, h1.inch);
      printf("\n The second height is: %d ft
   %d inch", h2.ft, h2.inch);
      break;
      case 3:
      h3 = add_height(&h1, &h2);
      printf("\n The sum of two heights is:
   %d ft %d inch", h3.ft, h3.inch);
```

```
        break;
        case 4:
        h3 = subtract_height(&h1, &h2);
        printf("\n The difference of two
     heights is: %d ft %d inch", h3.ft,
     h3.inch);
        break;
        }
     }while(option != 5);
     getch();
     return 0;
  }
  HEIGHT add_height(HEIGHT *h1, HEIGHT *h2)
  {
     HEIGHT sum;
     sum.inch = h1->inch + h2->inch;
     while(sum.inch > 12)
     {
        sum.inch -= 12;
        sum.ft++;
     }
     sum.ft = h1->ft + h2->ft;
     return sum;
  }
  HEIGHT subtract_height(HEIGHT *h1, HEIGHT *h2)
  {
     HEIGHT sub;
     if(h1->ft > h2->ft)
     {
        if(h1->inch < h2->inch)
        {
        h1->inch += 12;
        h1->ft--;
        }
        sub.inch = h1->inch - h2->inch;
        sub.ft = h1->ft - h2->ft;
     }
     else
     {
        if(h2->inch < h1->inch)
        {
        h2->inch += 12;
        h2->ft--;
        }
        sub.inch = h2->inch - h1->inch;
        sub.ft = h2->ft - h1->ft;
     }
     return sub;
  }
```

Output

```
******** MAIN MENU *********
1. Read height ");
2. Display height
3. Add
4. Subtract
5. EXIT
Enter your option: 1
Enter the first height in feet and inches: 2 3
Enter the second height in feet and inches:
4 5
******** MAIN MENU *********
1. Read height
2. Display height
3. Add
4. Subtract
5. EXIT
Enter your option: 3
The sum of two heights is: 6 ft 8 inch
```

8.15 Write a program that passes a pointer to a structure to a function.

```
#include <stdio.h>
#include <conio.h>
#include <alloc.h>
typedef struct student
{
   int r_no;
   char name[20];
   char course[20];
   int fees;
};

void display(struct student *);
main()
{
   struct student *ptr;
   ptr = (struct student *)malloc(sizeof
   (struct student));
   printf("\n Enter the data for the student ");
   printf("\n \t ROLL NO.: ");
   scanf("%d", ptr->r_no);
   printf("\n \t NAME: ");
   gets(ptr->name);
   printf("\n \t COURSE: ");
   gets(ptr->course);
   printf("\n \t FEES: ");
   scanf("%d", ptr->fees);
   display(ptr);
   getch();
   return 0;
}
```

```
void display(struct student *ptr)
{
    printf("\n DETAILS OF STUDENT");
    printf("\n ---------------------------");
    printf("\n ROLL NUMBER = %d", ptr->r_no);
    printf("\n NAME = ", puts(ptr->name));
    printf("\n COURSE  = ",
    puts(ptr->course));
    printf("\n FEES = %d", ptr->fees);
}
```

Output

```
Enter the data for the student
ROLL NO.: 01
NAME: Rahul
COURSE: BCA
FEES: 45000

DETAILS OF STUDENT
------------------------------------------
ROLL NUMBER = 01
NAME  = Rahul
COURSE  = BCA
FEES = 45000.00
```

8.16 Write a program to illustrate the use of arrays within a structure.

```
#include <stdio.h>
#include <conio.h>
#include <alloc.h>
typedef struct student
{
    char name[20];
    int roll_no;
    int marks[3];
};

void display(struct student* s)
{
    int i;
    printf("\n\n\n NAME: %s \n ROLL NO =
%d\n", s->name, s->roll_no);
    for(i = 0;i < 3;i++)

        printf(" %d", s->marks[i]);
}
main()
{
    struct student *s[2];
    int i,j;
    clrscr();
    for(i = 0;i < 2;i++)
    {
        s[i]=(struct student*)
        malloc(sizeof(struct student));
        printf("\n\n Enter the name of student
%d: ", i);
        gets(s[i]->name);
        fflush(stdin);
        printf("\n Enter the roll number of
student %d: ", i);
        scanf("%d", &s[i]->roll_no);
        printf("\n Enter the marks obtained in
three subjects by student %d: ", i);
        for(j = 0;j < 3;j++)
            scanf("%d",&s[i]->marks[j]);
        fflush(stdin);
    }
    printf("\n \n\n ******DETAILS*****");
    for(i=0;i<5;i++)
        display(s[i]);
    getch();
    return 0;
}
```

Output

```
Enter the name of student 1: Goransh
Enter the roll number of student 1: 01
Enter the marks obtained in three subjects
by student 1: 99 100 99
Enter the name of student 2: Pranjal
Enter the roll number of student 1: 02
Enter the marks obtained in three subjects
by student 2: 90 100 89
```

8.5 SELF-REFERENTIAL STRUCTURES

Self-referential structures are those structures that contain a reference to data of its same type, i.e., in addition to other data, a self-referential structure contains a pointer to a data that is of the same type as that of the structure. For example, consider the structure node given as follows.

> **Programming Tip:**
> It is an error to use a structure/union variable as a member of its own struct type structure or union type union, respectively.

```
struct node
{
    int val;
    struct node *next;
};
```

Here the structure node will contain two types of data—an integer `val` and `next`, which is a pointer to a node. You must be wondering why we need such a structure. Actually, self-referential structure is the foundation of other data structures. We will be using them throughout this book and their purpose will be clear to you when we will be discussing linked lists, trees, and graphs.

8.6 UNION

Similar to structures, a union is a collection of variables of different data types. The only difference between a structure and a union is that in case of unions, you can only store information in one field at any one time.

To better understand a union, think of it as a chunk of memory that is used to store variables of different types. When a new value is assigned to a field, the existing data is replaced with the new data.

Thus unions are used to save memory. They are useful for applications that involve multiple members, where values need not be assigned to all the members at any one time.

8.6.1 Declaring a Union

The syntax for declaring a union is the same as that of declaring a structure. The only difference is that instead of using the keyword `struct`, the keyword union would be used. The syntax for union declaration can be given as

Programming Tip:
Variable of a structure or a union can be declared at the time of structure/union definition by placing the variable name after the closing brace and before the semicolon.

```
union union-name
{
  data_type var-name;
  data_type var-name;
  ...
};
```

Again, the `typedef` keyword can be used to simplify the declaration of union variables.

The most important thing to remember about a union is that the size of a union is the size of its largest field. This is because a sufficient number of bytes must be reserved to store the largest sized field.

8.6.2 Accessing a Member of a Union

A member of a union can be accessed using the same syntax as that of a structure. To access the fields of a union, use the dot operator (`.`), i.e., the union variable name followed by the dot operator followed by the member name.

8.6.3 Initializing Unions

Programming Tip:
It is an error to initialize any other union member except the first member.

A striking difference between a structure and a union is that in case of a union, the fields share the same memory space, so fresh data replaces any existing data. Look at the following code and observe the difference between a structure and union when their fields are to be initialized.

```
#include <stdio.h>
typedef struct POINT1
{
   int x, y;
};

typedef union POINT2
{
   int x;
   int y;
};
main()
{
   POINT1 P1 = {2,3};
   // POINT2 P2 ={4,5}; Illegal with union

   POINT2 P2;
   P2.x = 4;
   P2.y = 5;
   printf("\n The co-ordinates of P1 are %d
   and %d", P1.x, P1.y);
   printf("\n The co-ordinates of P2 are %d
   and %d", P2.x, P2.y);
   return 0;
}
```

Output

```
The co-ordinates of P1 are 2 and 3
The co-ordinates of P2 are 5 and 5
```

In this code, `POINT1` is a structure name and `POINT2` is a union name. However, both the declarations are almost same (except the keywords—`struct` and `union`); in `main()`, you see a point of difference while initializing values. The fields of a union cannot be initialized all at once.

Programming Tip:
The size of a union is equal to the size of its largest member.

Look at the output carefully. For the structure variable the output is fine but for the union variable the answer does not seem to be correct.

To understand the concept of union, execute the following code. The code given below just re-arranges the `printf` statements. You will be surprised to see the result.

```
#include <stdio.h>
typedef struct POINT1
{
   int x, y;
};

typedef union POINT2
{
   int x;
   int y;
};
main()
{
   POINT1 P1 = {2,3};
   POINT2 P2;
printf("\n The co-ordinates of P1 are %d and
   %d", P1.x, P1.y);
   P2. x = 4;
printf("\n The  x co-ordinate of P2 is %d",
   P2.x);
   P2.y = 5;
   printf("\n The y co-ordinate of P2 is
   %d", P2.y);
   return 0;
}
```

Output

```
The co-ordinates of P1 are 2 and 3
The x co-ordinate of P2 is 4
The y co-ordinate of P2 is 5
```

Here although the output is correct, the data is still overwritten in memory.

8.7 ARRAYS OF UNION VARIABLES

Like structures we can also have an array of union variables. However, because of the problem of new data overwriting existing data in the other fields, the program may not display the accurate results.

```
#include <stdio.h>
union POINT
{
   int x, y;
};

main()
{
   int i;
   union POINT points[3];
   points[0].x = 2;
   points[0].y = 3;
   points[1].x = 4;
   points[1].y = 5;
   points[2].x = 6;
   points[2].y = 7;

   for(i=0;i<3;i++)
      printf("\n Co-ordinates of Point[%d]
   are %d and %d", i, points[i].x,
   points[i].y);
   return 0;
}
```

Output

```
Co-ordinates of Point[0] are 3 and 3
Co-ordinates of Point[1] are 5 and 5
Co-ordinates of Point[2] are 7 and 7
```

8.8 UNIONS INSIDE STRUCTURES

You must be wondering, why do we need unions? Generally, unions can be very useful when declared inside a structure. Consider an example in which you want a field of a structure to contain a string or an integer, depending on what the user specifies. The following code illustrates such a scenario.

```
#include <stdio.h>
struct student
{
   union
   {
      char name[20];
      int roll_no;
   };
   int marks;
};
main()
{
   struct student stud;
   char choice;
   printf("\n You can enter the name or roll
   number of the student");
   printf("\n Do you want to enter the name?
   (Y or N): ");
```

```
    gets(choice);
    if(choice=='y' || choice=='Y')
    {
        printf("\n Enter the name: ");
        gets(stud.name);
    }
    else
    {
        printf("\n Enter the roll number: ");
        scanf("%d", &stud.roll_no);
    }
    printf("\n Enter the marks: ");
    scanf("%d", &stud.marks);
    if(choice=='y' || choice=='Y')
       printf("\n Name: %s ", stud.name);
    else
       printf("\n Roll Number: %d ", stud.
    roll_no);
    printf("\n Marks: %d", stud.marks);
    return 0;
}
```

Now in this code, we have a union embedded within a structure. We know, the fields of a union will share memory, so in the main program we ask the user which data he/she would like to store and depending on his/her choice the appropriate field is used.

Note

Pointing to unions, passing unions to functions, and passing pointers to unions to functions are all done in the same way as that of structures.

8.9 ENUMERATED DATA TYPES

The enumerated data type is a user-defined type based on the standard integer type. An enumeration consists of a set of named integer constants. In other words, in an enumerated type, each integer value is assigned an identifier. This identifier (which is also known as an enumeration constant) can be used as a symbolic name to make the program more readable.

To define enumerated data types, we use the keyword `enum`, which is the abbreviation for ENUMERATE. Enumerations create new data types to contain values that are not limited to the values that fundamental data types may take. The syntax of creating an enumerated data type can be given as follows:

```
enum enumeration_name { identifier1,
identifier2, ......, identifiern };
```

The `enum` keyword is basically used to declare and initialize a sequence of integer constants. Here, `enumeration_name` is optional. Consider the following example, which creates a new type of variable called `COLORS` to store color constants.

```
enum COLORS {RED, BLUE, BLACK, GREEN,
YELLOW, PURPLE, WHITE};
```

Note that no fundamental data type is used in the declaration of `COLORS`. After this statement, `COLORS` has become a new data type. Here, `COLORS` is the name given to the set of constants. In case you do not assign any value to a constant, the default value for the first one in the list—`RED` (in our case), has the value of 0. The rest of the undefined constants have a value 1 more than its previous one. That is, if you do not initialize the constants, then each one would have a unique value. The first would be zero and the rest would count upwards. So, in our example,

```
RED = 0, BLUE = 1, BLACK = 2, GREEN = 3,
YELLOW = 4, PURPLE = 5, WHITE = 6
```

If you want to explicitly assign values to these integer constants then you should specifically mention those values shown as follows.

```
enum COLORS {RED = 2, BLUE, BLACK = 5, GREEN
= 7, YELLOW, PURPLE, WHITE = 15};
```

As a result of this statement, now `RED = 2, BLUE = 3, BLACK = 5, GREEN = 7, YELLOW = 8, PURPLE = 9, WHITE = 15`.

Look at the code which illustrates the declaration and access of enumerated data types.

```
#include <stdio.h>
main()
{  enum {RED=2, BLUE, BLACK=5, GREEN=7,
   YELLOW, PURPLE, WHITE=15};
   printf("\n RED = %d", RED);
   printf("\n BLUE = %d", BLUE);
   printf("\n BLACK = %d", BLACK);
   printf("\n GREEN = %d", GREEN);
   printf("\n YELLOW = %d", YELLOW);
   printf("\n PURPLE = %d", PURPLE);
   printf("\n WHITE = %d", WHITE);
   return 0;
}
```

Output

```
RED = 2
BLUE = 3
```

```
BLACK = 5
GREEN = 7
YELLOW = 8
PURPLE = 9
WHITE = 15
```

The value of an enumerator constant is always of the type **int**. Therefore, the storage associated with an enumeration variable is the storage required for a single **int** value. The enumeration constant or a value of the enumerated type can be used anywhere in the program where the C language permits an integer expression.

The following rules apply to the members of an enumeration list:

- An enumeration list may contain duplicate constant values. Therefore, two different identifiers may be assigned the same value, say 3.
- The identifiers in the enumeration list must be different from other identifiers in the same scope with the same visibility including ordinary variable names and identifiers in other enumeration lists.
- Enumeration names follow the normal scoping rules. So every enumeration name must be different from other enumeration, structure, and union names with the same visibility.

If we create an enumerated type without enumeration_name, it is known as an anonymous enumerated type. For example, enum {OFF, ON}; declares an enumerated type that has two constants OFF with a value 0 and ON with a value 1.

8.9.1 `enum` Variables

We have seen that enumerated constants are basically integers, so programs with statements such as `int fore_color = RED;` is considered to be a legal statement in C.

In extension to this, C also permits the user to declare variables of an enumerated data type in the same way as we create variables of other basic data types. The syntax for declaring a variable of an enumerated data type can be given as

```
enumeration_name variable_name;
```

So to create a variable of `COLORS`, we may write

```
enum COLORS bg_color;
```

This declares a variable called `bg_color`, which is of the enumerated data type, `COLORS`. Another way to declare a variable can be as illustrated in the following statement:

```
enum COLORS {RED, BLUE, BLACK, GREEN,
YELLOW, PURPLE, WHITE}bg_color, fore_color;
```

8.9.2 Using the `typedef` Keyword

C also permits to use the `typedef` keyword for enumerated data types. For example, if we write

```
typedef enum COLORS color;
```

Then, we can straight-away declare variables by writing

```
color forecolor = RED;
```

8.9.3 Assigning Values to Enumerated Variables

Once the enumerated variable has been declared, values can be stored in it. However, an enumerated variable can hold only declared values for the type. For example, to assign the color black to the back ground color, we will write,

```
bg_color = BLACK;
```

An important thing to note here is that once an enumerated variable has been assigned a value, we can store its value in another variable of the same type. The following statements illustrate this concept:

```
enum COLORS bg_color, border_color;
bg_color = BLACK;
border_color = bg_color;
```

8.9.4 Enumeration Type Conversion

Enumerated types can be implicitly or explicitly cast. For example, the compiler can implicitly cast an enumerated type to an integer when required. However, when we implicitly cast an integer to an enumerated type, the compiler will either generate an error or a warning message. To understand this, answer one question. If we write:

```
enum COLORS{RED, BLUE, BLACK, GREEN, YELLOW,
PURPLE, WHITE};
enum COLORS c;
c = BLACK + WHITE;
```

Here, c is an enumerated data type variable. If we write, `c = BLACK + WHITE`, then logically, it should be `2 + 6 = 8`, which is basically a value of type `int`. However, the left-hand side of the assignment operator is of the type `enum COLORS`. So the statement would report an error. To remove the error, you can do either of two things. First, declare `c` to be an `int`. Second, cast the right-hand side in the following manner:

```
c = enum COLORS(BLACK + WHITE);
```

To summarize,

```
enum COLORS(RED, BLUE, BLACK, GREEN, YELLOW,
PURPLE, WHITE};
enum COLORS c;
c = BLACK; //valid in C
c = 2;     // illegal in C
c = (enum COLORS)2; // Right way
```

8.9.5 Comparing Enumerated Types

C also allows using comparison operators on enumerated data type. Look at the following statements, which illustrate this concept.

```
bg_color = (enum COLORS)6;
if(bg_color == WHITE)
    fore_color = BLUE;
fore_color = BLACK;
if(bg_color == fore_color)
    printf("\n NOT VISIBLE");
```

Since enumerated types are derived from integer type, they can be used in a `switch case` statement. The following code demonstrates the use of the enumerated type in a `switch case` statement.

```
enum {RED, BLUE, BLACK, GREEN, YELLOW, PURPLE,
WHITE}bg_color;
switch(bg_color)
{
    case RED:
    case BLUE:
    case GREEN:
        printf("\n It is a primary color");
        break;
    case default:
        printf("\n It is not a primary color");
        break;
}
```

8.9.6 Input/Output Operations on Enumerated Types

Since enumerated types are derived types, they cannot be read or written using formatted input/output functions available in the C language. When we read or write an enumerated type, we read/write it as an integer. The compiler would implicitly do the type conversion as discussed earlier. The following statements illustrate this concept.

```
enum COLORS(RED, BLUE, BLACK, GREEN, YELLOW,
PURPLE, WHITE};
enum COLORS c;
scanf("%d", &c);
printf("\n Color = %d", c);
```

8.17 Write a program to display the name of the colors using an enumerated type.

```
#include <stdio.h>
enum COLORS {RED, BLUE, BLACK, GREEN, YELLOW,
    PURPLE, WHITE};
main()
{
    enum COLORS c;
    char *color_name[] = {"RED", "BLUE",
    "BLACK", "GREEN", "YELLOW", "PURPLE",
    "WHITE"};
    for(c = RED; c <= WHITE; c++)

        printf("\n %s", color_name[c]);
    return 0;
}
```

OR

```
#include <stdio.h>
#include <stdlib.h>
#include <conio.h>
enum COLORS {red, blue, black, green, yellow,
    purple, white};
main()
{
    enum COLORS c;
    c = rand()%7;
    switch(c)
    {
        case red: printf("\n RED"); break;
        case blue: printf("\n BLUE"); break;
        case black: printf("\n BLACK"); break;
        case green: printf("\n GREEN"); break;
        case yellow: printf("\n YELLOW");
    break;
        case purple: printf("\n PURPLE");
    break;
        case white: printf("\n WHITE"); break;
    }
    return 0;
```

Output

```
GREEN
```

POINTS TO NOTE

- A structure is similar to records. It stores related information about an entity. Structure is basically a user-defined data type that can store related information (even of different data types) together. The major difference between a structure and an array is that, an array contains related information of the same data type.
- A structure is declared using the keyword `struct` followed by a structure name. The structure definition however, does not allocate any memory or consume storage space. It just gives a template that conveys to the C compiler, how the structure is laid out in memory and gives details of the member names. Like any other data type, memory is allocated for the structure when we declare a variable of the structure.
- When we precede a `struct` name with `typedef` keyword, then the `struct` becomes a new data type.
- When the user does not explicitly initialize the structure C automatically does this. For `int` and `float` members, the values are initialized to zero and char and string members are initialized to `'\0'` by default.
- A structure member variable is generally accessed using a `'.'` (dot operator).

GLOSSARY

Copying structures Assigning a structure to another structure of the same type.

Nested structure A structure placed within another structure, i.e., a structure that contains another structure as its member.

Self-referential structures Structures that contain a reference to data of its same type. A self referential structure, in addition to other data, contains a pointer to a data that is of the same type as that of the structure.

Structure Structure is a user-defined data type that can store related information (even of different data types) together.

Structure initialization Initializing a structure means assigning some constants to the members of the structure. When the user does not explicitly initializes the structure C automatically does this. For `int` and `float` members, the values are initialized to zero and char and string members are initialized to the `'\0'` by default.

`typedef` declaration When we precede a `struct` name with `typedef` keyword, then the `struct` becomes a new data type. It is used to make the construct shorter with more meaningful names for types already defined by C or for types that you have declared. A `typedef` declaration, is a synonym for the type.

EXERCISES

Fill in the Blanks

1. Structure is a _______ data type.
2. A structure is similar to _______.
3. _______ contains related information of the same data type.
4. _______ contains related information of the same or different data type(s).
5. Memory is allocated for a structure when _______ is done.
6. _______ is just a template that will be used to reserve memory when a variable of type `struct` is declared.
7. A _______ is a collection of variables under a single name.
8. A structure is declared using the keyword `struct` followed by a _______.
9. When we precede a `struct` name with _______, then the `struct` becomes a new data type.
10. For `int` and `float` structure members, the values are initialized to _______.
11. `char` and `string` structure members are initialized to the _______ by default.
12. A structure member variable is generally accessed using a _______.
13. A structure placed within another structure is called a _______.
14. _______ structures contain a reference to data of their same type.
15. The keyword `typedef` is used to _______.

EXERCISES

16. _______ is a collection of data under one name in which memory is shared among the members.
17. The selection operator is used to _______.
18. _______ permits sharing of memory among different types of data.

Multiple Choice Questions

1. A data structure that can store related information together is
   (a) array (b) string
   (c) structure (d) all of these
2. A data structure that can store related information of different data types together is
   (a) array (b) string
   (c) structure (d) all of these
3. Memory for a structure is allocated at the time of
   (a) structure definition
   (b) structure variable declaration
   (c) structure declaration
   (d) function declaration
4. A structure member variable is generally accessed using the
   (a) address operator (b) dot operator
   (c) comma operator (d) ternary operator
5. A structure can be placed within another structure and is known as
   (a) self-referential structure
   (b) nested structure
   (c) parallel structure
   (d) pointer to structure
6. A union member variable is generally accessed using the
   (a) address operator (b) dot operator
   (c) comma operator (d) ternary operator
7. `typedef` can be used with which of these data types?
   (a) struct (b) union
   (c) enum (d) all of these
8. The enumerated type is derived from which data type?
   (a) int (b) float
   (c) double (d) char

State True or False

1. Structures contain related information of the same data type.
2. A `struct` type is a primitive data type.
3. Structure declaration reserves memory for the structure.
4. Initializing a structure means assigning some constants to the members of the structure.
5. When the user does not explicitly initialize the structure C automatically does this.
6. The dereference operator is used to select a particular member of a structure.
7. New variables can be created using the `typedef` keyword.
8. Memory is allocated for a structure only when we declare variables of the structure.
9. A nested structure contains another structure as its member.
10. C permits copying of one structure variable to another.
11. Union and structure are initialized in the same way.
12. A structure cannot have a union as its member.
13. C permits nested unions.
14. In an enumerated type, an integer value can be assigned to only one enumeration constant.
15. Declaring an enumerated type automatically creates a variable.
16. The identifiers in an enumerated type are automatically assigned values.
17. A field in a structure can itself be a structure.
18. No two members of a union should have the same name.
19. No two identifiers in an enumerated type must have the same value.
20. A union can have another union as its member.
21. A union can be a member of a structure.

Review Questions

1. Declare a structure(s) that represents the following hierarchical information:
   (a) Student
   (b) Roll Number
   (c) Name
      (i) First name
      (ii) Middle Name
      (iii) Last Name
   (d) Sex

EXERCISES

(e) Date of Birth
  (i) Day
  (ii) Month
  (iii) Year
(f) Marks
  (i) English
  (ii) Mathematics
  (iii) Computer Science

2. Define a structure to store the name, an array marks[] which stores marks of five different subjects and a character grade. Write a program to display the details of the student whose name is entered by the user. Use the structure definition of first question to make an array of student. Display the name of the students who have secured less than 40% of aggregate.
3. Modify question 2 to print each student's average marks, class average (that includes average of all the student's marks).
4. Make an array of student as illustrated in question 1 and write a program to display the details of the student with the given DOB.
5. Make an array of student as illustrated in question 1 and write a program to delete the record of the student with the given last name.
6. What is the advantage of using structures?
7. Differentiate between a structure and a union.
8. How is a structure name different from a structure variable?
9. Structure declaration reserves memory for the structure. Comment on this statement with valid justifications.
10. Differentiate between a structure and an array.
11. Write a short note on structures and inter process communication.
12. Explain the utility of `typedef` keyword in structures.
13. Explain with an example how structures are initialzed.
14. Is it possible to create an array of structure? Explain with the help of an example.
15. Write a program using structures to read and display the information about an employee.
16. Write a program to find the smallest of three numbers using structures.
17. Write a program to calculate the distance between the given points (6,3) and (2,2).
18. Write a menu-driven program to add and subtract 5+6i and 4-2i.
19. Write a short note on nested structures.
20. Write a program to read and display the information about an employee using nested structures.
21. Write a program to read and display the information about the entire faculty of a particular department.
22. Write a program to read and display the information about all the employees in a department. Edit the details of the ith employee and redisplay the information.
23. Write a program to add and subtract distances 6 km and 300 m and 4 Km and 700 m.
24. Write a program to add and subtract height 6'2" and 5'4".
25. Write a program to add and subtract 10hrs 20mins 50sec and 5hrs 30min 40sec.
26. Write a program that uses a structure called date that has is passed to an `isLeapYear` function to determine if the year is a leap year.
27. Write a program using pointer to structure to initialize the members in the structure. Use functions to print the student's information.
28. Write a program using pointer to structure to initialize the members in the structure using an alternative technique.
29. Define a structure date containing three integers—day, month, and year. Write a program using functions to read data, to validate the date entered by the user and then print the date on the screen. For example, if you enter 29,2,2010 then that is an invalid date as 2010 is not a leap year. Similarly 31,6,2007 is invalid as June does not have 31 days.
30. Using the structure definition of the above program, write a function to increment that. Make sure that the incremented date is a valid date.
31. Modify the above program to add a specific number of days to the given date.
32. Using the structure definition of 28th question, write a function to compare two date variables.
33. Write a program to define a structure vector. Then write functions to read data, print data, add two vectors and scale the members of a vector by a factor of 10.
34. Write a program to define a structure for a hotel that has members—name, address, grade, number

EXERCISES

of rooms, and room charges. Write a function to print the names of a hotel in a particular grade. Also write a function to print names of a hotel that have room charges less than the specified value.

35. What do you understand by a union?
36. Differentiate between a union and a structure.
37. Explain how members of a union are accessed using a program code.
38. In which applications union can be useful?
39. Write a program to define a union and a structure both having exactly the same members. Using the sizeof operator, print the size of structure variable as well as union variable and comment on the result.
40. Declare a structure time that has three field—hr, min, secs. Create two variables start_time and end_time. Input their values from the user. Then while start_time does not reach the end-time, display GOOD DAY on the screen.
41. Declare a structure fraction that has two fields—numerator and denominator. Create two variables and compare them using function. Return 0 if the two fractions are equal, –1 if the first fraction is less than the second and 1 otherwise. You may convert a fraction into a floating point number for your convenience.
42. Declare a structure POINT. Input the co-ordinates of a point variable and determine the quadrant in which it lies. The following table can be used to determine the quadrant

Quadrant	X	Y
1	Positive	Positive
2	Negative	Positive
3	Negative	Negative
4	Positive	negative

43. Write a program to calculate the area of one of the geometric figure—circle, rectangle or a triangle. Write a function to calculate the area. The function must receive one parameter which is a structure that contains the type of figure and the size of the components needed to calculate the area must be a part of a union. Note that a circle requires just one component, rectangle requires two components and a triangle requires the size of three components to calculate the area.
44. Write a program to create a structure with information given below. Then read and print the data.

Employee[10]
- (a) Emp_Id
- (b) Name
  - (i) First Name
  - (ii) Middle Name
  - (iii) Last Name
- (c) Address
  - (i) Area
  - (ii) City
  - (iii) State
- (d) Age
- (e) Salary
- (f) Designation

Find Errors in the Following Structure Definitions:

1.
```
struct
{
   int item_code;
   float price;
}
```

2.
```
struct product
{
   char prod_name[20];
   float price;
}product p[10];
```

Find Errors in the Following Statements:

1.
```
struct student
{
   char name[20];
   int id;
}name = "Ram", 9;
```

2.
```
union student
{
   char name[20];
   int id;
}s = {'Ram",01};
```

Give Output of the Following Codes:

1.
```
main()
{
struct values
{
     int i;
     float f;
}v;
```

EXERCISES

```
v.i = 2;
v.f = 2.3;
printf("\n %d %f", v.i, v.f);
}
```

2.
```
struct values
{
   int i;
   float f;
}v;
main()
{
i = 2;
f = 2.3;
printf("\n %d %f", i, f);
}
```

3.
```
struct values
{
   int i;
   float f;
}v;
main()
{
static values v = {5, 2.3};
printf("\n %d %f", v.i, v.f);
}
```

4.
```
struct values
{
   int i = 2;
   float f = 3.4;
}v;
main()
{
```

5.
```
static values v;
printf("\n %d %f", v.i, v.f);
}

struct values
{
   int i;
   float f;
}v={2, 3.4};
main()
{
printf("\n %d %f", v.i, v.f);
}
```

6.
```
struct first
{
   int i;
   float f;
};
struct second
{
   int i;
   float f;
};
main()
{
   struct first f = {7,4.5};
   struct second s = {4,3.4};
   int diff;
   diff = f.i - s.i;
printf("\n %d", diff);
}
```

7.
```
struct values
{
   int i;
   int val[10];
}v = {1,2,3,4,5,6,7,8,9}, *ptr = &v;
main()
{
printf("\n %d %d", v.i, ptr->i);
printf("\n %d %d %d", v.val[3],
   ptr->val[3], *(v.val+3));
}
```

8.
```
struct values
{
   int i;
   float f;
};
void change(values *v, int a, float b)
{
   v->i = a;
   v->f = b;
}
main()
{
values val = {2, 3.4};
printf("\n %d %f", val.i, val.f);
change(&val, 5, 7.9);
printf("\n %d %f", val.i, val.f);
}
```

ANNEXURE 6

A6.1 BIT FIELDS IN STRUCTURE

C facilitates the users to store integer members in memory spaces smaller than what the compiler would ordinarily allow. These space-saving structure members are called *bit fields.* In addition to this, C also permits the users to explicitly declare the width in bits. Bit fields are generally used in developing application programs that must force a data structure to correspond to a fixed hardware representation and are unlikely to be portable.

Therefore, besides having declarators for members of a structure or union, a structure declarator can also be a specified number of bits, generally known as a bit field. A bit field is interpreted as an integral type. The syntax for specifying a bit field can be given as,

```
type-specifier declarator: constant-
expression
```

In the syntax, the `constant-expression` is used to specify the width of the field in bits. The `type-specifier` for the declarator must be *unsigned int, signed int*, or *int*, and the `constant-expression` must be a non-negative integer value. If the value of the constant expression is zero, the declaration has no *declarator*.

Key Points About Bit Fields

- C does not permit arrays of bit fields, pointers to bit fields, and functions returning bit fields.
- C permits ordinary member variables along with bit fields as structure members.
- The *declarator* is optional and is used to name the bit field.
- Bit fields can only be declared as part of a structure.
- The `address-of` operator (&) cannot be applied to bit-field components. This means that you cannot use `scanf` to read values into a bit field. To read a value, you may use a temporary variable and then assign its value to the bit field.
- Bit fields that are not named cannot be referenced, and their contents at run time are unpredictable. However, they can be used as dummy fields, for alignment purposes.
- Bit fields must be long enough to contain the bit pattern. Therefore, the following statement is invalid in C language:

```
short num: 15
```

- When a value that is out of range is assigned to a bit field, the lower-order bit pattern is preserved and the appropriate bits are assigned.
- Although, the maximum bit field length is 64 bits, for portability reasons, do not use bit fields that are greater than 32 bits in size.
- Bit fields with a length of `0` must be unnamed.

Let us look at a structure that has bit fields.

```
struct
{
   unsigned short a: 2;
   unsigned short b: 1;
   int c: 7;
   unsigned short d: 4;
};
```

In the above structure, the size of the structure is 2 bytes. Bit fields have the same semantics as the integer type. This means a bit field is used in expressions in exactly the same way as a variable of the same base type would be used, regardless of how many bits are in the bit field.

The C99 standard requires the allowable data types for a bit field to include qualified and unqualified signed int and unsigned int in addition to the following types:

- int
- short, signed short, and unsigned short
- char, signed char, and unsigned char
- long, signed long, and unsigned long
- long long, signed long long, and unsigned long long

In all implementations, the default integer type for a bit field is unsigned.

Drawbacks

Bit fields are basically used to represent single bit flags, with each flag stored in a separate bit. However, bit members in structs have practical drawbacks.

- First, the ordering of bits in memory is architecture-dependent and memory padding rules vary from compiler to compiler. Moreover, many C compilers that are used today generate inefficient code for reading and writing bit members.
- Second, bit fields can require a surprising amount of run-time code to manipulate the values and therefore, the programs may end up using more space than they save.

A6.2 SLACK BYTE

In order to store any type of data in a structure, there is a minimum fixed byte which must be reserved by the memory. This minimum byte, which is usually machine-dependent is known as that *word boundary*. For example, TURBO C is based on the 8086 microprocessor and has two-byte word boundary. So any data type reserves at least two bytes of memory space. To understand it clearly, consider the following structure:

```
struct employee
{
    char grade;
    int id;
    int emp_code;
    float salary;
    char promotion_due;
};
```

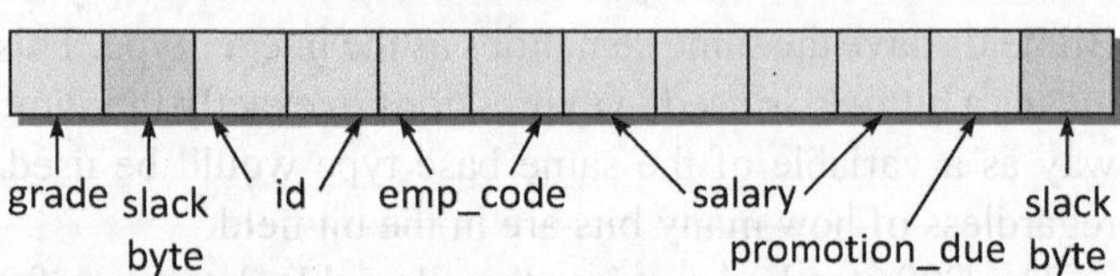

In the figure, char grade will reserve two bytes but store the data only in the first byte since size of char is one byte. Now int id has a size of two bytes and will search for two bytes but there is only one byte available so it will again reserve the next two byte of memory space. That one byte will be useless as it will not be used to store any data. Such a useless byte is known as *slack byte* and the structure is called an *unbalanced structure*.

Converting an unbalanced structure into a balanced structure

Now consider the same structure in which the sequence of fields has been altered.

```
struct employee_m
{
    char grade;
    char promotion_due;
    int id;
    int emp_code;
    float sal;
};
```

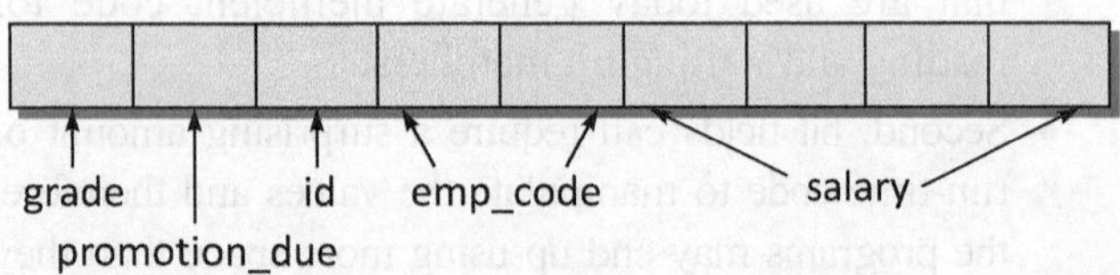

First char grade will reserve two bytes and store the data only in the first byte. Now char promotion_due will search for one byte and since one byte is available it will store the data in that byte. Now `int` id will reserve two bytes and store the data in the two bytes allocated to it. Similarly, `int emp_code` will reserve two bytes to store the data and float salary will reserve four bytes to do the same. Note that by re-arrangement of the fields, there is no slack byte, and we have saved the wastage of memory and structure `employee_m` is a balanced structure.

To understand the concept with clarity, execute the following code. However, before executing it, make sure that you first go to Options menu, then go to compiler, then to code generation, finally select word alignment, and press OK.

```
main()
{
struct employee
{
        char grade;
        int id;
        int emp_code;
        float salary;
        char promotion_due;
};
struct employee_m
{
        char grade;
        char promotion_due;
        int id;
        int emp_code;
        float sal;
};
clrscr();
    printf("\n Size of employee =
    %d",sizeof(struct employee));
    printf("\n Size of employee_m =
    %d",sizeof(struct employee_m));
    getch();
}
```

Output

```
Size of employee = 12
Size of employee_m = 10
```

Hence, slack byte is useful for speed optimization as it aligns bytes so that they can be read from the structure faster.

CHAPTER 9

Files

Takeaways

- Streams in C
- Command Line Arguments
- Creating Temporary Files
- Reading and Writing Data from Files
- Random Access of Data
- Error Handling
- Renaming Files

9.1 INTRODUCTION TO FILES

A *file* is a collection of data stored on a secondary storage device like hard disk. Till now, we had been processing data that was entered through the computer's keyboard. But this task can become very tedious especially when there is a huge amount of data to be processed. A better solution, therefore, is to combine all the input data into a file and then design a C program to read this data from the file whenever required.

Broadly speaking, a file is basically used because real-life applications involve large amounts of data and in such applications the console-oriented I/O operations pose two major problems:

- First, it becomes cumbersome and time-consuming to handle huge amount of data through terminals.
- Second, when doing I/O using terminal, the entire data is lost when either the program is terminated or computer is turned off. Therefore, it becomes necessary to store data on a permanent storage device (the disks) and read whenever necessary, without destroying the data.

In order to use files, we have to learn file input and output operations, i.e., how data is read or written to a file. Although file I/O operations is almost same as terminal I/O, the only difference is that when doing file I/O, the user must specify the name of the file from which data should be read/written.

9.1.1 Streams in C

In C, the standard streams are termed as pre-connected input and output channels between a text terminal and the program (when it begins execution). Therefore, *stream is a logical interface to the devices that are connected to the computer*.

Stream is widely used as a logical interface to a file where a file can refer to a disk file, the computer screen, keyboard, etc. Although files may differ in the form and capabilities, all streams are the same.

The three standard streams (Fig. 9.1) in C languages are as follows:

- standard input `(stdin)`
- standard output `(stdout)` and
- standard error `(stderr)`.

Standard input (`stdin`) Standard input is the stream from which the program receives its data. The program requests transfer of data using the *read* operation. However, not all programs require input. Generally, unless redirected, input for a program is expected from the keyboard.

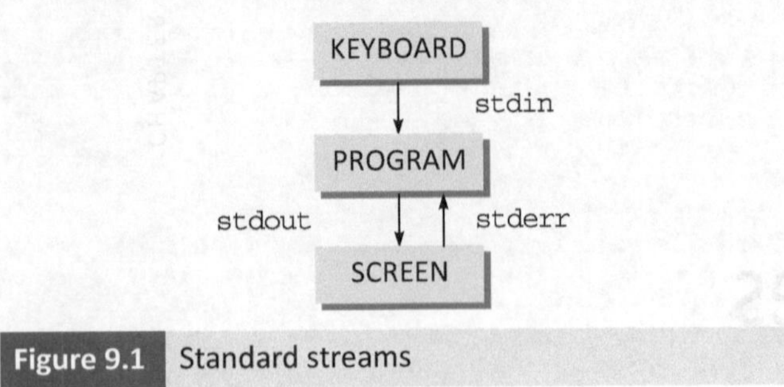

Figure 9.1 Standard streams

Standard output (`stdout`) Standard output is the stream where a program writes its output data. The program requests data transfer using the *write* operation. However, not all programs generate output.

Standard error (`stderr`) Standard error is basically an output stream used by programs to report error messages or diagnostics. It is a stream independent of standard output and can be redirected separately. No doubt, the *standard output* and *standard error* can also be directed to the same destination.

A stream is linked to a file using an open operation and disassociated from a file using a close operation.

9.1.2 Buffer Associated with File Stream

When a stream linked to a disk file is created, a buffer is automatically created and associated with the stream. A buffer is nothing but a block of memory that is used for temporary storage of data that has to be read from or written to a file.

Buffers are needed because disk drives are block-oriented devices as they can operate efficiently when data has to be read/written in blocks of certain size. An ideal buffer size is hardware dependent.

The buffer acts as an interface between the stream (which is character-oriented) and the disk hardware (which is block-oriented). When the program has to write data to the stream, it is saved in the buffer till it is full. Then the entire contents of the buffer are written to the disk as a block. This is shown in Fig. 9.2.

Similarly, when reading data from a disk file, the data is read as a block from the file and written into the buffer. The program reads data from the buffer. The creation and operation of the buffer is automatically handled by the operating system. However, C provides some functions for buffer manipulation. The data resides in the buffer until the buffer is flushed or written to a file.

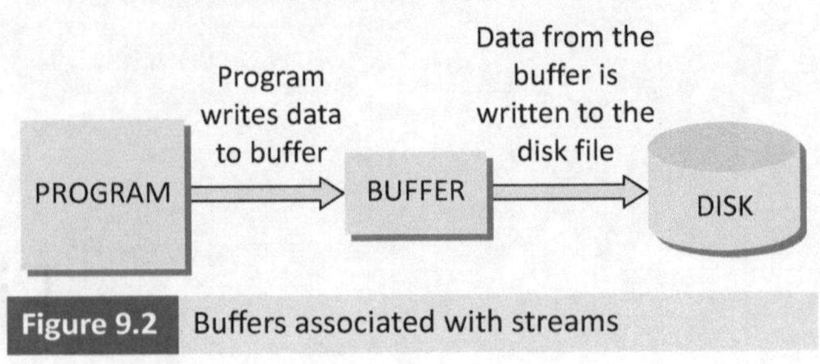

Figure 9.2 Buffers associated with streams

9.1.3 Types of Files

In C, the types of files used can be broadly classified into two categories—ASCII text files and binary files.

ASCII Text Files

A *text file* is a stream of characters that can be sequentially processed by a computer in forward direction. For this reason, a text file is usually opened for only one kind of operation (reading, writing, or appending) at any given time. Because text files only process characters, they can only read or write data one character at a time. In C, a text stream is treated as a special kind of file.

Depending on the requirements of the operating system and on the operation that has to be performed (read/write operation) on the file, `newline` characters may be converted to or from carriage return/line feed combinations. Besides this, other character conversions may also be done to satisfy the storage requirements of the operating system. However, these conversions occur transparently to process a text file.

In a text file, each line contains zero or more characters and ends with one or more characters that specify the end of line. Each line in a text file can have maximum of 255 characters. A line in a text file is not a C string, so it is not terminated by a null character. When data is written to a text file, each newline character is converted to a carriage return/line feed character. Similarly, when data is read from a text file, each carriage return/line feed character is converted into newline character.

> **Programming Tip:** The contents of a binary file are not human readable. If you want the data stored in the file to be human-readable, then store the data in a text file.

Another important thing is that when a text file is used, there are actually two representations of data—internal or external. For example, an `int` value will be represented as 2 or 4 bytes of memory internally, but externally the `int` value will be represented as a string of characters representing its decimal or hexadecimal value. To convert internal representation into external, we can use `printf` and `fprintf` functions. Similarly, to convert an external representation into internal `scanf` and `fscanf` can be used. We will read more about three functions in the coming sections.

In a text file, each line of data ends with a newline character. Each file ends with a special character called the end-of-file (EOF) marker.

Binary Files

A binary file may contain any type of data, encoded in binary form for computer storage and processing purposes. Like a text file, a binary file is a collection of bytes. In C, a byte and a character are equivalent. Therefore, a binary file is also referred to as a character stream with the following two essential differences:

- A binary file does not require any special processing of the data and each byte of data is transferred to or from the disk unprocessed.
- C places no constructs on the file, and it may be read from, or written to, in any manner the programmer wants.

While text files can be processed sequentially, binary files, on the other hand, can be either processed sequentially or randomly depending on the needs of the application. In C, to process a file randomly, the programmer must move the current file position to an appropriate place in the file before reading or writing data. For example, if a file is used to store records (using structures) of students, then to update a particular record, the programmer must first locate the appropriate record, read the record into memory, update it, and finally write the record back to the disk at its appropriate location in the file.

Binary files store data in the internal representation format. Therefore, an `int` value will be stored in binary form as a 2 or 4 byte value. The same format is used to store data in memory as well as in file. Like text file, binary file also ends with an EOF marker.

In a text file, an integer value 123 will be stored as a sequence of three characters—1, 2, and 3. So each character will take 1 byte and therefore, to store the integer value 123 we need 3 bytes. However, in a binary file, the `int` value 123 will be stored in 2 bytes in the binary form. This clearly indicates that binary files take less space to store the same piece of data and eliminates conversion between internal and external representations and are thus more efficient than the text files.

9.2 USING FILES IN C

To use files in C, we must follow the steps given below:

- declare a file pointer variable
- open the file
- process the file
- close the file

In this section, we will go through all these steps in detail.

9.2.1 Declaring a File Pointer Variable

There can be a number of files on the disk. In order to access a particular file, you must specify the name of the file that has to be used. This is accomplished by using a file pointer variable that points to a structure `FILE` (defined in `stdio.h`). The file pointer will then be used in all subsequent operations in the file. The syntax for declaring a file pointer is

Programming Tip: An error will be generated if you use the filename to access a file rather than the file pointer.

```
FILE *file_pointer_name;
```

For example, if we write

```
FILE *fp;
```

Then, `fp` is declared as a file pointer.

9.2.2 Opening a File

A file must first be opened before data can be read from it or written to it. In order to open a file and associate it with a stream, the `fopen()` function is used. The prototype of `fopen()` can be given as,

```
FILE *fopen(const char *file_name, const char
    *mode);
```

Using the above prototype, the file whose pathname is the string pointed to by `file_name` is opened in the mode specified using the mode. If successful, `fopen()` returns a `pointer-to-structure` and if it fails, it returns `NULL`.

Programming Tip: A file must be opened before any operation can be performed on it.

File Name

Every file on the disk has a name known as the file name. The naming convention of a file varies from one operating system to another. For example, in DOS the file name can have one to eight characters optionally followed by a period and an extension that has one to three characters. However, Windows and UNIX permit filenames having maximum of 256 characters. Windows also lays some restrictions on usage of certain characters in the filenames, i.e., characters such as /, \, :, *, ?, ", <, >, and ! cannot be part of a file name.

In C, the fopen() may contain the path information instead of specifying the filename. The path gives information about the location of the file on the disk. If a filename is specified without a path, it is assumed that the file is located in the current working directory. For example, if a file named Student.DAT is located on D drive in directory BCA, then the path of the file can be specified by writing,

```
D:\BCA\Student.DAT
```

In C, a backslash character has a special meaning with respect to escape sequences when placed in a string. So in order to represent a backslash character in a C program, you must precede it with another backslash. Hence, the above path will be specified as given below in the C program.

```
D:\\BCA\\Student.DAT
```

File Mode

The second argument in the fopen() is the *mode*. Mode conveys to C the type of processing that will be done with the file. The different modes in which a file can be opened for processing are given in Table 9.1.

Look at the code given below which opens a file using the fopen().

```
FILE *fp;
fp = fopen("Student.DAT", "r");
if(fp==NULL)
{
    printf("\n The file could not be opened");
    exit(1);
}
```

OR

```
char filename[30];
FILE *fp;
gets(filename);
fp = fopen(filename, "r+");
if(fp==NULL)
{
    printf("\n The file could not be opened");
    exit(1);
}
```

Table 9.1 File modes

Mode	Description
r	Open a text file for reading. If the stream (file) does not exist, then an error will be reported.
w	Open a text file for writing. If the stream does not exist, then it is created. If the file already exists, then its contents would be deleted.
a	Append to a text file. If the file does not exist, it is created.
rb	Open a binary file for reading. b indicates binary. By default this will be a sequential file in Media 4 format.
wb	Open a binary file for writing.
ab	Append to a binary file.
r+	Open a text file for both reading and writing. The stream will be positioned at the beginning of the file. When you specify 'r+', you indicate that you want to read the file before you write to it. Thus, the file must already exist.
w+	Open a text file for both reading and writing. The stream will be created if it does not exist, and will be truncated if it exists.
a+	Open a text file for both reading and writing. The stream will be positioned at the end of the file content.
r+b/rb+	Open a binary file for read/write.
w+b/wb+	Create a binary file for read/write.
a+b/ab+	Append a binary file for read/write.

We have already discussed that fopen() returns a pointer to FILE structure if successful and a NULL otherwise. So it is recommended to check whether the file was successfully opened before actually using the file. The fopen() can fail to open

Programming Tip: An error will be generated if you try to open a file that does not exist.

the specified file under certain conditions that are listed below:

- opening a file that is not ready for use
- opening a file that is specified to be on a non-existent directory/drive
- opening a non-existent file for reading
- opening a file to which access is not permitted

9.2.3 Closing a File Using `fclose ()`

To close an open file, the `fclose()` function is used which disconnects a file pointer from a file. After the `fclose()` has disconnected the file pointer from the file, the pointer can be used to access a different file or the same file but in a different mode. The `fclose()` function not only closes the file, but also flushes all the buffers that are maintained for that file.

Programming Tip: It is always recommended to close all the opened files when they are not going to be used further in the program.

If you do not close a file after using it, the system closes it automatically when the program exits. However, since there is a limit on the number of files which can be opened simultaneously; the programmer must close a file when it has been used. The prototype of the `fclose()` function can be given as

```
int fclose(FILE *fp);
```

Here, `fp` is a file pointer which points to the file that has to be closed. The function returns an integer value which indicates whether the `fclose()` was successful or not. A zero is returned if the function was successful; and a non-zero value is returned if an error occurred.

When the `fclose ()` is executed, any unwritten buffered data for the stream will be written to the file and any unread buffered data will be discarded.

In addition to `fclose()`, there is a function `fcloseall()` which closes all the streams that are currently opened except the standard streams (such as `stdin`, `stdout`, and `stderr`). The prototype of `fcloseall()` can be given as,

```
int fcloseall(void);
```

`fcloseall()` also flushes any stream buffers and returns the number of streams closed.

If a file's buffer has to be flushed without closing it then use `fflush()` or `flushall()` to flush the buffers of all open streams.

9.3 READ DATA FROM FILES

C provides the following set of functions to read data from a file:

- `fscanf()`
- `fgets()`
- `fgetc()`
- `fread()`

In this section, we will read about these functions.

9.3.1 `fscanf ()`

The `fscanf()` is used to read formatted data from the stream. The syntax of the `fscanf()` can be given as

```
int fscanf(FILE *stream, const char *format,...);
```

The `fscanf()` is used to read data from the `stream` and store them according to the parameter `format` into the locations pointed by the additional arguments. However, these additional arguments must point to the objects that have already occupied memory. These objects are of type as specified by their corresponding format tag within the `format` string.

Similar to the format specifiers used in `scanf()`, in `fscanf()` also the *format specifiers* is a C string that begins with an initial percentage sign (`%`). The format specifier is used to specify the type and format of the data that has to be obtained from the stream and stored in the memory locations pointed by the additional arguments. The prototype of a format specifier can be given as,

`[=%[*][width][modifiers]type=]`, where

`'*'` is an optional argument that suppresses assignment of the input field. It indicates that data should be read from the stream and ignored (not stored in the memory location).

width specifies the maximum number of characters to be read. However, fewer characters will be read if the `fscanf` function encounters a white space or an unconvertible character.

modifiers can be `h`, `l`, or `L` for the data pointed by the corresponding additional arguments. Modifier `h` is used for `short int` or `unsigned short int`, `l` is used for `long int`, `unsigned long int`, or `double` values. Finally, `L` is used for `long double` data values.

type specifies the type of data that has to be read. It also indicates how this data is expected to be read from the user.

The type specifiers for `fscanf` function are given in Table 9.2

Table 9.2 Type specifiers

Type	Qualifying Input
C	for single character
D	for decimal values
e, E, f, g, G	for floating point numbers
O	for octal number
S	for a sequence of (string of) characters
U	for unsigned decimal value
x, X	for hexadecimal value

The `fscanf` function has some additional arguments. Each of this additional argument must point to an object of the type specified by their corresponding `%` tag within the `format` string, in the same order.

The `fscanf` function is similar to the `scanf` function, except that the first argument of `fscanf` specifies a stream from which to read, whereas scanf can only read from standard input.

Let us look at an example which illustrates the use of `fscanf()`. Here, we will not give the complete program but just a partial program to demonstrate the use of `fscanf()`.

```
#include <stdio.h>
main()
{
   FILE *fp;
   char name[80];
   int roll_no;
   fp = fopen("Student.DAT", "r");
   if(fp==NULL)
   {
      printf("\n The file could not be opened");
      exit(1);
   }
   printf("\n Enter the name and roll number
   of the student: ");
   // READ FROM KEYBOARD
   fscanf(stdin, "%s %d", name, &roll_no);
   /* read from keyboard */
   printf("\n NAME: %s \t ROLL NUMBER =
   %d", name, roll_no);
   // READ FROM FILE Student.DAT
   fscanf(fp, "%s %d", name, &roll_no);
   printf("\n NAME: %s \t ROLL NUMBER =
   %d", name, roll_no);
   fclose(fp);
   return 0;
}
```

Output

```
Enter the name and roll number of the
   student: 01 Zubin
NAME: Zubin    ROLL NUMBER = 01
NAME: Goransh ROLL NUMBER = 03
```

If you want to use `fprintf ()` to write on the screen, then specify `stdout` instead of specifying any other file pointer.

9.3.2 fgets()

The function `fgets()` stands for *file get string*. The `fgets()` function is used to get a string from a stream. The syntax of `fgets()` can be given as,

```
char *fgets(char *str, int size, FILE *stream);
```

The `fgets()` function reads atmost one less than the number of characters specified by size (gets `size - 1` characters) from the given stream and stores them in the string `str`. The `fgets()` terminates as soon as it encounters either a newline character, EOF, or any other error. However, if a newline character is encountered it is retained. When all the characters are read without any error, a `'\0'` character is appended to the end of the string.

The `gets()` and `fgets()` functions are almost same except that `gets()` has an infinite size and a stream of `stdin`. Another difference is that when `gets()` encounters a newline character, it does not retain it, i.e., the newline character (if any) is not stored in the string.

On successful completion, `fgets()` will return `str`. However, if the stream is at EOF, the EOF indicator for the stream will be set and `fgets()` will return a null pointer. In case, `fgets()` encounters any error while reading, the error indicator for the stream will be set and null pointer will be returned. Look at the program code given below which demonstrates the use of `fgets()`.

```
#include <stdio.h>
main()
{
   FILE *fp;
   char str[80];
   fp = fopen("ABC.DAT", "r");
   if(fp==NULL)
   {
      printf("\n The file could not be opened");
      exit(1);
   }
   /* the file will read 79 characters
   during each iteration and prints them on
   the screen */
   while (fgets(str, 80, fp) != NULL)
      printf("\n %s", str);
   printf("\n\n File Read. Now closing the file");
   fclose(fp);
   return 0;
}
```

Output

```
Abdceweeferrttet gfejjherroiew tjketjer
   fddfgdfgfd
File Read. Now closing the file
```

9.3.3 fgetc()

The `fgetc()` function returns the next character from stream, `EOF` if the end of file is reached, or if there is an error. The syntax of `fgetc()` can be given as,

```
int fgetc(FILE *stream);
```

`fgetc` returns the character read as an `int` or return `EOF` to indicate an error or end of file.

`fgetc()` reads a single character from the current position of a file (file associated with `stream`). After reading the character, the function increments the associated file pointer (if defined) to point to the next character. However, if the stream has already reached the end of file, the EOF indicator for the stream is set. Look at the following program code which demonstrates the use of `fgets()` function:

```
#include <stdio.h>
main()
{
   FILE *fp;
   char str[80];
   int i, ch;
   fp = fopen("Program.C", "r");
   if(fp==NULL)
   {
      printf("\n The file could not be
         opened");
      exit(1);
   }
   // Read 79 characters and store them in str
      ch = fgetc(fp);
   for(i=0; (i < 79) && (feof(fp) == 0); i++)
      {
         str[i] = (char)ch;
         ch = fgetc(stream);
         // reads character by character
      }
      str[i] = '\0';
      // append the string with a null character
      printf("\n %s", str);
      fclose(fp);
}
```

Output

```
#include <stdio.h>
main()....
displays either first 79 characters or less
   characters if the file contains less than
   79 characters
```

The `feof()` is used to detect the end of file. We will read more on this function later in this chapter.

9.3.4 fread()

The `fread()` function is used to read data from a file. Its syntax can be given as,

```
int fread(void *str, size_t size, size_t num,
   FILE *stream);
```

The function `fread()` reads `num` number of objects (where each object is *size* bytes) and places them into the array pointed to by `str`. The data is read from the given input stream.

Upon successful completion, `fread()` returns the number of bytes successfully read. The number of objects will be less than `num` if a read error or `end-of-file` is encountered. If `size` or `num` is `0`, `fread()` will return `0` and the contents of `str` and the state of the stream remain unchanged. In case of error, the error indicator for the stream will be set.

The `fread()` function advances the file position indicator for the stream by the number of bytes read.

The `fread()` function does not distinguish between end-of-file and error. The programmer must use `feof` and `ferror` to determine which of the two has occurred.

Look at the program given below which illustrates the use of `fread()`.

```
#include <stdio.h>
main()
{
   FILE *fp;
   char str[11];
   fp = fopen("Letter.TXT", "r+");
   if(fp==NULL)
   {
      printf("\n The file could not be opened");
      exit(1);
   }
   fread(str, 1, 10, fp);
   /* In the str 10 objects of 1 byte are
   read from the file pointd by fp */
   str[10]= '\0';
   printf("\n First 9 characters of the file
   are: %s", str);
      fclose(fp);
}
```

Output

```
First 9 characters of the file are: Hello
   how
```

Since `fread()` returns the number of bytes successfully read, we can also modify the above program to print the number of bytes read. This would be helpful to know how many characters were read.

```
#include <stdio.h>
main()
{
   FILE *fp;
   char str[80];
   size_t bytes_read;
   fp = fopen("Letter.TXT", "r+");
   if(fp==NULL)
   {
      printf("\n The file could not be opened");
      exit(1);
   }
   bytes_read = fread(str, 1, 79, fp);
   str[bytes_read+1]= '\0';
   // explicitly store null character at the
   end of str
   printf("\n First %d characters of the
   file are: %s", bytes_read, str);
      fclose(fp);
}
```

Output

```
Output will depend on the contents of the
   file. Assuming 14 characters were read,
   the output can be given as
Hello how r u?
This program assumes that you have created
   a file Letter.TXT that conatins 14
   characters which has been displayed above
```

The function `fread()` does not check for overflow in the receiving area of memory. It is the programmer's job to ensure that the memory pointed to by `'str'` must be large enough to hold the number of objects being read.

If you have opened a stream for updating and later you want to switch from reading to writing or vice versa, you must first use the `fseek()` or `rewind()` function. However, if you have been reading and have reached end-of-file, then you can immediately switch to writing. We will discuss the `fseek()` and `rewind` functions later in this chapter.

9.4 WRITING DATA TO FILES

C provides the following set of functions to read data from a file:

- `fprintf()`
- `fputs()`
- `fputc()`
- `fwrite()`

In this section, we will read about these functions.

9.4.1 fprintf()

The `fprintf()` is used to write formatted output to stream. The syntax of the `fprintf()` can be given as

```
int fprintf (FILE * stream, const char * format, ...);
```

The function writes data that is formatted as specified by the format argument to the specified stream. After the format parameter, the function can have as many additional arguments as specified in format.

The parameter format in the `fprintf()` is nothing but a C string that contains the text that has to be written on to the stream. Although not mandatory, the `fprintf()` can optionally contain format tags, that are replaced by the values specified in subsequent additional arguments and are formatted as requested.

There must be enough arguments for format because if there are not, then result will be completely unpredictable. However, if by mistake you specify more number of arguments, the excess arguments will simply be ignored.

The prototype of the format tag can be given as

```
%[flags][width][.precision][length]specifier
```

Each format specifier must begin with a % sign. The % sign is followed by:

Flags which specifies output justification such as decimal point, numerical sign, trailing zeros, or octal or hexadecimal prefixes. Table 9.3 shows the different types of flags with their description.

Table 9.3 Flags in `printf()`

Flags	Description
-	Left justify within the data given field width
+	Displays the data with its numeric sign (either + or –)
#	Used to provide additional specifiers such as o, x, X, 0, 0x, or 0X for octa and hexadecimal values, respectively, for values except zero.
0	The number is left-padded with zeros (0) instead of spaces.

Width specifies the minimum number of characters to print after being padded with zeros or blank spaces.

Precision specifies the maximum number of characters to print.

- For integer specifiers (d, i, o, u, x, X): precision flag specifies the minimum number of digits to be written. However, if the value to be written is shorter than this number, the result is padded with leading zeros. Otherwise, if the value is longer, it is not truncated.
- For character strings, precision specifies the maximum number of characters to be printed.

Length field can be explained as given in Table 9.4.

Table 9.4 Length field in `printf()`

Length	Description
h	When the argument is a short `int` or unsigned short `int`
l	When the argument is a long int or unsigned long int for integer specifiers
L	When the argument is a long double (used for floating point specifiers)

Specifier is used to define the type and the interpretation of the value of the corresponding argument.

The `fprintf()` may contain some additional parameters as well depending on the `format` string. Each argument must contain a value to be inserted instead of each % tag specified in the `format` parameter, if any. In other words, the number of arguments must be equal to the number of % tags that expect a value.

Look at the program given below which demonstrates the use of `fprintf()`.

```
#include <stdio.h>
main()
{
    FILE *fp;
    int i;
    char name[20];
    float salary;
    fp = fopen("Details.TXT", "w");
    if(fp==NULL)
    {
        printf("\n The file could not be opened");
        exit(1);
    }
    for(i = 0;i < 10;i++)
    {
        puts("\n Enter your name: ");
        gets(name);
        fflush(stdin);
        puts("\n Enter your salary: ");
        scanf("%f", &salary);
        fprintf(fp, " (%d) NAME: [%-10.10s]
           \t SALARY %5.2f", i, name, salary);
    }
    fclose(fp);
}
```

Output

```
Enter your name: Aryan
Enter your salary: 50000
Enter your name: Anshita
```

```
Enter your salary: 65000
Enter your name: Saesha
Enter your salary: 70000
```

Programming Tip: If you open a file for writing using w mode, then the contents of the file will be deleted. If a file has to be used for reading as well as writing, then it must be opened in w+ mode.

This example asks the user to enter the name and salary of 10 people. Each time the user enters the name and salary, the data read is written to `Details.TXT`. The names are written on new lines in the file. In this example, we have used three format tags:

- `%d` to specify a signed decimal integer.
- `%-10.10s`. Here – indicates that the characters must be left aligned. There can be minimum of 10 characters as well as maximum of 10 characters (`.10`) in the strings.
- `%f` to specify a floating point number.

Note If you want to use `fprintf()` to write on the screen, then specify `stdout` instead of specifying any other file pointer.

9.4.2 fputs ()

The opposite of `fgets()` is `fputs()`. The `fputs()` is used to write a line to a file. The syntax of `fputs()` can be given as

```
int fputs(const char *str, FILE *stream);
```

The `fputs()` writes the string pointed to by `str` to the stream pointed to by stream. On successful completion, `fputs()` returns `0`. In case of any error, `fputs()` returns `EOF`.

```
#include <stdio.h>
main()
{
   FILE *fp;
   char feedback[100];
   fp = fopen("Comments.TXT", "w");
   if(fp==NULL)
   {
      printf("\n The file could not be opened");
      exit(1);
   }
   printf("\n Provide feedback on this book: ");
   gets(feedback);
   fflush(stdin);
   // feedback stored
   fputs(feedback, fp);
      fclose(fp);
}
```

Output

```
Provide feedback on this book: good
```

9.4.3 fputc ()

The `fputc()` is just the opposite of `fgetc()` and is used to write a character to the stream.

```
int fputc(int c, FILE *stream);
```

The `fputc()` function will write the byte specified by c (converted to an unsigned char) to the output stream pointed to by stream. On successful completion, `fputc()` will return the value it has written. Otherwise, in case of error, the function will return `EOF` and the error indicator for the stream will be set.

```
#include <stdio.h>
main()
{
   FILE *fp;
   char feedback[100];
   int i;
   fp = fopen("Comments.TXT", "w");
   if(fp==NULL)
   {
      printf("\n The file could not be opened");
      exit(1);
   }
   printf("\n Provide feedback on this book: ");
   gets(feedback);
   for(i = 0;i < feedback[i];i++)
   fputc(feedback[i], fp);
   fclose(fp);
}
```

Output

```
Provide feedback on this book: good
```

Note The standard file `stdout` is buffered in case the output unit is not the terminal. On the contrary, the standard file `stderr` is usually unbuffered. However, the settings of `stdout` and `stderr` can be changed using `setbuf`.

When an output stream is unbuffered, information appears on the destination device as soon as it is written.

> **Programming Tip:**
> EOF is an integer type defined in `stdio.h`and has a value '–1'.

When it is buffered, characters are saved internally and then written out as a group. In order to force buffered characters to be output before the buffer is full, use the `fflush()`.

9.4.4 fwrite()

The `fwrite()` is used to write data to a file. The syntax of `fwrite` can be given as

```
int fwrite(const void *str, size_t size,
    size_t count, FILE *stream);
```

The `fwrite()` function will write objects (number of objects will be specified by count) of size specified by size, from the the array pointed to by ptr to the stream pointed to by stream.

The file-position indicator for the stream (if defined) will be advanced by the number of bytes successfully written. If an error occurs, the resulting value of the file-position indicator for the stream is unspecified.

On successful completion, the `fwrite()` function returns the number of objects successfully written. The number of objects will be less than `count` if an error is encountered. If `size` or `count` is 0, `fwrite()` will `return 0` and the contents of the stream remains unchanged. In case of error, the error indicator for the stream will be set.

```
#include <stdio.h>
#include <string.h>
#include <stdlib.h>
main(void)
{
   FILE *fp;
   size_t count;
   char str[] = "GOOD MORNING";
   fp = fopen("Welcome.txt", "wb");
   if(fp==NULL)
   {
     printf("\n The file could not be opened");
     exit(1);
   }
   count = fwrite(str, 1, strlen(str), fp);
   printf("\n %d bytes were
     written to the file", count);
  fclose(fp);
   return 0;
}
```

Output

```
13 bytes were written to the file
```

> `fwrite()` can be used to write characters, integers, or structures to a file. However, `fwrite()` can be used only with files that are opened in binary mode.

9.5 DETECTING THE END-OF-FILE

When reading or writing data from files, we often do not know exactly how long the file is. For example, while reading the file, we usually start reading from the beginning and proceed towards the end of the file. In C, there are two ways to detect EOF:

- While reading the file in text mode, character by character, the programmer can compare the character that has been read with the `EOF`, which is a symbolic constant defined in `stdio.h` with a value `-1`. The following statement, does that

```
while(1)
{
   c = fgetc(fp);
   // here c is an int variable
   if (c==EOF)
     break;
   printf("%c", c);
 }
```

- The other way is to use the standard library function `feof()` which is defined in `stdio.h`. The `feof()` is used to distinguish between two cases:
  - When a stream operation has reached the end of a file
  - When the `EOF (end of file)` error code has returned an error indicator even when the end of the file has not been reached

The prototype of `feof()` can be given as

```
int feof(FILE *fp);
```

The function takes a pointer to the `FILE` structure of the stream to check as an argument and returns zero (false) when the end of file has not been reached and a one (true) if the EOF has been reached. Look at the following:

```
(The output assumes that a file Student.DAT
   already exists and conatins the following
   data: 1 Aditya 2 Chaitanya 3 Goransh)

#include <stdio.h>
main()
{
   FILE *fp;
```

```
    char str[80];
    fp = fopen("Student.DAT", "r");
    if(fp==NULL)
    {
        printf("\n The file could not be opened");
        exit(1);
    }
    /* The loop continues until fp reaches
        the end-of-file */
    while(!feof(fp))
    {
    fgets(str, 79, fp);
        // Reads 79 bytes at a time
        printf("\n %s", str);
    }
    printf("\n\n File Read. Now closing the file");
    fclose(fp);
    return 0;
}
```

Output

```
1 Aditya   2 Chaitanya   3 Goransh
```

9.6 ERROR HANDLING DURING FILE OPERATIONS

It is quite common that an error may occur while reading data from or writing data to a file. For example, an error may arise

> **Programming Tip:** An error will be generated if you try to read a file that is opened in w mode and vice versa.

- when trying to read a file beyond EOF indicator
- when trying to read a file that does not exist
- when trying to use a file that has not been opened
- when trying to use a file in an inappropriate mode, i.e., writing data to a file that has been opened for reading
- when writing to a file that is write-protected (i.e., trying to write to a read-only file)

If we fail to check for errors, then the program may behave abnormally. Therefore, an unchecked error may result in premature termination of the program or incorrect output.

In C, the library function `ferror()` is used to check for errors in the stream. Its prototype can be given as

```
int ferror (FILE *stream);
```

The `ferror()` function checks for any errors in the stream. It returns value zero if no errors have occurred and a non-zero value if there is an error. The error indication will last until the file is closed unless it is cleared by the `clearerr()` function. Look at the code given below which uses the `ferror()`.

```
#include <stdio.h>
main()
{
    FILE *fp;
    char feedback[100];
    int i;
   fp = fopen("Comments.TXT", "w");
   if(fp==NULL)
   {
      printf("\n The file could not be opened");
      exit(1);
   }
    printf("\n Provide feedback on this book: ");
    gets(feedback);
    for(i = 0; i < feedback[i];i++)
      fputc(feedback[i], fp);
    if(ferror(fp))
    {
      printf("\n Error writing in file");
      exit(1);
    }
    fclose(fp);
}
```

When you execute this code and an error occurs while writing the feedback, the program will terminate and a message indicating 'Error writing in file' will be displayed on the screen.

9.6.1 clearerr()

The function `clearerr()` is used to clear the `end-of-file` and error indicators for the stream. Its protoype can be given as

```
void clearerr(FILE *stream);
```

The `clearerr()` clears the error for the stream pointed to by stream. The function is used because error indicators are not automatically cleared; once the error indicator for a specified stream is set, operations on that stream continues to return an error value until `clearerr`, `fseek`, `fsetpos`, or `rewind` is called. Look at the code given below which use the `clearerr()`

```
#include <stdio.h>
#include <stdlib.h>
#include <errno.h>
main()
```

```
{
    FILE *fp;
    fp = fopen("Comments.TXT", "w");
    if(fp==NULL)
    {
       perror("OOPS ERROR");
       printf("\n error no = %d", errno);
       exit(1);
    }
    printf("\n Kindly give the feedback on
    this book: ");
    gets(feedback);
    for(i = 0; i < feedback[i];i++)
    {
       fputc(feedback[i], fp);
       if (ferror(fp))
       {
          clearerr(fp);
          break;
          /* clears the error indicators and
             jump out of for loop */
       }
    }
    // close the file
    fclose(fp);
}
```

9.6.2 perror()

The function `perror()` stands for print error. In case of an error, the programmer can determine the type of error that has occurred using the `perror()` function. The `perror()` function defined in `stdio.h` header file is used to handle errors in C programs. When called, `perror()` displays a message on `stderr` describing the most recent error that occurred during a library function call or system call. The prototype of `perror()` can be given as

```
void perror(char *msg);
```

The `perror()` takes one argument msg which points to an optional user-defined message. This message is printed first, followed by a colon, and the implementation-defined message that describes the most recent error.

If a call to `perror()` is made when no error has actually occurred, then a `'No error'` will be displayed. The most important thing to remember is that a call to `perror()` does nothing to deal with the error condition. It is entirely up to the program to take action. For example, the program may prompt the user to do something such as terminate the program.

Usually the program's action will be determined by checking the value of `errno` and the nature of the error. In order to use the external constant errno, you must include the header file `ERRNO.H`. The program given below illustrates the use of `perror()`. Here we assume that the file `Comments.TXT` does not exist.

```
#include <stdio.h>
#include <stdlib.h>
#include <errno.h>
main()
{
   FILE *fp;
   fp = fopen("Comments.TXT", "w");
   if(fp==NULL)
   {
      perror("OOPS ERROR");
      printf("\n error no = %d", errno);
      exit(1);
   }
   printf("\n Provide feedback on this book: ");
   gets(feedback);
   for(i=0; i<feedback[i];i++)
      fputc(feedback[i], fp);
   fclose(fp);
}
```

Output

```
OOPS ERROR: No such file or directory
errno =2
```

9.7 ACCEPTING COMMAND LINE ARGUMENTS

C facilitates its programmers to pass command arguments. Command line arguments are given after the name of a program in command-line operating systems like DOS or Linux, and are passed in to the program from the operating system.

Till now, no arguments were passed to the `main()`. But now in order to understand command-line arguments, you must first understand the full declaration of the main function. The `main()` can accept two arguments,

- The first argument is an integer value that specifies number of command-line arguments.
- The second argument is a full list of all of the command-line arguments.

The full declaration of `main()` can be given as

```
int main (int arg c, char *argv[])
```

The integer, arg c specifies the number of arguments passed into the program from the command line, including the name of the program.

The array of character pointers, argv contains the list of all the arguments. argv[0] is the name of the program, or an empty string if the name is not available. argv[1] to argv[argc - 1] specifies the command line argument. In the C program, every element in the argv can be used as a string. Moreover, elements of argv can also be accessed as a two-dimensional array. Note that argv[argc] is a null pointer.

In other words, each element of the array argv is a pointer where each pointer points to a string. Thus, argv[0] points to a string that contains the first parameter on the command line which is the program's name, argv[1] points to the next parameter, and so on. Look at the program given below which illustrates the use of command line arguments.

```
int main(int argc, char *argv[])
{
    int i;
    printf("\n Number of argumnets passed =
    %d",argc);
     for (i = 0; i < argc; i++)
            printf("\n arg[i] = %s",argv[i]);
     return 0;
}
```

In the program, the main() accepts command line arguments through argc and argv. In the main() function, the value of argc is printed which gives the number of arguments passed. Then each argument passed is printed in the for loop using the array of pointers, argv.

```
For example when you execute this program
    from dos prompt by writing
C:\>tc clpro.c Reema Thareja
Then argc = 3, where argv[0] = clpro.c
    argv[1] = Reema and argv[2] = Thareja
```

9.1 Write a program to read a file character by character, and display it simultaneously on the screen.

```
#include <stdio.h>
#include <string.h>
main()
{
    FILE *fp;
    int ch;
    char filename[20];
    printf("\n Enter the filename: ");
    fp = fopen(filename, "r");
    if(fp==NULL)
    {
        printf("\n Error Opening the File");
        exit(1);
    }
    ch= fgetc(fp);
    while(ch!=EOF)
    {
        putchar(ch);
        ch = fgetc(fp);
    }
    fclose(fp);
}
```

Output

```
Enter the filename: Letter.TXT
Hello how are you?
```

9.2 Write a program to count the number of characters and number of lines in a file.

```
#include <stdio.h>
#include <string.h>
main()
{
    FILE *fp;
    int ch,)no_of_characters = 0, no_of_lines = 1;
    char filename[20];
    printf("\n Enter the filename: ");
    fp = fopen(filename, "r");
    if(fp==NULL)
    {
        printf("\n Error Opening the File");
        exit(1);
    }
    ch= fgetc(fp);
    while(ch!=EOF)
    {
        if(ch=='\n')
            no_of_lines++;
        no_of_characters++;
        ch = fgetc(fp);
    }
    if(no_of_characters > 0)
    printf("\n In the file %s, there are %d
    lines and %d characters", filename, no_
    of_lines, no_of_characters);
    else
        printf("\n File is empty");
    fclose(fp);
}
```

Output

```
Enter the filename: Letter.TXT
In the file Letter.TXT, there are 1 lines
    and 18 characters
```

9.3 Write a program to print the text of a file on screen by printing the text line by line and displaying the line numbers before the text in each line. Use command line argument to enter the filename.

```
#include <stdio.h>
#include <conio.h>
int main()
{
   FILE *fp1;
   char text[100], ch;
   int line = 1;
   int i = 0;
   clrscr();
   if(argc != 2)
   {
      printf("\n Full information is not
         provided. Please provide a filename");
      return 0;
   }
   fp1 = fopen(argv[1], "r");
   if(fp1 == NULL)
   {
      printf("\n File Opening Error");
      return 0;
   }
   i = 0;
   while(feof(fp1) == 0)
   {
     fscanf(fp1, "%c", &ch);
     if (ch == '\n')
     {
        line++;
        text[i] = '\0';
        printf("%d %s", line, text);
        i = 0;
     }
        text[i] = ch;
        i++;
     }
     text[i] = '\0';
     printf("%s", text);
     fclose(fp1);
     getch();
     return 0;
}
```

Output

```
1 Hello how are you?
```

9.4 Write a program to compare two files to check whether they are identical or not.

```
#include <stdio.h>
#include <conio.h>
main()
{
   FILE *fp1, *fp2;
   int ch1, ch2;
   char filename1[20], filename2[20];
   clrscr();
   printf("\n Enter the name of the first file: ");
   gets(filename1);
   fflush(stdin);
   printf("\n Enter the name of the second file: ");
   gets(filename2);
   fflush(stdin);
   if((fp1=fopen(filename1, "r"))==0)
   {

      printf("\n Error opening the first file");
      exit(1);
   }
   if((fp2=fopen(filename2, "r"))==0)
   {
      printf("\n Error opening the second file");
      exit(1);
   }
   ch1 = fgetc(fp1);
   ch2 = fgetc(fp2);
   while(ch1!=EOF && ch2!=EOF && ch1==ch2)
   {
      /* Reading and comparing the contents
         of two files */
      ch1 = fgetc(fp1);
      ch2 = fgetc(fp2);
   }
   if(ch1==ch2)
   printf("\n Files are identical");
      else
   printf("\n Files are not identical");
   fclose(fp1);
   fclose(fp2);
   getch();
   return 0;
}
```

Output

```
Enter the name of the first filename:
   Comments.TXT
Enter the name of the second filename:
   Letter.TXT
Files are not identical
```

9.5 Write a program to copy one file into another. Copy one character at a time.

```
#include <stdio.h>
#include <conio.h>
```

```
main()
{
   FILE *fp1, *fp2;
   int ch;
   char filename1[20], filename2[20];
   clrscr();
   printf("\n Enter the name of the first file: ");
   gets(filename1);
   fflush(stdin);
   printf("\n Enter the name of the second
   file: ");
   gets(filename2);
   fflush(stdin);
   if((fp1=fopen(filename1, "r"))==0)
   {
      printf("\n Error opening the first file");
      exit(1);
   }
   if((fp2=fopen(filename2, "w"))==0)
   {
      printf("\n Error opening the second file");
      exit(1);
   }
      // Copy from fp1 to fp2
   ch = fgetc(fp1);
   while(ch!=EOF)
   {
      putc(ch, fp2);
      ch = fgetc(fp1);
   }
      printf("\n FILE COPIED");
   fclose(fp1);
   fclose(fp2);

      getch();
   return 0;
}
```

Output

```
Enter the name of the first filename:
   Comments.TXT
Enter the name of the second filename: User_
   Comments.TXT
FILE COPIED
```

9.6 Write a program to copy one file into another. Copy multiple characters simultaneously.

```
#include <stdio.h>
#include <conio.h>
main()
{
   FILE *fp1, *fp2;
   char filename1[20], filename2[20],
   str[30];
   clrscr();
   printf("\n Enter the name of the first
   filename: ");
   gets(filename1);
   fflush(stdin);
   printf("\n Enter the name of the second
   filename: ");
   gets(filename2);
   fflush(stdin);
   if((fp1=fopen(filename1, "r"))==0)
   {
      printf("\n Error opening the first file");
      exit(1);
   }
   if((fp2=fopen(filename2, "w"))==0)
   {
      printf("\n Error opening the second file");
      exit(1);
   }
   while((fgets(str, sizeof(str),
      fp1))!=NULL) fputs(str, fp2);
   fclose(fp1);
   fclose(fp2);
   getch();
   return 0;
}
```

Output

```
Enter the name of the first filename:
   Comments.TXT
Enter the name of the second filename:
   User_Comments.TXT
FILE COPIED
```

9.7 Write a program to read a file that contains characters. Encrypt the data in this file while writing it into another file. (For example while writing the data in another file you can use the formula ch = ch –2, i.e., if the data contains character 'red' the encrypted data becomes 'pcb'.

```
#include <stdio.h>
#include <conio.h>
int main(int argc, char *argv[])
{
```

```
    FILE *fp1, *fp2;
    char ch,
    clrscr();
    if(argc != 3)
    {
        printf("\n Full information is not
            provided");
        return 0;
    }
    fp1 = fopen(argv[1], "r");
    if(fp1 == NULL)
    {
        printf("\n File Opening Error");
        return 0;
    }
    fp2 = fopen(argv[2], "w");
    if(fp2 == NULL)
    {
        printf("\n File Opening Error");
        return 0;
    }
    while (feof(fp1) == 0)
    {
        fscanf(fp1, "%c", &ch);
        fprintf(fp2, "%c", ch - 2);
        /*encrypted character is printed on
            the screen */
    }
        printf("\n The encrypted data is
        written to the file");
    fclose(fp2);
    fcloseall();
    getch();
    return 0;
}
```

Output

```
The encrypted data is written to the file
```

9.8 Write a program to read a file that contains lower case characters. Then write these characters into another file with all lower case characters converted into upper case. (e.g., if the file contains data—'red' it must be written in another file as 'RED').

```
#include <stdio.h>
#include <conio.h>
int main(int argc, char *argv[])
{
    FILE *fp1, *fp2;
    char ch;
    clrscr();
    if(argc != 3)
    {
        printf("\n Full information is not
            provided");
        return 0;
    }
    fp1 = fopen(argv[1], "r");
    if(fp1 == NULL)
    {
        printf("\n File Opening Error");
        return 0;
    }
    fp2 = fopen(argv[2], "w");
    if(fp2 == NULL)
    {
        printf("\n File Opening Error");
        return 0;
    }
    while (feof(fp1) == 0)
    {
        fscanf(fp1, "%c", &ch);
        fprintf(fp2, "%c", ch - 32);
    }
    fcloseall();
    printf("\n File copied with upper case
    characters");
    getch();
    return 0;
}
```

Output

```
File copied with upper case characters
```

9.9 Write a program to merge two files into a third file. The names of the files must be entered using command line arguments.

```
#include <stdio.h>
#include <conio.h>
int main(int argc, char *argv[])
{
    FILE *fp1, *fp2, *fp3;
    char ch;
    clrscr();
    if(argc != 4)   // Read three filenames
    from the user
    {
        printf("\n Full information is not
            provided");
        return 0;
    }
    fp1 = fopen(argv[1], "r");
```

```
    if(fp1 == NULL)
    {
        printf("\n File Opening Error");
        return 0;
    }
    fp2 = fopen(argv[2], "r");
    if(fp2 == NULL)
    {
        printf("\n File Opening Error");
        return 0;
    }
    fp3 = fopen(argv[3], "w");
    if(fp3 == NULL)
    {
        printf("\n File Opening Error");
        return 0;
    }
    while (feof(fp1) != 0)
    {
        fscanf(fp1, "%c", &ch);
        fprintf(fp3, "%c", ch);
    }
    while (feof(fp2) != 0)
    {
        fscanf(fp2, "%c", &ch);
        fprintf(fp3, "%c", ch);
    }
    fcloseall();
    printf("\n File merged");
    getch();
    return 0;
}
```

Output

```
File merged
```

9.10 Write a program to read some text from the keyboard and store it in a file.

```
#include <stdio.h>
#include <string.h>
main()
{
    FILE *fp;
    char filename[20], str[100];
    printf("\n Enter the filename: ");
    fp = fopen(filename, "w");
    if(fp==NULL)
    {
        printf("\n Error Opening The File");
        exit(1);
    }
    printf("\n Enter the text: ");
    gets(str);
    fflush(stdin);
    fprintf(fp, "%s", str);
    fclose(fp);
}
```

Output

```
Enter the filename: Greet.TXT
Enter the text: Good Morning
```

9.11 Write a program to read the details of a student and then print it on the screen as well as write it into a file.

```
#include <stdio.h>
#include <conio.h>
int main()
{
    FILE *fp;
    typedef struct student
    {
        int roll_no;
        char name[80];
        float fees;
        char DOB[80];
    }STUDENT;
    STUDENT stud1;
    clrscr();
    fp = fopen("student_details.dat", "w");
    if(fp == NULL)
    {
        printf("\n File Opening Error");
        return 0;
    }
    printf("\n Enter the roll number: ");
    scanf("%d", &stud1.roll_no);
    printf("\n Enter the name: ");
    scanf("%s", stud1.name);
    printf("\n Enter the fees: ");
    scanf("%f", &stud1.fees);
    printf("\n Enter the DOB: ");
    scanf("%s", stud1.DOB);
    // PRINT ON SCREEN
    printf("\n *** STUDENT'S DETAILS ***");
    printf("\n ROLL No. = %d", stud1.roll_no);
    printf("\n NAME = %s", stud1.name);
    printf("\n FEES = %f", stud1.fees);
    printf("\n DOB = %s", stud1.DOB);
    // WRITE TO FILE
```

```
    fprintf(fp,"%d %s %f %s", stud1.roll_no,
    stud1.name, stud1.fees, stud1.DOB);

    fclose(fp);
    getch();
    return 0;
}
```

Output

```
Enter the roll number: 01
Enter the name: Aman
Enter the fees: 45000
Enter the DOB: 20-9-91
*******STUDENT'S DETAILS *******
ROLL No. = 01
NAME = Aman
FEES = 45000
DOB = 20-9-91
```

9.12 Write a program to read the details of a student from a file and then print it on the screen.

```
#include <stdio.h>
#include <conio.h>
int main()
{
    FILE *fp;
    typedef struct student
    {
        int roll_no;
        char name[80];
        float fees;
        char DOB[80];
    }STUDENT;

    STUDENT stud1;
    clrscr();
    fp = fopen("student_details.dat", "r");
    if(fp == NULL)
    {
        printf("\n File Opening Error");
        return 0;
    }
     // READ FROM FILE
    fscanf(fp,"%d %s %f %s", &stud1.roll_no,
    stud1.name, &stud1.fees, stud1.DOB);
    // PRINT ON SCREEN
    printf("\n *** STUDENT'S DETAILS ***");
    printf("\n ROLL No. = %d", stud1.roll_no);
    printf("\n NAME = %s", stud1.name);
    printf("\n FEES = %f", stud1.fees);
    printf("\n DOB = %s", stud1.DOB);

    fclose(fp);
    getch();
    return 0;
}
```

Output

```
*******STUDENT'S DETAILS *******
ROLL No. = 01
NAME = Aman
FEES = 45000
DOB = 20-9-91
```

9.13 Write a program to read the details of student until a '–1' is entered and simultaneously write the data to a file.

```
#include <stdio.h>
#include <conio.h>
int main()
{
    FILE *fp;
    typedef struct student
    {
        int roll_no;
        char name[80];
        float fees;
        char DOB[80];
    }STUDENT;
    STUDENT stud1;
    clrscr();
    fp = fopen("student_details.dat", "w");
    if(fp == NULL)
    {
        printf("\n File Opening Error");
        return 0;
    }
    printf("\n Enter the roll number: ");
    scanf("%d", &stud1.roll_no);
    while(stud1.roll_no != -1)
    {
        printf("\n Enter the name: ");
        scanf("%s", stud1.name);
        printf("\n Enter the fees: ");
        scanf("%f", &stud1.fees);
        printf("\n Enter the DOB: ");
        scanf("%s", stud1.DOB);
        fprintf(fp,"%d %s %f %s", stud1.roll_
           no, stud1.name, stud1.fees, stud1.
```

```
        DOB);
      fflush(stdin);
      printf("\n Enter the roll number: ");
      scanf("%d", &stud1.roll_no);
   }
   fclose(fp);
   getch();
   return 0;
}
```

Output

```
Enter the roll number: 01
Enter the name: Aman
Enter the fees: 45000
Enter the DOB: 20-9-91
Enter the roll number: 02
Enter the name: Divij
Enter the fees: 45000
Enter the DOB: 29-10-91
Enter the roll number: 03
Enter the name: Saransh
Enter the fees: 45000
Enter the DOB: 2-3-92
Enter the roll number: -1
```

9.14 Write a program to read characters until a '*' is entered. Simultaneously store these characters in a file.

```
#include <stdio.h>
#include <conio.h>
int main()
{
   file *fp;
   char ch;
   clrscr();
   fp = fopen("characters.dat", "w");
   if(fp == NULL)
   {
      printf("\n File Opening Error");
      return 0;
   }
   printf("\n Enter the characters: ");
   scanf("%c", &ch);
   while(ch != '*')
   {
      fprintf(fp, "%c", ch);
      scanf("%c", &ch);
   }
   printf("\n Written to the file");
   fclose(fp);
   getch();
   return 0;
}
```

Output

```
Enter the characters:  abcdef*
Written to the file
```

9.15 Write a program to count the number of lower case, upper case, numbers, and special characters present in the contents of a file. (Assume that the file contains the following data: 1. Hello, How are you?)

```
#include <stdio.h>
#include <conio.h>
int main(int arg c, char *argv[])
{
   FILE *fp;
   int ch, upper_case = 0, lower_case = 0.
   numbers = 0, special_chars = 0;
   clrscr();
   if(argc != 2)
   {
      printf("\n Full information is not
        provided");
      return 0;
   }
   fp = fopen(argv[1], "r");
   if(fp == NULL)
   {
      printf("\n File Opening Error");
      return 0;
   }
   i = 0;
   while(feof(fp) == 0)
   {
      fscanf(fp, "%c", &ch);
      if (ch >= 'A' && ch <= 'Z')
        upper_case++;
      if (ch >= 'a' && ch <= 'z')
        lower_case++;
      if (ch >= '0' && ch <= '9')
        numbers++;
      else
        special_chars++;
   }
   fclose(fp);
   printf("\n Number of upper case
   characters = %d", upper_case);
   printf("\n Number of lower case
   characters = %d", lower_case);
   printf("\n Number of digits = %d",
   numbers);
   printf("\n Number of special characters
     = %d", special_chars);
   getch();
   return 0;
```

```
}
```

Output

```
Number of upper case characters = 2
Number of lower case characters = 2
Number of digits = 1
Number of special characters = 2
```

9.16 Write a program to write record of students to a file using array of structures.

```
#include <stdio.h>
#include <conio.h>
int main()
{
   FILE *fp;
   typedef struct student
   {
      int roll_no;
      char name[80];
      int marks;
   }STUDENT;
   STUDENT stud1[5];
   int i;
   clrscr();
   fp = fopen("student_details.txt", "w");
   if(fp == NULL)
   {
      printf("\n File Opening Error");
      return 0;
   }
   for(i = 0; i < 5;i++)
   {
      printf("\n Enter the roll number: ");
      scanf("%d", &stud1[i].roll_no);
      printf("\n Enter the name: ");
      scanf("%s", stud1[i].name);
      printf("\n Enter the marks: ");
      scanf("%d", &stud1[i].marks);
   }
   // PRINT ON SCREEN
   for(i = 0;i < 5;i++)
   {
      printf("\n *** STUDENT'S DETAILS ***");
      printf("\n ROLL No. = %d", stud1[i].roll_no);
      printf("\n NAME = %s", stud1[i].name);
      printf("\n MARKS = %d", stud1[i].marks);
      // WRITE TO FILE
      fprintf(fp,"%d %s %d", stud1[i].roll_no,
              stud1[i].name, stud1[i].marks);
   }
   printf("\n Data Written to the file");
   fclose(fp);
   getch();
   return 0;
}
```

Output

```
********STUDENT'S DETAILS *******
ROLL No. = 01
NAME = Aditya
MARKS = 78
********STUDENT'S DETAILS *******
ROLL No. = 02
NAME = Goransh
MARKS = 100
********STUDENT'S DETAILS *******
ROLL No. = 03
NAME = Sarthak
MARKS = 81
Data Written to the file
```

9.17 Write a program to append a record to the student's file.

```
#include <stdio.h>
#include <conio.h>
int main()
{
   FILE *fp;
   typedef struct student
   {
      int roll_no;
      char name[80];
      int marks;
   }STUDENT;
   STUDENT stud1;
   clrscr();
   fp = fopen("student_details.txt", "a");
   if(fp == NULL)
   {
      printf("\n File Opening Error");
      return 0;
   }
   printf("\n Enter the Roll Number = ");
      scanf("%d", &stud1.roll_no);
   printf("\n Enter the Name = ");
      scanf("%s", stud1.name);
   printf("\n Enter the Marks = ");
      scanf("%d", &stud1.marks);
```

```
    fprintf("fp, "\n %d %s %d", stud1.
  roll_no, stud1.name, stud1.marks);
 /* After entering the record add a -1 to
  the file to denote the end of records */
    fprintf("fp, %d", -1);
    printf("\n Data Appended");
  fclose(fp);
  getch();
  return 0;
}
```

Output

```
Enter the Roll Number = 04
Enter the Name = Sanchita
Enter the Marks = 50
Data Appended
```

9.18 Write a program to read the record of a particular student.

```
#include <stdio.h>
#include <conio.h>
int main()
{
  FILE *fp1;
  typedef struct student
  {
    int roll_no;
    char name[80];
    int marks;
  }STUDENT;
  STUDENT stud1;
  int found =0, rno;
  clrscr();
  fp1 = fopen("student_details.txt", "r");
  if(fp1 == NULL)
  {
    printf("\n File Opening Error");
    return 0;
  }
  printf("\n Enter the roll number of the
  student whose record has to be read: ");
  scanf("%d", &rno);
  while(1)
  {
    fscanf(fp1, "%d %s %d", &stud1.roll_no,
      stud1.name, &stud1.marks);
    if(stud1.roll_no == -1)
    break;
    if(stud1.roll_no == rno)
    {
    found = 1;
      printf("\n The details of student are");

      printf(" %d %s %d", stud1.roll_no,
        stud1.name, stud1.marks);
     break;
      }
    }
     if (found==0)
      printf("\n Record not found in the file");
  fclose(fp1);
  return 0;
}
```

Output

```
Enter the roll number of the student whose
  record has to be read: 02
The details of student are - 02 Goransh 100
```

9.19 Write a program to edit the record of a particular student.

```
#include <stdio.h>
#include <conio.h>
int main()
{
  FILE *fp1, *fp2;
  typedef struct student
  {
    int roll_no;
    char name[80];
    int marks;
  }STUDENT;
  STUDENT stud1;
  int found =0, rno;
  clrscr();
  fp1 = fopen("student_details.txt", "r");
  if(fp1 == NULL)
  {
    printf("\n File Opening Error");
    return 0;
  }
  fp2 = fopen("temp.txt", "w");
  if(fp2 == NULL)
  {
    printf("\n File Opening Error");
    return 0;
  }
  printf("\n Enter the roll number of the
    student whose record has to be
    modified: ");
  scanf("%d", &rno);
  while(1)
  {
```

```
    fscanf(fp1, "%d", &stud1.roll_no);
    if(stud1.roll_no == -1)
    break;
    if(stud1.roll_no == rno)
    {
    found = 1;
    fscanf(fp1, "%s %d", stud1.name,
      &stud1.marks);
    printf("\n The details of existing
      record are ");
    printf(" %d %s %d", stud1.roll_no,
      stud1.name, stud1.marks);
    printf("\n Enter the modified name of
      the student: ");
    scanf("%s", stud1.name);
    printf("\n Enter the modified marks of
      the student: ");
    scanf("%d", &stud1.marks);
    /* Write the modified record to the
      temporary file */
    fprintf(fp2, "%d %s %d", stud1.roll_no,
      stud1.name, stud1.marks);
    }
    else
    {
      /* Copy the non-matching records to
          the temporary file */
      fscanf(fp1, "%s %d", stud1.name,
        &stud1.marks);
      fprintf(fp2, "%d %s %d", stud1.roll_no,
        stud1.name, stud1.marks);
    }
  }
  fprintf(fp2,"%d", -1);
  fclose(fp1);
  fclose(fp2);
  if(found==0)
  printf("\n The record with roll number &d
    was not found in the file", rno);
  else
  {
    fp1 = fopen("student_details.txt", "w");
    if(fp1 == NULL)
    {
    printf("\n File Opening Error");
    return 0;
    }
    fp2 = fopen("temp.txt", "r");
    if(fp2 == NULL)
    {
    printf("\n File Opening Error");
    return 0;
    }
      /* Copy the contents of temporary file
        into actual file */
      while(1)
      {
      fscanf(fp2,"%d",&stud1.roll_no);
      if(stud1.roll_no==-1)
      break;
      fscanf(fp2, "%s %d",stud1.name,
        &stud1.marks);
      fprintf(fp1, "%d %s %d", stud1.roll_
        no, stud1.name, stud1.marks);
      }
    }
    fclose(fp1);
    fclose(fp2);
    printf("\n Record Updated");
    getch();
    return 0;
}
```

Output

```
Enter the roll number of the student whose
  record has to be modified: 03
The details of exisitng record are - 03
  Sarthak 81
Enter the modified name of the student:
  Sarthak
Enter the modified marks of the student: 85
Record Updated
```

9.20 Write a program to delete the record of a particular student.

```
#include <stdio.h>
#include <conio.h>
int main()
{
  FILE *fp1, *fp2;
  typedef struct student
  {
    int roll_no;
    char name[80];
    int marks;
  }STUDENT;
  STUDENT stud1;
  int found =0, rno;
  clrscr();
  fp1 = fopen("student_details.txt", "r");
  if(fp1 == NULL)
  {
    printf("\n File Opening Error");
    return 0;
  }
```

```
fp2 = fopen("temp.txt", "w");
if(fp2 == NULL)
{
  printf("\n File Opening Error");
  return 0;
}
printf("\n Enter the roll number of the
  student whose record has to be
  deleted: ");
scanf("%d", &rno);
while(1)
{
  fscanf(fp1, "%d", &stud1.roll_no);
  if(stud1.roll_no == -1)
  break;
  if(stud1.roll_no == rno)
  {
  found = 1;
  fscanf(fp1, "%s %d", stud1.name,
    &stud1.marks);
  }
  // The matching record is not copied
    to temp file
  else
  {
  // Copy the non-matching records to
    the temporary file
  fscanf(fp1, "%s %d", stud1.name,
    &stud1.marks);
  fprintf(fp2, "%d %s %d ", stud1.roll_
    no, stud1.name, stud1.marks);
  }
}
fprintf(fp2," %d", -1);
fclose(fp1);
fclose(fp2);
if(found==0)
printf("\n The record with roll number &d
  was not found in the file", rno);
else
{
  fp1 = fopen("student_details.txt", "w");
  if(fp1 == NULL)
  {
  printf("\n File Opening Error");
  return 0;
  }
  fp2 = fopen("temp.txt", "r");
  if(fp2 == NULL)
  {
  printf("\n File Opening Error");
  return 0;
  }
  // Copy the contents of temporary file
     into actual file
  while(1)
  {
  fscanf(fp2,"%d",&stud1.roll_no);
  if(stud1.roll_no==-1)
  break;
  fscanf(fp2, "%s %d",stud1.name,
    &stud1.marks);
  fprintf(fp1, "%d %s %d ", stud1.roll_
    no, stud1.name, stud1.marks);
  }
}
fprintf(fp1, "%d ",-1);
fclose(fp1);
fclose(fp2);
 printf("\n Record Deleted");
 /* The programmer may delete the temp
file which will no longer be required */
getch();
return 0;
}
```

Output

```
Enter the roll number of the student whose
  record has to be deleted: 01
Record Deleted
```

9.21 Write a program to store records of an employee in employee file. The data must be stored using binary file.

```
#include <stdio.h>
#include <conio.h>
main()
{
  typedef struct employee
  {
    int emp_code;
    char name[20];
    int hra;
    int da;
    int ta;
  };
  FILE *fp;
  struct employee e[5];
  int i;
  fp = fopen("employee.txt", "wb");
  if(fp==NULL)
  {
    printf("\n Error opening file");
    exit(1);
  }
```

```
    printf("\n Enter the details ");
    for(i = 0;i < 5;i++)
    {
       printf("\n\n Enter the employee code:");
       scanf("%d", &e[i].emp_code);
       printf("\n\n Enter the name of the
          employee: ");
       scanf("%s", e[i].name);
       printf("\n\n Enter the HRA, DA, and TA: ");
       scanf("%d %d %d", &e[i].hra, &e[i].da,
          &e[i].ta);
       fwrite(&e[i], sizeof(e[i]), 1, fp);
    }
    fclose(fp);
    getch();
    return 0;
}
```

Output

```
Enter the employee code: 01
Enter the name of the employee: Gargi
Enter the HRA, DA and TA: 10000 2000 5000
Enter the employee code: 02
Enter the name of the employee: Nikita
Enter the HRA, DA and TA: 10000 2000 5000
```

9.22 Write a program to read the records stored in 'employee.txt' file in binary mode.

```
#include <stdio.h>
#include <conio.h>
main()
{
    typedef struct employee
    {
       int emp_code;
       char name[20];
       int hra;
       int da;
       int ta;
    };
    FILE *fp;
    struct employee e;
    int i;
    clrscr();
    fp =  fopen("employee.txt", "rb");
    if(fp==NULL)
    {
       printf("\n Error opening file");
       exit(1);
    }
    printf("\n THE DETAILS OF THE EMPLOYEES ARE ");
    while(1)
    {
       fread(&e, sizeof(e), 1, fp);
       if(feof(fp))
       break;
       printf("\n\nEmployee Code: %d", e.emp_code);
       printf("\n\n Name: %s", e.name);
       printf("\n\n HRA, DA, and TA: %d %d
          %d", e.hra, e.da, e.ta);
    }
    fclose(fp);
    getch();
    return 0;
```

Output

```
Employee Code: 01
Name: Gargi
HRA, DA and TA: 10000 5000 2000
Employee Code: 02
Name: Nikita
HRA, DA and TA: 10000 5000 2000
```

9.23 Write a program to append a record in the employee file (binary file).

```
#include <stdio.h>
#include <conio.h>
main()
{
    typedef struct employee
    {
       int emp_code;
       char name[20];
       int hra;
       int da;
       int ta;
    };
    FILE *fp;
    struct employee e;
    int i;
    fp = fopen("employee.txt", "ab");
    if(fp==NULL)
    {
       printf("\n Error opening file");
       exit(1);
    }
    printf("\n\n Enter the employee code:");
    scanf("%d", &e.emp_code);
    printf("\n\n Enter the name of employee: ");
    scanf("%s", e.name);
    printf("\n\n Enter the HRA, DA, and TA:");
    scanf("%d %d %d", &e.hra, &e.da, &e.ta);
    fwrite(&e, sizeof(e), 1, fp);
```

```
    fclose(fp);
    printf("\n Record Appended");
    getch();
    return 0;
}
```

Output

```
Enter the employee code: 06
Enter the name of employee: Tanya
Enter the HRA, DA and TA: 20000 10000 3000
```

9.24 Write a program to edit the employee record stored in a binary file.

```
#include <stdio.h>
#include <conio.h>
main()
{
  typedef struct employee
  {
    int emp_code;
    char name[20];
    int hra;
    int da;
    int ta;
  };
  FILE *fp1, *fp2;
  struct employee e;
  int i, ec, found = 0;
  clrscr();
  fp1 =  fopen("employee.txt", "rb");
  if(fp1==NULL)
  {
    printf("\n Error opening file");
    exit(1);
  }
  fp2 =  fopen("temp_emp.txt", "wb");
  if(fp2==NULL)
  {
    printf("\n Error opening file");
    exit(1);
  }
  printf("\n Enter the code of the employee
    whose information has to be edited:");
  scanf("%d",&ec);
  while(1)
  {
    fread(&e,sizeof(e),1,fp1);
    if(feof(fp1))
    break;
    if(e.emp_code==ec)
    {
      found=1;
      printf("\n The existing record is: %d
        %s %d %d %d", e.emp_code, e.name,
        e.hra, e.ta, e.da);
      printf("\n Enter the modified name: ");
      scanf("%s", e.name);
      printf("\n Enter the modified HRA, TA,
        and DA: ");
      scanf("%d %d %d", &e.hra, &e.ta, &e.da);
      fwrite(&e, sizeof(e),1,fp2);
      }
      else
      fwrite(&e, sizeof(e),1,fp2);
  }
  fclose(fp1);
  fclose(fp2);
  if(found==0)
  printf("\n Record not found");
  else
  {
    fp1 =  fopen("employee.txt", "wb");
    if(fp1==NULL)
    {
    printf("\n Error opening file");
    exit(1);
    }
    fp2 =  fopen("temp_emp.txt", "rb");
    if(fp2==NULL)
    {
    printf("\n Error opening file");
    exit(1);
    }
    while(1)
    {
    fread(&e, sizeof(e),1,fp2);
    if(feof(fp2))
    break;
    fwrite(&e, sizeof(e), 1, fp1);
    }
  }
  fclose(fp1);
  fclose(fp2);
    printf("\n Record Edited");
  getch();
  return 0;
}
```

Output

```
Enter the code of the employee whose
  information has to be edited: 01
The existing record is: 01 Gargi 10000 5000
  2000
Enter the modified name: Gargi
```

```
Enter the modified HRA, TA, and DA: 20000
   10000 30000
Record Edited
```

9.8 FUNCTIONS FOR SELECTING A RECORD RANDOMLY

In this section we will read about functions that are used to randomly access a record stored in a binary file. These functions include `fseek()`, `ftell()`, `rewind()`, `fgetpos()`, and `fsetpos()`.

9.8.1 fseek()

The function `fseek()` is used to reposition a binary stream. The prototype of `fseek()` function which is defined in `stdio.h` can be given as,

```
int fseek(FILE *stream, long offset, int
   origin);
```

`fseek()` is used to set the file position pointer for the given stream. The variable offset is an integer value that gives the number of bytes to move forward or backward in the file. The value of offset may be positive or negative, provided it makes sense. For example, you cannot specify a negative offset if you are starting at the beginning of the file. The `origin` value should have one of the following values (defined in `stdio.h`):

- `SEEK_SET`: to perform input or output on `offset` bytes from start of the file
- `SEEK_CUR`: to perform input or output on `offset` bytes from the current position in the file
- `SEEK_END`: to perform input or output on `offset` bytes from the end of the file
- `SEEK_SET`, `SEEK_CUR` and `SEEK_END` are defined constants with value `0`, `1`, and `2`, respectively.

Programming Tip: While using fseek (), if the third parameter is specified as SEEK_END, then you must provide a negative offset, otherwise it will try to access beyond EOF.

On successful operation, `fseek()` returns `zero` and in case of failure, it returns a non-zero value. For example, if you try to perform a seek operation on a file that is not opened in binary mode then a non-zero value will be returned. `fseek()` can be used to move the file pointer beyond a file, but not before the beginning.

If a file has been opened for update and later if you want to switch from reading to writing or vice versa, then you must use the `fseek()`.

Table 9.5 gives the interpretation of the `fseek()`.

Table 9.5 Origin field in `fseek()`

Function Call	Meaning
fseek (fp, 0L, SEEK_SET);	move to the beginning of the file
fseek (fp, 0L, SEEK_CUR);	stay at the current position
fseek (fp, 0L, SEEK_END);	go to the end of the file
fseek (fp, m, SEEK_CUR);	move forward by m bytes in the file from the current location
fseek (fp, -m, SEEK_CUR);	move backwards by m bytes in file from the current location
fseek (fp, -m, SEEK_END);	move backwards by m bytes from the end of the file

The `fseek()` is primarily used with binary files as it has limited functionality with text files.

9.25 Write a program to randomly read the nth records of a binary file.

```
#include <stdio.h>
#include <conio.h>
main()
{
   typedef struct employee
   {
      int emp_code;
      char name[20];
      int hra;
      int da;
      int ta;
   };
   FILE *fp;
   struct employee e;
   int result, rec_no;
   fp = fopen("employee.txt", "rb");
   if(fp==NULL)
   {
      printf("\n Error opening file");
      exit(1);
   }
```

```
printf("\n\n Enter the rec_no you want to
read: ");
scanf("%d", &rec_no);
if(rec_no >= 0)
{
    /* from the file pointed by fp read a
       record of the specified record
       starting from the beginning of the
       file*/
    fseek(fp, (rec_no-1)*sizeof(e), SEEK_SET);
    result = fread(&e, sizeof(e), 1, fp);
    if(result == 1)
    {
    printf("\n EMPLOYEE CODE: %d", e.emp_code);
    printf("\n Name: %s", e.name);
    printf("\n HRA, TA and DA: %d %d %d",
        e.hra, e.ta, e.da);
    }
    else
    printf("\n Record Not Found");
}
fclose(fp);
getch();
return 0;
}
```

Output

```
Enter the rec_no you want to read: 06
EMPLOYEE CODE: 06
Name: Tanya
HRA, DA and TA: 20000 10000 3000
```

9.26 Write a program to print the records in reverse order. The file must be opened in binary mode. Use `fseek()`.

```
#include <stdio.h>
#include <conio.h>
main()
{
  typedef struct employee
  {
    int emp_code;
    char name[20];
    int hra;
    int da;
    int ta;
  };
  FILE *fp;
  struct employee e;
  int result, i;
  fp =  fopen("employee.txt", "rb");
  if(fp==NULL)
  {
    printf("\n Error opening file");
    exit(1);
  }
  for(i=5;i>=0;i--)
  {
    fseek(fp, i*sizeof(e), SEEK_SET);
    fread(&e, sizeof(e) 1, fp);
    printf("\n EMPLOYEE CODE: %d", e.emp_code);
    printf("\n Name: %s", e.name);
    printf("\n HRA, TA, and DA: %d %d %d",
      e.hra, e.ta, e.da);
  }
  fclose(fp);
  getch();
  return 0;
}
```

Output

```
EMPLOYEE CODE: 06
Name: Tanya
HRA, DA and TA: 20000 10000 3000
EMPLOYEE CODE: 05
Name: Ruchi
HRA, DA and TA: 10000 6000 3000
```

9.27 Write a program to edit a record in binary mode using `fseek()`.

```
#include <stdio.h>
#include <conio.h>
main()
{
  typedef struct employee
  {
    int emp_code;
    char name[20];
    int hra;
    int da;
  int ta;
  };
  FILE *fp;
  struct employee e;
  int rec_no;
  fp = fopen("employee.txt", "r+");
  if(fp==NULL)
  {
    printf("\n Error opening file");
    exit(1);
```

```
    }
    printf("\n Enter record no. to be modified: ");
    scanf("%d", &rec_no);
    fseek(fp, (rec_no-1)*sizeof(e), SEEK_SET);
    fread(&e, sizeof(e), 1, fp);
    printf("\n Enter modified name of the employee: ");
    scanf("%s", e.name);
    printf("\n Enter the modified HRA, TA,
    and DA of the employee: ");
    scanf("%d %d %d", &e.hra, &e.ta, &e.da);
    fwrite(&e, sizeof(e), 1, fp);
    fclose(fp);
        printf("\n Record Edited");
    getch();
    return 0;
}
```

Output

```
Enter record no. to be modified: 04
Enter the modified HRA, TA, and DA of the
   employee: 30000 1000 5000
Record Edited
```

9.8.2 ftell()

The `ftell()` function is used to know the current position of file pointer. It is at this position where the next input or ouput operation will be performed. The syntax of `ftell()`, defined in `stdio.h`, can be given as

```
long ftell (FILE *stream);
```

Here, `stream` points to the file whose file position indicator has to be determined. If successful, `ftell()` function returns the current file *position* (in bytes) for stream. However, in case of error, `ftell()` returns `-1`.

When using `ftell()`, error can occur either because of two reasons:

- First, using `ftell()` with a device that cannot store data (e.g., keyboard).
- Second, when the position is larger than that can be represented in a long integer. This will usually happen when dealing with very large files.

Look at the program code which illustrates the use of `ftell()`.

/*The program writes data to a file, saves the number of bytes stored in it in a variable n (by using `ftell()`) and then re-opens the file to read n bytes from the file and simultaneously display it on the screen.*/

```
main()
{
   FILE *fp;
   char c;
   int n;
   fp=fopen("abc","w");
   if(fp==NULL)
   {
      printf("\n Error Opening The File");
      exit(1);
   }
   while((c=getchar())!=EOF)
   putc(c,fp);
   n = ftell(fp);
   fclose(fp);
   fp=fopen("abc","r");
   if(fp==NULL)
   {
      printf("\n Error Opening The File");
      exit(1);
   }
   while(ftell(fp)<n)
   {
      c= fgetc(fp);
      printf("%c", c);
   }
   fclose(fp);
}
```

Output

```
abcdefghijkjdqjdh
```

`ftell()` is useful when we have to deal with text files for which position of the data cannot be calculated.

9.8.3 rewind()

`rewind()` is used to adjust the position of file pointer so that the next I/O operation will take place at the beginning of the file. It is defined in stdio.h and its prototype can be given as

```
void rewind(FILE *f);
```

`rewind()` is equivalent to calling `fseek()` with following parameters:

```
fseek(f,0L,SEEK_SET);
```

We have seen earlier that if a file is opened for writing and you want to read it later, then you have to close the existing file and reopen it so that data can be read from the beginning of the file. The other alternative is to use the rewind(). Look at the program code given below which demonstrates the use of rewind().

```
#include <stdio.h>
main()
{
   FILE *fp;
   char feedback[80];
   int i=0;
   fp = fopen("comments.txt", "w+");
   if(fp==NULL)
   {
      printf("\n Error Opening The File");
      exit(1);
   }
   printf("\n Provide comments on this book: ");
   scanf("%s", feedback);
   while(feedback[i]!='\0')
   {
      fputc(feedback[i], fp);
      i++;
   }
   rewind(fp);
   printf("\n Contents of the file are: ");
   while(feof(fp)==0)
      printf("%c", fgetc(fp));
   fclose(fp);
   return 0;
}
```

Output

```
Provide comments on this book: Good
Contents of the file are: Good
```

However, you must prefer to use fseek() equivalent code rather calling rewind() because it is impossible to determine if rewind() was successful or not.

9.8.4 fgetpos()

The fgetpos() is used to determine the current position of the stream. The prototype of the fgetpos() as given in stdio.h is

```
int fgetpos(FILE *stream, fpos_t *pos);
```

Here, stream is the file whose current file pointer position has to be determined. pos is used to point to the location where fgetpos() can store the position information. In simple words, fgetpos() stores the file position indicator of the given file stream in the pos variable. The pos variable is of type fpos_t which is defined in stdio.h and is basically an object that can hold every possible position in a FILE.

On success, fgetpos() returns zero and in case of an error a non-zero value is returned. The value of pos obtained through fgetpos() can be used by the fsetpos() to return to this same position.

9.8.5 fsetpos()

The fsetpos() is used to move the file position indicator of a stream to the location indicated by the information obtained in 'pos' by making a call to the fgetpos(). Like fgetpos(), fsetpos() is defined in stdio.h and its prototype can be given as

```
int fsetpos(FILE *stream, const fpos_t pos);
```

Here, stream points to the file whose file pointer indicator has to be re-positioned. pos points to positioning information as returned by fgetpos.

On success, fsetpos() returns a zero and clears the EOF indicator. In case of failure it returns a non-zero value.

> **Programming Tip:** An error will be generated if you try to place the file position indicator before the first byte of the file.

After the successful call to fsetpos(), the next operation on a stream in update mode may be input or output. Look at the program code given below which illustrates the use of fgetpos() and fsetpos() functions.

// The program opens a file and reads bytes at several different locations.

```
#include <stdio.h>
main()
{
   FILE *fp;
   fpost_pos;
   char text[20];
   fp = fopen("practise.c", "rb");
   if(fp == NULL)
   {
      printf("\n Error opening file");
      exit(1);
   }
   /* Read some data and then check the
   position. */
   fread(text, sizeof(char), 20, fp);
   if(fgetpos(fp, &pos) != 0)
   {
      printf("\n Error in fgetpos()");
      exit(1);
   }
   fread(text, sizeof(char), 20, fp);
```

```
    printf("\n 20 bytes at byte %ld: %s",
    pos, text);

    /* Set a new random position and read
    more data */
    pos = 90;
    if(fsetpos(fp, &pos) != 0)
    {
        printf("\n Error in fsetpos()");
        exit(1);
    }
    fread(text, sizeof(char), 20, fp);
    printf("\n 20 bytes at byte %ld: %s",
    pos, text);
    fclose(fp);
  }
```

Output

```
20 bytes at byte 20: #include <conio.h>
ma
20 bytes at byte 90: getch();
return 0;
}
```

Only use values for fsetpos() that are returned from fgetpos().

9.9 remove()

The function `remove()` as the name suggests is used to erase a file. The prototype of `remove()` as given in `stdio.h` can be given as

```
int remove(const char *filename);
```

The `remove()` will erase the file specified by `filename`. On success, the function will return zero and in case of error, it will return a non-zero value.

If `filename` specifies a directory, then `remove (filename)` is the equivalent of `rmdir(filename)`. Otherwise, if filename specifies the name of a file then `remove (filename)` is the equivalent of `unlink(filename)`. Look at the program given below which deletes the file `"temp.txt"` from the current directory.

```
#include <stdio.h>
main()
{
    remove("temp.txt");
    return 0;
}
```

You may specify the path of the file which has to be deleted as the argument of `remove()`.

9.10 RENAMING THE FILE

The function `rename()` as the name suggests is used to rename a file. The prototype of the function is

```
int rename(const char *oldname, const char
    *newname)
```

Here, `oldname` specifies the pathname of the file to be renamed and `newname` gives the new pathname of the file.

On success, `rename ()` returns zero. In case of error, it will return a non-zero value and will set the `errno` to indicate the error. When an error occurs neither the file named by `oldname` nor the file named by `newname` shall be changed or created.

Points to remember about `rename()`

- If the `oldname` specifies pathname of a file that is not a directory, the `newname` shall also not point to the pathname of a directory.
- If the `oldname` specifies the pathname of a directory then the `newname` shall not point to the pathname of a file that is not a directory. In this case, if the directory named by the `newname` already exists then it shall be removed and `oldname` will be renamed to newname.

Look at the program code given below which illustrates the use of `rename()`.

```
#include <stdio.h>
main()
{
    int success=0;
    success = rename("comments.txt",
    "feedback.txt");
    if(success != 0)
    printf("\n The file could not be renamed");
    return 0;
}
```

9.11 CREATING A TEMPORARY FILE

The `tmpfile()` function is used to create a temporary file. The `tmpfile()` opens the corresponding stream with access parameters set as "w+". The file created with `tmpfile()` will be automatically deleted when all references to the file are closed, i.e., the file created will be automatically closed and erased when the program has been completely executed. The prototype of `tmpfile()` as given is `stdio.h` header file is

```
FILE * tmpfile(void);
```

On success, `tmpfile()` will return a pointer to the stream of the file that is created. In case of an error, the function will return a null pointer and set *errno* to indicate the error. The function can be used in the following manner:

```
FILE *tp = tmpfile();
```

Now the file created can be used in the same way as any other text or binary file.

POINTS TO NOTE

- A file is a collection of data stored on a secondary storage device such as a hard disk.
- When a stream linked to a disk file is created, a buffer is automatically created and associated with the stream.
- A file must be first opened before data can be read from it or written to it. In order to open a file and associate it with a stream, the `fopen()` function is used.
- To close an open file, the `fclose()` function is used which disconnects a file pointer from a file. `fclose()` function not only closes the file but also flushes all the buffers that are maintained for that file.
- If you have opened a stream for updating and later you want to switch from reading to writing or vice versa, you must first use the `fseek()` or `rewind()` function.
- When an output stream is unbuffered, information appears on the destination device as soon as it is written. When it is buffered, characters are saved internally and then written out as a group. In order to force buffered characters to be output on the destination device before the buffer is full, use the `fflush()`.
- `fseek()` is used to reposition a binary stream. The `ftell()` function is used to know the current position of file pointer. It is at this position at which the next input or output operation will be performed.
- The `fgetpos()` is used to determine the current position of the stream. The `rename()` function is used to rename a file. The `remove()` function is used to erase a file.
- The `tmpfile()` function is used to create a temporary file. The `tmpfile()` opens the corresponding stream with access parameters set as "w+". The file created with `tmpfile()` will be automatically deleted when all references to the file are closed.

GLOSSARY

Binary file A binary file is a file which may contain any type of data, encoded in binary form for computer storage and processing purposes.

Buffer A buffer is a block of memory that is used for temporary storage of data, that has to be read from or written to a file.

File A file is a collection of data stored on a secondary storage device like hard disk.

Standard error Standard error is basically an output stream used by programs to report error messages or diagnostics.

Standard input Standard input is the stream from which the program receives its data.

Standard output Standard output is the stream where a program writes its output data.

Stream Stream is a logical interface to the devices that are connected to the computer.

Text file A text file is a stream of characters that can be sequentially processed by a computer in the forward direction.

EXERCISES

Fill in the Blanks

1. __________ is a collection of data.
2. The standard streams in C are __________, __________, and __________.
3. __________ are pre-connected input and output channels between a text terminal and the program.
4. A file must be opened in __________ mode if it is being opened for updating.
5. __________ function can be used to move the file marker at the beginning of the file.
6. If a file is opened in 'wb' mode then it is a __________ file opened for writing.

EXERCISES

7. Block input in binary file is done using the __________ function.
8. __________ is the stream where a program writes its output data.
9. __________ is a block of memory that is used for temporary storage of data.
10. The creation and operation of the buffer is automatically handled by the __________.
11. __________ file can be processed sequentially as well as randomly.
12. __________ function closes the file and flushes all the buffers that are maintained for that file.
13. To use `fprintf()` to write on the screen specify __________ in place of the file pointer.
14. If you have opened a stream for updating and later you want to switch from reading to writing or vice versa, you must first use the __________ or __________ function.
15. The symbolic constant EOF is defined in __________ and has the value __________.

Multiple Choice Questions

1. Which function gives the current position of the file?
   (a) `fseek()` (b) `fsetpos()`
   (c) `ftell()` (d) `Rewind()`
2. Which function is used to perform block output in binary files?
   (a) `fwrite()` (b) `fprintf()`
   (c) `fputc()` (d) `fputs()`
3. Select the standard stream in C.
   (a) `stdin` (b) `stdout`
   (c) `stderr` (d) all of these
4. From which standard stream does a C program read data?
   (a) `stdin` (b) `stdout`
   (c) `stderr` (d) all of these
5. What acts as an interface between stream and hardware?
   (a) `file pointer` (b) `buffer`
   (c) `stdout` (d) `stdin`
6. Which function is used to associate a file with a stream?
   (a) `fread()` (b) `fopen()`
   (c) `floes()` (d) `fflush()`
7. Which function returns the next character from stream, EOF if the end of file is reached, or if there is an error?
   (a) `fgetc()` (b) `fgets()`
   (c) `fputc()` (d) `fwrite()`

State True or False

1. You can use a file without opening it.
2. It is mandatory to close all the files before exiting the program.
3. stderr is a standard stream in C.
4. An error will be generated if you try to position the file marker beyond EOF.
5. A file can be read if and only if it is opened in "r" mode.
6. Binary files are slower than text files.
7. In text files, the data is stored in internal format of the computer.
8. Text files can store only character data.
9. Standard output is an output stream used by programs to report error messages or diagnostics.
10. Each line in a text file can have maximum of 80 characters.
11. Binary file stores data in a human readable format.
12. `fread()` returns the number of elements successfully read.
13. `fseek()` is used to reposition a binary stream.
14. The `tmpfile()` opens the corresponding stream with access parameters set as "w+".
15. The value obtained by using `fgetpos()` can be used only with the `fsetpos()`.

Review Questions

1. What is a file?
2. Why do we need to store data in files?
3. Define the term stream.
4. Differentiate between a text file and a binary file.
5. Explain the different modes in which a file can be opened in a C program.
6. Under which circumstances does the `fopen()` fail?
7. Why should you close a file after it is used?
8. What is the impact of `fclose()` on buffered data?
9. Differentiate between `gets()` and `fgets()`.
10. What is the difference between a buffered output stream and an unbuffered output stream?

EXERCISES

11. With the help of a program code, explain the significance of `ftell()`.
12. Under what circumstances does the `ftell()` fail?
13. Where can `ftell()` be used?
14. With the help of a program, explain the significance of command line arguments.
15. Write a short note on `fgetpos()` and `fsetpos()`. Give a program to illustrate their usage in a C program.
16. What will happen if the argument to `remove()` specifies a directory? Also state its behaviour when the argument is a filename.
17. Give a program that uses a temporary file created using the `tmpfile()`.
18. Give the importance of associating a buffer with the stream.
19. Write a short note on functions that are used to: (a) read data from a file, (b) write data to a file.
20. Write a short note on the following functions. For each function, give a program code that demonstrates its usage.
    (a) `fopen()` (b) `fclose()`
    (c) `ferror()` (d) `clearerr()`
21. What do you understand by EOF?
22. How will you check for EOF when reading a file?
23. Why is it not possible to read from a file and write to the same file without resetting the file pointer?
24. Write a short note on error handling while performing operations.
25. Give the importance of `rewind()`.
26. Differentiate between `rewind()` and `fseek()`. Can `fseek()` work as an alternative to `rewind()`? If yes, how?
27. Write a program to write employees details in a file called `employee.dat`. Then read the record of the nth employee and calculate his salary.
28. Write a program to read the nth record and display it on screen. Repeat the procedure until –1 is entered.
29. Write a program to copy a file using `feof()`.
30. Create a file and store some names in it. Write a program read the names in the file in the reverse order without re-opening the file.
31. Why do we need `fflush()`?
32. Write a program to read the contents of a binary file.
33. Write a program to read the contents of a text file.
34. Write a program to write some contents into (a) a binary file (b) a text file.
35. Write a program to read a text file using `fscanf()`.
36. Write a program to read a text file using `fgetc()`.
37. Write a program to illustrate the use of `fprintf()`.
38. Write a program to illustrate the use of `fputc ()`.
39. Differentiate between `fscanf()` and `fread()`.
40. Write a program to count the number of characters in a file.
41. Write a program that reads the file name and text of 20 words as command line arguments. Write the text into a file whose name is given as the file name.
42. Assume that a file INTEGERS.TXT stores only integer numbers. A value '-1' is stored as the last value to indicate EOF. Write a program to read each integer value stored in the file. While reading the value, compute whether the value is even or odd. If it is even then write that value in a file called EVEN.TXT else write it in ODD.TXT. Finally display the contents of the two files— EVEN.TXT and ODD.TXT.

    Hint: You may use getw and putw functions. They are same as `getc()` and `putc()`. The prototypes of `getw()` and `putw()` are

    int getw(`FILE *fp`); and putw(int value, `FILE *fp`);
43. Write a program to read data from the keyboard and write it to a file. Read the contents stored in the file and display it on the screen.
44. Write a menu-driven program to read, insert, append, delete, and edit a record stored in a binary file.
45. Write a program to read data from a text file and store it in a binary file. Also read the data stored in the binary file and display it on the screen.
46. Write a program to read a text file, convert all the lower case characters into upper case and re-write the upper case characters in the file. Before the end of the program, all temporary files must be deleted.
47. Modify the above code fragment to allow the user three chances to enter a valid file name. If a valid file name is not entered after three chances, terminate the program.
48. Assume that there are two files—Names1 and Names2 that stores sorted names of students who would be participating in Activity1 and Activity2, respectively. Create a file `NAMES.TXT` which stores the names from both the files. Note that there should be no repetition of names in NAMES.TXT and while writing name into it, ensure that the file is also sorted.

EXERCISES

49. Write a program to create a file that stores only integer values. Append the sum of these integers at the end of the file.
50. Write a program that reads a binary file that stores employees records and prints, on the screen, the number of records that are stored in the file.
51. Write a program to append a binary file at the end of another.

Program output

Give the output of the following code.

1.
```
main()
{
    FILE *fp;
    char c;
    fp=fopen("abc","w");
    while((c=getchar())!=EOF)
        putc(c,fp);
    printf('\n No. of characters entered
    = %ld", ftell(fp));
    fclose(fp);
}
```

2.
```
main()
{
    FILE *fp;
    char comment[20];
    int i;
    fp=fopen("Feedbacks","w");
    for(i = 0;i < 5;i++)
    {
        fscanf(stdin, "%s", comment);
        fprintf(fp, "%s", comment);
    }
    fclose(fp);
}
```

3.
```
main()
{
    char c;
    FILE *fp;
    fp = fopen("temp","w+b"))
    for(c = 'A';c <= 'I', c++)
        fputc(c, fp);
    fseek(fp, 2, 0);
    c = fgetc(fp);
    printf("%c", c);
    fclose(fp);
}
```

4.
```
main()
{
    char c;
    FILE *fp;
    fp = fopen("temp","w+b"))
    for(c = 'A';c <= 'I', c++)
    fwrite(&c, 1, 1, fp);
    rewind(fp);
    fread(&c,1,1,fp);
    printf("%c", c);
fclose(fp);
}
```

5.
```
main()
{
    char c;
    FILE *fp;
    long int pos;
    fp = fopen("temp","w+b"))
    for(c = 'A';c <= 'I', c++)
    fwrite(&c, 1, 1, fp);
    pos = ftell(fp);
    pos = -3;
    fseek(fp, pos, SEEK_END);
    fread(&c,1,1,fp);
    printf("%c", c);
    fclose(fp);
}
```

6.
```
main()
{
    int i;
    FILE *fp;
    long int pos;
    fp = fopen("temp","w+b"))
    for(i = 1;i <= 10;i++)
        fwrite(&i, sizeof(int), 1, fp);
    fseek(fp, sizeof(int)*2, SEEK_SET);
    fread(&i,sizeof(int),1,fp);
    printf("%d", i);
    fclose(fp);
}
```

7.
```
main()
{
    int i;
    FILE *fp;
    long int pos;
    fp = fopen("temp","w+b"))
    for(i = 1;i <= 10;i++)
    fwrite(&i, sizeof(int), 1, fp);
    fseek(fp, -sizeof(int)*2, SEEK_CUR);
    fread(&i,sizeof(int),1,fp);
    printf("%d", i);
    fclose(fp);
}
```

CHAPTER 10

Preprocessor Directives

Takeaways

- Preprocessor Directives
- #error Directive
- Pragma Directives
- Predefined Macro Names
- Conditional Directives

10.1 INTRODUCTION

The preprocessor is a program that processes the source code before it passes through the compiler. It operates under the control of preprocessor directive which is placed in the source program before the `main()`. Before the source code is passed through the compiler, it is examined by the preprocessor for any preprocessor directives. In case the program has some preprocessor directives, appropriate actions are taken (depending on the directive) and the source program is handed over to the compiler.

Preprocessor directives are lines included in the C program that are not program statements but directives for the preprocessor. The preprocessor directives are always preceded by a hash sign `(#)` directive. The preprocessor directive is executed before the actual compilation of program code begins. Therefore, the preprocessor expands all the directives and takes the corresponding action before any code is generated by the program statements.

The preprocessor directives are only one line long because as soon as a newline character is found, the preprocessor directive is considered to end. No semicolon `(;)` can be placed at the end of a preprocessor directive. However, the preprocessor directives may contain a comment (which will be simply ignored).

Programming Tip: Preprocessor directives must start with a hash sign.

In order to extend a preprocessor directive to multiple lines; place a backslash character (\) as the last character of the line. This means that the line is continued in the line following it.

Although the preprocessor directive is usually placed before the `main()`, practically speaking, it can appear anywhere in the program code. However, if written in between, the directive will be applied only in the remainder of the source file. The advantages of using preprocessor directives in a C program include:

- Program becomes readable and easy to understand.
- Program can be easily modified or updated.
- Program becomes portable as preprocessor directives make it easy to compile the program in different execution environments.
- Due to the aforesaid reasons, the program also becomes more efficient to use.

10.2 TYPES OF PREPROCESSOR DIRECTIVES

We can broadly categorize the preprocessor directives into two groups—conditional and unconditional preprocessor directives. Figure 10.1 shows the categorization of preprocessor directives.

The conditional directives are used to instruct the preprocessor to select whether or not to include a chunk of code in the final token stream passed to the compiler. Such directives comprise directives such as `#if`, `#else`, `#elif`, `#ifdef`, `#ifndef`, and `#endif`.

The unconditional directives such as `#define`, `#line`, `#undef`, `#include`, `#error`, and `#pragma` perform well-defined task. In this chapter we will learn about all these directives in detail.

10.3 #define

To define preprocessor macros we use `#define`. The `#define` statement is also known as *macro definition* or simply a macro. There are two types of macros:

- object-like macro and
- function-like macro

10.3.1 Object-Like Macro

An *object-like macro* is a simple identifier which will be replaced by a code fragment. They are usually used to give symbolic names to numeric constants. Object-like macros do not take any argument. It is the same what we have been using to declare constants using `#define` directive. The general syntax of defining a macro can be given as

```
#define identifier string
```

The preprocessor replaces every occurrence of the identifier in the source code by a string. The macro must start with the keyword `#define` and should be followed by an identifier and a string with at least one blank space between them. The string may be any text, a statement, or anything. However, the identifier must be a valid C name. If we write,

```
#define PI 3.14
```

Then the above line defines a macro named `PI` as an abbreviation for the token `3.14`. If somewhere after this `#define` directive there comes a C statement of the form

```
area = PI * radius * radius;
```

Then the C preprocessor will recognize and *expand* the macro `PI`. The C compiler will see the same tokens as it would if you had written

```
area = 3.14 * radius * radius;
```

Programming Tip:
A semicolon (;) should not be placed at the end of a preprocessor directive.

A macro definition can also include an expression. However, when using expressions for replacement, make sure that the order of evaluation is correct. As a good programming habit, use parenthesis in the expression. For example, consider the following macro definitions:

```
#define ROWS 3
#define COLS 3
#define SIZE (ROWS * COLS)
```

Programming Tip:
In order to extend a preprocessor directive to multiple lines; place a backslash character (\) as the last character of the line.

Look at the following program which illustrates the use of `#define` for literal text substitution:

```
#include <stdio.h>
#include <conio.h>
#define INPUT printf("\n
   Enter a number: ");
scanf("%d", &num);
#define EQUALS ==
#define PRINT1 printf("\n GREAT")
#define PRINT2 printf("\n TRY AGAIN")
#define START main() {
#define END getch();\
   return 0; }
```

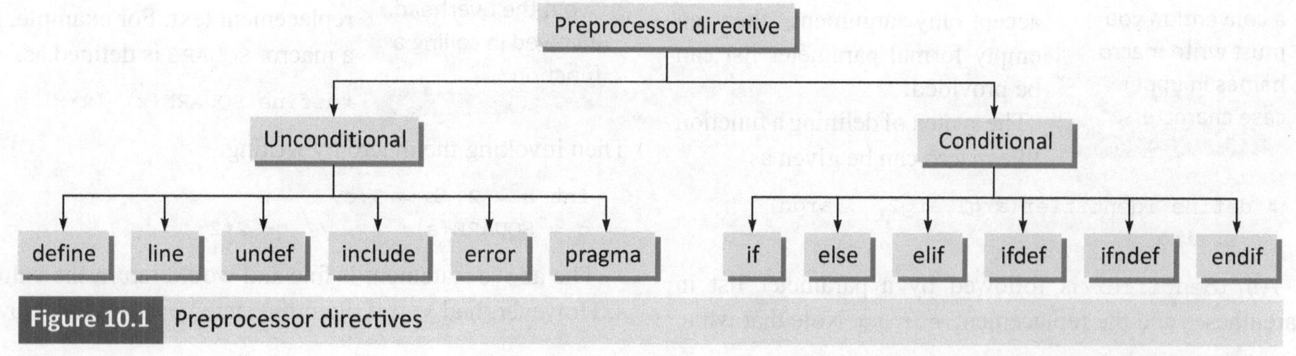

Figure 10.1 Preprocessor directives

```
START
   int num;
   INPUT
   if(num EQUALS 100)
      PRINT1;
   else
      PRINT2;
END
```

By convention, macro names are written in uppercase. This makes the program easy to read as anyone can tell at a glance which names are macros.

> **Note** An identifier is never replaced if it appears in a comment, within a string, or as part of a longer identifier.

10.3.2 Function-like Macros

Function-like macros are more complex than object-like macros. They are known as function-like macros because they are used to stimulate functions. When a function is stimulated using a macro, the macro definition replaces the function definition. The name of the macro serves as the header and the macro body serves as the function body. The name of the macro will then be used to replace the function call.

The function-like macro includes a list of parameters. References to such macros look like function calls. We have studied that when a function is called, control passes from the calling function to the called function at run time. However, when a macro is referenced, source code is inserted into the program at compile time. The parameters are replaced by the corresponding arguments, and the text is inserted into the program stream. Therefore, macros are considered to be much more efficient than functions as they avoid the overhead involved in calling a function.

> **Programming Tip:** Macro names can be in lower case characters. But as a convention you must write macro names in upper case characters.

A function-like macro definition declares the names of formal parameters within parentheses, separated by commas. In case the function-like macro does not accept any argument, then an empty formal parameter list can be provided.

The syntax of defining a function like macro can be given as

```
# define identifier(arg1,arg2,...argn)
   string
```

An `identifier` is followed by a parameter list in parentheses and the replacement `string`. Note that white space cannot separate the identifier (which is the name of the macro) and the left parenthesis of the parameter list. A comma must separate each parameter.

Invoking a Function-like Macro

A function-like macro is invoked by writing the identifier followed by a comma-separated list of arguments in parentheses. However, make sure that the number of arguments should match the number of parameters in the macro definition. One exception to this is if the parameter list in the definition ends with an ellipsis. In that case, the number of arguments in the invocation should exceed the number of parameters in the definition. The excess arguments are called *trailing arguments*.

When the preprocessor encounters a function-like macro invocation, argument substitution takes place. A parameter in the replacement code is replaced by the corresponding argument. If there are trailing arguments (as permitted by the macro definition), then they are merged with the intervening commas as if they were a single argument.

In case of nested macros (macro within another macro definition), i.e., if there are any macro invocations contained in the argument itself, they are completely replaced before the argument replaces its corresponding parameter in the replacement code.

The following line defines the macro `MUL` as having two parameters `a` and `b` and the replacement string `(a * b)`:

```
#define MUL(a,b) (a*b)
```

Look how the preprocessor changes the following statement provided it appears after the macro definition.

```
int a = 2, b = 3,c;
c = MUL(a,b);    // c = a*b;
```

> **Programming Tip:** Use macros instead of functions as macros are much more efficient than functions since they avoid the overhead involved in calling a function.

In the output of the preprocessor, the above statement would appear as: `c = a*b;`

While using function-like macros, you must use parentheses to ensure correct evaluation of replacement text. For example, if a macro `SQUARE` is defined as:

```
#define SQUARE(x) (x*x)
```

Then invoking the macro by writing,

```
int a = 2, b = 3,c;
c = SQUARE(a);      // c= 2*2;
```

The above statement is fine and would return the value 4. However, had you written the statements given below, you would have got incorrect results. For example, if had you written,

```
int a = 2, b = 3,c;
c = SQUARE(a+b);
    // c= 2+3*2+3; so c = 2+6+3 = 11
```

It is, therefore, very important that you put parentheses around each parameter in the definition to correctly evaluate an expression. So let us redefine our SQUARE macro by writing

```
#define SQUARE(x) ((x)*(x))
```

Now a statement like,

```
c = SQUARE(a+b);
```

would be expanded as

```
c = ((a + b) * (a + b));
```

Note For portability, you should not have more than 31 parameters for a macro.

10.3.3 Nesting of Macros

We can use a macro in the definition of another macro. For example, consider the following macro definitions:

```
#define SQUARE(x) ((x) * (x))
#define CUBE(x) (SQUARE(x) * (x))
#define FOURTH_POWER(x) (CUBE(x) * (x))
#define FIFTH_POWER(x) (FOURTH_POWER(x) * (x))
```

In these definitions, the preprocessor will expand each macro until all the macros do not exhaust in the text. For example, the macro CUBE will be expanded as

```
CUBE(x) => SQUARE(x) * (x) => ((x) * (x))* (x)
```

Generally, in C a macro can be nested to 31 levels.

10.3.4 Rules for Using Macros

Let us summarize some rules that must be used when specifying macro definitions and invoking them from an arbitrary place within the program.

- The macro name and the formal parameters are identifiers, so they must be specified in accordance with the rules for identifiers in the C language.
- Spaces, tabs, and comments are allowed to be used freely within a #define directive. All the spaces, tabs, and comments are replaced by a single space.
- White space in between the identifier and the left parenthesis that introduces the parameter list is not allowed.

Programming Tip: Although the preprocessor directive is usually placed before the main(), it can appear anywhere in the program code. However, if written in between, the directive will be applied only in the remainder of the source file.

- When referencing a macro, you may use comments and white-space characters freely. Comments are replaced with a single space. However, white-space characters (except leading and trailing white space) are preserved during the substitution.
- The number of arguments in the reference must match the number of parameters in the macro definition.

10.3.5 Operators Related to Macros

In this section, we will read about some operators that are directly or indirectly related to macros in C language.

Operator to Convert to String Literals

The # preprocessor operator which can be used only in a function-like macro definition is used to convert the argument that follows it to a string literal. For example:

```
#include <stdio.h>
#define PRINT(num) printf(#num " = %d", num)
main()
{
  PRINT(20);
}
The macro call expands to
printf("num" " = %d", num)
```

Finally, the preprocessor will automatically concatenate two string literals into one string. So the above statement will become

```
printf("num = %d", num)
```

Hence, the unary # operator produces a string from its operand. Consider another macro MAC which is defined as

```
#define MAC(x)    #x
```

MAC("10") gives a string literal equal to "10". Similarly, MAC("HI") would give a string literal "HI".

Programming Tip: Ensure that there is not more than one # operator in the replacement list of a macro definition because in such a case the order of evaluation of the operators is not defined.

Rules of using the # operator in a function-like macro definition

The # operator must be used in a function-like macro by following the rules mentioned below:

- A parameter following # operator in a function-like macro is converted into a string literal containing the argument passed to the macro.
- Leading and trailing white-space characters (those that appear before or after) in the argument passed to the macro are deleted.
- If the argument passed to the macro has multiple white-space characters, then they are replaced by a single-space character.
- If the argument passed to the macro contains a string literal and if a `\(backslash)` character appears within the literal, then on expansion of the macro, a second \ character is inserted before the original \.
- If the argument passed to the macro contains a `"` (double quotation mark) character, then on expansion of the macro, a \ character is inserted before the `"`.
- The conversion of an argument into a string literal occurs before macro expansion on that argument.
- If there is more than one # operator in the replacement list of a macro definition, the order of evaluation of the operators is not defined.
- If the result of the macro expansion is not a valid character string literal, the behaviour is undefined.

Merge Operator (##)

At times you need macros to generate new tokens. Using the merge operator you can concatenate two tokens into a third valid token. For example,

```
#include <stdio.h>
#define JOIN(A,B) A##B
main()
{
   int i;
   for(i = 1;i <= 5;i++)
   printf("\n HI JOIN(USER, i): ");
}
The above program would print
HI USER1
HI USER2
HI USER3
HI USER4
HI USER5
```

10.4 #include

An external file containing function, variables or macro definitions can be included as a part of our program. This avoids the effort to re-write the code that is already written. The `#include` directive is used to inform the preprocessor to treat the contents of a specified file as if those contents had already appeared in the source program at the point where the directive appears.

The `#include` directive can be used in two forms. Both the forms make the preprocessor insert the entire contents of the specified file into the source code of our program. However, the difference between the two is the way in which they search for the specified.

```
#include <filename>
```

This variant is used for system header files. When we include a file using angular brackets, a search is made for the file named `filename` in a standard list of system directories.

```
#include "filename"
```

This variant is used for header files of your own program. When we include a file using double quotes, the preprocessor searches the file named `filename` first in the directory containing the current file, then in the quote directories and then the same directories used for `<filename>`.

The filename can optionally be preceded by a directory specification. For example, you may specify the exact path by writing "c:\students\my_header.h".

Points to Remember

The preprocessor stops searching the directory as soon as it finds a file with the given name.

If a completely unambiguous path for the file is specified between double quotation marks (`" "`), then the preprocessor searches only that path specification and ignores the standard directories.

If an incomplete path is specified for the filename in double quotes, then the preprocessor first searches the parent file's directory (where a parent file is the one which contains the `#include` directive. For example, if you include a file named `file2` within a file named `file1`, `file1` is the parent file).

File inclusion can be 'nested'; i.e., a `#include` directive can appear in a file named by another `#include` directive. For example, `file1` can include `file2`, and in turn `file2` can include another file named `file3`. In this case, `file1` would be the parent of `file2` and the grandparent of `file3`.

When file inclusion is nested and when compiling is done from the command line, directory searching begins with the directories of the parent file and then proceeds through the directories of any grandparent files.

Nesting of include files can continue up to 10 levels.

10.5 #undef

As the name suggests, the `#undef` directive undefines or removes a macro name previously created with `#define`. Undefining a macro means to cancel its definition. This is done by writing `#undef` followed by the macro name that has to be undefined.

Like definition, undefinition also occurs at a specific point in the source file, and it applies starting from that point. Once a macro name is undefined, the name of the macro ceases to exist (from the point of undefinition) and the preprocessor directive behaves as if it had never been a macro name.

Therefore, the `#undef` directive removes the current definition of macro and all subsequent occurrences of macro name are ignored by the preprocessor.

If you had earlier defined a macro with parameters ,then when undefining that macro you do not have to give the parameter list. Simply specify the name of the macro.

You can also apply the `#undef` directive to a macro name that has not been previously defined. This can be done to ensure that the macro name is undefined.

The `#undef` directive when paired with a `#define` directive creates a region in a source program in which the macro has a special meaning. For example, a specific function of the source program can use certain constants to define environment specific values that do not affect the rest of the program.

The `#undef` directive can also be paired with the `#if` directive to control conditional compilation of the source program. We will read about the `#if` directive later in this section.

Consider the following example in which the `#undef` directive removes definitions of a symbolic constant and a macro.

```
#define MAX 10
#define MIN(X,Y) (((X)<(Y))?((X):(Y))
.
.
.
#undef MAX
#undef MIN
```

10.6 #line

Compile the following C program:

```
#include <stdio.h>
main()
{
   int a = 10:
   printf("%d", a);
}
```

The above program has a compile-time error because instead of a semicolon there is a colon that ends the line, `int a = 10`. So when you compile this program an error is generated during the compiling process and the compiler will show an error message with references to the name of the file where the error has happened and a line number. This makes it easy to detect the erroneous code and rectify it.

Programming Tip:
The filename in the `#line` directive must be enclosed in double quotes.

The `#line` directive enables the users to control the line numbers within the code files as well as the file name that appears when an error takes place. The syntax of `#line` directive is

```
#line line_number filename
```

Here, `line_number` is the new line number that will be assigned to the next line of code. The line numbers of successive lines will be increased one by one from this point onwards. The parameter `Filename` is an optional parameter that redefines the file name that will appear in case an error occurs. The filename must be enclosed within double quotes. If no filename is specified, then the compiler will show the original file name. For example:

```
#include <stdio.h>
main()
{
   #line 10 "Error.C"
   int a=10:
   #line 20
   printf("%d, a);
}
```

This code will generate an error that will be shown as error in file `"Error.C", lines 10 and 20. Please execute this program with the #line` directive and without the `#line` directive to visualize the difference.

Hence, we see that #line directive can be used to make the compiler provide more meaningful error messages.

> **Note** A *preprocessor line control directive* supplies line numbers for compiler messages. It tells the preprocessor to change the compiler's internally stored line number and filename to a given line number and filename.

10.7 PRAGMA DIRECTIVES

The #pragma directive is used to control the actions of the compiler in a particular portion of a program without affecting the program as a whole. You can include the pragma directive in your C program from the point where you want them to take effect. The effect of pragma will be applied from the point where it is included to the end of the compilation unit or until another pragma changes its status.

A #pragma directive is an instruction to the compiler and is usually ignored during preprocessing. The syntax of using a pragma directive can be given as

```
#pragma string
```

Here, string can be one of the instructions given to the compiler with any required parameters. Table 10.1 describes some pragma directives.

Table 10.1 Pragma directives

Instruction	Description
COPYRIGHT	To specify a copyright string
COPYRIGHT_DATE	To specify a copyright date for the copyright string
HP_SHLIB_VERSION	To create versions of a shared library routine
LOCALITY	To name a code subspace
OPTIMIZE	To turn the optimization feature on or off
OPT_LEVEL	To set the level of optimization
VERSIONID	To specify a version string

pragma COPYRIGHT

The syntax of pragma copyright can be given as:

```
#pragma COPYRIGHT "string"
```

Here, string specifies the set of characters included in the copyright message in the object file.

If no date is specified using pragma COPYRIGHT_DATE, then the current year is used in the copyright message. For example, if we write

```
#pragma COPYRIGHT "JRT Software Ltd"
```

Then the following string is placed in the object code (assuming the current year is 2011):

© Copyright JRT Software Ltd, 2011. All rights reserved. No part of this program may be photocopied, reproduced, or transmitted without prior written consent of JRT Software Ltd.

pragma COPYRIGHT_DATE

The syntax of pragma COPYRIGHT_DATE can be given as

```
#pragma COPYRIGHT_DATE "string"
```

Here, the string is a date which will be used by the COPYRIGHT pragma.

For example, consider the pragma given below

```
#pragma COPYRIGHT_DATE "1999-2011"
#pragma COPYRIGHT "JRT Software Ltd."
```

The above pragma will place the following string in the object code:

© Copyright JRT Software Ltd, 1999–2011. All rights reserved. No part of this program may be photocopied, reproduced, or transmitted without prior written consent of JRT Software Ltd.

pragma OPTIMIZE

The syntax of using the pragma OPTIMIZE can be given as

```
#pragma OPTIMIZE ON
#pragma OPTIMIZE OFF
```

The pragma optimize is basically used to turn on/off optimization in sections of a source program. However, when using this pragma you must specify one of the optimization options on the aCC command (while giving the command to compile the program), otherwise this pragma is ignored. Also remember that the pragma optimize cannot be used within a function.

For example,

```
aCC +O2 Prog.C   // Set optimization to level
                    2 for Prog.C
#pragma OPTIMIZE OFF
void Func1()
{                  // Turn off optimization for
                   this function
        .....
}
```

```
#pragma OPTIMIZE ON
void Func2()
{           // Restore optimization to level 2
    ...
}
```

pragma OPT_LEVEL

The syntax for `pragma OPT_LEVEL` which is used to set the optimization level to `1,2,3, or 4` can be given as

```
#pragma OPT_LEVEL 1
#pragma OPT_LEVEL 2
#pragma OPT_LEVEL 3
#pragma OPT_LEVEL 4
```

Like the optimization `pragma`, even this `pragma` cannot be used within a function. Finally, `OPT_LEVEL 3 and 4` are allowed only at the beginning of a file.
For example,

```
aCC -O prog.C
#pragma OPT_LEVEL 1
void Func1()
{ // Optimize Func1() at level 1.
   ...
}
#pragma OPT_LEVEL 2
void Func2()
{           // Optimize Func2() at level 2.
   ...
}
```

The kind of optimization done by the operating system at each level is beyond the scope of this book.

pragma HP_SHLIB_VERSION

The syntax for `pragma HP_SHLIB_VERSION` which is used to create different versions of a shared library routine can be given as

```
#pragma HP_SHLIB_VERSION ["]date["]
```

Here, the `date` argument is of the form `month/year`, optionally enclosed in quotes. The month must be specified using any number from `1` to `12`. The year can be specified as either the last two digits of the year `(99 for 1999)` or a full year specification `(1999)`. Here the two-digit year codes from `00` to `40` are used to represent the years from `2000` to `2040`, respectively.

The version number applies to all global symbols defined in the module's source file.

This pragma should be used only if incompatible changes are made to a source file.

pragma LOCALITY

The syntax of `pragma LOCALITY` which is used to specify a name to be associated with the code that is written to a re-locatable object module can be given as

```
#pragma LOCALITY "string"
```

Here, `string` specifies a name to be used for a code subspace. After this directive, all codes following the directive are associated with the name specified in string. The smallest scope of a unique `LOCALITY` pragma is a function.

pragma VERSIONID

The syntax of `pragma VERSIONID` can be given as

```
#pragma VERSIONID "string"
```

Here, `string` is a string of characters that is placed in the object file. For example, if we write,

```
#pragma VERSIONID "JRT Software Ltd.,
    Version 12345.A.01.10"
```

Then this pragma places the characters `JRT Software Ltd., Version 12345.A.01.10` into the object file.

pragma once

The `pragma once` specifies that the file, in which this pragma directive is specified will be included (opened) only once by the compiler in a building of a particular file. Its syntax can be given as

```
#pragma once
```

Conclusion: The pragma preprocessor directive is mainly used where each implementation of C supports some features unique to its host machine or operating system. For example, some programs may need to exercise precise control over the memory areas where data is placed or to control the way certain functions receive parameters. In such cases, `#pragma` directives provides machine- and operating system-specific features for each compiler while retaining overall compatibility with the C language.

10.8 CONDITIONAL DIRECTIVES

A conditional directive is used to instruct the preprocessor to select whether or not to include a chunk of code in the final token stream passed to the compiler. The preprocessor conditional directives can test arithmetic expressions, or whether a name is defined as a macro, etc.

Although the conditional preprocessor directive resembles an `if` statement, it is important to understand the difference between them. The condition in an `if` statement is tested when the program is executed. So the same C program may behave differently from run to run, depending on the data it is operating on. However, the condition in a preprocessing conditional directive is tested when the program is being compiled. This facilitates the programmer to allow different code to be included in the program depending on the situation at compile time.

However, in today's scenario the distinction is becoming less clear. Modern compilers usually test `if` statements during program compilation in order to check if their conditions are known not to vary at run time, and eliminate code which can never be executed. If you have such a modern compiler then the use of an `if` statement is recommended as the program becomes more readable if you use `if` statements with constant conditions.

Conditional preprocessor directives can be used in the following situations:

- A program may need to use different code depending on the machine or operating system it is to run on. This may be because in certain situations, the code for one operating system becomes erroneous on another operating system. For example, the program might refer to data types or constants that do not exist on the other system. When this happens, it is not enough to avoid executing the invalid code; as even the presence of such data types and constants will make the compiler reject the program. Therefore, in such situations the conditional preprocessing primitive is effective as with preprocessor the offending code can be effectively exercised from the program when it is not valid.
- The conditional preprocessor directive is very useful when you want to compile the same source file into two different programs. While one program might make frequent time-consuming consistency checks on its intermediate data, or print the values of those data for debugging, the other program, on the other hand can avoid such checks.
- The conditional preprocessor directives can be used to exclude code from the program whose condition is always false but is needed to keep it as a sort of comment for future reference.

10.8.1 #ifdef

`#ifdef` is the simplest sort of conditional preprocessor directive and is used to check for the existence of macro definitions. Its syntax can be given as

```
#ifdef MACRO
   controlled text
#endif
```

This block is called a conditional group. The controlled text will be included in the output of the preprocessor if and only if `MACRO` is defined. The `#ifdef` is said to be successful if the `MACRO` is defined. The controlled text will be executed only if the `#ifdef` succeeds.

Even if the `#ifdef` directive fails, the controlled text inside it is still run through initial transformations and tokenization. So, the programmer must ensure that the controlled text is lexically valid. For example, all comments and string literals inside a failing conditional group must still end properly.

As the statements under the controlled text of the `#ifdef` directive are not enclosed in braces, the `#endif` directive must be used to mark the end of the `#ifdef` block.

The following example defines a stack array if `MAX` is defined for the preprocessor.

```
#ifdef MAX
int STACK[MAX];
#endif
```

In the above example, the stack array will not be created if `MAX` had not been initially defined.

10.8.2 #ifndef

The `#ifndef` directive is the opposite of `#ifdef` directive. It checks whether the `MACRO` has not been defined or if its definition has been removed with **#undef**. `#ifndef` is successful and returns a non-zero value if the `MACRO` has not been defined. Otherwise in case of failure, that is when the `MACRO` has already been defined, `#ifndef` returns false (0).

Therefore, `#ifndef` directive is used to define code that is to be executed when a particular macro name is not defined. The general format to use `#ifndef` is the same as for `#ifdef`:

```
#ifndef MACRO
   controlled text
#endif
```

Here, `MACRO` and `controlled_text` have the same meanings they have in case of `#ifdef`. Again, the `#endif` directive is needed to mark the end of the `#ifndef` block.

You can also use `#else` directive with `#ifdef` and `#ifndef` directives like

```
#ifdef MACRO
   controlled_text1
#else
   controlled_text2
#endif
```

10.8.3 #if Directive

The #if directive is used to control the compilation of portions of a source file. If the specified condition (after the #if) has a non-zero value, the controlled text immediately following the #if directive is retained in the translation unit.

The #if directive in its simplest form consists of

```
#if condition
   controlled text
#endif
```

In the above syntax, condition is a C expression of integer type, subject to stringent restrictions, i.e., the condition may contain the following:

- Integer constants (which are all treated as either long or unsigned long).
- Character constants
- Arithmetic operators for addition, subtraction, multiplication, division, bitwise operations, shifts, comparisons, and logical operations.
- If an identifier used in the expression is not a macro and has not been currently defined, the compiler treats the identifier as though it were the constant zero.
- Macros which are actually expanded before computation of the expression's value begins.
- Defined operator can be used.
- The sizeof operator is not allowed in #if directives.
- Typecast operator is not allowed.
- Enumerated data types are not allowed.
- The condition must not perform any environmental inquiries and must remain insulated from implementation details on the target computer.
- Increment, decrement, and address operator are not allowed.

The controlled text inside the directive can include other preprocessing directives. However, any statement or any preprocessor directive in the controlled text will be executed if that branch of the conditional statement succeeds.

While using #if directive in your program, make sure that each #if directive must be matched by a closing #endif directive. Any number of #elif directives can appear between the #if and #endif directives, but at most one #else directive is allowed. However, the #else directive (if present) must be the last directive before #endif.

10.8.4 #else Directive

The #else directive can be used within the controlled text of a #if directive to provide alternative text to be used if the condition is false. The general format of #else directive can be given as

```
#if condition
      Controlled text1
#else
      Controlled text2
#endif
```

If condition evaluates to a non-zero value then controlled text1 becomes active and the #else directive acts like a failing conditional and the controlled text2 is ignored. On similar grounds, if the condition fails or evaluates to zero, then controlled text2 is considered included and controlled text1 is ignored.

The #else directive is usually used to delimit alternative source text to be compiled if the condition tested for in the corresponding #if, #ifdef, or #ifndef directive is false. However, a #else directive is optional.

10.8.5 #elif Directive

The #elif directive is used when there are more than two possible alternatives. The #elif directive like the #else directive is embedded within the #if directive and has the following syntax:

```
#if condition
      Controlled text1
#elif new_condition
      Controlled text2
#else
      Controlled text3
#endif
```

Here, when the if condition is non-zero then controlled text1 becomes active and the #elif and #else directives act like a failing conditional and the controlled text2 and controlled text3 are ignored. On similar grounds, if the condition fails or evaluates to zero, then new_condition is evaluated. If it is true controlled text2 is considered included and controlled text1 and controlled text3 is ignored. Otherwise, if condition and new_condition both are false then #else directive becomes active and controlled text3 is included.

The #elif directive is same as the combined use of the else-if statements. The #elif directive is used to delimit alternative source lines to be compiled if condition in the corresponding #if, #ifdef, #ifndef, or another #elif directive is false and if the new_condition in the #elif line is true. An #elif directive is optional.

```
#define MAX 10
#if OPTION == 1
    int STACK[MAX];
#elif OPTION == 2
    float STACK[MAX];
#elif OPTION == 3
    char STACK[MAX];
#else
    printf("\n INVALID OPTION");
#endif
```

The #elif does not require a matching '#endif' of its own. Every #elif directive includes a condition to be tested. The text following the #elif is processed only if the #if condition fails and the #elif condition succeeds.

In the above example, we have used more than one #elif directives in the same #if-#endif group. The text after each #elif is processed only if the #elif condition succeeds after the original #if and any previous #elif directives within it have failed.

If the condition specified with #if directive is false and if either no #elif directives appear or no #elif condition evaluated to true, then the preprocessor selects the text block after the #else clause. If the #else directive is also missing then no controlled text is selected.

10.8.6 #endif Directive

The general syntax of #endif preprocessor directive which is used to end the conditional compilation directive can be given as

```
#endif
```

The #endif directive ends the scope of the #if, #ifdef, #ifndef, #else, or #elif directives. The number of #endif directives that is required depends on whether the elif or #else directive is used. For example, consider the examples given below which although perform the same task, requires different number of #endif directives.

```
#if condition
    Controlled text1
#elif new_condition
Controlled text2
#endif
```

OR

```
#if condition
    Controlled text1
#else
#if new_condition
Controlled text2
#endif
#endif
```

10.9 defined OPERATOR

We have seen that we can check the existence of a macro by using #ifdef directive. However, there is another way to do the same. The alternative to #ifdef directive is to use the defined unary operator. The defined operator has one of the following forms:

```
defined MACRO

    or

defined (MACRO)
```

The above expression evaluates to 1 if MACRO is defined and to 0 if it is not. The defined operator helps you to check for macro definitions in one concise line without having to use many #ifdef or #ifndef directives. For example, consider the following macro checks:

```
#ifdef MACRO1
    #ifdef MACRO2
        Controlled text1
#else
    printf("\n MACROS not defined");
#endif
```

OR

```
#if defined (MACRO1) && defined (MACRO2)
    Controlled text1
#else
    printf("\n MACROS not defined");
#endif
```

As evident from the above example, the defined operator can be combined in any logical expression using the C logical operators. However, this operator can only be used in the evaluated expression of an #if or #elif preprocessor directive.

10.10 #error DIRECTIVE

The #error directive is used to produce compiler time error messages. The syntax of this directive is

```
#error string
```

The error messages include the argument string. The #error directive is usually used to detect programming inconsistencies and violation of constraints during preprocessing. When #error directive is encountered, the compilation process terminates and the message specified in string is printed to stderr. For example, consider the piece of codes given below which illustrates error processing during preprocessing:

```
#ifndef SQUARE
#error MACRO not defined.
#endif

#ifndef VERSION
   #error Version number is not specified.
   #endif

#ifdef WINDOWS
     ... /* Windows specific code */
#else
     #error "This code works only on WINDOWS
   operating system"
#endif
```

The #error directive causes the preprocessor to report a fatal error.

Here the string need not be enclosed within double quotes. It is a good programming practice to enclose the string in double quotes. The #error directive is a very important directive mainly because of two reasons:

- First, it helps you to determine whether a given line is being compiled or not.
- Second, when used within a heavily parameterized body of code, it helps to ensure that a particular MACRO has been defined.

Besides the #error directive, there is another directive—#warning, which causes the preprocessor to issue a warning and continue preprocessing. The syntax of #warning directive is same as that of #error.

```
#warning string
```

Here, string is the warning message that has to be displayed. One important place where #warning directive can be used is in obsolete header files. You can display a message directing the user to the header file which should be used instead.

10.11 PREDEFINED MACRO NAMES

There are certain predefined macros that are readily available for use by the C programmers. A list of such predefined macros is given in Table 10.2.

Table 10.2 Predefined macros

Macro	Value
__LINE__	A decimal integer constant which specifies the current line number in the source file being compiled. We have already studied that the line number can be altered with a #line directive.
__FILE__	A string literal which specifies the name of the source file being compiled.
__DATE__	Specifies the date of compilation of the current source file. It is a string literal of the form *mm dd yyyy*.
__TIME__	A string literal in the form "hh:mm:ss" which is used to specify the time at which the compilation process began.
_ STDC_	Specifies full conformance with ANSI C standard.
TIMESTAMP	A string literal in the form *Ddd Mmm Date hh:mm:ss yyyy*, where *Ddd* is the abbreviated day of the week and *Date* is an integer from 1 to 31. It is used to specify the date and time of the last modification of the current source file.

```
#include <stdio.h>
 void main(void)
 {
        printf("\n Current File's Path Name:
%s", __FILE__);
        printf("\n Line Number in the
 current file: %d", __LINE__);
        printf("\n Date of Compilation: %s",
 __DATE__);
```

```
    printf("\n Time of Compilation: %s",
__TIME__);
    #ifdef __STDC__
        printf("\n Your C compiler
conforms with the ANSI C standard");
    #else
        printf("\n You C compiler
doesn't conform with the ANSI C
standard");
    #endif
}
```

POINTS TO NOTE

- The preprocessor is a program that processes the source code before it passes through the compiler.
- Preprocessor directives are lines included in the C program that are not program statements but directives for the preprocessor. The preprocessor directives are always preceded by a hash sign (#) and are executed before the actual compilation of program code begins.
- To define preprocessor macros, we use `#define` directive. An object-like macro is a simple identifier which will be replaced by a code fragment. They are usually used to give symbolic names to numeric constants. Function-like macros are used to stimulate functions.
- The merge operator is used to concatenate two tokens into a third valid token.
- The `#include` directive is used to inform the preprocessor to treat the contents of a specified file as if those contents had appeared in the source program at the point where the directive appears.
- `#undef` directive removes a macro name previously created with `#define`. The `#line` directive enables the users to control the line numbers within the code files as well as the file name that appears when an error takes place.
- The `#pragma` directive is used to control the actions of the compiler in a particular portion of a program without affecting the program as a whole.
- A conditional directive is used to instruct the preprocessor to select whether or not to include a chunk of code in the final token stream passed to the compiler.
- `#ifdef` is used to check for the existence of macro definitions. The `#ifndef` directive is the opposite of `#ifdef` directive. It checks whether the MACRO has not been defined or if its definition has been removed with `#undef`. The `#if` directive is used to control the compilation of portions of a source file.
- The `#else` directive is used within the controlled text of a `#if` directive in order to provide alternative text to be used if the condition is false. The `#elif` directive is used when there are more than two possible alternatives. The `#elif` directive like the `#else` directive is embedded within the `#if` directive.
- The `#error` directive is used to produce compile-time error messages.

GLOSSARY

Function-like macro It is used to stimulate functions.

Object-like macro It is a simple identifier which will be replaced by a code fragment. They are usually used to give symbolic names to numeric constants.

Preprocessor It is a program that processes the source code before it passes through the compiler.

Preprocessor directives These are lines included in the C program that are not program statements but directives for the preprocessor. They are always preceded by a hash sign (#).

Self-referential macro A macro whose name appears in its definition.

Trailing arguments A function-like macro definition declares the names of formal parameters within parentheses, separated by commas. If the number of arguments in the invocation exceeds the number of parameters in the definition, the excess arguments are called trailing arguments.

EXERCISES

Fill in the Blanks

1. ________ is a program that processes the source code before it passes through the compiler.
2. ________ operates under the control of preprocessor directive.
3. Before the source code is passed through the compiler, it is examined by the preprocessor for any ________.
4. ________ are lines included in the program that are not program statements but directives for the preprocessor.
5. The ________ is also known as a macro.
6. The `#define` directive is used to ________.
7. ________ is used to give symbolic names to numeric constants.
8. Trailing arguments are ________.
9. ________ preprocessor operator is used to convert the argument that follows it to a string literal.
10. The ________ operator is used to concatenate two tokens into a third valid token.
11. When we include a file using ________, a search is made for the file in a standard list of system directories.
12. File inclusion can be nested to ________ levels.
13. The `#undef` directive removes a macro name previously created with ________.
14. The ________ directive is used to control the actions of the compiler in a particular portion of a program without affecting the program as a whole.
15. ________ is used to instruct the preprocessor to select whether or not to include a chunk of code in the final token stream passed to the compiler.
16. Each `#if` directive must be matched by the ________ directive.
17. The `#elif` directive and the `#else` directive are embedded within the ________ directive.
18. When ________ directive is encountered, the compilation process terminates.
19. ________ causes the preprocessor to issue a warning and continue preprocessing.
20. ________ specifies full conformance with `ANSI C` standard.

Multiple Choice Questions

1. The preprocessor directives must be preceded by which symbol?
   (a) * (b) &
   (c) @ (d) #
2. In order to extend a preprocessor directive to multiple lines; which character is placed as the last character of the line?
   (a) \ (b) /
   (c) ^ (d) !
3. Which directive is used to control the line numbers within the code files as well as the file name that appears when an error takes place?
   (a) `#pragma` (b) `#define`
   (c) `#line` (d) `#filename`
4. Which directive is used to check for the existence of macro definitions?
   (a) `#if` (b) `#define`
   (c) `#ifdef` (d) `#undef`
5. Choose the operator which can be used in the conditional expression of `#if` directive.
   (a) defined (b) sizeof
   (c) typecast (d) address
6. Which predefined macro is used to specify the date and time of the last modification of the current source file?
   (a) `_TIME_` (b) `_DATE_`
   (c) `_TIMESTAMP_` (d) `_STDC_`

State True or False

1. Preprocessor directives are executable statements in a C program.
2. The preprocessor is executed before the actual compilation of program code begins.
3. Preprocessor directives can only be one line long.
4. Preprocessor directives can appear anywhere in the program.
5. Object-like macros takes one argument.
6. A macro definition can include an expression.
7. It is compulsory to write macro names in uppercase.
8. The # preprocessor operator can be used only in a function-like macro definition.
9. The conversion of an argument into a string literal occurs before macro expansion on that argument.
10. File inclusion cannot be nested.
11. While undefining a macro, you have to specify the parameters, if any.

EXERCISES

12. `#ifdef` checks whether the MACRO has not been defined or if its definition has been removed with `#undef`.
13. We can use enumerated data types in the expressions of conditional directives.
14. The `#endif` directive is used to end the conditional compilation directive.
15. `_TIMESTAMP_` is used to specify the time at which the compilation process began.

Review Questions

1. What do you understand by the term preprocessor directive?
2. Can we have a C program that does not use any preprocessor directive?
3. Why should we incorporate preprocessor directives in our programs? Give at least one example to support your answer.
4. Explain the importance of the `#define` preprocessor directive.
5. How are trailing arguments, if any, handled by the preprocessor?
6. What happens when the argument passed to the macro has multiple white-space characters?
7. Why should we not use more than one # operator in the replacement list of a macro definition?
8. How can `#include` directive be used in your C program? Illustrate with respect to both the forms available for usage.
9. File inclusion can be nested. Justify this statement with the help of a suitable example.
10. Can the `#undef` directive be applied to a macro name that has not been previously defined? If yes, why?
11. Explain in detail the `#pragma` directive.
12. Write a short note on conditional directives.
13. Compare an `if` statement with the #if directive.
14. In which situations will you recommend to use conditional directives in a program?
15. Comment on the restrictions imposed on the conditional expression of `#if` directive.
16. Give the importance of `#error` and `#warning` directive.
17. Give the rules for using macros.
18. Enumerate the rules for using the # operator in a function-like macro definition.

ANNEXURE 7

A7.1 INTRODUCTION TO DATA STRUCTURES

A data structure is nothing but an arrangement of data either in computer's memory or on the disk storage. Some common examples of data structure include arrays, linked lists, queues, stacks, binary trees, and hash tables. Data structures are widely applied in areas such as

- Compiler design
- Operating system
- Statistical analysis package
- Database Management System (DBMS)
- Numerical analysis
- Simulation
- Artificial intelligence
- Graphics

While studying DBMS you will realize that the major data structures used in the Network data model are graphs, Hierarchical data model are trees, and RDBMS are arrays.

A7.2 DIFFERENT TYPES OF DATA STRUCTURES

There are a variety of data structures that we can have in C language. In this section, we will just have an introduction to them and in further chapters we will learn about them in detail.

Arrays An array is a collection of similar data elements. These data elements have the same data type. The elements of the array are stored in consecutive memory locations and are referenced by an index (also known as the subscript). Arrays are declared using the following syntax:

```
type name[size];
```

For example

```
int marks[1];
```

This statement declares an array `marks` that contains 10 elements. In C, the array index starts from zero. This means that the array `marks` will contain 10 elements in all. The first element will be stored in `marks[0]`, second element in `marks[1]`, and so on. Therefore, the last element, i.e., the 10th element will be stored in `marks [9]`. In memory, the array will be stored as shown in Fig. A7.1.

The limitations with arrays are as follows:

- Arrays are of fixed size.
- Data elements are stored in continuous memory locations which may not be available always.
- Adding and removing of elements is difficult because of shifting the elements from their positions.

However, these limitations can be solved by using the linked list. We have already read about arrays in Chapter 5.

Linked lists Linked list is a very flexible and dynamic data structure in which elements can be added to or deleted from anywhere at will. In contrast to using static arrays, a programmer need not worry about how many elements will be stored in the linked list. This feature enables the programmers to write robust programs which require much less maintenance.

In a linked list, each element (called a *node*) is allocated space as it is added to the list. Every node in the list points to the next node in the list. Therefore, in a linked list every node contains two types of information:

- The value of the node or any other data that corresponds to that node.
- A pointer or link to the next node in the list.

The last node in the list contains a `NULL` pointer to indicate that it is the end or *tail* of the list. Since memory for a node is dynamically allocated when it is added to the list, the total number of nodes that may be added to a list is limited only by the amount of memory available. Figure A7.2 shows a linked list of seven nodes.

1st element	2nd element	3rd element	4th element	5th element	6th element	7th element	8th element	9th element	10th element
marks[0]	marks[1]	marks[2]	marks[3]	marks[4]	marks[5]	marks[6]	marks[7]	marks[8]	marks[9]

Figure A7.1 Memory representation of an array of 10 elements

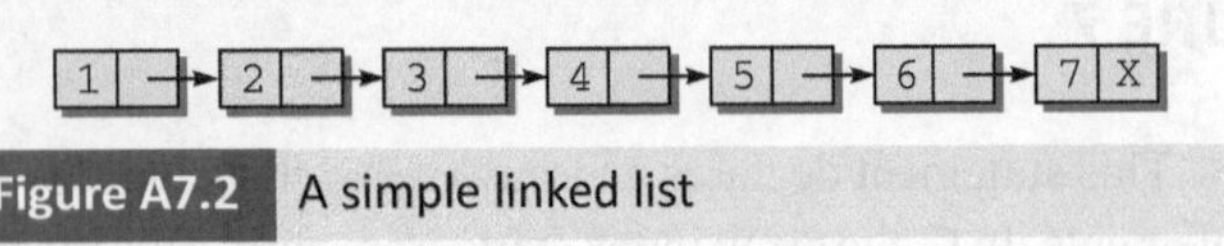

Figure A7.2 A simple linked list

Advantage: Provides quick insert and delete operations.
Disadvantage: Slower search operation and requires more memory space.
We will read more about linked lists in Chapter 11.

Stacks In computer memory, stacks can be represented as a linear array. Every stack has a variable `TOP` associated with it. `TOP` is used to store the address of the topmost element of the stack. It is this position from where the element will be added or deleted. There is another variable `MAX` which will be used to store the maximum number of elements that the stack can store.
If `TOP = NULL`, then it indicates that the stack is empty and if `TOP = MAX`, then the stack is full.

The stack in Fig. A7.3 shows that `TOP = 4`, so insertions and deletions will be done at this position. Here, the stack can store at most 10 elements where the indices range from 0 to 9. In this stack, five more elements can be stored.

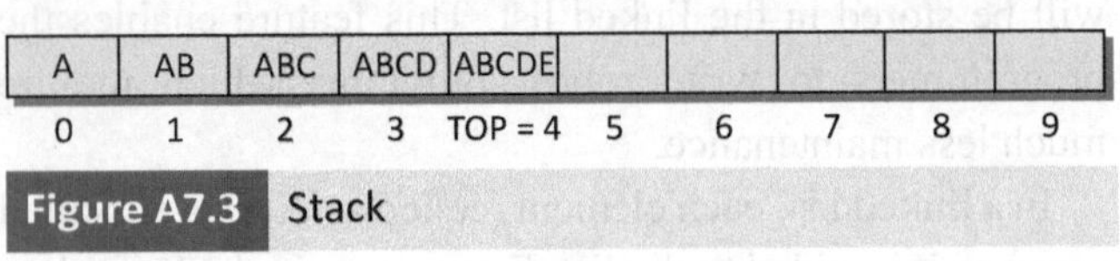

Figure A7.3 Stack

A stack has three basic operations: `push`, `pop`, and `peek`. The `push` operation adds an element to the top of the stack. The pop operation removes the element from the top of the stack. Finally, the peek operation returns the value of the topmost element of the stack.

However, before inserting an element in the stack we must check for *overflow* condition. An overflow will occur when we will try to insert an element into a stack that is already full.

Similarly, before deleting an element from the stack, we must check for *underflow* condition. An underflow condition occurs when we try to delete an element from a stack that is already empty. If `TOP = -1`, it indicates that there is no element in the stack.

Advantage: Last-in, first-out access `(LIFO)`

Disadvantage: Slow access to other elements

Queue A queue is a `FIFO` (First In First Out) data structure in which the element that inserted first is the first one to be taken out. The elements in a queue are added at one end called the `rear` and removed from the other end called `front`. Similar to stacks, queues can be implemented using either arrays or linked lists.

Every queue will have `front` and `rear` variables that will point to the position from where deletions and insertions can be done, respectively. Consider a queue as given in Fig. A7.4.

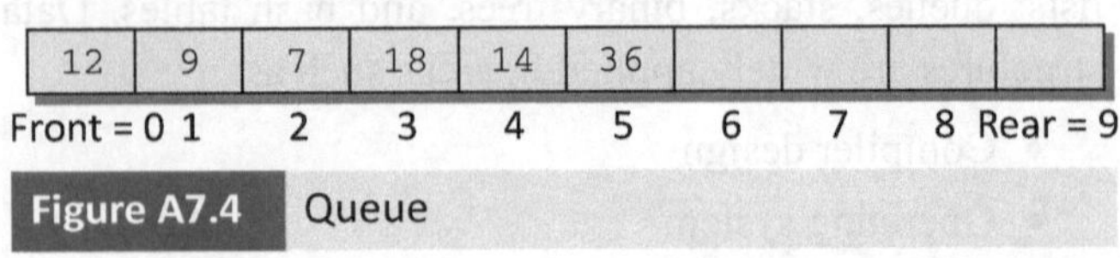

Figure A7.4 Queue

Here, `front = 0` and `rear = 5`. If we want to add one more value in the list say, if we want to add another element with value 45, then `rear` would be incremented by 1 and the value would be stored at the position pointed by `rear`. The queue after addition would be as shown in Fig. A7.5.

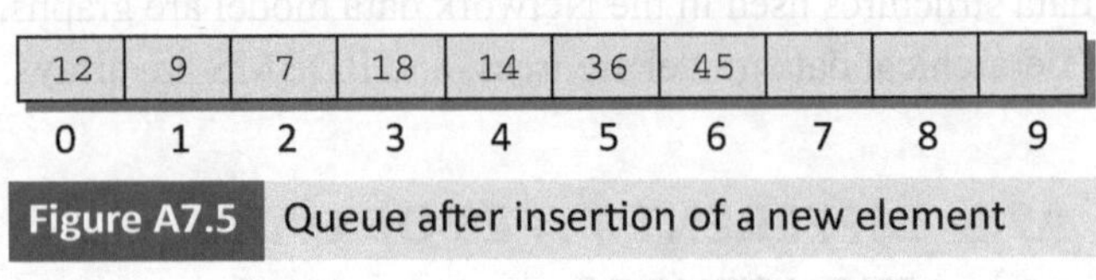

Figure A7.5 Queue after insertion of a new element

Here, `front = 0` and `rear = 6`. Every time a new element has to be added, we will repeat the same procedure.

Now, if we want to delete an element from the queue, then the value of `front` will be incremented. Deletions are done from only this end of the queue. The queue after deletion will be as shown in Fig. A7.6.

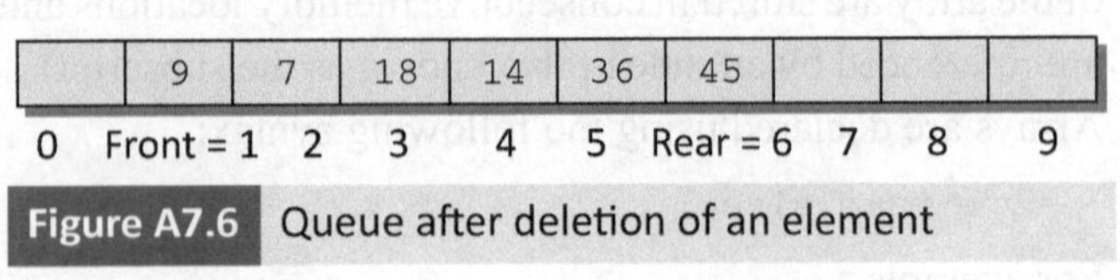

Figure A7.6 Queue after deletion of an element

However, before inserting an element in the queue we must check for overflow conditions. An overflow will occur when we try to insert an element into a queue that is already full. When `rear = MAX - 1`, where `MAX` is the size of the queue, i.e., `MAX` specifies the maximum number of elements in the queue. Note that we have written `MAX - 1`, because the index starts from 0.

Similarly, before deleting an element from the queue, we must check for underflow condition. An underflow condition occurs when we try to delete an element from a queue that is already empty. If `front = -1 and rear = -1`, this means there is no element in the queue.

Advantage: Provides first-in, first-out data access.

Disadvantage: Slow access to other items.

Trees A binary tree is a data structure which is defined as a collection of elements called nodes. Every node contains a `left pointer`, a `right pointer`, and a data element. Every binary tree has a root element pointed by a root pointer. The root element is the topmost node in the tree. If `root = NULL`, then it means the tree is empty.

Figure A7.7 shows a binary tree. If the root node `R` is not `NULL`, then the two trees T_1 and T_2 are called the left and right subtrees of `R`. If T_1 is non-empty, then T_1 is said to be the left successor of `R`. Likewise, if T_2 is non-empty, then it is called the right successor of `R`.

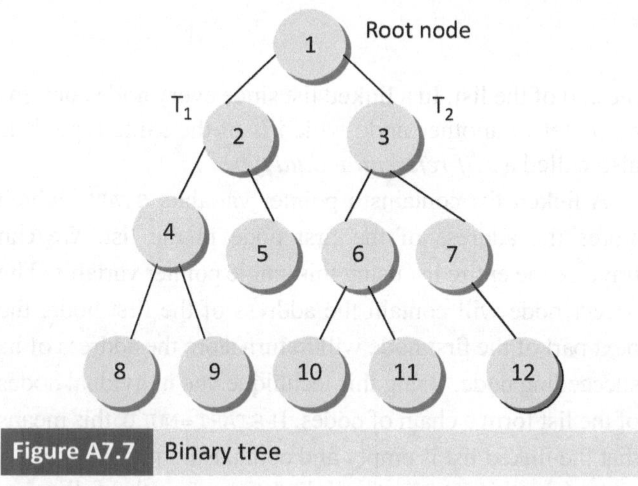

Figure A7.7 Binary tree

In Fig. A7.7, node 2 is the `left successor` and node 3 is the `right successor` of the root node 1. The `left subtree` of the root node consists of the nodes 2, 4, 5, 8, and 9. Similarly, the `right subtree` of the root node consists of nodes 3, 6, 7, 10, 11, and 12.

Advantages: Provides quick search, insert, and delete operations.

Disadvantage: Complicated deletion algorithm.

Graphs A graph is an abstract data structure that is used to implement the graph concept in mathematics. A graph is basically a collection of vertices (also called nodes) and edges that connect these vertices. A graph is often viewed as a generalization of the tree structure, where instead of having a purely parent-to-child relationship between the tree nodes, any kind of complex relationships between the nodes can be represented.

In trees, the nodes can have many children but only one parent, a graph on the other hand doesn't have such kinds of restrictions. Figure A7.8 shows a graph with five nodes.

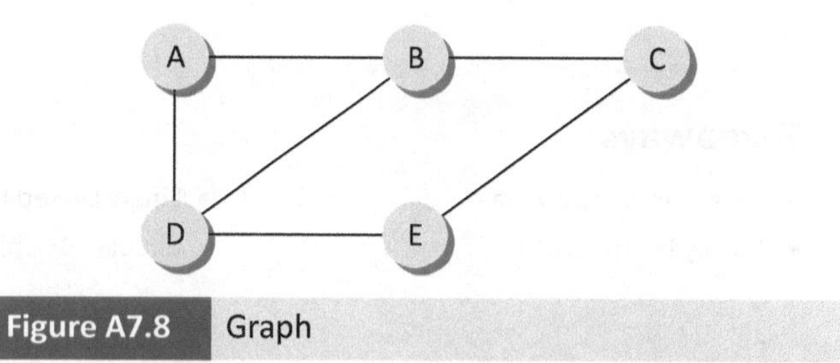

Figure A7.8 Graph

Every node in the graph may be considered to represent a city and the edges connecting the nodes could represent the roads. A graph can also be used to represent a computer network where the nodes are workstations and the edges are the network connections. Graphs have so many applications in computer science and mathematics that several algorithms have been written to perform the standard graph operations such as searching the graph and finding the shortest path between nodes of a graph.

Unlike trees, graphs do not have any root node.

Rather, every node in the graph can be connected with any other node in the graph. When two nodes are connected via an edge, the two nodes are known as neighbours. For example, node `A` above has two neighbours: `B and D`.

Advantages: Best models real-world situations.

Disadvantages: Some algorithms are slow and very complex.

CHAPTER 11

Linked Lists

Takeaways

- Linked List versus Arrays
- Doubly Linked List
- Singly Linked List
- Circular Doubly Linked List
- Circular Linked List
- Header Linked List

11.1 INTRODUCTION

A *linked list*, in simple terms, is a linear collection of data elements. These data elements are called *nodes*. Linked lists are data structures which can be used to implement other data structures. Thus, they act as building blocks for other data structures such as stacks, queues, and their variations. A linked list can be perceived as a train or a sequence of nodes in which each node contains one or more data fields and a pointer to the next node. In Fig. 11.1, we see a linked list in which every node contains two parts—an integer and a pointer to the next node.

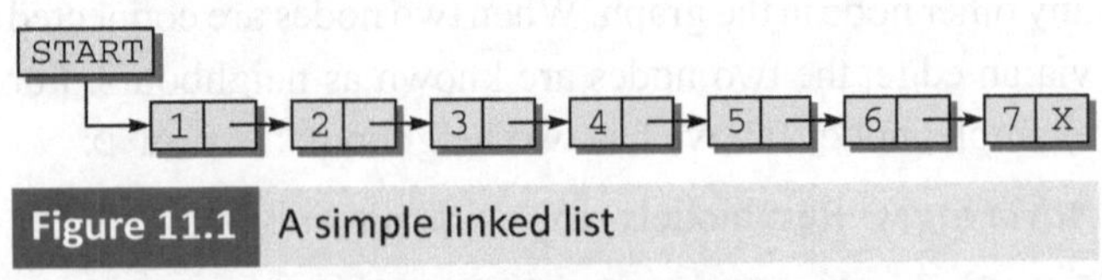

Figure 11.1 A simple linked list

The left part of the node which contains data may include a simple data type, an array, or a structure. The right part of the node contains a pointer to the next node (or the address of the next node in sequence). The last node will have no next node connected to it, so it will store a special value called NULL. In Fig. 11.1, the NULL pointer is represented by X. However, when we do programming we usually define NULL as −1. Hence, a NULL pointer denotes the end of the list. In a linked list since every node contains a pointer to another node which is of the same type, it is also called a *self-referential data type*.

A linked list contains a pointer variable, START, which stores the address of the first node in the list. We can traverse the entire list using this single pointer variable. The START node will contain the address of the first node; the next part of the first node will in turn store the address of its succeeding node. Using this technique, the individual nodes of the list form a chain of nodes. If START=NULL, this means that the linked list is empty and contains no nodes.

In C, we implement a linked list using the following code:

```
struct node
{
  int data;
  struct node *next;
};
```

Let us see how a linked list is maintained in memory. In order to form a linked list we need a structure called node that has two fields—DATA and NEXT, where DATA will store the information part and NEXT will store the address of the next node in the sequence. Consider Fig. 11.2.

From the figure we can see that the variable START is used to store the address of the first node. Here, in this example, START=1, so the first data is stored at address

1, which is 'H'. The corresponding variable NEXT stores the address of the next node, which is 4. So, we will look at address 4 to fetch the next data item. The second data element obtained from address 4 is 'E'. Again, we see the corresponding NEXT, to go to the next node. From the entry in the NEXT field, we get the next address, i.e., 7 and fetch 'L' as the data. We repeat this procedure until we reach a position where the NEXT entry contains –1 or NULL, as this would denote the end of the linked list. When we traverse fields the DATA and NEXT fields in this manner, we will finally see that the linked list in this example stores characters which when put together form the word "HELLO".

START = 1

	DATA	NEXT
1	H	4
2		
3		
4	E	7
5		
6		
7	L	8
8	L	10
9		
10	O	–1

Figure 11.2 START pointing to the first element of the linked list in memory

This figure shows a chunk of memory locations whose addresses range from 1 to 10. The shaded portion contains data for other applications. Remember that the nodes of a linked list need not be in consecutive memory locations. In our example, the nodes for the linked list are stored at addresses 1, 4, 7, 8, and 10.

11.2 LINKED LISTS VERSUS ARRAYS

An array is linear collection of data elements and a linked list is a linear collection of nodes. But unlike an array, a linked list does not store its nodes in consecutive memory locations. Another point of difference between an array and a linked list is that a linked list does not allow random access of data. Nodes in a linked list can be accessed only in a sequential manner, but like an array, insertions and deletions can be done at any point in the list in constant time.

Another advantage of a linked list over an array is that, we can add any number of elements in the list. This is not possible in case of an array. For example, if we declare an array as `int marks[10]`, then the array can store a maximum of ten data elements and not even one more than that. There is no such restriction in the case of a linked list.

Thus, linked lists provide an efficient way of storing related data and perform basic operations such as insertion, deletion, and updating of information at the cost of the extra space required for storing the address of the next node.

11.3 MEMORY ALLOCATION AND DEALLOCATION FOR A LINKED LIST

We have seen how a linked list is represented in memory. If we want to add a node to an already existing linked list, we will first find free space in the memory and then use it to store the information. For example, consider the linked list given in Figs 11.3(a) and (b). The linked list contains the roll numbers of the students, marks obtained by them in Biology, and finally a NEXT field which stores the address of the next node in sequence. Now, if a new student joins the class and is asked to appear for the same test that the other students had given, then the new student's marks should also be recorded in the linked list. For this purpose, we will find a free space and store the information there. If, the grey shaded portions show free spaces, then we see that we have 4 locations of memory available and we can use any one of them to store our data.

START = 1 (Biology)

	Roll No	Marks	Next
1	S01	78	2
2	S02	84	3
3	S03	45	5
4			
5	S04	98	7
6			
7	S05	55	8
8	S06	34	10
9			
10	S07	90	11
11	S08	87	12
12	S09	86	13
13	S10	67	15
14			
15	S11	56	–1

Figure 11.3(a) Memory representation of a linked list storing the marks obtained by students in Biology

START: 1 (Biology)

Address	Roll No	Marks	Next
1	S01	78	2
2	S02	84	3
3	S03	45	5
4	S12	75	–1
5	S04	98	7
6			
7	S05	55	8
8	S06	34	10
9			
10	S07	90	11
11	S08	87	12
12	S09	86	13
13	S10	67	15
14			
15	S11	56	4

Figure 11.3(b) Memory representation of a linked list storing the marks obtained by students in Biology after the new student's record has been added

Now the big question is who will take care of the memory—which part of the memory is available and which part is occupied. When we delete a node from a linked list then who will change the status of the memory occupied by it from occupied to available. The answer is the operating system. Discussing the mechanism of how the operating system does all this is out of the scope of this book. So, in simple language, we can say that the computer takes care of this without any intervention from the user or the programmer. As a programmer, you just have to take care of the code to perform insertions and deletions in the list.

However, to have an overview of the mechanism, we will briefly discuss the basic concept. The computer maintains a list of all free memory cells. This list of available space is called the *free pool*.

We have seen that every linked list has a pointer variable `START` which stores the address of the first node of the list. Likewise, for the free pool (which is a linked list of all free memory cells), we have a pointer variable `AVAIL` which stores the address of the first free space. Let us revisit the memory representation of the linked list storing the students' marks in Biology. We have another pointer variable `AVAIL` here which stores the address of the first free space.

Now, when a new student's record has to be added, the memory address pointed by `AVAIL` is taken and used to store the desired information. After the insertion, the address of the next available free space is stored in `AVAIL`. For example, in Fig. 11.4, when the first free memory space is utilized for inserting the new node, the `AVAIL` pointer will be set to contain address 6.

This was all about inserting a new node in an already existing linked list. Now we will talk about deleting a node or the entire linked list. When we delete a particular node from an existing linked list or delete the entire linked list for some reason, the space occupied by it must be given back to the free pool so that the memory can be reused by some other program that needs memory space.

The operating system does this task of adding the freed memory to the free pool. The operating system will perform this operation whenever it finds the CPU idle or whenever programs fall short of memory. The operating system scans through all the memory cells and marks the cells being used by some other programs. Then, it collects all those cells which are not being used and adds their address to the free pool so that they can be reused by the programs. This process is called garbage collection. The whole process of collecting unused memory cells (garbage collection) is transparent to the programmer.

START: 1 (Biology)
AVAIL: 4

Address	Roll No	Marks	Next
1	S01	78	2
2	S02	84	3
3	S03	45	5
4			6
5	S04	98	7
6			9
7	S05	55	8
8	S06	34	10
9			12
10	S07	90	11
11	S08	87	14
12			13
13			16
14	S09	86	15
15	S10	67	17
16			18
17	S11	56	–1
18			19
19			–1

Figure 11.4 Memory representation of a linked list with AVAIL and START pointers

11.4 DIFFERENT TYPES OF LINKED LISTS

There are different types of linked lists which we will discuss in the following sections. These are

- Singly linked list
- Doubly linked list
- Circular linked list
- Circular doubly linked list
- Header linked list

11.5 SINGLY LINKED LIST

A singly linked list is the simplest type of linked list in which every node contains some data and a pointer to the next node of the same data type. By saying that the node contains a pointer to the next node we mean that the node stores the address of the next node in sequence. Fig. 11.5 shows a singly linked list.

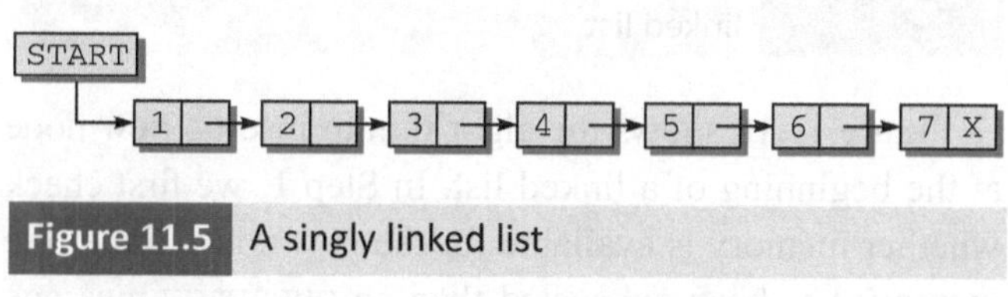

Figure 11.5 A singly linked list

A singly linked list allows traversal of data only in one way.

11.5.1 Traversing a Singly Linked List

Traversing a linked list means accessing the nodes of the list in order to perform some operations on them. Remember, a linked list always contains a pointer variable START which stores the address of the first node of the list. The end of the list is marked by storing NULL or -1 in the NEXT field of the last node. For traversing the linked list, we also make use of another pointer variable PTR, which will point to the node that is currently being accessed. The algorithm to traverse a linked list is shown in Fig. 11.6.

In this algorithm, we first initialize PTR with the address of the START. So now, PTR points to the first node of the linked list. Then in Step 2, a while loop is executed which is repeated till PTR processes the last node, that is, until it encounters NULL. In Step 3, we apply the process (for ex, print) to the current node, i.e., the node pointed by PTR. In Step 4, we move to the next node by making the PTR variable point to the node whose address is stored in the NEXT field.

```
Step 1: [INITIALIZE] SET PTR = START
Step 2: Repeat Steps 3 and 4 while PTR != NULL
Step 3:                 Apply process to PTR->DATA
Step 4:                 SET PTR = PTR->NEXT
        [END OF LOOP]
Step 5: EXIT
```

Figure 11.6 Algorithm to traverse a linked list

11.5.2 Searching a Linked List

Searching a linked list means to find a particular element in the linked list. As already discussed, a linked list consists of a node which is divided into two parts—the DATA part and the NEXT part, where DATA stores the relevant information and NEXT stores the address of the next node in sequence. So obviously, searching means finding whether a given value is present in the information part of the node or not. If it is present, the searching algorithm returns the address of the node that contains that value.

There are two variants of the searching algorithm. While one algorithm is used to search for a value in a sorted linked list, the other works for an unsorted linked list. Let us first have a look at the algorithm used to search for a value in an unsorted linked list given in Fig. 11.7.

```
Step 1: [INITIALIZE] SET PTR = START
Step 2: Repeat Step 3 while PTR != NULL
Step 3:         IF VAL = PTR->DATA
                     SET POS = PTR
                     Go To Step 5
                ELSE
                     SET PTR = PTR->NEXT
                [END OF IF]
        [END OF LOOP]
Step 4: SET POS = NULL
Step 5: EXIT
```

Figure 11.7 Algorithm to search an unsorted linked list

In Step 1, we initialize a pointer variable PTR with START. In Step 2, a while loop is executed which will compare every node's DATA with the VAL for which the search is being made. If the search is successful, that is, the VAL has been found, then the address of that node is stored in POS and the control jumps to the last statement of the algorithm. However, if the search is unsuccessful, `POS` is set to `NULL`, which indicates that the `VAL` is not present in the linked list.

Consider the linked list shown in Fig. 11.8. If we have `VAL = 4`, then the flow of the algorithm can be explained as shown in this figure.

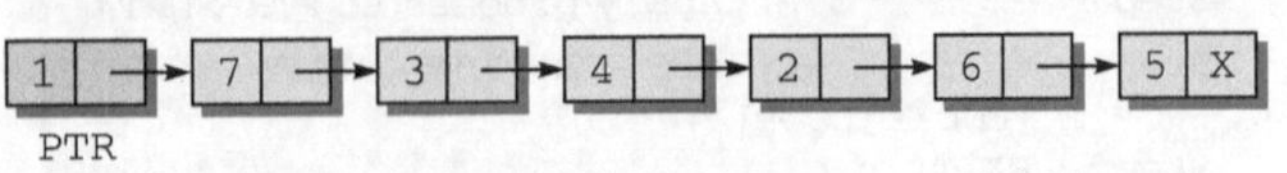

Here, `PTR->DATA = 1`. Since `PTR->DATA != 4`, We move to the next node because `PTR = PTR->NEXT`.

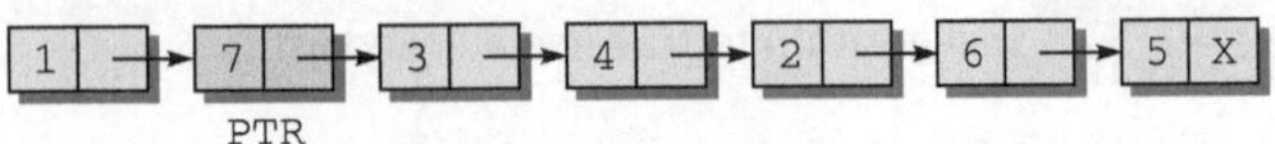

Here, `PTR->DATA = 7`. Since `PTR->DATA != 4`, We move to the next node because `PTR = PTR->NEXT`.

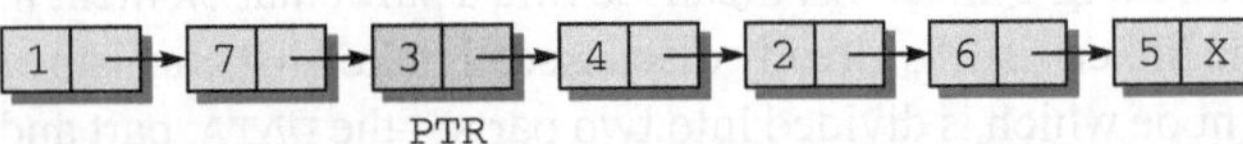

Here, `PTR->DATA = 3`. Since `PTR->DATA != 4`, We move to the next node because `PTR = PTR->NEXT`.

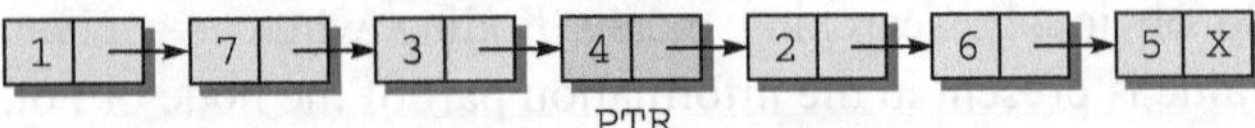

Here, `PTR->DATA = 4`. Since `PTR->DATA = 4`, `POS = PTR.POS` Now stores the address of the node that contains the `VAL`.

Figure 11.8 Searching a linked list

11.5.3 Inserting a New Node in a Linked List

In this section, we will see how a new node is added into an already existing linked list. To illustrate this, we will take five cases and see how the insertion is done in each case.

Case 1: The new node is inserted at the beginning of a linked list

Case 2: The new node is inserted at the end of a linked list

Case 3: The new node is inserted after a given node

Case 4: The new node is inserted before a given node

Before we begin with the algorithms to do the insertion in all these five cases, let us first discuss an important term—`OVERFLOW`. Overflow is a condition that occurs when `AVAIL = NULL` or no free memory space is present in the system. This means that we want to add data to the data structure, but there is no memory space available to do so. When this condition prevails, the programmer must give an appropriate message.

Case 1 Consider the linked list shown in Fig. 11.9. Suppose we want to add a new node with data 9 that as the first node of the list. Then the following changes will be done in the linked list.

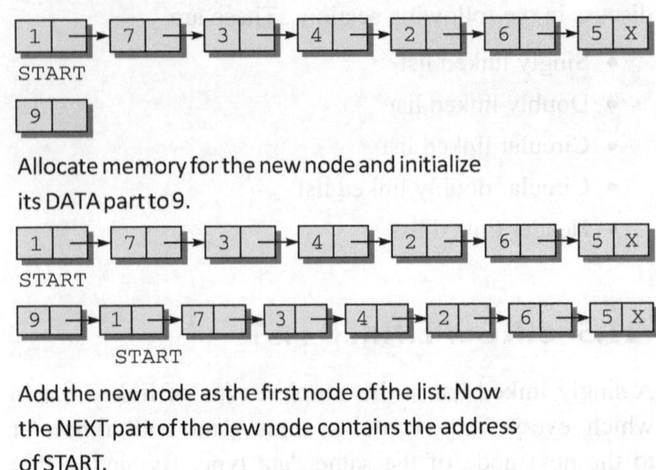

Figure 11.9 Inserting an element at the beginning of a linked list

Figure 11.10 shows the algorithm to insert a new node at the beginning of a linked list. In Step 1, we first check whether memory is available for the new node. If the free memory has been exhausted then an `OVERFLOW` message is printed. Otherwise, if a free memory cell is available then we allocate space for the new node. Its `DATA` part is set with the given `VAL` and its `NEXT` part is initialized with the address of the first node of the list, which is stored in `START`. Now, since the new node is added as the first node of the list, it will now be known the `START` node, that is, the `START` pointer variable will now hold the address of the `New_Node`.

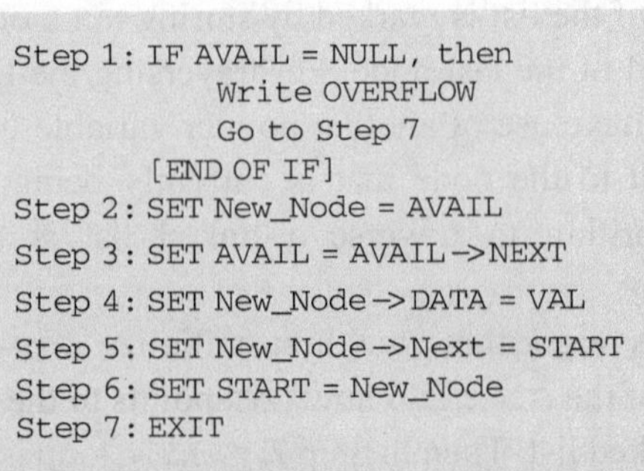

```
Step 1: IF AVAIL = NULL, then
            Write OVERFLOW
            Go to Step 7
        [END OF IF]
Step 2: SET New_Node = AVAIL
Step 3: SET AVAIL = AVAIL->NEXT
Step 4: SET New_Node->DATA = VAL
Step 5: SET New_Node->Next = START
Step 6: SET START = New_Node
Step 7: EXIT
```

Figure 11.10 Algorithm to insert a new node at the beginning of a linked list

Note the two steps—

```
Step 2: SET New_Node=AVAIL
Step 3: SET AVAIL = AVAIL->NEXT
```

These steps allocate memory for the new node. In C, functions such as `malloc()`, `alloc()`, and `calloc()` do this automatically on behalf of the user.

Case 2 Consider the linked list shown in Fig. 11.11. Suppose we want to add a new node with data 9 as the last node of the list. Then the following changes will be done in the linked list.

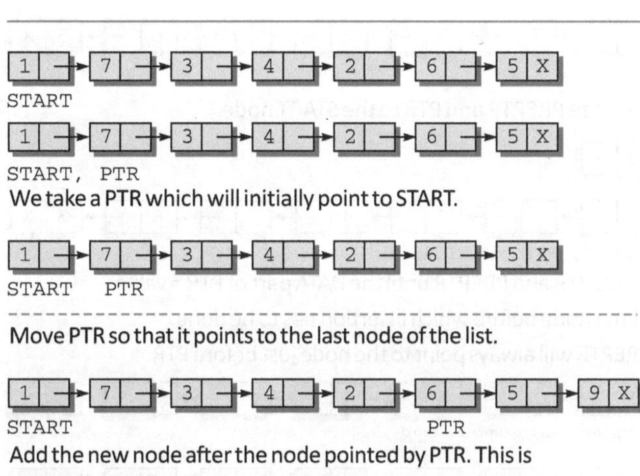

Figure 11.11 Inserting an element at the end of a linked list

Figure 11.12 shows the algorithm to insert a new node at the end of the linked list. In Step 1, we first check whether memory is available for the new node. If the free memory has been exhausted then an OVERFLOW message is printed. Otherwise, if a free memory cell is available then we allocate space for the new node. Its DATA part with the given VAL and its NEXT part is initialized with NULL because this is the last node of the linked list.

In Step 6, we take a PTR and initialize it with START. That is, PTR now points to the first node of the linked list. In the `while` loop, we traverse through the linked list to reach the last node. Once we reach the last node, in Step 9, we change the NEXT pointer of the last node to store the address of the new node. Remember that the NEXT field of the new node contains NULL which signifies the end of the linked list.

Case 3 Consider the linked list shown in Fig. 11.13. Suppose that we want to add a new node with value 9 after the node containing data 3. Let us look at changes that will be done in the linked list; the algorithm to add the new node is given in Fig. 11.14.

```
Step 1: IF AVAIL = NULL, then
            Write OVERFLOW
            Go to Step 10
        [END OF IF]
Step 2: SET New_Node = AVAIL
Step 3: SET AVAIL = AVAIL->NEXT
Step 4: SET New_Node->DATA = VAL
Step 5: SET New_Node->Next = NULL
Step 6: SET PTR = START
Step 7: Repeat Step 8 while PTR->NEXT != NULL
Step 8:            SET PTR = PTR->NEXT
        [END OF LOOP]
Step 9: SET PTR->NEXT = New_Node
Step 10: EXIT
```

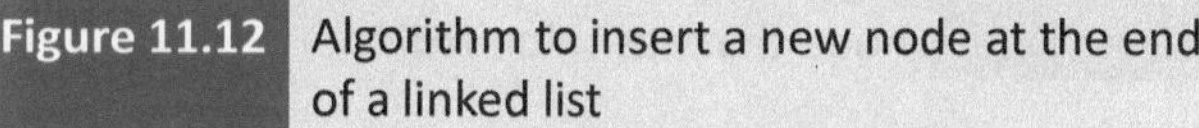

Figure 11.12 Algorithm to insert a new node at the end of a linked list

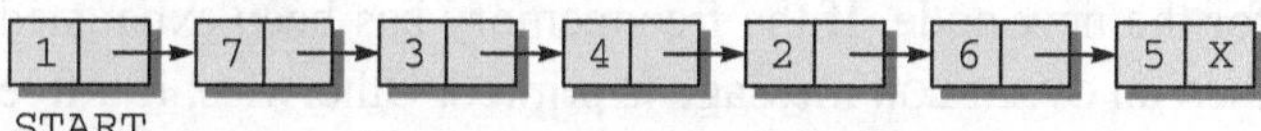

Take two pointer variables PTR and PREPTR and initialize them with START so that START, PTR, and PREPTR all point to the first node of the list.

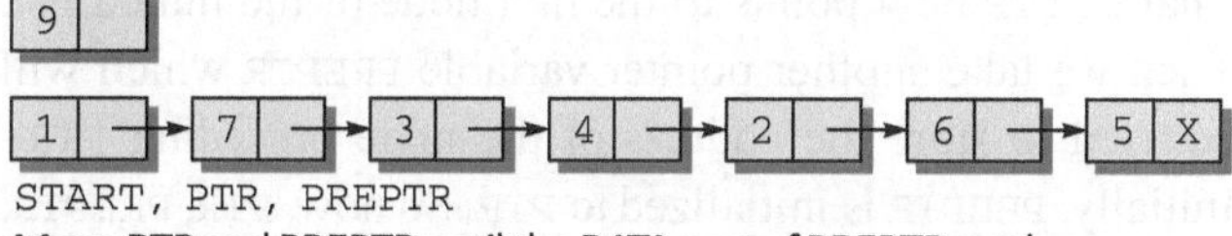

Move PTR and PREPTR until the DATA part of PREPTR = value of the node after which insertion has to be done. PREPTR will always point to the node just before PTR.

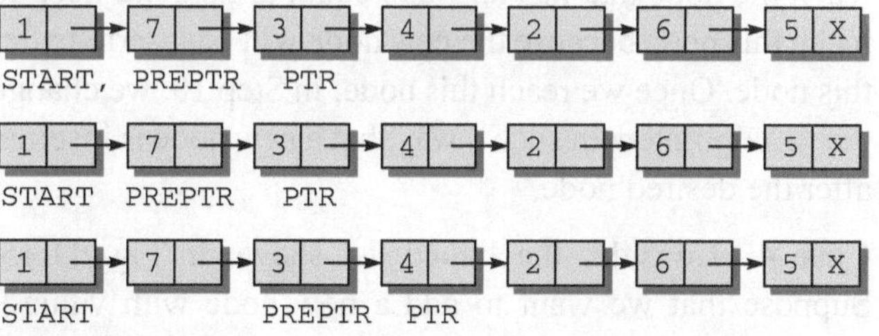

Add the new node in between the nodes pointed by PREPTR and PTR.

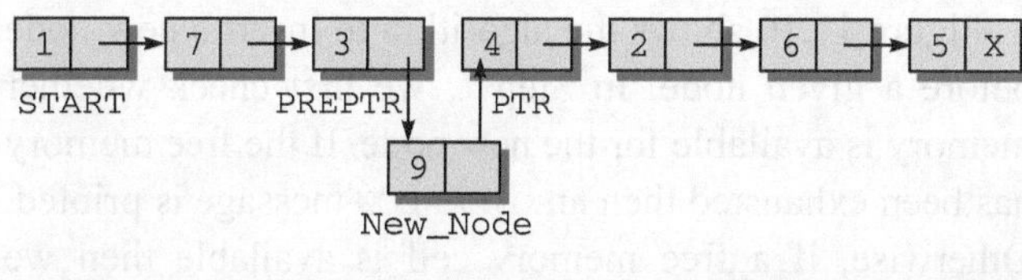

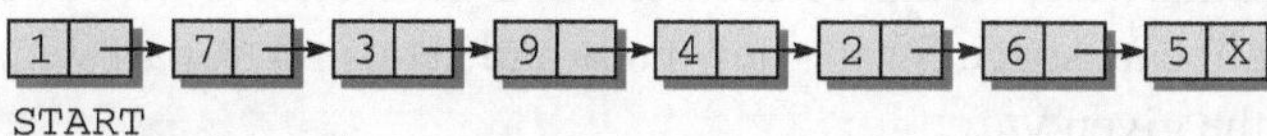

Figure 11.13 Inserting an element after a given node in the linked list

```
Step 1: IF AVAIL = NULL, then
            Write OVERFLOW
            Go to Step 12
        [END OF IF]
Step 2: SET New_Node = AVAIL
Step 3: SET AVAIL = AVAIL->NEXT
Step 4: SET New_Node->DATA = VAL
Step 5: SET PTR = START
Step 6: SET PREPTR = PTR
Step 7: Repeat Steps 8 and 9 while PREPTR->DATA != NUM
Step 8:             SET PREPTR = PTR
Step 9:             SET PTR = PTR->NEXT
        [END OF LOOP]
Step 10: PREPTR->NEXT = New_Node
Step 11: SET New_Node->NEXT = PTR
Step 12: EXIT
```

Figure 11.14 Algorithm to insert a new node after a node that has value NUM

In Step 1, we first check whether memory is available for the new node. If the free memory has been exhausted then an OVERFLOW message is printed. Otherwise, if a free memory cell is available then we allocate space for the new node and set its DATA part with the given VAL.

In Step 5, we take a PTR and initialize it with START. That is, PTR now points to the first node of the linked list. Then we take another pointer variable PREPTR which will be used to store the address of the node preceding PTR. Initially, PREPTR is initialized to PTR. So now, PTR, PREPTR, and START all point to the first node of the linked list.

In the while loop, we traverse through the linked list to reach the node that has its value equal to NUM. We need to reach this node because the new node will be inserted after this node. Once we reach this node, in Step 10, we change the NEXT pointers in such a way that a new node is inserted after the desired node.

Case 4 Consider the linked list shown in Fig. 11.15. Suppose that we want to add a new node with value 9 before the node containing 3. Let us discuss the changes that will be done in the linked list.

Figure 11.16 shows the algorithm to insert a new node before a given node. In Step 1, we first check whether memory is available for the new node. If the free memory has been exhausted then an OVERFLOW message is printed. Otherwise, if a free memory cell is available then we allocate space for the new node and set its DATA part with the given VAL.

In Step 5, we take a pointer variable PTR, and initialize it with START. That is, PTR now points to the first node of the linked list. Then we take another pointer variable PREPTR and initialize it with PTR. So now, PTR, PREPTR, and START all point to the first node of the linked list.

In the while loop, we traverse through the linked list to reach the node that has its value equal to NUM. We need to reach this node because the new node will be inserted before this node. Once we reach this node, in Step 10, we change the NEXT pointers in such a way that new node is inserted after the desired node.

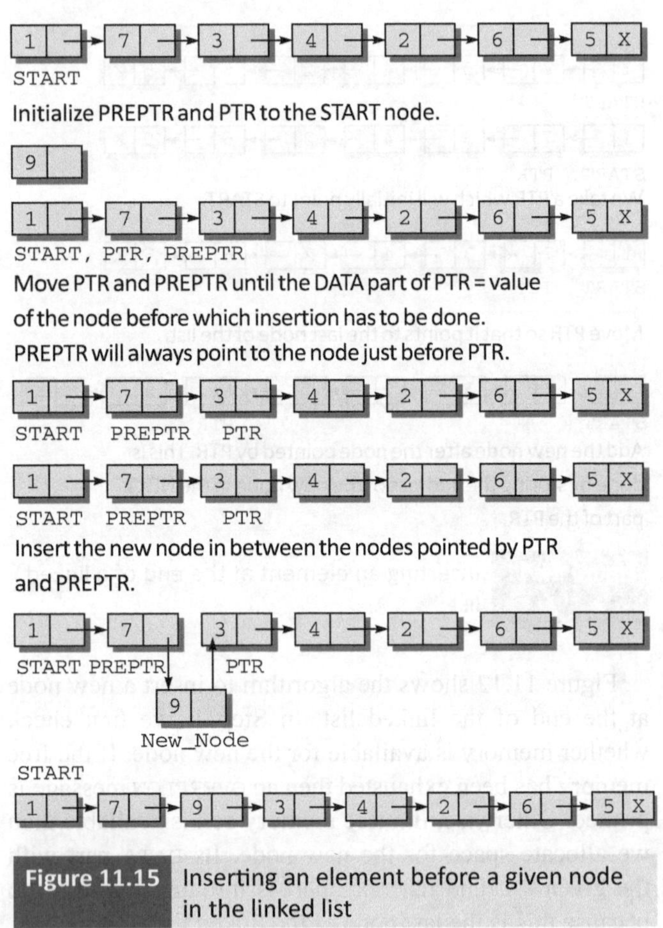

Figure 11.15 Inserting an element before a given node in the linked list

Deleting a Node from a Linked List

In this section we will see how a new node is deleted from an already existing linked list. To illustrate this we will take five cases and see how the deletion is done in each case.

Case 1: The first node is deleted

Case 2: The last node is deleted

Case 3: The node after the given node is deleted

Before we begin with the algorithms to do the deletions in all these five cases, let us first discuss an important term—UNDERFLOW. Underflow is a condition that occurs when we try to delete a node from a linked list that is empty. This happens when START=NULL or when there are no more nodes to delete.

```
Step 1: IF AVAIL = NULL, then
              Write OVERFLOW
              Go to Step 12
        [END OF IF]
Step 2: SET New_Node = AVAIL
Step 3: SET AVAIL = AVAIL->NEXT
Step 4: SET New_Node->DATA = VAL
Step 5: SET PTR = START
Step 6: SET PREPTR = PTR
Step 7: Repeat Steps 8 and 9 while PTR->DATA != NUM
Step 8:           SET PREPTR = PTR
Step 9:           SET PTR = PTR->NEXT
        [END OF LOOP]
Step 10: PREPTR->NEXT = New_Node
Step 11: SET New_Node->NEXT = PTR
Step 12: EXIT
```

Figure 11.16 Algorithm to insert a new node before a node that has value NUM

When we delete a node from the linked list, we have to free the memory occupied by that node. The memory is returned back to the free pool so that it can be used to store other data. Whatever be the case of deletion, we always change the AVAIL pointer so that it points to the address which has been recently freed.

Case 1 Consider the linked list in Fig. 11.17. When we want to delete a node from the beginning of the list, then the following changes will be done in the linked list.

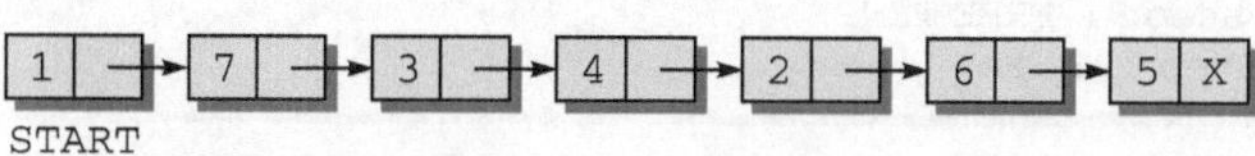

Move the START pointer so that it now points to the second node of the list. Delete the first node. Now the list begins from the node with data 7 as it is the node pointed by START.

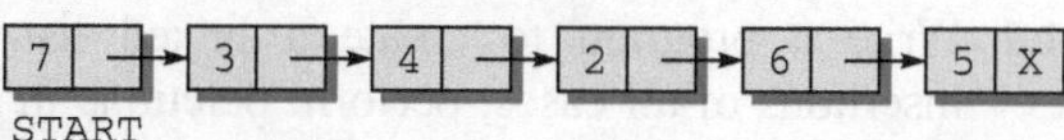

Figure 11.17 Deleting the first node of a linked list

Figure 11.18 shows the algorithm to delete the first node from the linked list. In Step 1 of the algorithm, we check if the linked list exists. If START=NULL, then it signifies that there are no nodes in the list and the control is transferred to the last statement of the algorithm.

```
Step 1: IF START = NULL, then
                Write UNDERFLOW
                Go to Step 5
           [END OF IF]
Step 2: SET PTR = START
Step 3: SET START = START->NEXT
Step 4: FREE PTR
Step 5: EXIT
```

Figure 11.18 Algorithm to delete the first node from a linked list

However, if there are nodes in the linked list, then we use a pointer variable that is set to point to the first node of the list. For this, we initiate PTR with START which stores the address of the first node of the list. In Step 3, START is made to point to the next node in sequence and finally the memory occupied by the node pointed by PTR (initially the first node of the list) is freed and returned to the free pool.

Case 2 Consider the linked list shown in Fig. 11.19. Suppose we want to delete the last node from the linked list, then the following changes will be done in the list.

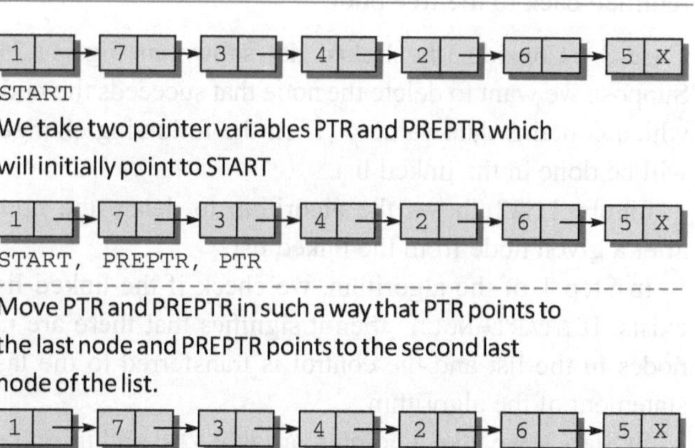

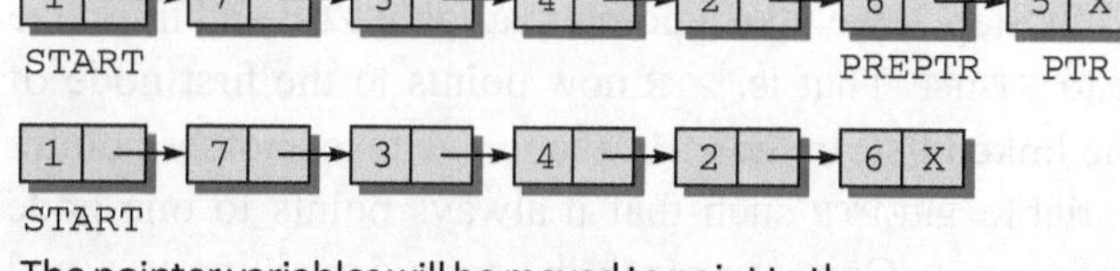

The pointer variables will be moved to point to the last node of the list so that the memory occupied by it can be freed. We also store NULL in the last node (which was initially the second last node).

Figure 11.19 Deleting the last node of a linked list

Figure 11.20 shows the algorithm to delete the first node from a linked list. In Step 1 of the algorithm, we check if the linked list exists. If START=NULL, then it signifies that there are no nodes in the list and the control is transferred to the last statement of the algorithm.

```
Step 1: IF START = NULL, then
              Write UNDERFLOW
              Go to Step 8
        [END OF IF]
Step 2: SET PTR = START
Step 3: Repeat Steps 4 and 5 while PTR->NEXT != NULL
Step 4:            SET PREPTR = PTR
Step 5:            SET PTR = PTR->NEXT
        [END OF LOOP]
Step 6: SET PREPTR->NEXT = NULL
Step 7: FREE PTR
Step 8: EXIT
```

Figure 11.20 Algorithm to delete the last node from a linked list

In Step 2, we take a pointer variable, PTR and initialize it to START. That is, PTR now points to the first node of the linked list. In the while loop, we take another pointer variable PREPTR such that it always points to on node before PTR. Once we reach the last and the second last nodes, we set the next pointer of the second last node to NULL, so that it now becomes the (new) last node of the linked list. The memory of the initial last node is freed and returned back to the free pool.

Case 3 Consider the linked list shown in Fig. 11.21. Suppose we want to delete the node that succeeds the node which contains data value 4. Then the following changes will be done in the linked list.

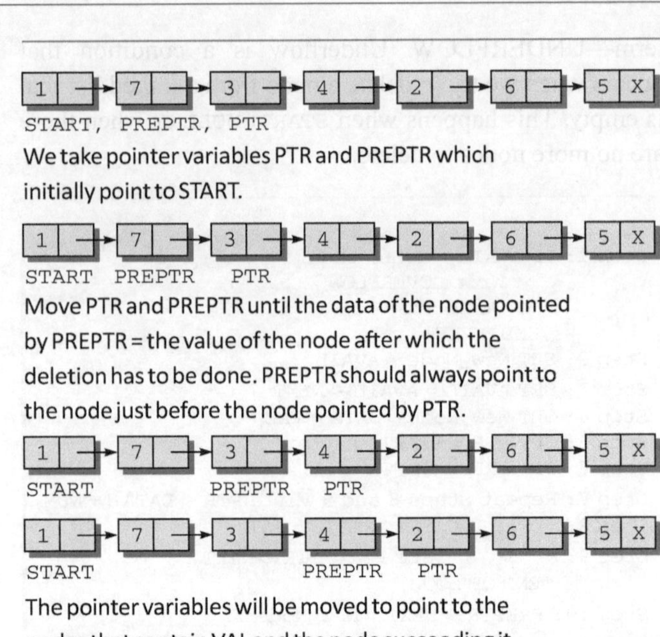

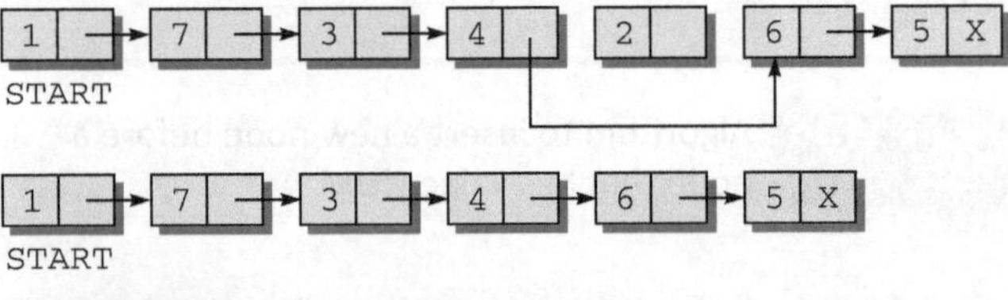

Figure 11.21 Deleting the node after a given node in a linked list

Figure 11.22 shows the algorithm to delete the node after a given node from the linked list.

In Step 1 of the algorithm, we check if the linked list exists. If START=NULL, then it signifies that there are no nodes in the list and the control is transferred to the last statement of the algorithm.

In Step 2, we take a pointer variable PTR and initialize it to START. That is, PTR now points to the first node of the linked list. In the while loop, we take another pointer variable PREPTR such that it always points to one node before PTR. Once we reach the node containing VAL and the node succeeding it, we set the NEXT pointer of the node containing VAL to the address contained in NEXT field of the node succeeding it. The memory of the node succeeding the given node is freed and returned back to the free pool.

```
Step 1: IF START = NULL, then
              Write UNDERFLOW
              Go to Step 10
        [END OF IF]
Step 2: SET PTR = START
Step 3: SET PREPTR = PTR
Step 4: Repeat Steps 5 and 6 while PRETR->DATA != NUM
Step 5:            SET PREPTR = PTR
Step 6:            SET PTR = PTR->NEXT
        [END OF LOOP]
Step7:  SET TEMP = PTR->NEXT
Step 8: SET PREPTR->NEXT = TEMP->NEXT
Step 9: FREE TEMP
Step 10: EXIT
```

Figure 11.22 Algorithm to delete the node after a given node from the linked list

11.1 Write a program to create a linked list, perform insertions of all cases, perform deletions in all cases, sort the linked list, and finally delete the entire list at once.

```
#include <stdio.h>
#include <conio.h>
```

```
struct node
{
   int data;
   struct node *next;
};
struct node *start=NULL;
struct node *create_ll(struct node *);
struct node *display(struct node *);
struct node *insert_beg(struct node *);
struct node *insert_end(struct node *);
struct node *insert_before(struct node *start);
struct node *insert_after(struct node *start);
struct node *insert_sorted(struct node *start);
struct node *delete_beg(struct node *);
struct node *delete_end(struct node *);
struct node *delete_node(struct node *start);
struct node *delete_after(struct node *start);
struct node *delete_sorted(struct node *start);
struct node *delete_list(struct node *start);
struct node *sort_list(struct node *start);
main()
{
   int option;
   clrscr();
   do
   {
      printf("\n\n ***** MAIN MENU *****");
      printf("\n 1: Create a list");
      printf("\n 2: Display the list");
      printf("\n 3: Add a node in the beginning");
      printf("\n 4: Add a node at the end");
      printf("\n 5: Add a node before a given node");
      printf("\n 6: Add after a given node");
      printf("\n 7: Delete from the beginning");
      printf("\n 8: Delete from the end");
      printf("\n 9: Delete a given node");
      printf("\n 10: Delete before a given node");
      printf("\n 11: Delete the entire list");
      printf("\n 12: Sort the list");
      printf("\n 13: EXIT");
      printf("\n ***************************");
      printf("\n\n Enter your option: ");
      scanf("%d", &option);
      switch(option)
      {
      case 1:
         start=create_ll(start);
         printf("\n LINKED LIST CREATED");
         break;
      case 2:
         start=display(start);
         break;
      case 3:
         start=insert_beg(start);
         break;
      case 4:
         start=insert_end(start);
         break;
      case 5:
         start=insert_before(start);
         break;
      case 6:
         start=insert_after(start);
         break;
      case 7:
         start=delete_beg(start);
         break;
      case 8:
         start=delete_end(start);
         break;
      case 9:
         start=delete_node(start);
         break;
      case 10:
         start=delete_after(start);
         break;
      case 11:
         start=delete_list(start);
         printf("\n List is EMPTY");
         break;
      case 12:
         start=sort_list(start);
         break;
      }
   }while(option !=15);
   getch();
   return 0;
}
struct node *create_ll(struct node *start)
{
   struct node *new_node;
   int num;
   printf("\n Enter -1 to end");
   printf("\n Enter the data: ");
   scanf("%d", &num);
   while(num!=-1)
   {
      new_node=(struct node*)
      malloc(sizeof(struct node*));
      new_node->data = num;
      if(start == NULL)
      {
```

```
        new_node->next = NULL;
        start = new_node;
      }
      else
      {
        new_node->next = start;
        start=new_node;
      }
      printf("\n Enter the data: ");
      scanf("%d", &num);
    }
    return start;
}
struct node *display(struct node *start)
{
    struct node *ptr;
    ptr = start;
    printf("\n");
    while(ptr!=NULL)
    {
      printf("\t %d", ptr->data);
      ptr=ptr->next;
    }
    return start;
}

struct node *insert_beg(struct node *start)
{
    struct node *new_node;
    int num;
    printf("\n Enter the data: ");
    scanf("%d", &num);
    new_node= (struct node *);malloc
    (sizeof(struct node *));
    new_node->data = num;
    new_node->next = start;
    start = new_node;
    return start;
}

struct node *insert_end(struct node *start)
{
    struct node *ptr, *new_node;
    int num;
    printf("\n Enter the data: ");
    scanf("%d", &num);
    new_node= (struct node *);
    malloc(sizeof(struct node *));
    new_node->data = num;
    ptr = start;
    while(ptr->next! = NULL)
      ptr = ptr->next;
    ptr->next = new_node;
    new_node->next = NULL;
    return start;
}

struct node *insert_before(struct node *start)
{
    struct node *new_node, *ptr, *preptr;
    int num, val;
    printf("\n Enter the data: ");
    scanf("%d", &num);
    printf("\n Enter the value before which
    the data has to be inserted: ");
    scanf("%d", &val);
    new_node = (struct node *);
    malloc(sizeof(struct node *));
    new_node->data = num;
    ptr = start;
    while(ptr->data! = val)
    {
      preptr = ptr;
      ptr=ptr->next;
    }
    new_node->next = ptr;
    preptr->next = new_node;
    return start;
}

struct node *insert_after(struct node *start)
{
    struct node *new_node, *ptr, *preptr;
    int num, val;
    printf("\n Enter the data: ");
    scanf("%d", &num);
    printf("\n Enter the value after which
    the data has to be inserted: ");
    scanf("%d", &val);
    new_node= (struct node *);
    malloc(sizeof(struct node *));
    new_node->data = num;
    ptr = start;
    while(preptr->data != val)
    {
      preptr=ptr;
      ptr=ptr->next;
    }
    new_node->next = ptr;
    preptr->next = new_node;
    return start;
}
struct node *delete_beg(struct node *start)
{
```

```
    struct node *ptr;
    ptr = start;
    start = start->next;
    free(ptr);
    return start;
}
struct node *delete_end(struct node *start)
{
    struct node *ptr, *preptr;
    ptr = start;
    while(ptr->next != NULL)
    {
        preptr = ptr;
        ptr = ptr->next;
    }
    preptr->next = NULL;
    free(ptr);
    return start;
}
struct node *delete_node(struct node *start)
{
    struct node *ptr, *preptr;
    int val;
    printf("\n Enter the value of the node
    which has to be deleted: ");
    scanf("%d", &val);
    ptr = start;
    if(ptr->data == val)
    {
        start = delete_beg(start);
        return start;
    }
    else
    {
        while(ptr->data != val)
        {
        preptr = ptr;
        ptr = ptr->next;
        }
        preptr->next = ptr->next;
        free(ptr);
        return start;
    }
}
struct node *delete_after(struct node *start)
{
    struct node *ptr, *preptr;
    int val;
    printf("\n Enter the value after which
    the node has to deleted: ");
    scanf("%d", &val);
    ptr = start;
    while(preptr->data != val)
    {
        preptr = ptr;
        ptr = ptr->next;
    }
    preptr->next = ptr->next;
    free(ptr);
    return start;
}

struct node *delete_list(struct node *start)
{
    struct node *ptr;
    ptr = start;
    while(ptr->next != NULL)
    {
        printf("\n %d is to be deleted next",
        ptr->data);
        start = delete_beg(ptr);
        ptr = ptr->next;
    }
    return start;
}

struct node *sort_list(struct node *start)
{
    struct node *ptr1, *ptr2;
    int temp;
    ptr1 = start;
    while(ptr1->next != NULL)
    {
        ptr2 = ptr1->next;
        while(ptr2 != NULL)
        {
            if(ptr1->data > ptr2->data)
            {
                temp = ptr1->data;
                ptr1->data = ptr2->data;
                ptr2->data = temp;
            }
            ptr2 = ptr2->next;
        }
        ptr1 = ptr1->next;
    }
    return start;
}
```

Output

```
***** MAIN MENU *****
1: Create a list
2: Display the list
3: Add a node in the beginning
```

```
4: Add a node at the end
5: Add a node before a given node
6: Add after a given node
7: Delete from the beginning
8: Delete from the end
9: Delete a given node
10: Delete before a given node
11: Delete the entire list
12: Sort the list
13: EXIT
***************************
Enter your option : 1
Enter –1 to end
Enter the data : 1
Enter the data : 2
Enter the data : 3
Enter the data : 4
Enter the data : 5
Enter the data : –1
***** MAIN MENU *****
1: Create a list
2: Display the list
3: Add a node in the beginning
4: Add a node at the end
5: Add a node before a given node
6: Add after a given node
7: Delete from the beginning
8: Delete from the end
9: Delete a node after a given node
10: Delete before a given node
11: Delete the entire list
12: Sort the list
13: EXIT
***************************
Enter your option : 2
5 4 3 2 1
```

11.6 CIRCULAR LINKED LIST

In a *circular linked list*, the last node contains a pointer to the first node of the list. We can have a circular singly listed list as well as a circular doubly linked list. While traversing a circular linked list, we can begin at any node and traverse the list in any direction forward or backward until we reach the same node where we started. Thus, a circular linked list has no beginning and no end. Figure 11.23 shows a circular linked list.

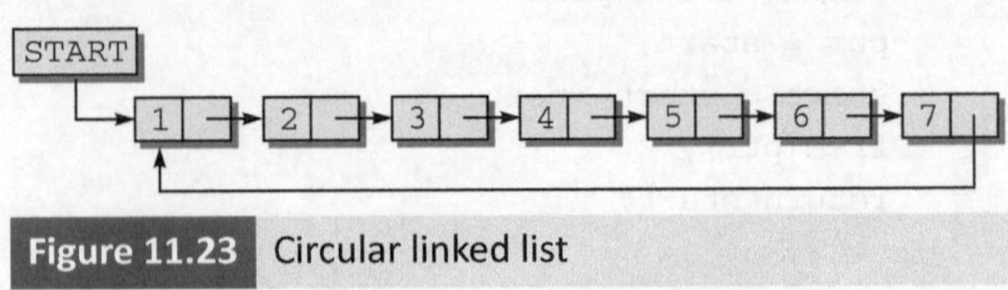

Figure 11.23 Circular linked list

The only disadvantage of a circular linked list is the complexity of iterations. Note that there is no storing of NULL values in the list.

Circular linked lists are widely used in operating systems for task maintenance. Let us consider another example where a circular linked list is used. When we are surfing the Internet, we can use the Back and the Forward buttons to move to the earlier visited previous and the next pages, respectively. How is this done? The answer is simple. A circular linked list is used to maintain the sequence of the web pages visited. Traversing this circular linked list either in the forward or backward direction helps to revisit the pages again using the Forward and Back buttons. Actually this is done using either a circular stack or a circular queue. We will read more about it in Chapter 12.

Let us view how a linked list is maintained in memory. In order to form a linked list we need a structure called node that has two fields—DATA and NEXT. The DATA field will store the information part and the NEXT field will store the address of the node in sequence. Consider Fig. 11.24.

START = 1

	DATA	NEXT
1	H	4
2		
3		
4	E	7
5		
6		
7	L	8
8	L	10
9		
10	O	1

Figure 11.24 Memory representation of a circular linked list

In the figure, we see that a variable START is used to store the address of the first node. Here in this example, START=1, so the first data is stored at address 1, which is

'H'. The corresponding `NEXT` stores the address of the next node, which is 3. So, we will look at address 3 to fetch the next data item. The second data element obtained from address 3 is `'E'`. Again we see the corresponding `NEXT`, to go to the next node. From the entry in the `NEXT`, we get the next address, that is 7 and fetch `'L'` as the data. We repeat this procedure until we reach a position where the `NEXT` entry contains 1 or the address of the first node of the list. This denotes the end of the linked list, that is, the node that contains the address of the first node is actually the last node of the list. When we traverse the `DATA` and `NEXT` fields in this manner, we will finally see that the linked list in this example stores characters which when put together form the word `"HELLO"`.

The figure shows a chunk of memory locations whose addresses range from 1 to 10. The shaded portion contains data for other applications. Remember that the nodes of a linked list need not be in consecutive memory locations. In our example, the nodes for the linked list are stored at addresses 1, 4, 7, 8, and 10.

11.7 DOUBLY LINKED LIST

A *doubly linked list* or a two-way linked list is a more complex type of linked list which contains a pointer to the next as well as the previous node in sequence. Therefore, it consists of three parts and not just two. The three parts are data, a pointer to the next node, and a pointer to the previous node (refer Fig. 11.25).

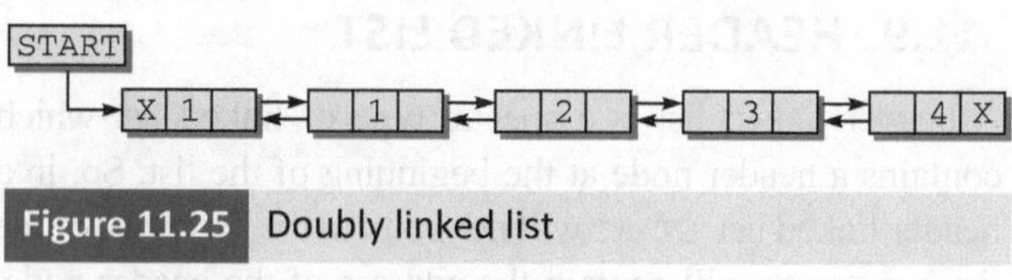

Figure 11.25 Doubly linked list

In C, the structure of a doubly linked list is given as,

```
struct node
{
   struct node *prev;
   int data;
   struct node *next;
};
```

The `prev` field of the first node and the `next` field of the last node contain `NULL`. The `prev` field is used to store the address of the preceding node. This would enable one to traverse the list in the backward direction as well.

Thus, we see that a doubly linked list calls for more space per node and for more expensive basic operations. However, a doubly linked list provides the ease to manipulate the elements of the list as it maintains pointers to nodes in both the directions (forward and backward). The main advantage of using a doubly linked list is that it makes searches twice as efficient. Let us view how a doubly linked list is maintained in memory. Consider Fig. 11.26.

START = 1

	DATA	PREV	NEXT
1	H	−1	3
2			
3	E	1	7
4			
5			
6			
7	L	3	8
8	L	7	10
9			
10	O	8	−1

Figure 11.26 Memory representation of a doubly linked list

In the figure, we see that a variable `START` is used to store the address of the first node. Here in this example, `START=1`, so the first data is stored at address 1, which is `'H'`. Since this is the first node, it has no previous node and hence stores `NULL` or −1 in the `PREV` field. The corresponding `NEXT` stores the address of the next node, which is 3. So, we will look at address 3 to fetch the next data item. The `prev` field will contain the address of the first node. The second data element obtained from address 3 is `'E'`. Again we see the corresponding `NEXT`, to go to the next node. From the entry in the `NEXT` field, we get the next address, that is 7 and fetch `'L'` as the data. We repeat this procedure until we reach a position where the `NEXT` entry contains −1 or `NULL`. This denotes the end of the linked list, that is, the node that contains the address of the first node is actually the last node of the list. When we traverse the `DATA` and `NEXT` fields in this manner, we will finally see that the linked list in this example stores characters which when put together form the word "HELLO".

The figure shows a chunk of memory locations whose addresses range from 1 to 10. The shaded portion contains data for other applications. Remember that the nodes of a linked list need not be in consecutive memory locations. In our example, the nodes for the linked list are stored at addresses 1, 3, 7, 8, and 10.

11.8 CIRCULAR DOUBLY LINKED LIST

A circular doubly linked list or a circular two-way linked list is a more complex type of linked list which contains a pointer to the next as well as the previous node in sequence. The difference between a doubly linked and a circular doubly linked list is the same as that between a singly linked list and a circular linked list. The circular doubly linked list does not contain `NULL` in the previous field of the first node and the next field of the last node. Rather, the next field of the last node stores the address of the first node of the list, i.e., `START`. Similarly, the previous field of the first field stores the address of the last node. A circular doubly linked list is shown in Fig. 11.27.

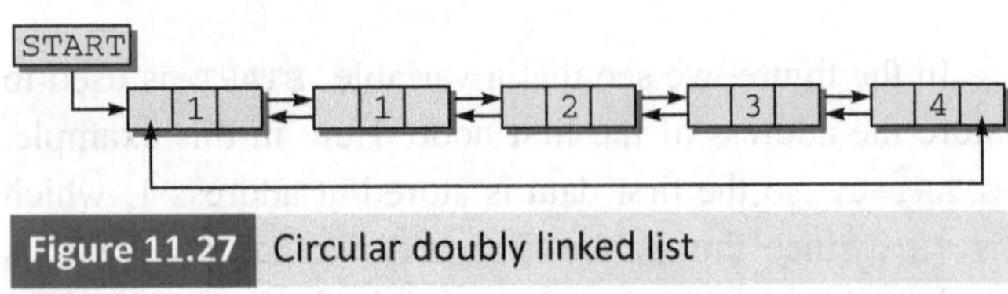

Figure 11.27 Circular doubly linked list

Since a circular doubly linked list contains three parts in its structure, it calls for more space per node and for more expensive basic operations. However, a circular doubly linked list provides the ease to manipulate the elements of the list as it maintains pointers to nodes in both the directions (forward and backward). The main advantage of using a circular doubly linked list is that it makes searches twice as efficient.

Let us view how a circular doubly linked list is maintained in memory. Consider Fig. 11.28.

In the figure, we see that a variable `START` is used to store the address of the first node. Here in this example, `START=1`, so the first data is stored at address 1, which is `'H'`. Since this is the first node, it stores the address of the last node of the list in its previous field. The corresponding `NEXT` field stores the address of the next node, which is 3. So, we will look at address 3 to fetch the next data item. The previous field will contain the address of the first node. The second data element obtained from address 3 is `'E'`. Again we see the corresponding `NEXT`, to go to the next node. From the entry in the `NEXT` field, we get the next address, that is 7 and fetch `'L'` as the data. We repeat this procedure until we reach a position where the `NEXT` entry stores the address of the first element of the list. This denotes the end of the linked list, that is, the node that contains the address of the first node is actually the last node of the list. When we traverse the `DATA` and `NEXT` fields in this manner, we will finally see that the linked list in the above example stores characters which when put together form the word "HELLO".

START: 1

	DATA	PREV	NEXT
1	H	10	3
2			
3	E	1	7
4			
5			
6			
7	L	3	8
8	L	7	10
9			
10	O	8	1

Figure 11.28 Memory representation of a circular doubly linked list

11.9 HEADER LINKED LIST

A header linked list is a special type of linked list which contains a header node at the beginning of the list. So, in a header linked list `START` will not point to the first node of the list but `START` will contain the address of the header node. There are basically two variants of a header linked list:

- grounded header linked list which stores `NULL` in the next field of the last node, and
- circular header linked list which stores the address of the header node in the next field of the last node. Here, the header node will denote the end of the list.

Look at Fig. 11.29 which shows both these types of header linked lists.

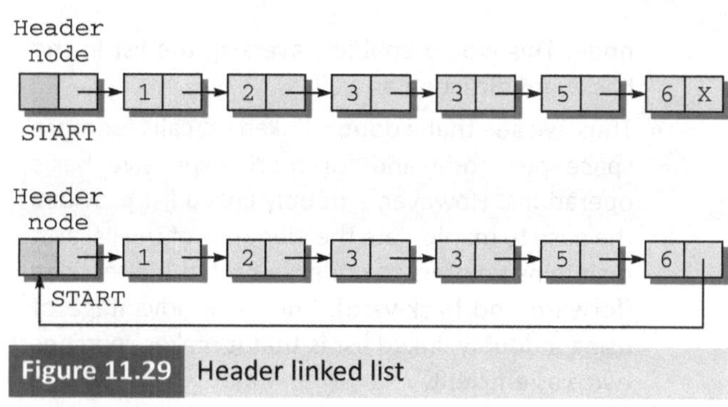

Figure 11.29 Header linked list

Header Node

Similar to the other linked lists, if START=NULL, then this denotes an empty header linked list. Let us see how a grounded header linked list is stored in memory. In order to form a grounded header linked list we need a structure called node that has two fields—DATA and NEXT. The DATA field will store the information part and the NEXT field will store the address of the node in sequence. Consider Fig. 11.30.

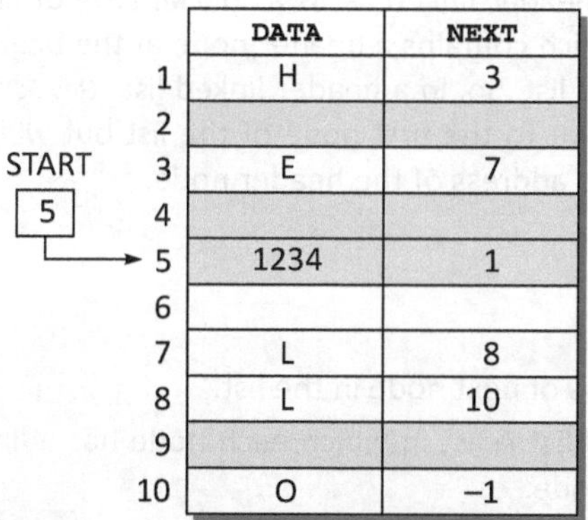

	DATA	NEXT
1	H	3
2		
3	E	7
4		
5	1234	1
6		
7	L	8
8	L	10
9		
10	O	–1

Figure 11.30 Memory representation of a header linked list

START stores the address of the header node. The shaded row denotes a header node. The NEXT field of the header node stores the address of the first node of the list. This node stores 'H'. The corresponding NEXT field stores the address of the next node, which is 3. So, we will look at address 3 to fetch the next data item. The second data element obtained from address 3 is 'E'. Again we see the corresponding NEXT field, to go to the next node. From the entry in the NEXT, we get the next address, that is 7 and fetch 'L' as the data. We repeat this procedure until we reach a position where the NEXT entry contains –1 or NULL, as this would denote the end of the linked list. When we traverse the DATA and NEXT in this manner, we will finally see that the linked list in the above example stores characters which when put together form the word "HELLO".

Hence, we see that the first node can be accessed by writing first_node = START->NEXT and not writing START = first_node. Because START points to the header node and the header node points to the first node of the header linked list.

Let us now see how a circular header linked list is stored in memory. Look at Fig. 11.31.

START: 5

	DATA	NEXT
1	H	3
2		
3	E	7
4		
5	1234	1
6		
7	L	8
8	L	10
9		
10	O	5

Figure 11.31 Memory representation of a circular header linked list

START stores the address of the header node. The shaded row denotes a header node. The NEXT field of the header node stores the address of the first node of the list. This node stores 'H'. The corresponding NEXT field stores the address of the next node, which is 3. So, we will look at address 3 to fetch the next data item. The second data element obtained from address 3 is 'E'. Again we see the corresponding NEXT, to go to the next node. From the entry in the NEXT, we get the next address, that is 7 and fetch 'L' as the data. We repeat this procedure until we reach a position where the NEXT entry contains 5 or the address of the header node as this would denote the end of the circular header linked list. When we traverse the DATA and NEXT fields in this manner, we will finally see that the linked list in this example stores characters which when put together form the word 'HELLO'.

Hence, we see that the first node can be accessed by writing first_node = START->NEXT and not writing START = first_node as START points to the header node and the header node points to the first node of the header linked list.

POINTS TO NOTE

- A linked list is a data structure which in turn can be used to implement other data structures such as stacks, queues, and their variations. Linked lists contain a pointer variable `START`, which stores the address of the first node in the list.
- `AVAIL` stores the address of the first free space.
- Before we insert a new node in a linked list, we need to check for `OVERFLOW` condition, which occurs when `AVAIL=NULL` or no free memory cell is present in the system.
- Before we delete a node from a linked list, we must first check for the `UNDERFLOW` condition which occurs when we try to delete a node from a linked list that is empty. This happens when `START = NULL` or when there are no more nodes to delete when we attempt deletion.
- Note that when we delete a node from the linked list, we have to actually free the memory occupied by that node. The memory is returned to the free pool so that it can be used to store other useful programs and data. So whatever be the case of deletion, we always change the `AVAIL` pointer so that it points to the address that has been recently vacated.
- The `PREV` field of the first node and the `NEXT` field of the last node will contain `NULL`. The `PREV` field is used to store the address of the preceding node. This would enable traversing the list in the backward direction as well.
- Thus, we see that a doubly linked list calls for more space per node and for more expensive basic operations. However, a doubly linked list provides the ease to manipulate the elements of the list as it maintains pointers to nodes in both the directions (forward and backward). The main advantage of using a doubly linked list is that it makes searches twice as efficient.
- A circular doubly linked list or a circular two-way linked list is a more complex type of linked list which contains a pointer to the next as well as the previous nodes in the sequence. The difference between a doubly linked and a circular doubly linked list is the same as that which exists between a singly linked list and a circular linked list. The circular doubly linked list does not contain `NULL` in the previous field of the first node and the next field of the last node. Rather, the next field of the last node stores the address of the first node of the list, i.e., `START`. Similarly, the previous field of the first field stores the address of the last node.
- A header linked list is a special type of linked list which contains a header node at the beginning of the list. So, in a header linked list `START` will not point to the first node of the list but will contain the address of the header node.

GLOSSARY

Circular linked list A type of a linked list in which the last node is linked to the head. The nodes of the list may be accessed starting at any item and following the links until one comes to the starting item again.

Doubly linked list A type of a linked list in which each node has a link to the previous item as well as the next. This enables ease of accessing the nodes backward as well as forward and deleting any node.

Head The first node of the list.

Link A reference, pointer, or access handle to another part of the data structure. It usually stores the memory address of next node in the list.

Linked list A list in which each node has a link to the next node.

Searching a linked list Searching means to find a particular element in a linked list. The worst case complexity of searching an unsorted or a sorted linked list is `O(n)`.

Traversing a linked list Traversing means accessing the nodes of the list in order to perform some processing on them.

EXERCISES

Fill in the Blanks

1. ________ is used to store the address of the first free memory location.
2. The complexity to insert a node at the beginning of a linked list is ________.

EXERCISES

3. The complexity to delete a node from the end of a linked list is ________.
4. Inserting a node in the beginning of a doubly linked list needs modification of ________ pointers.
5. Inserting a node in the middle of a singly linked list needs modification of ________ pointers.
6. Inserting a node at the end of a circular linked list needs modification of ________ pointers.
7. Inserting a node in the beginning of a circular doubly linked list needs modification of ________ pointers.
8. Deleting a node from the beginning of a singly linked list needs modification of ________ pointers.
9. Deleting a node from the middle of a doubly linked list needs modification of ________ pointers.
10. Deleting a node from the end of a circular linked list needs modification of ________ pointers.
11. Each element in a linked list is known as a ________.
12. The first node in the linked list is called the ________.
13. Data elements in a linked list are known as ________.
14. Overflow occurs when ________.
15. In a circular linked list, the last node contains a pointer to the ________ node of the list.

Multiple Choice Questions

1. A linked list is a
   (a) random access structure
   (b) sequential access structure
   (c) both
   (d) none of these
2. An array is a
   (a) random access structure
   (b) sequential access structure
   (c) both
   (d) none of these
3. Linked list is used to implement data structures such as
   (a) Stacks (b) Queues
   (c) Trees (d) all of these
4. Which type of linked list contains a pointer to the next as well as the previous nodes in sequence?
   (a) singly linked list
   (b) circular linked list
   (c) doubly linked list
   (d) all of these

State True or False

1. A linked list is a linear collection of data elements.
2. A linked list can grow and shrink during run time.
3. A node in a linked list can point to only one node at a time.
4. A node in the singly linked list can reference the previous node.
5. A linked list can store only integer values.
6. Linked list is a random access structure.
7. Deleting a node from a doubly linked list is easier than deleting it from a singly linked list.
8. Every node in a linked list contains an integer part and a pointer.
9. `START` pointer stores the address of the first node in the list.
10. Underflow is a condition that occurs when we try to delete a node from a linked list that is empty.

Review Questions

1. Make a comparison between a linked list and a linear array. Which one will you prefer to use and when?
2. Why is a doubly linked list more useful than a singly linked list?
3. Give the advantages and uses of a circular linked list.
4. Specify the use of a header node in a header linked list.
5. Explain the difference between a circular linked list and a singly linked list.
6. Write a program that removes all nodes that have duplicate information.
7. Write a program to print the total number of occurrences of a given item in the linked list.
8. Write a program to multiply every element of the linked list with 10.
9. Write a program to print the number of non-zero elements in the list.
10. Write a program that prints whether the given linked list is sorted (in ascending order) or not.
11. Write a program that copies a circular linked list.
12. Write a program to merge two linked lists.
13. Write a program to sort the values stored in a doubly circular linked list.
14. Form a linked list to store student's details.
15. Use the linked list of the above question to insert the record of a new student in the list.

EXERCISES

16. Delete the record of a student with a specified roll number from the list maintained in question 14.
17. Write a program to merge two sorted linked lists. The resultant list must also be sorted.
18. Write a program to delete the first, last and middle node of a header linked list.
19. Write a program to create a linked list from an already given list. The new linked list must contain every alternate element of the existing linked list.
20. Given a linked list that contains alphabets. The alphabets may be in upper case or in lower case. Create two linked lists—one which stores upper case alphabets and the other that stores lower case characters.
21. Write a program to concatenate two doubly linked lists.
22. Write a program to delete the first element of a doubly linked list. Add this node as the last node of the list.
23. Write a program to
    (a) Delete the first occurrence of a given character in a linked list
    (b) Delete the last occurrence of a given character
    (c) Delete all the occurrences of a given character
24. Write a program to reverse a linked list using recursion.
25. Write a program to input an n digit number. Now break this number into its individual digits and then store every single digit in a separate node thereby forming a linked list. For example, if you enter `12345`, now there will `5` nodes in the list containing nodes with values—`1, 2, 3, 4, 5`.
26. Write a program to sum the values of the nodes of a linked list and then calculate the mean.
27. Write a program that prints minimum and maximum value in a linked list that stores integer values.
28. Write a program to interchange the value of the first element with the last element, second element with second last element, so on and so forth of a doubly linked list.
29. Write a program to make the first element of singly linked list, the last element of the list.
30. Write a program to count the number of occurrences of a given value in a linked list.
31. Write a program that adds 10 to the values stored in the nodes of a doubly linked list.
32. Write a program to form a linked list of floating point numbers. Display the sum and mean of these numbers.
33. Write a program to delete the `k`th node from a linked list.
34. Write a program to perform deletions in all the cases of a circular header linked list.
35. Write a program to multiply a polynomial with a given number.
36. Write a program to count the number of non-zero values in a circular linked list.
37. Write a program to create a linked list which stores the details of a student. Read and print the information stored in such a list.
38. Modify program 29 so that it displays the record of a given student only.
39. Create a linked list which stores names of the employees. Then sort these names and re-display the contents of the linked list.
40. Write a program to create a linked list which stores the details of employees in a department. Insert information about a new employee. Using the structure created in program 29, write a program to delete a student's information from the list.
41. Use the linked list of Question 40 and delete information about an existing employee.
42. Why are linked lists more preferred than using arrays?
43. Write a program to create a singly linked list and reverse the list by interchanging the links and not the data.
44. Write a program that prints the nth element from the end of a linked list in a single pass.
45. Write a program that creates a singly linked list. Use a function isSorted that returns 1 if the list is sorted and 0 otherwise.
46. Write a program to interchange the kth and the (k+1)th node of a circular doubly linked list.
47. Write a program to create a header linked list.
48. Write a program to delete a node from a circular header linked list.
49. Write a program to delete all nodes from a header linked list that has negative values in its data part.
50. Consider the linked list given below and deduce the correct option:

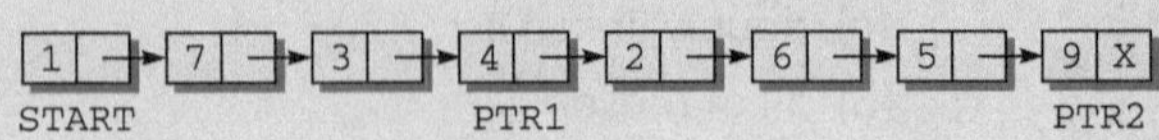

EXERCISES

(a) `PTR1->NEXT->NEXT->DATA = ?`

- 3
- 4
- 2
- 6

(b) `To delete a linked list, set START = ?`

- PTR1
- PTR2
- NULL
- START->NEXT

51. Given following names of students in a class, show the memory representation of the linked list in memory provided that the names should be sorted in alphabetical order.

NAMES = Mary, Joe, Adam, Navya, Arshiya, Karan, Sehej, Riyansh, Priya

Hint: Set the START and NEXT pointer accordingly

52. Look at the figure given below and find out the names of countries that are stored in memory using linked lists.

Country

Country
0
1
4
16

	DATA	NEXT
0	I	2
1	C	5
2	N	6
3	A	
4	J	14
5	H	12
6	D	9
7	N	13
8	A	−1
9	I	8
10	M	20
11	P	15
12	I	7
13	A	−1
14	A	11
15	A	17
16	B	18
17	N	−1
18	U	19
19	R	10
20	A	−1

54. Given the memory representation of a linked list of student shown below, give the changes that will have to be done to the representation when a new record is added. Also show the changes when the record of `S04` is deleted.

START = 1

	Roll No	Marks	Next
1	S01	78	2
2	S02	84	3
3	S03	45	5
4			
5	S04	98	7
6			
7	S05	55	8
8	S06	34	10
9			
10	S07	90	11
11	S08	87	12
12	S09	86	13
13	S10	67	15
14			
15	S11	56	−1

Case Study for Chapters 8, 9, and 11

In Chapter 8, we have seen how related information can be grouped and stored together using structures. In Chapter 11 we have seen that a number of records that are related to each other can be stored using a linked list. Storing records using linked lists helps to preserve memory space and is much more efficient.

Finally to store the records on a persistent storage area we can use files. The files are stored on the hard disk of the computer and can be brought into the memory as and when their need arises.

1. **Using all this information, write a program for implementing a telephone directory. Write an application for storing the names and phone numbers in a file. Use a linked list to store and retrieve data.**

```
# include <conio.h>
# include <stdio.h>
# include <alloc.h>
# include <string.h>

struct node
{
   int num;
   char name[15];
   struct node *next;
};

struct node *start;
FILE *fp;

struct node *get_record()
{
   struct node *ptr;
  ptr = (struct node*)malloc(sizeof(struct
   node));
   fread(&ptr,sizeof(struct node),1,fp);
   printf("\n NUM = %d \t NAME =
   %s",ptr->num, ptr->name);
   ptr->next = NULL;
   return ptr;
}
struct node *get_node()
{
struct node *ptr;
  ptr = (struct node*)malloc(sizeof(struct
   node));
   printf("\n Enter the phone number : ");
   scanf("%d",&ptr->num);
   printf("\n Enter the Name : ");
   scanf("%s",&ptr->name);
   ptr->next = NULL;
   return ptr;
}
struct node *search_record(int id,int *flag)
{
   struct node *cur = start,*prev = NULL;
        *flag = 0;
        if(start == NULL)
        return NULL;
   while(start! = NULL)
   {
        if(cur->num == id)
        {
          *flag = 1;
          break;
        }
        prev = cur;
        cur = cur->next;
   }
   return prev;
}

int insert_node(struct node *new_node)
{
        struct node *prev;
        int flag;
```

```
        prev = search_record(new_node->num,
&flag);
        if(start == NULL)
        {
            start = new_node;
            return -1;
        }
        if(flag == 1)
    return -1;
    else
    {
        new_node->next = prev->next;
        prev->next = new_node;
    }
    return 0;
}
void display()
{
        struct node *ptr;
        int i = 0;
        if(start == NULL)
        {
            printf("\n LIST IS EMPTY");
            return;
        }
        printf("\n RECORDS : ");
        ptr = start;
        while(ptr! = NULL)
        {
            printf("\n Record no. %d",i+1);
            printf("\n \t PHONE NUMBER:
            %d",ptr->num);
        printf("\n \t NAME :
        %s",ptr->name);
            i++;
            ptr = ptr->next;
        }
}
int delete_node(int id)
{
    struct node *prev,*ptr, *temp;
    int flag = 0;
    if(start==NULL)
        return -1;
    prev = search_record(id,&flag);
    if(flag==0)
      return -1;
    if(prev==NULL)
    {
                    ptr = start;
      start = start->next;
      free(ptr);
    }
    else
    {
        temp = prev->next;
        prev->next = temp->next;
        free(temp);
    }
    return 0;
}

struct node *query_record(int id, char
*flag,int option)
{
    struct node *cur,*prev = NULL;
    int x = 0;
    if(start == NULL)
    return NULL;
    cur = start;
    if(option)
    {
      while(cur! = NULL)
      {
        if(cur->num == id)
        {
            x = 1;
            break;
        }
        prev = cur;
        cur = cur->next;
      }
    }
    else
    {
      while(cur! = NULL)
      {
        if(!strcmp(cur->name,flag))
        {
            x=1;
            break;
        }
        prev = cur;
        cur = cur->next;
      }
    }
      if(x == 0)
      {
            printf("\n The record does not
            exist");
            return NULL;
      }
    return cur;
}
void backup()
{
        FILE *fp;
        struct node *ptr;
        fp = fopen("PHONE_NUMBERS.TXT","w");
```

```
    ptr=start;
    if(ptr==NULL)
    {
       printf("The list is empty, nothing
         to write back...");
       return;
    }
    while(ptr! = NULL)
    {
       fprintf(fp,"%d
         %s",ptr->num,ptr->name);
       ptr = ptr->next;
    }
    fclose(fp);
}
void main()
{
    int option = 0, pno;
    int flag = 0;
    char str[15], search_name[20];
    struct node *new_node;
    clrscr();

    fp = fopen("PHONE_NUMBERS.TXT","r");

    if(fp == NULL)
    {
      printf("File cant be opened!");
      getch();
      exit(1);
    }
    while(!feof(fp))
    {
          new_node=get_record();
          if(insert_node(new_node) == -1)
             printf("\n The new node could
                  not be inserted");
          else
             printf("\n Record Added.");
    }
    getch();
    fclose(fp);
   do
   {
      clrscr();
      printf("\n\n ****** MAIN MENU
       *******");
      printf("\n 1. Add Record");
      printf("\n 2. Delete Record");
      printf("\n 3. Display Records");
      printf("\n 4. Edit Record");
      printf("\n 5. Exit.");
      printf("\n Enter your option : ");
      scanf("%d",&option);
      switch(option)
      {
         case 1:
            new_node = get_node();
            flag = insert_node(new_node);
            if(flag== -1)
              printf("\n Record already
                exists");
            else
              printf("\n Record Added");
            break;
       case 2:
            printf("\n Enter the phone
              no. to be deleted");
            scanf("%d",&pno);
            flag = delete_node(pno);
            if(flag == -1)
              printf("\n Record does not
                exist");
            if(flag == 0)
              printf("Record deleted !");
            break;
         case 3:
            display();
            break;
         case 4:
           printf("\n Search by phone
              no. or Name ? (1/2)");
           scanf("%d",&option);
           if(option == 1)
           {
              printf("\n Enter the phone
                no. to be searched:");
              scanf("%d",&pno);
              new_node = query_
                record(pno,&str,1);
           }
           else
           {
              printf("\n Enter the name
                to be searched : ");
              scanf("%s",&str);
              new_node = query_
                record(0,&str,0);
           }
           if(new_node)
           {
              printf("\n Enter the new
                name : ");
             scanf("%s",&new_node->name);
             printf("\n Enter new phone
                no. : ");
              scanf("%d",&new_node->num);
              printf("\n Record modified
                successfully !");
```

```
    }
    break;

  case 5:
    printf("\n Copying the
          database to the file");
    backup();
    getch();
    free(start);
    exit(1);
    break;
  }
  getch();
  }while(1);
}
```

Output

```
****** MAIN MENU *******
1. Add Record
2. Delete Record
3. Display Records
4. Edit Record
5. Exit.
Enter your option : 1
Enter the phone number : 9871123456
Enter the Name : Goransh Bathla
Record Added
```

Answers to Objective Questions

CHAPTER 1

Fill in the Blanks

1. software; 2. software; 3. programming; 4. programming language; 5. compiler; 6. driver software; 7. operating system; 8. system software; 9. cryptographic utilities; 10. label, an operation code, and one or more operands

Multiple Choice Questions

1. ROM; 2. FORTRAN; 3. assembly language; 4. all of these; 5. machine language; 6. linker; 7. anti-virus; 8. BIOS; 9. computer hardware; 10. operating system

True or False

1. true	2. true	3. true	4. false	5. false
6. true	7. false	8. true	9. false	10. true

CHAPTER 2

Fill in the Blanks

1. Dennis Ritchie; 2. function; 3. main() ; 4. ASCII codes; 5. operating system; 6. modulus operator; 7. logical NOT; 8. unary; 9. type casting; 10. number of values that are successfully read 11. default case; 12. printf(); 13. abs() in math.h; 14. single quotes; 15. closing bracket; 16. math.h; 17. \n; 18. double; 19. const; 20. he sign of the first operand is positive; 21. the direction in which the operator having the same precedence acts on the operands; 22. parenthesis; 23. sizeof; 24. %hd; 25. x; 26. –

Multiple Choice Questions

1. relational; 2. Logical AND and Logical OR; 3. 3; 4. Bitwise NOT; 5. comma; 6. %hd; 7. ‘bb’, “A”,; 8. ‘a’, “1”, pi; 9. Initial.Name, A+B, $amt, 1st_row, Col Amt; 10. % 11. res = /4

State True or False

1. false	2. false	3. true	4. false	5. true
6. false	7. true	8. false	9. false	10. false
11. true	12. true	13. false	14. false	15. false
16. true	17. true	18. false	19. false	20. false
21. false	22. true	23. false	24. false	25. true
26. true				

CHAPTER 3

Fill in the Blanks

1. there is no matching else; 2. integral; 3. n for every if statement; 4. break/continue; 5. infinite; 6. loop; 7. decision control; 8. integral; 9. iterative; 10. post test loops; 11. sentinel controlled; 12. goto; 13. goto

State True or False

1. false	2. false	3. true	4. true	5. true
6. true	7. true	8. false	9. true	10. true
11. true	12. false	13. false	14. true	15. false
16. true	17. true	18. false	19. true	20. true
21. true	22. true	23. true	24. false	25. false

CHAPTER 4

Fill in the Blanks

1. function name; 2. calling function; 3. calling function; 4. arguments/parameters; 5. operating system; 6. function header and function body; 7. call-by-reference; 8. goto label; 9. recursive; 10. system stack; 11. recursive; 12. zero or no; 13. global; 14. main(); 15. int; 16. arguments; 17. local variable

Multiple Choice Questions

1. called function; 2. all of these; 3. void; 4. defined; 5. static; 6. extern; 7. static; 8. auto

State True or False

1. false	2. true	3. true	4. true	5. true
6. false	7. true	8. false	9. true	10. true
11. true	12. false	13. true	14. false	15. false
16. true	17. true			

CHAPTER 5

Fill in the Blanks

1. collection of similar data elements; 2. subscript/index; 3. integral; 4. consecutive; 5. n; 6. pointer; 7. data type, name and size; 8. the element being referenced; 9. index; 10. array name; 11. the number of elements stored in it; 12. traversing; 13. sorted array; 14. O(n); 15. consecutive; 16. constant; 17. array of arrays; 18. fourth; 19. linear;

Multiple Choice Questions

1. 10; 2. 7; 3. 200; 4. 50; 5. 25; 6. greater; 7. O(log n); 8. best case; 9. all of these

State True or False

1. true	2. false	3. true	4. true	5. false
6. false	7. true	8. false	9. true	10. false
11. false	12. false	13. true	14. true	15. false
16. true	17. true	18. true	19. true	20. true
21. false	22. false	23. false	24. false	25. false
26. false				

CHAPTER 6

Fill in the Blanks

1. a null-terminated character array; 2. null character; 3. 5; 4. zero; 5. consecutive; 6. 99; 7. scanf(); 8. zero; 9. 65-91; 10. convert a character into upper case; 11. when in dictionary order S1 will come after S2; 12. strrev(); 13. ORNING; 14. 15; 15. index; 16. stdlib.h; 17. Appends the string pointed to by str2 to the end of the string pointed str2 to the end of the string pointed; 18. if str1 is greater than str2 respectively x; 19. strlen(); 20. puts();

Multiple Choice Questions

1. 0; 2. 97-123; 3. XPPPXXYYYZZZ; 4. XXXYZZ; 5. world; 6. string.h; 7. all of these; 8. XXABYYZZZ; 9. 7; 10. strcat(s,1(strcat(s2,s3))); 11. 23; 12. strcat();

State True or False

1. false	2. false	3. false	4. true	5. false
6. false	7. true	8. false	9. false	10. false
11. true	12. true	13. false	14. true	15. false
16. false	17. false			

CHAPTER 7

Fill in the Blanks

1. 1 byte; 2. dynamic memory allocation; 3. address, pointer; 4. null; 5. data type; 6. 2; 7. rvalue; 8. memory addresses; 9. pointers; 10. *; 11. main memory; 12. stack; 13. stack; 14. executable image of shared libraries that are being used by the program; 15. a pointer (of cast type) to an area of memory with size byte-size; 16. free(), heap; 17. void pointer, null pointer; 18. to change the memory size already allocated by calloc() and malloc(); 19. pointer-to-pointer-to-int; 20. garbage value; 21. address of a pointer variable; 22. 0; 23. pointer-to-pointer-to-int; 24. pointers; 25. free(); 26. arrays of varying sizes;

Multiple Choice Questions

1. Dereferencing operator; 2. num; 3. all of these; 4. address; 5. &; 6. stack; 7. heap; 8. stdlib.h; 9. calloc();

State True or False

1. true	2. true	3. true	4. true	5. true
6. false	7. true	8. false	9. true	10. false
11. true	12. false	13. true	14. true	15. false
16. true	17. true	18. false	19. true	20. true
21. false	22. false	23. false	24. false	25. true
26. true	27. true			

CHAPTER 8

Fill in the Blanks

1. user defined; 2. records; 3. array; 4. structure; 5. structure variable declaration; 6. structure declaration; 7. structure; 8. structure name; 9. typedef; 10. 0; 11. \0; 12. dot operator; 13. nested structure; 14. self referential; 15. create a new data type name for an existing data type; 16. union; 17. refer to the individual members for the actual parameters; 18. union;

Multiple Choice Questions

1. all of these; 2. structure; 3. Structure variable declaration; 4. dot operator; 5. nested structure; 6. dot operator; 7. all of these; 8. int;

State True or False

1. false	2. false	3. false	4. true	5. true
6. false	7. false	8. true	9. true	10. true
11. false	12. false	13. true	14. false	15. false
16. true	17. false	18. true	19. false	20. true
21. true				

CHAPTER 9

Fill in the Blanks

1. file; 2. stderr, stdin, stdout; 3. standard stream; 4. w/a; 5. rewind(); 6. binary; 7. fread(); 8. stdout; 9. buffer; 10. operating system; 11. binary files; 12. flushall(); 13. stdout; 14. fseek() or rewind(); 15. stdio.h, -1;

Multiple Choice Questions

1. ftell(); 2. fwrite(); 3. all of these; 4. stderr; 5. buffer; 6. fopen(); 7. fgetc();

State True or False

1. false	2. false	3. true	4. true	5. false
6. false	7. false	8. false	9. true	10. false
11. false	12. true	13. true	14. true	15. true

CHAPTER 10

Fill in the blanks

1. pre-processor; 2. pre-processor; 3. preprocessor directives; 4. preprocessor directives; 5. #define statement; 6. give symbolic names to numeric constants; 7. #define directive; 8. arguments in the invocation that exceed the number of parameters in the definition; 9. #; 10. merge operator; 11. angular brackets; 12. 10; 13. #define; 14. #pragma; 15. conditional directive; 16. a closing #endif; 17. #if directive; 18. #error directive; 19. #warning directive; 20. _STDC_;

Multiple Choice Questions

1. #; 2. \; 3. #line; 4. #ifdef; 5. defined; 6. _TIMESTAMP_;

State True or False

1. false	2. true	3. false	4. true	5. false
6. true	7. false	8. true	9. true	10. false
11. false	12. true	13. false	14. true	15. false

CHAPTER 11

Fill in the Blanks

1. AVAIL; 2. O(1); 3. O(n); 4. two; 5. one; 6. two; 7. two; 8. one; 9. two; 10. one; 11. node; 12. START; 13. node; 14. there is no memory that can be allocated for the new node to be inserted; 15. first;

Multiple Choice Questions

1. Sequential access structure; 2. both; 3. all of these; 4. doubly linked list;

State True or False

1. true	2. true	3. false	4. false	5. false
6. false	7. true	8. false	9. true	10. true

Index

Related Titles

DATA STRUCTURES USING C (SECOND EDITION)
9780198099307

Reema Thareja, *University of Delhi*

The book starts off with a brief overview of C programming concepts, which is followed by the study of various data structures such as arrays, linked lists, stacks, queues, trees, and graphs.

Key Features

- Provides a brief recapitulation of C programming basics before delving into the analysis of data structures
- Makes use of numerous algorithms, programs, and illustrations to explain the concepts
- Improved explanation of algorithms and a greater variety of in-text examples

DATA STRUCTURES USING C++
9780198066231

Varsha H. Patil, *Matoshri College of Engineering, Nashik*

The book begins with a discussion on the fundamentals of data structures and algorithms, and moves on to the concepts of linear data structures, recursion, searching and sorting.

Key Features

- Provides a thorough overview of the fundamental concepts
- Includes numerous algorithms and program codes in C++ to illustrate the topics discussed
- Provides several illustrations and flowcharts to help understand the subject effectively

PROGRAMMING WITH ANSI C++ (SECOND EDITION)
9780198083962

Bhushan Trivedi, *GLS Institute of Computer Technology, Ahmedabad*

This textbook provides a fine balance between theory and practice and an in-depth coverage of both elementary as well as advanced topics.

Key Features

- Detailed discussion on advanced topics such as RTTI, Casting operators, MIL, Reference variables, and Templates
- Programs are followed by a detailed analysis section that decodes the logic behind the programs
- Accompanied with a CD that contains the codes of all the programs as well as case studies

PROGRAMMING IN JAVA (SECOND EDITION)
9780198094852

Sachin Malhotra, *IMS Ghaziabad* and **Saurabh Choudhary,** *IT Consultant and Corporate Trainer*

Thoroughly updated for Java Standard Edition 7 (Java SE 7), this textbook provides greater topical coverage and more programming examples in every chapter.

Key Features

- Provides a quick recap of object-oriented programming concepts before getting started with Java
- Includes plenty of user-friendly programs with line-by-line explanations and comments in them to encourage self-study
- Contains a Lab Manual with useful program codes and a set of interview questions with answers as appendices

OTHER RELATED TITLES

- 9780198097402 Harsh Bhasin: *Programming in C #*
- 9780198082163 B. M. Harwani: *Unix and Shell Programming*
- 9780195696561 Subhajit Datta: *Software Engineering*
- 9780198082873 Naresh Chauhan: *Principles of Operating Systems*
- 9780198070887 Srimanta Pal: *Systems Programming*
- 9780198061847 Naresh Chauhan: *Software Testing: Principles and Practices*
- 9780198066774 Bhushan Trivedi: *Computer Networks*